Introduction to Mariology

Introduction to Mariology

Manfred Hauke

Translated by
RICHARD CHONAK

The Catholic University of America Press
Washington, D.C.

Originally published in Italian as *Introduzione alla Mariologia* (2008)
ISBN 978-88-88446-52-3
EUpress FTL, Lugano

The paper used in this publication meets the minimum requirements of American National Standards for Information Science–Permanence of Paper for Printed Library Materials, ANSI Z39.48-1984.
∞

Art on page ii and front cover: Mary, Mother of God, as "Seat of Wisdom" (Sedes Sapientiae), with the divine child. The statue, probably made in the thirteenth century, is venerated in the Monastery of Thalbach in the Austrian city of Bregenz. Photograph by J. Güfel, Feldkirch-Gisingen (Austria). Courtesy of the Spiritual Family "The Work" (Familia spiritualis opus).

Cataloging-in-Publication Data available
from the Library of Congress
ISBN 978-0-8132-3337-6

Contents

Sedi Sapientiae

Preface to the English Edition

The present volume was written as a handbook for students in the first cycle of studies at the Theological Faculty of Lugano, in the Italian-speaking part of Switzerland. The Faculty is an academic setting serving students from all over the world.

This publication has benefited from the author's experience as president of the German Society for Mariology (*Deutsche Arbeitsgemeinschaft für Mariologie*). Originally, the study was published in Italian (2008); it was translated, with some updates, into Spanish (2015). Other translations into Portuguese and Korean are on the way. The book presents the treasure of Marian doctrine for a first comprehensive view; for specialists in Mariology it offers basic information with bibliographical references for further study.

The Italian original, updated for the English edition, is the second volume of a series begun in 2002 (*Collana di Mariologia*). The first volume of this series publishes selected texts from the German Cardinal Leo Scheffczyk (1920–2005), whom St. John Paul II awarded the dignity of cardinal for his theological merits.[1] The theological perspective of the present volume has been considerably influenced by Scheffczyk, who directed the doctoral thesis of the author (on "Women in the Priesthood?"), and by Anton Ziegenaus, who published, together with Scheffczyk, a dogmatic theology in eight volumes (in German; an Italian translation is available). My profound

1. Leo Scheffczyk, *Il mondo della fede Cattolica: Verità e forma; Con un'intervista a Benedetto XVI* [The World of the Catholic Faith: Truth and Form; Including an Interview with Benedict XVI], trans. Alessio Musio (Milan: Vita e Pensiero, 2007); Scheffczyk, *Ecumenismo: La ripida via della verità* [Ecumenism: The Steep Way of Truth], Memoria via 1 (Vatican City: Lateran University Press, 2007). See also Manfred Hauke, *Essere cattolico? Un primo sguardo all'opera teologica del Cardinale Leo Scheffczyk* [To Be a Catholic? A First Look at the Theological Work of Cardinal Leo Scheffczyk], Mane nobiscum 10 (Vatican City: Lateran University Press, 2007).

gratitude to Richard Chonak, who translated my *Mariology* into English, and to John B. Martino, who followed the publication in the name of the Catholic University of America Press.

I hope that the present volume will foster an increase in love for the Mother of God and Companion of the Redeemer, the Blessed Virgin Mary, "Seat of Wisdom."

Lugano, May 13, 2020, Memorial of Our Lady of Fatima
Manfred Hauke

Abbreviations

AAS	*Acta Apostolicae Sedis*
AMI	Academia Mariana Internationalis (since 1959: PAMI)
AMII	Associazione Mariologica Interdisciplinaria Italiana
ANF	*Ante-Nicene Fathers 1885–1887*
BTC	Biblioteca della Teologia Contemporanea
BVM	Blessed Virgin Mary (Beata Virgo Maria)
CCC	*Catechism of the Catholic Church*
CChr. SL	*Corpus Christianorum,* Latin series.
CdM	Collana di Mariologia
CM	John Paul II, Marian Catecheses (Catechesi Mariane)
COD	Giuseppe Alberigo et al., eds., *Conciliorum Oecumenicorum Decreta*
CR	*Catechismus Romanus*
CSEL	*Corpus Scriptorum Ecclesiasticorum Latinorum*
DH	Heinrich Denzinger and Peter Hünermann, *Enchiridion Symbolorum, definitionum et declarationum de rebus fidei et morum*
DLCA	Siegmar Döpp and Wilhelm Geerlings, eds., *Dizionario di letteratura cristiana antica*
DMar	Stefano De Fiores, Valeria Ferrari Schiefer, and Salvatore M. Perrella, eds., *Mariologia* (Dizionari San Paolo)
DPPL	Congregation for Divine Worship and the Discipline of the Sacraments, *Directory on Popular Piety and the Liturgy*
DThC	*Dictionnaire de Théologie catholique*
EE	*Enchiridion delle encicliche*
EMTheo	*Enciclopedia mariana "Theotokos"*
EV	*Enchiridion Vaticanum: Documenti ufficiali della Santa Sede*

FKTh	*Forum Katholische Theologie*
GdT	*Giornale di Teologia*
GCS	*Die Griechischen Christlichen Schriftsteller der ersten drei Jahrhunderte*
JB	*The Jerusalem Bible*
LG	Vatican Council II, Dogmatic Constitution on the Church *Lumen gentium*
Mansi	J. D. Mansi, *Sacrorum conciliorum nova et amplissima collectio*
MBVM	Congregation for Divine Worship, *Collectio Missarum de beata Maria Virgine* and *Lectionarium pro missis de beata Maria Virgine*
MCu	Paul VI, Apostolic Exhortation *Marialis cultus*
MD	John Paul II, Apostolic Letter *Mulieris dignitatem.* August 15, 1988.
ML	Remigius Bäumer and Leo Scheffczyk, eds., *Marienlexikon*
NDM	Stefano De Fiores and S. Meo, eds., *Nuovo dizionario di mariologia*
NPNF1	Philip Schaff, ed., *Nicene and Post-Nicene Fathers*, First Series
NPNF2	Philip Schaff, ed., *Nicene and Post-Nicene Fathers*, Second Series
NT	New Testament
OT	Old Testament
PAMI	Pontificia Academia Mariana Internationalis
PBC	Pontifical Biblical Commission
PE	Claudia Carlen, ed., *The Papal Encyclicals*
PG	J.-P. Migne, Patrologiae cursus completus, Series graeca
PL	J.-P. Migne, Patrologiae cursus completus. Series latina
RC	John Paul II, Apostolic Exhortation *Redemptoris Custos*
RM	John Paul II, Encyclical *Redemptoris Mater*
RSV2CE	*The Holy Bible*, Revised Standard Version, 2nd Catholic ed.
RTLu	*Rivista Teologica di Lugano*
RVM	John Paul II, Apostolic Letter *Rosarium Virginis Mariae*
SC	*Sources chrétiennes*
ST	*Summa Theologiae*
TD	Louis-Marie Grignion de Montfort, *True Devotion to the Blessed Virgin*
TMPM	Georges Gharib et al., eds., *Testi mariani del primo millennio*
TMSM	Angelo Amato et al., eds., *Testi mariani del secondo millennio*
TU	*Texte und Untersuchungen zur Geschichte der altchristlichen Literatur*

Introduction to

Mariology

Introduction

MARY, "FOCAL POINT" OF CATHOLIC THEOLOGY

The broadest lexicographical work of contemporary theology about the Mother of God is a dictionary of Mariology that appeared from 1988 to 1994 in Germany. The text comprises six volumes and about 8,500 entries.[1] To date there is no comparable work on the Holy Trinity, and not even one on Christology. At first glance, this fact might seem excessive. Would it not have been better to dedicate the same effort to a ten-volume dictionary on the Holy Trinity first? Aren't there perhaps more important topics than Mariology, such as God, Jesus Christ, and man?

Another question: Mary is certainly a great saint, but wouldn't it be enough to save a place for her in works of hagiography, together with the apostles Peter and Paul, for example, and together with St. Lucy and St. Edith Stein? What reason is there for a distinct treatise on Mariology? There is no such thing as a "Petrology" or a "Paulology."

One German Catholic theologian engaged in dialogue with Protestants, taking the universe of saints, so abundant and fascinating, as his starting point, maintains that, since "it is a good and useful thing" to invoke the saints, according to the Council of Trent,

1. Remigius Bäumer and Leo Scheffczyk, eds., *Marienlexikon* [Encyclopedia of Mary], 6 vols. (St. Ottilien: EOS, 1988–94), hereinafter abbreviated as *ML*; see also the List of Abbreviations. Regarding this resource, see Manfred Hauke, "Introduzione all'opera teologica e alla mariologia del cardinale Leo Scheffczyk" [Introduction to the Theological Works and the Mariology of Cardinal Leo Scheffczyk], in Scheffczyk, *Maria, crocevia della fede cattolica* [Mary, Crossroads of the Catholic Faith], Collana di Mariologia (hereinafter CdM) 1, (Lugano: Eupress FTL, 2002), 31f; Hauke, "La mariologia di Leo Scheffczyk" [The Mariology of Leo Scheffczyk], *Scripta de Maria*, 2nd ser., 8 (2011): 65–91.

but it is not obligatory,[2] then for the Catholic faith it should not be necessary to invoke Mary.[3] Is that author right?

We can find an answer in the texts of the Second Vatican Council. The last ecumenical Council was, as it were, "the Council of the Church about the Church."[4] In the Dogmatic Constitution *Lumen gentium,* the "iron core" of the conciliar texts, the church is placed in the larger context of salvation history. It begins from Jesus Christ and from the Most Holy Trinity and reaches all the way to eschatology, to the future life. In this great panorama a Marian chapter is inserted under the title "The Blessed Virgin Mary, Mother of God in the Mystery of Christ and the Church." *Lumen gentium* ends with this chapter. According to the authoritative words of Pope Paul VI, the pages dedicated to the Madonna are the "summit" and "crowning" of the whole Dogmatic Constitution on the Church.[5] They are the first overview of Mariology formulated by a Council. The Marian chapter, like the whole Dogmatic Constitution on the Church, places the topic in the larger context of the faith. And here we find an emblematic phrase: "Mary ..., since her entry into salvation history unites in herself and re-echoes the greatest teachings of the faith."[6]

Mary, virgin Mother of the Savior, is closely united with the work of salvation. God made the Incarnation depend on the "yes" of this woman, who deeply becomes part of the mystery of the Covenant. The fathers described the role of Mary as a "new Eve" beside the "new Adam," Jesus Christ.[7] So it is apparent that a unique role, a

2. Heinrich Denzinger and Peter Hünermann, *Enchiridion Symbolorum, definitionum et declarationum de rebus fidei et morum*, Bilingual Latin-English ed. (hereinafter DH) (San Francisco: Ignatius, 2012), 1821.

3. Wolfgang Beinert, "Maria in Leben und Lehre der römisch-katholischen Kirche" [Mary in the Life and Teaching of the Roman Catholic Church], in *Maria, die Mutter unseres Herrn: Eine evangelische Handreichung* [Mary, Mother of Our Lord: A Protestant Handbook], ed. Manfred Kiessig (Lahr: Verlag Ernst Kaufmann, 1991), 99.

4. See, for example, the summary in Claudio Delpero, *La Chiesa del Concilio: L'ecclesiologia del Vaticano II* [The Church of the Council: The Ecclesiology of Vatican II] (Florence: Libreria Editrice Fiorentina, 2004).

5. Paul VI, Allocution *Post duos menses* [After Two Months], on the close of the third session of the Second Vatican Council, November 21, 1964: *Acta Apostolicae Sedis (AAS)* 56 (1964): 1014; *Enchiridion Vaticanum: Documenti ufficiali della Santa Sede* (hereinafter *EV*) (Bologna: EDB, 1966–) 1:300*.

6. Second Vatican Council, Dogmatic Constitution on the Church *Lumen gentium* (hereinafter *LG*) 65. Vatican translations are used for Vatican II documents unless otherwise indicated.

7. See Luigi Gambero, *Mary and the Fathers of the Church: The Blessed Virgin Mary in Patristic*

role placed at the center of salvation history, belongs to Mary, and in a sense, the entire content of the faith is gathered up in this center.

Anyone who participates in the liturgy of the church automatically meets the Mother of God as well, above all in the context of the Incarnation. Mary appears in the professions of the faith (such as the Credo) and in the Eucharistic Prayer. She is mentioned with particular tenderness in the Christmas cycle and at the Annunciation of the Lord. Numerous feasts and two months (May and October) are dedicated particularly to her. Vatican II affirms, in regard to the liturgical year:

In celebrating this annual cycle of Christ's mysteries, holy Church honors with especial love the Blessed Mary, Mother of God, who is joined by an inseparable bond to the saving work of her Son. In her the Church holds up and admires the most excellent fruit of the redemption, and joyfully contemplates, as in a faultless image, that which she herself desires and hopes wholly to be.[8]

A few years before the Council, Michael Schmaus wrote the following words in the introduction to his Mariology:

In Mariology nearly all the theological lines are found together: the Christological line, the ecclesiological, the anthropological, and the eschatological. Add to that the fact that in Mariology the methodological questions of theology develop with particular clarity and sharpness. Nearly all the theological discussions of the present time flow together in it. Mariology shows itself to be the intersection of the most important theological affirmations.[9]

Let us present some examples regarding the central place of Mariology. The Council of Ephesus (which we will discuss later) defined the title "Theotokos" (Mother of God) in 431:[10] Jesus Christ is not merely the temple of God; rather, the very Son of God assumed a human nature. Because of this, Mary gave birth not merely to the man in whom God dwelt (as Nestorius described him), but to the

---

Thought, trans. Thomas Buffer (San Francisco: Ignatius Press, 1999), 425 (index, under the term "Eve-Mary parallel").

8. Second Vatican Council, *Sacrosanctum concilium* (December 4, 1963), 103.

9. Michael Schmaus, *Katholische Dogmatik*, vol. 5, *Mariologie* [*Catholic Dogmatics*, vol. 5, *Mariology*], 2nd ed. (Munich: Hueber, 1961), 8.

10. See the section "The Council of Ephesus (431)," in chapter 4.

Son of God. In the person of the divine Word, the divine nature and human nature are united without separation and without confusion. Therefore, the true faith in Jesus Christ shows itself in the title "Theotokos." This is why St. Cyril of Alexandria, in his sermon to the Council of Ephesus, called Mary the "scepter of orthodoxy": the true faith is shown in Mary; in her we see who is Jesus Christ.[11]

In 449, shortly before the Council of Chalcedon, Pope Leo the Great summarized Christian doctrine in three points: (1) faith in God, the almighty Father; (2) in Jesus Christ, his only-begotten Son, our Lord; (3) who was born by the Holy Spirit of the Virgin Mary. As the Pope commented, "By these three phrases, the schemes of nearly all the heretics are destroyed."[12]

Because of this experience, the Western liturgy, in the divine office, has known the invocation of Mary since the eighth century as the "conqueror of all heresies." In the liturgical reform the corresponding antiphon was deleted,[13] perhaps because it seemed exaggerated in the opinion of liturgists. On this subject it is interesting to hear the voice of Cardinal Ratzinger, who later became supreme pontiff:

> As a young theologian in the time before (and also during) the Council, I had, as many did then and still do today, some reservations in regard to certain ancient formulas, as for example, that famous 'De Maria nunquam satis,' "concerning Mary one can never say enough." It seemed exaggerated to me. So it was difficult for me later to understand the meaning of another famous expression ... that designated the Virgin as "the conqueror of all heresies." Now—in this confused period where truly every type of heretical

11. Cyril of Alexandria, *Homily IV against Nestorius*, in J.-P. Migne, Patrologiae cursus completus, Series graeca (hereinafter PG) 77 (Paris: 1857–66), 992–96: "We hail you, O Mary Mother of God, venerable treasure of the entire world, inextinguishable lamp, crown of virginity, scepter of orthodoxy, imperishable temple, container of him who cannot be contained, Mother and Virgin, through whom it is said in the Gospels, 'Blessed is He who comes in the name of the Lord.'" See Gambero, *Mary and the Fathers*, 248.

12. *Epist.* 28:2 (ad Flavianum), in J.-P. Migne, Patrologiae cursus completus, Series latina (hereinafter PL) 54 (Paris: 1841–64), 757 B. See DH 290–95.

13. "Gaude, Maria Virgo, cunctas haereses sola interemisti, quae Gabrielis archangeli dictis credidisti" [Rejoice, Virgin Mary, You Have Destroyed All the Heresies, You Who Believed What Was Said by the Archangel Gabriel]. See Anton Ziegenaus, "Häresie" [Heresy], in *ML* 3:67–69; René Laurentin, *Marie, clé du mystère chrétien* [Mary, Key of the Christian Mystery] (Paris: Fayard, 1994), epilogue.

aberration seems to be pressing upon the doors of the authentic faith—now I understand that it was not a matter of pious exaggerations, but of truths that today are more valid than ever.[14]

Mary is like a focal point in which the central truths of the Catholic faith can be seen. To point out another example, this is also true for ecumenism. In Protestantism Mariology does not exist as a scholarly discipline, although we do also find essays on the Mother of the Lord from Protestant theologians. A statement of Karl Barth, the most famous Protestant theologian of the twentieth century, is emblematic:

Marian dogma is neither more nor less than the critical, central normative dogma of the Roman Catholic Church, the dogma from the standpoint of which all their important positions are to be regarded and by which they stand or fall.... The "mother of God" of Roman Catholic Marian dogma is quite simply the principle, type and the essence of the human creature co-operating servantlike (ministerialiter) in its own redemption on the basis of prevenient grace, and to that extent the principle, type, and the essence of the Church.[15]

For Barth, Mariology is suspect because it upholds the fact that man collaborates in the process of justification: hence it is contrary to the Protestant principle of sola gratia, according to which God alone brings man to salvation. Therefore, according to Barth, Mariology is "a tumor; i.e., a diseased construct of theological thought. Tumors must be excised."[16]

In the ecumenical dialogue between Catholics and Lutherans, a document was signed on October 31, 1999, that asserts a fundamental (but not total) consensus on the topic of justification (of man before God).[17] However, many Protestant theologians objected to this

14. Joseph Ratzinger and Vittorio Messori, *The Ratzinger Report: An Exclusive Interview on the State of the Church*, trans. Graham Harrison (San Francisco: Ignatius Press, 1985), 105–6.

15. Karl Barth, *Church Dogmatics*, vol. 1, part 2, *The Doctrine of the Word of God* (Edinburgh: T. and T. Clark, 1956), 143.

16. Barth, *Die Kirchliche Dogmatik*, vol. 1, part 2 (Zurich: Theologischer Verlag, 1975), 6th ed., 153; see Cándido Pozo, SJ, *María en la obra de la salvación* [Mary in the Work of Salvation], 2nd ed. (Madrid: Biblioteca de Autores Cristianos, 1990), 4; Pozo, *María, nueva Eva* [Mary, the New Eve] (Madrid: Biblioteca de Autores Cristianos, 2005), xviii.

17. See the documentation in (inter alia) Fulvio Ferrario and Paolo Ricca, eds., *Il Consenso*

statement, as did some Catholics.[18] Such a consensus needs to be verified (or disproved) in the realities that depend on the doctrine of justification, such as ecclesiology and Mariology. Otherwise we run the risk of finding only a verbal consensus that is more apparent than real.[19] For this reason, the Protestant theologian Cornelis A. de Ridder had urged more than forty years ago that attention be paid first of all to Mariology, excluding from it any human cooperation in justification.[20]

The subject of ecumenism will be studied in later chapters.[21] But these indications already suffice to make clear the central position of Mariology. The cooperation of Mary in salvation brings into play the value of anthropology and ecclesiology.

---

cattolico-luterano sulla dottrina della giustificazione [The Catholic-Lutheran Agreement on the Doctrine of Justification] (Turin: Claudiana, 1999).

18. See the information in Hauke, "Die Antwort des Konzils von Trient auf die Reformatoren" [The Council of Trent's Response to the Reformers], in *Der Mensch zwischen Sünde und Gnade* [Man between Sin and Grace], ed. Anton Ziegenaus (Buttenwiesen: Stella-Maris-Verlag, 2000), 75–109; Hauke, "Maria, 'compagna del Redentore': La cooperazione di Maria alla salvezza come pista di ricerca" [Mary, "Companion of the Redeemer": The Cooperation of Mary in Salvation as a Pathway of Research], *Rivista Teologica di Lugano* (hereinafter *RTLu*) 7 (2002): 62–64; Hauke, "Die 'Gemeinsame Erklärung' zur Rechtfertigung und die Norm des Glaubens" [The Joint Declaration on Justification and the Norm of Faith], *Forum Katholische Theologie* (hereafter *FKTh*) 22, no. 2 (2006): 127–34; Angelo Maffeis, *Dossier sulla giustificazione: La Dichiarazione congiunta cattolico-luterana, commento e dibattito teologico* [Dossier on Justification: The Joint Catholic-Lutheran Declaration, Commentary and Theological Debate] (Brescia: Queriniana, 2000); Christopher J. Malloy, *Engrafted into Christ: A Critique of the Joint Declaration* (New York: Peter Lang, 2005); Malloy, "Marian Coredemption and the Joint Declaration on the Doctrine of Justification," in *Mary at the Foot of the Cross*, vol. 8, *Coredemption as Key to a Correct Understanding of Redemption* (New Bedford, Mass.: Academy of the Immaculate, 2008), 351–409.

19. See Pozo, *María en la obra de salvación*, 9; Pozo, *María, nueva Eva*, xxiii.

20. See Cornelis A. de Ridder, *Maria als Miterlöserin?* [Mary as Coredemptrix?] (Göttingen: Vandenhoeck and Ruprecht, 1965), 164.

21. On ecumenical aspects, see "Reformation and Counter-Reformation," in chapter 2, "Ecumenical Aspects," in chapter 4, "The Ecumenical Debate," in chapter 6, "The Dogma in the Ecumenical Context," in chapter 7, and "Maria: *Mater Unitatis*," in chapter 8.

For an overview, see among others, Konrad Algermissen, "Bekenntnisse und Bekenntnisschriften" [Confessions and Confessional Writings] in *ML* 1:407–14; Brunero Gherardini, *La Madre: Maria in una sintesi storico-teologica* [The Mother: Mary in Historical-Theological Synthesis] (Frigento: Casa Mariana, 1989), 345–75; Ziegenaus, *Katholische Dogmatik*, vol. 5, *Maria in der Heilsgeschichte: Mariologie* [Catholic Dogmatics, vol. 5, Mary in Salvation History: Mariology] (Aachen: MM-Verlag, 1998), 43–74; Salvatore M. Perrella, OSM, *"Non temere di prendere con te Maria" (Matteo 1,20): Maria e l'ecumenismo nel postmoderno; Dalla "Mater divisionis" alla "Mater unitatis"* ["Fear Not to Take Mary with You" (Mt 1:20): Mary and Ecumenism in the Postmodern; From "Mother of Division" to "Mother of Unity"] (Milan: San Paolo, 2004); Jean Galot, SJ, *Maria, La donna nell'opera della salvezza* [Mary, Woman in the Work of Salvation], 3rd ed. (Rome: Ed. Pontificia Università Gregoriana, 2005), 379–415; Pozo, *María, nueva Eva*, 41–100.

A particularly current topic in anthropology is the role of woman in the church. Here too Mariology is a key discipline, and Pope John Paul II has expressed himself on the subject with a strongly Marian perspective.[22] Conversely, the issue of feminism, with its various shadings, is present in an exemplary way in the Marian field. If Marian devotion is lacking, the churches become empty. In a bitter critique, Hans Urs von Balthasar observes:

> Without mariology Christianity threatens imperceptibly to become inhuman. The Church becomes functionalistic, soulless, a hectic enterprise without any point of rest, estranged from her true nature by the planners. And because, in this manly-masculine world, all that we have is one ideology replacing another, everything becomes polemical, critical, bitter, humorless, and ultimately boring, and people in their masses run away from such a Church.[23]

To sum up, Mariology is a focal point, a "crossroads" of Catholic theology.[24] Looking at the figure of Mary, we reach the entirety of the faith with more persistence and clarity. This explains the particular attention given to her in a visible and exemplary way by the great Mariological-Marian congresses and by the dictionary mentioned earlier.

THE IMPORTANCE OF A DISTINCT TREATISE ON MARIOLOGY

Even once we recognize the central place of Mariology, we still need to clarify its role within dogmatic theology as a whole. In theology we find two diverse schools of thought, visible above all during the

22. See the section "Mary the Woman, in the Context of Anthropology," in chapter 3.

23. Hans Urs von Balthasar, *Elucidations*, trans. John Kenneth Riches (San Francisco: Ignatius Press, 1998), 112–13.

24. This formulation comes from Pozo, "María en la encrucijada de la Teología católica" [Mary at the Crossroads of Catholic Theology], in *María en los Caminos de la Iglesia* [Mary on the Roads of the Church], ed. Centro de Estudios de Teología Espiritual (Madrid: Centro de Estudios de Teologia Espiritual, 1982), 31–53, cited in Ziegenaus, "Häresie," in *ML* 3:68f. See also Scheffczyk, *Maria, crocevia;* Scheffczyk, "Maria: Punto focale dei misteri della fede" [Mary: Focal Point of the Mysteries of the Faith], *RTLu* 9, no. 2 (2004): 283–94; Scheffczyk, *Il mondo della fede Cattolica: Verità e forma; Con un'intervista a Benedetto XVI* [The World of the Catholic Faith: Truth and Form; including an Interview with Benedict XVI], trans. Alessio Musio (Milan: Vita e Pensiero, 2007), 249–74.

1950s and at the beginning of Vatican II: a somewhat Christocentric tendency and another that is ecclesiocentric.[25] The Christocentric (or "Christotypical") tendency insists above all on the divine maternity of Mary and derives from this principle all the other privileges of our Lady. Here Mary appears intimately associated with Jesus Christ and faces us along with him. The ecclesiocentric (or "ecclesiotypical") tendency, in contrast, describes Mary most of all as a "type of the Church": in the Blessed Virgin, in her openness to Christ, we find the essential traits of the reality of the church.

Both tendencies have their advantages and their risks. The Christotypical tendency clearly emphasizes the distinction between Mary and the other members of the church, but it risks obscuring the exemplary role of the Mother of our Lord for the whole church. Mary is not only our spiritual mother, but also the example of faith, hope, and charity that we need during our earthly journey. The ecclesiotypical tendency, on the other hand, highlights the solidarity of Mary with the church and her particular position in the mystery of the covenant; the risk is one of forgetting the transcendence of Mary vis-à-vis the church: our Lady is not a member of the church like all the others, but exercises a maternal role for the whole ecclesial community. To underscore this: Mary is not only our "sister" as a type of the church, but is also the "Mother of the Church."

Later we will study how the confrontation between these two tendencies influenced the work of the Council. The fruit in each case is a sort of healthy compromise: on one hand Mariology is placed in the Dogmatic Constitution of the Church; on the other hand, Paul VI solemnly proclaimed the title "Mary, Mother of the Church." And the title of the last chapter of *Lumen gentium* refers to Mary "in the mystery of Christ and of the Church."

For a scholarly presentation, placing this field neither within Christology nor in ecclesiology is advisable. A distinct treatise is better, one that highlights on one hand the transcendence of Mary vis-à-vis the church and, on the other hand, highlights her own role in the mystery of Christ. Mary, simply by being nearest to the per-

25. See "The Contribution of Vatican II," in chapter 2.

son and work of the Redeemer, is redeemed (preserved from original sin); at the same time, by the same nearness to the Redeemer, Mary is the spiritual mother for the whole church because of her cooperation in the work of salvation.[26]

A particularly important document for the teaching of Mariology was published on March 25, 1988, by the Congregation for Catholic Education: the Letter on the Virgin Mary in intellectual and spiritual formation.[27] This letter, a fruit of the Marian Year 1987–88, vigorously reaffirms the place owed to mariological teaching:

The teaching of Mariology is to be conveyed in a "systematic treatment" that will be (a) organic—that is, "inserted adequately in the program of studies of the theological curriculum"; (b) "complete, so that the person of the Virgin be considered in the whole history of salvation, that is, in her relation to God; to Christ, the Word incarnate, Saviour and Mediator; to the Holy Spirit, the Sanctifier and Giver of life; to the Church, sacrament of salvation; to man—in his origins and his development in the life of grace, and his destiny to glory"; and (c) "suited to the various types of institution … and to the level of the students."[28]

It does not state explicitly that Mariology must be a distinct course, but that is an almost natural consequence. The Congregation for Education "has clearly opted for a unitary course on Mariology."[29] Otherwise it would be difficult to implement the concept of

26. See Ziegenaus, "Der Weg zu einem geschlossenen mariologischen Traktat in den dogmatischen Handbüchern des deutschsprachigen Raumes" [The Way to a Self-Contained Treatise on Mariology in the Dogmatic Handbooks of the German-Speaking Countries], *FKTh* 12, no. 2 (1996): 102–26. See also Ziegenaus, *Maria in der Heilsgeschichte*, 10–28; Scheffczyk, *Maria, crocevia*, 51–68.

27. Congregation for Catholic Education, Letter *The Virgin Mary in Intellectual and Spiritual Formation*, March 25, 1988 (Italian text in *EV* 11, n. 283–324). A point-by-point analysis is provided by Ignazio Calabuig, OSM, "L'insegnamento della mariologia nei documenti ecclesiali dal decreto conciliare 'Optatam totius' alla lettera circolare (25-III-1988) della Congregazione per l'Educazione Cattolica" [The Teaching of Mariology in Church Documents, from the Conciliar Decree *Optatam totius* to the Circular Letter (March 25, 1988) of the Congregation for Catholic Education], in *La Mariologia nell'organizzazione delle discipline teologiche: Collocazione e metodo* [Mariology in the Organization of the Theological Disciplines: Locus and Method], ed. E. Peretto (Rome: Marianum, 1992), 194–255. See also Perrella, *L'insegnamento della mariologia ieri e oggi* [The Teaching of Mariology Yesterday and Today] (Padua: Messaggero, 2012), 142–75.

28. Congregation for Catholic Education, *Virgin Mary*, n. 28 (*EV* 11, n. 314).

29. Calabuig, "L'insegnamento," 250.

a systematic treatment that is organic, complete, and adapted to the various levels of instruction. The unitary course, obviously, would not be isolated from numerous relations with other theological disciplines that contain various references to the Mother of God. The curial document cites in particular Christology, ecclesiology, pneumatology, supernatural anthropology, and eschatology: "Mariology is closely connected with these fields."[30]

METHODOLOGICAL PLAN

The study proposed here is intended as an introduction to Mariology. It concentrates on dogmatic aspects that integrate the biblical basis, historical investigation, and systematic reflection. It is intended for anyone interested in exploring the topic at a scholarly level, but in a simple and clear manner. Among readers, students of theology will probably be foremost, but also priests, deacons, and other people involved in the pastoral or catechetical spheres. An introduction, obviously, does not provide a treatment of all the aspects one can think of, but offers basic concepts as well as a springboard for higher explorations, thanks above all to the bibliographical references.[31] Through the critical bibliography, various linguistic regions are present: first of all, the Italian, but also the Spanish, French, English, and (with a particular emphasis, because of the author's origin) the German. This linguistic variety corresponds to the lived experience at the Faculty of Theology at Lugano that brings together students of many and varied nations, as do the theological faculties in Rome.

There are handbooks that offer a systematic plan without taking an interest in the biblical basis and the historical genesis of the dogmatic teachings, and there are also texts that furnish a historical journey without deepening the systematic view. The present intro-

30. Congregation for Catholic Education, *Virgin Mary*, n. 22 (EV 11, n. 308).

31. A virtually complete bibliography of recent decades is available, thanks to the "Marianum" Theological Faculty in Giuseppe Maria Besutti, OSM, ed., *Bibliografia mariana*, 8 vols. (Rome: Marianum, 1950–93); Ermanno M. Toniolo, OSM, ed., *Bibliografia mariana*, vol. 9 (1990–1993) (Rome: Marianum, 1998); Silvano M. Danieli, ed., *Bibliografia mariana*, vols. 10–14 (1994–2011) (Rome: Marianum, 2005–13). Volumes 1–13 are available online at http://www.culturamariana.com/.

duction will seek to unite the diachronic (historical) view with the synchronic (systematic) view. In this way we will use both "eyes" of theology, the "historical" and the "philosophical."[32] Furthermore, after more than fifty years, it seems worthwhile to reaffirm the precious request of Vatican II regarding Mariology in its decree on the formation of future priests, one that by its nature applies to all theology students:

> Dogmatic theology should be so arranged that these biblical themes are proposed first of all. Next there should be opened up to the students what the Fathers of the Eastern and Western Church have contributed to the faithful transmission and development of the individual truths of revelation. The further history of dogma should also be presented, account being taken of its relation to the general history of the Church. Next, in order that they may illumine the mysteries of salvation as completely as possible, the students should learn to penetrate them more deeply with the help of speculation, under the guidance of St. Thomas, and to perceive their interconnections. They should be taught to recognize these same mysteries as present and working in liturgical actions and in the entire life of the Church. They should learn to seek the solutions to human problems under the light of revelation, to apply the eternal truths of revelation to the changeable conditions of human affairs and to communicate them in a way suited to men of our day.[33]

A first consequence of this very demanding program is a distinct presentation of biblical teaching. In this way, the revealed basis of doctrine in the word of God is emphasized. This biblical presentation is also important for ecumenical dialogue. Yet the word of God is conveyed authoritatively by the community of the church of roughly two thousand years. For this reason, sacred Scripture and sacred Tradition "are to be accepted and venerated with the same sense of loyalty and reverence."[34] In an introductory presentation, it is not possible to cover all the stages of the history of Mariology in

32. On this image from Ignaz von Döllinger, see Scheffczyk, *Katholische Dogmatik,* vol. 1, *Grundlagen des Dogmas: Einleitung in die Dogmatik* [Catholic Dogmatics, vol. 1, Foundations of Dogma: Introduction to Dogmatic Theology] (Aachen: MM-Verlag, 1997), 204.

33. Second Vatican Council, *Optatam totius* (October 28, 1965), 16.

34. Second Vatican Council, *Dei Verbum* (November 18, 1965), 9.

which Tradition makes itself manifest. Notwithstanding that, at least a global tour of the development of Mariology will be offered in its own chapter. Later, some particularly important elements will be integrated into the study of the various systematic views.

In 2000, the Pontifical International Marian Academy (PAMI) published an extensive Letter that offers "a discussion of the Marian questions currently investigated, discussed, and debated."[35] In this reflection there are also some clues about method. It is appropriate, the authors hold, to keep "a constant reference to the history of salvation," as called for by Vatican II in *Optatam totius*, no. 16.[36] The relationship of Mary with Christ and the church, reaffirmed by the Council, extends "in its vertical and horizontal dimensions: vertically Mary is viewed in a Trinitarian perspective because of the threefold relation ... which she has with the three Divine Persons; horizontally, Mary is viewed in her relation, first to the Church, and then to humanity and the universe."[37] There is also serious consideration of the "way of beauty" that shows the splendor of truth and grace in the blessed Virgin by means of the artistic and symbolic view.[38] Then an invitation to the "way of experience" follows, drawing on the lives of the saints, authentic witnesses of the faith.[39] Finally, PAMI makes note of interdisciplinary and narrative views in the "priority of 'the experience of Mary' over 'reasoning about Mary.'"[40]

We will take these precious clues into account within the limits of this doctrinal introduction. Still, it also seems appropriate that we point out the need to develop the speculative view that a systematic

35. Pontificia Academia Mariana Internationalis (hereinafter PAMI), *La Madre del Signore: Memoria presenza speranza; Alcune questioni attuali sulla figura e la missione della beata Vergine Maria* (Vatican City: PAMI, 2000), 5. Available online in Italian at https://www.pami.info/copia-di-maiora-in-dies. English translation: PAMI, *The Mother of the Lord: Memory, Presence, Hope* (Staten Island, N.Y.: St. Paul, 2007), ix.

36. PAMI, *Mother of the Lord*, n. 31.

37. Ibid., n. 32.

38. Ibid., n. 33. For a deeper view of this aspect, see Alfonso Langella, ed., *Via pulchritudinis et Mariologia* [The Way of Beauty and Mariology] (Rome: AMII, 2003). Also see the section "Fullness of Grace," in chapter 6.

39. PAMI, *Mother of the Lord*, nn. 34–35.

40. Ibid., nn. 36–37. For a critical appraisal of PAMI's presentation, see the review by Hauke, "Pontificia Accademia Mariana Internationalis, La Madre del Signore. Memoria Presenza Speranza," *RTLu* 9, no. 2 (2004): 500–504.

overview of Mariology provides. We will take into account the philosophical basis of each dogmatic exposition and the "analogy of faith" or, rather, the "coherence of the truths of faith among themselves and within the whole plan of Revelation."[41] In this study of Mariology the greatest works of the "Marian era" are also integrated, from the time of Pius IX to Pius XII—such as, for example, the great contribution of Gabriele Maria Roschini, OSM,[42] and the magisterial synthesis by the Belgian theologian Benoît-Henri Merkelbach, OP.[43] Vatican II is not seen as a rupture that puts all the works of the past into the wastebasket,[44] but as an important stage in a development that adds value to studies done before and discovers new directions for the future. This way between *nova et vetera* takes particular inspiration from the magisterium of Pope John Paul II, who left an immense heritage to be appraised through the work of mariologists.[45]

41. *Catechism of the Catholic Church* (hereinafter *CCC*), 2nd ed. (Vatican City: Libreria Editrice Vaticana, 2000), n. 114.

42. See Pietro Parrotta, "La cooperazione di Maria alla Redenzione in Gabriele Maria Roschini" [Mary's Cooperation in the Redemption in Gabriele Maria Roschini], CdM 3 (Lugano: Eupress FTL, 2002); "Atto accademico nel venticinquesimo della morte di fra Gabriele M. Roschini, OSM" [Symposium on the Twenty-Fifth Anniversary of the Death of Friar Gabriele M. Roschini, OSM], *Marianum* 64, no. 161–62 (2002): 549–606 (essays, inter alia, by A. Amato and M. Hauke). Consider Gabriele M. Roschini, *La Madonna: Secondo la fede e la teologia* [The Madonna: According to the Faith and Theology], 4 vols. (Rome: Libreria Editrice Francesco Ferrari, 1953–54); Roschini, *Maria Santissima nella storia della salvezza: Trattato completo di mariologia alla luce del Concilio Vaticano II* [Mary Most Holy, in the History of Salvation: Complete Treatise on Mariology in Light of the Second Vatican Council], 4 vols. (Isola del Liri: Pisani, 1969).

43. Benoît-Henri Merkelbach, OP, *Mariologia* (Paris: Desclée, 1939). See Richard Schenk, "Merkelbach," in *ML* 4:424; Hauke, "Merkelbach, Benoît Henri," in *Thomistenlexikon* [Encyclopedia of Thomists], edited by D. Berger and J. Vijgen (Bonn: Nova et Vetera, 2006), 458–63.

44. See Benedict XVI, *Christmas Address to the Roman Curia*, December 22, 2005 [Italian text in *Insegnamenti di Benedetto XVI*, vol. 1 (Vatican City: Libreria Editrice Vaticana, 2006), 1018–32; Hauke, "Das Zweite Vatikanum und die Überlieferung: Eine wichtige Wegweisung von Papst Benedikt XVI" [The Second Vatican Council and Tradition: An Important Guidepost by Pope Benedict XVI], *Theologisches* 36, no. 3–4 (2006): 90–94.

45. See also Ziegenaus, ed., *Totus tuus: Maria in Leben und Lehre Johannes Pauls II* [Totally Yours: Mary in the Life and Teaching of John Paul II], Mariologische Studien 1 (Regensburg: Friedrich Pustet, 2004); Arthur B. Calkins, *Totus tuus: John Paul II's Program of Marian Consecration and Entrustment* (New Bedford, Mass.: Academy of the Immaculate, 1992); Perrella, *Ecco tua Madre (Gv 19,27): La Madre di Gesù nel magistero di Giovanni Paolo II e nell'oggi della Chiesa e del mondo* [Behold Your Mother (Jn 19:27): The Mother of Jesus in the Magisterium of John Paul II and in the Church and the World Today] (Cinisello Balsamo: San Paolo, 2007); and see "The Post-Conciliar Period," in chapter 2.

THE STRUCTURE OF THE FOLLOWING PRESENTATION

After the introduction we will turn our attention to the biblical foundations of Mariology. In a brief historical run-through, we will try to see the grand lines of development of Marian devotion and of Mariology. The principal part of the study will be dedicated to the systematic synthesis, which will also deepen the biblical background (where necessary) and the historical development of the topics under consideration.

The "nucleus," which can be found in all contemporary handbooks on Mariology, consists of explaining the four (principal) "Marian dogmas": her divine maternity, her virginity, her Immaculate Conception (that is, freedom from original sin), and her bodily Assumption into Heaven; also, we will remember to include some signposts for Marian devotion, to distinguish the honor due to our Lady (and to the saints) from adoration that is rendered only to God.

The current treatise, respecting the need to present this "nucleus," will seek to build the topics into an organic structure, to understand better how Mary "since her entry into salvation history unites in herself and re-echoes the greatest teachings of the faith."[46] This is why we will begin by considering some starting points for systematic reflection. We will pose the question of the "fundamental principle" and of the role of Mary in the mystery of the Covenant, a particularly valuable theme in the renewal of Mariology in the twentieth century. Inasmuch as the theme of the Covenant gives value to feminine symbolism as an expression of creation's self-giving to God, we will add an anthropological reflection that points to the role of Mary as woman in the mystery of salvation.

The "four Marian dogmas" will be presented in this way: first the divine maternity and the perpetual virginity; then the Immaculate Conception, which appears in the more global context of the "holiness" of Mary; finally, the Assumption into Heaven, which integrates

46. *LG* 65.

in itself the eschatological aspect of Mariology and queenship. The theme of the Immaculate Heart will conclude the chapter on holiness.

While the "four Marian dogmas" have been given a precise magisterial formulation, other propositions no less central have need of more theological work. This applies above all to the mediation of Mary, which is articulated on two levels: first, that of cooperation in the work of salvation, concentrating on her consent to the Incarnation and at the foot of the cross; then the intercession of Mary for the distribution of graces. The first level relates to objective redemption (the offering of salvation on the part of Jesus Christ), the second level to subjective redemption (the coming of salvation to individual persons). Debate, often controversial, revolves around the titles of "mediatrix" and "co-redemptrix." A theme very near to that of mediation, and therefore treated in the context of mediation, is the spiritual motherhood of Mary.

The mediation of Mary can also be described as participation in the three ministries of Christ as prophet, king, and priest. The chapter on mediation sets forth the maternal priesthood of Mary, her queenship in the context of the Assumption, while her prophetic role expresses itself particularly compellingly in apparitions. It is a delicate topic, but one of great systematic and pastoral importance. Marian apparitions are rightly called "the field most neglected, unknown, and least researched, in a scholarly manner, in all of theology."[47] It will not be possible to present this "unknown continent" exhaustively; but we will give some indications of the systematic value of Marian apparitions in regard to the faith and of the criteria to be applied in specific cases.

Chapter 10 is dedicated to the cult of Mary—that is, to the veneration of Mary and its diverse forms. The theological value of the principal devotions will also be studied—such as, for example, the consecration to Mary according to Louis-Marie Grignion de Mont-

47. René Laurentin, "Die Marienerscheinungen: Ihre Bedeutung, ihr Wert, ihre wesentliche Botschaft" [Marian Apparitions: Their Meaning, Their Value, and Their Relevant Message], in *Maria in Leben und Lehre der Kirche* [Mary in the Life and Teaching of the Church], ed. Franz Breid (Steyr: Ennsthaler Verlag, 1995), 11.

fort, particularly recommended by John Paul II in his encyclical *Redemptoris Mater.*[48]

For Marian devotion we also need a certain ecumenical sensitivity that does not diminish Marian piety, but at the same time keeps in mind possible misunderstandings on the part of separated brethren. Ecumenical difficulties, above all on the part of Protestants, will be presented in the appropriate chapters, as well as the possibility of promoting the unity of Christians in the fullness of Catholic truth.

Finally, we will offer an appendix with various interesting internet addresses for those wishing to keep up to date on our field. We will list the bibliography of sources used in this work and various indexes (biblical passages, names, and topics).

48. John Paul II, Encyclical *Redemptoris Mater* (hereinafter *RM*) (March 25, 1987), n. 48; English: *Mother of the Redeemer*, anniversary ed. (Boston: Pauline Books and Media, 2012).

One

Biblical Foundations

OLD TESTAMENT PREPARATIONS

Introductory Note

Mary is a personage of the *New* Testament. Yet, as the coming of Jesus Christ was prepared in many ways in the history of Israel and in the OT, the coming of the mother of the Messiah was also foretold in the old covenant. Certainly, these threads only become visible thanks to the revelation of the NT.[1]

The theological relationship between the OT and the NT is anything but a simple topic. For this reason we find rather diverse assessments of the role of the OT for Mariology. Many textbooks begin their biblical overview abruptly with the NT, without reviewing the topic of Old Testament preparation. According to another school of thought, less common today, the presence of Mary can be found in almost every page of the OT. For a balanced presentation, we need to make some distinctions first.

For the interpretation of Scripture, the literal sense is funda-

1. Irenaeus declared, "The treasure hid in the Scriptures is Christ, since He was pointed out by means of types and parables. Hence his human nature could not be understood, prior to the consummation of those things which had been predicted, that is, the advent of Christ"; Irenaeus, *Adversus haereses* IV.26, in *Sources chrétiennes* (hereinafter *SC*) (Paris: *Éditions du Cerf*, 1941–), 100:712; English trans. Alexander Roberts and James Donaldson, eds., *Ante-Nicene Fathers 1885–1887* (hereinafter *ANF*) (Peabody, Mass.: Hendrickson, 1994), 1:496; Anton Ziegenaus, *Katholische Dogmatik*, vol. 5, *Maria in der Heilsgeschichte: Mariologie* [Catholic Dogmatics, vol. 5, Mary in Salvation History: Mariology] (Aachen: MM-Verlag, 1998), 161–64, differentiates this approach (which implies a history of revelation) from that of Justin (Is 7:14 as a direct prophecy of the virgin birth) and that of Origen (the OT as allegory; in that way a history of revelation does not exist, but only a history of the revelation of its hidden meaning).

mental; only by means of the literal sense can anyone prove an argument.[2] The literal sense of Scripture "is that which has been expressed directly by the inspired human authors. Since it is the fruit of inspiration, this sense is also intended by God, as principal author. One arrives at this sense by means of a careful analysis of the text, within its literary and historical context."[3]

The literal sense, in turn, can be a sign of another reality foreseen in the plan of God. In this case one speaks of the "spiritual sense," the sense "expressed by the biblical texts when read under the influence of the Holy Spirit, in the context of the paschal mystery of Christ and of the new life which flows from it."[4] According to the Pontifical Biblical Commission, the literal sense and the spiritual sense can be identical if the Old Testament text is referring to the mystery of Christ and to the new life coming from it. The *sensus plenior*, in contrast, is the deeper sense willed by God, even if its content is not clearly expressed by the human author. This "full(er)" sense is revealed when the texts are contemplated in the light of subsequent passages or in their relation to the development of Revelation. As an example of the *sensus plenior*, the Biblical Commission mentions the prophecy of Isaiah 7:14 as seen from Matthew 1:23 ("the virgin will conceive and bear a son").[5]

The *sensus plenior* as a "spiritual sense" is to be distinguished from "accommodation." Accommodation is the interpretation of a biblical passage with regard to a content that per se has nothing to do with the text itself, but can be illustrated with the scriptural example. As an example, we can take the analogy of the intercession of Mary with the ladder reaching up to heaven (Gn 28:12), or the analogy of the virginal motherhood of Mary with the burning bush that was not consumed (Ex 3:2).[6] The "Litany of Loreto" and the *Akathist*

2. See Thomas Aquinas, *ST* I, q. 1, a. 10, ad 1. For biblical hermeneutics, see, in addition to Vatican II, *Dei Verbum* (November 18, 1965), 12, the document of the Pontifical Biblical Commission (hereinafter PBC), *The Interpretation of the Bible in the Church* (Vatican City: Libreria Editrice Vaticana, 1993), especially II.B and III.A. See also, more briefly, *CCC* 109–19.

3. PBC, *Interpretation of the Bible in the Church,* II.B.1 (Ital. text in *EV* 13, n. 2997).

4. PBC, II.B.2 (*EV* 13, n. 3003).

5. PBC, II.B.3 (*EV* 13, nn. 3010f).

6. See, for example, in the Liturgy of the Hours, Evening Prayer II of January 1, third antiphon:

Hymn are loaded with Old Testament images; we also find an impressive list in the bull *Ineffabilis Deus* of Pius IX from 1854 (definition of the Immaculate Conception).[7] The illustrative method of accommodation appears numerous times in liturgical texts. Some examples: the recitation of Psalm 87 (86) with the concluding verse "All my springs are in you" (Ps 87:7);[8] the analogy with Judith who is honored (Jdt 15:9)[9] "above all women" for having struck "the head of the leader of our enemies" (Jdt 13:18);[10] the intercession of Esther; the bride of the messianic king of Psalm 45 (44) and the bride

"Moses saw the thornbush which was on fire yet was not burnt up. In it we see a sign of your virginity which all must honour; Mother of God, pray for us." English text from *Morning and Evening Prayer* (Dublin: Talbot Press, 1976), 80. Or Ez 44:2: the glory of God enters the temple through closed doors. See also the reference to closed doors as a symbol of Mary's virginity *in partu* at p. 188.

7. "Accordingly, the Fathers have never ceased to call the Mother of God the lily among thorns, the land entirely intact, the Virgin undefiled, immaculate, ever blessed, and free from all contagion of sin, she from whom was formed the new Adam, the flawless, brightest, and most beautiful paradise of innocence, immortality and delights planted by God himself and protected against all the snares of the poisonous serpent, the incorruptible wood that the worm of sin had never corrupted, the fountain ever clear and sealed with the power of the Holy Spirit, the most holy temple, the treasure of immortality, the one and only daughter of life—not of death—the plant not of anger but of grace, through the singular providence of God growing ever green." English translation available online at clerus.va (website of the Congregation for the Clergy). See *Enchiridion delle encicliche* (hereinafter *EE*) (Bologna: EDB, 1994–98), 2, nn. 751f.

8. In the Liturgy of the Hours, this text appears as the third psalm of the Office of Readings, in the Common of the Blessed Virgin Mary (hereinafter BVM): *Liturgia Horarum* (Vatican City: Libreria Editrice Vaticana, 2000), 3:1427; in the Mass, it appears as the responsorial psalm for the Marian Mass "Our Lady of the Cenacle," in Congregation for Divine Worship, *Lectionarium pro missis de beata Maria Virgine* (Vatican City: Libreria Editrice Vaticana, 1987), n. 17; also, "The Blessed Virgin Mary, Queen of Apostles" (n. 18), and "The Blessed Virgin Mary, Image and Mother of the Church" (n. 26). The text of the psalm refers to Jerusalem, which will be "the sacred metropolis and mother of all peoples," Jerusalem Bible (hereinafter JB), note. Jerusalem is a type representing the Church, that finds its exemplary realization in Mary. Because of this we can speak of an "accommodation with a basis in reality," while the analogy with the burning bush is a "merely verbal accommodation."

9. Common of the BVM, Morning Prayer, antiphon 2: *Liturgia Horarum*, 3:1435; also, *Morning and Evening Prayer*, 299*.

10. See the Roman Missal, the Common of the BVM, Mass 3, introit verse: *The Roman Missal* (Washington: USCCB, 2011), 1041. See also John Paul II, "Woman's Indispensable Role in Salvation History," in Marian Catecheses (Catechesi Mariane) (hereinafter CM) 15 (March 27, 1996), in, among other places, John Paul II, *Theotokos: Woman, Mother, Disciple: A Catechesis on Mary, Mother of God* (Boston: Pauline, 2000). The pope recalls in particular Miriam, sister of Moses and Aaron; Deborah, Jael, Huldah, Judith, Esther (the last two more extensively), and Abigail, concluding, "the Old Testament tradition frequently emphasizes the decisive action of women in the salvation of Israel.... In this way the Holy Spirit ... sketches with ever greater precision the characteristics of Mary's mission in the work of salvation for the entire human race." Esther in particular, "playing the role of mediator, intercedes for those who are threatened with destruction."

of the Song of Songs;[11] the use of texts about wisdom (Sir 24:3–21; Prv 8:22–35).[12]

In some cases there is room to debate whether there is a "spiritual sense" (or "typological sense") or instead an "accommodation" *cum fundamento in re* (with a basis in the reality itself). It seems that the spousal images have a typological sense, inasmuch as they bring out the "feminine" aspect of the church that finds its type in Mary. The figure of Wisdom appears with feminine traits, as a mediatrix of creation and salvation history. The twofold character of Wisdom is important for theological explanation. On one hand, she appears as a personification of closeness to God; on the other hand, she is found among the creatures, expressing response to the call of God. While passages on Wisdom are adopted in the NT to illustrate the figure of Christ,[13] the fathers of the church also make use of them to make known the pneumatological dimension[14] and the mariological view. The pure response of creation to the divine call is perfectly realized in the Mother of God. The beauty of divine Wisdom shines in her maternal mediation.[15]

11. See Joseph Scharbert, "Hoheslied" [Song of Songs], in *ML* 3:232–34; Pozo, "La consagración a los Corazones de Jesús y María en Juan Pablo II," 138–46; Pozo, *María, nueva Eva*, 140–45; L. Manicardi, "Il Salmo 45 (44) e il Cantico dei Cantici" [Psalm 45 (44) and the Song of Songs], *Theotokos* 8, no. 2 (2000): 569–600.

12. See Lectionary index in Congregation for Divine Worship, *Lectionarium pro missis de beata Maria Virgine*; English edition: *Collection of Masses of the Blessed Virgin Mary* (hereinafter *MBVM*). 2 vols. (Collegeville, Minn.: Liturgical Press, 2012).

13. In the prologue of John, for example, the divine Word dwells among us as though he had pitched a tent (Jn 1:14)—an image that looks back to Sir 24:8. For the adoption of the traits of Wisdom into the Christology of the NT, see the various commentaries and Christologies—for example, Ziegenaus, *Katholische Dogmatik*, vol. 4, *Jesus Christus: Die Fülle des Heils* [Catholic Dogmatics, vol. 4, Jesus Christ: The Fullness of Salvation; Christology and Doctrine of the Redemption] (Aachen: MM-Verlag, 2000), 140–45.

14. See Yves Congar, *Je crois en l'Esprit Saint* (Paris: Éditions du Cerf, 1995), 28–32; English translation: *I Believe in the Holy Spirit* (New York: Seabury, 1983), 1:9–12 (repr. New York: Crossroads, 1997).

15. See Louis Bouyer, *Le Trône de la Sagesse: Essai sur la signification du culte marial* (Paris: Éditions du Cerf, 1957); English translation: *The Seat of Wisdom: An Essay on the Place of the Virgin Mary in Christian Theology* (London: Darton, Longman and Todd, 1960); Joseph Ratzinger, *Daughter Zion: Meditations on the Church's Marian Belief* (San Francisco: Ignatius Press, 1983), 25–29; Aristide Serra, "Sapiente" [Wise], in Stefano De Fiores and Salvatore Meo, OSM, eds. *Nuovo dizionario di mariologia* (hereinafter *NDM*) (Milan: San Paolo, 1985), 1272–85; Serra, *La Donna dell'Alleanza: Prefigurazioni di Maria nell'Antico Testamento* [The Woman of the Covenant: Prefigurations of Mary in the Old Testament] (Padua: Messaggero, 2006), 261–308; Leo Scheffczyk, "'Sitz der Weisheit': Maria–Bild vollendeten Menschseins" ["Seat of Wisdom": Mary, Image

In any case, two central texts that the church's tradition has interpreted as foretelling the Savior and his mother are not considered accommodations: Genesis 3:15 and Isaiah 7:14. Before reflecting on these passages, let us cite an important text from *Lumen gentium*:

The Sacred Scriptures of both the Old and the New Testament, as well as ancient Tradition show the role of the Mother of the Saviour in the economy of salvation in an ever clearer light and draw attention to it. The books of the Old Testament describe the history of salvation, by which the coming of Christ into the world was slowly prepared. These earliest documents, as they are read in the Church and are understood in the light of a further and full revelation, bring the figure of the woman, Mother of the Redeemer, into a gradually clearer light. When it is looked at in this way, she is already prophetically foreshadowed in the promise of victory over the serpent which was given to our first parents after their fall into sin. Likewise she is the Virgin who shall conceive and bear a son, whose name will be called Emmanuel. (cf. Is 7:14; Mi 5:2–3; Mt 1:22–23). She stands out among the poor and humble of the Lord, who confidently hope for and receive salvation from Him. With her the exalted Daughter of Sion, and after a long expectation of the promise, the times are fulfilled and the new Economy established, when the Son of God took a human nature from her, that He might in the mysteries of His flesh free man from sin.[16]

To distinguish the various types of Old Testament preparation for the person of Mary, we can use a threefold schema.[17] We find:

---

of Humanity Fulfilled], *Sedes Sapientiae: Mariologisches Jahrbuch* 2, no. 1 (1998): 48–69; Raymund Noll, *Die mariologischen Grundlinien im exegetischen Werk des Cornelius a Lapide (1567–1637)* [Mariological Outlines in the Exegetical Work of Cornelius a Lapide, SJ], Mariologische Studien 16 (Regensburg: Friedrich Pustet, 2003), 142–51 (explanation of Cornelius a Lapide); Philippe Lefebvre, *La Vierge au Livre: Marie et l'Ancien Testament* [The Virgin of the Book: Mary and the Old Testament] (Paris: Les Éditions du Cerf, 2004), 185–207; Stefano M. Manelli, FI, *All Generations Shall Call Me Blessed: Biblical Mariology*, 2nd ed. (New Bedford, Mass.: Academy of the Immaculate, 2005), 88–91; Nuria Calduch-Benages, "Sapienza" [Wisdom], in Stefano De Fiores, Valeria Ferrari Schiefer, and Salvatore M. Perrella, eds., *Mariologia* (hereinafter *DMar*), Dizionari San Paolo (Cinisello Balsamo: San Paolo, 2009), 1059–72; Gisbert Greshake, *Maria–Ecclesia: Perspektiven einer marianisch grundierten Theologie und Kirchenpraxis* [Mary– Church: Perspectives of a Marian-Based Theology and Church Praxis] (Regensburg: Pustet, 2014), 301–42.

16. *LG* 55.

17. See René Laurentin, *A Short Treatise on the Virgin Mary* (Washington, N.J.: Ave Maria Institute, 1991), 267–71; Miguel Ponce Cuéllar, *María, Madre del Redentor y Madre de la Iglesia* [Mary, Mother of the Redeemer and Mother of the Church], 2nd ed. (Barcelona: Herder, 2001), 53–67.

1. a *moral preparation.* In the history of Israel, God traces a line of faith and holiness that leads to the mother of the Messiah.[18] The *Magnificat* hints at this circle of the faithful when it speaks of the "poor" of Israel who depend on the intervention of the Lord for everything (Lk 1:48, 1:52). The conciliar text affirms that Mary is the first "among the poor and humble of the Lord."

2. a *typological preparation.* The OT brings us "sketches," "figures" that lead to fulfillment in the New Testament. "Throughout the Old Covenant the mission of Mary was *prepared for* by the mission of holy women. At the beginning there was Eve; despite her disobedience, she receives the promise of a posterity that will be victorious over the evil one, and the promise that she will be the mother of all the living. By virtue of this promise, Sarah conceives a son in spite of her old age. Against all human expectation God chooses what was considered powerless and weak to show his faithfulness to his promise: Hannah, the mother of Samuel; Deborah; Ruth; Judith and Esther; and many other women."[19] Most prominent among the feminine figures are the "daughter of Zion" (a symbolic figure to which we shall return), the great mothers of Israel, women involved with the salvation of the people, and women favored with miraculous births. We will see how the infancy narrative according to Luke particularly alludes to such antecedent events.

3. a *prophetic preparation.* This deals with prophetic texts that look directly at the mother of the Messiah, hence at Mary. The Council lists three for us: Genesis 3:15; Isaiah 7:14; and Micah 5:2–3. Since the last of these is close to the second, we will study in the following pages only Genesis 3:15 (the "Protoevangelium") and Isaiah 7:14 (the birth of Emmanuel).

18. See John Paul II, CM 16 (Apr. 10, 1996), "The ideal woman is a precious treasure."

19. *CCC* 489; See John Paul II, CM of Mar. 27 and Apr. 10, 1996. On the "mothers of Israel" in preparation for the Mother of God, see Serra, *La Donna dell'Alleanza*, 19–94; Giorgio Paximadi, "L'importanza salvifica della donna nell'Antico Testamento" [The Salvific Importance of Woman in the Old Testament], in *La donna e la salvezza: Maria e la vocazione femminile* [Woman and Salvation: Mary and the Feminine Vocation], ed. Manfred Hauke, CdM 7 (Lugano: Eupress FTL, 2006) 11–27; Alberto Valentini, *Maria secondo le Scritture: Figlia di Sion e Madre del Signore* [Mary according to the Scriptures: Daughter of Zion and Mother of the Lord] (Bologna: EDB, 2007), 394–98.

The "Protoevangelium" (Genesis 3:15)

As its first text the Council cites Genesis 3:15, the so-called "Protoevangelium."[20] According to this verse, God said to the serpent, "I will put enmity between you and the woman, between your seed and her seed: he will bruise your head and you will bruise his heel."

This passage, seen in its original context, describes the struggle between the forces of evil and humanity, the offspring of the woman. The serpent attacks the heel—that is, tries to do harm to men—but ultimately will be defeated.

The implicit biblical tradition has already set the ancient promise in a context of messianic salvation.[21] Following this path, the Septuagint (= LXX, the most important Greek translation of the OT) makes the victorious "seed" of the woman concrete in a personal way: *autós*, "he," will bruise the serpent's head. Here the use of a masculine pronoun (*autós*) for the neuter noun *tò spérma* (the seed, the offspring) is significant. "He" is a concrete person, not simply humanity in general. The messianic context appears more clearly here, and it is also present in the Hebrew interpretation of the Targum.[22] But the two interpretations for "offspring" (the Messiah/humanity) do not exclude one another, because the Messiah also represents humanity before God.

The Vulgate (the Latin translation of the Bible developed by Je-

20. See, among others, Laurentin, "L'interprétation de Genèse 3,15 dans la tradition jusqu'au début du XIII siècle" [The Interpretation of Genesis 3:15 in Tradition, up to the Beginning of the 13th Century], *Études Mariales* 12 (1954): 79–156; Pozo, "La consagración a los Corazones de Jesús y María en Juan Pablo II," 147–75; Pozo, *María, nueva Eva*, 146–75; Ziegenaus, *Maria in der Heilsgeschichte*, 167–74; Heinz-Lothar Barth, *Ipsa conteret: Maria die Schlangenzertreterin; Philologische und theologische Überlegungen zum Protoevangelium* [She Herself Will Crush: Mary the Treader of the Serpent; Philological and Theological Considerations on the Protoevangelium] (Ruppichteroth: Canisius-Werk, 2000); Ponce Cuéllar, *María*, 58–63; Galot, *Maria, La donna*, 189–91; Stefano M. Manelli, *All Generations*, 2–19; Settimio M. Manelli, "Gen 3,15 e l'Immacolata Corredentrice" [Gen. 3:15 and the Immaculate Coredemptrix], *Immaculata Mediatrix* 5 (2005): 17–63; Serra, *La Donna dell'Alleanza*, 249–59.

21. Specifically: the "Yahwist," one strain of the Pentateuch that tends to use the name "Yahweh" for God. The Yahwist, according to current exegetical theories, wrote during the Davidic kingdom, in the tenth century B.C. The books of Moses were formed in a long process of redaction from the time of Moses (thirteenth century B.C.) until about 400 B.C. The "Yahwist" knows well the promise of God given to David through the prophet Nathan: a descendant of David will have a kingdom that will last forever (2 Sm 7).

22. See Ziegenaus, *Maria in der Heilsgeschichte*, 168f.; Serra, *La Donna dell'Alleanza*, 250f.

rome) preferred a Marian interpretation of the passage: *Ipsa conteret caput tuum*, "She will crush your head."[23] Philologically, this translation is usually considered mistaken, and it was corrected by the recent Neo-Vulgate. But the reference to the woman contains the truth that one cannot separate the Messiah from his Mother, the "new Eve."[24] This perspective arises in the time of the fathers: alongside the parallelism "Adam–Christ," Justin and Irenaeus set another: "Eve–Mary." The "woman" of Genesis is Eve in an imperfect sense, but the meaning of the prophecy is fulfilled perfectly in Mary, the "new Eve," who is radically opposed to the serpent, as mother of the Messiah.[25]

Already in Genesis 3:15 there is talk of "enmity" between the serpent and the woman (even while the two are associated in the sin and in the act of punishment). "The aspects of messianic motherhood, of the woman's transcendence in comparison to Eve, and of the text's victorious tone give the text a mariological meaning."[26]

23. The introduction of the *ipsa* probably did not originate with Jerome, but is a later reading. And it is not at all sure that this version developed through a Marian interpretation of the Protoevangelium; the Jew Philo already opposed the woman (*auté* instead of *autós*) to the serpent: *Allegorical Interpretations* 3:188, in *Philo*, trans. F.H. Colson and G.H. Whittaker (Cambridge, Mass.: Harvard University Press, 1981), 1:428–29; Pozo, "La consagración a los Corazones de Jesús y María en Juan Pablo II," 168f.; Pozo, *María, nueva Eva*, 168. The translation in the old Vulgate is defended by Settimio M. Manelli, "Gen 3,15," 36–62; see also Stefano M. Manelli, *All Generations*, 3–4. Note also that the tradition of the Greek fathers attributes the victory over the serpent to Christ, an interpretation also shared by the ancient Latin authors. The saints and the entire church can also participate in this victory. According to Prudentius, who first reads the *ipsa* in the Vulgate (as did Ephrem in the Syrian sphere), Mary crushed the serpent's head because she became the Mother of Christ who conquered the devil; Cathemerinon, hymn. 3: *Corpus Christianorum*, Latin series (hereinafter *CChr. SL*) (Turnhout and Paris: Brepols, 1953f), 126:15f. Only from the Middle Ages onward (eleventh century, with Fulbert of Chartres) is the "crushing" of the serpent's head attributed directly to Mary. Yet the older translation closely connects the Mother of God to the victory of the Redeemer over the diabolical serpent. For the patristic point of view, see Laurentin, "L'interprétation de Genèse 3,15"; Leo Scheffczyk, "Protoevangelium II: Dogmengeschichte" [Protoevangelium II: History of Dogma], in *ML* 5:343–44.

24. See John Paul II, CM 12 ("Victory over Sin Comes through a Woman"), 3 (Jan. 25, 1996): "Exegetes now agree in recognizing that the text of Genesis, according to the original Hebrew, does not attribute action against the serpent directly to the woman, but to her offspring. Nevertheless, the text gives great prominence to the role she will play in the struggle against the tempter: the one who defeats the serpent will be her offspring."

25. See also the references made by John Paul II, *RM*, n. 7, 11, 24 (also Jn 2:4 and Jn 19:27f.; see later, "Mary at the Foot of the Cross"); John Paul II, *Mulieris dignitatem*, 2f., 11. Other texts of the preceding magisterium in Ziegenaus, *Maria in der Heilsgeschichte*, 171f.; Settimio Manelli, "Gen 3,15," 32–36.

26. Ziegenaus, *Maria in der Heilsgeschichte*, 174.

The Prophecy of Isaiah 7:14

The gospel according to Matthew expressly cites Isaiah 7:14 as a proclamation of the virginal origin of Jesus (Mt 1:22f.),[27] and the account of the Annunciation according to Luke also contains some reference to this prophecy.[28] Its historical environment is well known.[29] In 740 B.C. the Assyrian king Tiglat-Pilèzer III entered into the northern part of Syria and (in 734) reached as far as the end of Palestine and the frontier with Egypt. He controlled the Mediterranean coast and the western part of Israel, making it an Assyrian province. Facing this menace, several states of Syria and Palestine made a coalition under the guidance of Rezìn, king of Aram, and Pekach, king of Israel (kingdom of the North). They were also pressing Ahaz, king of Judah, to enter into this alliance against the Assyrians. Ahaz refused, probably motivated by political prudence. The army of the allies marched toward Jerusalem to depose Ahaz and set up a successor allied with them, "the son of Tabeèl" (Is 7:6), therefore a king not coming from the dynasty of David. Ahaz instead considers asking Tiglat-Pilèzer for help.

In this situation Isaiah was given the task of putting Ahaz on guard against an alliance with the Assyrians. The king must trust in the help of God, not in that of the Assyrians. To make the king's decision in favor of God easier, the prophet offered a sign, which Ahaz refused so that he could carry out his alliance with the Assyrians. Then Isaiah announced that God himself will give a sign:

27. See, among others, Aristide Serra, "Bibbia" [Bible], in *NDM*, 241f.; Pozo, "La consagración a los Corazones de Jesús y María en Juan Pablo II," 175–201; Pozo, *María, nueva Eva*, 175–201; Giovanni Odasso, "Il segno dell'Emmanuele nella tradizione dell'Antico Testamento" [The Sign of Emmanuel in the Tradition of the Old Testament], *Theotokos* 4, no. 1 (1996): 151–88; Ziegenaus, *Maria in der Heilsgeschichte*, 174–85; Lefebvre, *La Vierge au Livre*, 143–49; Manelli, *All Generations*, 21–36; Serra, *La Donna dell'Alleanza*, 231–37; Franz Sedlmeier, "Jes 7,14—Überlegungen zu einem umstrittenen Vers und zu seiner Auslegungsgeschichte" [Is. 7:14: Considerations on a Disputed Verse and the History of Its Exegesis], in "*Geboren aus der Jungfrau Maria*": *Klarstellungen* ["Born of the Virgin Mary": Elucidations], ed. A. Ziegenaus, Mariologische Studien 19 (Regensburg: Pustet, 2007), 13–43.

28. See Is 7:14, with Lk 1:26f., 31.

29. See (besides Is) 2 Kgs 15–16. R. Kilian, "Die Geburt des Immanuel aus der Jungfrau: Jes 7,14" [The Birth of Emmanuel from the Virgin: Is. 7:14], in *Zum Thema Jungfrauengeburt* [On the Topic of the Virgin Birth], ed. Karl Suso Frank (Stuttgart: Katholisches Bibelwerk, 1970), 9f.

(14) Behold, a virgin (Hebrew *alma*; LXX: *parthénos*) shall conceive and bear a son, and shall call his name Immanu-el. (15) He shall eat curds and honey when he knows how to refuse the evil and choose the good. (16) For before the child knows how to refuse the evil and choose the good, the land before whose two kings you are in dread will be deserted. (17) The Lord will bring upon you and upon your people and upon your father's house such days as have not come since the day that Ephraim departed from Judah. (Is 7:14–17)

The exegesis of this passage is very diverse. It seems that Isaiah 7:14 is the verse most commented on in the entire OT, and the Jewish philosopher Martin Buber considers it the most controversial biblical passage of all.[30] Nonetheless, a few firm points can be established. There are two levels superimposed in this prophecy. First, we can consider the birth of a son of Ahaz: namely, Hezekiah, who guarantees the permanence of the dynasty of David, promised by the prophet Nathan (2 Sm 7).[31] Otherwise, v. 16 would be incomprehensible: before the boy reaches the age of discretion,[32] the countries allied against Judea will be devastated (which indeed happened in 732). For the other part, the prophecy goes beyond the immediate horizon and toward the birth of the Messiah. This fact is signaled with the name "Emmanu-el" ("God with us") and by the passage's connection with other texts that speak of definitive salvation (Is 8:8, 9:1–6, 11:1–9).[33]

It is typical for prophecy that various future events are seen in the same perspective, as when a view of the starry sky looks as though there were a single light from distinct stars. This unity of prophetic perspective is present not only at various times in the OT, but also in the prophetic proclamation of Jesus: the destruction of Jerusalem and the end of the world are presented as if seen in the same perspective, particularly in the gospel according to Mark (Mk 13). In

30. See Ziegenaus, *Maria in der Heilsgeschichte*, 175.

31. This applies above all if v. 14d is read in this way: "And you will call him Emmanuel"; it would be Ahaz who is to name him, according to the LXX and the first scroll of Isaiah found in the first cave of Qumran: Serra, "Bibbia," 302f., n. 13. Serra, *La Donna dell'Alleanza*, 234: it is an "'indirectly messianic' interpretation, inasmuch as it considers Hezekiah a type of Christ."

32. In this context it amounts to saying: when he is about two years old (see Is 8:4: before he can say "papa" and "mama"). See Serra, "Bibbia," 242.

33. Chapters 6–12 are often called "The Book of Emmanuel" (e.g., as in the Jerusalem Bible).

brief, the prophecy of Isaiah contains a dynamic oriented toward the future, toward the birth of Jesus, the Messiah of the line of David.[34]

The Hebrew term *alma* means "young woman," not necessarily "virgin," although there are no references that call a woman *alma* after a childbirth. An unequivocal term would be *betula*; *alma* can be used as a synonym for *betula*.[35] A clear specification of the term as "virgin" comes with the Septuagint (*parthénos*). Of the seven Hebrew references to *alma* in the OT only two are translated by *parthénos*: Genesis 24:43 (Rebecca, who in v. 16 was called *betula* = "virgin") and Isaiah 7:14. In contrast, it does not seem clear whether the passage is stating the virginity of the mother or not.

The messianic coming is only realized with the birth of Jesus from the Virgin Mary; it is not something one can deduce in its concreteness out of the chiaroscuro of Old Testament prophecy. Nonetheless, in the light of the New Testament, the text of Isaiah finds an impressive correspondence with the Incarnation and the birth of Jesus of the Virgin Mary.[36]

34. This solution is, however, not without problems itself. It seems that Hezekiah was born already before the Syro-Ephraimite war against Judea; so one can ask (as did Justin and Jerome) whether the birth of a boy, by itself, could be a sign (see Ziegenaus, *Maria in der Heilsgeschichte*, 182f.). For this reason it would be possible to consider the text (at least in the final redaction of the book of Isaiah) a prophecy of the birth of the future Messiah, without a connection to the historical situation at the time of Ahaz (e.g., Manelli, *All Generations*, 21–36, although the author also makes reference to the "prophetic perspective" to fend off an objection: 34). To this author, nonetheless, the hypothesis described earlier seems more convincing, even if the text doubtless remains mysterious. Perhaps it was that way for Isaiah, too (see Sedlmeier, "Jes 7,14," 54).

35. As in Gn 24:16, 43. Perhaps not in Sg 6:8, where the *alamot* ("girls") form part of an immense harem; they are distinguished from the "queens" and "brides" (secondary wives). The other passages are Ex 2:8, Ps 68:26, Sg 1:3, Prv 30:18f.

36. John Paul II also speaks on the prophecy in CM 13 (Jan. 31, 1996), concluding the catechesis on "Isaiah's prophecy fulfilled in Incarnation": "The Old Testament does not contain a formal announcement of the virginal motherhood, which was fully revealed only by the New Testament. Nevertheless, Isaiah's prophecy (Is 7:14) prepared for the revelation of this mystery" (n. 7). The papal position corresponds to Galot, *Maria, La donna*, 54, 124.

A certain link with the prophecy of Isaiah seems to be located in Mi 5:2–3, a text also cited by Vatican II (see previously): "(2) But you, O Bethlehem Ephrathah, who are little to be among the clans of Judah, from you shall come forth for me one who is to be ruler in Israel, whose origin is from of old, from ancient days. (3) Therefore he shall give them up until the time when she who has labor pains has brought forth; then the rest of his brethren shall return to the sons of Israel. (4) And he shall stand and feed his flock in the strength of the Lord, in the majesty of the name of the Lord his God. And they shall dwell secure, for now he shall be great to the ends of the earth." On the messianic prophecy of Micah, see Stefano M. Manelli, *All Generations*, 37–42.

The "Daughter of Zion"

Vatican II calls Mary the "exalted daughter of Zion."[37] First, "Zion" refers to the small hill with the fortress of the Jebusites, conquered by David (2 Sm 5:6–9). Thereafter "Zion" becomes a symbol for Jerusalem and for the entire people that finds its center there. It becomes associated with the temple that bears the special protection of God. The pre-exilic prophets denounce a mistaken reliance on the protection of Zion. They foretell the judgment and devastation of the "daughter of Zion." Then the reversal is prophesied: the exiles can return to their country, and on the horizon definitive salvation for the entire world is shining. The third layer of the book of Isaiah (Trito-Isaia) announces the pilgrimage of the people to Jerusalem.[38] "Zion" is described with the image of a mother, full of joy, who gives birth without suffering.[39] Other passages of post-exilic prophecy invite the "daughter of Zion" to rejoice at the presence of God in her midst and at peace for all the peoples.[40]

37. On "daughter of Zion" in general, see Nunzio Lemmo, "Maria, 'Figlia di Sion,' a partire da Lc 1,26–38: Bilancio esegetico dal 1939 al 1982" [Mary, "Daughter of Zion," with Reference to Lk 1:26–38: Exegetical Assessment from 1939 to 1982], *Marianum* 45, no. 130 (1983): 175–258; E. G. Mori, "Figlia di Sion" [Daughter of Zion], in *NDM*, 580–89; Ziegenaus, *Maria in der Heilsgeschichte*, 186–91; Galot, *Maria, La donna*, 42–44; Manelli, *All Generations*, 86f; Serra, *La Donna dell'Alleanza*, 175–220; Elena L. Bartolini, "Figlia di Sion" [Daughter of Zion], in *DMar*, 551–56.

On "daughter of Zion" according to Vatican II, see *LG* 55. See also John Paul II, CM 17 (Apr. 24, 1996), "God Is Ever Faithful to His Covenant."

38. See also Is 2.

39. See Is 66:7–11: "Before she was in labor she gave birth; before her pain came upon her she was delivered of a son. Who has heard such a thing? Who has seen such things? Shall a land be born in one day? Shall a nation be brought forth in one moment? For as soon as Zion was in labor she brought forth her sons.… Rejoice with Jerusalem, and be glad for her, all you who love her; rejoice with her in joy, all you who mourn over her; that you may suck and be satisfied with her consoling breasts."

40. See Zep 3:14–17 ("Sing aloud, O daughter of Zion; shout, O Israel! Rejoice and exult with all your heart, O daughter of Jerusalem! The Lord has taken away the judgments against you, he has cast out your enemies. The king of Israel, the Lord, is in your midst; you shall fear evil no more. On that day it shall be said to Jerusalem: 'Do not fear, O Zion; let not your hands grow weak. The Lord, your God, is in your midst, a warrior who gives victory; he will rejoice over you in gladness, he will renew you in his love; he will exult over you with loud singing as on a day of festival'"); Zec 2:10f. ("Sing and rejoice, O daughter of Zion; for behold, I come and I will dwell in the midst of you"); 9:9f. ("Rejoice greatly, O daughter of Zion! Shout aloud, O daughter of Jerusalem! Behold, your king comes to you; triumphant and victorious is he, humble and riding on a donkey.… I will cut off the chariot from Ephraim …, and the battle bow shall be cut off, and he shall command peace to the nations; his dominion shall be from sea to sea, and from the River to the ends of the earth.")

MARY IN THE NEW TESTAMENT

Mary, Mother of the Son of God (Paul)

The oldest text of the NT regarding Mary is found in the letter to the Galatians:[41]

When the time had fully come, God sent forth his Son, born of woman, born under the law, to redeem those who were under the law, so that we might receive adoption as sons. (Gal 4:4–5)

Paul is not interested in biographical details about the life of Jesus;[42] besides the Incarnation,[43] the Apostle places the cross and the resurrection at the center.[44] This approach leads Paul to be equally sparing in regard to information on the mother of Jesus; he does not even mention her name. The aim of the previous passage is to highlight the true humanity of Jesus (Son of God, "born of woman")[45] and his submission to the law of Moses. The Son of God makes the human and Jewish condition his own in order to make us sharers in the life of God as adoptive sons.

Whereas Paul touches only briefly on the figure of Mary, we can say that Galatians 4:4–5, from the dogmatic point of view, "is the mariologically most significant text of the NT;"[46] the reason is that

41. Written in 57 or perhaps a year or so earlier; see, for example, the commentary of Franz Mussner, *La lettera ai Galati* [The Letter to the Galatians] (Brescia: Paideia, 1987), 50–53. German original: *Der Galaterbrief* (Freiburg im Breisgau: Herder, 1974); 5th ed., 1988; reprinted 2002.

42. See 2 Cor 5:16: now we no longer know Christ "according to the flesh." On this passage see, for example, the comment of Vincenzo Scippa, "Lettere ai Corinzi" [Letters to the Corinthians], in *La Bibbia*, ed. Luciano Pacomio (Casale Monferrato: Piemme, 1995), 2777.

43. Also see in particular Phil 2:5–11.

44. 1 Cor 15:3–8 is emblematic here.

45. The *genómenon* indicates his human origin, not only his birth.

46. Georg Söll, *Storia dei dogmi mariani* [History of Marian Dogmas] (Rome: Libreria Ateneo Salesiano, 1981). German original: *Mariologie* [Handbuch der Dogmengeschichte, vol. 3, part 4] (Freiburg im Breisgau: Herder, 1978), 31. See also Albert Vanhoye, "La Mère de Dieu selon Gal 4,4" [The Mother of God according to Gal 4:4], *Marianum* 40 (1978): 237–47; Aristide Serra, "Galati 4,4: Una mariologia in germe" [Galatians 4:4: A Mariology in Germ], *Theotokos* 1, no. 2 (1993): 7–25; Bruno Forte, *Maria, la donna icona del Mistero: Saggio di mariologia simbolico-narrativa* [Mary the Woman, Icon of the Mystery: Essay in Symbolic-Narrative Mariology], 3rd ed. (Cinisello Balsamo: Ed. Paoline, 1996), 46–49; Ziegenaus, *Maria in der Heilsgeschichte*, 76f.; Franco Manzi, "Tratti mariologici del 'vangelo' di Paolo" [Mariological Features of the "Gospel" of Paul], *Theotokos* 8, no. 2 (2000): 649–89; Manelli, *All Generations*, 125–30; Juan Luis Bastero, *Mary, Mother of the Redeemer* (Dublin: Four Courts, 2006), 81–83; Valentini, *Maria secondo le Scritture*, 29–38.

we implicitly find in it the fundamental dogma of Marian doctrine: the divine maternity. The Son of God is sent into this world; his mission begins with his birth of a woman; hence this woman is the Mother of God. Already in this oldest NT passage Mary is closely linked with the Incarnation; one cannot separate her from her son.

In Paul we find no explicit reference to the virginity of Mary. The true humanity of Jesus, his participation in the human condition, is emphasized.[47] While many modern exegetes are content with this fact,[48] a certain number of interpreters, both ancient and contemporary, also see in Galatians 4:4 an implicit reference to the virginal motherhood of Mary.[49] The fact that it only mentions "the woman," while there is no reference to a human father, is significant. At least it is evident that one cannot invoke the silence of Paul against the virginal conception of Jesus.

The "Son of God" as "Son of Mary" (Mark)

The gospel according to Mark has the aim of highlighting Jesus Christ as "Son of God" (Mk 1:1; see also 1:11, 9:7, 15:39).[50] In contrast to Matthew and Luke, Mark does not hand down any account of the infancy, but begins his presentation with the baptism of Jesus. Mary appears in two passages (Mk 3:20f., 31–35, 6:1–6a).

The first passage describes how the relatives of Jesus ("his own") come out to take him away, because people were saying that the

47. "Born of woman" can also have this meaning elsewhere, e.g., in Mt 11:11: "Among those born of women there has arisen no one greater than John the Baptist." Further references in Salvatore M. Perrella, OSM, *Maria, Vergine e Madre: La verginità feconda di Maria tra fede, storia e teologia* [Mary, Virgin and Mother: The Fruitful Virginity of Mary, in Faith, History, and Theology] (Cinisello Balsamo: San Paolo, 2003), 106.

48. For example, Mussner, *Galati* (on Gal 4:4).

49. On the history of the exegesis, see Emile de Roover, "*La maternité virginale de Marie dans l'interprétation de Gal 4,4*" [The Virginal Motherhood of Mary in the Interpretation of Gal 4:4], in *Studiorum Paulinorum Congressus Internat. Cath. II* [Second International Catholic Congress in Pauline Studies], Analecta Biblica 18 (Rome: Pontifico Istituto Biblico, 1963), 17–37.

50. See Serra, "Bibbia," 233–37; Aristide Serra, "Vergine II: Testimonianza biblica," in *NDM*, 1424–29; Bastero, *Mary, Mother of the Redeemer*, 83–88; Forte, *Maria, la donna icona*, 49–53; Ziegenaus, *Maria in der Heilsgeschichte*, 83–88; Ermenegildo Manicardi, "La madre di Gesù nel Vangelo secondo Marco" [The Mother of Jesus in the Gospel according to Mark], *Theotokos* 8, no. 2 (2000): 691–707; Valentini, *Maria secondo le Scritture*, 39–62.

Lord was acting strangely. When "his mother and brothers" arrive, the Lord calls his disciples—that is, those who fulfill the will of God—"mother" and "brothers."[51]

The gospel according to John also attests to the incomprehension of the "brothers":[52] "Even his brethren did not believe in him" (Jn 7:5). However, the text of Mark does not exclude Mary (or the "brothers") from the believers; instead the evangelist affirms a closeness to Christ that is not determined by family relationship, but by promptness in fulfilling the will of God. Certainly, this is not a polemic against Jesus' relatives, because after Easter the "brothers of the Lord" are members of the Christian community, and James becomes the head of the church of Jerusalem.[53] We know from other sources (in particular Luke 1–2) the exemplary faith of Mary from the beginning. One cannot interpret this episode in an "anti-marian" sense, as happens at times in Protestant exegesis. Also, we need to take account of the fact that the primitive community at Jerusalem met in the house of Mark's mother (Acts 12:12); and Mary, at least between the Ascension and Pentecost, was in Jerusalem (Acts 1:14).

The second passage in Mark presents the rejection of Jesus by the inhabitants of Nazareth.[54] They know Jesus' occupation and his family; they put him in a "normal" context and do not understand his high mission. In this context a rather strange designation appears:

51. Mk 3:20f., 31–35: "He went home, and the crowd came together again, so that they could not even eat. And when his friends heard it, they went out to seize him, for they said, 'He is beside himself.'... And his mother and his brethren came, and standing outside they sent for him and called him. And a crowd was sitting about him, and they said to him, 'Your mother and your brethren are outside, asking for you.' And he replied, 'Who are my mother and my brothers?' And looking around on those who sat about him, he said, 'Here are my mother and my brethren! Whoever does the will of God is my brother, and sister, and mother.'"

52. On the relatives of Jesus (cousins), see "Virginitas post partum," in chapter 5.

53. Acts 1:14; 1 Cor 9:5, 15:7; Gal 1:19, 2:9, 2:12.

54. Mk 6:1–6a: "He went away from there and came to his own country; and his disciples followed him. And on the sabbath he began to teach in the synagogue; and many who heard him were astonished, saying, 'Where did this man get all this? What is the wisdom given to him? What mighty works are wrought by his hands! Is not this the carpenter, the son of Mary and brother of James and Joses and Judas and Simon, and are not his sisters here with us?' And they took offense at him. And Jesus said to them, 'A prophet is not without honor, except in his own country, and among his own kin, and in his own house.' And he could do no mighty work there, except that he laid his hands upon a few sick people and healed them. And he marveled because of their unbelief."

"the son of Mary" (Mk 6:3). A son was identified according to his father. To tie his identity to his mother is unusual, even if we presuppose that Joseph had already died.[55] Moreover, in the parallel passages (Mt 13:55; Lk 4:22; see Jn 6:42), Matthew and Luke speak of Joseph also. So a sign of Mary's widowhood is not very probable here.

The title "son of Mary," seen in itself, is interpreted in the later polemics of the Talmud as a reference to an illegitimate birth of Jesus.[56] The other possibility is a sign of the virgin birth of the Lord (as, e.g., later in the Quran: Jesus as "son of Mary"). This interpretation is more plausible.[57] Mark does not present an infancy narrative, but seems to point here discreetly to a knowledge of the virgin birth.[58]

Preliminary Note on the "Infancy Gospels"

The first two chapters of the gospel, both according to Matthew and according to Luke, are called "infancy gospels." They constitute a sort of prologue to the public life of Jesus; they highlight the birth and childhood of the Lord. Their aim is not simply biographical, but theological, even if that fact does not compromise the historicity of their accounts. Luke, in the prologue, clearly affirms the reliability of the information that he is presenting (Lk 1:4). He reports events from the perspective of Mary, who directly (or indirectly) is the source of the narration. According to many exegetes, linguistic observations suggest that Luke found a tradition formulated in the Hebrew-Christian community. At the same time, the Lucan account

55. Indeed, Joseph does not appear again in the NT after the time of the infancy of Jesus; the fact that the Lord entrusted his mother to John only makes sense if Joseph was already deceased.

56. Also see in Chapter 5, "Early Opposition (Judaism, Paganism)."

57. See also Ignace de la Potterie, SJ, *Maria nel mistero dell'alleanza* [Mary in the Mystery of the Covenant] (Genoa: Marietti, 1988), 100f.; Ziegenaus, *Maria in der Heilsgeschichte*, 85–88; Perrella, *Maria, Vergine e Madre*, 165.

58. A similar explanation consists in the thesis that Mark did not want to call Jesus "son of Joseph," because he is emphasizing the fact that Jesus Christ is the "son of *God*" (Mk 1:1, 15:39): thus O. Knoch and F. Mussner, "Maria in der Heiligen Schrift" [Mary in Sacred Scripture], in *Handbuch der Marienkunde* [Handbook of Mariology], ed. W. Beinert and H. Petri (Regensburg: Pustet, 1996), 1:26.

contains many implicit references to the OT; in the narrative, for example, the prophecy of Isaiah (7:14) resonates (Lk 1:31), as do texts that recall the joy of the "daughter of Zion" (Zep 3:14f. and others, in Lk 1:28).

Matthew's account, on the other hand, is presented from the perspective of Joseph; the evangelist may be drawing on the family circle of the "brethren of the Lord." While Luke tends to make allusions to the fulfillment of the OT, Matthew makes explicit citations. Exegetical analysis shows that the evangelists do not depend on each other; in particular, the content of Matthew 2 is not found in Luke 2, and vice versa. Precisely because of this literary independence the common kernel seems important: the name of Mary and her virginal state; the marriage with Joseph of the house of David; Mary conceives when she does not yet live with Joseph; the virginal conception by the work of the Holy Spirit; an angelic annunciation (in Matthew, to Joseph; in Luke, to Mary); the duty of naming the boy "Jesus"; the birth at Bethlehem; the delivery when Joseph and Mary are living together in lawful matrimony; the time of Herod the Great; last, the location of the home of the Holy Family at Nazareth.

It seems impossible to frame the infancy gospels in a specific "literary genre." In particular, the denomination of "midrash" (as some have proposed) does not seem suitable: a "midrash" is a homiletic account based on a specific Old Testament text. Luke and Matthew, however, do not want to narrate a commentary on an OT text but vice versa; they start out from New Testament events and add in various Old Testament references.[59]

59. For further information, we refer the reader to commentaries and specialized works, particularly to René Laurentin, *I Vangeli dell'infanzia di Cristo* [The Gospels of the Infancy of Christ] (Turin: Paoline, 1985). French original: *Les Évangiles de l'Enfance du Christ: Vérité de Noël au-delà des mythes; Exégèse et sémiotique, historicité et théologie*, 2nd ed. (Tournai-Paris: Desclée de Brouwer, 1982); and Salvador Muñoz Iglesias, *Los evangelios de la infancia* [The Infancy Gospels], 4 vols. (Madrid: Biblioteca de Autores Cristianos, 1986–90); Muñoz Iglesias, "Lo histórico en los Evangelios de la infancia" [The Historical Component in the Infancy Gospels], *Estudios Marianos* 64 (1998): 3–36; Tarcisio Stramare, *Vangelo dei Misteri della Vita Nascosta di Gesù (Matteo e Luca I-II)* [Gospel of the Mysteries of the Hidden Life of Jesus (Matthew and Luke 1–2)] (Bornato in Franciacorta [BS]: Sardini, 1998); Mauro Orsatti, "Storicità e vangeli dell'infanzia" [Historicity and the Infancy Gospels], *RTLu* 9, no. 3 (2004): 603–22. Other bibliographical references in Perrella, *Maria, Vergine e Madre*, 68–77; Valentini, *Maria secondo le Scritture*, 63–69, 449f.

The Virgin Mother of Jesus according to Matthew

The Genealogy

While the gospel according to Mark is destined for Christians originating in paganism, the gospel according to Matthew is definitely written for Christians of Jewish origin.[60] Matthew's specificity regarding Mary is found especially in the first two chapters, the "infancy narrative."

In the genealogy of Jesus, Matthew makes Jesus' connection with Abraham and with David stand out. The connection with David is given by Joseph as the legal father: legal paternity (by adoption, the Levirate law) "sufficed to confer all hereditary rights: in this case, those of the offspring of David."[61] At the same time, the evangelist is referring to the subsequent account of the virginal birth of Jesus; Matthew breaks the long list of generations ("A begat B, B begat C"), saying, "Jacob begat Joseph, the husband of Mary, of whom was born Jesus who is called Christ" (Mt 1:16).

An unusual trait for a genealogy is the reference to four additional women, despite the fact that women were not listed in Hebrew genealogies. Tamar (v. 3) became the mother of Perez and Zerah in a peculiar way: she conceived from her father-in-law through a trick, because the brothers of her deceased husband had not granted her right to have legal offspring for him (Gn 38). Tamar thus prevented the race of Judah, from which the Messiah was to arise, from being extinguished (Gn 49:10). Rahab and Ruth (v. 4) are women of pagan origin. Rahab, a prostitute at Jericho, helped the Israelites to conquer the city (Jos 2:1f, 6:22–25). The Moabite Ruth, married to a Hebrew husband, is exalted because of her faithfulness and becomes the great-grandmother of David. The book of Ruth (4:11f.) praises Ruth and Tamar (alongside Leah and Rachel) as women who will found the house of Israel. Then Matthew mentions the wife of Uriah (v. 6)—that is, Bathsheba, with whom David committed adultery, but who nevertheless then became the mother of Solomon.

60. See, among others, the syntheses of research in Serra, "Bibbia," 237–43; Bastero, *Mary, Mother of the Redeemer*, 89–102; Forte, *Maria, la donna icona*, 53–64; Ziegenaus, *Maria in der Heilsgeschichte*, 88–96; Valentini, *Maria secondo le Scritture*, 71–87.

61. Jerusalem Bible, note on Mt 1:1.

The conduct of these women is not reproved in the OT. Therefore, the evangelist does not want to highlight sin,[62] but divine providence, which reaches its ends in unusual ways. In a way the relations of these women were outside the rules, but were still instruments of the divine plan. In that sense, the four women prepare for the role of Mary, who becomes the virginal mother of the Messiah.[63]

The Virgin Birth

The stylistic "breach" in the genealogy (Mt 1:16) is explained directly by the account of the virgin birth of Jesus. "Birth" (*génesis*) indicates origin and provenance. The evangelist describes it as a fulfillment of Isaiah 7:14 (Mt 1:18–25). Jesus is the true "God with us" ("Emmanuel"), as Matthew reaffirms at the end of his gospel: "Behold, I am with you always, to the close of the age" (Mt 28:20). And the "sign" promised by Isaiah now is revealed to be a virginal conception by the work of the Holy Spirit. "Is 7:14 is the first of the Old Testament oracles to be understood in a Marian sense by a New Testament author."[64] But only the light of New Testament events could clearly reveal the messianic (and Marian) meaning of Isaiah's prophecy. Based on Matthew's testimony, Mary is called "the Virgin" (*he parthénos*).

The events presuppose Jewish marriage customs of the time. A wedding took place in two phases:

1. The matrimonial contract was established by the parents of the spouses and determined the amount of the dowry that the husband had to present. Such a "betrothal" (in quotes) juridically constituted marriage, even if the bride was still living with her parents for a year and was not yet permitted sexual relations with the husband. The age of such a betrothal for the children was about twelve years or twelve and a half.

2. The wedding indicated the bride's relocation to the house of the husband and their cohabitation with marital relations.

62. According to a current interpretation following St. Jerome.

63. See Joachim Gnilka, *Das Matthäusevangelium* [The Gospel of Matthew] (Freiburg im Breisgau: Herder, 1986), 1:8f.; Serra, "Bibbia," 240. One may also note that the women are foreigners: Tamar and Rahab are of Canaanite origin, Ruth is a Moabite, and Bathsheba was wife of the Hittite Uriah, and therefore perhaps pagan too.

64. Serra, "Bibbia," 243.

The virginal conception of Jesus comes in the first phase of matrimony, and Joseph "being a just man and unwilling to put her to shame, resolved to send her away quietly" (Mt 1:19).[65] The angel's appearance resolves the difficulty and presents the assignment to Joseph: to accept Mary as his bride and to name the child "Jesus." Through Joseph, Jesus is "son of David" (Mt 1:1, 1:20), bearer of the prophetic promises.

"He did not know her until (*héos*) the birth of the son, and he named him Jesus" (Mt 1:25). This phrase affirms that Joseph had no sexual relations with Mary until the birth of Jesus. "Until" (*heos* [*hou*]) does not imply, however, that they had such relations afterward; the meaning of the word is affirmative, marking the ends or limits under consideration. When it is written that "Michal the daughter of Saul had no child to [LXX: *héos*] the day of her death" (2 Sm 6:23), it is obvious that she also did not have any afterward.[66]

"The Child and His Mother"

The visit of the Magi also contains a Marian dimension. In the redaction of the text Joseph does not appear (although he obviously was present at the events), but only "the child" is named—the newborn King-Messiah—"with Mary his mother" (Mt 2:11). This attention to Mary finds a certain precedent in the role of the mother of the king (*gebiráh*) in the dynasty of David. The mother of the king had specific duties, such as imposing the crown on the new king (Sg 3:11) and administering the inheritance of the king after his passing. Solomon had a throne set at his right for his mother (1 Kg 2:19). In the visit of the Magi, Mary appears "as the new *gebiráh* of the messianic kingdom which Jesus will establish now that he has come into the world."[67]

65. On hypotheses regarding Joseph's motivations, see, for example, Bastero, *Mary, Mother of the Redeemer*, 93f.; Manelli, *All Generations*, 222–26: Is the passage describing a suspicion of infidelity, or fear and humility in face of the mystery of the virginal conception, or perplexity in face of an inexplicable fact? The best arguments support the third interpretation, as in P. Barbagli, "Joseph, noli timere accipere Mariam coniugem tuam" ["Joseph, Fear Not to Accept Mary as Your Wife"], in *Maria in Sacra Scriptura*, ed. C. Balić (Rome: PAMI, 1967), 4:445–63.

66. See Johannes Brinktrine, *Die Lehre von der Mutter des Erlösers* [Doctrine of the Mother of the Redeemer] (Paderborn: F. Schöningh, 1959), 69f.; Laurentin, *I Vangeli dell'infanzia*, 360.

67. Bastero, *Mary, Mother of the Redeemer*, 102. See Valentini, *Maria secondo le Scritture*, 83–87.

"There is a dominant image at the center of Mt 2: the child with Mary his mother (2:11)."[68] Four times over, the formula "the child and his mother" comes back (2:13, 2:14, 2:20, 2:21). The formula may be inspired by Exodus 4:20: "Moses took his wife and his children [or rather: his son]" to return to Egypt. Yet Matthew mentions the child first to emphasize his dignity. Only twice does Matthew (in chap. 1–2) mention the name "Mary" (Mt 1:18; 2:11); both times he adds "his mother"; the other four passages (2:13, 2:14, 2:20, 2:21) only mention her maternity, which is more important than her name. Joseph, in contrast, is always presented with his name. Jesus, the "God with us," surpasses his mother in dignity, though she cannot be separated from him.

While Exodus 4:20 underscores the family relation between Moses and his son (his children), Matthew does not put Jesus in such a relation with Joseph. Thus, it is emphasized: Jesus is not the son of Joseph.[69]

Redactional Peculiarities

A few small changes in the text handed on by Mark are significant for Matthew. Matthew leaves out the passage in which Jesus' relatives (or the crowd) were saying that Jesus had been "beside himself" (Mk 3:20f.) This change may have been motivated by a superior respect for the relatives of Jesus, in particular for his mother. From the phrase that a prophet is disrespected "in his own country, among his family, and in his house" (Mk 6:4), Matthew omits the "family," the closest relatives (while "house" has a broader meaning).[70] In the account of Jesus' visit to Nazareth, Matthew removes the expression "son of Mary" and writes instead, "Is he not the son of the carpenter?

68. Ernst Nellessen, *Das Kind und seine Mutter: Struktur und Verkündigung des 2. Kapitels im Matthäusevangelium* [The Child and His Mother: Structure and Proclamation in the Gospel of Matthew 2] (Stuttgart: Verlag Katholisches Bibelwerk, 1969), 94. See Giuseppe Segalla, "Il bambino con Maria sua madre in Matteo 2" [The Child with Mary His Mother in Matthew 2], *Theotokos* 4, no. 1 (1996): 15–27.

69. See Nellessen, *Das Kind und seine Mutter*, 95. The formula "son of the carpenter" (Mt 13:55) is found on the lips of people who do not understand the mystery of Jesus. We will return to the real, but not biological, fatherhood of Joseph in Chapter 5 at "The Role of the Marriage of Mary and the Figure of Joseph."

70. See Ziegenaus, *Maria in der Heilsgeschichte*, 116.

Isn't his mother's name Mary?" (Mt 13:55). The evangelist can speak calmly (from the mouth of the people) of Jesus as "son" of Joseph, because the reader already knows the reality of the virgin birth.

In short, Matthew's references to the virginal conception and the maternity of Mary (the mother of "God with us") are important for Mariology. In the infancy gospel, "the child and his mother" are indivisible. Whoever believes in the Messiah also encounters his mother.

The Virgin Mother of the Lord according to Luke

The Importance of the Lucan Testimony

According to a sixth-century legend, the evangelist Luke[71] once made a painting of the Madonna.[72] This reference does not prove anything about historical authenticity, but at least it expresses the fact that Luke reports the greater part of the information on Mary in the NT. Walter Delius, a Protestant scholar and author of a rather critical work on the history of Marian devotion, was able to affirm, about the first two chapters of the gospel according to Luke, "With the hand of a master, Luke has constructed an image of Mary that contains in itself nearly all the essential elements of Marian devotion during the centuries."[73] In fact, the veneration of Mary had already begun with the greetings given by the angel and by Elizabeth.

Note on the Structure of Luke 1–2

The "infancy gospel" according to Luke constitutes a sort of "diptych" that highlights the parallelism between John the Baptist and Jesus:

71. Among others, see the syntheses of Serra, "Bibbia," 243–74; Bastero, *Mary, Mother of the Redeemer*, 103–34; Forte, *Maria, la donna icona*, 64–87; Ziegenaus, *Maria in der Heilsgeschichte*, 96–115; Valentini, *Maria secondo le Scritture*, 89–274. The Lucan pericopes are also commented upon by John Paul II, in particular CM 18 (May 1, 1996), "Mary Responds to God with Spousal Love"; CM 25 (July 3, 1996), "Mary Freely Co-operated in God's Plan"; CM 27 (July 24, 1996), "Our Lady Intended to Remain a Virgin"; CM 34 (Oct. 2, 1996), on the Visitation; CM 35 (Nov. 6, 1996), on the *Magnificat*; CM 36 (Nov. 20, 1996), "Nativity Shows Mary's Closeness to Jesus"; CM 39 (Dec. 11, 1996), "Simeon Was Open to the Lord's Action"; CM 40 (Dec. 18, 1996), "Mary Has a Role in Jesus' Saving Mission"; CM 42 (Jan. 15, 1997), "Mary Co-operates by Personal Obedience."

72. See Florian Trenner, "Lukasbild" [Image in Luke], in *ML* 4:183–86.

73. Walter Delius, *Geschichte der Marienverehrung* [History of Marian Veneration] (Munich and Basel: E. Reinhardt, 1963), 26.

Annunciation of John the Baptist	*Annunciation of Jesus*
presentation of the parents	presentation of the parents
apparition of the angel	apparition of the angel
the worry of Zechariah	the fear of Mary
communication of the message	communication of the message
the incredulity of Zechariah	the question by Mary
punishment	response of the angel
departure of Zechariah	departure of the angel
	Visitation by Mary to Elizabeth
	Song of the *Magnificat*
Birth of John the Baptist	*Birth of Jesus*
birth of John the Baptist	birth of Jesus
rejoicing at his birth	rejoicing at his birth / song of the angels
circumcision	circumcision
the song *Benedictus*	the song *Nunc dimittis*
John the Baptist growing up	Jesus growing up
	the child Jesus lost and found in the temple[74]

With this parallel structure, Luke emphasizes the superior dignity of Jesus with respect to John the Baptist. While, for example, the Baptist is announced as "great before the Lord" (Lk 1:15), Jesus will be "great and will be called Son of the Most High" (Lk 1:32). Mary also participates in this parallelism: while Zechariah remains incredulous at the message of the angel, the "mother of the Lord" (see Lk 1:43) gives the generous response of faith (Lk 1:38, 1:45).

The Annunciation

(26) In the sixth month the angel Gabriel was sent from God to a city of Galilee named Nazareth, (27) to a virgin betrothed to a man whose name was Joseph, of the house of David, and the virgin's name was Mary. (28) And he came to her and said, "Hail, full of grace, the Lord is with you!" (29) But she was greatly troubled at the saying, and considered in her mind what sort

74. See Bastero, *Mary, Mother of the Redeemer*, 103f.

of greeting this might be. (30) And the angel said to her, "Do not be afraid, Mary, for you have found favor with God. (31) And behold, you will conceive in your womb and bear a son, and you shall call his name Jesus. (32) He will be great, and will be called the Son of the Most High; and the Lord God will give to him the throne of his father David, (33) and he will reign over the house of Jacob for ever, and of his kingdom there will be no end."

(34) And Mary said to the angel, "How can this be, since I have no husband?" (35) And the angel said to her, "The Holy Spirit will come upon you and the power of the Most High will overshadow you; therefore the child to be born will be called holy, the Son of God. (36) And behold, your kinswoman Elizabeth in her old age has also conceived a son; and this is the sixth month with her who was called barren. (37) *For with God nothing will be impossible.*" (38) And Mary said, "Behold, I am the handmaid of the Lord; let it be to me according to your word." And the angel departed from her. (Lk 1:26–38)

The apparition of the angel Gabriel (v. 26) connects the passage with the preceding account (v. 19). The presentation suggests that the messenger belongs to the supreme class of angels: they stand before the celestial throne ("I am Gabriel who stand in the presence of God," v. 19).[75] The name "Gabriel" recalls the prophecy of Daniel, according to which the angel's appearance is connected to the eschatological fulfillment of the history of Israel (Dn 9).

Gabriel is sent to Nazareth, a small town in Galilee, and hence into a half-pagan environment. "Can anything good come out of Nazareth?" asks Nathaniel (Jn 1:46).

Luke affirms that Mary was a virgin at the time of the Annunciation and "betrothed" (*emneustemé̂ne*) (v. 27). With the term "virgin" (twice) the account refers to Isaiah 7:14, as also appears a few verses later: "Behold, you will conceive in your womb and bear a son, and you shall call his name Jesus" (v. 31). As in Isaiah, it will be the mother who gives the name to the child.[76] The meaning of the name "Jesus" ("Yahweh saves") is close to the name "Emmanuel" ("God with us").

75. According to the apocalyptic tradition, seven angels stand before the throne of God; see, e.g., Tb 12:15; Rv 8:2, 8:6; Heinz Schürmann, *Il Vangelo di Luca* [The Gospel of Luke] (Brescia: Paideia, 1985), 1:125.

76. In the LXX, however, as we have seen, this task is carried out by Ahaz ("you will name").

Equally important is the fact that Joseph comes from the house of David (v. 27), because by means of his legal paternity the prophecy of Nathan is realized, as pointed out subsequently (2 Sm 7: vv. 32–33). It is not important for the biblical context whether Mary is of the line of David or not.[77] "The virgin's name was Mary" (v. 27).[78]

"Hail (*chaîre*), full of grace (*kecharitoméne*), the Lord is with you!" (v. 28). The very first word of the angelic salutation deserves particular attention. *Chaîre* is the habitual greeting of the Greek world; later the Vulgate translates the word with the corresponding Latin greeting: *Ave*. The semitic equivalent could have been *shalom*, "peace."

Nonetheless, we also can see a deeper meaning. Stanislas Lyonnet was the first to show (in 1939) that *chaîre* appears in the LXX only four times, and that three of these references point to the messianic joy promised to Jerusalem or, respectively, to the daughter of Zion (to Jerusalem as personification of the people).[79] In this case the ordinary greeting more clearly receives the content of "rejoice"; besides that, Mary appears as the concrete personification of Israel, an interpretation that can also find support from other evidence in Lk 1–2. Here are the three referenced passages in their context:

77. Her belonging to the line of David was affirmed later by the patristic tradition, starting from Tertullian, *De carne Christi* 21:5 (PL 2:833f.). From the biblical context a theory also arose of her belonging to a priestly family; at least Elizabeth, a relative of Mary (Lk 1:36) was "a descendant of Aaron" (Lk 1:5) (according to Pozo, *María, nueva Eva*, 212). On the other hand, there is the custom of taking a wife only within one's own tribe. On this, see Josef Schmid, "Abstammung Mariens" [Lineage of Mary], in *ML* 1:21f.; M. Rehm and J. Scharbert, "David," in *ML* 2:150; Maria-Luisa Rigato, "Maria di Nazaret di stirpe levitico sacerdotale" [Mary of Nazareth of the Levitical Priestly Line], *Theotokos* 8, no. 1 (2000): 275–304.

78. Note: the name "Mary" corresponds in the original (in Hebrew/Aramaic; in Greek in Lk 1) to *Mariam*; only the Masoretes (Hebrew exegetes of c. 500 to 900) later placed the vowels into the Hebrew OT text as *Mirjam* for the sister of Moses, the first bearer of the name in Sacred Scripture (*Maria*, on the other hand, is an abbreviation in the Greek context). The etymology of *Mariam* is uncertain. If an Egyptian origin is chosen (as with "Moses"), the name could mean "to be loved" (by the god Amun). Comparisons between the sister of Moses and Mary are rare in the history of theology; but more often, Mariam as the singer of the song of victory (Ex 15) is compared with Mary, singer of the *Magnificat*. See Richard Kugelman, CP, "El santo nome de María" [The Holy Name of Mary], in *Mariología*, ed. J. Carol (Madrid: Biblioteca de Autores Cristianos, 1964), 386–98 [English original: "The Holy Name of Mary," in *Mariology*, ed. J. Carol (Milwaukee: Bruce, 1954), 1:411–24]; "Mirjam," in *ML* 4:467–69. The Quran seems to confuse the sister of Moses and the mother of Jesus (see Sura 19:16–29).

79. See Stanislas Lyonnet, SJ, "Chaíre, Kecharitoméne" [Hail, Full of Grace], *Biblica* 20, no. 2 (1939): 131–41; Valentini, *Maria secondo le Scritture*, 129f.

- "Sing aloud, O daughter of Zion; shout, O Israel! Rejoice and exult with all your heart, O daughter of Jerusalem! The Lord has taken away the judgments against you, he has cast out your enemies. The King of Israel, the Lord is in your midst; you shall fear evil no more. On that day it shall be said in Jerusalem: 'Do not fear, O Zion; let not your hands grow weak. The Lord, your God, is in your midst; a warrior who gives victory'" (Zep 3:14–17).
- "Fear not, O land; be glad and rejoice, for the Lord has done great things! ... Be glad, O sons of Zion, and rejoice.... You shall know that I am in the midst of Israel" (Jl 2:21–27).
- "Rejoice greatly, O daughter of Zion! Shout aloud, O daughter of Jerusalem! Behold, your king comes to you" (Zec 9:9).

The similarity between the Lucan text and Zephaniah (joy, "fear not," the presence of the Lord) seems particularly suggestive. At the least the Old Testament source makes us think of Mary as a feminine representative of the people, as the "daughter of Zion" in person. Moreover, it emphasizes that Mary "asked what meaning such a greeting would have" (v. 29). It would be too banal to see in the *chaîre* merely a normal "Good day."[80]

Kecharitoméne is translated by the Vulgate, with good reason, as *gratia plena*. The verb *charitóo* bears a causal sense (*óo*) and indicates abundance: "filling to the rim with grace."[81] Hence the passive past participle of the verb signifies "made abundantly the object of divine grace and benevolence."[82] "Full of grace" is used as a title: "It is the first title attributed to the Virgin, in light of which those that follow are to be understood and explained."[83] The title forms a play on words with the greeting (*chaîre kecharitoméne*). The title is commented upon by the angel's subsequent observation that Mary has "found

80. See Ziegenaus, *Maria in der Heilsgeschichte*, 97f.

81. See Eph 1:6: God "has filled us with grace" (*echarítosen hemâs*).

82. See Pozo, *María, nueva Eva*, 215–19. See also Bastero, *Mary, Mother of the Redeemer*, 106–8, taking up an interesting work by Ignace de la Potterie, SJ, "Kecharitomene en Lc. 1,28: Étude philologique" [Kecharitomene in Lk 1:28: Philological Study], *Biblica* 68, no. 3 (1987): 357–82; de la Potterie, "Étude exégétique et théologique" [Exegetical and Theological Study], *Biblica* 68, no. 4 (1987): 480–506. In addition, Mario Cimosa, "Il senso del titolo *kecharitoméne*" [The Meaning of the Title *Kecharitomene*], *Theotokos* 4, no. 2 (1996): 589–97.

83. Valentini, *Maria secondo le Scritture*, 93.

favor with God" (v. 30). It is a matter of "divine benevolence in view of the mission to be completed, but which profoundly affects the person to whom that benevolence is directed."[84]

The affirmation "the Lord is with you" refers not only to the subsequent conception, but also to the dignity of Mary, to the divine presence in her. *Kecharitoméne* thus means more than "elect," as Protestant exegetes interpret at times.

There is a vigorous exegetical controversy about Mary's question: "How is it possible? I do not know man" (v. 34). To "know" refers to sexual relations. Gregory of Nyssa and Augustine interpreted the question as the expression of a preceding vow of virginity.[85] Such a question would not have made sense if a few months later Mary was going to begin having matrimonial relations with Joseph. The principal difficulty for this solution, according to many authors, is the Jewish environment that emphasized the duty of devoting oneself to procreation. For this reason, v. 34 is interpreted often as a simple literary means so as to put the angel's explanation in context.[86] But this interpretation has to confront the difficulty that Mary, in that case, would have been posing a question with no particular sense.[87]

As regards the Jewish environment, one needs to take into account the influence of the Essenes. The Essene monks (e.g., at Qumran) did not condemn procreation, but abstained from sexual relations. There were other members of the community who lived the ascetic ideal without being monks. The presence of the Essenes could have prepared the ground for a intention to live in virginity, supported by divine grace in Mary (and Joseph).[88] John the Baptist also lived such an ascetic ideal.[89] The better arguments seem to sup-

84. Ibid.

85. See "A Plan of Virginity," in chapter 5.

86. E.g., Perrella, *Maria, Vergine e Madre*, 89f.

87. Pozo, *María, nueva Eva*, 225f.

88. See Pozo, *María, nueva Eva*, 226f.

89. According to another solution (Audet/Craghan), Mary (having heard the message of the angel) recalls the prophecy of Is 7:14 that announces the birth of the Messiah by a virgin; because of this, she asks how the birth will come to be, if (in this case) she will not have relations with her husband. This solution faces the linguistic difficulty that *epei* ("seeing that" I do not know man) does not support the meaning proposed, and that no evidence exists of a messianic interpretation for Is 7:14 in the Jewish religion of the time: J. P. Audet, "L'Annonce à Marie," *Revue biblique* 63

port the "classic" interpretation of the fathers, also reaffirmed multiple times recently by John Paul II.[90]

But even if v. 34 were explained in another way, it would be necessary to clear up Mary's preparation for her mission: "Mary is taken so profoundly by the mission of being the virgin mother of God ... that she remains constantly influenced by this plan.... It is inconceivable that Mary, before the angel's coming, had felt and thought of her future like all the other Jewish girls of her time and that the angel had totally destroyed her plans for the future.... In Mary there was a profound desire for virginity ... which was then clarified by means of the angel and consciously accepted by Mary."[91]

"The Holy Spirit will come upon you and the power of the Most High will overshadow you" (v. 35a). This announcement seems to allude to the narrative of Genesis: the spirit of God that hovered over the waters at the beginning of the creation (Gn 1:2); in this perspective, the virginal origin appears almost like a new creation. The same verse also implicitly refers to the presence of God during the Exodus: "The cloud covered the tent of meeting and the glory of the Lord filled the tabernacle" (Ex 40:34). The cloud that casts its shadow on the tent is a sign of the glory (*kabod*) of God, of his majestic presence. The glory of God that accompanied Israel in the desert takes up a dwelling in Mary as in a new tabernacle, or rather before the Ark of the Covenant.

Referring to Elizabeth, the angel underscores the omnipotence of God, which can intervene even by means of miracles. "Nothing will be impossible for God" (v. 37): this phrase also appears in Genesis 18:14 in the prophecy to Sarah about the birth of Isaac. The cre-

(1956): 362–72; J. F. Craghan, *Mary, the Virginal Wife and the Married Virgin: The Problematic of Mary's Vow of Virginity* (Rome: Typis Pontificiae Universtatis Gregorianae, 1967), 71–99.

Another interpretation (Gächter, e.g.) thinks that the question refers only to the immediate situation: P. Gächter, *Maria im Erdenleben: Neutestamentliche Marienstudien*, 3rd ed. (Innsbruck: Tyrolia, 1955), 96–102; Gächter, *Marjam, die Mutter Jesu,* 2nd ed. (Einsiedeln: Johannes Verlag, 1981), 30–32. In any case, seeing the nearness of the wedding, such a question, according to Pozo, *María, nueva Eva*, 223, "would be one of incredible naïveté."

90. We will return to the "Plan for Virginity," in chapter 5.

91. Ziegenaus, *Maria in der Heilsgeschichte*, 274f., inspired by Romano Guardini, *Die Mutter des Herrn: Ein Brief und darin ein Entwurf* [The Mother of the Lord: A Letter and Therein a Sketch], 2nd ed. (Würzburg: Werkbund-Verlag, 1956), 31–37.

ative power of God also constitutes the basis for the virginal conception of Jesus, an event that surpasses Old Testament antecedents that only describe overcoming sterility.

"Behold, I am the handmaid of the Lord; let it be to me according to your word" (v. 38). With this answer Mary shows her full availability for the plan of the Lord. Mary's collaboration implies free obedience, joined to the commitment of understanding what is happening (vv. 29, 34). It is the answer of faith without reserve.

The Visitation

(39) In those days Mary arose and went with haste into the hill country, to a city of Judah, (40) and she entered the house of Zechariah and greeted Elizabeth. (41) And when Elizabeth heard the greeting of Mary, the child leaped in her womb; and Elizabeth was filled with the Holy Spirit (42) and she exclaimed with a loud cry, "Blessed are you among women, and blessed is the fruit of your womb! (43) And why is this granted me, that the mother of my Lord should come to me? (44) For behold, when the voice of your greeting came to my ears, the child in my womb leaped for joy. (45) And blessed is she who believed that there would be a fulfillment of what was spoken to her from the Lord." (Lk 1:39–45)

Mary's visit to Elizabeth confirms the content of the Annunciation. The first encounter between Jesus and his precursor takes place in the wombs of their mothers. The account contains a few elements that may recall the transfer of the Ark of the Covenant to Jerusalem by David (2 Sm 6:2–11).[92] "Jesus is on a journey, the destination is the temple in Jerusalem, Mary (who carries him) is the type of the Ark of the Covenant." [Or better, vice versa: the Ark of the Covenant is

92. See René Laurentin, *Structure et théologie de Luc I-II* [Structure and Theology of Lk 1–2] (Paris: Gabalda, 1957), 79–81; Laurentin, *I Vangeli dell'infanzia*, 82–85, 218, 226: both times, there is a journey in Judea; the arrival provokes joy; they enter a house (2 Sm 6:10 / Lk 1:40); a similar exclamation comes at the arrival (2 Sm 6:9: "How can the ark of the Lord come to me?"; Lk 1:43: "And why is this granted me, that the mother of my Lord should come to me?"); a stay of three months at the house (2 Sm 6:11 / Lk 1:56). Nevertheless, it is not a mechanical parallelism (or an ahistorical symbolism): Mary remains with Elizabeth "about" three months; the "about" is missing in 2 Sm 6:11. The aim of Lk 1–2 is the "ascent" of Jesus to Jerusalem (Lk 2:4, 2:42), and the Ark of the Covenant in 2 Sm is also carried into the holy city. The Lucan intention of establishing a parallelism between the Ark of the Covenant and Mary is questioned by Muñoz Iglesias, *Los evangelios de la infancia*, 2:240–45; Valentini, *Maria secondo le Scritture*, 119.

the type of Mary.][93] Mary's "haste" seems to be a sign of the joy that is expressed later in the *Magnificat*. The whole account is permeated by a profound joy, present in the boy John who exults in the womb of his mother (vv. 41, 44). The greeting of Elizabeth (v. 42) recalls the greeting addressed to Judith for having slain the chief of their enemies: "You are blessed by the Most High God above all women on earth; and blessed (LXX: *eulógetos*) be the Lord God" (Jdt 13:18).[94] If we compare the greeting "Blessed are you among women, and blessed (*eulogetós*) is the fruit of your womb!" (v. 42) with the words addressed to Judith, it points to the divine character of the son.

This observation is confirmed in the Lucan text itself: "And why is this granted me, that the mother of my Lord should come to me?" (v. 43) In the Septuagint, the "Lord" (*kyrios*) is an expression that describes God himself, replacing the tetragrammaton ("Yahweh"). Indeed, Jesus is not great "before the Lord" like John the Baptist (Lk 1:15) but "great" in the absolute sense, "son of the Most High" (Lk 1:32), the "Lord" himself (Lk 1:43). Hence "mother of the Lord" appears as synonymous with the later title "Mother of God." In this way, Luke leads to the same faith attested by Paul when he affirms that the "Son of God" is "born of woman" (Gal 4:4).

The last phrase of the passage recalls the end of the Annunciation, the believing response to the angel's message: "Blessed is she who believed that there would be a fulfillment of what was spoken to her from the Lord" (v. 45). Mary appears thus as the first person in the NT who believes, the first concrete realization of faith in Jesus Christ.

Also noteworthy is the presence of the Holy Spirit in all the protagonists, a sign of the arrival of the messianic age: Mary (Lk 1:35), John the Baptist (Lk 1:15, 1:41, 1:44), Elizabeth (Lk 1:41), Zechariah (Lk 1:67) and Simeon (Lk 2:25) become prophetic bearers of the Spirit.

93. Laurentin, *Structure et théologie*, 80f.

94. This phrase may perhaps resonate with the exaltation formulated by Deborah: "Most blessed of all women be Jael, the wife of Heber the Kenite" (Jgs 5:24) for having slain Sisera, enemy of the Israelites.

The Magnificat

(46) And Mary said, "My soul magnifies the Lord, (47) and my spirit rejoices in God my Savior, (48) for he has regarded the low estate of his handmaiden. For behold, henceforth all generations will call me blessed; (49) for he who is mighty has done great things for me, and holy is his name. (50) And his mercy is on those who fear him from generation to generation. (51) He has shown strength with his arm, he has scattered the proud in the imagination of their hearts, (52) he has put down the mighty from their thrones, and exalted those of low degree; (53) he has filled the hungry with good things, and the rich he has sent empty away. (54) He has helped his servant Israel, in remembrance of his mercy, (55) as he spoke to our fathers, to Abraham and to his posterity for ever." (Lk 1:46–55)

Mary's canticle of praise, the *Magnificat*, highlights the grace received by the singer, but at the same time, opens itself to the community: the lifting of the poor, the mercy offered to Israel, the fulfillment of the promise made to Abraham. The *Magnificat* is particularly rich in allusions to Old Testament texts, and there is a particular resemblance to the canticle of Hannah, the great thanksgiving for the birth of Samuel (1 Sm 2:1–10). The plan of the canticle is clearly tied to the personal situation of Mary; first of all, the declaration "henceforth all generations will call me blessed" (Lk 1:48) is not suited to be an "interchangeable framework" for just any speaker.[95]

We have already noted the implicit allusions to the "daughter of Zion" in the angel's greeting. A similar interweaving between Mary and Israel is also found in the *Magnificat*. Mary exalts God as "my" savior (an unusual personalization, corresponding to the personal grace given to the Mother of the Lord); God "has regarded the low estate of his handmaiden" (v. 48). But with the coming of salvation God has also "exalted those of low degree" (v. 52). The haughty, powerful, and rich are set in opposition to the humble and hungry (vv. 51–53). Mary belongs to the "little ones" to whom is promised salvation in the Old Testament.[96]

95. For other exegetical questions we refer the reader to specialized works, e.g., Elio Peretto, "Magnificat," in *NDM*, 853–65; Manelli, *All Generations*, 187–215; Valentini, *Maria secondo le Scritture*, 133–64; Alberto Valentini, "Magnificat," in *DMar*, 785–90.

96. See, for example, the prayer of Judith: "Your power depends not upon numbers, nor your

The first Beatitude, formulated by Luke, follows along the same lines: "Blessed are the poor" (Lk 6:20). It is speaking of those who are open to receive salvation from God; this spiritual attitude is not identical to social poverty, but may find sustenance in it. At least it is worth noting that Mary and Joseph belonged to the poor class of society, as follows from the sacrifice they brought to the temple (Lk 2:24): doves constituted the offering of the poor (cf. Lv 5:7, 12:8).[97]

With the grace addressed to Mary, God has "reminded" himself of the promise made to Abraham. Mary, in sum, appears as the representative of Israel, of the church being born. Mary and the church are presented as closely linked in this view, though they are not interchangeable.

The salvific events are formulated in the aorist tense, which refers to the past, but the linguistic form of the past can also describe what God is always working and what is happening in the last days. Future things can be described as if they had already happened. The canticle ends with a look to the future: "for ever" (v. 55).

The Birth of Jesus

After the account of the birth of John the Baptist (Lk 1:57–80), Luke presents the account of the birth of Jesus (Lk 2:1–20). The message shines through in the angels' proclamation: "To you is born this day in the city of David a Savior, who is Christ the Lord" (v. 11).

Joseph goes to Bethlehem "to be enrolled with Mary his betrothed (*emnesteuméne*), who was with child" (v. 5). The verb *mnesteúein* ("to betroth") is also found in Matthew 1:18 and Luke 1:27. The expression "betrothed" recalls the account of the virginal conception: Mary, after having conceived, still finds herself in the state described in the account of the Annunciation (Lk 1:27: virgin, betrothed). In any case, the mother of the Messiah is presented in the most human condition, that of an expectant mother, exposed to difficult conditions.

---

might upon men of strength; for you are God of the lowly, helper of the oppressed, upholder of the weak, protector of the forlorn, savior of those without hope" (Jdt 9:11). See inter alia Ps 9:19; Is 57:15.

97. See Alois Stöger, "Armut Mariens" [The Poverty of Mary], in *ML* 1:242f.

At Bethlehem "the time came for her to be delivered. And she gave birth to her first-born son and wrapped him in swaddling cloths, and laid him in a manger, because there was no place for them in the inn" (v. 7). "The expression 'for them' unites the Son and the Mother in the same rejection and shows how Mary was already associated with the Son's destiny of suffering and was made a participant in his redeeming mission."[98] The term "first-born" simply indicates the first one born, without implying subsequent births. This fact is clear enough, for instance, thanks to a funerary inscription of a Jewish woman, found in Egypt and dated to the fifth century B.C.: "In the pains of giving birth to my first-born, Fate brought me to the end of life."[99]

The shepherds "found Mary and Joseph and the baby, lying in a manger" (v. 16). The order of this list gives a particular prominence to Mary.

Toward the end of the passage, the evangelist notes, "But Mary kept all these things [literally: these words] pondering them [moving them] in her heart" (v. 19). Later, after the finding of Jesus in the temple, at the age of twelve, a similar formula appears: "His mother kept all these things in her heart" (Lk 2:51). Mary interiorly preserves the event and the message of salvation. Thus, the Virgin appears as "the model disciple, a profound and not superficial hearer of the word."[100]

The Presentation of Jesus in the Temple

After the account of the birth of Jesus, the infancy gospel according to Luke concentrates on events that took place at the temple in Jerusalem: the presentation of Jesus, the testimony of the prophets Simeon and Anna, the finding of Jesus at age twelve. For the structure of the Lucan work this placement is important: the gospel concludes in Jerusalem, while the Acts of the Apostles begin there, then to lead the reader to the missionary journeys as far as Rome.

98. John Paul II, CM 36 ("The Nativity Shows Mary's Closeness to Jesus"), 3 (Nov. 20, 1996).
99. See Laurentin, *I Vangeli dell'infanzia*, 270, n. 4.
100. Forte, *Maria, la donna icona*, 80.

When the time came for their purification according to the law of Moses, they brought him up to Jerusalem to present him to the Lord (as it is written in the law of the Lord, "*Every male that opens the womb shall be called holy to the Lord*") and to offer a sacrifice according to what is said in the law of the Lord, "*a pair of turtledoves, or two young pigeons.*" (Lk 2:22–24)

The journey to Jerusalem was motivated by prescriptions of the Mosaic law regarding the first-born male. But first the text speaks of the "time for their purification" (v. 22). According to Leviticus 12:2–8, a woman was considered "unclean" after giving birth. "Childbirth, like menstruation or the masculine seminal emission (chap. 15) is considered a loss of vitality for the individual, who can, with certain rites, restore his integrity and thus his union with God the source of life."[101] The most typical consequence of this state of "uncleanness" (ritual, not moral) was the prohibition of participating in worship and entering the sanctuary. After forty days (for a male) or eighty days (for a female) the postpartum mother was to go to the priest to carry out the rite of "purification" ("from the shedding of blood": Lv 12:7). In the temple, she had to offer "a lamb a year old for a burnt offering, and a young pigeon or a turtledove for a sin offering" (Lv 12:6). "If she cannot afford a lamb, then she shall take two turtledoves or two young pigeons, one for a burnt offering and the other for a sin offering; and the priest shall make atonement for her, and she shall be clean" (Lv 12:8).

The presentation of Jesus at the temple appears as the principal reason for the journey to Jerusalem. According to the Mosaic law,[102] every first-born male, whether human or animal, was to be offered to God. The first-born son had to be "redeemed"[103] after the first month.[104] It was not required that the rite be carried out at Jerusalem and in the temple. Moreover, the Lucan text does not speak of "redeeming": Jesus "is presented and offered to God as one consecrated to him, like ... Samuel."[105]

While Leviticus 12:6 speaks only of "her purification," Luke mentions "their" purification (v. 22), despite the fact that the new-

101. Jerusalem Bible, note on Lv 12.

102. Ex 22:28f., 13:2, 13:12, 13:15, 34:19; Nm 3:13, 8:17.

103. Ex 13:13–16.

104. Nm 18:16 (with 5 silver shekels—that is, 20 denari).

105. Valentini, *Maria secondo le Scritture*, 170, note 12.

born could not have been considered unclean. To explain this surprising formulation, various solutions are proposed:[106]

1. According to Raymond E. Brown, Luke is making a mistake, producing a strange mixture between his knowledge of the Hebrew religion and errors in details. Salvador Muñoz Iglesias, however, observes that the author of Luke 1–2 is profoundly immersed in the Old Testament mentality and in a priestly or levitical environment; it would be strange to accept a mistake here regarding the law of Moses.

2. René Laurentin thinks that "their purification" does not refer to Jesus and Mary, but to the entire people of Israel, which needed redemption. The French mariologist connects the initial verse of the account (v. 22) to the concluding verse (v. 38) that speaks of the "redemption of Jerusalem" (which represents the whole of Israel). Then the theologian refers to Malachi 3:1f: "Behold, I send my messenger to prepare the way before me, and the Lord whom you seek will suddenly come to his temple ..., and he will purify the sons of Levi." It seems a somewhat artificial solution.

3. Muñoz Iglesias, in view of a hypothetical Hebrew text that Luke would have used in writing his gospel, maintains that "their" (*autôn*) does not refer to a person, but to the verb "fulfill." However, in this case, Luke's translation is erroneous.

4. There is also debate about the exact meaning of the term *katharismós*, which means "purification," but the Greek text of the Mosaic law uses another similar word (*kátharsis*) in the passages cited. For this reason M.-J. Lagrange proposes an interpretation of the term as the "redemption" of the son. The terms used in the law on redemption (Ex 13:2, 13:13, 13:15 LXX) relate to sanctification and expiation. The word *katharismós* can appear in a linguistic context that expresses these ideas.[107]

To this author, a solution of type (1) seems most convincing, even if it seems exaggerated to speak of an "error." And one can-

106. See the summary in Bastero, *Mary, Mother of the Redeemer*, 126f., and Valentini, *Maria secondo le Scritture*, 168–76 (who describe yet other "solutions").

107. See Valentini, *Maria secondo le Scritture*, 174f.

not exclude the possibility in (4), which sets "purification" alongside sanctification and an atoning offering. Heinz Schürmann maintains that with "their purification," "the narrator, so it appears, intends to refer, in imprecise and general terms, to everything that happens in the temple, above all to the 'presentation' of the first-born ... which proves to be the determining motive (cf. also v. 27) for the journey to Jerusalem."[108] Thus John Paul II writes, with some caution, that Luke intends "perhaps, to indicate together the prescriptions regarding the mother and the first-born Son."[109] The context points "toward the sacrificial dimension of the presentation of Jesus at the temple and the role Mary his mother had in it."[110]

The reference to the law of Moses on the purification of the mother is not an argument against *virginitas in partu*, a topic we will analyze later.[111] It is simply emphasizing her obedience to the Mosaic law, a theme dear to the infancy gospel (see Lk 1:6, 1:59, 2:21).

In the temple Simeon approaches, thanking God with the *Nunc dimittis* (2:29–32), and proclaims a prophecy regarding Jesus; a Marian aspect comes into it, also:

> This child is set for the fall and rising of many in Israel, and for a sign that is spoken against (and a sword will pierce through your own soul also). (Lk 2:34–35)[112]

Jesus becomes a "sign of contradiction": everyone has to make a decision. The decision leads a part of the people to rise, while the other part falls. The fall, which appears first, is accentuated, and the end of the oracle (in the Greek text) may also be going in this direc-

108. Schürmann, *Il Vangelo de Luca*, 1:244.

109. CM 39 (Nov. 14, 1996), 2. Along the same line, see also Galot, *Maria, La donna*, 254: Luke "unites ... the two actions, purification of the mother and redemption of the first-born."

110. Valentini, *Maria secondo le Scritture*, 174.

111. See "Virginitas in partu," in chapter 5.

112. For a deeper examination, see Settimio M. Manelli, "E una spada trapasserà anche la tua stessa anima" (Lc 2,35): Esegesi del versetto e il suo sviluppo dottrinale in riferimento alla cooperazione di Maria all'opera salvifica di Gesù ["And a Sword Will Also Pierce Your Soul" (Lk 2:35): Exegesis of the Verse and Its Doctrinal Development in Reference to Mary's Cooperation with the Salvific Work of Jesus], *Maria Corredentrice* 6 (2003); Serra, "*Una spada trafiggerà la tua vita" (Lc 2,35a): Quale spada? Bibbia e tradizione giudaico-cristiana a confronto* ["A Sword Will Pierce Your Life" (Lk 2:35a): Which Sword? Bible and Jewish-Christian Tradition in Contrast] (Rome: Marianum, 2003); Valentini, *Maria secondo le Scritture*, 176–89.

tion: "that thoughts of many hearts may be revealed." Schürmann comments, "God has set this sign so that the evil hidden in the world by the thoughts of men may be unmasked. The greater part of Israel will be opposed to this sign of salvation. Messianic salvation will be for the greater part of Israel the cause of a fall ... the passion of Jesus casts its shadow even over 'prehistory.'"[113]

The image of the "sword" means that the soul of the mother will be transfixed by a deep sorrow. Indirectly the future suffering of the child is announced. Through compassion, the mother finds herself associated with the Savior, a sign contradicted by his people. Origen's interpretation, which interprets the "sword" as unbelief and doubt in Mary at the foot of the cross, is out of bounds.[114]

And the interpretation of the "sword" as the word of God (as in Heb 4:12) "as it is expressed in the teaching of Jesus" seems improbable. In this case "the image of Mary would be that of a believer who, like all Israel his people, will have to confront the word of the Son, mystically symbolized by the sword."[115] This idea (as such) is right, but in the context, the interpretation of the "sword" as the sorrow of the mother who participates in the fate of her Son seems closer.[116]

A linguistic influence may be coming from Ezekiel 14:17: "If I bring a sword upon that land" (*romphaia dieltáto dià tes gês* LXX; see Lk 2:35: *soû autês tèn psychèn dieleúsetai romphaía*). Some interpreters (such as Benoit and Laurentin) see behind this allusion the "daughter of Zion" who experiences compassion for the fate of the people.[117]

"Simeon's reference to the redeeming sacrifice, absent at the Annunciation, has shown in his prophecy almost a 'second Annunciation' (*Redemptoris Mater*, n. 16), which will lead the Virgin to a deeper understanding of her Son's mystery."[118]

113. Schürmann, *Il Vangelo de Luca*, 1:254f. However, a "neutral" interpretation of the thoughts is also possible: Serra, "Bibbia," 337.

114. On this interpretation and its replacement in Eastern patristics, see Hauke, "Begierlichkeit" [Concupiscence], in *ML* 1:403; Serra, "*Una spada*," 98–170; and see "Patristic Development and the Importance of the Council of Ephesus," in chapter 6.

115. Thus Serra, "Bibbia," 265; see Serra, "*Una spada*," 304–6.

116. See Settimio Manelli, "E una spada," 138–43, 175–79; Valentini, *Maria secondo le Scritture*, 181–86.

117. See Manelli, "E una spada," 73–74.

118. John Paul II, CM 40 (Dec. 18, 1996), 1.

In the context of the "second Annunciation" to Mary, John Paul II sees in the two doves offered at the temple a sacrifice that "prefigured the sacrifice of Jesus, 'for I am gentle and lowly in heart' (Mt 11:29); in it the true 'presentation' would be made (see Lk 2:22), which would see the Mother associated with her Son in the work of Redemption."[119]

The Finding of Jesus in the Temple

His parents went to Jerusalem every year at the feast of the Passover. And when he was twelve years old, they went up according to custom; and when the feast was ended, as they were returning, the boy Jesus stayed behind in Jerusalem. His parents did not know it, but supposing him to be in the company they went a day's journey, and they sought him among their kinsfolk and acquaintances; and when they did not find him, they returned to Jerusalem, seeking him. After three days they found him in the temple, sitting among the teachers, listening to them and asking them questions; and all who heard him were amazed at his understanding and his answers. And when they saw him they were astonished; and his mother said to him, "Son, why have you treated us so? Behold, your father and I have been looking for you anxiously." And he said to them, "How is it that you sought me? Did you not know that I must be in my Father's house?" And they did not understand the saying which he spoke to them. (Lk 2:41–52)

In the temple, Jesus, aged twelve, reveals himself as bearer of wisdom and as son of the Father. Mary and Joseph have to set out in search of Jesus—a first realization of the prophecy of Simeon ("a sword will pierce through your soul"). Finding the twelve-year-old in the temple, they meet him among the teachers, "and all who heard him were amazed at his understanding and his answers" (v. 47). When the passage speaks of the "amazement" of his parents,[120] it is not referring to an expression of joy at seeing the child again, but at amazement in the face of the presence of God. "They recognize anew that Jesus comes from another world altogether."[121]

"Son, why have you treated us so? Behold, your father and I have been looking for you anxiously" (v. 48). Mary's question expresses the

119. CM 40 (Dec. 18, 1996), 3.

120. *Exeplágesan* comes from *explésso*, "going out of oneself, being stunned (by fear)." The same word appears in Lk 4:32, 9:43; Acts 13:12.

121. Josef Ernst, *Il Vangelo secondo Luca* [The Gospel according to Luke], 2nd ed. (Brescia: Morcelliana, 1990), 1:168.

sorrow she felt during the search for her son. It is too much to call it a "reproof." Rather, here we can see the bewilderment of Mary in the face of an event that was apparently not consistent with the usual behavior of the child Jesus at Nazareth. The question is posed in a respectful tone.

The response of Jesus establishes the center of the pericope: "How is it that you sought me? Did you not know that I must be in my Father's house?" (v. 49).

Jesus compares the claim of the fourth commandment with his superior bond to the heavenly Father. In a way, he also corrects Mary's formulation "your father and I have been looking for you," recalling "my Father." The true father of Jesus is not Joseph, but the heavenly Father. The divine sonship, of which the account of the Annunciation had spoken first, is made manifest.

"And they did not understand the saying" (v. 50). At first glance, these words seem strange, because the divine sonship of Jesus has already been presented. On the other hand, even the faith of Mary found itself on a journey and needed support from above. The same incomprehension appears when Jesus speaks to his disciples of the sorrowful mission that awaits him (Lk 9:45, 18:34, 24:25). Nonetheless there is a difference between the behavior of those disciples and that of Mary: while they were afraid to return to the question (see Lk 9:45), Mary "kept all these things in her heart" (Lk 2:51); she "preserved this enigma in her heart, with reverent and active silence. She strains to decipher the meaning, remains open to the mystery and lets herself enter into it."[122] Therefore it is not correct to speak of a complete incomprehension.

In addition, we have to take account of the paschal perspective.[123] The finding "after three days" may be alluding to the resurrection "after three days" (Lk 24:21).[124] "Having to be in the Father's house" is

122. Serra, "Bibbia," 270.

123. See the various signs collected in Valentini, *Maria secondo le Scritture*, 225–35.

124. See Jerusalem Bible, note on Lk 2:46; Manelli, *All Generations*, 325. Similarly, John Paul II, CM 42 (Jan. 15, 1997), 2: "Through this episode, Jesus prepares his Mother for the mystery of the Redemption. During those three dramatic days when the Son withdraws from them to stay in the temple, Mary and Joseph experience an anticipation of the triduum of his Passion, Death and Resurrection."

also interpreted by some authors as a return from this world to the Father, by means of his death and resurrection. Thus, the finding in the temple would show a paschal depth. Mary's incomprehension would refer above all to the paschal mystery, which was still veiled.[125] John Paul II speaks of this point with a certain caution: "Mary and Joseph do not perceive the sense of his answer, nor the way (apparently a rejection) he reacts to their parental concern. With this attitude, Jesus intends to reveal the mysterious aspects of his intimacy with the Father, aspects which Mary intuits without knowing how to associate them with the trial she is undergoing."[126]

Other Texts in the Gospel

In the patrimony specific to Luke we find a saying of the Lord on true blessedness:

> As he said this, a woman in the crowd raised her voice and said to him, "Blessed is the womb that bore you, and the breasts that you sucked!" But he said, "Blessed rather are those who hear the word of God and keep it!" (Lk 11:27f.)

In his answer, Jesus does not deny the woman's praise for Mary (a praise whose purpose is to acclaim Him), although he corrects it: what counts to God is not the bond of nature, but obedience to the word of God. Luke has already strongly highlighted the obedience and faith of Mary. In this way, seen in the "macro-context," this beatitude clearly applies to the Mother of the Lord.[127]

In using the story from Mark about the encounter between Jesus and his relatives, Luke shows a tendency similar to Matthew. He is handing on Mark 3:20f. The relatives do not come to "seize" Jesus, but to see him (Lk 8:19–21; see Mk 3:31–35). The Lord is rejected by his "country" (Nazareth), but Luke does not mention (as does Mark)

125. See, for example (along with Laurentin and others), Serra, "Bibbia," 270; Manelli, *All Generations*, 324–27. This deeper meaning remains even if one were to leave the interpretation of the literal sense unresolved.

126. John Paul II, CM 42 (Jan. 15, 1997), 4.

127. See also Franz Mussner, *Maria, die Mutter Jesu im Neuen Testament* [Mary the Mother of Jesus in the New Testament] (St. Ottilien: EOS Verlag, 1993), 51–55; Ziegenaus, *Maria in der Heilsgeschichte*, 117; Stefano M. Manelli, *All Generations*, 365–68.

the "relatives" or their "house" (Lk 4:24; see Mk 6:4). Perhaps the presence of the Lord's relatives in the primitive community led to more moderate formulations.

Mary in the Newborn Church at Jerusalem (Acts 1:14)

Mary is found at the beginning of the "first book" (Acts 1:1) of Luke's works, the gospel, and also at the beginning of the second part. The Acts of the Apostles mention Mary amid the disciples in prayer, awaiting the coming of the Holy Spirit: the Apostles "devoted themselves to prayer, together with the women and Mary, the mother of Jesus and with his brethren" (Acts 1:14). As the Holy Spirit descended on Mary for the Incarnation, so He descends on the newborn church for Pentecost, called by prayer. In the works of Luke, we find various points of contact between the Annunciation and Pentecost:

> On one hand, there is Mary: overshadowed by the Holy Spirit in the interior of her own self (Lk 1:35), she nearly bursts out into the external world, onto the hills of Judea (v. 39), to proclaim the great things the Almighty has done in her (vv. 46,49). On the other, there is the apostolic church of Jerusalem: validated by the power of the Spirit (Lk 24:49; Acts 1:8) while they were all together inside the house (Acts 2:2), it leaves its retreat to publicly proclaim the great works of the Lord (Acts 2:4, 6, 7, 11, 12). The illumination of the Spirit allows both Mary and the church to be prophetic witnesses of what God has done for his people (cf. Acts 2:4, 11, 17, 18)."[128]

The account of those gathered in prayer links together four components: the eleven apostles (with their names), Mary (by name and with the addition "the mother of Jesus"), several women, and the brethren (Acts 1:14). Immediately thereafter Luke describes the replacement of Judas by Matthias, a qualified witness of the public ministry of Jesus. It seems that all the persons named (out of about 120 present: Acts 1:15) had a particular role in regard to testimony. This is obvious for the apostles, but is real also for the women who accompany the Lord during his travels (Lk 8:2f.) and who are witnesses of both the crucifixion and the empty tomb (Lk 23:49, 23:55, 24:1–11). It is mentioned that James, one of the "brethren" of the

128. Serra, "Bibbia," 273 (see the table of linguistic coincidences there).

Lord, received an appearance of the risen Christ (1 Cor 15:7; after the appearances, the "brethren" come to believe in Jesus). Mary is mentioned twice (Lk 2:19, 2:51) as a witness in the infancy gospel. The persons named constitute the continuity between the pre-paschal circle around Jesus and the post-paschal community.[129]

Besides the apostles, only Mary is mentioned with her proper name; her central role is added: "the mother of Jesus." Her maternal mission begins to extend itself to become mother of the church, as John Paul II observes:

> Mary "prays for the gift of the Spirit for herself and for the community.
>
> "It was appropriate that the first outpouring of the Spirit upon her, which had happened in view of her divine maternity, should be repeated and reinforced. Indeed, at the foot of the cross Mary was entrusted with a new motherhood which was concerned with Jesus' disciples. It was precisely this mission that demanded a renewed gift of the Spirit. The Blessed Virgin therefore desired it for the fruitfulness of her spiritual motherhood."[130]

At Pentecost, "Mary also was fully illuminated by the Spirit about what Jesus did and said. From then on, it is reasonable to think that she began to pour out on the Church the treasures which she had until then enclosed in the casket of her sapiential meditations. In this way, the Virgin also ... became a witness of the things she had seen and heard (cf. Lk 1:2)."[131]

The Presence of Mary in the Gospel according to John

References to the Virgin Birth

In the gospel according to John,[132] Mary is present in two central events: at the wedding of Cana, when her intercession obtains the

129. See Josef Zmijewski, *Die Apostelgeschichte* [Acts of the Apostles] (Regensburg: Pustet, 1994), 76f.

130. John Paul II, CM 52 (May 28, 1997), 3; cf. Galot, *Maria, La donna*, 360f. See *RM* 24 (correspondence between the Annunciation and Pentecost).

131. Serra, "Bibbia," 273.

132. See, inter alia, Serra, *Maria a Cana e presso la croce: Saggio di mariologia giovannea* [Mary at Cana and at the Foot of the Cross: Essay in Johannine Mariology] (Rome: Centro di cultura mariana "Madre della Chiesa," 1985); Serra, "Bibbia," 274–92; Serra, *Le nozze di Cana (Gv 2,1–12): Incidenze cristologico-mariane del primo "segno" di Gesù* [The Wedding of Cana (Jn 2:1–12):

first miracle, and below the cross, when the "hour" toward which Jesus' activity is directed is fulfilled. Both passages are well known, correspond to each other (they form a narrative framework),[133] and possess a notable depth.

Less known are the references (hypothetical or factual) to the virgin birth. A first allusion to this reality perhaps appears in the prologue.[134] We find two versions of textual witness for John 1:13, manuscript and patristic. The former is presented, for example, in the text of the *Revised Standard Version*, Second Catholic Edition:

> (12) But to all who received him, who believed in his name, he gave power to become children of God; (13) who were born (*eghennéthesan*), not of blood nor of the will of the flesh nor of the will of man but of God.

The other version, preferred, for instance, by the Jerusalem Bible, presents v. 13 in the singular:

> [the Word] who was born (*eghennéthe*) not out of human stock or urge of the flesh of will of man but of God (*ek theoû*) himself.

The reading in the plural is found in all of the Greek manuscripts, including papyri of the third century. These witnesses are concentrated in the area of Egypt. The reading in the singular, although the number of witnesses handed down is smaller, nonetheless seems more ancient and geographically dispersed. It appears in the patristic writings starting from Irenaeus—that is, starting from the second century. It is present in manuscripts of the *Vetus latina* and in other Syriac sources. We find it in Syria (Letter of the Twelve Apostles), Egypt (Origen), North Africa (Tertullian), in Rome (Hippolytus), and in Gaul (Irenaeus). The transition from the singular reading to

Christological-Marian Implications of the First "Sign" of Jesus] (Padua: Messaggero, 2009); Serra, *Maria presso la Croce: Solo l'addolorata? Verso una rilettura dei contenuti di Giovanni 19,25–27* [Mary at the Foot of the Cross: Only the Lady of Sorrows? Toward a Re-reading of the Content of Jn 19:25–27] (Padua: Messaggero, 2011); de la Potterie, *Maria nel mistero*; Bastero, *Mary, Mother of the Redeemer*, 135–53; Ziegenaus, *Maria in der Heilsgeschichte*, 119–33; Stefano M. Manelli, *All Generations*, 331–53, 371–90; Valentini, *Maria secondo le Scritture*, 275–324.

133. The account of the wedding at Cana is found near the start of the gospel (Jn 2); in contrast, the account of Mary at the foot of the Cross is near the end (Jn 19). In both texts Mary is called by the unaccustomed appellation "woman."

134. See, for example, the brief *status quaestionis* in Serra, "Vergine II," *NDM*, 1431–36.

the plural reading probably took place for an anti-Docetist reason: the formula "not of blood" (literally, "not of bloods"), referring to Jesus, could support the misunderstanding that the humanity of Jesus was not true flesh, because blood was considered the material of conception. On the other hand, it seems more difficult to theorize about the motive for a change from the plural to the singular. The singular version also finds a certain support in a similar passage: "We know that anyone who has been begotten by God does not sin, because the begotten Son of God (*ho ghennetheìs ek toû theoû*) protects him" (1 Jn 5:18).

A reading in the singular expresses the virginal conception of Jesus. In the process of the Incarnation sexual instinct is excluded ("not by the will of the flesh"), as is the intervention of man ("nor by the will of man"). The only fatherhood was that of God ("but was born of God"). The classic interpretation of the expression "of bloods," maintained today by Jean Galot, among others, is found in Augustine: "The bloods" are the blood of the father and the mother that run together to form the new creature.[135] Ignace de la Potterie, in contrast, thinks it is implied that the birth of Jesus took place without a loss of blood that caused ritual impurity in every childbearing mother.[136] In the Hebrew parts of the OT and in rabbinical texts, the word "bloods" (*damîn*) refers to blood shed by the woman during birth and during menstruation (see Lv 12:4, 12:7, 20:18; Ez 16:6, 16:9).[137]

135. See Augustine, *In Johannem* 2.1.14 (*CChr. SL* 36:8.18); Jean Galot, SJ, *Être né de Dieu: Jean 1,13* [Being Born of God: Jn 1:13], Analecta biblica 37 (Rome: Pontifical Biblical Institute, 1969); Galot, *Maria, La donna*, 127f.

136. The exegete adds to this thesis an interpretation of Lk 1:35 that affirms: "He who is to be born holy will be called Son of God." "Holiness," in this context, would be the absence of contamination according to the "holiness code" in Leviticus (Lv 17–26). See the summary of the debate in Serra, "Vergine II," *NDM*, 1445–48; Perrella, *Maria, Vergine e Madre*, 101–5. Thus we will have in Lk 1:35 and Jn 1:13 a biblical testimony of the *virginitas in partu;* see also in Chapter 2, "Patristic Motifs through the Sixth Century."

The author of a monograph on Jn 1:13 holds, similarly, that the verse denies an origin in ritually impure blood from the woman and implies instead a conception prior to the first menstruation (thus by a virgin before the matrimonial cohabitation): Peter Hofrichter, "Jungfräulichkeit I. 4" (Jn), in *ML* 3:468f.; see Hofrichter, *Nicht aus Blut, sondern monogen aus Gott geboren: Textkritische, dogmengeschichtliche und exegetische Untersuchung zu Joh 1,13–14* [Not of Blood, but Only-Begotten of God: Text-Critical, Dogmatic-Historical, and Exegetical Investigation on Jn 1:13–14] (Würzburg: Echter, 1978).

137. See de la Potterie, SJ, "Il parto verginale del Verbo incarnato: 'Non ex sanguinibus ...

The outcome of the exegetical controversy (whether the text has a singular or plural reading) remains open.[138] The better arguments seem inclined toward the singular reading.[139] Even Pope John Paul II has written on this point:

> The Church has constantly held that Mary's virginity is a truth of faith, as she has received and reflected on the witness of the gospels of Luke, of Matthew and probably also of John.... This truth, according to a recent exegetical discovery, would be explicitly contained in verse 13 of the Prologue of John's Gospel, which some ancient authoritative authors (for example, Irenaeus and Tertullian) present, not in the usual plural form, but in the singular: "He, who was born, not of blood nor of the will of the flesh nor of the will of man, but of God." This version in the singular would make the Johannine Prologue one of the major attestations of Jesus' virginal conception, placed in the context of the mystery of the Incarnation.[140]

In addition to this (hypothetical) passage regarding the virginal conception, we must also take account of another clue. During the discourse on the bread of life, the Jews murmur and say, "Surely this is Jesus son of Joseph.... We know his father and mother. How can he now say, 'I have come down from heaven'?" (Jn 6:42) In response, Jesus speaks of the (heavenly) "Father" four times (Jn 6:43–47); He seems to be discreetly correcting the origin from a human father.

The same observation applies to the encounter with Philip and Nathanael. At first Philip presents Jesus to Nathanael as "son of Joseph" (Jn 1:45); but the scene ends with the awareness of the superhuman dignity of Jesus. The title "son of man" recalls the heavenly origin of the anonymous figure of the book of the prophet Daniel (Jn 1:49–51; Dn 7).[141]

---

sed ex Deo natus est'" [The Virginal Birth of the Incarnate Word: "Born not of Bloods ... but of God"], *Marianum* 45, no. 130 (1983): 139–50; de la Potterie, *Maria nel misterio*, 131–37. Perrella, *Maria, Vergine e Madre*, 103, in support of this interpretation, reports a study made by a medical doctor and rabbi: Riccardo Di Segni, "'Colei che non ha mai visto il sangue': Alla ricerca delle radici ebraiche dell'idea della concezione verginale di Maria" ["She Who Never Saw Blood": In Search of the Hebrew Roots of the Idea of Mary's Virginal Conception], *Quaderni Storici* 75, no. 3 (1990): 757–89.

138. The summary in Ziegenaus, *Maria in der Heilsgeschichte*, 123, speaks of a "balance."

139. See Perrella, *Maria, Vergine e Madre*, 101–5.

140. John Paul II, CM 26 (July 10, 1996), 1, 3; Galot, *Maria, La donna*, 127f. (without "probably").

141. See Ziegenaus, *Maria in der Heilsgeschichte*, 123f.

Mary at the Wedding of Cana

(1) On the third day, there was a marriage at Cana in Galilee, and the mother of Jesus was there; (2) Jesus also was invited to the marriage, with his disciples. (3) When the wine failed, the mother of Jesus said to him, "They have no wine." (4) And Jesus said to her, "O woman, what have you to do with me? My hour has not yet come." (5) His mother said to the servants, "Do whatever he tells you." (6) Now six stone jars were standing there, for the Jewish rites of purification, each holding twenty or thirty gallons. (7) Jesus said to them, "Fill the jars with water." And they filled them up to the brim. (8) He said to them, "Now draw some out, and take it to the steward of the feast." So they took it. (9) When the steward of the feast tasted the water, now become wine, and did not know where it came from (though the servants who had drawn the water knew), the steward of the feast called the bridegroom (10) and said to him, "Every man serves the good wine first; and when men have drunk freely, then the poor wine; but you have kept the good wine until now." (11) This, the first of his signs, Jesus did at Cana in Galilee, and manifested his glory; and his disciples believed in him. (12) After this he went down to Capernaum, with his mother and his brethren and his disciples; and there they stayed for a few days. (Jn 2:1–12)

In the episode of the wedding at Cana, St. John presents Mary's first intervention in the public life of Jesus and highlights her co-operation in her Son's mission.[142]

The account of the wedding of Cana is set in the "inaugural week" of the public life of Jesus (Jn 1:19–2:12). This week begins at the Jordan and concludes with the manifestation of glory at Cana (Jn 2:12).

The initial setting on "the third day" (v. 1) is counting from the fourth day of the inaugural week (the call of Philip and Nathanael).[143] Some exegetes support a symbolic meaning: a similarity to the creation (Gn 1:1–2:4a), to the theophany at Sinai,[144] or to the

142. John Paul II, CM 44 ("Jesus Works Miracle at Mary's Request," Feb. 26, 1997), 1.

143. Since it would be counting from the fourth day inclusive, this would refer to the sixth day of the inaugural week.

144. Ex 19:11: "Let them ... hold themselves in readiness for the third day, because on the third day Yahweh will descend on the mountain of Sinai in the sight of all the people." Ex 19:16: "Now at daybreak on the third day there were peals of thunder on the mountain and lightning flashes, a dense cloud, and a loud trumpet blast" (the theophany).

resurrection on the third day (see Jn 2:19–21). Of these, a connection with the event on Sinai, the revelation of the divine glory, the giving of the law and the Covenant, seems most suggestive.[145] This view leads to the interpretation "As Yahweh revealed his glory on Sinai giving the law to Moses, so at Cana Jesus reveals his glory, giving a better wine, symbol of the new law which is his gospel."[146]

The "third day" seems to be connected with the "hour" of Jesus to which v. 4 refers. The "hour" of Jesus in the gospel according to John is the passage from this world to the Father (Jn 13:1), and the passion and death on the cross, and the resurrection that follows, are designated by this "hour."[147] Augustine suggests identifying this "hour" with the event of the Passion, while others relate it to the fitting time for the first miracle.[148] Just as Jesus accepts Mary's suggestion to work the miracle, it seems that this event already anticipates, in a sense, the "hour" of the glorification of Jesus. Thus "we can ... say that a thread runs through the theological weave of the fourth gospel from the 'third day' of Sinai, to the 'third day' of Cana, and the 'third day' of the glorifying passion of Christ: three milestones on the one itinerary leading to salvation."[149] Still, it does not seem that the "hour" of Jn 2:4 can be identified with the "hour" of the final glorification.

John never mentions the name of Mary, but speaks of the "mother of Jesus" (vv. 1–2; see 12: "mother"), while Jesus designates his mother as "woman" (Jn 2:4, 19:26). This is a strange title; there is no literary parallel in antiquity in which a son speaks to his mother in this way.[150] It might be a sign of distance, because the Lord, in his messianic work, depends solely on the heavenly Father.[151]

145. See Ex 24:17.

146. Serra, "Bibbia," 276.

147. See Jn 7:30, 8:20, 12:23, 12:27, 13:1, 17:1.

148. John Paul II, CM 44 (Feb. 26, 1997), 4, mentions this; see Galot, *Maria, La donna*, 64f., which prefers the second version.

149. Serra, "Bibbia," 276.

150. See J. Michl, "Frau" [Woman], in *ML* 2:520.

151. See John Paul II, CM 44 (Feb. 26, 1997), 3: "According to one interpretation, from the moment his mission begins Jesus seems to call into question the natural relationship of son to which his mother refers. The sentence, in the local parlance, is meant to stress a distance between the persons, by excluding a communion of life. This distance does not preclude respect and esteem"

At the same time, another interpretation has been offered that connects the title "woman" with the "woman" of the Protoevangelium, the mother of the Messiah (Gn 3:15). This connection is obvious, at least for Rv 12:1–6: the "woman" clothed with the sun, and opposed, along with her son, to the dragon, clearly recalls the account of Genesis. Not all exegetes consider the apostle John the author of the book of Revelation, but in any case, an interpretation that gives a symbolic depth to the title "woman" does seem possible: Mary as the "new Eve," as representative of the new Israel. Following the prophet Hosea, we have to take into account the fact that the mystery of the Covenant is compared with marriage; woman is a sign of Israel, "married" to Yahweh. Woman becomes a symbol for man in general, inasmuch as he is open to salvation or refuses it.

"They have no more wine" (v. 3). The lack of wine is explained by the length of the wedding ceremony, which was celebrated for an entire week with the participation of as many guests as possible. Still, it is an annoyance when the wine starts to run out. In this observation offered to Jesus, "we see a woman's attention to detail."[152]

This observation, like other details of the story, invites a symbolic perspective (beyond the immediate meaning of a lack of wine). A lack of wine is considered a sign of divine punishment,[153] while abundance of excellent wine illustrates messianic riches.[154] The miraculous transformation of water into wine, therefore, can appear as a prophetic announcement of the new covenant. Mary, representative of Israel, shows her son the lack of wine that symbolizes messianic salvation.

In this context we should also note what kind of water is transformed into wine. There are "six stone water jars standing there,

---

(the Pope notices the recurrence of the term "woman" in the dialogues with the Canaanite woman [Mt 15:25], with the Samaritan woman [Jn 4:2], with the woman caught in adultery [Jn 8:10], and with Mary Magdalen [Jn 20:13]). "With the expression: 'O woman, what have you to do with me?,' Jesus intends to put Mary's co-operation on the level of salvation which, by involving her faith and hope, requires her to go beyond her natural role of mother."

152. Forte, *Maria, la donna icona*, 91.

153. As in Is 24:8–11.

154. Is 25:6–9. And the benefits of Wisdom (Prv 9:5); the Targum uses "wine" as one of the preferred symbols of the Mosaic law: Serra, "Bibbia," 278.

meant for the ablutions that are customary among the Jews" (v. 6). So there was water destined for the ablutions prescribed by the law of Moses. "Purification" no longer comes from observance of the Mosaic law but from the salvation brought by Jesus Christ. "You are clean already, by means of the word that I have spoken to you" (Jn 15:3).

"What have you to do with me?" (*tì emoì kaì soí*) (v. 4b). This phrase is a common formula for indicating a difference in viewpoints. Ignace de la Potterie interprets it this way: Jesus and Mary are thinking from different perspectives; "she is thinking of wine for the feast, while Jesus is thinking of the messianic mission that is beginning."[155] "While ... Mary is making known the shortage of material wine, Jesus raises the conversation to the level of the spiritual realities that concern his hour."[156]

The interpretation of the question ("What have you to do with me, woman?") is tied to the next phrase, which can be read as a statement or as a rhetorical question: "My hour has not come" or "Has not my hour come?" If it is read as a question, "Has not my hour come?," the whole verse gets this meaning: "What do you want? My hour has already come!" In this case, "hour" signifies messianic action determined by the Father. The "hour" cannot be interpreted as a reference to the final glorification, as elsewhere in the gospel,[157] but only as an anticipation or a foretaste (not a realization) of it.[158]

If instead the phrase is read as a statement (the hour has not come), a difficulty arises: Mary's suggestion is not refused, but accepted, as is shown by what follows. And therefore, the reading of the phrase as a rhetorical question is preferable.[159]

Mary's response shows a total readiness to orient herself to the

155. De la Potterie, "La Madre de Jesús en el misterio de Caná" [The Mother of Jesus in the Mystery of Cana], *Scripta di Maria* 1st ser., 4 (1981): 13, cited in Bastero, *Mary, Mother of the Redeemer*, 142; see de la Potterie, *Maria nel mistero*, 202.

156. Serra, "Bibbia," 280.

157. See Jn 7:30, 8:20: the hour had not yet come.

158. See Salvatore A. Panimolle, *Lettura pastorale del vangelo di Giovanni* [Pastoral Reading of the Gospel of John], 3rd ed. (Bologna: EDM, 1988), 1:220.

159. For example, Panimolle, *Lettura pastorale*, 220; Hofrichter, "Hochzeit zu Kana" [Wedding at Cana], in *ML* 3:218f. Conversely Valentini, *Maria secondo le Scritture*, 279n5.

will of Jesus: "His mother said to the servants, 'Do whatever he tells you'" (v. 5). This phrase also finds a notable parallel in the story of the events of Sinai. "Indeed, in the immediacy of making a pact with Yahweh at the foot of the holy mountain, all the assembly of Israel broke out three times in a unanimous choral response: 'what the Lord has spoken, we will do' (Ex 19:8; 24:3, 7). This profession of fidelity was the spousal 'yes' of the chosen nation to its bridegroom Yahweh.... Here we have an identification, be it but indirect and allusive, between *the community of Israel and the mother of Jesus.*"[160]

For this reason, too, it is appropriate to address Mary with the term "woman." "In more explicit terms: Jesus sees in his mother the personification of ancient Israel just at the threshold of the messianic redemption. And as the gift of the ancient Mosaic law was preceded by a prompt declaration of faith by Israel, so too the gift of wine at Cana—a prophetic symbol of the new law of Christ—is preceded by the total abandonment of Mary to the will of the Son: 'Do whatever he tells you.'"[161] It is the last word handed on by Mary in the gospels, a testimony of the radical Christocentric orientation that should proceed from venerating the mother of Jesus.

Mary at the Foot of the Cross

(25) Standing by the cross of Jesus were his mother, and his mother's sister, Mary the wife of Clopas, and Mary Magdalene. (26) When Jesus saw his mother, and the disciple whom he loved standing near, he said to his mother, "Woman, behold, your son!" (27) Then he said to the disciple: "Behold, your mother!" And from that hour the disciple took her to his own home. (Jn 19:25–27)

Mary is present at the wedding of Cana, at the beginning of the public activity of Jesus in the gospel according to John. In addition, the mother of the Lord is mentioned at the foot of the cross, when the "hour" of Jesus is realized, that of his passage from this world to the Father. The importance of the scene is emphasized by the following verse: "After this, Jesus, knowing that all was now finished"

160. Serra, "Bibbia," 280.
161. Serra, "Bibbia," 281.

(v. 28). Having consigned the disciple to his mother and vice versa, the work for which Jesus was sent is completed.

Mary is presented together with a group of women.[162] This group is also mentioned in the synoptic gospels, but those do not mention the presence of the mother of Jesus.[163] While the women in the synoptics look on "from afar" (Mk 15:40), John describes the presence of the little group "by the cross."

When Jesus saw his mother and the disciple whom he loved, standing near, he said to his mother, "Woman, behold, your son!" Then he said to the disciple: "Behold, your mother!" And from that hour the disciple took her to his own home. (Jn 19:26f.)

Jesus, even in his agony, is concerned for the future of his mother and his favorite disciple. The fact that the mother is entrusted to John is an argument against the interpretation of "brethren of Jesus" as brothers in the strict sense.

It seems interesting that the first phrase of Jesus is not about the fate of his mother, but about committing Mary to the good of John: "Woman, behold, your son!" The unusual appellation "woman" reappears, as in the story of the wedding at Cana. This term is linked to a reading that goes beyond the immediate sense of the passage: Mary appears as a "new Eve," as a representative of Israel, of the newborn church, of those who seek salvation, even if the nuances of the symbolism are debated among exegetes.

Both at the wedding of Cana and below the cross, the title

162. There is debate about whether there are three or four women. According to Rudolf Schnackenburg, *Il Vangelo di Giovanni* [The Gospel of John], vol. 3 (Brescia: Paideia, 1981) (and others), there were four: two are mentioned without their names (the mother of Jesus and her sister), two by name. In the rabbinic tradition is a recurring idea of the four mothers of Israel: Sarah (seen as a new Eve), Rebecca, Rachel, and Leah (or perhaps Eve, Sarah, Rebecca, and Rachel): Frédéric Manns, "Esegesi di Gv 19,25–27" [Exegesis of Jn 19:25–27], *Theotokos* 7 (1999): 333–36.

If there are three women, "Mary of Clopas" would be the "sister" (= relative) of the mother of Jesus; the fact that the gospels mention two or three names of the women (in regard to the cross and the empty tomb) seems connected with judicial testimony that calls for two or three witnesses (even if the testimonies of women were not accepted in a trial): Dt 19:15, cited several times in the NT (Mt 18:16; Jn 8:16; 2 Cor 13:1; Heb 10:28; 1 Tm 5:19).

163. Mk and Mt highlight three names: Mk 15:40 names Mary Magdalen, Mary the mother of James the lesser and of Joses, and Salome, and also refers to "many other women"; Mt 27:56 replaces "Salome" with "the mother of the sons of Zebedee"; see Lk 23:49: "The women who had come with him from Galilee" were watching from a distance.

"woman" is connected to the "hour" of Jesus (Jn 2:4, 13:1, 17:1) Mary therefore is carrying out a particular role in salvation history.

The fact that John takes Mary *eis tà ídia* (literally "among his own things") means not only "to his own home." Seeing the Johannine context of the expression,[164] there is more: "Among those 'own things' we would principally see 'spiritual goods,' 'values of the faith'; those goods, those values which the love of Jesus made into a gift to the disciples: such as his word (Jn 17:8), the eucharistic bread (Jn 6:51), peace (Jn 14:27), the Holy Spirit (Jn 20:22).... Hence in substance, those 'own things' amount to *the disciple's faith in the Master*, and *the vital environment in which he has now situated his own existence.*"[165]

The disciple "whom Jesus loved" is identified by tradition with the apostle John. There is a confirmation of this interpretation in the closeness between Peter and John in the Acts of the Apostles,[166] corresponding to the link between the favorite disciple and Peter in the Gospel according to John.[167] The fact that John is not mentioned by name may have a deeper meaning: "The disciple 'whom Jesus loved' would be ... *the 'type' of every other disciple who, for reasons of faith, is loved by Christ.*"[168]

Seeing the symbolic depth of the passage, Mary and John appear as representatives of spiritual values even beyond the historical sense (which is presupposed). The true disciple must accept Mary "among his goods," and Mary, accepting care and concern for John, becomes spiritual mother to all the disciples. This spiritual motherhood of Mary as the "new Eve" is underscored by recent exegetical works.[169] On the other hand, this interpretation does not seem obvious to everyone (at the level of the literal sense), and explicit conviction of

164. See Serra, "Bibbia," 291, with reference to Jn 1:11, 8:44, 15:19, 16:32.

165. Serra, "Bibbia," 292. See also Valentini, *Maria secondo le Scritture*, 320–23.

166. Acts 3–4, 8:14. According to Luke, Peter and John prepare the Last Supper together (Lk 22:8). In the synoptic gospels Peter, James, and John already appear as a "nucleus" of the apostles (present, inter alia, at the Transfiguration and on the Mount of Olives).

167. Jn 13:23, 20:2, 21:7, 21:20.

168. Serra, "Bibbia," 290.

169. Especially by Ignace de la Potterie, famous specialist on Johannine theology, including in *Maria nel mistero*, 229–51.

finding the spiritual motherhood of Mary for all the faithful in this passage only arrives centuries later. In any case, this reading finds in the Johannine account a point of contact that invites us to a deeper understanding.[170] John Paul II, following the path of Tradition, sees in John 19 a prefiguration of the universal mediation of Mary[171] as well as a basis for the Marian devotion willed by Christ himself.[172]

The "Woman" of the Apocalypse

The Apocalypse,[173] the book of Revelation, brings a message of hope in a difficult situation, probably during the persecution of Domitian (c. 95).[174] The book uses a strongly symbolic language, rich with references to the OT. We find certain parallels with the Gospel according to John, even if there are notable differences of style. For this reason, its attribution to the Apostle John is often contested today, although the better arguments (including the testimony of the first tradition) seem to favor an apostolic origin.[175]

Chapter 12 sets a woman, who is giving birth to a son, in opposition to a dragon. The passage is divided into three parts: the woman, her son, and the dragon are presented (vv. 1–6); Michael's victorious

170. See "La Madre di Gesù presso la Croce" [The Mother of Jesus at the Foot of the Cross], *Theotokos* 7, no. 2 (1999); Antonio García Moreno, "María en el Calvario (Jn 19,25–27)" [Mary at Calvary (Jn 19:25–27)], *Scripta de Maria* 2nd ser., 2 (2005): 217–19.

171. Among others, see John Paul II, *RM* 23f; CM 49 (Apr. 23, 1997), 3: "Even if in God's plan Mary's motherhood was destined from the start to extend to all humanity, only on Calvary, by virtue of Christ's sacrifice, is its universal dimension revealed." The topic will be explored in more depth in chap. 8.

172. See, for example, John Paul II, *RM* 45 (Origin of Consecration to Mary at the Foot of the Cross); CM 50 (May 7, 1997), 2: "The words 'Behold, your mother!' express Jesus' intention to inspire in his disciples an attitude of love for and trust in Mary, leading them to recognize her as their mother, the mother of every believer." On Marian devotion (including consecration to the Blessed Virgin), see chap. 10.

173. See, among others, de la Potterie, *Maria nel mistero*, 255–78; Mussner, *Maria, die Mutter Jesu*, 119–55; Pavol Farkaš, *La "Donna" di Apocalisse 12: Storia, bilancio, nuove prospettive* [The "Woman" of Revelation 12: History, Summary, New Perspectives] (Rome: Pontificia Università Gregoriana, 1997); Giancarlo Biguzzi, "La donna, il drago e il Messia in Ap 12" [The Woman, the Dragon, and the Messiah in Rv 12], *Theotokos* 8, no. 1 (2000): 17–66; Stefano M. Manelli, *All Generations*, 405–25; Valentini, *Maria secondo le Scritture*, 325–58.

174. Other exegetes propose a dating around the persecution of Nero (after 64).

175. For more, see the commentaries. The difference in language may come from the fact that the gospel underwent a redaction by the Johannine school, but the Revelation (written in exile on the isle of Patmos) did not.

battle against the dragon (vv. 7–13); the flight of the woman into the desert and the aggression of the dragon (vv. 14–17).

> (1) And a great sign appeared in heaven, a woman clothed with the sun, with the moon under her feet, and on her head a crown of twelve stars; (2) she was with child and she cried out in her pangs of birth, in anguish for delivery. (3) And another sign appeared in heaven; behold, a great red dragon, with seven heads and ten horns, and seven diadems upon his heads. (4) His tail swept down a third of the stars of heaven, and cast them to the earth. And the dragon stood before the woman who was about to bear a child, that he might devour her child when she brought it forth; (5) she brought forth a male child, one who is to rule all the nations with a rod of iron, but her child was caught up to God and to his throne, (6) and the woman fled into the wilderness, where she has a place prepared by God, in which to be nourished for one thousand two hundred and sixty days. (Rv 12:1–6)

The Old Testament source is indisputable: the opposition between the "woman" and the "serpent" in Genesis 3:15 (Rv 12:9: "the great dragon … that ancient serpent"). The figure of the "woman" evokes the new Jerusalem, mother of the messianic people (see Is 66:7), and in general Israel (see, for instance, the reference to "twelve stars," v. 1).[176]

The woman is "clothed with the sun," the source of light, image of the glory of God who is "robed with light as with a cloak" (Ps 104:2). The "daughter of Zion," too, is "clothed" with "beautiful garments" (Is 52:1) and "garments of salvation" (Is 61:10) in the messianic age. Since the moon is the star by which the seasons are measured,[177] the woman with the moon at her feet may symbolize a superiority to the events of this life. The "crown" is a sign of victory and also appears in other passages of Revelation (Rv 3:11, 4:4, 4:10, 6:2, 14:14).

The woman with the crown of twelve stars is a figure of the ancient people of Israel. At the same time, she bears traits of the new Israel, the newborn church: the woman appears as mother of the Messiah raised to the throne of God (v. 5) and of those who

176. See Gn 37:9: in the dream, Joseph sees the sun, the moon (father, mother), and eleven stars (his brothers) that bow down before him.

177. See Gn 1:14–19.

bear witness to Christ (v. 17); moreover, at the end of the book, the "woman" takes on the outlines of the "bride of the Lamb" (Rv 21:2, 21:9). She is "the holy city Jerusalem coming down out of heaven from God.... It had a great, high wall, with twelve [!] gates, and at the gates twelve angels, and on the gates the names of the twelve tribes of the sons of Israel were inscribed.... And the wall of the city had twelve foundations, and on them the twelve names of the twelve apostles of the Lamb" (Rv 21:10, 21:12, 21:14). Obviously, this description is moving from Israel to the church (the twelve apostles of the Lamb).

"She was with child and she cried out in her pangs of birth, in anguish for delivery" (v. 2). Labor pains were already, in the OT, a sign of the affliction and difficulty experienced by Israel.[178] Birth-pangs appear in various passages of the NT as a sign of the last days.[179] In this perspective the woman's birth-pangs point to the last days, which began with the birth of the Messiah.[180] In a Marian perspective, the pain of the "woman" can be compared with the suffering presence of the Mother of God below the cross.[181]

Set in opposition to the woman is the satanic power of the dragon. His wrath is aimed against the woman's son, scarcely born. But the son is lifted up to the throne of God, a sign of the heavenly dominion of Jesus Christ after the Ascension. This dominion brings victory against the dragon, which is then described with Michael's battle (vv. 7–13). The woman flees to the desert, the place of testing,[182] for a limited time (vv. 6, 14)[183] that lasts until the parousia. It is the time of persecution, even if the dragon cannot defeat the woman and her "offspring" (vv. 13–17).

178. For example, Jer 4:31 ("I heard a cry as of a woman with labor pains, anguish as of one bringing forth her first child, the cry of the daughter of Zion"); see Jer 6:24, 13:21, 22:23, 30:6.

179. See Mk 13:8; Mt 24:8; 1 Thes 5:3.

180. The "pangs of birth" seem to also imply the passion of Jesus; see Jn 16:21f.: "When a woman is in labor, she has pain, because her hour has come; but when she is delivered of the child, she no longer remembers the anguish, for joy that a child is born into the world. So you have sorrow now, but I will see you again and your hearts will rejoice, and no one will take your joy from you."

181. See Laurentin, *Short Treatise*, 41f.; Manelli, *All Generations*, 419–21.

182. See Dt 8:2: "You shall remember all the way which the Lord your God has led you these forty years in the wilderness, that he might humble you, testing you."

183. Verse 14: 3.5 is half of 7, a perfect number.

The apocalyptic woman primarily represents the old and the new people of God. The situation described in the chapter corresponds to the entire age of the church. Nonetheless, a Marian significance is implicit. Not all of her traits can be applied to Mary, but the identification of the newborn son with Jesus (v. 5) hardly allows for excluding the mother of the Lord from the symbolism. The placement of the woman in the desert does not represent the Assumption into heavenly glory[184] or her bodily transfiguration, but divine protection in the passage toward her final destiny. The mother of the Messiah is a sign and type of the church in her spiritual maternity and her invincibility despite persecutions. Divine protection and the opposition between the dragon and the woman indicate the immaculate sanctity of the new Eve. The church is "painted" with Marian "colors," and Mary appears as the prototype of the church.[185]

Looking at the Apocalypse underscores the presence of the mother of the Messiah in the whole arc of biblical history, from the "Protoevangelium" of Genesis until the last days described prophetically in the symbolism of the Revelation of John.[186] Mary, subordinate to her Son, belongs to the "golden thread" that passes throughout the history of salvation, from predestination to heavenly glorification. Much of its content still waits for greater expression and clarification, as happens in the history of the church. But Sacred Scripture already brings an immense treasure, a broad base on which Marian dogma rests.

REFERENCES

Old Testament Preparations

Ecclesiastical Texts

Catechism of the Catholic Church (CCC). 2nd ed., nn. 410–11, 489. Vatican City: Libreria Editrice Vaticana, 2000.

Graber, Rudolf and Anton Ziegenaus, eds. *Die Marianischen Weltrundschreiben der Päpste von Pius IX, bis Johannes Paul II (1849–1988)* [The Marian Encyclicals of the

184. We will return to this in Chapter 7: see "Biblical Foundations."

185. See Ziegenaus, "Apokalyptische Frau" [Woman of the Apocalypse], in *ML* 1:191.

186. See John Paul II, *RM* 24: Mary is present in the mystery of Christ as "'the woman' spoken of by the Book of Genesis (3:15) at the beginning and by the Apocalypse (12:1) at the end of the history of salvation."

Popes, from Pius IX to John Paul II *(1849–1988)*]. Regensburg: Institutum Marianum Regensburg, 1997. Biblical index. Also available in large part in *Enchiridion delle Encicliche* [Handbook of Encyclicals] (=*EE*), 8 vols. Bologna: EDB, 1994–98. In addition, some are available in Carlen, Claudia, ed. *The Papal Encyclicals* (= *PE*). 4 vols. Raleigh, N.C.: Pierian, 1990.

John Paul II. Marian Catecheses (CM) of Jan. 25, Jan. 31, Mar. 6, Mar. 27, Apr. 10, and Apr. 24, 1996. In *Theotokos: Woman, Mother, Disciple, A Catechesis on Mary, Mother of God.* Boston: Pauline, 2000.

Vatican Council II. Dogmatic Constitution on the Church *Lumen gentium* (November 21, 1964), 55.

Other Sources

Bastero, Juan Luis. *Mary, Mother of the Redeemer*, 63–80. Dublin: Four Courts, 2006.

Bea, Augustin. "Das Marienbild des Alten Bundes" [The Image of Mary in the Old Covenant]. In *Katholische Marienkunde* [Catholic Doctrine of Mary], edited by Paul Sträter, 1:23–43. Paderborn: F. Schöningh, 1947. Italian trans. Sträter, Paul, ed. *Mariologia*, 21–40. Torino: Marietti, 1952.

De Fiores, Stefano. "Microstoria della salvezza" [Micro-History of Salvation]. In *Maria. Nuovissimo dizionario*, 2:1143–69. Bologna: Dehoniane, 2006.

Haffner, Paul. *The Mystery of Mary*. 25–51. Leominster (England): Gracewing, 2004.

Hauke, Manfred, ed. *Maria und das Alte Testament*. Regensburg: Friedrich Pustet, 2015.

Laurentin, René. *A Short Treatise on the Virgin Mary*, 267–83. Washington, N.J.: AMII, 1991.

Lefebvre, Philippe. *La Vierge au Livre: Marie et l'Ancien Testament*. Paris: Cerf, 2004.

Manelli, Stefano Maria. *All Generations Shall Call Me Blessed: Biblical Mariology*, 2nd ed., 2–104. New Bedford, Mass.: Academy of the Immaculate, 2005.

May, Eric, OFM. "María en el Antiguo Testamento." In *Mariología*, edited by Juniper B. Carol, 54–81. Madrid: Biblioteca de Autores Cristianos, 1964. English original: "Mary in the Old Testament." In *Mariology*, edited by J. Carol, 1:51–79. Milwaukee: Bruce, 1954.

Noll, Raymund. *Die mariologischen Grundlinien im exegetischen Werk des Cornelius a Lapide (1567–1637)* [Mariological Principles in the Exegetical Work of Cornelius a Lapide, SJ (1567–1637)]. Mariologische Studien 16. Regensburg: Friedrich Pustet, 2003.

Paximadi, Giorgio. "L'importanza salvifica della donna nell'Antico Testamento" [The Salvific Importance of Woman in the Old Testament]. In *La donna e la salvezza: Maria e la vocazione femminile* [Woman and Salvation: Mary and the Feminine Vocation], edited by M. Hauke, CdM 7, 11–27. Lugano: Eupress FTL, 2006.

Piazza, Alessandro. "Maria nell'Antico Testamento" [Mary in the Old Testament]. In *EMTheo* (1958 ed.), 14–29.

Ponce Cuéllar, Miguel. *María: Madre del Redentor y Madre de la Iglesia* [Mary: Mother of the Redeemer and Mother of the Church], 2nd ed., 51–67. Barcelona: Herder, 2001.

Pozo, Cándido, SJ. *María en la obra de la salvación* [Mary in the Work of Salvation], 2nd ed., 126–201. Madrid: Biblioteca de Autores Cristianos, 1990.

———. *María, nueva Eva* [Mary, the New Eve], 125–201. Madrid: Biblioteca de Autores Cristianos, 2005.

Robert, André. "La Sainte Vierge dans l'Ancien Testament" [The Holy Virgin in the Old Testament]. In *Maria. Études sur la sainte vierge*, edited by H. du Manoir, 1:21–39. Paris: Beauchesne, 1949.

Serra, Aristide M. *La Donna dell'Alleanza: Prefigurazioni di Maria nell'Antico Testamento* [The Woman of the Covenant: Prefigurations of Mary in the Old Testament]. Padua: Messaggero, 2006.

Valentini, Alberto. *Maria secondo le Scritture: Figlia di Sion e Madre del Signore* [Mary according to the Scriptures: Daughter of Zion and Mother of the Lord], 393–404. Bologna: EDB, 2007.

Ziegenaus, Anton. *Katholische Dogmatik*. Vol. 5, *Maria in der Heilsgeschichte: Mariologie* [Catholic Dogmatics, vol. 5, Mary in Salvation History: Mariology], 160–92. Aachen: MM-Verlag, 1998.

Mary in the New Testament

Ecclesiastical Texts

Graber and Ziegenaus. *Weltrundschreiben*, biblical index (pontifical Magisterium).

John Paul II. CM of Sept. 6, 1995; May 1, May 8, July 3, July 10, July 24, Sep. 4, Oct. 2, Nov. 6, Nov. 20, Nov. 27, Dec. 4, Dec. 11, and Dec. 18, 1996; Jan. 8, Jan. 15, Jan. 29, Feb. 26, Mar. 5, Mar. 12, Apr. 2, Apr. 23, May 7, and May 28, 1997 (and passim).

John Paul II. Encyclical *Redemptoris Mater* (March 25, 1987), 7–24.

Vatican II. *Lumen gentium*, 56–59.

Other Sources

Balić, Carolus, ed. *Maria in sacra Scriptura* [Mary in Sacred Scripture]. 6 vols. Rome: PAMI, 1967.

Bastero. *Mary, Mother of the Redeemer*, 81–153.

Brown, Raymond E., ed. *Mary in the New Testament*. New York: Paulist Press, 1978.

Cantinat, Jean. *La Madonna nella Bibbia* [The Madonna in the Bible]. 3rd ed. Cinisello Balsamo: San Paolo, 1987.

Da Spinetoli, Ortensio. *Maria nella Bibbia* [Mary in the Bible]. 2nd ed. Bologna: EDB, 1988.

De Fiores, Stefano. *Maria, Madre di Gesù: Sintesi storico-salvifica* [Mary, Mother of Jesus: A Salvation-Historical Synthesis], 35–106. Bologna: EDB, 1992.

———. *Maria sintesi di valori: Storia culturale della mariologia* [Mary, Synthesis of Values: Cultural History of Mariology], 55–77. Cinisello Balsamo: Paoline, 2005.

———. "Bibbia." In *Maria: Nuovissimo dizionario* 1:291–321. Bologna: EDB, 2006.

de la Potterie, Ignace. *Maria nel mistero dell'alleanza* [Mary in the Mystery of the Covenant]. Genoa: Marietti, 1988.

Feuillet, A. "La Vierge Marie dans le Nouveau Testament" [The Virgin Mary in the New Testament]. In *Maria*, edited by H. du Manoir, 6:15–69. Paris: Beauchesne, 1961.

Forte, Bruno. *Maria, la donna, icona del Mistero: Saggio di mariologia simbolico-narrativa* [Mary the Woman, Icon of the Mystery: Essay in Symbolic-Narrative Mariology], 45–103. Cinisello Balsamo: Ed. Paoline, 1989 (3rd ed., 1996).
Gächter, Paul, SJ. *Maria im Erdenleben: Neutestamentliche Marienstudien* [Mary in Earthly Life: New Testament Marian Studies]. 3rd ed. Innsbruck: Tyrolia, 1955.
———. *Marjam, die Mutter Jesu* [Mariam, the Mother of Jesus]. 2nd ed. Einsiedeln: Johannes Verlag, 1981.
García Paredes, José Cristo Rey. *Mariología*. 3–169. Madrid: Biblioteca de Autores Cristianos, 1995.
Haffner. *Mystery of Mary*. 48–72.
Hilion, G. "La Sainte Vierge dans le Nouveau Testament" [The Holy Virgin in the New Testament]. In *Maria*, edited by H. du Manoir, 1:41–68. 1949.
Knoch, Otto, and Franz Mussner. "Maria in der Heiligen Schrift" [Mary in Sacred Scripture]. In *Handbuch der Marienkunde* [Handbook of Marian Doctrine], edited by Wolfgang Beinert and Heinrich Petri, 1:15–98. Regensburg: Friedrich Pustet, 1996.
Laconi, Mauro, OP. "Maria nel Nuovo Testamento" [Mary in the New Testament]. In *EMTheo* (1958 ed.), 30–43.
Laurentin, *Short Treatise*, 19–56, 318–21.
Manelli, Stefano. *All Generations Shall Call Me Blessed*, 109–436.
"Maria secondo le Scritture" [Mary according to the Scriptures]. *Theotokos* 8, no. 2 (2000): 377–905.
May. "María en el Antiguo Testamento."
Merk, A. "Das Marienbild des Neuen Bundes" [The Image of Mary in the New Covenant]. In *Katholische Marienkunde*, 3rd ed., edited by P. Sträter, 1:44–84.
Mussner, Franz. *Maria, die Mutter Jesu im Neuen Testament* [Mary, the Mother of Jesus, in the New Testament]. St. Ottilien: EOS Verlag, 1993.
Ponce Cuéllar. *María, Madre del Redentor*, 69–197.
Pozo, *María en la obra*, 202–46.
———. *María, nueva Eva*, 203–59.
Scheffczyk, Leo. *Maria, Mutter und Gefährtin Christi* [Mary, Mother and Companion of Christ], 14–82. Augsburg; Sankt Ulrich, 2003.
Serra, Aristide. "Bibbia" [Bible]. In *NDM*, 231–311.
———. *E c'era la Madre di Gesù ... Saggi di esegesi biblico-mariana (1978–1988)* [And the Mother of Jesus Was There ... Essays of Biblical-Marian Exegesis (1978–1988)]. Milan and Rome: CENS and Marianum, 1989.
———. *Maria secondo il Vangelo* [Mary according to the Gospel]. Brescia: Queriniana, 1987.
———. *Nato da donna ... Ricerche bibliche su Maria di Nazaret (1989–1992)* [Born of Woman ... Biblical Research on Mary of Nazareth (1989–1992)]. Milan and Rome: CENS and Marianum, 1992.
Söll, Georg. *Storia dei dogmi mariani* [History of Marian Dogmas]. Rome: Libreria Ateneo Salesiano, 1981, §1.
Stock, Klemens. *Maria, la Madre del Signore, nel Nuovo Testamento* [Mary, Mother of the Lord, in the New Testament]. 2nd ed. Rome: Ediziones ADP, 2003.

Valentini, Alberto. "Bibbia" [Bible]. In *DMar*, 199–216.

———. *Maria secondo le Scritture: Figlia di Sion e Madre del Signore* [Mary according to the Scriptures: Daughter of Zion and Mother of the Lord]. Bologna: EDB, 2007.

Ziegenaus, Anton. *Maria in der Heilsgeschichte: Mariologie*, 75–143.

Zmijewski, Josef. *Die Mutter des Messias: Maria in der Christusverkündigung des Neuen Testaments* [The Mother of the Messiah: Mary in the New Testament's Proclamation of Christ]. Kevelaer: Butzon and Bercker, 1989.

Two

A Short Historical Overview

INTRODUCTORY NOTE

The broad lines of development of Mariology are profiled in the following overview. In this way it will be easier to grasp the material presented later in the systematic section in its historical context. There we will take up the history of each of the principal topics in turn. This chronological run-through also illustrates the fact that Mariology is "the exemplary case of the development of dogma in Catholicism."[1]

MARY IN THE PATRISTIC ERA

The First Mariological Witnesses of the Tradition (Ignatius of Antioch, Justin, Irenaeus)

Ignatius, one of the "apostolic fathers," was bishop of Antioch in Syria, starting from approximately the year 70. His letters, written around 116 at the latest, during his journey to Rome where the bishop suffered martyrdom, testify to the ecclesial tradition at the beginning of the second century. Ignatius defends Christology (and Mariology) against Docetism (which denied the true humanity of Christ) and against Judaism (which denied the true divinity of Jesus).[2] Both

1. Georg Söll, *Storia dei dogmi mariani* [History of Marian Dogmas] (Rome: Libreria Ateneo Salesiano, 1981), 15.

2. "Doceti" comes from *dokein*, "to seem, to appear": in this doctrine, Jesus was a man and had only appeared to suffer.

challenges are visible in an exemplary way in the following affirmation:

There is only one Physician, having both flesh and spirit, born and unborn, God become man, true life in death, from Mary and from God, first passible and then impassible—Jesus Christ our Lord.[3]

Without the technical terminology that arose later, this expresses the content of the hypostatic union—that is, the union between the divine nature and human nature in the hypostasis or the person of the Word. Mary is intimately connected to the mystery of the Incarnation:

For our God, Jesus Christ, was ... conceived in the womb by Mary.... Now the virginity of Mary was hidden from the prince of this world, as was also her offspring, and the death of the Lord; three mysteries of renown which were wrought in silence.[4]

Jesus was "truly (*aletôs*) born of a virgin" and was "truly" crucified under Pontius Pilate.[5]

While Matthew and Luke recount the virgin birth of Jesus at the beginning of their gospels, Ignatius places it as an integral and central part of the history of salvation. The Redemption began with the Incarnation, and here Mary possesses an undeniable role. Jesus' birth from Mary underscores his true humanity. Her virginity is affirmed equally strongly, and the profession of that virginity forms part of the tradition to which the bishop refers, already making use of fixed formulas.[6]

In writings that are lost today, Justin (around 165) addresses Marcion, who rejected the entire Old Testament;[7] according to Marcion,

3. Ignatius of Antioch, *To the Ephesians* 7:2; English translation from Luigi Gambero, *Mary and the Fathers of the Church: The Blessed Virgin Mary in Patristic Thought*, trans. Thomas Buffer (San Francisco: Ignatius Press, 1999), 31.

4. *In Eph.* 18:2–19:1 (English trans., *ANF* 1:57); see Luigi Gambero, *Mary and the Fathers of the Church: The Blessed Virgin Mary in Patristic Thought*, trans. Thomas Buffer (San Francisco: Ignatius Press, 1999), 31.

5. *To the Smyrnaeans* 1:1f (English trans., Gambero, *Mary and the Fathers*, 32); see *To the Trallians* 9:1f.

6. *In Eph.* 7:2; 18:2; *In Trall.* 9:1; *In Smyrn.* 1:1 (English trans., *ANF* 1:52, 57, 70, 86).

7. See C. P. Vetten, "Giustino Martire" [Justin Martyr], in *Dizionario di letteratura cristiana antica* [Dictionary of Ancient Christian Literature] (abbreviated hereafter as *DLCA*), ed. Siegmar Döpp and Wilhelm Geerlings (Rome: Urbaniana, 2006), 455.

Jesus did not have human parents, but appeared as an adult (hence in the one gospel retained by Marcion, that of Luke, the first two chapters were deleted).[8] In the "Dialogue with Trypho, a Jew," Justin discusses the OT signs that lead to Christ. This opens a broad discussion on the prophecy of Isaiah 7:14 (on the Virgin, *parthénos*) and—for the first time in history—presents the analogy between Eve and Mary:

For Eve, who was virgin and undefiled, gave birth to disobedience and death after listening to the serpent's words. But the Virgin Mary conceived faith and joy; for when the angel Gabriel brought her the glad tidings that the Holy Spirit would come upon her and that the power of the Most High would overshadow her, so that the Holy One born of her would be the Son of God.[9]

Justin does battle with nearly all the arguments raised today against the virgin birth: some thought that the prophecy of Isaiah 7:14 had nothing to do with the birth of the Messiah and that a virgin birth was an influence from pagan mythology.[10]

Irenaeus of Lyons († 202) left us a short summary of the "apostolic preaching" ("Demonstratio," *Epídeixis toû apostolikoû kerúgmatos*) and, above all, a broad work in five books against the Gnostic heresies ("Adversus haereses," *Élenchos kaì anastropè tês pseudonúmou gnóseos*). In his works we find the first great attempt to show the tradition of the faith in a complete overview of the history of salvation. Often Irenaeus is called the "father of Christian theology" or "of Catholic dogmatics."[11] Irenaeus comes from Asia Minor and is proud of his historic closeness to the apostolic tradition.

While the Gnostics separated the Old Testament from the New

8. See Antonio Orbe and Manlio Simonetti, eds., *Il Cristo*, vol. 1, *Testi teologici e spirituali dal I al IV secolo* [The Christ, vol. 1, Theological and Spiritual Texts of the First to Fourth Centuries], 6th ed. (Milan: A. Mondadori, 2005), xv–xvii, 197.

9. *Dial.* 100:5, English trans., Gambero, *Mary and the Fathers*, 47. See Edgar J. Goodspeed, ed., *Die ältesten Apologeten* [The Earliest Apologists] (Göttingen: Vanderboeck and Ruprecht, 1914); reprint 1984, 215.

10. *Dial.* 68, 71, 77, 84, 67:2–3, 70:5. See Michael Durst, "Justin der Martyrer" [Justin the Martyr], in *ML* 3:489–91.

11. See Manfred Hauke, *Heilsverlust in Adam: Stationen griechischer Erbsündenlehre; Irenäus—Origenes—Kappadozier* [Salvation Lost in Adam: Stages of Greek Teaching on Original Sin; Irenaeus, Origen, the Cappadocians] (Paderborn: Bonifatius, 1993), 195.

Testament, Irenaeus highlights the unity of Scripture: the Old Testament comes to its fulfillment in the New. In this context the concept of *recapitulation* (*anakefalaíosis*) appears: renewal and fulfillment (of the beginning in paradise). The term comes from rhetoric, and it means the summary of a discourse. Thanks to the prefix *aná-*, it can also have the meaning of "returning to the origin" and "taking things over from the beginning and going through to the end." It presupposes ideas from the Letter to the Ephesians (1:10), according to which the entire creation is submitted to Christ as its head (*kefalé*) (Eph 1:22). Jesus Christ is the new Adam who leads us back to paradise, but at the same time he guides creation to its end, being the head of the universe. The "recapitulation of Adam" began with the origin of Jesus: as Adam was formed from virgin earth (which had never been worked), so Christ's origin is from the Virgin Mary.[12] The coming of Jesus therefore constitutes a new beginning comparable to the first creation. Yet unlike Adam, Jesus stands against the temptation of the devil.[13] While Adam was disobedient at the tree (of paradise), Jesus obeyed even unto death on the cross.[14]

The antithesis between Eve and Mary,[15] already outlined in Justin, corresponds to the parallelism between Adam and Christ. Irenaeus describes Eve's disobedience as the universal cause of "death" and Mary's obedience as the cause of "salvation" (*causa salutis*) "for herself and for the whole human race."[16] The image appears of the knot tied by Eve but loosed by Mary. To describe Mary's reparative activity, Irenaeus does not use the term "recapitulation," but "recircu-

12. Irenaeus, *Adversus haereses* III.18.7; 21.10; *Dem.* 33 (*SC* 211:368–70; 428:220–28; English: Irenaeus, "The Demonstration of the Apostolic Preaching," in Iain MacKenzie, *Irenaeus's Demonstration of the Apostolic Preaching: A Theological Commentary and Translation*, trans. J. Armitage Robinson, (Burlington, Vt.: Ashgate, 2002), 11. See Hauke, *Heilsverlust*, 261–65.

13. *Adversus haereses* V.21.2 (*SC* 153:266–70).

14. *Adversus haereses* V.16.3; see V.17.4; V.23.2 (*SC* 153:40–42, 232, 292).

15. See Gambero, *Mary and the Fathers*, 51–58; Hauke, *Heilsverlust*, 265–67.

16. *Adversus haereses* III.22.4 (*SC* 211:441; see Gambero, *Mary and the Fathers*, 58). The translation is based on the Latin text, since the Greek original has been lost, except for a few fragments in the work cited previously. But probably the Latin expression *sibi facta est salutis*, with the preposition *sibi*, does not refer to Mary but to Eve, noting the fact that the Latin translator often translated the Greek preposition *ei* in the same incorrect way. See José A. de Aldama, "'Sibi causa facta est salutis' (S. Ireneo, Adv. Haereses 3,22,4)" ["Became the Cause of Salvation for Herself" (St. Irenaeus, Against the Heresies III.22.4)], *Ephemerides Mariologicae* 16 (1966): 291–321; Galot, *Maria, La donna*, 89.

lation" (in Latin "recirculatio" = in Greek *anakúklesis*).[17] "What Eve bound through her unbelief, Mary loosed by her faith."[18] "And just as through a disobedient virgin man was stricken down and fell into death, so through the Virgin who was obedient to the Word of God man was reanimated and received life."[19]

Mary appears totally allied to Christ, opposed to the evil forces of the devil and sin. In her the freshness of original holiness reappears. The parallelism between Eve and Mary later becomes a starting point for the dogma of the Immaculate Conception, according to which the Blessed Virgin was free from original sin from the first moment of her existence. This privilege has a decisive role for salvation history.

Beside the parallelism of Eve and Mary there is a strong connection between Mary and the church, particularly demonstrated by a passage that links them both with the virgin birth and the rebirth wrought by Baptism:

> The prophets, in particular Is 7:14, point to "the union of the Word of God with His own workmanship, that the Word should become flesh, and the Son of God the son of man, the pure one opening purely that pure womb which regenerates men unto God, and which He Himself made pure (*purus pure puram aperiens vulvam eam quae regenerat homines in Deum, quam ipse puram fecit*); and having become this which we also are, He is the Mighty God, and possesses a generation which cannot be declared."[20]

In this passage Baptism wrought by "mother" church and the virgin birth by Mary come together; at the same time the purity of Mary's person and her bodily integrity are affirmed. The fact that the bodily aspect is strongly implicit (as in John!) is directed against Gnosticism, according to whose doctrine the "spirit" of man could be virginal while physical virginity would be unimportant. Moreover, it is clear that Irenaeus does not declare created reality (such as, for example, marriage) "impure."[21]

17. *Adversus haereses* III.22.4 (*SC* 211:440; Gambero, *Mary and the Fathers*, 58).

18. *Adversus haereses* III.22.4 (*SC* 211:442–44; Gambero, *Mary and the Fathers*, 58).

19. *Dem.* 33; English: MacKenzie, *Irenaeus's Demonstration of the Apostolic Preaching*, trans. Robinson, 11.

20. *Adversus haereses* IV.33.11 (*SC* 100:830f.; *ANF* 1:509).

21. See, for example, *Adversus haereses* I.6.1–4 (*SC* 264:90–100; *ANF* 1:323–25).

The mediating role of Mary is clearly expressed in the title "advocate" ("advocata" = *parákletos*?): "While the former [Eve] was seduced into disobeying God, the latter was persuaded to obey God, so that the Virgin Mary became the advocate (*advocata*) of the virgin Eve."[22]

Probably the function of "advocate" indicates a "running to aid" (and not yet intercession). In any case, it is obvious that Mary intervenes not exclusively for "Eve," but for the whole human race.[23] From these observations an important path is opening to appreciate the cooperation of Mary in the work of salvation.

The Contribution of Apocryphal Writings

The word "apocrypha" ("hidden") designates writings that claim to be the work of biblical authors but are not so and do not belong to the list of the Sacred Scriptures (the Canon).[24] In our case we are speaking of apocrypha of the New Testament. The document with the greatest influence is the "Protoevangelium of James" (*Protoevangelium Jacobi*), which is cited for the first time at the beginning of the third century by Clement of Alexandria and Origen; therefore, it probably originated in the second half of the second century.[25]

22. *Adversus haereses* V.19.1 (*SC* 153:248; Gambero, *Mary and the Fathers*, 54); see *Dem.* 33; English: MacKenzie, *Irenaeus's Demonstration of the Apostolic Preaching*, trans. Robinson, 11.

23. See Manfred Hauke, *Heilsverlust in Adam: Stationen griechischer Erbsündenlehre; Irenäus—Origenes—Kappadozier* [Salvation Lost in Adam: Stages of Greek Teaching on Original Sin; Irenaeus, Origen, the Cappadocians] (Paderborn: Bonifatius, 1993), 267.

24. See Edouard Cothenet, "Marie dans les Apocryphes" [Mary in the Apocrypha], in *Maria: Études sur la sainte vierge*, ed. H. du Manoir (Paris: Beauchesne, 1961), 6:71–156; Alfred C. Rush, CSSR, "Mary in the Apocrypha of the New Testament," in *Mariology*, edited by J. Carol (Milwaukee: Bruce, 1954), 1:156–84; Söll, *Storia dei dogmi mariani*, §2; E. Elio Peretto, "Apocrifi" [Apocrypha], in De Fiores and Meo, *NDM*, 106–25; Gambero, *Mary and the Fathers*, 33–42; Michael O'Carroll, CSSp, *Theotokos: A Theological Encyclopedia of the Blessed Virgin Mary* (Eugene, Ore.: Wipf and Stock, 2000), 37–44; Stefano De Fiores, *Maria sintesi di valori: Storia culturale della mariologia* [Mary, Synthesis of Values: Cultural History of Mariology] (Cinisello Balsamo: San Paolo, 2005), 75–85; De Fiores, *Maria: Nuovissimo dizionario* (abbreviated hereafter as "De Fiores, *Dizionario*") (Bologna: EDB, 2006), 2:1616–19; Angelo M. Gila, "Apocrifi," in *DMar*, 128–35; E. Norelli, "Maria nella Letteratura apocrifa cristiana antica" [Mary in Ancient Christian Apocryphal Literature], in *Storia della Mariologia* [History of Mariology], ed. E. Dal Covolo and A. Serra (Rome: Città Nuova, 2009), 1:143–254. Selected texts: Georges Gharib et al., eds. *Testi mariani del primo millennio* (hereinafter *TMPM*) (Rome: Città Nuova, 1988–1991), 1:861–903.

25. See A. Keller, "Über die Bedeutung der Apokryphen und der Transituslegenden" [On the Meaning of the Apocrypha and Transitus Legends], in *Volksfrömmigkeit und Theologie* [Popular Piety and Theology], ed. A. Ziegenaus (Regensburg: Pustet, 1998), 57–73.

A brief summary: the parents of Mary, Joachim and Anne, lament their childlessness. When an angel announces to Anne that she will conceive and give birth, she promises to offer the daughter as a sacrifice to God (4:1). When the girl is born, she receives the name "Mary." At her second birthday she is blessed by the priest in front of the entire people, and at the age of three her parents bring her to the temple where there are other virgins [an imaginary "fact" not confirmed by Jewish sources]. When Mary reaches the age of twelve, the priests discuss what should be done with her. They receive advice from an angel to summon widowers from all the people and give each one of them a stick. As a dove alights on Joseph's stick, Mary is entrusted to him. He argues that he already has children and that he is old, but the priests calm him down and warn him not to rebel against the will of God (9:2).

After some time, Joseph has to travel for his work as a carpenter. He leaves Mary at home alone. In the meantime, the Annunciation and the virginal conception take place. When Joseph returns and finds Mary pregnant, he rebukes her. Mary defends herself (13:1–3). As the priests are informed of Joseph's long absence and of Mary's pregnancy, they subject both to a divine trial. But both drink the water of ordeal without result, "and all the people marveled" (16:2).

When Mary gives birth in a cave, all of nature comes to a standstill. Joseph has gone looking for a midwife, and admits to her that the child was conceived by the Holy Spirit. At the birth, first a bright cloud appears and then a great light, until the child arrives and he is nursed by Mary. The midwife, amazed by the events, goes and tells Salome, "A virgin has given birth, a thing that nature knows nothing of!" Salome [like Thomas in John 20] does not believe this and wants to test the virginity of Mary with a finger (19:3). Mary allows the investigation, and Salome's hand is cut off as if burned by fire. Through Mary's intercession, the woman recovers her hand and is ordered to tell no one until the boy reaches Jerusalem (20:3).[26]

We find other apocryphal writings in the second century. Those

26. See *ANF* 8:361–367. For the critical text, see Gerhard Schneider, ed., *Evangeliae infantiae apocrypha* [Apocryphal Infancy Gospels], Fontes christiani 18 (Freiburg im Breisgau: Herder, 1995).

with any Marian interest arise neither from Judaism nor from Gnosticism. They typically want to highlight the virginity of Mary, including the *virginitas in partu.* The influence of the "Protoevangelium of James" was great, especially in the East; the text appears as a reading in the Byzantine calendar of Marian feasts. Two Eastern feasts (the presentation of Mary in the temple and the passive conception of Mary by Anne) are derived from this apocalyptic writing. The Eastern conviction that the "brethren of Jesus" are sons of Joseph, born of a first marriage, comes from this source. In any case, the "Protoevangelium" was never made part of the Canon.

The West was more skeptical. Jerome rejects the idea that Joseph was a widower and had children before his marriage with Mary; from him comes the expression *deliramenta apocryphorum.*[27] The apocrypha are like cloudy waters that still carry nuggets of gold, in this case especially the conviction of the perpetual virginity of Mary. Mary is "the Virgin"; this attribute highlights the personal identity of the Mother of God.

While the first apocrypha that relate to Mary focus on her birth, another set of apocrypha contemplates the earthly end of Mary: legends about her passing and the assumption into heaven, which first appeared in the fifth century.[28]

Patristic Motifs through the Sixth Century

The Christological Councils of the ancient church are important for the development of Mariology.[29] At the Council of Nicea (325),

27. *Adversus Helvidium* 13–19 (PL 23:195–203); see also Hieronymus, *La perenne verginità di Maria* [The Perpetual Virginity of Mary], ed. Maria Ignazia Danieli, Collana di testi patristici 70 (Rome: Città Nuova, 1988); English: "On the Perpetual Virginity of the Blessed Mary against Helvidius," trans. John N. Hritzu, in St. Jerome, *Dogmatic and Polemical Works*, Fathers of the Church 53 (Washington, D.C.: The Catholic University of America Press, 1965), 28–39. Hauke, "Deliramenta apocryphorum: Die theologischen Klarstellungen des Hieronymus zu den Maria betreffenden Apokryphen" [Deliramenta apocryphorum: Jerome's Theological Explications on the Apocrypha Regarding Mary], in *Volksfrömmigkeit und Theologie: Die eine Mariengestalt und die vielen Quellen* [Piety and Theology: The One Figure of Mary and Its Many Sources], ed. Anton Ziegenaus (Regensburg: Friedrich Pustet, 1998), 63–69.

28. On the Assumption of Mary, see "Interpretation of the Apocrypha," in chapter 7.

29. See Angelo Amato, *Gesù il Signore: Saggio di cristologia* [Jesus the Lord: Essay in Christology] (Bologna: EDB, 1999), 215–367.

the true divinity of Jesus is reaffirmed, contrary to Arius. The creed of Nicea is completed at the Council of Constantinople (381), which principally defends the divinity of the Holy Spirit; the "Nicene-Constantinopolitan Creed," the Credo used in the Holy Mass, comes from these Councils.

The Council of Ephesus (431) defines the title *Theotokos*: Mary is truly "Mother of God" for having borne the Word of God made man. The designation *Theotokos*, known from at least the beginning of the fourth century (at first in the Church of Alexandria), defends the hypostatic union—that is, the unity in Jesus Christ whose basis is the hypostasis (= the person, the subject, the "who"). The Council of Ephesus becomes the starting point for a strong flowering of Mariology.[30]

Christological development came to its height with the Council of Chalcedon (451), which defined the relation of the two natures in Jesus Christ: the human nature and the divine nature are neither separated from each other nor mixed, but united in the person of the Son. While Ephesus is directed against Nestorius (who maintained a duality of subjects in Christ), Chalcedon opposed the Monophysites, in particular Eutyches, who dissolved the duality of the natures into a single nature. Instead, it is necessary to maintain that the two natures in Jesus Christ are neither mixed (against the Monophysites) nor separated (against the Nestorians).

In this era we find the virgin birth as a constant part of the creeds of the faith (*virginitas ante partum*). The first testimonies derive from the second century (Hippolytus and Tertullian on the baptismal creed at Rome). Then the *virginitas post partum* and *in partu* were also clarified and defended in the fourth century against some denials.[31] The title "ever-virgin" ("semper virgo," *aeiparthénos*) comes to the fore. The parallelism "Eve/Mary" and the title "holy Virgin" (in Origen, who does not use it for any other women) testify to the holiness of Mary. The faith of Mary is praised, as is her role as an exemplar of Christian life, in particular for virgins. Nonetheless, we still find statements that attribute imperfections or minor sins to

30. See "The Council of Ephesus," in chapter 4, and "Interpretation of the Apocrypha," in chapter 7.

31. See Chapter 5.

Mary—a tendency that was disappearing, especially after the Council of Ephesus. The interrelationship between Mary and the church is important: both can be called "holy Virgin"; Ambrose calls Mary *typus Ecclesiae*.[32]

A direct invocation of Mary is attested for the first time by Gregory of Nazianzus in 379. In a sermon he recounts the story of Justina, a beautiful maiden harassed by Cyprian (of Antioch), "beseeching the Virgin Mary to bring her aid, since the pure girl was a virgin and was in danger; she entrusted herself to the remedy of fasting and sleeping on the ground." "The virgin was victorious, and the evil spirit suffered a defeat."[33] The episode refers to the end of the third century, since the martyrdom of Justina and also of Cyprian took place under Diocletian (285–302).

Also from the third or fourth century comes the most ancient Marian prayer known, widespread both in the East and West:

> "We fly to your patronage, O holy Mother of God; despise not our petitions in our necessities, but deliver us always from all dangers, O glorious and blessed Virgin." (*Sub tuum praesidium confugimus, sancta Dei Genitrix; nostras deprecationes ne despicias in necessitatibus, sed a periculis cunctis libera nos semper, Virgo gloriosa et benedicta*).[34]

A new element appears in the conviction of Mary's bodily assumption into heaven. At the time of the Byzantine emperor Maurice (582–602) the feast of the Dormition of Mary (*koímesis*) was introduced for the whole church on August 15. At its basis, most probably, is not a historical tradition (although it does take account of the empty tomb of the Blessed Virgin at Jerusalem), but the maturing of the faith as it contemplates the consequences of the dignity of Mary as Virgin and Mother of God.[35]

32. Ambrose, *Expositio in Lucam* 2:7 (PL 15:1635–36); adopted by Vatican II, *LG* 63.

33. *Oratio* 24:10–11 (PG 35:1180 C–81 A). English trans. in *Nicene and Post-Nicene Fathers* (hereafter *NPNF2*), ed. Philip Schaff, Second Series, 14 vols. (1886–89; repr. Peabody, Mass.: Hendrickson, 1994), 7.

34. See T. Maas-Ewerd, "Sub tuum praesidium," in *ML* 6:327f.; De Fiores, *Maria sintesi di valori*, 138f. The oldest papyrus text is in Greek: see the reconstruction reported in De Fiores, *Maria sintesi di valori*, 138. English trans. from Apostolic Penitentiary, *Manual of Indulgences* (Washington, D.C.: USCCB, 2006), 62.

35. See "Development of the Doctrine in the Eastern Church," in chapter 7.

In the fifth century, especially after the Council of Ephesus (431), in various particular churches, we find a liturgical memorial of Mary, with various dates, usually connected with Christmas. Soon this anamnesis also includes the departure of Mary from earthly life, analogously to the feasts of the martyrs (considered as a *dies natalis*, a birthday, into heavenly glory).[36] In the sixth century these are added:

1. the memorial of the Annunciation, at first as a feast of the Lord set on March 25 (nine months before December 25, Christmas);

2. the commemoration of the birth of Mary (September 8), which brought with it the memorial of the conception by Anne (December 9), which precedes the later feast of the Immaculate Conception;

3. the feast of the *Hypapante* (= "encounter" of the Lord with his people), called "Presentation of the Lord" in the West (February 2, forty days after Christmas). The first traces of the feast lead back to Jerusalem in the fourth century.

4. the feast of the Dormition, already mentioned (August 15).

MEDIEVAL DEVELOPMENT

With the Middle Ages we arrive at a more systematic reflection on the deposit of the faith. In the *Summa Theologiae* of St. Thomas, to present an example with particular influence, Mariology is treated in the Christological context (see *ST* III, qq. 27–35). The Eastern tradition does not include a corresponding systematic presentation, but transmits the Byzantine heritage with a strongly poetic dimension, as, for example, the *Akáthistos* hymn (eighth century) demonstrates.[37]

36. On the development of the first Marian feasts, see Hansjörg Auf der Maur, "Feste und Gedenktage der Heiligen" [Feasts and Memorials of the Saints], in *Feiern im Rhythmus der Zeit* [Celebrations in the Rhythm of Time], part 2, vol. 1, edited by H. Auf der Maur and Philipp Harnancourt, Gottesdienst der Kirche, vol. 6, part 1 (Regensburg: Friedrich Pustet, 1994), 2:123–30; see also "Mary in the Liturgical Calendar," in chapter 10.

37. See Ermanno M. Toniolo, OSM, *Akathístos: Saggi di critica e di teologia* [Akathistos: Critical and Theological Essays] (Rome: Centro di cultura mariana "Madre della Chiesa," 2000); Toniolo, "Maria 'donna nuova' nella testimonianza liturgica: Maria nella liturgia orientale" [Mary, 'New Woman' in the Liturgical Witness: Mary in the Eastern Liturgy], in *La donna e la salvezza: Maria e la vocazione femminile* [Woman and Salvation: Mary and the Feminine Vocation], ed. Hauke, 100–11.

Even before Scholasticism, we find important contributions by St. Bernard of Clairvaux († 1153), honored as a "Marian doctor" as well as *doctor mellifluus*.[38] These are generally homilies on biblical episodes and liturgical feasts for the Mother of the Lord. A prayer that later inspired the famous *Memorare* is typical (and also typical for "inculturation" in the feudal epoch):

Our lady, our mediatrix, our advocate, reconcile us to thy Son, commend us to thy Son, present us to thy Son.[39]

Closer to scholastic thought is St. Anselm of Aosta (of Canterbury) († 1109). He emphasizes the compassion of Mary, her intercession, her maternal role in regard to men, and her perfect holiness. Among his disciples the first writings in support of the Immaculate Conception flowered—especially the works of the English Benedictine Eadmer, who first formulated the statement that Mary was conceived without original sin.[40]

Toward the end of the eleventh century we find a greater accent on the role of Mary at the foot of the cross and in the present life of the church. Previously interest had been concentrated almost exclusively on the role of our Lady in the mystery of the infancy of Jesus. Now they "discover her compassion, her active union with the offer-

38. See Luigi Gambero, *Maria nel pensiero dei teologi latini medievali* [Mary in the Thought of the Medieval Latin Theologians] (Cinisello Balsamo: Ed. Paoline, 2000), 155–68; English translation: *Mary in the Middle Ages: The Blessed Virgin Mary in the Thought of Medieval Latin Theologians*, trans. Thomas Buffer (San Francisco: Ignatius Press, 2005), 131–41; A. Montanari, "San Bernardo di Clairvaux e la sua scuola" [St. Bernard of Clairvaux and His School], in *Storia della Mariologia* [History of Mariology], ed. Enrico Dal Covolo and Aristide Serra (Rome: Città Nuova, 2009), 1:637–61.

39. Bernard of Clairvaux, *De adventu Domini, Sermo 2* (PL 183:43 C); English from *St. Bernard's Sermons* (Westminster, Md.: Newman (Carroll), 1921), 1:21. The most developed text comes from the fifteenth century: see T. Maas-Ewerd, "*Memorare*," in *ML* 4:411. Here is the full text of the prayer: "Remember, O most gracious Virgin Mary, that never was it known that anyone who fled to your protection, implored your help, or sought your intercession was left unaided. Inspired with this confidence, I fly unto you, O Virgin of virgins, my Mother. To you I come, before you I stand, sinful and sorrowful. O Mother of the Word Incarnate, despise not my petitions, but in your mercy hear and answer me. Amen." See James Socias, ed., *Daily Roman Missal* (Woodridge, Ill.: Midwest Theological, 2011), 2437.

40. See René Laurentin, *A Short Treatise on the Virgin Mary* (Washington, N.J.: Ave Maria Institute, 1991), 105, 108; Stefano M. Cecchin, *L'Immacolata Concezione: Breve storia del dogma* [The Immaculate Conception: A Short History of the Dogma] (Vatican City: PAMI, 2003), 31–34; also see "Development in the West up to the 12th Century," in chapter 6.

ing of her Son, the ecclesial dimension of her faith during the three days of his death (*triduum mortis*). They finally grasp the implications of the dying Christ's words: 'This is your mother.' ... Mary was given to be the mother of men. Little by little the idea dawns that in her own way she cooperated in the sacrifice of Calvary."[41]

A synthesis of medieval Mariology is presented by the famous *Mariale super missus est*, which was considered until 1954 to be a work of St. Albert the Great, while the text originated with an anonymous author of the thirteenth century. In the *Mariale* the principle of the "omnicontinence" of Marian grace—that is, the thesis that Mary includes the graces of all creatures— is problematic: "the universality of human knowledge, the properties of the angels, and the grace of the seven sacraments, including penance, which she is held actually to have received, and holy orders, whose dignity, grace, and powers she is held to have possessed eminently."[42] There is a risk here of losing sight of the specific place of Mary in the church.

However, what the author says on the cooperation of Mary in the work of salvation is more fruitful: Mary is the companion of Christ (*socia Christi*) and, by analogy to Eve with respect to Adam, is "a helper similar to him" (Gn 2:18).[43]

THE ROAD TO THE DEFINITIONS OF THE IMMACULATE CONCEPTION AND THE ASSUMPTION

The doctrinal development of Mariology is most commonly described in terms of the Immaculate Conception and the Assumption of Mary into heaven.[44] On the first topic, the English Franciscan Duns Scotus (†1308) stands out: he formulated the idea of the *praeredemptio* (the redemption of Mary took place in such a way that the Mother of God was protected from original sin). The debate on Mary's exemption from original sin lasted for centuries, and when

41. Laurentin, *Short Treatise*, 110f.

42. Laurentin, *Short Treatise*, 117.

43. See (Pseudo-) Albert the Great, *Mariale*, q. 42, Opera omnia 37 (Paris: ed. Borgnet, 1898), 81.

44. See chaps. 6–7.

the dogma of the Immaculate Conception was solemnly proclaimed in 1854, it was already part of the profound conviction of the church. The debate on the Assumption of Mary into heaven was less intense: the idea was already present in a liturgical feast since the patristic era; but the formal dogma was only proclaimed in 1950.

REFORMATION AND COUNTER-REFORMATION

The Protestant reformation finds its theological core in the doctrine of justification: man becomes "just" before God only by means of divine grace, without involving any human cooperation.[45] Hence the principle of *sola gratia* is its starting point. Furthermore, the absolutely gratuitous gift of justification happens in an extrinsic manner: God pardons man without infusing sanctifying grace. Because of this, man remains a sinner even immediately after Baptism. The axiom is *simul iustus et peccator* ("simultaneously just and a sinner"). The exclusion of human cooperation in justification and the extrinsic vision of sanctification fail to recognize the difference of the justified, while the veneration of saints in the Catholic Church sheds light on the heroic example of persons who have given a particularly generous response to grace. The Protestant doctrine of justification renders the veneration of saints problematic and is shown later in the conviction, shared by all the Reformers, of excluding on principle any invocation of the Virgin in prayer. Thus the role of Mary is greatly diminished. Luther's example is typical: at the beginning he still preached about the Immaculate Conception and the Assumption of Mary, but afterward lost sight of these doctrines.[46] Anglicanism, too,

45. For the positions of Karl Barth and C. A. de Ridder on Mary's cooperation, pp. 5–6.

46. See "The Ecumenical Debate," in chapter 6; and "Ecumenical Dialogue with the Ecclesial Communities Arising from the Reformation," in chapter 7. On Luther and the reformers, see Eduard Stakemeier, "De Beata Maria Virgine eiusque cultu iuxta reformatores" [On the Blessed Virgin Mary and Her Cult, according to the Reformers], in *De Mariologia et oecumenismo* [Mariology and Ecumenism], ed. PAMI (Rome: PAMI, 1962), 423–77; Brunero Gherardini, *La Madonna in Lutero* [The Madonna in Luther] (Rome: Città Nuova, 1967); Gherardini, *Lutero–Maria: Pro o contro?* [Luther and Mary: For or Against?] (Pisa: Giardini, 1985); Achim Dittrich, *Protestantische Mariologie-Kritik: Historische Entwicklung bis 1997 und dogmatische Analyse* [Protestant Criticism of Mariology: Historical Development to 1997 and Dogmatic Analysis], Mariologische Studien 11 (Regensburg: Pustet, 1998), 15–45; O'Carroll, *Theotokos*, 94f, 227f, 338; De Fiores, *Maria sintesi di*

while maintaining a greater openness to veneration of the Blessed Virgin, rejects the invocation of saints on principle.[47]

The Council of Trent did not deal with the Marian question but was satisfied to clarify the doctrine of justification and to defend the cult of saints. But its clause relative to the Immaculate Conception is important: the conciliar fathers did not wish to include Mary in the transmission of original sin.[48] In any case, the Counter-Reformation era brought a strong defense of Marian devotion: "Disparaged by Protestantism, the Virgin Mary is going to be systematically exalted in Catholicism, under the force of an impulse without precedent."[49]

The new Marian surge arose above all in the countries not touched by the Reformation: Italy and especially Spain, where the Jesuit Francisco Suárez presented in 1592 (after a first rough outline in 1584–85) what is considered the first systematic mariology in his commentary on the *Summa Theologiae* of Thomas.[50] A few years later, in 1602, the Sicilian Placido Nigido coined the term "Mariology," composing a systematic independent treatise on Mary for the first time: *Summae sacrae mariologiae*.[51] A widespread and valuable contribution came in Germany from St. Peter Canisius, SJ (*De Maria Virgine incomparabili*, 1577). The author concentrates on her virginity, the divine maternity, the Immaculate Conception, and the Assumption into heaven.[52]

---

valori, 234–43; Giancarlo Bruni and M. Wirz, "Maria nella teologia di Martin Lutero" [Mary in the Theology of Martin Luther], in *Storia della Mariologia*, ed. Emanuele Boaga and Luigi Gambero, 2:215–29 (Rome: Città Nuova, 2012).

47. See "Anglicanism," in chapter 8.

48. DH 1516.

49. Laurentin, *Short Treatise*, 124–25.

50. Francisco Suárez, *De mysteriis vitae Christi* (ad *ST* III, qq. 27–37): published at Alcalà in 1592, available in *Francisci Suarez … Opera omnia* 19, ed. Vivès (Paris: 1856–78), 1–336. See Laurentin, *Short Treatise*, 126; Johann G. Roten, "Suarez," in *ML* 6:323–25. De Fiores, *Dizionario* 3:761–99; Stefano De Fiores, "La nascita della mariologia come trattazione sistematica" [The Birth of Mariology as a Systematic Discipline], in *Storia della Mariologia*, ed. E. Boaga and L. Gambero (Rome: Città Nuova, 2012), 2:352–59; Enrique Llamas, "Il Concilio di Trento e la mariologia spagnola nel XVI e XVII secolo" [The Council of Trent and Spanish Mariology in the 16th and 17th Centuries], in Boaga and Gambero, *Storia della Mariologia* 2:300–302.

51. N. Nigidus [= P. Nigido], *Summa sacrae mariologiae pars prima*, Palermo, 1602; see De Fiores, *Dizionario* 2:1645. The term "mari*a*logia," instead, appears first in the works of the Dominican Guillaume-Vincent de Contenson (†1674): see Otto Stegmüller and Richard Schenk, "Contenson," in *ML* 2:92; De Fiores, *Dizionario* 2:1647; De Fiores, *Dizionario* 3: 695–727; De Fiores, "La nascita della mariologia," 2:359–63.

52. Leo Scheffczyk, "Canisius," in *ML* 1:647f; Luigi Gambero, "La riflessione mariologica

DEVELOPMENT FROM THE SEVENTEENTH CENTURY UNTIL THE EVE OF VATICAN II

In the seventeenth century a genuine "Marian movement" arose: "a desire to know Mary better and to glorify her in all kinds of ways."[53] Among the important and memorable authors are St. John Eudes († 1680; *Le Coeur admirable de la Mère de Dieu*), St. Louis-Marie Grignion de Montfort († 1716; *Traité de la vrai dévotion à la Sainte Vierge*, discovered in 1842),[54] and St. Alphonsus de Liguori, whose 1750 work *Le Glorie di Maria* was the most highly published Marian work of all time.[55] Enlightenment philosophy brought a notable decrease in Marian devotion and theology (from about 1780 to 1830).[56] The sign of a turning point was in the apparitions of the Virgin to St. Catherine Labouré in the Rue du Bac, Paris, in 1830. The miraculous medal, which shows "the Virgin 'conceived without sin,' with arms stretched downward, seemed to set forth the program that was to guide the Marian movement for a whole century: Mary's Immaculate Conception and her Mediation."[57]

In 1854 the Immaculate Conception was proclaimed a dogma of the faith. Four years later, with the apparitions at Lourdes in 1858, came a sign of heavenly support for the dogma, and a focal point for Marian devotion to this day was created.[58] Among the pearls

---

post-tridentina in area italo-germania" [Mariological Reflection after Trent in the Italo-German Area], in Boaga and Gambero, *Storia della Mariologia* 2:340–46.

53. Laurentin, *Short Treatise*, 128.

54. Some recent English editions: Louis-M. Grignion De Montfort, *True Devotion to the Blessed Virgin* (hereinafter *TD*) (Rockford, Ill.: TAN, 1985); *God Alone: The Collected Writings of St. Louis Marie de Montfort* (anthology), (Bay Shore, N.Y.: Montfort, 1995 (2010). See "Marian Consecration as Proposed by Grignion de Montfort," in chapter 10 (consecration to Mary as a perfect renewal of baptismal vows).

55. Laurentin, *Short Treatise*, 130. See, e.g., the recent editions: Alfonso M. De Liguori, *Le glorie di Maria: Presentazione di Giovanni Velocci*, 2nd ed. (Cinisello Balsamo [Milan]: San Paolo, 2002). See also Angelo Amato et al., eds. *Testi mariani del secondo millennio* (hereafter *TMSM*) (Rome: Città Nuova, 2000–2012), 5:291–318.

56. See "Aufklärung" [Enlightenment], in *ML* 1:270–76; De Fiores, *Maria sintesi di valori*, 265–83; De Fiores, *Dizionario* 2:1652–56; De Fiores, "Criticismo e movimiento illuministico" [Enlightenment Critique and Movement], in Boaga and Gambero, *Storia della mariologia*, 2:561–87.

57. Laurentin, *Short Treatise*, 135.

58. Regarding the Marian apparition at Lourdes, see pp. 394–95.

of Marian theology of the nineteenth century, we can count a text of John Henry Newman in defense of the "new" dogma, the "Letter to Pusey" (1866).[59] The contribution of the most famous German dogmatic theologian of the 1800s, Matthias Joseph Scheeben,[60] is also notable. Scheeben takes into account, among other things, the monumental work (in four volumes with 1,887 pages) of the Franciscan Ludovico da Castelplanio,[61] "author of the most powerful mariological synthesis of the 1800s."[62]

Notable theological progress came with the twentieth century. In 1900 the era of international Marian congresses opened. Particular credit belongs to the Pontificia Academia Mariana Internationalis (PAMI), founded (initially as a private effort) in 1946 by the Croatian Franciscan Carl Balić, who organized international Mariological-Marian congresses every four years and published their acts, eventually extending to over 100 volumes.[63] The academy became a pontifical institution in 1959. The first congress in 1900 (bringing together prior initiatives from the 1800s) gave a notable impulse to the movement for the definition of the Assumption, which came in 1950.[64]

59. See Lutgart Govaert, "Newman," in *ML* 4:608–10; John Henry Newman, *Mary: The Virgin Mary in the Life and Writings of John Henry Newman*, ed. Philip Boyce (Leominster, Herefordshire: Gracewing; Grand Rapids, Mich.: Eerdmans, 2001); *TMSM* 5:725–43; J. Morales, "Il movimento di Oxford e John Henry Newman" [The Oxford Movement and John Henry Newman], in Boaga and Gambero, *Storia della mariologia*, 2:715–27.

60. See Hauke, "Die Mariologie Scheebens: Ein zukunftsträchtiges Vermächtnis" [Scheeben's Mariology: A Seminal Legacy], in *Donum Veritatis: Theologie im Dienst der Kirche; Festschrift zum 70. Geburtstag von Anton Ziegenaus*, ed. Manfred Hauke and Michael Stickelbroeck (Regensburg: Pustet, 2006), 255–74; in Boaga and Gambero, *Storia della Mariologia*, vol. 3 (Rome: Città Nuova, 2016); *TMSM* 5:712–24; Hauke, "Matthias Joseph Scheeben (†1888) nella mariologia tedesca del XIX secolo" [Scheeben in the German Mariology of the 19th Century], in Boaga and Gambero, *Storia della mariologia*, 2:696–714.

61. Ludovico da Castelplanio, *Maria nel consiglio dell'Eterno, ovvero la Vergine predestinata alla missione medesima con Gesù Cristo* [Mary in the Counsels of Eternity, or the Virgin Predestined to Share the Mission of Jesus Christ], 4 vols. (Naples: Tipografia editrice degli accattoncelli, 1872–73). See *TMSM* 5:593–608.

62. De Fiores, *Dizionario* 2:1659; see Stefano M. Cecchin, *Maria Signora Santa e Immacolata nel pensiero francescano: Per una storia del contributo francescano alla mariologia* [Mary, Holy and Immaculate Lady in Franciscan Thought: Toward a History of the Franciscan Contribution to Mariology] (Vatican City: PAMI, 2001), 383–98.

63. See Pontificia Academia Mariana Internationalis, https://pami.info/atti-dei-congressi.

64. For a short piece on the congresses, see Franz Courth, "Kongresse" [Congresses], in *ML* 3:629f. The first congresses are described with more detail in Emilio Campana, *Maria nel culto*

A great proliferation of studies took place from the 1920s to the 1950s on the topic of the cooperation of Mary in the work of salvation (as "Co-redemptrix") and on her mediation, terms still in need of further clarification. A first stimulus to the development of these topics came with the fiftieth anniversary of the dogma of the Immaculate Conception in 1904; another through the efforts of the Belgian cardinal Mercier, who, starting in 1915, launched a worldwide effort for the definition of the universal mediation of Mary. Theological work was propelled forward by the introduction of the optional feast of "Mary Mediatrix of all graces" by Benedict XV in 1921.[65]

The high point of Marian devotion and theology was reached during the pontificate of Pius XII. After some years of study and a consultation with the episcopate, in 1950 the pope defined the Assumption of Mary, body and soul, into heavenly glory. In the Marian Year of 1954, the centenary of the definition of the Immaculate Conception, the Feast of the Queenship of Mary was proclaimed. In 1958 the centenary of the apparitions at Lourdes was celebrated.

Theological work produced great manuals that collected the fruit of studies (for instance, the works of Gabriele Maria Roschini, founder of the "Marianum" pontifical institute and the journal of the same name).[66] We also find stimuli based on a new reading of the fathers, in particular studies of Mariology in an ecclesiological key (as in René Laurentin, Heinrich Maria Köster, SAC, Hugo Rahner, SJ).

---

cattolico [Mary in Catholic Worship], 2nd ed. (Turin: Marietti, 1944), 2:487–652. On the development of specialized centers, see Maria Marcellina Pedico, "Centri mariani di studio" [Marian Study Centers], in De Fiores and Meo, *NDM*, 332–50; Cecchin and Jean-Pierre Sieme Lasoul, "Centri mariologici" [Mariological Centers], in *DMar*, 244–56.

65. See Hauke, *Mary, "Mediatress of Grace": Mary's Universal Mediation of Grace in the Theological and Pastoral Works of Cardinal Mercier* (New Bedford, Mass.: Academy of the Immaculate, 2004); Hauke, "Maria, 'Mediatrice di tutte le Grazie' nell'Archivio Segreto Vaticano del Pontificato di Pio XI: Rapporto intermedio sulle tracce trovate," *Immaculata Mediatrix* 7 (2007): 118–29; Hauke, "Riscoperta: La petizione del Cardinale Mercier e dei Vescovi belgi a Papa Benedetto XV per la definizione dogmatica della Mediazione universale delle grazie da parte di Maria (1915): Introduzione teologica e testo originale francese," *Immaculata Mediatrix* 10, no. 3 (2010): 305–38; *TMSM* 7:116–27.

66. See the list in Pietro Parrotta, *La cooperazione di Maria alla Redenzione in Gabriele Maria Roschini* [Mary's Cooperation in the Redemption in Gabriele Maria Roschini], CdM 3 (Lugano: Eupress FTL, 2002), 213–16; Francesco Scanziani, "*Il manuale di mariologia dagli inizi dell'ottocento al Vaticano II*" [The Manual of Mariology, from its Beginnings in the 1800s to Vatican II], in Boaga and Gambero, *Storia della mariologia* 2:795–801; *TMSM* 7:558–65.

Ecumenical dialogues with Protestants (with a certain tendency to declare Mary *only* "the typical case" of every Christian) are following this trail.[67] Before the Second Vatican Council we found two theological currents: one more classical, which we might call "Christotypical" (or Christocentric), and another more innovative, the "ecclesiotypical" (or ecclesiocentric). The "Christotypical" tendency studies the figure of Mary in her analogous sharing in the unique mediation of Christ, while the "ecclesiotypical" view points to the blessed Virgin as a type of the church, which opens itself to Christ. Köster describes the encounter between the two tendencies at the International Mariological Congress at Lourdes in 1958 in these terms.[68]

THE CONTRIBUTION OF THE SECOND VATICAN COUNCIL

The two currents mentioned earlier will clash animatedly during Vatican II, when the insertion of the Marian treatise into the Dogmatic Constitution on the Church is debated.

> One group [adherents to the ecclesiotypical current] wanted integration. It was their intention to treat of the Blessed Virgin in her place both within the communion of saints and within salvation history. They hoped thereby to bring remedy to a Mariology that too easily closed in on itself and to reduce the separation between theology and Marian devotion.
>
> The other group [adherents to the Christological tendency] held that this kind of integration was a minimizing enterprise reducing the Virgin Mary to the level of other Christians.[69]

In the voting the decision to integrate the text into the schema on the church prevailed, but only by a little (1,114 votes in favor, 1,074 against). Afterward the new approaches were accepted without forgetting the essence of the existing teaching. The eighth chapter of

67. See Stefano De Fiores, *Maria nella teologia contemporanea* [Mary in Contemporary Theology], 3rd ed. (Rome: Centro di Cultura Mariana "Madre della Chiesa," 1991), 38–107; PAMI, ed., *De cultu mariano saeculis XIX–XX*, 7 vols. (Rome: PAMI, 1988–91).

68. See Franz Courth, "Heinrich Maria Köster (1911–1993): Forscher und Künder Mariens," *Marianum* 55 (1993): 435f.

69. Laurentin, *Short Treatise*, 142–43.

Lumen gentium (1964) was prepared decisively by the Belgian theologian Gérard Philips, principal editor of the whole dogmatic constitution, who was of the "ecclesiotypical" tendency, and by Croatian Franciscan Carl Balić, president of the Pontificia Academia Mariana Internationalis, of a rather "Christotypical" tendency.[70] So a kind of healthy compromise was produced, visible even in the title of the Marian chapter: "The Blessed Virgin Mary, Mother of God, in the Mystery of Christ and the Church."

The result is the fullest presentation of the figure of Mary by a Council, with a particular accent on her salvific mission, as Pope John Paul II notes, having been present in the council hall: "For the first time, the conciliar Magisterium offered the Church a doctrinal exposition of Mary's role in Christ's redemptive work and in the life of the Church."[71]

As the Council preferred a pastoral approach, it did not wish to proceed to any dogmatic definitions and did not accept the numerous proposals to formulate a dogma on the universal mediation of Mary.[72] This pastoral character also shows itself in the choice of terminology that often leaves aside the technical language of mariological studies. Another motive for presenting a less elaborated mariological doctrine was the attention being paid to separated Christians, especially Protestants.[73] For this reason, the titles "Coredemptrix" and "Mother of unity" were avoided, and even the ancient title of "Mediatrix," well established in the Christian East, enters the text only with great discretion.[74] Terminological concerns also did not

70. See Ermanno M. Toniolo, OSM, *La Beata Vergine Maria nel Concilio Vaticano II: Cronistoria del capitolo VIII della costituzione dogmatica "Lumen gentium" e sinossi di tutte le relazioni* [The Blessed Virgin Mary at the Second Vatican Council: Chronicle of Chapter Eight of the Dogmatic Constitution "Lumen gentium" and Synopsis of All the Reports] (Rome: Centro di cultura Mariana "Madre della Chiesa," 2004), 198–339.

71. John Paul II, CM 9 (Dec. 13, 1995), n. 3.

72. See Antonio Escudero Cabello, *La cuestión de la mediación mariana en la preparación del Vaticano II: Elementos para una evaluación de los trabajos preconciliares* [The Question of Marian Mediation in the Preparation for Vatican II: Elements toward an Evaluation of Preconciliar Works] (Rome: LAS, 1997).

73. See pp. 323–24 and 359–60.

74. *LG* 62. See Carolus Balić, "De titulo 'Mediatrix' B. Virgini Mariae adscripto" [The Title 'Mediatrix' Ascribed to the Blessed Virgin Mary], in *De cultu mariano saeculis VI–XI* [The Cult of Mary in the Sixth to Eleventh Centuries] (Rome: PAMI, 1972), 4:277–80.

allow for the use of the title "Mother of the Church," for the purpose of clearly teaching the saving mission of Mary for all the other members of the ecclesial community. However, Paul VI, acting as the bearer of the Petrine ministry, officially proclaimed Mary as "Mother of the Church" during the Council itself (November 21, 1965).[75]

Notwithstanding the limits of the conciliar document due to its pastoral and irenic position, the eighth chapter of *Lumen gentium* bears "a very rich and positive presentation of basic doctrine, an expression of faith and love for her whom the Church acknowledges as Mother and Model."[76] The text begins with an introduction that highlights the Incarnation of the Son of God by the Virgin Mary[77] as well as the relations of the Mother of God with the Trinity and with the body of Christ that is the church.[78] Also importantly, the document notes that the Council does not "have it in mind to give a complete doctrine on Mary, nor does it wish to decide those questions which the work of theologians has not yet fully clarified."[79]

A second section describes the "role of the blessed Virgin in the economy of salvation."[80] It begins with the Old Testament preparation for the mother of the Messiah.[81] The document's gaze turns to the Annunciation, with commentary from the fathers, who see Mary in the Annunciation as a new Eve, associated with the new Adam in an active cooperation for the salvation of man in the liberty of faith and obedience.[82] The Annunciation is preceded by the predestination of Mary to be the Mother of the divine Son, and by the holiness that was hers from the beginning of her earthly existence.[83] Other phases of salvation history show Mary during the infancy of Jesus,[84] in the public ministry of the Lord, and after the Ascension of Jesus Christ to heaven.[85] At the foot of the Cross, Mary is associated

75. See in chap. 8, "Mary as 'Mother of the Church.'"
76. John Paul II, CM 9 (Dec. 13, 1995), n. 4.
77. *LG* 52.
78. *LG* 53.
79. *LG* 54.
80. *LG* 55–59.
81. *LG* 55.
82. *LG* 56.
83. *LG* 56.
84. *LG* 57.
85. *LG* 58 and *LG* 59, respectively.

with the sacrifice of her Son with a mother's heart and receives her maternal mission on behalf of the disciples of Jesus.[86] Assumed into heaven body and soul, Mary has become "queen of the universe," fully conformed to Christ, "conqueror of sin and death."[87]

The third section is dedicated to the relation between the blessed Virgin and the church.[88] The first topic is Mary's maternal role (or her mediation), which "in no wise obscures or diminishes this unique mediation of Christ, but rather shows His power."[89] Mary is made the "companion" (*socia*) of the Redeemer and "cooperated in a singular way in the work of the Savior." Therefore she "is our mother in the order of grace."[90] This maternity endures because "the unique mediation of the Redeemer does not exclude but rather gives rise to a manifold cooperation which is but a sharing in this one source."[91] Mary is a personal prefiguration of the church (*typus Ecclesiae*, according to an expression of St. Ambrose) "in the order of faith, charity and perfect union with Christ."[92] The maternity and virginity of Mary appear as a model for Christian life in the spiritual generation of the faithful by means of Baptism and in her integral preservation of faith, hope, and charity.[93] The church imitates the holiness of Mary who, "since her entry into salvation history unites in herself and re-echoes the greatest teachings of the faith."[94]

The fourth section deals with "the cult of the Blessed Virgin in the Church."[95] The cult of Mary is "altogether singular," but different from the adoration due exclusively to the incarnate Word together with the Father and the Holy Spirit.[96] The faithful are exhorted to promote the cult of Mary, "especially the liturgical cult," and to assure that "the practices and exercises of piety, recommended by the magisterium of the Church toward her in the course of centuries, be

86. *LG* 58.
87. *LG* 59.
88. *LG* 60–65.
89. *LG* 60.
90. *LG* 61.
91. *LG* 62.
92. *LG* 63.
93. *LG* 63–64.
94. *LG* 65.
95. *LG* 66–67.
96. *LG* 66.

made of great moment." Theologians and preachers should "abstain zealously both from all gross exaggerations as well as from petty narrow-mindedness in considering the singular dignity of the Mother of God."[97]

Last, the fifth section describes Mary as a "sign of sure hope and solace to the people of God during its sojourn on earth."[98] Under this heading is also the exhortation to all the Christian faithful, including separated brethren, to have recourse in prayer to the Mother of God and mother of all men, so that all men "may be happily gathered together in peace and harmony into one people of God."[99]

To evaluate the importance of Vatican II for Mariology, René Laurentin, author of an authoritative work on the conciliar debate,[100] offers a summary in seven points. He writes:

> 1. The *biblical movement*[101] has restored some essential features to the spiritual portrait of Mary: her faith, her charity, her humility, her "poverty" that had been too much forgotten in a too exclusive emphasis on her glory. It recognized in her life the "Daughter of Zion," ... the personification of the Church and the mother of Christ's disciples.... [*LG* 55–59, 60, 66]
>
> 2. Likewise, the *patristic movement* has brought back into the foreground the importance and meaning of the Annunciation: the faith of the Virgin who "conceived in her heart before she conceived in her body." The meaning the new Eve has in a theological anthropology was rediscovered.... [*LG* 56, 63, 64]
>
> 3. The *ecclesiological movement* has thrown light again on the meaning that Mary in her exemplary role has for the Church.... It has not destroyed our Lady's privileges, but rather has given back to them their functional meaning. [*LG* 52–53,60–65]
>
> 4. The theology built around the *history of salvation* has likewise

97. *LG* 67.
98. *LG* 68–69.
99. *LG* 69.
100. Laurentin, *La Madonna del Vaticano II: Storia, esegesi e testo del capitolo ottavo della costituzione "De Ecclesia"* (Bergamo: Priorato di Sant'Egidio, 1965). French original: *La Vierge au concile* [The Virgin at the Council] (Paris: P. Lethielleux, 1965).
101. Emphasis added.

helped restore the historical, ecclesial, and anthropological meaning that the Virgin Mary has as new Eve. [*LG* 55–60]

5. Similarly, the *liturgical movement* has restored the essential that [was] being neglected in favor of the accessory. A sometimes-mediocre proliferation has been brought back to unity and sobriety. New value has been discovered especially in what is the ancient traditional root and center of true Marian devotion: the place the Virgin has in the Advent and Christmas mystery—in a word, in the mystery of salvation itself. The liturgical movement has neither condemned nor destroyed popular devotions; the conciliar texts say this very explicitly [*Sacrosanctum Concilium* 13; *LG* 67]. It has reinstated them and classified them anew according to a proper gradation, purifying them also in function of the essential....

6. The *missionary movement* made its own contribution ... to what is most important and most authentic—namely, the Annunciation and Visitation mystery seen as exemplifying the Christian life. The Virgin appears there as the type of the Church's apostolate, an apostolate inspired by the Holy Spirit.... [*LG* 65]

7. the *ecumenical movement* ... invites everyone to a renewed appreciation of the essential, but also leads us to a deeper perception and integration of values that had in some way been neglected: the gratuitous character of God's grace toward Mary ..., her exemplary faith and her poverty.... In the direction of the Orthodox, an immense field of work has been opened: the task of exploring together the Tradition of Fathers and Byzantine authors that is held in common....

All these movements converge in reemphasizing a central truth: Mary's place is at the point of departure and the very center of the mystery of salvation.[102]

THE POST-CONCILIAR PERIOD

In the wake of deviations among the "movements" mentioned earlier (in particular 1, 5, and 7: exegesis, liturgy, and ecumenism), the de-

102. Laurentin, *Short Treatise*, 148–50.

cade immediately after the Council brought on a powerful "Marian crisis."[103] A biblicist trend tended to undervalue doctrinal expressions grown from tradition. A liturgical extremism considered the manifestation of Marian devotion valid only within public worship, discounting forms of popular piety (for example, in the Rosary). A misunderstood ecumenism sought to carry on only those Marian concepts that are shared with Protestants.

A certain recovery was signaled by the apostolic exhortation *Marialis cultus* of Paul VI (1974).[104] Paul VI "sets a course for the future of Marian devotion. Starting from the liturgical renewal decided by the council, he explains the position of Mary in the general cycle of the year and the meaning of the specifically Marian feasts. Then he specifies the characteristics a true devotion for our time must have. Doctrinally the mystery of Mary must be understood as a trinitarian, Christological, ecclesial, and pneumatological mystery. Devotion will respond to contemporary needs if it follows the four orientations given: biblical, liturgical, ecumenical, and anthropological, proposed to 'emphasize and accentuate the bond which unites us to her who is the Mother of Christ and our Mother in the communion of saints.'"[105]

A marked resurgence in Marian life begins decisively with the pontificate of John Paul II (1978–2005).[106] The most visible fruit of

103. Antonio Maria Calero, *La Vergine Maria nel mistero di Cristo e della Chiesa: Saggio di mariologia* [The Virgin Mary in the Mystery of Christ and the Church: Essay in Mariology] (Leumann [Turin]: Elle Di Ci, 1995), 57–60; Spanish original: *María en el misterio de Cristo y de la Iglesia* (Madrid: CCS, 1990); see De Fiores, *Maria nella teologia contemporanea*, 123–36.

104. We will return to this in chap. 10.

105. T. Koehler, "Storia della mariologia" [History of Mariology], in De Fiores and Meo, *NDM*, 1402, citing Paul VI, Apostolic exhortation *Marialis cultus* (hereinafter *MCu*), 1974, 29.

106. See De Fiores, *Maria nella teologia contemporanea*, 533–77; Arthur B. Calkins, *Totus tuus: John Paul II's Program of Marian Consecration and Entrustment* (New Bedford, Mass.: Academy of the Immaculate, 1992); Aurelio Fusi, *Ha creduto meglio degli altri: Maria modello della Chiesa nell'insegnamento di Giovanni Paolo II* [She Believed Better Than Others: Mary, Model of the Church in the Teaching of John Paul II] (Milan: Ed. Paoline, 1999); Antoine Nachef, *Mary's Pope: John Paul II, Mary, and the Church since Vatican II* (Franklin, Wisc.: Sheed and Ward, 2000); Anton Ziegenaus, ed., *Totus tuus: Maria in Leben und Lehre Johannes Pauls II* [Totally Yours: Mary in the Life and Teaching of John Paul II], Mariologische Studien 1 (Regensburg: Friedrich Pustet, 2004); Salvatore M. Perrella, OSM, *Ecco tua Madre (Gv 19,27): La Madre di Gesù nel magistero di Giovanni Paolo II e nell'oggi della Chiesa e del mondo* [Behold Your Mother (Jn 19:27): The Mother of Jesus in the Magisterium of John Paul II and in the Church and the World Today] (Cinisello Balsamo: San Paolo, 2007), 179–259; Perrella, "La ricezione e l'approfondimento del capitolo VIII

his Marian teaching is the encyclical *Redemptoris Mater* (1987).[107] Also notable is the apostolic letter *Mulieris dignitatem* (1988) on the dignity and the vocation of woman, on the occasion of the Marian Year (1987–88). The anthropological approach to Mariology is strongly integrated into this Letter.[108] The Marian Year also brought the publication of the *Masses of the Blessed Virgin Mary* (= *MBVM*) in which a rich spiritual patrimony of forty-six liturgical formulas, in part concentrated on specific religious orders and local traditions, is placed at the disposition of the universal church.[109] New challeng-

della 'Lumen gentium' nel Magistero di Paolo VI, Giovanni Paolo II e Benedetto XVI" [The Reception and Deepening of Chapter Eight of "Lumen gentium" in the Magisterium of Paul VI, John Paul II, and Benedict XVI], in *Mariologia in tempore Concilii Vaticani II* [Mariology at the Time of the Second Vatican Council] (Vatican City: PAMI, 2013), 63–111; Hauke, "La mediazione materna di Maria secondo Papa Giovanni Paolo II" [Mary's Maternal Mediation according to Pope John Paul II], *Maria Corredentrice* 7 (2005):35–91; Ermanno M. Toniolo, ed., *Il magistero mariano di Giovanni Paolo II: Percorsi e punti salienti* [The Marian Magisterium of John Paul II: Pathways and Salient Points] (Rome: Centro di cultura mariana "Madre della Chiesa," 2006); Teofil Siudy, ed., *La Vergine Maria nel magistero di Giovanni Paolo II* [The Virgin Mary in the Magisterium of John Paul II] (Vatican City: PAMI, 2007); Lázaro Ilzo Daniel, *La mediazione materna di Maria in Cristo negli insegnamenti di Giovanni Paolo II* [The Maternal Mediation of Mary in Christ in the Teachings of John Paul II], CdM 9 (Lugano and Gavirate [Varese]: Eupress FTL, 2011); *TMSM* 7:29–36, 914–40.

107. See, among others, Angelo Amato, "L'Enciclica mariana 'Redemptoris Mater' di Giovanni Paolo II. Problemi e interpretazioni" [John Paul II's Marian Encyclical 'Redemptoris Mater': Problems and Interpretations], *Salesianum* 49 (1987): 813–33; De Fiores, *Maria nella teologia contemporanea*, 551–69; Perrella, *Ecco tua Madre*, 187–201; Pozo, *María, nueva Eva*, 403–27; Hauke, "La mediazione materna," 42–46, 59–91.

108. See, for example, Sandro Maggiolini, ed., *Profezia della donna: Lettera apostolica "Mulieris dignitatem": Testo e commenti* [Prophecy of the Woman: Apostolic Letter "Mulieris dignitatem": Text and Comments] (Rome: Città Nuova, 1988); Mario Toso, ed., *Essere donna: Studi sulla lettera apostolica "Mulieris dignitatem" di Giovanni Paolo II* [Being a Woman: Studies on John Paul II's Apostolic Letter "Mulieris dignitatem"] (Turin: Elledici, 1989); Aristide Serra, "La 'Mulieris dignitatem': Consensi e dissensi" ["Mulieris dignitatem": Agreements and Dissents], *Marianum* 53, no. 141 (1991): 144–82; (No author), "El misterio de María y la mujer (Intorno a la 'Mulieris dignitatem')" [The Mystery of Mary and of Woman (in "Mulieris dignitatem")], *Estudios Marianos* 62 (1996); José A. Riestra, "Bibliografia sobre la 'Mulieris dignitatem,'" *Estudios Marianos* 62 (1996): 267–90; Hauke, *Das Weihesakrament für die Frau—eine Forderung der Zeit? Zehn Jahre nach der päpstlichen Erklärung "Ordinatio Sacerdotalis"* [The Ordination of Women: A Demand of the Times?], Respondeo 17 (Siegburg: F. Schmitt, 2004), 86–94; Carla Rossi Espagnet, "*La dignità della donna* (Mulieris dignitatem—1988)" [The Dignity of Woman (Mulieris dignitatem, 1988)], in *Prendere il largo con Cristo: Esortazioni e lettere di Giovanni Paolo II*, ed. G. Borgonovo and A. Cattaneo (Siena: Cantagalli, 2005), 182–92.

109. Congregation for Divine Worship, *Collection of Masses of the Blessed Virgin Mary* (New York: Catholic Book Pub., 1992); 2nd ed. (Collegeville, Minn.: Liturgical Press, 2012). For an introduction and bibliography, see Nereo Zamberlan, "La Collectio Missarum de B. Maria Virgine: Bibliografia ragionata (1986–2001)" [The "Collection of Masses of the BVM": Critical Bibliography], *Marianum* 65, no. 163–64 (2003): 49–99; A. Catella, "La Collectio Missarum de Beata Maria

es to confront came in liberation theology and in feminism.[110] Then various other paths of research opened up: the role of Mary in popular piety, Marian apparitions, the contribution of the Western and Eastern traditions of approaching Mary, the relation between Mary and the Holy Spirit.... The 1992 *CCC* offers a reliable summary of the church's doctrine, including on the Mother of God;[111] the same is true for the "Compendium" of the *CCC* (2005).[112] From 1995 to 1997, John Paul II held seventy Marian catecheses that constituted a magisterial synthesis of all of Mariology.[113]

The great Jubilee of 2000 (and its preparation) brought with itself a strong Marian dimension, described in the apostolic letter *Tertio millennio adveniente* of 1994. Describing in the letter the fi-

---

Virgine: Analisi della eucologia" [The Collection of Masses of the BVM: Analysis of Euchology], in Hauke, *La donna e la salvezza*, 43–73.

110. On feminism, see "The Application of Feminism to Mariology," in chapter 3. Liberation theology brought some extreme expressions influenced by Marxism, and some more balanced approaches that are summarized in Clodovis M. Boff, *Mariologia sociale: Il significato della Vergine per la società* [Social Mariology: The Significance of the Virgin for Society], BTC 136 (Brescia: Queriniana, 2007). See also J. G. Piepke, "Befreiungstheologie" [Liberation Theology], in *ML* 1:400f.; Bertrand de Margerie, "Mary in Latin American Liberation Theologies," in *Kecharitoméne: Mélanges René Laurentin*, ed. Charles Augrain (Paris: Desclée, 1990), 365–76; De Fiores, *Maria nella teologia contemporanea*, 374–91; Stefano De Fiores, "Impegno sociale" [Social commitment] in *Dizionario* 1:906–11; Javier Losano Barragan, "La figura de María en la teología de la liberación" [The Figure of Mary in Liberation Theology], *Ephemerides Mariologicae* 42, no. 3–4 (1992): 317–41.

111. *CCC*, in particular 484–511; 721–26; 963–75. See also J. Ibáñez and F. Mendoza, "La Santísima Virgen en el Catecismo Romano y en el Nuevo Catecismo de la Iglesia Católica" [The Most Holy Virgin in the Roman Catechism and in the New Catechism of the Catholic Church], *Estudios Marianos* 59 (1994): 213–28; Enrico Dal Covolo, "Maria 'associata' a Gesù: La catechesi mariologica del *CCC*" [Mary, "Associated" with Jesus: The Marian Catechesis of the *CCC*], in *La catechesi al traguardo: Studi sul Catechismo della Chiesa Cattolica*, ed. A. Amato, E. Dal Covolo, and A. M. Triacca (Rome: LAS, 1997), 283–300; Perrella, *Ecco tua Madre*, 211–14; Perrella, *Le apparizioni mariane* (Cinisello Balsamo: San Paolo, 2007), 189–97.

112. *Compendium of the Catechism of the Catholic Church* (Washington, D.C.: USCCB, 2005), nn. 94–100, 142, 196–99.

113. John Paul II, *Maria Madre di Cristo e della Chiesa: Catechesi mariane* [Mary Mother of Christ and of the Church: Marian Catechesis], ed. Vincenzo Fagiolo (Casale Monferrato: Piemme, 1998). An English edition is in *Theotokos: Woman, Mother, Disciple; A Catechesis on Mary, Mother of God* (Boston: Pauline, 2000). On the importance of these catecheses and the role of Jean Galot, SJ, in their preparation, see Hauke, "Die Unbefleckte Empfängnis bei den griechischen Vätern: Die Hinweise Johannes Pauls II. im ökumenischen Disput," *Sedes Sapientiae: Mariologisches Jahrbuch* 8, no. 2 (2004): 17–20 (testimony of the Eastern tradition for the doctrine of the Immaculate Conception as acceptance of Galot's research); abbreviated version in English: "The Immaculate Conception of Mary in the Greek Fathers and in an Ecumenical Context," *Chicago Studies* 45 (2006): 330–33; Hauke, "La mediazione materna," 46–59 (dependence on Galot for the doctrine on mediation); see also Perrella, *Le apparizioni mariane*, 230–76; Daniel, *La mediazione materna*, 51–105.

nal three years of preparation he envisioned for the Jubilee, the pope meditated on the mystery of the divine maternity (1997), on Mary's openness to the Holy Spirit (1998), and on the perfect example of love in Mary, "chosen daughter of the Father" (1999).[114] He closes the Letter with the wish that Mary become, on the road toward the third millennium, "the Star which safely guides their steps to the Lord. May the unassuming Young Woman of Nazareth, who two thousand years ago offered to the world the Incarnate Word, lead the men and women of the new millennium towards the One who is 'the true light that enlightens every man' (Jn 1:9)."[115] The Marian perspective also resounds in the apostolic letter that calls for a new evangelization after the celebrations of the Great Jubilee of 2000, *Novo millennio ineunte* (2001).[116] For 2002–3, the pope proclaimed a Year of the Rosary, with a preparatory apostolic letter *Rosarium Virginis Mariae*.[117] The encyclical *Ecclesia de Eucharistia* (2003) also contains an appropriate Marian chapter (chap. 6).[118]

Pope Benedict XVI has distinguished himself with an intense and clear magisterium, prepared by various earlier theological contributions (including in the mariological field).[119] The theologian Joseph Ratzinger particularly affirmed the connection between Mary

114. John Paul II, *Tertio millennio adveniente*, 43, 48, and 54, respectively.

115. John Paul II, *Tertio millennio adveniente*, 59. See Perrella, *Ecco tua Madre*, 214–17; Perrella, *Le apparizioni mariane*, 310–14.

116. See Perrella, *Ecco tua Madre*, 221–26; *Le apparizioni mariane*, 314–23.

117. See Stefano M. Cecchin, ed., *Contemplare Cristo con Maria: Atti della Giornata di studio sulla Lettera apostolica Rosarium Virginis Mariae di Giovanni Paolo II: Roma, 3 maggio 2003* [Contemplating Christ with Mary: Acts of the Study Day on the Apostolic Letter "Rosarium Virginis Mariae" by John Paul II: Rome, May 3, 2003] (Vatican City: PAMI, 2003); Krzysztof (Cristoforo) Charamsa, *Il Rosario: Riflessioni sulla Lettera Apostolica Rosarium Virginis Mariae* [The Rosary: Reflections on the Apostolic Letter Rosarium Virginis Mariae] (Vatican City: Libreria Editrice Vaticana, 2003); Perrella, *Ecco tua Madre*, 227–38; *Le apparizioni mariane*, 380–401.

118. See Hauke, "L'eucaristia: Fonte e culmine della vita Cristiana; L'enciclica Ecclesia de Eucaristia" [The Eucharist: Source and Summit of Christian Life; The Encyclical Ecclesia de Eucharistia], in *Il papa teologo: Nel segno delle encicliche*, ed. G. Borgonovo and A. Cattaneo (Milan: Mondadori, 2003), 269f.; Perrella, *Ecco tua Madre*, 238–59; *La Madre di Gesù*, 405–35.

119. See, in particular, Joseph Ratzinger, *Daughter Zion: Meditations on the Church's Marian Belief* (San Francisco: Ignatius Press, 1983); Hans Urs von Balthasar and Joseph Ratzinger, *Mary: The Church at the Source* (San Francisco: Ignatius, 2005). A general overview: Michele G. Masciarelli, *Il segno della donna: Maria nella teologia di Joseph Ratzinger* [The Sign of the Woman: Mary in the Theology of Joseph Ratzinger] (Cinisello Balsamo: San Paolo, 2007); *TMSM* 7:1005–18; Perrella, "La ricezione e l'approfondimento," 111–27.

and the church. His mariological doctrine has been influenced since then by the teaching of his predecessor, in particular on the mediation of Mary.[120] The ecclesiotypical variation on Mariology is manifest in the encyclical *Sacramentum Caritatis* (2007), which affirms that Mary "received Christ's sacrifice for the whole Church"; as an "icon of the nascent Church, [She] is the model for each of us, called to receive the gift that Jesus makes of himself in the Eucharist."[121] Notwithstanding that, Mary is not only a model for us, but also assumes a maternal role in our challenges. Among other points in the pontiff's teaching, we can note two characteristics consonant with the doctrine of his predecessor, but not yet visible with the same clarity in his own body of theological work prior to assuming the Petrine ministry: the awareness that Mary is associated with Christ at his sacrifice on Calvary[122] and the recognition of the fact that the Mother of God participates in the distribution of all graces.[123] A

120. See Ratzinger, "Un'interpretazione dei segni dei tempi per il cammino della Chiesa e dell'umanità" [An Interpretation of the Signs of the Times for the Journey of the Church and of Humanity], in *Una luce sul cammino dell'uomo: Per una lettura della "Redemptoris Mater,"* Quaderni de "L'Osservatore Romano" 6 (Vatican City: 1988), 3–12; von Balthasar and Ratzinger, *Mary: The Church at the Source*, in the section "Marian Mediation"; Masciarelli, *Il segno*, 100–122.

121. Benedict XVI, *Sacramentum caritatis*, 33.

122. See, among others, the sermon at Ephesus, November 29, 2006: "We have listened to a passage from Saint John's Gospel that invites us to contemplate the moment of the Redemption when Mary, united to her Son in the offering of his sacrifice, extended her motherhood to all men and women, and in particular to the disciples of Jesus"; *Insegnamenti di Benedetto XVI*, vol. 2, book 2 (Vatican City: Libreria Editrice Vaticana, 2007), 711; English translation from https://w2.vatican.va/content/benedict-xvi/en/homilies/2006/documents/hf_ben-xvi_hom_20061129_ephesus.html. Or his discourse at the Angelus, September 17, 2006: "The Evangelist recounts: Mary was standing by the Cross (cf. Jn 19:25–27). Her sorrow is united with that of her Son. It is a sorrow full of faith and love. The Virgin on Calvary participates in the saving power of the suffering of Christ, joining her 'fiat,' her 'yes,' to that of her Son"; *Insegnamenti di Benedetto XVII*, vol. 2, book 2 (Vatican City: Libreria Editrice Vaticana, 2007), 304; English translation from https://w2.vatican.va/content/benedict-xvi/en/angelus/2006/documents/hf_ben-xvi_ang_20060917.html. See Hauke, "Die Lehre von der 'Miterlösung' im geschichtlichen Durchblick: Von den biblischen Ursprüngen bis zu Papst Benedikt XVI" [The Theory of "Coredemption" in Historical Perspective; From the Biblical Sources to Benedict XVI], *Sedes Sapientiae: Mariologisches Jahrbuch* 11 (2007): 58–60.

123. See the homily for the canonization of Frei Galvão (Brazil), May 11, 2007: "There is no fruit of grace in the history of salvation that did not have as its necessary instrument the mediation of Our Lady.... Let us give thanks to God the Father, to God the Son, to God the Holy Spirit from whom, through the intercession of the Virgin Mary, we receive all the Blessings of Heaven"; *L'Osservatore Romano*, May 16, 2007, 5. See the *Act of Entrustment and Consecration of Priests to the Immaculate Heart of Mary* on the Occasion of the Year for Priests on May 12, 2010 at Fatima: "Advocate and Mediatrix of grace, you who are fully immersed in the one universal mediation of Christ, invoke upon us, from God, a heart completely renewed."

discreet inspiration may have come from the teaching of his predecessor and from the influence of Hans Urs von Balthasar, who had emphasized the participation of Mary in the sacrifice of her Son,[124] and who would have wished to see clearer formulations about this idea in the texts of Vatican II.[125]

In the Apostolic Exhortation *Verbum Domini* (2010),[126] Pope Benedict XVI draws a strong parallel between the Christian faith and the reception of the Word by Mary. This theme is present also in the encyclical by Pope Francis on faith, *Lumen fidei* (2013),[127] prepared in large part by his predecessor. In the Apostolic Exhortation *Evangelii gaudium* (2013),[128] Maria appears as a "most pure icon of the Church" and "star of the new evangelization."

REFERENCES

An Anthology of Texts: The Series *TMPM* and *TMSM*

Marian Texts of the First Millennium

Testi mariani del primo millennio (hereinafter *TMPM*) [Marian Texts of the First Millennium]. Vol. 1, *Padri ed altri autori greci* [Greek Fathers and Other Authors]. Edited by Georges Gharib. Rome: Città Nuova, 1988; 2nd ed. 2001.

———. Vol. 2, *Padri ed altri autori bizantini (VI–XI sec.)* [Byzantine Fathers and Other Authors, 6th–11th Centuries]. Edited by Georges Gharib. Rome: Città Nuova, 1989.

———. Vol. 3, *Padri e altri autori latini* [Latin Fathers and Other Authors]. Edited by Luigi Gambero. Rome: Città Nuova, 1990.

———. Vol. 4, *Padri e altri autori orientali* [Eastern Fathers and Other Authors]. Edited by Georges Gharib. Rome: Città Nuova, 1991.

124. Hans Urs von Balthasar, *Teodrammatica* (Milan: Jaca, 1986), 4:369 [German original: *Theodramatik* (Einsiedeln: Johannes Verlag, 1980), 3:369]: the "yes" of Mary, a condition for the Incarnation, becomes below the Cross an integral part (*Mitbestandteil*) of the sacrifice of Christ, even if the consent of the new Eve depends on Christ, the new Adam. See Aidan Nichols, "Von Balthasar and the Coredemption," in *Mary at the Foot of the Cross* (New Bedford, Mass.: Academy of the Immaculate, 2000), 1:301–15; Hilda Steinhauer, *Maria als dramatische Person bei Hans Urs von Balthasar: Zum marianischen Prinzip seines Denkens* [Mary as a Dramatic Figure in Hans Urs von Balthasar: The Marian Principle of His Thought], Salzburger Theologische Studien 17 (Innsbruck: Tyrolia, 2001), 407–9; Vittoria Marini, *Maria e il Mistero di Cristo nella teologia di Hans Urs von Balthasar* (Vatican City: PAMI, 2005), 304–8.

125. Hans Urs von Balthasar, *Theodramatik*, vol. 2, book 2 (Einsiedeln: Johannes Verlag, 1978), 291f. Italian: *Teodrammatica* (Milan: Jaca, 1983), 3:293–295; Steinhauer, *Maria*, 498f.

126. See L. F. Mateo-Seco, "Dimension mariana de la Exhortacion apostólica Verbum Domini," *Scripta de Maria* 2nd ser., no. 8 (2011): 183–204; Perrella, "La ricezione e l'approfondimento," 117–25.

127. See Francis, Encyclical *Lumen fidei*, nn. 58–60.

128. Apostolic Exhortation *Evangelii Gaudium*, nn. 284–88.

Marian Texts of the Second Millennium

Testi mariani del secondo millennio (hereinafter *TMSM*) [Marian Texts of the Second Millennium]. Vol. 1, *Autori orientali: Sec. XI–XX* [Eastern Authors, 11th–20th Centuries]. Edited by Georges Gharib and Ermanno M. Toniolo. Rome: Città Nuova, 2008.

———. Vol. 2, *Autori dell'area russa: Sec. XI–XX* [Authors from the Region of Russia, 11th–20th Centuries]. Edited by Tomáš Špidlík et al. Rome: Città Nuova, 2008.

———. Vol. 3, *Autori medievali dell'Occidente: Sec. XI–XII* [Western Medieval Authors, 11th–12th Centuries] Edited by Luigi Gambero. Rome: Città Nuova, 1996.

———. Vol. 4, *Autori medievali dell'Occidente: Sec. XIII–XV* [Western Medieval Authors, 13th–15th Centuries]. Edited by Luigi Gambero. Rome: Città Nuova, 1996.

———. Vol. 5, *Autori moderni dell'Occidente: Sec. XVI–XVII* [Modern Western Authors, 16th–17th Centuries]. Edited by Luigi Gambero and Stefano De Fiores. Rome: Città Nuova, 2003.

———. Vol. 6, *Autori moderni dell'Occidente: Sec. XVIII–XIX* [Modern Western Authors, 18th–19th Centuries]. Edited by Luigi Gambero and Stefano De Fiores. Rome: Città Nuova, 2005

———. Vol. 7, *Autori contemporanei dell'Occidente: Sec. XX* [Contemporary Western Authors, 20th Century]. Edited by Angelo Amato. Rome: Città Nuova, 2012.

———. Vol. 8, *Poesia e prosa letteraria* [Poetry and Literary Prose]. Edited by Ferdinando Castelli. Rome: Città Nuova, 2002.

Works Containing Historical Articles

Bäumer, Remigius, and Leo Scheffczyk, eds. *Marienlexikon*. 6 vols. St. Ottilien: EOS, 1988–94.

O'Carroll, Michael, CSSp. *Theotokos: A Theological Encyclopedia of the Blessed Virgin Mary*. Eugene, Ore.: Wipf and Stock, 2000.

Pontificia Academia Mariana Internationalis (PAMI), ed. *De primordiis cultus mariani* [Origins of the Cult of Mary], 6 vols. Rome: Pontificia Academia Mariana Internationalis, 1970.

———. *De cultu mariano saeculis VI–XI* [The Cult of Mary in the 6th–9th Centuries]. 5 vols. Rome: PAMI, 1972.

———. *De cultu mariano saeculis XII–XV*. 6 vols. Rome: PAMI, 1979–81.

———. *De cultu mariano saeculo XVI*. 6 vols. Rome: PAMI, 1983–86.

———. *De cultu mariano saeculis XVII–XVIII*. 7 vols. Rome: PAMI, 1987.

———. *De cultu mariano saeculis XIX–XX*. 7 vols. Rome: PAMI, 1989.

———. *De cultu mariano saeculo XX a concilio Vaticano II usque ad nostros dies*. 6 vols. Vatican City: PAMI, 1998–2001.

Historical Overview

Auer, Johann. *Gesù il Salvatore: Soteriologia–Mariologia* [Jesus the Savior: Soteriology–Mariology]. Assisi: Cittadella, 1993, § 3.

Bastero, Juan Luis. *Mary, Mother of the Redeemer*, 32–62. Dublin: Four Courts, 2006.

Boaga, Emanuele, and Luigi Gambero, eds. *Storia della mariologia*. Vol. 2. Rome: Città Nuova, 2012. (A third volume is forthcoming.)

Calero, Antonio Maria. *La Vergine Maria nel mistero di Cristo e della Chiesa: Saggio di mariologia* [The Virgin Mary in the Mystery of Christ and the Church: Essay in Mariology], 14–66. Leumann (Turin): Editrice Elle di CI, 1995.

Colzani, Gianni. *Maria: Mistero di grazia e di fede* [Mary, Mystery of Grace and Faith]. 3rd ed. 79–159. Cinisello Balsamo: Paoline, 2006.

Dal Covolo, Enrico, and Aristide Serra, eds. *Storia della mariologia* [History of Mariology]. Vol. 1. Rome: Città Nuova, 2009.

Delius, Walter. *Geschichte der Marienverehrung* [History of Marian Veneration]. Munich and Basel: Reinhardt, 1963.

De Fiores, Stefano. *Maria, Madre di Gesù: Sintesi storico-salvifica* [Mary, Mother of Jesus: Salvation-Historical Synthesis], 107–87. Corso di teologia sistematica 6. Bologna: EDB, 1992.

———. *Maria sintesi di valori: Storia culturale della mariologia* [Mary, Synthesis of Values: Cultural History of Mariology]. Cinisello Balsamo: San Paolo, 2005.

———. "Storia della Mariologia." In *Maria: Nuovissimo dizionario* 2:1613–1715. Bologna: EDB, 2006.

———. "Storia della mariologia." In *DMar*, 1162–77.

Graef, Hilda C. *Maria: Eine Geschichte der Lehre und Verehrung*. Freiburg im Breisgau: Herder, 1964. (English editions: *Mary: A History of Doctrine and Devotion*. London: Sheed and Ward, 1963; Notre Dame, Ind.: Christian Classics, 2009.)

Holböck, Ferdinand. *Geführt von Maria: Marianische Heilige aus allen Jahrhunderten der Kirchengeschichte* [Led by Mary: Marian Saints from All Centuries of Church History]. Stein am Rhein (Switzerland): Christiana, 1987.

Holstein, Henri, SJ. "Le développement du Dogme Marial" [The Development of Marian Dogma]. In *Maria*, edited by H. du Manoir, 6:241–93. Paris; Beauchesne, 1961.

Koehler, T. "Storia della mariologia" [History of Mariology]. In De Fiores and Meo, *NDM*, 1385–1405.

Laurentin, René. *A Short Treatise on the Virgin Mary*. Washington, N.J.: Ave Maria Institute, 1991, 57–175.

Manelli, Stefano M. "La Mariologia nella storia della salvezza" [Mariology in Salvation History]. *Immaculata Mediatrix* 1 (2002): 43–78, 139–76, 285–322; 3 (2003): 19–57; 6 (2006): 17–62; 7 (2007): 13–62.

Pelikan, Jaroslav. *Mary through the Centuries*. New Haven, Conn.: Yale University Press, 1996.

Roschini, Gabriele Maria. *La Madonna: Secondo la fede e la teologia* [The Madonna, according to the Faith and Theology], 1:135–66. Rome: Libreria Editrice Francesco Ferrari, 1953–54.

———. *Maria Santissima nella storia della salvezza: Trattato completo di mariologia alla luce del Concilio Vaticano II* [Mary Most Holy in the History of Salvation: Complete Treatise on Mariology in Light of the Second Vatican Council], 1:235–542. Isola del Liri: Pisani, 1969.

———. "Storia della Mariologia" [History of Mariology]. In *Enciclopedia mariana "Theotocos"* (hereinafter *EMTheo*). Genoa-Milan: Editrice Massimo, 1954 (2nd ed. 1958), 81–98.

Söll, Georg. *Storia dei dogmi mariani* [History of Marian Dogmas]. Rome: Libreria Ateneo Salesiano, 1981. German original: *Mariologie: Handbuch der Dogmengeschichte*. Vol. 3, part 4. Freiburg im Breisgau: Herder, 1978.

Stöhr, Johannes. "Mariologie." In *ML* 4:320–26.

Sträter, Paul., ed. *Katholische Marienkunde* [Catholic Marian Doctrine], 1:85–375. Paderborn: F. Schöningh, 1947 (3rd ed. 1962). Italian translation: *Mariologia*. Vol. 1. Turin: Marietti Editori Pontifici, 1952.

Toniolo, Ermanno M., ed. *La Vergine Madre nella Chiesa delle origini* [The Virgin Mother in the Early Church]. Rome: Centro di cultura mariana, 1996.

———, ed. *La Vergine Madre dal secolo VI al secondo millennio* [The Virgin Mother from the 6th Century to the Second Millennium]. Rome: Centro di cultura mariana, 1998.

———, ed. *La Madre del Signore dal Medioevo al Rinascimento* [The Mother of the Lord from the Middle Ages to the Renaissance]. Rome: Centro di cultura mariana, 1998.

———, ed. *La Vergine Madre dal Rinascimento ad oggi* [The Virgin Mother from the Renaissance to Today]. Rome: Centro di cultura mariana, 1999.

Ziegenaus, Anton. *Katholische Dogmatik.* Vol. 5. *Maria in der Heilsgeschichte: Mariologie* [Catholic Dogmatics. Vol. 5. Mary in Salvation History: Mariology], 142–60, 192–203 (sec. IV). Aachen: MM-Verlag, 1998.

Mary in the Patristic Era

"Maria." In *Nuovo dizionario patristico e di antichità cristiane*, edited by Angelo Di Berardino, 2:3035–55. Genoa and Milano: Marietti, 2007. English edition: *Encyclopedia of Ancient Christianity*. Downers Grove: IVP Academic, 2014.

"Maria in scrittori del II secolo" [Mary in Authors of the Second Century]. *Theotokos* 10, no. 1 (2002).

"Maria in scrittori orientali del IV secolo" [Mary in Eastern Authors of the Fourth Century]. *Theotokos* 10, no. 2 (2002); 11, no. 1 (2003).

"Maria nei Concili ecumenici e in scrittori dei secoli IV–V" [Mary in the Ecumenical Councils and in Authors of the Fourth and Fifth Centuries]. *Theotokos* 12 (2004).

"Maria in scrittori del V–VIII secolo" [Mary in Authors of the Fifth to Eighth Centuries]. *Theotokos* 14, no. 1 (2006); 15, no. 1 (2007).

"Maria nell'area culturale latina: Da Tertulliano († 240 ca.) a sant'Ildefonso di Toledo († 667)" [Mary in the Latin Cultural Area, from Tertullian to St. Ildefonso of Toledo]. In Dal Covolo and Serra, *Storia della Mariologia*, 1:143–502.

Burghardt, Walter J. "María en la patristica occidental." In *Mariología*, edited by J. Carol, 111–55. Madrid: Biblioteca de Autores Cristianos, 1964. English original: "Mary in Western Patristic Thought," in *Mariology*, edited by J. Carol, 1:109–55. Milwaukee: Bruce, 1954.

———. "María en el pensamiento de los Padres orientales." In *Mariología*, edited by

J. Carol, 2:488–547. English original: "Mary in Eastern Patristic Thought," in *Mariology*, edited by J. Carol, 2:88–153. Milwaukee: Bruce, 1957.

De Fiores. *Maria sintesi di valori*, 78–152.

———. *Maria: Nuovissimo dizionario*, 1:1615–28. Bologna: EDB, 2006.

Felici, Sergio, ed. *La mariologia nella catechesi dei padri (età prenicena)* [Mariology in the Catechesis of the Fathers (Pre-Nicene Period)]. Rome: Università Pontificia Salesiana, 1989.

———, ed., *La mariologia nella catechesi dei padri (età postnicena)* [Mariology in the Catechesis of the Fathers (Post-Nicene period)]. Rome: Università Pontificia Salesiana, 1991.

Gambero, Luigi. *Mary and the Fathers of the Church: The Blessed Virgin Mary in Patristic Thought*. Translated by Thomas Buffer. San Francisco: Ignatius Press, 1999.

———. "Maria negli antichi concili" [Mary in the Ancient Councils]. In Dal Covolo and Serra, *Storia della Mariologia*, 1:451–502.

Jouassard, G. "Marie à travers la patristique: Maternité, virginité, sainteté" [Mary in Patristics: Motherhood, Virginity, Holiness]. In *Maria*, edited by H. du Manoir, 1:69–157. Paris: Beauchesne, 1949.

Hauke, M. "Marienlehre und Marienfrömmigkeit bei den Heiligen der Väterzeit" [Marian Doctrine and Piety in the Saints of the Patristic Era]. *Sedes Sapientiae: Mariologisches Jahrbuch* 6, no. 1–2 (2002): 49–68.

Manelli, Stefano M. "La mariologia nella storia della salvezza: Età antica" [Mariology in Salvation History: Ancient Period]. *Immaculata Mediatrix* 2 (2002), 139–76.

Maritano, M. "Maria nei Padri della Chiesa" [Mary in the Fathers of the Church]. In *Letteratura patristica*, edited by A. Di Berardino, G. Fedalto, and M. Simonetti, 838–46. Cinisello Balsamo: San Paolo, 2007.

———. "Padri della Chiesa" [Fathers of the Church]. In *DMar*, 917–27.

PAMI, ed. *De cultu mariano saeculis VI–XI*. 5 vols. Rome: PAMI, 1972.

———. *De primordiis cultus mariani*. 6 vols. Rome: PAMI, 1970.

Peretto, Elio. "Maria nell'area culturale greca: Da san Giustino (†165 ca.) a san Giovanni Damasceno (†749)" [Mary in the Greek Cultural Area, from St. Justin to St. John Damascene]. In Dal Covolo and Serra, *Storia della Mariologia*, 1:263–305.

———. *Percorsi mariologici nell'antica letteratura cristiana* [Paths of Mariology in Ancient Christian Literature]. Vatican City: Libreria Editrice Vaticana, 2001.

Ponce Cuéllar, Miguel. *María: Madre del Redentor y Madre de la Iglesia* [Mary: Mother of the Redeemer and Mother of the Church]. 2nd ed., 201–82. Barcelona: Herder, 2001.

Reynolds, Brian. *Gateway to Heaven: Marian Doctrine and Devotion, Image and Typology in the Patristic and Medieval Periods*. Hyde Park, N.Y.: New City Press, 2012.

Söll. *Storia dei dogmi mariani*, §§ 3–8.

Toniolo, Ermanno M. *La Vergine Madre di Dio nei primi padri della Chiesa* [The Virgin Mother of God in the Early Church Fathers]. Rome: Centro di cultura mariana "Mater Ecclesiae," 1988.

———. *La Vergine Madre nella Chiesa delle origini*.

———. "Padri della Chiesa" [Fathers of the Church]. In De Fiores and Meo, *NDM*, 1044–80.

Anthologies of Patristic Sources

Alvarez Campos, Sergius. *Corpus marianum patristicum*. 8 vols. Burgos: Ediciones Aldecoa, 1970–1985.

Casagrande, Domenico. *Enchiridion marianum biblico-patristicum*. Rome: Cor unum, 1974.

Pons Pons, Guillermo. *Textos marianos de los primeros siglos*. Madrid: Ciudad nueva, 1994.

TMPM I–IV.

Medieval Development

Bäumer, Remigius. "Mittelalter" [Middle Ages]. In *ML* 4:486.

Cecchin, Stefano M. *Maria: Signora Santa e Immacolata nel pensiero francescano; Per una storia del contributo francescano alla mariologia* [Mary: Holy and Immaculate Lady in Franciscan Thought; Toward a History of the Franciscan Contribution to Mariology], 43–228. Vatican City: PAMI, 2001.

Dal Covolo, E., and A. Serra, eds. *Storia della Mariologia*, 1:505–840.

De Fiores. *Maria: Nuovissimo dizionario*, 2:1628–40. Bologna: EDB, 2006.

———. *Maria sintesi di valori*, 155–208.

Gambero, Luigi. *Fede e devozione mariana nell'impero bizantino* [Marian Faith and Devotion in the Byzantine Empire]. Cinisello Balsamo: San Paolo, 2012.

———. "Il XIII secolo e la fioritura della scholastica" [The 13th Century and the Flowering of Scholasticism]. In Dal Covolo and Serra, *Storia della Mariologia*, 1:774–829.

———. *Maria nel pensiero dei teologi latini medievali* [Mary in the Thought of the Medieval Latin Theologians]. Cinisello Balsamo: San Paolo, 2000.

Langella, A. "La figura di Maria nel XIV secolo (con bibliografia)" [The Figure of Mary in 14th-Century Theology (with Bibliography)]. *Theotokos* 20 (2012): 7–32.

———. "Maria nella teologia del XIII secolo (con bibliografia)" [Mary in 13th-Century Theology (with Bibliography)]. *Theotokos* 19 (2011): 3–48.

Manelli, Stefano M. "La mariologia nella storia della salvezza. Età medievale." *Immaculata Mediatrix* 2 (2002): 285–322.

———. "Maria, hl." [St. Mary]. In *Lexikon des Mittelalters*, 6:243–75.

Müller, M. "Maria: Ihre geistige Gestalt und Persönlichkeit in der Theologie des Mittelalters" [Mary: Spiritual Figure and Personality in Medieval Theology]. In *Katholische Marienkunde*, edited by P. Sträter, 1:268–316.

PAMI, ed. *De cultu mariano saeculis VI–XI*. 5 vols. Rome: PAMI, 1972.

———. *De cultu mariano saeculis XII–XV*. 6 vols. Rome: PAMI, 1979–81.

Scheffczyk, Leo. *Das Mariengeheimnis in Frömmigkeit und Lehre der Karolingerzeit* [The Mystery of Mary in Piety and Doctrine of the Carolingian Era]. Leipzig: St. Benno-Verlag, 1959.

———. "Scholastik" [Scholasticism]. In *ML* 6:57–59.

———. "Tendenzen und Entwicklungslinien der Marienlehre im Mittelalter" [Schools of Thought and Lines of Development of Marian Doctrine in the Mid-

dle Ages]. In *Das Zeichen des Allmächtigen: Die jungfräuliche Gottesmutterschaft Mariens in ihrer Verbindlichkeit für das christliche Leben* [The Sign of the Almighty: The Virginal Motherhood of Mary, in its Bindingness for the Christian Life], edited by G. Rovira, 118–38. Würzburg: Naumann, 1981.
Shea, George W. "Historia de la mariología en la Edad Media y en los tiempos modernos." In Carol, *Mariología*, 267–306. English original: "Outline History of Mariology in the Middle Ages and Modern Times." In Carol, *Mariology*, 1:281–327.
Söll. *Storia dei dogmi mariani*, 227–318.
TMSM III–IV. Toniolo, ed. *La Madre del Signore Dal Medioevo al Rinascimento.*

Second Vatican Council

Ecclesiastical Texts

John Paul II, CM 9 (Dec. 13, 1995) ("The Council's Teaching on Mary Is Rich and Positive").

Other Sources

Antonelli, Carlo. *Il debattito su Maria nel Concilio Vaticano II: Percorso redazionale sulla base di nuovi documenti di archivio* [The Debate on Mary at Vatican II: The Redactional Path, on the Basis of New Archive Documents]. Padua: Messaggero, 2009.
Balić, Carolus, OFM. "El capitolo VIII de la constitución 'Lumen gentium' comparado con el primer esquema de la Virgen Madre de la Iglesia" [Chapter Eight of the Constitution "Lumen gentium" Compared with the First Schema on the Virgin Mother of the Church]. *Estudios Marianos* 27 (1966): 135–83.
Besutti, Giuseppe Maria, OSM. *Lo schema mariano al Concilio Vaticano II: Documentazione e note di cronaca* [The Marian Schema at Vatican II: Documentation and Notes]. Rome: Desclée, 1966.
De Fiores, Stefano. *Maria: Nuovissimo dizionario*, 1:324–58.
———. *Maria nella teologia contemporanea* [Mary in Contemporary Theology]. 3rd ed., 108–22. Rome: Centro della cultura mariana "Madre della Chiesa," 1991.
Greco, Angelico. *"Madre dei viventi": La cooperazione salvifica di Maria nella "Lumen gentium"; Una sfida per oggi* ["Mother of the Living": The Salvific Cooperation of Mary, in "Lumen gentium"; A Challenge for Today]. CdM 10. Lugano and Gavirate (Varese): Eupress FTL, 2011.
Hauke, Manfred. "Die marianischen Aussagen des Zweiten Vatikanischen Konzils und ihre Interpretation durch Johannes Paul II" [The Marian Statements of Vatican II and Their Interpretation by John Paul II]. *Sedes Sapientiae: Marianisches Jahrbuch* 16, no. 1 (2012): 58–88.
———. "Die trinitarischen Beziehungen Mariens als Urbild der Kirche auf dem Zweiten Vatikanischen Konzil" [The Trinitarian Relationships of Mary as an Archetype of the Church at Vatican II]. *Sedes Sapientiae: Mariologisches Jahrbuch* 4, no. 2 (2000): 78–114 (bibliography).
Lanzetta, Serafino M. *Il Vaticano II, un Concilio pastorale: Ermeneutica delle dottrine conciliari* [Vatican II, a Pastoral Council: Hermeneutic of the Conciliar Doc-

trines], 369–419. Siena: Cantagalli, 2014. English translation, *Vatican II, A Pastoral Council*. Leominster, UK: Gracewing, 2016.
Laurentin, René. *La Madonna del Vaticano II*. Bergamo (Sotto il Monte): Centro Giovanni XXIII, 1965.
Manelli, Stefano M. "La mariologia nella storia della salvezza: L'età contemporanea; Dal Concilio Ecumenico Vaticano II dal 2000." *Immaculata Mediatrix* 7 (2007): 13–30.
Meo, Salvatore Maria. "Concilio Vaticano II." In De Fiores and Meo, *NDM*, 379–94.
O'Carroll. *Theotokos*, 351–56.
Perrella, Salvatore M., OSM. "Concilio Vaticano II." In *DMar*, 308–19.
———. *La Madre di Gesù nella coscienza ecclesiale contemporanea* [The Mother of Jesus in Contemporary Ecclesial Awareness], 1–140. Rome: PAMI, 2005.
Philips, Gérard. *La Chiesa e il suo mistero nel Concilio Vaticano II: Storia, testo e commento della Costituzione Lumen gentium* [The Church and Her Mystery in Vatican II: History, Text, and Commentary on the Constitution Lumen gentium]. Milan: Jaca, 1975.
———. "La Vierge au IIe Concile du Vatican et l'avenir de la mariologie" [The Virgin at Vatican II and the Future of Mariology]. In *Maria*, edited by H. du Manoir, 8:41–88. Paris: Beauchesne, 1971.
Roschini. *Maria Santissima*, 1:16–102.
Scheffczyk, Leo. "Vaticanum II." In *ML* 6:567–71.
Söll. *Storia dei dogmi mariani*, 388–93.
TMSM, 7:340–51.
Toniolo, Ermanno M. *La Beata Vergine Maria nel Concilio Vaticano II: Cronistoria del capitolo VIII della costituzione dogmatica "Lumen gentium" e sinossi di tutte le relazioni* [The Blessed Virgin Mary in Vatican II: Chronicle of Chapter Eight of the Dogmatic Constitution "Lumen gentium" and Synopsis of Reports]. Rome: Centro "Madre della Chiesa," 2004.
———, ed. *Maria nel Concilio: Approfondimenti e percorsi*. Rome: Centro "Madre della Chiesa," 2005.

The Post-Conciliar Period

Amato, Angelo. "Maria nell'insegnamento del magistero dal Concilio Vaticano II a oggi." In *Fons lucis: Miscellanea di studi in onore di Ermanno M. Toniolo*, edited by R. Barbieri et al., 437–72. Rome: Marianum, 2004.
Bastero, Juan Luis. *Virgen singular: La reflexión teológica mariana en el siglo XX*. Madrid: Rialp, 2001.
De Fiores. "Attualità." In *Maria: Nuovissimo dizionario* 1:123–63.
———. *Maria nella teologia contemporanea*.
———. *Maria sintesi di valori*, 306–548.
———. "Storia della mariologia." In *Maria: Nuovissimo dizionario* 2:1667–77.
Görg, P. H. *"Sagt an, wer ist doch diese": Inhalt, Rang und Entwicklung der Mariologie in dogmatischen Lehrbüchern und Publikationen deutschsprachiger Dogmatiker des 19. und 20. Jahrhunderts* ["Say Then, Who Is She?": Content, Rank, and Development

of Mariology in Dogmatic Manuals and Publications of German-Language Dogmatic Theologians of the 19th and 20th Centuries], 317–95. Bonn: Nova et Vetera, 2007.

Manelli, Stefano M. "La mariologia nella storia della salvezza: L'età contemporanea; Dal Concilio Ecumenico Vaticano II dal 2000." *Immaculata Mediatrix* 7 (2007): 30–62.

PAMI, ed. *De cultu mariano saeculo XX a concilio Vaticano II usque ad nostros dies.*

———. *La Madre del Signore: Memoria presenza Speranza; Alcune questioni attuali sulla figura e la missione della beata Vergine Maria*, 49–120. Vatican City: PAMI, 2000. English translation: *The Mother of the Lord: Memory, Presence, Hope*, 33–112. Staten Island, N.Y.: St. Paul, 2007.

———. *Mariologia a tempore Concilii Vaticani II: Receptio, ratio et prospectus; Acta Congressus Mariologici-mariani Internationalis in civitate Romae anno 2012 celebrati; Studia in sessionibus plenariis exhibita* [Mariology at the Time of Vatican II ...]. Vatican City: PAMI, 2013.

Perrella. *La Madre di Gesù*, 141–296.

Scanziani, Francesco. "Da Lumen gentium VIII ad oggi: Il trattato di mariologia; Scelte di metodo; Rassegna bibliografica in campo italiano" [From Lumen gentium VIII to Today: The Treatise on Mariology; Choice of Method; Bibliographic Review in the Italian Milieu]. *La scuola cattolica* 132 (2004): 75–122.

Söll. *Storia dei dogmi mariani*, 393–409.

TMSM VII.

Three

Starting Points for Systematic Reflection

In the realm of philosophy, the contemporary world suffers from the defects of "weak thinking," the kind of thinking that is satisfied to observe empirical phenomena without thoroughly examining ontological aspects—that is, the truth of being.[1] There is an analogous weakness in some sectors of contemporary theology that devote attention to salvation history (a laudable emphasis, per se) and to narrow issues (such as inculturation), but without devoting itself to the hard work of a complete systematic reflection on the various topics. To compensate a little for these defects, which are also found within the field of Mariology, our doctrinal elaboration begins with a deeper look at the starting points for systematic reflection. We will (1) integrate the fruits of the debate on the "fundamental Marian principle" and (2) analyze the importance of the Mother of God for the theology of the covenant, which constitutes a "golden thread" through Sacred Scripture. Since Mary appears as the "woman of the covenant," a figure standing for the people of God in its spousal response to the divine initiative, we must not neglect (3) the anthropological foundations for which femininity is a basic datum.

1. On this challenge of "weak thinking," see Joseph Ratzinger, *Truth and Tolerance: Christian Belief and World Religions*, trans. Henry Taylor (San Francisco: Ignatius Press, 2004); Giorgio Sgubbi, *Dio di Gesù Cristo, Dio dei filosofi: Il cristico e il critico* [God of Jesus Christ, God of the Philosophers: The Christic and the Critical] (Bologna: EDB: 2004), 197–232; Carmelo Dotolo, "Pensiero debole kenosi" [Weak Thought/Kenosis], in De Fiores, Schiefer, and Perrella, *DMar*, 927–34.

THE DEBATE ON THE "FUNDAMENTAL MARIAN PRINCIPLE"

The person of Mary possesses many characteristics that are intrinsically connected with God's plan as a whole. *Lumen gentium* reminds us, "Mary, … since her entry into salvation history unites in herself and re-echoes the greatest teachings of the faith."[2]

For a systematic reflection, however, it is important to establish a starting point: where to begin in describing the role of Mary? It is not a matter of finding a "first principle" from which one could deduce, *more geometrico*, all the details about our Lady. Yet it is important to notice the personal core around which all the mariological descriptions "revolve." The systematic debate is relatively recent and is characterized by the term "first principle," or better, the "fundamental mariological principle." The most notable initial push is found in an essay by the Belgian theologian Jacques Bittremieux from 1931.[3] His reflection starts from a greater attention to the epistemological status of Mariology and from the publication of specialized systematic treatises on the Mother of God. But the search for a fundamental perspective or for a "first principle" precedes all that. The most typical reference highlights the divine maternity of Mary, called the "first principle of the nobility and dignity of Mary" by the Capuchin theologian Lawrence of Brindisi († 1619); the Jesuit Suárez, too († 1617), holds that the dignity of the Mother of God is "the foundation from which we must draw the reason for everything that we say about the Virgin."[4] Eadmer already in the twelfth century († 1141) deduces all his statements about Mary from the root of being *Theotokos* (Mother of God). In the Greek Byzantine world, the poet John

2. *LG* 65.

3. Jacques Bittremieux, "De principio supremo Mariologiae" [The Supreme Principle of Mariology], *Ephemerides Theologiae Lovanienses* 8 (1931): 249–51. See Manfred Hauke, "La questione del 'Primo principio' e l'indole della cooperazione di Maria all'opera redentrice di Cristo: Due temi rilevanti nella mariologia di Gabriele M. Roschini" [The Question of the "First Principle" and the Contribution of Mary to Christ's Work of Redemption: Two Relevant Themes in the Mariology of Roschini], *Marianum* 64, no. 161–62 (2002): 572–75.

4. Francisco Suárez, *Mysteria vitae Christi* (Venezia, 1605), disp. I, p. 2, cited in Stefano De Fiores, *Maria, Madre di Gesù: Sintesi storico-salvifica* [Mary, Mother of Jesus: Salvation-Historical Synthesis], Corso di teologia sistematica 6 (Bologna: EDB, 1992), 189.

Geometres describes the virginity of Mary as the central idea. In the *Mariale* of Pseudo-Albert that role is assigned to the principle of omnicontinence (fullness of grace). Jean Gerson (†1429) holds Mary to be the most perfectly redeemed creature.[5]

It is obvious that every reflection on the "first principle" must start in some way from the divine maternity, the fundamental task of Mary. On the other hand, we need to make clear that this maternity is extended analogously to all the faithful and that Mary possesses an exemplary role within the church. In other words, it is important to take into account both the relation of Mary with Christ and her relation with the church. This requirement is well demonstrated in an article of Bittremieux that proposes two principles (or a double principle): Mary as "Mother of God" and "companion of the Redeemer" (*mater Dei/consors Filii sui Redemptoris*). Mary's divine maternity and her association with the Redeemer, says Bittremieux, are connected with each other: being a companion of the Redeemer presupposes as its basis the divine maternity, while the divine maternity is oriented toward making Mary the companion of the Redeemer. Nevertheless, being a mother and being a companion are two formally distinct realities.

Bittremieux recalls the example from Christology that, as early as the *Summa Theologiae* of St. Thomas, distinguishes between the mystery of the Incarnation and the mystery that Christ has acted and suffered for us.[6] In a similar way, Christology and soteriology become distinguished later (*De Verbo Incarnato–De Christo Redemptore*). Among the premises of Christology there is a distinction between the Incarnation and the Redemption (even if the Redemption begins with the Incarnation). Analogously, two fundamental principles (or a double principle) can be presented for Mariology: Mary is Mother of God and companion of the Redeemer.[7]

Other authors have not been satisfied with this duality and only take the divine maternity as a starting point. Gabriele Maria Roschi-

5. See Leo Scheffczyk, "Fundamentalprinzip, mariologisches" [Fundamental Principle of Mariology], in *ML* 2: 566.

6. *ST* III, prologue.

7. See Bittremieux, "De principio," 250f.

ni, for example, accepts Bittremieux's thesis early on but later (after 1947) speaks of "universal motherhood" as a first principle or central idea, though supported by other secondary principles.[8] Similarly, Narciso García Garcés, founder of the Spanish Mariological Society, describes Mary as "Mother of the whole Christ" (the head and the members of the mystical body of Christ) (1940).[9]

Moreover, there are other proposals that start from a "single" principle. Descriptions of Mary as the prototype of liberation or as the "perfect disciple of Christ" (Wolfgang Beinert) are somewhat insufficient;[10] the former does not take the divine maternity into account (in the first principle as such). The same difficulty follows from the proposal of Karl Rahner, which points to Mary as the "radically (or: most perfectly) redeemed" person; the theologian also includes the divine maternity as part of being redeemed (seeing it as the most perfect reception of redemption.)[11] In the latter, the active contribution of Mary seems undervalued. The thesis of Xavier Pikaza, which describes Mary as the "first person in history," is interesting but equally inadequate. He starts with the observation (highlighted by Scheeben in the nineteenth century) that Mary is the only human person totally free from sin (Jesus, on the other hand, while being man, is a divine person inasmuch as he is the eternal Son of God).[12]

8. See Hauke, "La questione del 'Primo principio,'" 570–91. In the last edition of Roschini's Mariology, the Servite theologian shows four "universal" secondary principles, valid for the entire sphere of Marian doctrine: transcendent uniqueness, suitability, eminence, and analogy (see his earlier Roschini, *La Madonna* [1953], 1:116–34); he adds, as "particular" secondary principles (in certain spheres) association with Christ, solidarity with Adam the sinner, the "recapitulation" (It., *recircolazione*) (of Eve) and exemplarity: Roschini, *Maria Santissima*, 1:145–99.

9. See Hauke, "La questione del 'Primo principio,'" 581f.

10. Wolfgang Beinert, "Die mariologischen Dogmen und ihre Entfaltung" [Mariological Dogmas and Their Evolution], in *Handbuch der Marienkunde*, 2nd ed., ed. W. Beinert and H. Petri, (Regensburg: F. Pustet, 1996), 299–305.

11. See Karl Rahner, "Le principe fondamental de la théologie mariale" [The Fundamental Principle of Marian Theology], *Recherches de science religieuse* 42, no. 4 (1954): 481–522; Ziegenaus, *Maria in der Heilsgeschichte*, 39.

12. See De Fiores, *Maria, Madre di Gesù*, 193. An analogous proposal is developed in Ernesto Piacentini, *Nuovo corso sistematico di Mariologia sub luce Immaculatae* [New Systematic Course of Mariology in Light of the Immaculate] (Frascati [Rome]: Bannò, 2002), 65–97, where he declares the Immaculate Conception the "first principle," making reference to St. Maximilian Kolbe, who calls the words of the apparition at Lourdes ("I am the Immaculate Conception") a "definition" of Mary: the conception relates to her being a creature, and the adjective "immaculate," in turn, to her exceptional sanctity; Maximilian Kolbe, *Scritti* [Writings], new ed., trans. Cristoforo Zambelli

Mary's similarity to Christ is underemphasized by one-sidedly ecclesiotypical proposals, such as those of Semmelroth (Mary as "type of the Church") and Köster (Mary as "the representative and apex of humanity to be saved and already saved").[13] The idea of starting from Mary as the "new Eve" seems more significant, since Eve is the companion of Adam, is similar to him (Gn 2:18) and is "mother of the living" (Gn 3:20).[14]

In short, mariologists are not all in agreement on the "fundamental principle." A few suggest giving up the effort as too reminiscent of Cartesian rationalism (for instance, Hans Urs von Balthasar,[15] Jean Galot,[16] and René Laurentin).[17] Some others believe that it would be adequate to describe Mary as the synthesis of all the mysteries of the faith: according to Bruno Forte, Mary is the "iconic woman of the mystery."[18] On the other hand, Leo Scheffczyk observes that the

(Rome: Assoc. Rel. Centro Nazionale Milizia dell'Immacolata, 1997), 2149 and elsewhere. If these words should be accepted as the real and proper "fundamental principle," one would arrive at a minimalist Mariology, foreign to Padre Kolbe, that would not shed light on the active cooperation of the Mother of God. On Kolbe, see Stefano M. Cecchin, *Maria Signora Santa e Immacolata nel pensiero francescano: Per una storia del contributo francescano alla mariologia* [Mary, Holy and Immaculate Lady in Franciscan Thought: Toward a History of the Franciscan Contribution to Mariology] (Vatican City: PAMI, 2001), 410–13; Z. J. Kijas, "L'apostolo dell'Immacolata: Massimiliano Kolbe" [Apostle of the Immaculate: Maximilian Kolbe], in *La "Scuola Francescana" e l'Immacolata Concezione*, ed. S. Cecchin (Vatican City: PAMI, 2005), 568–72.

13. See De Fiores, *Maria, Madre di Gesù*, 192.

14. The proposal of S. Alameda, "El primer principio mariologico según los padres" [The First Mariological Principle according to the Fathers], *Estudios Marianos* 3 (1944): 163–86, is significant. See also René Laurentin, "Nuova Eva I. Il cammino storico del parallelismo Eva-Maria" [New Eve (I): The Historical Trail of the Eve-Mary Parallelism], in *NDM*, 1021.

15. Hans Urs von Balthasar, *Teodrammatica* (Milan: Jaca, 1992), 3:272f.: Woman, like Mary, would become part of a process of movement, that in Mary takes shape as the passage from Virgin-Spouse to Mother of the church. Only an exasperated masculinism would attempt to restrict this flow into a fixed principle. For this reason, the recent attempts, at all costs, to find a "fundamental principle" from which the main aspects can all be deduced would have to fail. Yet note that even Balthasar speaks of a "Marian principle" (see "Critical Evaluation," in chapter 3).

16. Galot, *Maria, La donna*, 12, presents the attempts as if it were a matter of needing to deduce all the Marian attributes from a single principle. This impression could arise from some writings of the past but does not correspond to the most influential proposals. In fact, Galot also arrives at a type of "fundamental principle" when he affirms at the start of chapter 1 of his manual: "Defined in her most essential role, Mary is the woman with whom God has made a covenant." With this mission the Madonna is connected with all that follows (23).

17. Laurentin, *Short Treatise*, 165–70.

18. See Forte, *Maria, la donna icona*, 153–68. De Fiores, *Maria, Madre di Gesù*, 197–99, wants to uncover the "salvation-historical laws" of the respective "biblical schemas of understanding": De Fiores, *Dizionario* 1:137.

various suggestions lead to a dual structure: they set out to accentuate the divine maternity (which cannot be reduced to the biological fact) and Mary's cooperation in the work of salvation, which is centered on the Annunciation and on the presence of Mary at the foot of the Cross. "This dual structure corresponds to the order of the Redemption, with the Incarnation and the death on the Cross; this order likewise cannot be deduced from a single principle."[19]

Already in the nineteenth century, Matthias Joseph Scheeben tried to describe this duality as a single principle. He speaks of the "spousal motherhood," or rather the "maternal spousality" (*gottesbräutliche Mutterschaft, gottesmütterliche Brautschaft*). The theologian states that the two characteristics of being Mother and companion of the Son of God are not separate, but united. Mary is "spouse" inasmuch as she cooperates in the work of salvation; inasmuch as she is mother, Mary is also "spouse" because the service of motherhood bears within itself—through the *fiat*—a spousal character.[20] Laurentin observes that "spousal motherhood" would be a "rather strange expression, but a deep insight as he explains it. The divine motherhood, he shows, differs from any other motherhood in being concerned with a preexisting Son. It is this eternal Son who chose his Mother. He proposed this motherhood, proposed himself to her consent. Thus the matter is one of a free association, a bond between two persons who freely commit themselves to each other, whence the expression 'spousal motherhood.'"[21]

The expression "fundamental Marian principle" (*marianisches Fundamentalprinzip*) comes from a German theologian, Carl Feckes, who in 1935 reproposed Scheeben's approach.[22] Scheeben himself does not speak of a "first principle" or of a "fundamental principle," but of a "personal character" (*Personalcharakter*). This character, or

19. Scheffczyk, "Fundamentalprinzip," 2:567.

20. See Ziegenaus, *Maria in der Heilsgeschichte*, 32–35; Hauke, "Die Mariologie Scheebens", 261–63.

21. Laurentin, *Short Treatise*, 171, n. 12.

22. See Carl Feckes, "Das Fundamentalprinzip der Mariologie: Ein Beitrag zu ihrem organischen Aufbau" [The Fundamental Principle of Mariology: A Contribution toward Its Organic Growth], in *Scientia sacra, theologische Festgabe für Kardinal Schulte* (Cologne and Düsseldorf: Bachem, 1935), 252–76; Hauke, "La questione del 'Primo principio,'" 574.

personal imprint, consists of the grace of the divine maternity, which in turn is oriented toward the hypostatic union in Jesus Christ, a fundamental characteristic for understanding Christology. The *Personalcharakter* is similar to the sacramental character (conferred in Baptism, in Confirmation, and in Holy Orders), inasmuch as it provides a permanent imprint and a specific connection with Jesus Christ. Spousal motherhood, according to Scheeben, is the focal point of all the other Marian attributes and is, as it were, the essential form that conveys the accidents.[23] Anton Ziegenaus affirms, "The most profound things said on the organic unity in Mary come from M. J. Scheeben."[24]

MARY IN THE MYSTERY OF THE COVENANT

To situate Mariology within the whole context of theology, it is important to find a "starting point." This is true about the search for the "fundamental principle," but also about attempts to place Mary in connection with one of the central categories of biblical theology, that of the "covenant" or (as it is called in some languages) the "alliance." An alliance (in a general secular sense) is "the union of two or more parties with a promise of mutual aid."[25] The Hebrew word *berit*, as such, cannot be translated by "alliance," because in this context it refers to a commitment undertaken by God. Inasmuch as man accepts that commitment, a certain reciprocity comes about, and we can speak of a covenant. There are unconditional commitments by God (such as the *berit* with Abraham and with Noah), but also conditional commitments that depend on the human response (the *berit* on Sinai). The "new covenant" (Jer 31:31–34; Lk 22:50/1 Cor 11:25; Heb 8:7, 8:13) is no longer based on human frailty (expressed in the sacrifice of animals at Sinai), but on the sacrifice of Jesus, mediator of the New Covenant (Heb 8:7, 8:13). In the priesthood of Jesus, "ac-

23. Anton Ziegenaus, "Charakter Marias [The Character of Mary]," in *ML* 2:22f.

24. Ziegenaus, *Maria in der Heilsgeschichte*, 32.

25. See Albert Vanhoye, "Discussioni sulla Nuova Alleanza" [Debates on the New Covenant], *RTLu* 1, no. 2 (1996): 165–67. See also Vanhoye, *La lettre aux Hébreux: Jésus-Christ, médiateur d'une nouvelle alliance* [The Letter to the Hebrews: Jesus Christ, Mediator of a New Covenant], Jésus et Jésus-Christ 84 (Paris: Desclée, 2002), 127–29.

cording to the order of Melchizedek," the divine conditions and the human conditions unite, rendering the New Covenant stable forever. Jesus is the mediator, inasmuch as he brings divine grace to men and offers humanity to God.

Jesus is the only mediator, inasmuch as he connects man with God, but his mediation is prepared and conveyed by other "secondary mediators."[26] In this context the contribution of Mary becomes part of the mystery of the Covenant. This contribution is prepared in the Old Testament, which—following the prophet Hosea—describes the Covenant with the image of marriage.[27] The most central reality in the communion between human persons becomes a window into the communion between God and man. The sexual symbolism present in the Canaanite religion for describing the "divine couple" and the process of fecundity is transformed by Hosea (at God's request): masculine and feminine symbolism is no longer centered on the divine level, but points to the relationship between God and humanity, called to friendship with him in the people of Israel. Here woman becomes the symbol of the human person before God, in her receptivity and cooperation. That symbolism can be seen, for example, in the "daughter of Zion," an image that appears in the Gospel of Luke as the background for approaching the figure of Mary.[28]

The bonds between Mary and the church, visible in the New Testament and even more in the fathers of the church, cannot be separated from feminine traits. Human receptivity (the capacity to receive, which is not to be confused with "passivity,") is seen more strongly in woman's being. This characteristic, central to the human situation before God, is underscored by the characteristic of Mary as Virgin, while the titles of Spouse and Mother indicate her active cooperation more.[29]

In the New Testament, the human part of the Covenant between God and man is established by Jesus Christ inasmuch as he is a man.

26. See chap. 8 (the mediation of Mary).

27. Hos 1:2, 2:4f.; Is 1:21–26, 5:1f., 54:6f., 62:4f.; Jer 2:2, 3:1, 3:6–12, 31:22; Ez 16; Ez 23.

28. Regarding "Daughter of Zion" in Luke, see "The Annunciation," in chapter 1.

29. See Hauke, *Die Problematik um das Frauenpriestertum vor dem Hindergrund der Schöpfungs- und Erlösungsordnung*, 4th ed. (Paderborn: Bonifatius, 1995), 292–304; English translation: *Women in the Priesthood?* (San Francisco: Ignatius Press, 1988), 297–309.

"Being God and man, Christ has the metaphysical capacity to represent all of humanity and to influence the destiny of all men by transforming it radically."[30] On the other hand, the Covenant is made concrete in the relation between Christ and the church (Eph 5:21–33). The church is described as "immaculate" (Eph 5:27), but how can it ever be so if all its members are sinners? This dilemma is resolved by the holiness of Mary, the one *human* person never touched by sin. In her, human fidelity to the Covenant becomes concrete and the Old Testament preparation that describes this fidelity (and also infidelity) in "feminine" terms is fulfilled.

Mary's characteristic as the "new Eve" also becomes part of this perspective on the Covenant, as many of the fathers emphasize. It seems that the contribution of Eve and of the new Eve has a strong anthropological foundation in the sense that the attitude of woman is more rooted in the unity of the person. To illustrate this reality, we can point to a midrash on Genesis:

> Once upon a time, a devout man married a devout woman. But they did not have any children. So people said: they don't count for much before God. And they separated. The husband went and took an impious woman and she made him impious. The wife went and took an impious man, and she made him righteous. Here you see how everything depends on the woman.[31]

An exegete notes that woman does "everything she does with a greater spiritual commitment than man. The prospect of pulling the whole visible creation away from God was greater for the devil if he succeeded in bringing the woman over."[32]

As the "new Eve," Mary acts in the name of humanity as a whole, coming before the intervention of the "new Adam." St. Thomas affirms: the annunciation of the angel was needed "so that a kind of spiritual marriage between the Son of God and the human race could be made manifest; and thus by the Annunciation the consent

30. Galot, *Maria, La donna*, 46.

31. Bereschit Rabbah [The Great Midrash], 17 (on Gn 2:21). See Hauke, *Gott oder Göttin? Feministische Theologie auf dem Prüfstand* (Aachen: MM Verlag, 1993), 11; English translation: *God or Goddess? Feminist Theology: What Is It? Where Does It Lead?* (San Francisco: Ignatius Press, 1995), 9.

32. Theodor Schwegler, *Die biblische Urgeschichte* [Biblical Primeval History], 2nd ed. (Munich: Friedrich Pustet, 1962), 122.

of the Virgin was besought, in place of the whole human race (*loco totius humanae naturae*)."[33]

The vicarious action of Mary toward humanity indicates not only that she did something for the good of the human race, but also that she acted in its place. It is a reality analogous to the vicarious substitution by Jesus Christ: he acted and suffered in our place and for our good. John Paul II, in the encyclical *Redemptoris Mater*, emphasizes:

> *In Mary's faith*, first at the Annunciation and then fully at the foot of the Cross, an *interior space* was reopened within humanity which the eternal Father can fill "with every spiritual blessing." It is the space "of the new and eternal Covenant," and it continues to exist in the Church, which in Christ is "like a sacrament or as a sign and instrument both of a very closely knit union with God and of the unity of the whole human race' [*LG* 1]."[34]

MARY THE WOMAN, IN THE CONTEXT OF ANTHROPOLOGY

The veneration of Mary as the only *human* person *perfectly redeemed* has profound repercussions on anthropology. This influence is articulated in the vision of the human person as such, and also in the image of woman. Conversely, there is also an influence of anthropological ideas on Mariology. Some reflection on the relationship between Mariology and anthropology is found in specialized presentations dedicated to Marian spirituality.[35] As a particularly debated example, the significance of Mary as a feminine subject will be developed here.

The Teaching of St. Paul VI (and His Predecessors)

In his encyclical *Pacem in terris* (1963), John XXIII lists "three things which characterize our modern age": "a progressive improvement in

33. *ST* III, q. 30, a. 1. The text is cited, among others, by Leo XIII (*Octobri mense*, 1891) and Pius XII (*Mystici Corporis*, 1943): Galot, *Maria, La donna*, 45f.

34. *RM* 28.

35. See, for example, Elio Peretto, ed., *La Spiritualità Mariana: Legittimità, natura, articolazione* [Marian Spirituality: Legitimacy, Nature, Articulation] (Rome: Marianum, 1994); Juan Esquerda Bifet, *Spiritualità mariana della Chiesa: Esposizione sistematica* [Marian Spirituality of the Church] (Rome: Centro di Cultura Mariana "Madre della Chiesa," 1994).

the economic and social condition of working men," the approaching political independence of all peoples, and "the part that women are now playing in political life."[36] Pius XII had already pointed out the new situation which demanded a greater participation of woman in public life. At the same time he had affirmed the specificity of the sexes that leads to different emphases in their particular involvement.[37] Paul VI turns to the situation of woman in the apostolic exhortation *Marialis cultus* (1974) when he describes the example of Mary for women.[38] Mary is an example, not because of the social environment of 2,000 years ago, but because she was the first and most perfect disciple of Christ. The pope observes the mother of Jesus as a constant factor in the various eras, "as the New Woman and perfect Christian ... as a virgin, wife and mother ... summing up the most characteristic situations in the life of a woman" (*Marialis cultus* 36). As regards the greater responsibility of woman for family, political, and social life, Paul VI presents Mary in her active and responsible consent (to the Incarnation), being involved in dialogue with God. She dedicated herself totally to the will of the Lord. But this is not about a passive religiosity: Mary did not hesitate to proclaim that God will vindicate the lowly and the oppressed, casting the mighty of this world from their thrones (*Magnificat*: Lk 1:51–53). She is a humble woman, but also a strong woman, knowing poverty and suffering, flight and exile (see Mt 2:13–23). Through her action, she built up the faith of the apostolic community in Christ (see

36. *EE* 7, nn. 580–81. John XXIII, *Pacem in terris*, 39–42. [Note: paragraph numbering in some encyclicals varies across the languages.]

37. Especially in the allocution of October 21, 1945, considered "classic, touching on all the problems": Pius XII, *Ruf an die Frau* [Call to Women], 2nd ed., ed. Käthe Seibel-Royer (Graz: Styria, 1956), 193; *AAS* 37 (1945) 284–95. We also recall a passage cited by Pope John Paul II (Address to the Tenth National Congress of the Italian Professional Association of Family Collaborators, April 29, 1979): "Woman has to contribute with man to the good of the 'civitas,' in that she is in dignity equal to him. Either sex must take the part that belongs to it according to its nature, characteristics, physical, intellectual and moral attitudes. Both have the right and the duty to cooperate for the total good of society. However it is clear that if man is by temperament more inclined to deal with exterior affairs, public activities, woman has, generally speaking, greater insight and finer tact to know and solve the delicate problems of domestic and family life, the basis of all social life; that does not prevent some women from showing great skill also in every field of public activity."

38. On the message of *Marialis cultus*, see "Mary, Model of the Worshipping Church," in chapter 10.

Jn 2:1–12), and her maternal mission was amplified to universal dimensions on Mount Calvary (*Marialis cultus* 37).

Feminist Mariology

Before looking at the magisterium of John Paul II, let us take a look at the challenge of modern feminism. The extreme solutions it has proposed can help us understand the importance of the topic.[39]

The Demands of Modern Feminism

The term "feminism" derives, it appears, from the socialist Charles Fourier, who lived at the beginning of the nineteenth century. The communities he established called for an absolute equality of the sexes. Two disciples of another socialist of the era (Henri de Saint-Simon) anticipated even then the central demands of modern theological feminism. Saint-Amand Bazard and Barthélemy-Prosper Enfantin expected a female Messiah (a sort of "Jesa Christa"). To find this person, some disciples of Saint-Simon made an excursion to the East, searching in Turkish harems for the "free woman," the woman-messiah. In the church of Saint-Simon's supporters, God was called "Mapah" ("mama/papa"). Analogously, they proposed a mixing of man and woman, an androgyne, at the start of creation: "Evadam."[40]

"Feminism" is a term whose meaning does not seem to be clearly defined. The word can indicate a radical commitment in favor of the rights of women, but it can also refer to the aim of abolishing every social difference between the sexes. The latter meaning, arising from the student revolution of the 1960s, is the more common one: it tries to eliminate difference in social roles. Under this approach, it is im-

39. For the following, see Hauke, *Gott oder Göttin*, 17–59 (= *God or Goddess*, 180–204). See also José A. Riestra, "Los movimientos feministas y su significación teológica: La mariología feminista" [Feminist Movements and Their Theological Significance: Feminist Mariology], *Estudios Marianos* 72 (1996): 3–42; Riestra, "La contestación de la paternidad de Dios y la mariología feminista" [The Debate on the Fatherhood of God and Feminist Mariology], *Estudios Marianos* 66 (2000): 389–430; Riestra, "La maternidad de María en la mariología feminista" [The Motherhood of Mary in Feminist Mariology], *Estudios Marianos* 68 (2002): 221–76.

40. The roots of androgynous thought lead back to Platonic myth (*Symposium* 189d–91e).

portant to call for a "quota" of (at least) 50 percent female participation in every kind of work activity.

While this type of feminism can be called "egalitarian" or "androgynous," another approach accentuates a necessary predominance by woman and (in contrast to the first approach) defends typically feminine qualities. In the field of religion, this tendency is expressed in wanting to venerate a "goddess," while the other tendency led rather to finding 50 percent feminine attributes in the realm of the divine (even alternating between an "our Father" and an "our Mother").

Both tendencies have, as their root, the Marxist model according to which the husband and father, as head of the family, is the oppressor, whereas the wife and mother is the oppressed person. Karl Marx wanted to overcome "the dominion of man over man," holding that man was only "the sum of social conditions." Therefore, everything can be changed by means of education. Biological givens do not count.

It fell to Friedrich Engels to apply Marxist principles to the family and to woman. Family corresponded to a society of social classes: as the working class was oppressed by capitalists, so in the family man would be the *bourgeois* (the "citizen," the oppressor) and woman the proletariat who must be liberated from domestic slavery. They would have to abolish the family, integrate man and woman into the process of labor in the same way, and leave the education of children to public institutions.

The influence of Marxism joined that of Sartre's existentialism in Simone de Beauvoir's 1949 work *Le deuxième sexe* (The Second Sex), a book sometimes called a "Bible of feminism." According to Sartre's concepts, existence precedes essence, which is to say, personal choice precedes natural conditions. Hence there is no creation or Creator that would limit autonomous choice. Simone de Beauvoir, Sartre's life companion, applies this concept to the situation of woman. This phrase is typical: "A woman is not born, but becomes one." There is no "feminine essence." The bodily conditions that oppose a detached choice (pregnancy, menstruation, etc.) are firmly lamented by Beauvoir. As many critical voices note, even within feminism itself, Beauvoir's ideal appears to be masculine existence.

The Application of Feminism to Mariology

From Beauvoir comes an emblematic criticism of Mariology: "'I am the handmaiden of the Lord.' For the first time in the history of humanity a mother is kneeling before her son and freely recognizes her inferiority. The supreme victory of masculinity is fulfilled with the cult of Mary: it means that woman is rehabilitated by perfecting her defeat."[41]

The most important author for the beginning of feminist theology is the American Mary Daly.[42] In 1968 she published a book whose very title bore the influence of Simone de Beauvoir: *The Church and the Second Sex*. According to Daly, too, woman is not born, but becomes one. Because of evolution one cannot speak of an "essence" of man and woman, still less of an immutable God who establishes an immutable order.

In 1973 Daly proclaimed a radical departure from Christianity (*Beyond God the Father*). Christianity cannot be reformed, she writes, because its symbology is sexist: if the Son of God becomes incarnate in the masculine sex, woman is excluded from the Incarnation. In turn, Mary is subordinated to Christ. Such a fact is poison to the absolute equality of the sexes desired by Daly in 1973. For Daly, Mary is a remnant of the old mother goddess, subordinated and shackled. In the face of this fact it becomes necessary to place feminine symbols at the divine level in the same way as masculine symbols.

In the 1978 book *Gyn/Ecology*, Daly bids farewell to the earlier ideal of "androgyny" and becomes the most noted representative of "Goddess feminism." The theologian transitions from "androgynous" to "gynocentric" feminism. But regarding Mary, she repeats more or less the same ideas: Mary is a pale symbol that hides the vanquished goddess. Her role as a servant at the Incarnation is nothing more than rape.

41. Simone de Beauvoir, *Le deuxième sexe* (Paris: Gallimard, 1949) (reprint 1965), 1:275f.; English trans., *The Second Sex*, trans., ed. H. M. Parshley (London: Knopf, 1953).

42. See Hauke, *Gott oder Göttin*, 68–75, 157–62 (= *God or Goddess*, 78–86, 181–86).

Daly proposes a "reinterpretation" of the Marian dogmas: the virginity of Mary stands for feminine autonomy (not depending on any male); the divine maternity is not addressed, because the title "mother" (which implies offspring and removes autonomy) is not welcome; the Immaculate Conception means a denial of female sin and a rejection of patriarchy (woman has no need to be redeemed by a male; on the other hand, Daly wants to integrate negative traits into Mary); the Assumption of Mary indicates the ascent of woman to the divine level. And it would be a mistake to make a distinction between the assumption of Mary, which declares her assumed by someone else (by God), and the ascension of Jesus who raises himself by his own divine power.

Daly is an extreme example, but significant for the approach of feminist "Mariology."[43] But all these theses have a common presupposition: they deny the complementarity of the sexes.[44] The egalitarian approach denies everything distinctively feminine in the example of Mary, while the gynocentric tendency explains Mary as a representative of feminine attributes of God that need to be rediscovered.

Critical Evaluation

How can we evaluate feminist Mariology?[45]

First of all, we can say that even extreme responses hide a kernel of truth:

1. *The importance of the symbolism of the sexes.* The symbolism of being man or woman is an important reality even in the realm of religion. We need to reflect on the fact that Scripture and Tradition describe the image of God (not exclusively, but predominantly) with

43. On other feminist approaches, see Hauke, *Gott oder Göttin*, 162–67 (= *God or Goddess*, 186–92).

44. By way of example, an author very typical of the "Catholic" feminism in the United States, Elizabeth A. Johnson, *Truly our Sister: A Theology of Mary in the Communion of Saints* (New York and London: Continuum, 2003), 47f., sets up an opposition between "(a) dualistic anthropology or an anthropology of complementarity" (bad) and "an egalitarian anthropology of partnership," proposed by means of "feminist liberation theology" (good). As supporters of the complementarity of the sexes she cites Leonardo Boff (!), Hans Urs von Balthasar, and John Paul II (54–64).

45. See Hauke, *Gott oder Göttin*, 168–78 (= *God or Goddess*, 193–204).

masculine symbols, while the human response to God is indicated more prominently with feminine symbols (for example, God as a bridegroom and Israel as a bride; the covenant between Christ and the church in Ephesians 5; the human soul as a "bride" in mysticism).

2. *The relevance of the masculinity of Jesus and the femininity of Mary.* It is not a matter of indifference that the Son of God became incarnate as a male and that the prototype of the church, of humanity redeemed, is found in Mary, a woman.

3. *Mary as a revelation of the "feminine" traits of God.* Mary also makes visible the "feminine" tenderness of God, to which Scripture has pointed (for instance, Is 49:14–15, 66:13). The specialty of Mary, however, does not consist in manifesting the "motherhood" of God, but in her cooperation in the work of salvation as Mother of God. She represents the dignity of the creature redeemed.

4. *Mary as the fulfillment of human desires.* Mary is not a "hidden goddess," but she attracts to herself the psychological energies that, in paganism, were directed toward feminine divinities. Still, the Mother of God constitutes a purification and a change: she is not both a sinner and holy, but the All-Holy woman who makes man grow toward God. She is not a screen upon which any need can be projected, but a historical personage who gives a firm root to human desire. It does not seem negative that feminine symbolism thus moves from the divine realm (paganism) into the human realm: in this way the dignity of the creature is valued, especially that of woman.

5. *The human closeness of Mary as "sister."* Often in the feminist realm the title of "sister" (already traditional) is recommended to underscore the closeness of Mary. But we need to note that this name, justified as it is, does not grasp the specific nature of Mary's position as Virgin and Mother of God.

6. *The "liberating" importance of Mary.* From Paul VI, we have already come to recognize the stress on Mary's active role, an example for feminine responsibility in a changed world. But surely we cannot identify virginity with "autonomy," since we cannot say that the virginity of Mary is self-sufficient: it relates to Christ and to the church in the spirit of service. An idea of Gertrud von le Fort (who was not

a feminist) seems more appropriate: the consecrated virgin "has her place, not within the generation, but rather closes the generation.... From this situation, she exacts faith in the ultimate value of the individual as such ... her formal meaning is the religious exaltation and affirmation of a person's value, as directly and immediately related to God."[46]

Having shed light on the contribution that even these extreme positions can offer, in the final analysis, we need to equally emphasize their limitations:

1. Feminism as an overall concept is confused. Feminist anthropology rejects the complementarity of man and woman, a fundamental premise of any Christian anthropology: man and woman are equal as persons, but complementary as man and woman.[47] The "androgynous" or "gynocentric" image is a diversion for Mariology: either it fails to value at all Mary's specific exemplary role for woman or it interprets the Mother of God only as a representative of what she is not: as a sign of divinity. Moreover, feminist Mariology does not bring us anything that was not already available to Catholic doctrine from its own sources.

2. The fundamental significance of feminine religious symbolism is ecclesiological. All the feminists are outraged about the fact that in the biblical symbolism of the Covenant the feminine part is subordinated to the masculine part, especially in the relation of Christ and the church. But they fail to recognize that in this case feminine symbolism is also the measure for the male. For man's attitude toward God, the desired qualities have more "feminine" nuances in the symbolism than "masculine": receptivity, but also active cooperation. Woman symbolizes a reality identical with herself. The situation of masculine symbolism, however, is different: for example, if the man in matrimony represents Christ the bridegroom, it is obvious that the husband is not Christ, but only represents him. A man, even in

46. Gertrud von le Fort, *Die ewige Frau* (1934; repr. Munich: Kösel, 1962), 38; English translation: *The Eternal Woman* (San Francisco: Ignatius Press, 2010), 26.

47. See *CCC* 372.

his relationship with God, has to measure himself by the "Marian" attitude. The church *as* church, says von Balthasar, as the one who receives Christ and cooperates with him, is primarily "feminine" and not "masculine."[48]

3. The "masculine" mission of Jesus the "head" is given for service. This reflection from a Protestant theologian seems interesting, even if a certain exaggerated nuance is felt: "It is not irrelevant that a male refused the temptations of power.... A woman could not take the place of the oppressed because her place always had been there.... Jesus, the male, brings down what is above. Jesa [instead of Jesus], the woman, would have been already down for ever.... What would Jesa Christa be? No redemption for women, and for males, a temptation to subjugate God."[49]

4. Mary is the type of the church and of man redeemed. The decisive importance of Mary is not in revealing the "feminine" traits of God, but in showing human cooperation in the work of salvation. For this reason, it does not seem to be a coincidence that feminist theology has won much greater success in the Protestant sphere (than in the Catholic and Orthodox): if human cooperation is excluded, religious symbolism is expressed only within the divine realm. This is what led the Reformation to a loss of the Christian symbolism of motherhood.

A valid example, to grasp the difference between a feminine divinity and Mary, is the Marian image in the shrine of Guadalupe (Mexico). On this image are seen elements known in the divine world of the Aztecs: sun, moon, stars, and serpent.[50] But the placement of these symbols is completely reversed: Mary is placed in front of the sun; she is therefore more powerful than the feared god of the

48. See Antonio Baldini, *Principio petrino e principio mariano ne "Il complesso antiromano" di Hans Urs von Balthasar* [Petrine Principle and Marian Principle in von Balthasar's "The Anti-Roman Attitude"], CdM 4 (Lugano: Eupress FTL, 2003); Roberto Carelli, *L'uomo e la donna nella teologia di H. U. von Balthasar* [Man and Woman in the Theology of Hans Urs von Balthasar], Collana Balthasariana 2 (Lugano: Eupress FTL, 2007), 495–565.

49. Susanne Heine, *Wiederbelebung der Göttinnen? Zur systematischen Kritik einer feministischen Theologie* [Revival of the Goddesses? Toward a Systematic Critique of a Feminist Theology] (Göttingen: Vandenhoeck and Ruprecht, 1987), 156f., 162.

50. We will return to this in the section on "Modern Apparitions Recognized by Ecclesiastical Authority," in chapter 9.

sun. The Mother of God places a foot on the crescent-moon, a sign of the terrible serpent god to whom thousands of human victims were offered. Then she is more powerful than all the masculine and feminine divinities symbolized by the stars. But Mary is not a goddess, because she folds her hands in prayer and bows her head before someone greater than her. She does not wear a mask to hide her divinity (like the Aztec gods; this is something a "hidden goddess" would do), but clearly shows the fact that she is human. In the image of Guadalupe, the desires and the heritage of the pre-Colombian peoples are accepted on one hand, and on the other are transformed and directed to God.

The Contribution of *Mulieris Dignitatem*

In 1988 John Paul II published his apostolic letter *Mulieris dignitatem* (*MD*) on the dignity and vocation of woman on the occasion of the Marian Year. The papal "meditation" describes the role of woman with a strong Marian influence.[51] The "*fullness of grace* that was granted to the Virgin of Nazareth, with a view to the fact that she would become *Theotokos, also signifies the fullness of the perfection of what is characteristic of woman*, of *what is feminine*. Here we find ourselves, in a sense, at the culminating point, the archetype, of the personal dignity of women."[52]

The pope is describing virginity and motherhood as two particular dimensions of the fulfillment of the female personality.[53] Motherhood, in its internal psychophysical character, implies a greater capacity by woman to pay attention to another person.[54] Here the feminine "genius" is seen.[55] "The moral and spiritual strength of a woman is joined to her awareness *that God entrusts the human being to her in a special way*."[56] As a mother, woman is the prime edu-

51. John Paul II, Apostolic Letter *Mulieris Dignitatem* (hereafter *MD*), 2, August 15, 1988.

52. Ibid., 5.

53. Ibid., 17.

54. Ibid., 18.

55. Ibid., 31.

56. Ibid., 30. Earlier the pope points to "a special *sensitivity that is characteristic* of their *femininity*," a sensitivity demonstrated in the acceptance of Jesus by women (ibid., 16).

cator of the human person and therein exercises a precedence over man.[57] Virginity is joined to spousal love, without which it cannot be understood. Virginity freely chosen points to the value of the person in himself and becomes at the same time dedication to Christ, "Redeemer of humanity and the Spouse of souls."[58] Virginity in the sense of the gospel renounces physical motherhood but opens itself to spiritual motherhood: being "open *to all people, who are embraced by the love of Christ the Spouse.*"[59] In Mary the Protoevangelium that speaks of the "woman" is fulfilled (Gn 3:15);[60] she is "the representative and the archetype of the whole human race" at the moment of the Annunciation.[61]

Based on the Letter to the Ephesians (Eph 5:21–33), the pope sees being a bride and woman as a symbol of human love. "*Christ is the Bridegroom.* This expresses the truth about the love of God who 'first loved us' (cf. 1 Jn 4:19) and who, with the gift generated by this spousal love for man, has exceeded all human expectations.… *The symbol of the Bridegroom is masculine.* This masculine symbol represents the human aspect of the divine love which God has for Israel, for the Church, and for all people."[62]

The call of the apostles, who act in a particular way as representatives of Christ, finds its continuation above all in the Eucharist. "Since Christ, in instituting the Eucharist, linked it in such an explicit way to the priestly service of the Apostles, it is legitimate to conclude that he thereby wished to express the relationship between man and woman, between what is 'feminine' and what is 'masculine.' It is a relationship willed by God both in the mystery of creation and in the mystery of Redemption. It is *the Eucharist* above all that expresses *the redemptive act of Christ the Bridegroom towards the Church the Bride.* This is clear and unambiguous when the sacramental ministry of the Eucharist, in which the priest acts '*in persona Christi*' [as head of the Church], is performed by a man. This explanation con-

57. Ibid., 19.
58. Ibid., 20.
59. Ibid., 21.
60. Ibid., 22.
61. Ibid., 4.
62. Ibid., 25.

firms the teaching of the Declaration *Inter Insigniores*, published at the behest of Paul VI in response to the question concerning the admission of women to the ministerial priesthood."[63]

Citing Hans Urs von Balthasar in a footnote,[64] the pope affirms that "the Church is *both* 'Marian' and 'Apostolic-Petrine.'" The hierarchical structure (in the apostolic succession) is placed at the service of the holiness of the body of Christ. But in the hierarchy of holiness (the one that really counts before God), the image of the church consists of Mary, "type" of the church (*MD* 27). The greatest gift is love (1 Cor 13:13).[65]

REFERENCES

The "Fundamental Marian Principle"

Bastero, Juan Luis. *Mary, Mother of the Redeemer*, 24–29. Dublin: Four Courts, 2006.

Beinert, Wolfgang. "Die mariologischen Dogmen und ihre Entfaltung" [Mariological Dogmas and Their Evolution]. In *Handbuch der Marienkunde*, 2nd ed., edited by W. Beinert and H. Petri, 267–363. Regensburg: F. Pustet, 1996.

Bittremieux, Joseph. "De principio supremo Mariologiae" [The Supreme Principle of Mariology]. *Ephemerides Theologiae Lovanienses* 8 (1931): 249–51.

Colzani, Gianni. *Maria: Mistero di grazia e di fede* [Mary: Mystery of Grace and Faith], 3rd ed., 26–28. Cinisello Balsamo: Paoline, 2006.

———. "Mariologia." In *Teologia*, edited by Giuseppe Barbaglio, Giampiero Bof, and Severino Dianich, 941–43. Cinisello Balsamo: San Paolo, 2002.

de Broglie, Guy, SJ. "Le 'principe fondamental' de la théologie mariale" [The "Fundamental Principle" of Marian Theology]. In *Maria*, edited by H. du Manoir, 6:297–365. Paris: Beauchesne, 1961.

De Fiores, Stefano. *Maria, Madre di Gesù: Sintesi storico-salvifica* [Mary, Mother of

63. Ibid., 26.

64. The passage cited (note 55) is this: "This Marian profile is also—even perhaps more so—fundamental and characteristic for the church as is the apostolic and Petrine profile to which it is profoundly united.... The Marian dimension of the church is antecedent to that of the Petrine, without being in any way divided from it or being less complementary. Mary Immaculate precedes all others, including obviously Peter himself and the Apostles. This is so, not only because Peter and the Apostles, being born of the human race under the burden of sin, form part of the church that is 'holy from out of sinners,' but also because their triple function has no other purpose except to form the church in line with the ideal of sanctity already programmed and prefigured in Mary. A contemporary theologian has rightly stated that Mary is 'Queen of the Apostles without any pretensions to apostolic powers: she has other and greater powers.'" Address to the Cardinal and Prelates of the Roman Curia (December 22, 1987), *L'Osservatore Romano*, December 23, 1987, citing H. U. von Balthasar, *Neue Klarstellungen* (Einsiedeln: Johannes Verlag, 1979), 114; see also English trans., *New Elucidations* (San Francisco: Ignatius, 1986), 196.

65. *MD* 30.

Jesus: Salvation-Historical Synthesis]. Corso di teologia sistematica 6. 190–97. Bologna: EDB, 1992.
Dillenschneider, Clément. *Il principio primo della teologia mariana*. Rome: Edizioni Ates, 1957. French original: *Le principe premier d'une théologie mariale organique. Orientations*. Paris: Ed. Alsatia, 1956.
Feckes, Carl. "Das Fundamentalprinzip der Mariologie: Ein Beitrag zu ihrem organischen Aufbau" [The Fundamental Principle of Mariology: A Contribution to Its Organic Growth]. In *Scientia sacra: Theologische Festgabe für Kardinal Schulte*, 252–76. Cologne and Düsseldorf: Schwann, 1935.
Hauke, M. "La questione del 'Primo principio' e l'indole della cooperazione di Maria all'opera redentrice di Cristo: Due temi rilevanti nella mariologia di Gabriele M. Roschini" [The Question of the "First Principle" and the Character of Mary's Cooperation in the Redemptive Work of Christ: Two Themes Relevant in the Mariology of G. M. Roschini]. *Marianum* 64 (2002): 569–97.
Laurentin, René. *A Short Treatise on the Virgin Mary*, 161–70. Washington, N.J.: Ave Maria Institute, 1991.
Müller, Alois. "La posizione e la cooperazione di Maria nell'evento di Cristo" [The Position and the Cooperation of Mary in the Christ Event]. *Mysterium salutis* 6 (1971): 511–528.
O'Carroll, Michael, CSSp. *Theotokos: A Theological Encyclopedia of the Blessed Virgin Mary*, 152f. Eugene, Ore.: Wipf and Stock, 2000.
Piacentini, Ernesto. *Nuovo corso sistematico di mariologia sub luce Immaculatae* [New Systematic Course in Mariology in Light of the Immaculate], 18–97. Frascati (Rome): Bannò, 2002.
Rahner, Karl. "Le principe fondamental de la théologie mariale" [The Fundamental Principle of Marian Theology]. *Recherches de science religieuse* 42 (1954): 481–522.
Roschini, Gabriele M. *Dizionario di mariologia* [Dictionary of Mariology], 406–11. Rome: Editrice Studium, 1961.
———. *La Madonna: Secondo la fede e la teologia* [The Madonna, according to the Faith and Theology], 1:97–116. Rome: Libreria Editrice Francesco Ferrari, 1953–54.
———. *Maria Santissima nella storia della salvezza: Trattato completo di mariologia alla luce del Concilio Vaticano II* [Mary Most Holy in the History of Salvation: Complete Treatise on Mariology in Light of the Second Vatican Council], 1:112–45. Isola del Liri: Pisani, 1969.
———. *Mariologia*, 1:429–44. Milan: Belardetti, 1941.
Royo Marin, A. *La Virgen María: Teología y espiritualidad marianas*. 2nd ed. [The Virgin Mary. Marian Theology and Spirituality], 38–46. Madrid: Biblioteca de Autores Cristianos, 1997.
Scheffczyk, Leo. "Fundamentalprinzip, mariologisches" [Fundamental Principle, Mariological]. In *ML* 2:565–67.
Vollert, Cyril, SJ. "Principio fundamental de la mariología" [Fundamental Principle of Mariology]. In *Mariología*, edited by J. Carol, 431–87. Madrid: Biblioteca de Autores Cristianos, 1964. English original: "Mary and the Church." In *Mariology*, edited by J. Carol, 2:30–87. Milwaukee: Bruce, 1957.

Ziegenaus, Anton. *Maria in der Heilsgeschichte: Mariologie* [Mary in Salvation History: Mariology], 28–43. Katholische Dogmatik 5. Aachen: MM-Verlag, 1998.

Mary in the Mystery of the Covenant

de la Potterie, Ignace, SJ. *Maria nel mistero dell'alleanza* [Mary in the Mystery of the Covenant]. Genoa: Marietti, 1988.

Galot, Jean, SJ. *Maria, La donna nell'opera della salvezza* [Mary, the Woman in the Work of Salvation]. 3rd ed., 23–47. Rome: Ed. Pontificia Università Gregoriana, 2005. 2nd ed., 1991.

Hauke, Manfred. *Die Problematik um das Frauenpriestertum vor dem Hindergrund der Schöpfungs- und Erlösungsordnung* [The Issue of the Priesthood of Women, in Light of the Order of Creation and Redemption]. Paderborn, 1995, 4th ed., passim. English translation: *Women in the Priesthood?* San Francisco: Ignatius Press, 1988.

———. ed. *La donna e la salvezza: Maria e la vocazione femminile* [Woman and Salvation: Mary and the Feminine Vocation]. CdM 7. Lugano: Eupress FTL, 2006.

Scola, Angelo. *Il mistero nuziale* [The Nuptial Mystery]. 2 vols. Vatican City, 1998–2000. English translation: *The Nuptial Mystery*. Grand Rapids, Mich.: William B. Eerdmans, 2005.

Serra, Aristide. "Alleanza." In De Fiores, Schiefer, and Perrella, *DMar*, 40–48.

Ziegenaus, Anton. "Stellvertretung (der Menschheit durch Maria)" [Representation (of Humanity by Mary)]. In *ML* 6:292f.

Mary the Woman, in the Context of Anthropology

Ecclesiastical texts

John Paul II. Apostolic Letter *Mulieris dignitatem* (*MD*). August 15, 1988.

———. *Letter to Women*. June 29, 1995.

The Monks of Solesmes, ed. *La femme dans l'enseignement des Papes* [Woman in the Teachings of the Popes]. Sablé-sur-Sarthe: Abbaye Saint-Pierre de Solesmes, 1982.

Other Sources

Amato, Angelo. "Maria, paradigma dell'antropologia Cristiana" [Mary, Paradigm of Christian Anthropology]. In *Maria la Theotokos: Conoscenza ed esperienza*, 369–90. Vatican City, LEV, 2011.

Bonetti, Renzo, ed. *La reciprocità uomo-donna via di spiritualità coniugale e familiare* [The Reciprocity of Man and Woman, A Way of Conjugal and Family Spirituality]. Rome: Città Nuova, 2001.

Düren, Sabine. *Die Frau im Spannungsfeld von Emanzipation und Glaube* [Woman in the Voltage Field of Emancipation and Faith]. Regensburg; Roderer, 1998.

De Fiores, Stefano. *Maria nella teologia contemporanea* [Mary in Contemporary Theology]. 3rd ed., 400–37. Rome: Centro di Cultura Mariana "Madre della Chiesa," 1991.

Hauke, Manfred. "Antropologia e mariologia nel dibattito teologico contemporaneo: Temi condivisi e nodi problematici" [Anthropology and Mariology in Contemporary Theological Debate: Shared Themes and Problematic Knots]. *Rivista teologica di Lugano* 19 (2014): 233–55.

———. *Die Problematik um das Frauenpriestertum*, 292–321, 508f (see *Women in the Priesthood?*, 297–325).

———. *Gott oder Göttin? Feministische Theologie auf dem Prüfstand*, 155–78. Aachen: MM Verlag, 1993. English translation: *God or Goddess? Feminist Theology: What Is It? Where Does It Lead?* 180–204. San Francisco: Ignatius Press, 1995.

———. "Il sacerdozio femminile nel recente dibattito teologico" [Female Priesthood in Recent Theological Debate]. *RTLu* 1 (1996): 257–81.

———. "La Chiesa ha demonizzato il sesso e disprezzato la donna? La questione femminile e l'amore matrimoniale *nel Codice da Vinci* alla luce della fede Cattolica" [Has the Church Demonized Sex and Despised Woman? The Question of Woman and Marital Love in *The Da Vinci Code* in Light of the Catholic Faith]. In *La frode del Codice da Vinci*, edited by A. Cattaneo, 121–50. Torino: Leumann, 2006.

———. "Maria–Mutter Gottes oder domestizierte Göttin? Zum Marienbild der Feministischen Theologie" [Mary: Mother of God or a Domesticated Goddess? The Image of Mary in Feminist Theology]. In *De cultu mariano s. XX*, vol. 4. Rome: PAMI, 429–58.

———. "Mariologie und Frauenbild: Wachstumskräfte für einen neuen Aufbruch" [Mariology and the Image of Woman: Forces of Growth for a New Starting Point]. In *Das Marianische Zeitalter: Entstehung—Gehalt—bleibende Bedeutung*, edited by A. Ziegenaus, Mariologische Studien 14, 229–54. Regensburg, 2002.

———. ed. *La donna e la salvezza*.

Twents, Simone. *Frau sein ist mehr: Die Würde der Frau nach Johannes Paul II* [Being a Woman Is More: The Value of Woman according to John Paul II]. Buttenwiesen: Stella-Maris-Verlag, 2002.

Four

The Divine Maternity of Mary

THE SYSTEMATIC IMPORTANCE OF THE DOGMA

The "Virgin Mary ... is acknowledged and honored as being truly the Mother of God and Mother of the Redeemer. Redeemed by reason of the merits of her Son and united to Him by a close and indissoluble tie, she is endowed with the high office and dignity of being the Mother of the Son of God, by which account she is also the beloved daughter of the Father and the temple of the Holy Spirit. Because of this gift of sublime grace she far surpasses all creatures, both in heaven and on earth."[1]

These words of the Second Vatican Council highlight well the central importance of the divine maternity. As the previous discussion on the "fundamental principle" of Mariology has made clear,[2] the title "Mother of God" is the most important root of all the mariological affirmations. "All the other assertions about Mary derive from it, not by logical necessity, but in an evolution motivated by it."[3] In turn, the most notable Marian dogma is closely united with the most important Christological dogma, the hypostatic union: the divine nature and human nature are joined in the person (or the hypostasis) of the Son of God. As we shall see, the definition of the

1. *LG* 53.

2. See "The Debate on the 'Fundamental Marian Principle,'" in chapter 3.

3. Michael Schmaus, "Maria," in *Sacramentum mundi*, ed. K. Rahner (Brescia: Morcelliana, 1976), 5:61. German original: "Maria," in *Sacramentum mundi*, ed. Rahner, vol. 3 (Freiburg: Herder, 1969).

title *Theotokos* at the Council of Ephesus (431) had a clearly Christological aim.

It is obvious that Mary does not bring forth God as such, but the result of her generation is the Son of God. Thus Mary is truly "Mother of God."

BIBLICAL FOUNDATIONS

Our understanding of the role of Mary depends on the person of Jesus Christ, the Word of God made flesh (Jn 1:14). Hence all the assertions that connect the divinity of Jesus with the maternity of Mary are worthy of note. The most important passage is in the Letter to the Galatians: "When the time had fully come, God sent forth his Son, born of woman, born under the law, to redeem those who were under the law, so that we might receive adoption as sons" (Gal 4:4–5). The Son of God, preexisting, is "born of woman."[4] In the infancy gospel according to Luke two verses are particularly significant: "The child to be born will be called holy, the Son of God." (Lk 1:35). "Why is this granted me, that the mother of my Lord should come to me?" (Lk 1:43). The "Lord" is the *Kyrios*, therefore the divine Lord.[5]

PATRISTIC DEVELOPMENT TO THE END OF THE FOURTH CENTURY

In the era of the fathers, the maternity of Mary was initially highlighted against Gnostic tendencies that denied the true humanity of Jesus. Ignatius of Antioch, at the beginning of the second century, emphasized the true birth and true death of Jesus against the idea of the Docetists, according to whom our Lord was not truly born of Mary and died on the cross only in appearance. Ignatius also makes clear that Jesus Christ is a single subject who unites divine and human properties in himself. Even without terminological precision,

4. For an analytical exegesis of the passage, see "Mary, Mother of the Son of God (Paul)," in chapter 1.

5. See "The Annunciation," in chapter 1.

St. Ignatius expresses the truth of the hypostatic union, the systematic basis for the divine maternity of Mary.[6]

According to the Gnostics Apelles and Valentinus, Jesus passed through the womb of Mary as through a channel, without truly assuming flesh from his mother, but possessing a heavenly body. Irenaeus opposes this explanation,[7] and Cyril of Jerusalem (fourth century) states: the Incarnation of the Word took place "not in seeming and mere show, but in truth; nor yet by passing through the Virgin as through a channel; but was of her made truly flesh, and truly nourished with milk, and did truly eat as we do, and truly drink as we do."[8] Because of this, the formulation in the creeds stated that the Son of God was born *ex Maria Virgine* (in Greek *ek*), and not *per Maria Virgine* (in Greek *dià*).[9]

Therefore, the maternity of Mary secures the true humanity of Christ. Yet Mary, as Mother of God, also underscores the divinity of Jesus. This most central truth of the Christian faith was defended by the Council of Nicea (325) against the heresy of Arius. Even before Nicea, in the Alexandrian sphere we encounter the term *Theotokos* —that is, "genitrix of God." This word, as such, appeared first in paganism (second century A.D.) and referred to the divine mother of the gods, usually called *méter theíon* (mother of the gods).[10] But the Christian use of this word was not taking up pagan mythology; the connection with biblical roots is very clear: Mary has not given birth to God as such (we do not speak of "mother of the divinity"), but to Jesus Christ, who is the incarnate Son of God. To keep a distance from paganism, the more common title "mother of God" was even avoided at first, preferring (in the Greek environment) "genitrix of God" (*Theotokos*).

6. See "The First Mariological Witnesses of the Tradition (Ignatius of Antioch, Justin, Irenaeus)," in chapter 2.

7. *Adversus haereses* III.11.3; 22.1–2 (*SC* 211:334–36; 430–36).

8. *Catechesis* IV:9 (PG 33:465B –468A); English trans. in Philip Schaff, ed. *Nicene and Post-Nicene Fathers*, Second Series (hereinafter *NPNF2*), 14 vols., 1886–89. Repr. Peabody, Mass.: Hendrickson, 1994), 7:21. See also the title *Theotókos*, in *Catechesis* X:19 (PG 33:685A).

9. See DH 10–30; 150.

10. See Epiphanius, *Panarion* 79, in *Die Griechischen Christlichen Schriftsteller der ersten drei Jahrhunderte* (hereinafter *GCS*) (Leipzig: Hinrichs, 1897–), 37, 475–85); Gerhard L. Müller, "Gottesmutter" [Mother of God], in *ML* 2:684.

There is a contentious debate about the first appearances of the title *Theotokos*. Its first appearance, which is undisputed, is in Alexander of Alexandria around 320, a few years before the Council of Nicea. The bishop, in a circular letter sent to other bishops, explains the creed of the Church of Alexandria: "Our Lord Jesus Christ did truly, and not in appearance, receive a body of the *Theotokos* Mary."[11] Therefore it is not an innovation, but an already established conviction of the faith. In the same era, the synod of Antioch against Arius in 324/325 cites the Alexandrian creed and states, "The Son of God, the Word, was born of the *Theotokos* Mary and became flesh."[12] The title was already so habitual that it was also used by the Arians, though they changed the meaning of the term: Jesus would be "god" in an improper sense, undergoing the birth and passion as a "god" (that is, as a creature preexisting his earthly existence). In the preceding historical chapter we studied the most ancient Marian prayer, found in Egypt on a papyrus buried in sand, and tracing back to the third or fourth century. In this prayer appears the title *Theotokos*.[13]

These observations lead us to the third century as the first origin of the title. In fact, the historian Socrates († 450) states that Origen († 254) explained it at length in his commentary on the Letter to the Romans.[14] Other signs point to Peter of Alexandria († 311).[15]

In any case, the title spread widely during the fourth century. Athanasius used it a dozen times.[16] Gregory of Nazianzus explains the reality of the hypostatic union in his famous letter to Cledonius:

> If anyone does not believe that Holy Mary is the Mother of God, he is severed from the Godhead. If anyone should assert that He passed through

11. *Ep. ad Alex. Const.* 12 (PG 82:908A–B).

12. See Müller, "Gottesmutter," 2:684.

13. Regarding the prayer *"Sub tuum praesidium,"* see "Patristic Motifs through the Sixth Century," in chapter 2.

14. *Hist. Eccl.* 7:32 (PG 67:812B). See Galot, *Maria, La donna*, 93.

15. See Marek Starowieyski, "Le titre Theotokos avant le concile d'Éphèse" [The Title Theotokos before the Council of Ephesus], in *Studia Patristica* 19 (1989): 237–42; L. F. Mateo-Seco, "Der Titel 'Gottesmutter' in der Theologie der Kirchenväter vor dem Konzil von Ephesus" [The Title "Mother of God" in Patristic Thought before Ephesus], *Sedes Sapientiae: Mariologisches Jahrbuch* 8, no. 1 (2004): 6–8.

16. For example, Athanasius, *De incarnatione Dei* 8 (PG 26:696); *In virginitatem* 3 (PG 28:256); *Contra Arianos* III:29 (PG 26:385).

the Virgin as through a channel, and was not at once divinely and humanly formed in her (divinely, because without the intervention of a man; humanly, because in accordance with the laws of gestation), he is in like manner godless. If any assert that the Manhood was formed and afterward was clothed with the Godhead, he too is to be condemned.... If any introduce the notion of Two Sons, one of God the Father, the other of the Mother, and discredits the Unity and Identity, may he lose his part in the adoption promised to those who believe aright. For God and Man are two natures, as also soul and body are; but there are not two Sons or two Gods.[17]

The title also spread into the region of Antioch, although the theology there was somewhat unfavorable to it.[18] Antiochian Christology highlights the duality in Jesus Christ and prefers the model "Word/man" (*Logos/anthropos*). Alexandrian theologians, instead, point to the unity of Jesus Christ with the model "Word/flesh" (*Logos/sarx*). The Antiochians risk neglecting the unity of the subject in Jesus Christ, the Alexandrians the distinction between the two natures, the divine and the human. While the Alexandrians are more disposed to accept Mary as "Mother of God," the Antiochians have difficulty with it, because they tend to separate the Son of God from Jesus Christ, in whom the Son lives as in a temple. This tendency goes back to Diodorus of Tarsus (†394), teacher of John Chrysostom (in whose writings the title *Theotokos* never appears) and of Theodore of Mopsuestia (†428, and therefore before the Council of Ephesus, 431). Theodore (later upheld by the Nestorians as their theological "father") distributes the actions of Jesus to two different subjects, to the man and to God living in him. There is a sort of moral (and not ontological) union between the divine nature and the human. According to Theodore, only the Word can be adored, and birth is attributed only to the man. He does not reject the title *Theotokos*, but states that Mary was genitrix of God inasmuch as God was in Jesus, according to the direction of Jesus' will. "We cannot say that God was born of the Virgin."[19] Theodore is somewhat hostile to the

17. *Ep*. 101:4 (PG 37:177A–80A).

18. See Manfred Hauke, "Maria in alexandrinischer und antiochenischer Denkform" [Alexandrian and Antiochian Concepts of Mary], in *De cultu mariano* s. XX, ed. PAMI (Vatican City: PAMI, 2000), 2:203–31.

19. See *In Joh*. (PG 66:997B–C); Ziegenaus, *Maria in der Heilsgeschichte*, 210.

divine maternity, because in Christology, he never was able to understand the hypostatic union.

Despite the skepticism of the Antiochian theologians, the title *Theotokos* spread universally in the East by the end of the fourth century. In the West the term appears for the first time in the writings of the Spaniard Prudentius († 405), who speaks of the *Dei genitrix.*[20] Ambrose, however, uses the expression *mater Dei* and is able to declare, "Mary has borne God."[21]

DOES THE CHRISTIAN DOCTRINE OF THE DIVINE MATERNITY HAVE A PAGAN ORIGIN?

As we indicated earlier, the term *Theotokos* has a pagan origin. Because of this, at the end of the 1800s and the beginning of the 1900s, the liberal school of thought in the history of religion (*religionsgeschichtliche Schule*) took the pagan origin of the word "genitrix of God" as evidence for the thesis that early Christianity was a syncretism derived from different religions. Cults with mother goddesses would then be the source of Marian devotion and the doctrine of the divine maternity. Theologians of this school observed that the dogma of the *Theotokos* was proclaimed at the Council of Ephesus (431), in a city known in the past as a center for the cult of the goddess Artemis (Diana), who combined maternal and virginal traits. This theory has been "recycled" in feminist publications and in Protestant circles. As we have seen,[22] some feminists present Mary as a hidden goddess and declare that the feminine traits of the Mother of God should be transferred to God, who would be our true mother in heaven.

20. Prudentius, *Psychomachia* (PL 60:52A). See Ziegenaus, *Maria in der Heilsgeschichte*, 213. The other Latin translation is *Deipara.*

21. Ambrose, *De virg.* II.2:13 (PL 16:210C). The title *Mater Dei* appears in *De virg.* II.2:7 (PL 16:209A); *In Hexaemeron* V:65 (PL 14:333C). See Georg Söll, *Storia dei dogmi mariani* [History of Marian Dogmas] (Rome: Libreria Ateneo Salesiano, 1981), 152f.; J. Huhn, "Ambrosius von Mailand" [Ambrose of Milan], in *ML* 1:126; Luigi Gambero, *Mary and the Fathers of the Church: The Blessed Virgin Mary in Patristic Thought*, trans. Thomas Buffer (San Francisco: Ignatius Press, 1999), 194.

22. See "Mary, the Woman, in the Context of Anthropology," in chapter 3.

From the systematic point of view Mary does reveal some symbolically "feminine" traits in God, but her identity does not consist of this, but rather in her cooperation in the redemptive work of Christ. Mary is the Mother of God and not the divine Mother. St. Ambrose summarizes this situation with the phrase "Mary is the temple of God, but not the God of the temple."[23] Mary, a type of the church and of humanity redeemed, can take part in the process of salvation.

From a historical point of view, the theses of the *religionsgeschichtliche Schule* are simply erroneous.[24] The doctrine of the divine maternity originates, as the biblical chapter demonstrated, from Revelation itself. Theologians of the early church were not sympathetic to an indiscriminate reception of pagan elements into Christianity, but held the pagan religions primarily as manifestations of the devil. Tertullian, for example, calls Cybele (the mother of the gods) *magna mater daemonum* (the great mother of the demons).[25] In a sense, Marian devotion and the cult of goddesses do have in common that they give importance to feminine symbolism in religion. Therefore, we can observe a natural respect for maternity and (in a less obvious way) for virginity. In the early church, the religious importance of feminine symbolism is emphasized to show human cooperation in the process of salvation: the church, for example, appears as a moon that receives the light of the sun, Jesus Christ. The heavenly body whose light is gentle and maternally fruitful receives the "masculine" rays of the sun and hands them on, in a gentler way, to the earth.[26]

The church was able to incorporate feminine symbolism, present even in the pagan goddesses, but only in a specifically Christian context wherein the relation between man and woman would appear as a sign of the covenant between Christ and the church (Eph 5:21–33).

23. Ambrose, *De Spiritu Sancto* III:80 (PL 16:795A).

24. See, for example, Jean Daniélou, "Le culte marial et le paganisme" [The Cult of Mary and Paganism], in *Maria: Études sur la sainte vierge*, ed. H. du Manoir (Paris: Beauchesne, 1949), 1:159–81; Söll, *Storia dei dogmi mariani*, 120–22; Müller, "Gottesmutter," 2:690–92; Stefano De Fiores, *Maria, Madre di Gesù: Sintesi storico-salvifica* [Mary, Mother of Jesus: Salvation-Historical Synthesis], Corso di teologia sistematica 6 (Bologna: EDB, 1992), 27–30.

25. Tertullian, *De spectaculis* VIII:5 (*SC* 332:162).

26. See Hugo Rahner, *Symbole der Kirche: Die Ekklesiologie der Väter* [Creeds of the Church: The Ecclesiology of the Fathers] (Salzburg: Müller, 1964), 99; Italian trans., *Simboli della Chiesa: L'ecclesiologia dei Padri*, 2nd ed. (Cinisello Balsamo: San Paolo, 1995).

Thus it was able to take in, for example, statues of a mother nursing a boy; this type of image could refer to a pagan goddess (such as Isis), but also to the Mother of God. Let us note, moreover, that Christians remained attentive to terminology: instead of the term *méter theou*, frequently used in paganism (in particular in the cult of Isis), the lesser known term of *Theotokos* was favored, with a change in its meaning. "The difference between Mary and Isis was very clear: Mary was also 'the handmaid of the Lord,' the chaste virgin whose Son was true God and true man, while Isis was known as a goddess who conceived her son in passion and was utterly distant from the mysterious designs of the Incarnation."[27]

In regard to the title *Theotokos* at Ephesus, some Protestant authors suggest an influence of the cult of the mother goddess Artemis on the dogmatic definition. In fact, in the primitive church the Apostle Paul confronted this cult (Acts 19:28). Artemis, called the "great Mother," was venerated as a symbol of fertility and as the exaltation of motherly traits. The enthusiasm of the people of Ephesus at the proclamation of the title *Theotokos* appears, according to this band of Protestant authors, as "evidence" of pagan influence on the dogmatic definition of the Council.

These speculations are contrary to the historical reality. The title *Theotokos* did not originate in Ephesus, but in Alexandria. The cult of Artemis had already been dead since 263, when the city of Ephesus was sacked by the Goths.[28] The figure of Mary was able to attract religious sentiments that were moved to exalt the feminine reality, sentiments present in the people before their conversion to Christianity, but the Christian faith carried out a profound transformation of symbolism: feminine qualities became the expression of the creature's cooperation in the process of salvation. The Mother of God is not at all a hidden goddess, but the holiest created person, called to collaborate with God.

27. Michael O'Carroll, *Theotokos: A Theological Encyclopedia of the Blessed Virgin Mary* (Eugene, Ore.: Wipf and Stock, 2000), 342.

28. See W. Gessel, *Ephesos*, in *ML* 2:367f.

THE COUNCIL OF EPHESUS (431)

At the end of the fourth century, the title *Theotokos* was already widespread and was considered, especially in Alexandria, as part of the treasury of the faith. Therefore an "ecumenical scandal" arose (in the words of Cyril of Alexandria), when Nestorius, patriarch of Constantinople, cast doubt on the use of the title. Elected patriarch in 428, Nestorius entered into debate about whether Mary should be called *Theotokos* (genitrix of God) or *anthropotokos* (genitrix of the man). As a compromise formula, Nestorius proposed the title of *Christotokos* (genitrix of Christ). According to him, the use of *Theotokos* was connected with the Arian theology that considered the Word passible (that is, subject to the passions, and hence a creature). He spoke of a single "person" (*prósopon*) in Jesus Christ, but by that he only intended a moral union between two subjects. His difficulties are those typical of the Antiochian school from which the patriarch had come: it did not accept the hypostatic union in Christ, in whom the one person is bearer of divine and human attributes. In Theodore of Mopsuestia and Nestorius, a correct interpretation of the Blessed Virgin is impeded by their Christology: in their approach, "the humanity of Christ assumes the position attributed in traditional theology to Mary, 'temple' or rather genitrix of God."[29]

The title was defended by Cyril of Alexandria: if we say that the Word was born and suffered, that does not mean that the divinity was born or suffered; it intends to refer to the man united to God. Mary is Genitrix of God, because she bore the eternal Son who assumed flesh—that is, she caused God to be born according to the flesh.

Both Nestorius and Cyril appealed to Pope Celestine, who took Cyril's side. The Council of Ephesus (431),[30] called by the emperor, accepted Cyril's second letter to Nestorius as fundamental:

29. Anton Ziegenaus, *Jesus Christus: Die Fülle des Heils* [Jesus Christ: The Fullness of Salvation; Christology and Doctrine of the Redemption], Katholische Dogmatik 4 (Aachen: MM-Verlag, 2000), 144. On the Christological doctrine of Nestorius (who according to some theologians never professed any heresy), see also the balanced presentation and the justification of the council's condemnation in Leo Scheffczyk, "Nestorius," in *ML* 4:598f.

30. On the Council, see Söll, *Storia dei dogmi mariani*, 152–64; Basil Studer, "Il concilio di Efeso (431) nella luce della dottrina Mariana di Cirillo di Alessandria" [The Council of Ephesus

We do not say, in fact, that the nature of the Word underwent a transformation and became flesh or that it was changed into a complete man composed of soul and body.[31] Rather, we say that the Word, hypostatically uniting to himself the flesh animated by a rational soul, became man in an ineffable and incomprehensible manner and was called Son of man, not merely by will or good pleasure or because he only assumed a [another] person.[32] Furthermore, (we say) that the natures brought together in real union (are) different and from these two only one Christ and Son results.... For this was not an ordinary man who was at first begotten of the holy Virgin, and then the Word descended upon him: rather, (the Word) united flesh to himself from his mother's womb and is said to have undergone begetting in the flesh in order to take to himself flesh of his own.... For this reason [the holy fathers] have not hesitated to speak of the holy Virgin as the Mother of God, not certainly because the nature of the Word or his divinity had the origin of its being from the holy Virgin, but because from her was generated his holy body, animated by a rational soul, a body hypostatically united to the Word, and thus it is said that (the Word) was begotten according to the flesh.[33]

In sum: *Jesus Christ, God and man, is one, and therefore Mary must be recognized as mother of God. Theotokos* literally means "she who has given birth to God." It is clear that this refers exclusively to the human generation of Jesus, not to his eternal generation within the Most Holy Trinity. From Mary, the Word "was born according to the flesh."

---

in Light of the Marian Doctrine of Cyril of Alexandria], in *La Mariologia nella catechesi dei Padri (età postnicena)*, ed. S. Felici (Rome: LAS, 1991), 49–67; L. F. Mateo-Seco, "La Maternidad divina de María: La lección de Efeso" [The Divine Maternity of Mary: The Lesson of Ephesus], *Estudios Marianos* 64 (1998): 269–92; Angelo Amato, *Gesù il Signore: Saggio di cristologia* [Jesus the Lord: Essay in Christology] (Bologna: EDB, 1999), 267–84; Miguel Ponce Cuéllar, *María, Madre del Redentor y Madre de la Iglesia* [Mary, Mother of the Redeemer and Mother of the Church], 2nd ed. (Barcelona: Herder, 2001), 307–13; Pietro Rosa, "Aspetti della mariologia di Cirillo Alessandrino e di Nestorio" [Aspects of Mariology in Cyril of Alexandria and in Nestor], *Theotokos* 12 (2004): 255–85; Luigi Gambero, "Maria negli antichi concili" [Mary in the Ancient Councils], in Dal Covolo and Serra, *Storia della mariologia*, 1:472–79; critical edition of the acts of the Council: E. Schwarz, ed., *Acta conciliorum oecumenicorum* (hereinafter *ACO*), vol. 1, part 1.18 (Berlin 1927–30). The essential parts have been translated into French: André Marie Jean Festugière, ed., *Ephèse et Calcédoine: Textes des conciles* (Paris: Beauchesne, 1982).

31. Note by Hauke: Not like a stick that changes into a serpent.

32. Translation corrected by Hauke. Literally, "assumed one person."

33. DH 250–51. The anathemas of Cyril against Nestorius (DH 252–63) were included in the formal acts of the Council, but not formally approved; their approval only came later at the Second Council of Constantinople in 553.

Moreover, this specifies that Mary is not mother "of the Trinity," but of the Son who is God. "God" therefore refers only to the person of the Word. Mary is not called the "mother of the divinity."

Cyril of Alexandria began the Council before the arrival of the papal legates and the Syriac bishops (and therefore of the Antiochians). The papal legates (and the pope) swiftly consented, but a *formula of union* between Cyril of Alexandria and the Antiochian bishops was established only two years later, in 433:

> Consequently, we acknowledge that our Lord Jesus Christ, the only begotten Son of God, perfect God and perfect man, composed of a rational soul and body, was begotten of the Father before the ages in respect to his divinity, but in the final days the same was born for our sake and for our salvation of the Virgin Mary in respect to his humanity; he is of the same being as the Father in respect to his divinity and of the same being as we in respect to his humanity. For a union of two natures has taken place: due to it we acknowledge one Christ, one Son, one Lord. In accordance with the understanding of the unmixed union, we acknowledge that the holy Virgin is the God-bearer (*tèn hagían parthénon theotókon*) because the God-Word took flesh and became man, and, from his very conception, he made one with himself the temple taken from her.[34]

This formula also clarifies the terminology, because Cyril had previously spoken of "one nature of the incarnate Word" and of "a hypostasis" of the Word (the difference between nature and hypostasis was not obvious). Then Cyril also accepted the terminology of the "two natures," united in the one subject of the Son. Notice also the typical formula, of Alexandrian origin, of the "holy Virgin *Theotokos* Mary."

The formula of union of 433 prepared the way for the definition by the *Council of Chalcedon in 451*: the hypostatic union of Christ is highlighted, with the duality of natures neither separated nor confused. In this context the title *Theotokos* appears anew: "one and the same Son ... begotten from the Father before the ages as to the divinity and in the latter days for us and our salvation was born as to his humanity from Mary the Virgin Mother of God."[35]

34. DH 272.
35. DH 301.

We find a summary of the anti-Nestorian requirements in a letter of Pope John II to the senate of Constantinople (534)[36] and in the *Second Council of Constantinople* (553), whose canons declare,[37] among other things:

> If anyone says that the glorious holy Mary, ever virgin, is not Mother of God in the true sense but only by an abuse of language … let him be anathema.[38]

FURTHER DEVELOPMENTS OF DOCTRINE AFTER EPHESUS

The Council of Ephesus set forth the essence of Catholic dogma on the Mother of God. Since the Council, this doctrine has been maintained as a precious treasure and deepened further. A good dogmatic synthesis at the end of the patristic era is found in the works of St. John Damascene, for whom the term *Theotokos* expresses the entire mystery of salvation, the whole *oikonomia*, because it reveals the single divine hypostasis of the Son in the two natures.[39]

In the Middle Ages, the divine maternity was usually presented in the systematic context of the Incarnation.[40] For example, Thomas Aquinas treats the whole figure of Mary in the *Summa theologiae* between the questions on the mediation of Christ, God and man,[41] and his birth.[42] The exposition is integrated at the beginning of the redemptive work of Christ.[43] To illustrate the divine maternity of Mary, the *doctor angelicus* uses the analogy of human birth. Our parents did not generate our souls (which are given directly by God), but only our bodies. Notwithstanding this, they are called our father and our mother. Just as any woman is called "mother" because her son took his body from her, the Blessed Virgin also can be called

36. DH 401.
37. DH 421–38.
38. DH 427.
39. John Damascene, *De fide orthodoxa* III:12 (PG 94:1028B–29A).
40. For an overview, see Gambero, *Maria nel pensiero dei teologi latini medievali* [Mary in the Thought of the Medieval Latin Theologians] (Cinisello Balsamo: Ed. Paoline, 2000).
41. *ST* III, q. 26.
42. *ST* III, q. 35.
43. See Richard Schenk, "Thomas v. Aquin," in *ML* 6:404.

"Mother of God" because the Son of God took his body from her. Whoever professes that the Son of God has assumed human nature into the unity of his divine person must also recognize that the Blessed Virgin Mary is the Mother of God.[44]

An important development of doctrine relates to the concept of person. Maternity as such does not relate to a nature, but to a person. Conception and birth are attributed to the person, according to the nature in which the person is conceived or born. A human mother bears a person, not a nature. When the divine person of the Word assumes human nature, it is clear that the Son of God was conceived and born of the Virgin. For this reason, she is truly called "Mother of God."[45]

Thomas Aquinas states that the Son of God was begotten eternally of the Father and was born in time of the Blessed Virgin. Thus we find in Jesus Christ two sonships, but there is only one Son. Since there is no change in God through the Incarnation, the relation between Mary and her Son is real in Mary (because it constitutes a new reality), but not in the divine Son. It is a real temporal relation of the Son with Mary only with respect to the human nature of Jesus.[46] This ontological clarification underscores the divine transcendence of the person of Christ and the situation of Mary as a creature.

Another important contribution comes from Francisco Suárez, who speaks of the relation of Mary to the hypostatic union: the Blessed Virgin cannot be separated from the Son of God who assumed a human nature in the hypostatic union. Mary, obviously, is not part of the hypostatic union, but "the dignity of the mother is of a higher order, for it belongs in some way to the order of the hypostatic union."[47] The most notable theological contribution of the

44. See Thomas Aquinas, *Compendium Theologiae*, chap. 222. The idea was already developed in various passages of Cyril of Alexandria—for example, *Ep. 4 ad Nestorium* (PG 77:480); see Hubert du Manoir, "Cyrill," in *ML* 2:116.

45. See Thomas Aquinas, *ST* III, q. 35, a. 4.

46. See *ST* III, q. 35, a. 5; Quodlib. 9, a. 2, ad 1. See also Gregorio Alastruey, *Tratado de la Virgen Santisima* [Treatise on the Most Holy Virgin], 3rd ed. (Madrid: Editorial catolica, 1952), 99–101, and the defense of metaphysical doctrine against the "weak thinking" of contemporary criticism in Gherardini, *La Madre*, 84–89.

47. Francisco Suárez, *De mysteriis vitae Christi*, sec. 2:4, Opera omnia 19 (Paris 1856), 8

1800s is by Scheeben, who speaks of the "personal character" and the "spousal motherhood" of Mary.[48]

Among magisterial documents, we mention Paul IV's Bull in 1555 against the sect of the Unitarians, who denied the divinity of Christ and thus also the title "Mother of God,"[49] as well as the encyclical *Lux veritatis* of Pius XI, written on the occasion of the 1,500th anniversary of the Council of Ephesus (December 25, 1931).[50] The supreme pontiff provides a broad description of the doctrinal importance of the divine maternity. In the face of modern attempts to "rehabilitate" Nestorius, Pius XI emphasizes:

> against such an attempt, as vain as it is temerarious, arises the protest of all the Church, which in every age has recognized the condemnation of Nestorius as rightly pronounced, which holds the doctrine of Cyril orthodox, which will always number and venerate the Council of Ephesus among the ecumenical councils celebrated under the inspiration of the Holy Spirit.[51]

Pius XI also explains the pastoral aspects of the divine maternity of Mary. For example, he notes the veneration of the dignity of Mary as Virgin Mother of God among Christians separated from the church, even among Protestants, and expresses the hope that these Christians will want to return to the one flock of Christ guided by his vicar on earth; the Blessed Virgin embraces all her wandering sons with maternal love and sustains our prayer for unity with her intercession.[52]

Vatican II deals with the divine maternity of Mary in the mystery of Christ and the church. The "Council of the Church about the Church" emphasizes the similarity between the Mother of God, who as a Virgin bore the Son of God, and the church. In the expression of St. Ambrose, Mary is the "type of the church" (*typus Ecclesiae*).

(cited in Gherardini, *La Madre*, 81, note 43): "Haec dignitas matris est altioris ordinis, pertinet enim quodammodo ad ordinem unionis hypostaticae, illam enim intrinsece respicit, et cum illa necessariam conjunctionem habet." See also Roschini, *Maria Santissima*, 2:72–74; O'Carroll, *Theotokos*, 258, 334f.

48. On Scheeben and the question of a "fundamental principle" of Mariology, see pp. 120–21.

49. DH 1880.

50. *AAS* 23 (1931) 493–517; Italian trans. in *EE* 5, nn. 820–78.

51. *AAS* 23 (1931) 504; *EE* 5, n. 846.

52. See *AAS* 23 (1931) 513; *EE* 5, n. 868.

The church becomes "mother" through her believing acceptance of the divine Word. She gives birth to her sons, conceived by the Holy Spirit, by means of the preaching of the Gospel and Baptism.[53] She is also Virgin inasmuch as she holds to the promise given by her divine Spouse, preserving "with virginal purity an entire faith, a firm hope and a sincere charity."[54]

The 1969 reform of the liturgical calendar introduced the solemnity of Mary, the Holy Mother of God, placing it on January 1. The solemnity replaces the feast of the Divine Maternity, introduced by Pius XI in 1931 and placed on October 11. The date of January 1 underscores the connection of Mary, Mother of God, with the mystery of the Nativity and corresponds to the most ancient tradition. In the Byzantine churches, the solemnity of the *Theotokos* is celebrated on December 26.[55]

Pope John Paul II, in his encyclical *Redemptoris Mater* (1987), recalls that "the dogma of the divine motherhood of Mary was for the Council of Ephesus and is for the Church like a seal upon the dogma of the Incarnation, in which the Word truly assumes human nature into the unity of his person, without canceling out that nature."[56] In his apostolic letter on the dignity of woman in the light of Mary (*Mulieris dignitatem*, 1988), the Holy Father shows the relation of the divine maternity with the vocation of every woman. The mystery of the Incarnation involves the believing response of Mary, involving her fully as a person and as a woman.[57] The pope reaffirms the perennial importance of the title *Theotokos* in his letter on the occasion of the 1,600th anniversary of the First Council of Constantinople and the 1,550th anniversary of the Council of Ephesus (1981).[58] John Paul II also criticized the proposal of some theologians (reviving the old heresies of Arius and Nestorius) to speak of Jesus as a human

53. *LG* 63.

54. *LG* 64. See Salvatore Meo, "Madre di Dio. II. Dogma, storia, e teologia," in *NDM*, 822–25.

55. See Danilo Maria Sartor, "Madre di Dio. III. Celebrazione liturgica," in *NDM*, 825–28.

56. *RM* 4.

57. John Paul II, *Mulieris dignitatem*, 4. See also Arthur B. Calkins, ed., *Totus tuus: Il magistero mariano di Giovanni Paolo II* (Siena: Cantagalli, 2006), 88–94.

58. John Paul II, Apostolic Letter *A Concilio Constantinopolitano I* (March 25, 1981).

person; in that case Mary could not be called the Mother of God.[59] The supreme pontiff affirmed with vigor the divine maternity during the preparations for the Great Jubilee of the Incarnation in 2000.[60] Pope Benedict XVI makes reference to it as well during his visit to Ephesus, focusing on Mary as Mother of God, Mother of the church, and Mother of unity.[61]

ECUMENICAL ASPECTS

The Council of Ephesus, generally speaking, has the agreement of all the Christian confessions. This is obvious for the Catholic Church and the Orthodox Church, which count Ephesus among the ecumenical Councils. The Council is also accepted by the Coptic churches (Egypt, Ethiopia), which greatly esteem the tradition of St. Cyril of Alexandria, although they have been separated from the universal church since the Council of Chalcedon in 451 that condemned Monophysitism.

However, the title *Theotokos* is not used by the spiritual heirs of the Antiochian tradition who had not accepted the Council of Ephesus, and who today constitute the Assyrian Church of the East, a group that has become very small (approx. 400,000 members). They call Mary "Mother of the Lord" and "Mother of Christ."[62] In 1994, the Assyrian patriarch Mar Dinkha IV and Pope John Paul II signed a joint Christological Declaration, according to which Catholics and Assyrians today are united in profession of the same faith

59. See General audience, April 13, 1988, "Le definizioni cristologiche dei concili e la fede della Chiesa oggi" [The Christological Definitions of the Councils and the Faith of the Church Today], n. 4, in *Insegnamenti di Giovanni Paolo II*, vol. 11, part 1 (Vatican City: Libreria Editrice Vaticana, 1989), 878f. The theological context is explained in Ponce Cuéllar, *María*, 316–18; Juan Luis Bastero, *Virgen singular: La reflexión teológica mariana en el siglo XX* [Singular Virgin: Theological Reflection on Mary in the 20th Century] (Madrid: Rialp, 2001), 17–57.

60. John Paul II, Apostolic Letter *Tertio Millennio Adveniente* (1994), 43.

61. Benedict XVI, Homily at the Marian shrine of Meryem Ana Evì, Nov. 29, 2006, *Insegnamenti di Benedetto XVI*, vol. 2, part 2 (Vatican City: Libreria Editrice Vaticana, 2007), 710–14. Similarly, John Paul II, Homily at Ephesus, Nov. 30, 1979, *Insegnamenti di Giovanni Paolo II*, vol. 2, part 2 (Vatican City, Libreria Editrice Vaticana, 1980), 1287–92.

62. See Ronald Roberson, "Assira, Chiesa, d'Oriente" [Assyrian Church of the East], in *Dizionario enciclopedico dell'Oriente cristiano*, ed. E. G. Farrugia (Rome: Pontificio Istituto Orientale, 2000), 82f.

in the Son of God. The document uses the Christological formulas of Chalcedon: the divinity and the humanity of Christ are united in one person, without mixing and without separation. The Assyrians venerate Mary as Mother of Christ, our God and Savior. "In the light of this same faith the Catholic tradition addresses the Virgin Mary as 'the Mother of God' and also as 'the Mother of Christ.' We both recognize the legitimacy and rightness of these expressions of the same faith."[63]

In regard to Protestantism, especially among Lutherans more connected to the tradition, the *consensus quinquesaecularis* ("consensus of the [first] five centuries") is sometimes invoked, in the sense that the Trinitarian and Christological Councils of the early church are accepted. The theologians of the Reformation do accept the title of *Theotokos* because it expresses the Christological dogma of the hypostatic union (and of the communication of properties—that is, the use of human and divine attributes in regard to Jesus Christ—on account of the unifying principle, the one subject of the Word).

Yet the principal Reformers led the way to a devaluation of the maternal role of Mary. In an explanation of the *Regina coeli*, which contains the expression *quem meruisti portare* ("whom you merited to bear"),[64] Luther compares the dignity of Mary to that of the wood of the cross that bore Jesus: everything is by grace, and there is no need to attribute any merit to Mary.[65] For Catholic doctrine, however, the primary factor of grace does not exclude human cooperation, while the Protestant principle of *sola gratia* establishes that man is justified before God without any merit sustained by grace.[66]

63. Common Christological Declaration of the Catholic Church and the Assyrian Church of the East, Nov. 11, 1994, in *Insegnamenti di Giovanni Paolo II*, vol. 17, part 2 (Vatican City: Libreria Editrice Vaticana, 1996), 745.

64. *Regina coeli, laetare, alleluia, quia quem meruisti portare, alleluia, resurrexit sicut dixit, alleluia, ora pro nobis Deum, alleluia.*

65. See Luther, Exposition of the Magnificat (1521) (Weimar edition 7, 573); Achim Dittrich, *Protestantische Mariologie-Kritik: Historische Entwicklung bis 1997 und dogmatische Analyse* [Protestant Criticism of Mariology: Historical Development to 1997 and Dogmatic Analysis], Mariologische Studien 11 (Regensburg: Pustet, 1998), 29–37.

66. See Council of Trent, *Decree on Justification* (DH 1520–83); Hauke, "Die Antwort des Konzils von Trient auf die Reformatoren" [The Council of Trent's Response to the Reformers], in *Der Mensch zwischen Sünde und Gnade* [Man between Sin and Grace], ed. Anton Ziegenaus (Buttenwiesen: Stella-Maris-Verlag, 2000).

While on one hand the results of the Council of Ephesus are accepted in general, on the other hand the active contribution of Mary to the redemption is rejected. This ambiguity in Protestant theology has continued to this day. The most renowned Calvinist theologian of the twentieth century, Karl Barth, maintains that the title *Theotokos* is an "auxiliary christological proposition" (*ein christologischer Hilfssatz*) that has a biblical basis (Gal 4:4; Lk 1:43) and rightly underscores the true unity between the two natures in the one subject of Christ.[67] However, the influence of liberal theology, with its departure from the true divinity of Christ and from the Trinity, sweeps away the divine maternity for other authors. For this reason, modern Protestant theology is divided about the title of *Theotokos* and usually refuses to speak of the "Mother of God," arguing that the word tends to suggest a natural power of Mary to produce the divine nature of the Son. Some authors insist that mythology has entered into Mariology with the term *Theotokos*. "Counter to the orthodox desire [that is, within 'Protestant orthodoxy'] to maintain the Credo of the early Church, and even the doctrine of Ephesus on the Mother of God, Protestant theology [today] includes varying and often contradictory evaluations of Marian doctrine [on the Mother of God]."[68]

In Anglicanism we find a greater acceptance of the Marian doctrine formulated in the early church. This fact is shown with clarity in the Joint Declaration on "Mary: Grace and Hope in Christ," formulated in 2004 by the official international Commission composed of Anglican and Roman Catholic theologians (ARCIC = *Anglican-Roman Catholic International Commission*): "In receiving the Council of Ephesus and the definition of Chalcedon, Anglicans and Roman Catholics together confess Mary as *Theotokos*."[69]

67. Barth, *Church Dogmatics*, vol. 1, part 2, 138; see Dittrich, *Protestantische Mariologie-Kritik*, 305f.

68. Dittrich, *Protestantische Mariologie-Kritik*, 305. This ambiguity also reappears, a little softened, in the Anglo-Saxon school of thought among evangelicals (conservative Protestants who defend the divinity of Christ): Dwight Longenecker and David Gustafson, *Mary: A Catholic-Evangelical Debate* (Grand Rapids, Mich.: Brazos Press, 2003), 37, 43, 189–207.

69. Anglican-Roman Catholic International Commission, *Mary: Grace and Hope in Christ* (Harrisburg, Pa.: Morehouse, 2005), n. 34, cited at https://iarccum.org/doc/?d=16.

SYSTEMATIC ASPECTS

The Title "Mother of God" Is Important for Understanding the Person of Jesus Christ

The primary intention of the Council of Ephesus was not Marian devotion, but the defense of faith in Jesus Christ, against Nestorius. The title *Theotókos* clearly highlights the unity of the personal subject in Jesus Christ, the Son of God incarnate. The Nestorian danger is present today as well, when Jesus Christ is described as a human person.[70]

The Divine Maternity Originates in the Eternal Plan of God (Predestination)

Mary was prepared for her motherly role according to the plan of God:[71] "predestined from eternity by that decree of divine providence which determined the incarnation of the Word."[72] Popes Pius IX and Pius XII, in their bulls to define the Immaculate Conception and the bodily Assumption into heaven of the Blessed Virgin, affirm that God "by one and the same decree, had established the origin of Mary and the Incarnation of Divine Wisdom."[73] In the plan of God, the salvific role of Mary and the mission of the Savior are closely united. The Old Testament texts on Wisdom can also be read in this perspective of predestination, inasmuch as they affirm the created response to the divine call, a response with feminine traits (in particular Proverbs 8:22–31; Sir 24).[74] The angelic salutation and the

70. As the Dutch theologian Piet Schoonenberg has proposed. See the critical notes by Galot, *Maria, La donna*, 98; Ponce Cuéllar, *María*, 316–18; Bastero, *Virgen singular*, 17–57.

71. On the predestination of Mary, see Benoît-Henri Merkelbach, *Mariologia* (Paris: Desclée, 1939), 93–104; Alastruey, *Tratado*, 51–66; Accademia Mariana Internazionale, ed., *Alma Socia Christi*, vol. 3, *De praedestinatione et regalitate B. Virginis Mariae* (Rome: AMI, 1952); Roschini, *La Madonna*, 2:3–46; John F. Bonnefoy, OFM, "The Predestination of Our Blessed Lady," in *Mariology*, ed. J. Carol (Milwaukee: Bruce, 1957), 2:154–56; Anton Ziegenaus, "Auserwählung" [Election], in *ML* 1:302f.; O'Carroll, *Theotokos*, 291, 296.

72. *LG* 61. See also John Paul II, *RM* 7–11.

73. Pius IX, *Ineffabilis Deus* (1854) (*EE* 2, n. 740), which is followed by Pius XII, *Munificentissimus Deus* (1950) (DH 3902).

74. See Pius IX, *Ineffabilis Deus* (1854) (*EE* 2, n. 740): "The very words with which the Sacred

name "full of grace" (Lk 1:28) "refer first of all to the election of Mary as Mother of the Son of God," an election "wholly exceptional and unique. Hence also the singularity and uniqueness of her place in the mystery of Christ."[75]

According to the Scotist vision, the Incarnation of the Son of God would have taken place even if Adam had never sinned, while the Thomist school states that the Incarnation was contingent on sin (which was not its cause, but the occasion for divine intervention). The Thomist solution, which takes the biblical texts as its starting point, is more sober, while Scotus provides a theory that is consistent in itself, but cannot be demonstrated from Sacred Scripture.[76] The Thomist thesis, "while it shows more respect for the freedom of the Incarnation—and as a consequence its merciful character toward man—better explains the historicity of salvation. This is not a simple, automatic realization of ideal necessity; rather it is carried out by unforeseeable divine interventions and no less unforeseeable decisions of human freedom."[77]

The question of the motive of the Incarnation, or rather of the "absolute primacy of Christ" (as the Scotists formulate it), also touches upon the way the figure of Mary is presented. In the Thomist view, the blessed Virgin appears essentially as Mother of the Redeemer. Pius IX, without deciding the theological controversy, describes the predestination of Mary in its contingency on sin: "God Ineffable ... having foreseen from all eternity the lamentable wretchedness of the entire human race which would result from the sin of Adam, decreed, by a plan hidden from the centuries, to complete the first work of his goodness by a mystery yet more wondrously sublime through the Incarnation of the Word.... From the very beginning,

---

Scriptures speak of Uncreated Wisdom and set forth his eternal origin, the church, both in its ecclesiastical offices and in its liturgy, has been wont to apply likewise to the origin of the Blessed Virgin, inasmuch as God, by one and the same decree, had established the origin of Mary and the Incarnation of Divine Wisdom." On the mariological use of the wisdom texts, see pp. 19–20.

75. John Paul II, *RM* 9.

76. For a review of positions regarding the motive for the Incarnation, see Jean Galot, SJ, *Gesù Liberatore: Cristologia*, 2nd ed. (Firenze: Fiorentina, 1983), 2:11–31; Jean-Hervé Nicolas, *Sintesi dogmatica* [Dogmatic Synthesis], vol. 1 (Vatican City: Libreria Editrice Vaticana, 1991), nn. 425–30; Amato, *Gesù il Signore*, 439–43.

77. Nicolas, *Sintesi dogmatica*, n. 430, 1:590.

and before time began, the eternal Father chose and prepared for his only-begotten Son a Mother."[78]

There Was Preparation for the Divine Maternity in the Holiness of Mary

Mary's protection from original sin occurs in view of the Incarnation. The consent that was asked of Mary is given with the theological virtue of faith, which can be compared with the divine maternity itself. Augustine explains this relation in a sermon that comments on the encounter between Jesus and his relatives: his brothers and his mother are all those who obey the heavenly Father (Mt 12:48–50):

> Didn't the Virgin Mary do the will of the Father? I mean, she believed by faith, she conceived by faith, she was chosen to be the one from whom salvation in the very midst of the human race would be born for us, she was created by Christ before Christ was created in her. Yes, of course, holy Mary did the will of the Father. And therefore it means more for Mary to have been a disciple of Christ than to have been the mother of Christ.[79]

In this perspective, patristic thought also describes the "maternity" of consecrated virgins and of every disciple of Christ as a "conception" of the Word.[80] "Like conception, faith is, on the spiritual level, fruitful acceptance of a seed of life. Receiving the word ... every Christian conceives God in his heart. In this perspective, faith implies a type of spiritual maternity; and the divine, physical maternity of Mary appears like the radiance, in the flesh, of her faith."[81]

The holiness of Mary is a gratuitous gift, like the grace of the divine maternity itself. Mary could not "merit," in the strict sense, the fact of being the Mother of God. There is no *meritum de condigno*, no merit in strict justice. And yet, we can speak of a *meritum de congruo*—that is, a merit of fittingness: with her holiness, sustained

78. Pius IX, *Ineffabilis Deus* (1854) (*EE* 2, n. 739).

79. Augustine, *Sermo* 72.A.7 (PL 46:937), English trans. from http://www.vatican.va/spirit/documents/spirit_20001208_agostino_en.html.

80. For example, Augustine, *De sancta virginitate* 6 (PL 40:399).

81. René Laurentin, *A Short Treatise on the Virgin Mary* (Washington, N.J.: Ave Maria Institute, 1991), 192.

by the grace of God, Mary went to meet the intentions of the divine plan.[82] The merit of Mary is described impressively by St. Bernard of Clairvaux. He contemplates the responsibility of the answer she gave to the angel, and he imagines all the human race, starting from Adam and Eve, in a state of anxious waiting for the consent asked of her:

> Behold the entire human race prostrate at your feet in expectation. And rightly, for on your word depend the consolation of the wretched, the redemption of the captive, the freedom of the condemned, the salvation of your entire race, of all the children of Adam.[83]

The Divine Maternity Brings with It a Transforming Relationship

The descent of the Holy Spirit upon Mary, according to the account of Luke (Lk 1:26–38),[84] evoked the act of the Creation (Gn 1:2) and the presence of God in the Ark of the Covenant (Ex 40:34). With the Incarnation, which came at the Annunciation, Mary comes to "a new degree of purity and of assimilation to God, something like the last passing of an already pure metal through the crucible in order to bring out its temper and brilliance."[85]

82. See Thomas Aquinas, III Sent., d. 4, a. 1, ad 5; *ST* III, q. 2, a. 11, ad 3. On the merit of Mary, see Benoît-Henri Merkelbach, OP, *Mariologia* (Paris: Desclée, 1939), 204–13, 327–36; Roschini, *Maria Santissima*, 2:47–52; Johannes Stöhr, "Verdienst Marias" [Merit of Mary], in *ML* 6:593–96; O'Carroll, *Theotokos*, 246f.; Hauke, "La cooperazione attiva di Maria alla Redenzione: Prospettiva storica (patristica, medievale, moderna, contemporanea)" [The Active Cooperation of Mary in the Redemption: Historical (Patristic, Medieval, Modern, Contemporary) Perspective], in *Maria, "Unica Cooperatrice alla Redenzione"* (New Bedford, Mass.: Academy of the Immaculate, 2005), 171–219; also in Immaculata Mediatrix 6 (2006): 157–89, passim.

83. Bernard of Clairvaux, *Super missus est* I.7 (PL 183:59D); English trans. in *Sermons of St. Bernard on Advent and Christmas, London 1909*, available at http://archive.org/details/sermonsofstbernaoobernuoft.

84. Regarding the Holy Spirit's "overshadowing" of Mary in the Annunciation, see p. 40.

85. Laurentin, *Short Treatise*, 210. The Byzantine theologian Nicholas Cabasilas (fourteenth century) affirms it expressly (ibid.). The idea of "purification" (*kátharsis*), upheld by various Eastern authors, may be intended in this manner: 313f.; see Manfred Hauke, *Heilsverlust in Adam: Stationen griechischer Erbsündenlehre; Irenäus—Origenes—Kappadozier* [Salvation Lost in Adam: Stages of Greek Teaching on Original Sin; Irenaeus, Origen, the Cappadocians] (Paderborn: Bonifatius, 1993), 560; Hauke, "Die Unbefleckte Empfängnis bei den griechischen Vätern: Die Hinweise Johannes Pauls II. im ökumenischen Disput," *Sedes Sapientiae: Mariologisches Jahrbuch* 8, no. 2 (2004): 52f.

The divine maternity, as the basic relationship of Mary with Christ, can be compared to a sacramental character, distinct from grace, but given in view of the supernatural life.[86] The indelible character in the sacraments (of Baptism, Confirmation, and Orders) constitutes the consecration of the Christian to the Most Holy Trinity and a conformation to Christ. Similarly, the divine maternity, prepared in the grace of the Immaculate Conception at the beginning of Mary's existence, consecrates our Lady to God for the sake of her relation with her Son, who assumes human nature from her by the power of the Holy Spirit. According to Scheeben, the grace of the divine maternity is already present in Mary from the beginning of her life. He, the most famous German dogmatic theologian of the 1800s, describes the maternal relation of the Holy Virgin with Christ by means of the expression "personal character" and identifies it with her spiritual marriage with the divine Word. The "personal character" involves being Mother and "Spouse" of Christ, who asks her consent before becoming her Son. Thus the theologian arrives at the concept of "spousal motherhood."[87]

This systematic concept of Scheeben confirms the Catholic conviction that the divine maternity cannot be separated from Mary's mediation, a function that is not limited to the physical birth of Jesus. In the divine maternity, the whole person is consecrated to Christ forever, which implies cooperation in the process of salvation. The "spousal" maternity of Mary finds its expression already in the fathers of the church and in a famous affirmation of Thomas Aquinas, repeatedly cited in the pontifical magisterium:

> The event of the Annunciation was fitting "in order to show that there is a certain spiritual wedlock between the Son of God and human nature. Wherefore in the Annunciation the Virgin's consent was besought in lieu of that of the entire human nature (*loco totius humanae naturae*)."[88]

86. See Laurentin, *Short Treatise*, 201–10.

87. See pp. 120–21; Hauke, "Matthias Joseph Scheeben († 1888) nella mariologia tedesca del XIX secolo" [Scheeben in the German Mariology of the 19th Century]. In Boaga and Gambero, *Storia della mariologia*, 2:261f.

88. Thomas Aquinas, *ST* III, q. 30, a. 1; also see pp. 123–24. The text is cited in Leo XIII, Encyclical *Octobri mense* (1891) (DH 3274); Pius XII, Encyclical *Mystici Corporis* (1943) (*AAS* 35 [1943] 247); John Paul II, "Mary, the New Eve, Freely Obeyed God," Marian Catechesis of Sep. 18, 1996, in *Theotókos: Mother, Woman, Disciple* (Boston: Pauline, 2000), 137 (*CCC* 511).

Christ also represents the whole human race, but does so as a divine person and as head of the church. Mary represents the human race as a created person and, in a way, as the "heart" of the mystical body of Christ. She does so as woman in her "spousal" receptivity, united to her active response to the initiative of God.

With the Divine Maternity, Mary Takes an Active Role in the Work of Salvation

The Incarnation is not only a premise that precedes the work of salvation, but forms part of it. Therefore, Mary's consent has a salvific quality, rendered possible by the grace of Christ given ever since the beginning of the life of the Blessed Virgin.[89] Mary's cooperation is directed toward the redemptive work of Christ that began at the Incarnation, as we can deduce from the Letter to the Hebrews: "When Christ came into the world, he said, 'Sacrifices and offerings you have not desired, but a body have you prepared for me'" (Heb 10:5). While Christ appears as the "new Adam," Mary acts as the "new Eve." Both are united to renew humanity fallen in sin.[90]

The Divine Maternity Is the Beginning of Mary's Spiritual Maternity for the Church

The divine maternity has a close relationship with the person of the Incarnate Word as head of the mystical body. A milestone for the development of doctrine on the spiritual maternity of Mary is found in a famous text of Augustine, cited in the documents of Vatican II:

Physically, Mary "is only the mother of Christ, but after the Spirit she is both his sister and mother. And on this account, that one female, not only in the Spirit, but also in the flesh, is both a mother and a virgin. And a mother indeed in the Spirit, not of our Head, which is the Saviour himself, of whom rather she was born after the Spirit: for as much as all who have

89. See "Biblical Foundation," in chapter 8 (Mary's cooperation in the work of salvation).

90. See Stefano M. Manelli, "Maria Corredentrice nella Sacra Scrittura" [Mary Coredemptrix in Sacred Scripture], in *Maria Corredentrice* 1 (1998): 73–82.

believed in Him, among whom is herself also, are rightly called children of the Bridegroom: but clearly the mother of his members, which are we: in that she wrought together by charity, that faithful ones should be born in the Church, who are members of that head."[91]

Mary's cooperation in the spiritual birth of the members of the church is open to a universal dimension. This spiritual maternity, based on the Incarnation, is confirmed and fully constituted at the foot of the Cross, when Jesus Christ reveals the vocation of Mary as "mother" of John, the type of every faithful disciple.[92] During his visit to Ephesus, Pope Benedict XVI underscored this relation between the divine maternity of Mary and her maternal function for the church: "We have listened to a passage from Saint John's Gospel which invites us to contemplate the moment of the Redemption when Mary, united to her Son in the offering of his sacrifice, extended her motherhood to all men and women, and in particular to the disciples of Jesus."[93]

The Divine Maternity Exalts Mary above All Other Creatures

The NT itself alludes to the most high dignity of Mary as mother of the Lord. This becomes evident in the greeting of the angel (Lk 1:28: "Hail, full of grace, the Lord is with you"), but also in the words of Elizabeth (Lk 1:42: "Blessed are you among women and blessed is the fruit of your womb! And why is this granted me, that the mother of my Lord should come to me?") and in the praise of the *Magnificat* (Lk 1:48: "Henceforth all generations will call me blessed").

In the third century, Mary's greater grace than the apostles is not yet clear, as, for example, Origen's notes on the alleged sins of the

91. Augustine, *De sancta virginitate* 5–6 (PL 40:399). English translation from *NPNF2*, 3:418–19. The last phrase is cited in *LG* 53.

92. The explanation of spiritual maternity appears more vigorously from the twelfth century on; see below, pp. 316–18 (mediation); for information, see first Michael O'Carroll, CSSp, *Theotokos: A Theological Encyclopedia of the Blessed Virgin Mary* (Eugene, Ore.: Wipf and Stock, 2000), 238–45, 253–56; Ponce Cuéllar, *María*, 467–69.

93. Benedict XVI, Homily of Nov. 29, 2006, in *Insegnamenti di Benedetto XVI*, vol. 2, part 2 (Vatican City: Libreria Editrice Vaticana, 2007), 711.

Madonna bear witness.[94] But in the fourth century we find explicit witnesses that highlight the greater nobility of Mary as Mother of God with respect to all other creatures. With the Council of Ephesus this conviction becomes universal. The echo of this faith can be noticed in Vatican II: by the gift of the divine maternity, Mary "far surpasses all creatures, both in heaven and on earth."[95]

Her personal relationship with God, which comes from the divine maternity, is the most profound that can exist between a created person and the Creator. Certainly this relationship is less profound than the relation of the humanity of Jesus Christ with the Word who assumes it: that relation makes human nature subsist in the divine person of the Son of God, according to the systematic expression of St. Thomas. Notwithstanding that, Mary bore her own Creator, according to human nature, a fact that constitutes a virtually infinite dignity.[96] Following Suárez (sixteenth century), many theologians express the dignity of the Mother of God with the idea that this dignity belongs to the order of the hypostatic union, which is to say that she cannot be separated from the incarnate Word.[97]

The Divine Maternity Constitutes a Special Relationship with the Most Holy Trinity

A theological work of the seventeenth century calls Mary "mirror and revelation of the Trinity"[98] and, referring to the Annunciation,

94. See "Patristic Development and the Importance of the Council of Ephesus," in chapter 6.

95. *LG* 53.

96. *ST* I, q. 25, a. 6, ad 4: "Beata Virgo ex hoc, quod est mater Dei, habet quandam dignitatem infinitam ex bono infinito, quod est Deus; et ex hac parte non potest aliquid fieri melius ea, sicut non potest aliquid melius esse Deo."

97. Regarding the contribution of Suárez, see p. 151; Francisco Suárez, *De mysteriis vitae Christi*, sec. 2:4, Opera omnia 19 (Paris 1856), 8 (cited in Gherardini, *La Madre*, 81, note 43): "Haec dignitas matris est altioris ordinis, pertinet enim quodammodo ad ordinem unionis hypostaticae, illam enim intrinsece respicit, et cum illa necessariam conjunctionem habet." On the whole question, see Severino M. Ragazzini, OFM Conv., *La Divina Maternità di Maria nel suo concetto teologico integrale* [The Divine Maternity of Mary in Its Integral Theological Concept] (Frigento: Casa Mariana Editrice, 1986), 214–38.

98. For a more explicit treatment, see Benoît Henri Merkelbach, OP, *Mariologia* (Paris: Desclée, 1939), 58–64; M.-J. Nicolas, "Marie et la Trinité," in *Maria*, ed. H. du Manoir (Paris: Beauchesne, 1964), 7:421–30; Joaquin María Alonso, "Trinità," in De Fiores and Meo, *NDM*, 1406–17; Karl Wittkemper, "Dreifaltigkeit I. Dogmatik" [Trinity. I. Dogmatics], in *ML* 2:233–39; Hauke, "Die

says that the Father has sent the Son, while the Son became man by the power and the working of the Holy Spirit.[99] The mystery of the Annunciation sheds light on the mystery of God One and Three. Vatican II provides a precise summary of the relation of Mary with the Most Holy Trinity:

> Redeemed by reason of the merits of her Son and united to Him by a close and indissoluble tie, she is endowed with the high office and dignity of being the Mother of the Son of God, by which account she is also the beloved daughter of the Father and the temple of the Holy Spirit. Because of this gift of sublime grace she far surpasses all creatures, both in heaven and on earth.[100]

Mary is the "favored daughter of the Father" and "temple of the Holy Spirit" already before becoming Mother of God; and yet these relations with the Father and the Holy Spirit are closely connected with the divine maternity, the starting point for describing her relationship with the Most Holy Trinity.

The title "daughter" is the one most frequently used for describing her relation with the heavenly Father. Already we find a prefiguration in the Old Testament type of the "daughter of Zion." At the same time, the daughterhood of Mary resembles the adoptive sonship of all the baptized, who are able to pray "Abba, Father!" (see Gal 3:26, 4:4–7). The aim of our life is to receive "adoption as sons" (Gal 4:5). In this very context, the Apostle Paul speaks of the divine maternity of Mary: "God sent his Son, born of woman" (Gal 4:4).

---

trinitarischen Beziehungen Mariens als Urbild der Kirche auf dem Zweiten Vatikanischen Konzil" [The Trinitarian Relations of Mary as a Model of the Church at the Second Vatican Council], *Sedes Sapientiae: Mariologisches Jahrbuch* 4, no. 2 (2000): 78–114; Angelo Amato, *Maria e la Trinità* (Cinisello Balsamo: San Paolo, 2000); Juan Luis Bastero, "El Padre y María en el magisterio post-conciliar" [The Father and Mary in the Post-Conciliar Magisterium], *Estudios Marianos* 66 (2000): 343–65; Bastero, "El Espiritu Sancto y María en el Concilio Vaticano II y en Pablo VI" [The Holy Spirit and Mary in Vatican II and Paul VI], *Scripta theologica* 38 (2006): 701–35; Leo Scheffczyk, *Maria, crocevia della fede cattolica*, CdM 1 (Lugano: Eupress FTL, 2002), 69–79; Rosa Lombardi, *Maria icona della Trinità* [Mary, Icon of the Trinity] (Rome: Edizioni pro sanctitate, 2003); De Fiores, *Dizionario*, 2:1717–43; De Fiores, "Trinità," in *DMar*, 1219–32; Eloy Bueno de la Fuente, "La revelación entre la Trinidad y la Virgen María desde la perspectiva de Lumen gentium" [Revelation between the Trinity and the Virgin Mary, from the Perspective of Lumen gentium], *Ephemerides mariologicae* 64, no. 4 (2014): 403–26.

99. See Josephus de la Cerda, *Maria effigies revelatioque trinitatis* [Mary, Image and Revelation of the Trinity], Almeria, 1640.

100. *LG* 53.

Certainly, Mary is also the "favored" daughter of the Father. This exclusive relation became the object of reflection by the fathers of the church, who described Christ as the common Son of God the Father and of the Virgin Mary. We find this idea also in the Council of Chalcedon: "begotten from the Father before the ages as to the divinity and in the latter days for us and our salvation was born as to his humanity."[101]

The awareness of a "spousal" relation of Mary with God the Father also began in the early church, as in a passage of St. John Damascene cited in the Apostolic Constitution *Munificentissimus Deus* (1950). In that document Pope Pius XII defined the Assumption of Mary, soul and body, into heavenly glory and affirmed, "It was fitting that the spouse, whom the Father had taken to himself, should live in the divine mansions."[102] The title "spouse" became more widespread in the Middle Ages—for example, in Rupert of Deutz and in the seventeenth century in the French school of spirituality, particularly in Bérulle and Olier.[103] According to Olier, the Father chose Mary as his spouse so that she could become, together with him, the principle of the temporal generation of the Word in the Incarnation. Notwithstanding this, the title "spouse of the Father" is not very common because of the possible misunderstanding of attributing to Mary the eternal generation of the Son of God, while her contribution clearly remains in the temporal sphere.

The title "daughter" implies a similarity to the Father. For this reason the divine maternity is also compared with the active generation of the Son by the Father. The eternal source of the Son in the Father is reflected in the Son's temporal origin from Mary as mother. According to Grignion de Montfort, "God the Father imparted to Mary his fruitfulness as far as a mere creature was capable of receiving it, to enable her to bring forth his Son and all the members of his mystical body."[104]

101. DH 301.

102. John Damascene, *Hom. II in Dormit.* 14 (PG 96: 741); see *AAS* 42 (1950): 768; *EE* 6, n. 1951.

103. See O'Carroll, *Theotokos*, 333f.; Wittkemper, "Braut IV. Dogmatik" [Bride. IV. Dogmatics], in *ML* 1:568f.

104. *TD* n. 17.

The similarity of the divine maternity with the eternal fatherhood of God can also shed light on the importance of the virginity of Mary: "If one maintains that the divine Motherhood is the most perfect created assimilation to the divine Paternity, it would seem to indicate that Mary's divine Motherhood is necessarily a virginal motherhood."[105]

Mary, in a way, could be called the "feminine face" of the Father, revealing in particular his mercy and tenderness. Note, however, that the Blessed Virgin does not directly represent the "motherhood" of God; instead she is the Mother of God who represents the summit of created reality.[106]

To point to her relation with the Son, the title "Mother" is fundamental above all else. Yet already in the era of the fathers and more so in the Middle Ages, we find the description of Mary as the "bride" of Christ, understood as his companion in the work of salvation. The commentaries on the Song of Songs especially, starting with St. Ambrose, practically put Mary, the church, and the human soul in the same position, as a "bride" of Christ opening herself to the love of the divine "bridegroom."[107] The title "bride of Christ" is used somewhat for the church, following the biblical sources (among others, Ephesians 5:21–33).

Today the title "spouse" is more widespread for Mary's relation with the Holy Spirit. The first to present Mary as "spouse of the Holy Spirit" was St. Francis.[108] It is a reasonable custom, inasmuch as Mary is highlighted as a "cooperator" of the third divine person. Yet, on the other hand, the Holy Spirit is not called "bridegroom" of Mary, to avoid the idea that there was any begetting on his part.

105. Paul Haffner, *The Mystery of Mary* (Leominster, UK: Gracewing; Mundelein, Ill.: Hillenbrand, 2004), 128. This "necessity" should be seen, however, not as a metaphysical necessity, but as fittingness.

106. See "Mary, the Woman, in the Context of Anthropology," in chapter 3, with the notes on feminist theology.

107. See Scharbert, "Hoheslied," in *ML* 3:233.

108. Antiphon *Sancta Maria Virgo*, v. 2: "filia et ancilla altissimi summi Regis Patris caelestis, mater sanctissimi Domini nostri Jesu Christi, sponsa Spiritus Sancti." See Octavian Schmucki, "Franz v. Assisi," in *ML* 2:510; Johannes Schneider, *Virgo Ecclesia facta: La presenza di Maria nel crocifisso di San Damiano e nell'Officium Passionis di san Francesco d'Assisi* [The Virgin, Made Church: The Presence of Mary in the San Damiano Crucifix and in the Passion Office of St Francis] (Assisi: Porziuncola, 2003), 223–72.

The Spirit is not the Father of Jesus.[109] His action in the Incarnation is compared in the Gospel of Luke with the first Creation and not with begetting. More recent Mariology that finds its reflection in *Lumen gentium* 53 tends to avoid this title and prefers to speak of Mary as "temple," "dwelling-place," or "sanctuary" of the Holy Spirit.[110]

On the other hand, the description "temple of the Holy Spirit" does not describe a specific relation of Mary with the Holy Spirit, but only reflects what it means for every Christian. The expression "spouse of the Holy Spirit" has the advantage of showing a specific trait of the Blessed Virgin. This can be seen already in the works of St. Francis, who uses the title exclusively for Mary (and not for consecrated virgins).[111] John Paul II has renewed this title neglected by Vatican II.[112] In one of the Marian catecheses, the supreme pontiff clearly affirms that, as "spouse of the Holy Spirit," Mary enjoys a special relationship with the Spirit, in addition to being simply a "temple of God" like every Christian.[113]

Paul VI, in the apostolic exhortation *Marialis cultus* (1974), emphasized the trinitarian character of Marian devotion. Mary helps us to turn to the Father through his Son in the Holy Spirit.[114] John Paul II recalls that the Annunciation brings us a revelation of the Trinity in its relation to Mary.[115] In this way Mary realizes the supreme vocation of a creature, a vocation in which all the members of

109. See the Eleventh Synod of Toledo (DH 533).

110. See Hauke, "Die trinitarischen Beziehungen Mariens als Urbild der Kirche auf dem Zweiten Vatikanischen Konzil" [The Trinitarian Relations of Mary as a Model of the Church at the Second Vatican Council], *Sedes Sapientiae: Mariologisches Jahrbuch* 4, no. 2 (2000): 87–90.

111. See Lorenzo M. Ago, *La "Salutatio Beatae Mariae Virginis" di san Francesco di Assisi* [St. Francis' "Salutation of the Blessed Virgin Mary"] (Rome: Edizioni Monfortane, 1998), 228.

112. See, for example, *RM* 9 and *RM* 26: Mary is the "temple of the Holy Spirit" and "faithful spouse" of the Holy Spirit.

113. John Paul II, CM 11 (Jan. 10, 1996), n. 4: "Again, every Christian is a 'temple of the Holy Spirit.' ... But this assertion takes on an extraordinary meaning in Mary. In her the relationship with the Holy Spirit is enriched with a spousal dimension. I recalled this in the encyclical *Redemptoris Mater*: 'The Holy Spirit had already come down upon her, and she became his faithful spouse at the annunciation, welcoming the Word of the true God' (n. 26)." See Hauke, "La mediazione materna di Maria secondo Papa Giovanni Paolo II" [Mary's Maternal Mediation according to Pope John Paul II], in *Maria Corredentrice* 7 (2005): 70f. See also Étienne Richer, "Marie, Epouse du Saint-Esprit? Le point de vue de la mariologie des saints et des papes" [Mary, Spouse of the Holy Spirit? The Mariological Viewpoint of the Saints and the Popes], *RTLu* 12 (2007): 257–77.

114. See *MCu* 25.

115. See John Paul II, *Mulieris dignitatem*, 3.

the church share. On the other hand, the title "Mother of God" can be attributed uniquely to Mary; the special use of the expressions "spouse of the Holy Spirit" and "*favored* daughter of the Father" illuminates this also. "Here we see the authentic meaning of Mary's privileges and of her extraordinary relationship with the Trinity. Their purpose is to enable her to cooperate in the salvation of the human race."[116]

REFERENCES

Ecclesiastical Texts

CCC 466, 495, 2677.

Collantes, Justo, ed. *La fede della Chiesa Cattolica: Le idee e gli uomini nei documenti dottrinali del Magistero* [The Faith of the Catholic Church: Ideas and Men in the Doctrinal Documents of the Magisterium], 298–301. Vatican City: Libreria Editrice Vaticana, 1993.

Council of Ephesus (431): DH 250f.

John II, Letter *Olim quidam* (534): DH 401.

John Paul II. CM of Nov. 27, 1996 ("Church Proclaims Mary Mother of God").

———. *RM* 4.

LG 52–53.

Paul IV. Bull *Cum quorumdam* (1555): DH 1880.

Pius XI. Encyclical *Lux veritatis* (1931, 15th Centenary of the Council of Ephesus): *EE* 5, nn. 820–78 and *AAS* 23 (1931): 493–517.

Other Sources

La Maternidad divina de María [The Divine Maternity of Mary]. *Estudios Marianos* 68 (2002).

Auer, Johann. *Gesù il Salvatore: Soteriologia–Mariologia* [Jesus the Savior: Soteriology, Mariology]. Translated by Carlo Molari. § 6. Assisi: Cittadella, 1993. German original: *Jesus Christus—Heiland der Welt: Maria, Christi Mutter im Heilsplan Gottes*. Regensburg: Friedrich Pustet, 1988.

Bastero, Juan Luis. *Mary, Mother of the Redeemer*, 154–65. Dublin: Four Courts, 2006.

Bastero de Eleizalde, Juan Luis. *Virgen singular: La reflexión teológica mariana en el siglo XX* [Singular Virgin: Theological Reflection on Mary in the 20th Century]. 17–57. Madrid: Rialp, 2001.

Calero, Antonio Maria. *La Vergine Maria nel mistero di Cristo e della Chiesa: Saggio di mariologia* [The Virgin Mary in the Mystery of Christ and the Church: Essay in Mariology], 108–18. Leumann (Turin): Elle Di Ci, 1995. Spanish original: *María en el misterio de Cristo y de la Iglesia*. Madrid: CCS, 1990.

Colzani, Gianni. *Maria: Mistero di grazia e di fede* [Mary: Mystery of Grace and Faith], 184–99. Cinisello Balsamo: Ed. Paoline, 1996. 3rd ed., 2006.

116. John Paul II, CM 11 (Jan. 10, 1996), n. 5.

De Fiores, Stefano. *Maria, Madre di Gesù: Sintesi storico-salvifica* [Mary, Mother of Jesus: Salvation-Historical Synthesis], 122–29. Corso di teologia sistematica 6. Bologna: EDB, 1992.

———. *Maria nella teologia contemporanea* [Mary in Contemporary Theology]. 3rd ed., 480–97. Rome: Centro di Cultura Mariana "Madre della Chiesa," 1991.

———. *Maria sintesi di valori: Storia culturale della mariologia* [Mary, Synthesis of Values: Cultural History of Mariology], 96–107. Cinisello Balsamo: San Paolo, 2005.

Dittrich, Achim. *Protestantische Mariologie-Kritik: Historische Entwicklung bis 1997 und dogmatische Analyse* [Protestant Criticism of Mariology: Historic Development until 1997 and Dogmatic Analysis]. Mariologische Studien 11, 305–7. Regensburg: Friedrich Pustet, 1998.

Galot, Jean, SJ. *Maria, La donna nell'opera della salvezza* [Mary, the Woman in the Work of Salvation]. 3rd ed., 91–112. Rome: Ed. Pontificia Università Gregoriana, 2005. 2nd ed., 1991.

Gherardini, Brunero. *La Madre: Maria in una sintesi storico-teologica* [The Mother: Mary in a Historical-Theological Synthesis], 57–92. Frigento: Casa Mariana, 1989.

Haffner, Paul. *The Mystery of Mary*, 107–33. Leominster, UK: Gracewing; Mundelein, Ill.: Hillenbrand, 2004.

Laurentin, René. *A Short Treatise on the Virgin Mary*, 187–226, 276–79. Washington, N.J.: Ave Maria Institute, 1991.

Meo, Salvatore, OSM. "Madre di Dio II. Dogma, storia e teologia" [Mother of God II: Dogma, History, and Theology]. In *NDM*, 812–25.

Merkelbach, Benoît Henri. *Mariologia*. 19–104. Paris: Desclée, 1939.

Müller, Gerhard L. "Gottesmutter" [Mother of God]. In *ML* 2:684–92 = Müller, *Maria: Die Frau im Heilsplan Gottes*. Mariologische Studien 15, 231–50. Regensburg: Friedrich Pustet, 2002.

O'Carroll, Michael, CSSp. *Theotokos: A Theological Encyclopedia of the Blessed Virgin Mary*, 257–59. Eugene, Ore.: Wipf and Stock, 2000.

Petrillo, Francisco. "Theotokos/Madre di Dio." In *DMar*, 1211–19.

Philippe, Marie-Dominique, OP. "Le mystère de la Maternité Divine de Marie" [The Mystery of the Divine Maternity of Mary]. In *Maria*, edited by H. du Manoir, 6:367–416. Paris: Beauchesne, 1961.

Ponce Cuéllar, Miguel. *María: Madre del Redentor y Madre de la Iglesia* [Mary, Mother of the Redeemer and Mother of the Church]. 2nd ed., 298–322. Barcelona: Herder, 2001.

Pozo, Cándido, SJ. *María en la obra de la salvación* [Mary in the Work of Salvation]. 2nd ed., 285–95. Madrid: Biblioteca de Autores Cristianos, 1990.

———. *María, nueva Eva* [Mary, the New Eve], 301–13. Madrid: Biblioteca de Autores Cristianos, 2005.

Ragazzini, Severino M., OFM Conv. *La Divina Maternità di Maria nel suo concetto teologico integrale* [The Divine Maternity of Mary in Its Integral Theological Concept]. Frigento: Casa Mariana Editrice, 1986.

Roschini, Gabriele M. *La Madonna: Secondo la fede e la teologia* [The Madonna, according to the Faith and Theology], 2:150–218. Rome: Libreria Editrice Francesco Ferrari, 1953–54.

———. *Maria Santissima*, 2:9–110.

Sartor, Danilo Maria. "Madre di Dio III: Celebrazione liturgica." In De Fiores and Meo, *NDM*, 825–28.

Scheffczyk, Leo. *Maria, Mutter und Gefährtin Christi* [Mary, Mother and Companion of Christ], 94–105. Augsburg: Sankt Ulrich, 2003.

Serra, Aristide. "Madre di Dio I: Fondamenti biblici." In De Fiores and Meo, *NDM*, 806–12.

Söll, Georg. *Storia dei dogmi mariani* [History of Marian Dogmas], 90f, 108–13, 152–64. Rome: Libreria Ateneo Salesiano, 1981. German original: *Mariologie* [Handbuch der Dogmengeschichte III/4]. Freiburg i.Br.: Herder, 1978.

Van Ackeren, Gerald, SJ. "Maternidad divina de María" [Mary's Divine Motherhood]. In *Mariología*, edited by J. Carol, 570–618. English original: "Outline History of the Mariology of the Middle Ages and Modern Times." In Carol, *Mariology*, 1:177–227.

Villar, José Ramón. "La madre di Dios en la teologia ortodoxa" [The Mother of God in Orthodox Theology]. *Scripta de Maria* 2nd ser., 7 (2010): 27–73.

Ziegenaus, Anton. *Maria in der Heilsgeschichte: Mariologie* [Mary in Salvation History: Mariology], 204–18. Katholische Dogmatik 5. Aachen: MM-Verlag, 1998.

Five

The Virginity of Mary

THE IMPORTANCE OF THE DOCTRINE

From the beginning, the divine maternity of Mary was believed to be a virginal maternity: the human origin of Jesus took place without the intervention of a human father. Such an origin makes manifest the gratuitous gift of God and the new beginning it makes in salvation history, comparable to the first Creation. On the other hand, Mary too was marked forever by the event of the Incarnation: virginity is the bodily expression of her openness to God. In the perpetual virginity of Mary we find an interleaving of bodily reality and spiritual virtue. The Church professes Mary "ever Virgin": virgin before giving birth, while giving birth, and after giving birth (*virginitas ante partum, in partu, post partum*). The systematic exposition here will be organized according to this schema.

The virginity of Mary and the resurrection of Jesus are elements of the faith that particularly conflict with a secularized mentality that rejects the bodily concreteness of God's intervention in history. Certainly this fact is not new, but has been present since the beginning, with Jewish and pagan polemics against the virginity of Mary. Today this polemic feeds on a deism that denies any miraculous intervention of God in this world; this ideology is often joined, in the exegetical environment, with a tendency that considers the infancy narratives in the Gospels a product of legend. Moreover there is the suspicion that the exaltation of virginity is a sign of the church's hostility toward sexual life. Against these trends we need to show that faith in the virginity of Mary finds its root in history and that it is anything but a disparagement of marriage and the sexual condition.

The church's faith in the virginity of Mary is even older than the explicit formulation of the divine maternity. While the title *Theotókos* was applied in the fourth century and then found its solemn approval at the Council of Ephesus, the designation "Virgin" for Mary is found as early as the second century and is present in all the ancient creeds of the faith (e.g., in our Nicene-Constantinopolitan Creed and the Apostles' Creed). We also recall the contemporaneous formula, especially following the Council of Ephesus, of the "Holy Virgin Mother of God."

In the early church, the virginity of Mary was the distinguishing mark of the true divinity of Jesus Christ. Athanasius, for example, states, "When He [the Son of God] came among us, He formed Himself a body, taking it from a Virgin to offer a proof of His divinity which could not be ignored."[1]

Had Jesus been conceived in the natural way, it would have been necessary to attribute all the Marian titles to Joseph also: the divine paternity, Immaculate Conception, etc. There would only have been veneration for the Holy Family, but not for the specific role of Mary.

VIRGINITAS ANTE PARTUM

Biblical References

On the biblical side, we have already seen the testimonies of Sacred Scripture on the virginal origin of Jesus. We find a direct affirmation in the accounts of the infancy of Jesus (Mt 1; Lk 1). This double testimony, despite the independent redaction of the two texts, is notable. In both cases there is a reference to the prophecy of Isaiah 7:14 LXX: the Virgin will conceive and give birth (a literal reference in Matthew, one by allusion in Luke). A debated witness is that of John 1:13: the Christological version of this verse points to the virgin birth of Jesus.

1. *De incarn.* 18 (PG 25:128C); English trans. in Luigi Gambero, *Mary and the Fathers of the Church: The Blessed Virgin Mary in Patristic Thought*, trans. Thomas Buffer (San Francisco: Ignatius Press, 1999), 103.

Furthermore, in John, when people speak of the fatherhood of Joseph, John seems to discreetly correct the opinion (Jn 1:45, 1:49–51, 6:42–47). When Paul points to the human origin of Jesus, the Apostle only speaks of the mother ("born of woman": Gal 4:4). Mark, in contrast to Matthew and Luke, calls Jesus "son of Mary"; this unconventional term can be seen as an allusion to the virginal origin of the Lord.

Early Opposition (Judaism, Paganism)

From the beginning, the testimony of Sacred Scripture clashed with Jewish and pagan opposition. According to the Jew Trypho (who debated with St. Justin), Christians should have felt ashamed of the doctrine of the virgin birth of Jesus, since it was based on pagan myths, according to which a god procreated a son with a human woman (as in the birth of Perseus from the union of Zeus and Danae; Zeus had approached Danae in the form of golden rain).[2] It would be better, says Trypho, "for you to say that this Jesus had been generated humanly as a man and declare ... that he had been called Christ because of his perfect conduct according to the law." The Jews categorically denied that Isaiah 7:14 had anything to do with a virginal origin of Jesus, and their abandonment of the Septuagint also seems to have been motivated by this debate. In the second century there was a widespread Jewish opinion, according to which Mary had been driven out by Joseph, on the ground that she had conceived the son of a soldier named Pantera (*Pántera* seemed to be a twist on the term *parthénos*, virgin).[3]

The virginity of Mary was derided by the pagan world. The philosopher Celsus (circa 180) willingly accepted the calumnies of the Jews,[4] and Porphyry (third century) considered it undignified on the part of God to enter the womb of a virgin to be born, be wrapped in swaddling clothes, and be soiled.[5] Celsus also accepted

2. Justin, *Dialogue with Trypho* 67 (PG 6:629A–B). See *1 Apol.* 22:5, 54:8 (PG 6:361B; 409C). On Justin, see Anton Ziegenaus, "Jungfräulichkeitsgelübte" [Vow of Virginity], in *ML* 469f.

3. See Origen, *Contra Celsum* 1:32, 1:69 (*SC* 132:162–64, 270).

4. Origen, *Contra Celsum* 1:28, 1:32 (*SC* 132:150, 164).

5. See Ziegenaus, *Maria in der Heilsgeschichte: Mariologie* [Mary in Salvation History: Mariology], Katholische Dogmatik 5 (Aachen: MM-Verlag, 1998), 151.

the Jewish opinion comparing the virgin birth of Jesus with Greek myths that were no longer taken seriously.[6]

Modern Criticism

The ancient objections are found again within modern criticism, which adds other and very different perspectives. Let us present some significant examples.

(1) The denial of the virgin birth has become habitual in liberal Protestantism, especially since the time of David Friedrich Strauss, a student of Hegel and author of a book on "The Life of Jesus" (1835). According to him, the biblical accounts were *the historicization of an idea* contrary to historical facts—namely, the idea of a supernatural origin of Jesus. Such an event would be impossible because miracles do not exist. Moreover, the virgin birth would not be necessary to explain the divinity of Jesus, which Strauss did not accept anyway. Mark, Paul, and John are silent on the virgin birth; the genealogies, in their original form, according to Strauss, testify to the biological fatherhood of Joseph. The idea of the virgin birth would have come from Hellenism, accepted in a purified form through the influence of Isaiah 7:14. Heinrich Maria Köster, in a review of the criticism of the virgin birth based on Strauss, observes that this author anticipated nearly all the critical observations of later exegesis.[7]

In the biblical section earlier, we have already considered the argument about the silence of Mark and Paul on the virgin birth. They do not mention it because it does not enter into their purpose of presenting the public life of Jesus (Mark) or the death and resurrection of the Lord (Paul). Nevertheless we can find allusions to the virgin birth in them, as in John. In any case, Paul and Mark do not point to a biological paternity on Joseph's part, and they highlight only the origin of Jesus from Mary. We will return to other argu-

6. See Origen, *Contra Celsum* 1:37, 1:67 (*SC* 132:176–80, 264–66).

7. Heinrich M. Köster, "Die Jungfrauengeburt als theologisches Problem seit D. F. Strauß" [The Virgin Birth as a Theological Problem since Strauss], in *Jungfrauengeburt gestern und heute*, ed. H. J. Brosch and J. Hasenfuss, Mariologische Studien 4 (Essen: Hans Driewer, 1969), 40. See Gerhard L. Müller, *Maria: Die Frau im Heilsplan Gottes* [Mary: The Woman in God's Plan of Salvation], Mariologische Studien 15 (Regensburg: Friedrich Pustet, 2002), 122f.

ments from Strauss later. The theses of this author are typically idealistic, inasmuch as they eliminate the importance of the historical event, which is fundamental for Christian revelation.

(2) Adolf von Harnack, the most famous representative of liberal Protestantism in the nineteenth century, held that the origin of belief in the virgin birth was in the *Christian reading of Isaiah 7:14 LXX*. Unlike Strauss, Harnack rules out an origin from pagan myth: the most ancient tradition of Christianity is free from such myths. Instead it would be necessary to look for an origin in the Judaism of the time, in an interpretation of Isaiah 7:14. Such an interpretation would have taken place with Matthew and Luke, while the oldest New Testament texts (Paul, Mark) would not have presented it. Harnack contends that the first proclamation of the primitive community would have taken into consideration only the time between the Baptism of Jesus and Pentecost. Even John would not have been a clear witness. Moreover, in Harnack the idea of the God-man would not depend on the virgin birth. The theories of preexistence and of the virginal origin of Jesus would be two distinct (and mutually contrary) attempts to uncover the mystery of Jesus. Attributing a virginal origin to Jesus would be the fruit of a post-paschal elogy.[8]

Such an explanation clashes with a difficulty—namely, the Jewish exegesis of Isaiah 7:14. We do not find contemporaneous sources that interpret the text of Isaiah as a reference to the virgin birth of the Messiah. It is obvious that Isaiah's prophecy is not the starting point for the infancy narratives, but vice versa: in order to accept the already existing message of the virgin birth of Jesus, the narratives refer to the Old Testament, which prepares for what happens in the New Testament. If the historical message had not existed, it would have been counterproductive to add to the difficulties that already existed vis-à-vis the Jews because of the divinity of Jesus.

8. On Harnack, see inter alia Anton Ziegenaus, "Die Jungfrauengeburt im Apostolischen Glaubensbekenntnis: Ihre Interpretation bei Adolf von Harnack" [The Virgin Birth in the Apostles' Creed: Its Interpretation by Adolf von Harnack], in *Divergenzen in der Mariologie: Zur ökumenischen Diskussion um die Mutter Jesu*, ed. H. Petri, Mariologische Studien 7 (Regensburg: Pustet, 1989), 35–55; Ziegenaus, *Maria in der Heilsgeschichte*, 236f.

(3) To explain the New Testament message on the virgin birth of Jesus, the liberal literature proposed the most varied hypotheses;[9] the only "hypothesis" it absolutely excluded was that of historical truth. A particularly drastic attempt was made, for example, by a certain H. E. G. Paulus, according to whom someone would have come to Mary and made her a mother; and Mary would have considered him the archangel Gabriel.[10]

With Strauss a turning point arrived, conjecturing a pagan influence on faith in the virgin birth of Jesus. The willingness to propose this was rather strange, since it meant accepting a reproach made by opponents of early Christianity: that Christians had adopted a myth that no one took seriously any more, even within paganism itself. For example, Herman Gunkel (1903), like Trypho, thought of the *influence of the Greek myth of carnal union between gods and human women.* Eduard Meyer, in a commentary on the Gospels widely used among Protestants (1924), stated that according to Matthew and Luke the divinity himself had mated with Mary to make her pregnant. Such an account would find its model in the stories of heroes, considered sons of a god and a human woman.[11]

These hypotheses met considerable opposition within their own liberal environment, because the primitive church did not really offer an atmosphere inclined to the acceptance of pagan myths. Moreover, the Holy Spirit is not the father of Jesus, but instead he causes a creative act, similar to the creation of the world in Genesis 1:2 (Lk 1:35). Justin makes this point in his polemic against Trypho, and the eleventh synod of Toledo (675) formulated expressly that the Holy Spirit is not the father of Jesus.[12] While myth speaks of a mating, the gospel account indicates a creative act by the Holy Spirit.

Another difference is that between the being of Jesus, God and

9. See Albert Schweitzer, *Geschichte der Leben-Jesu-Forschung* [The History of Research into the Life of Jesus], 9th ed. (1913; repr. Tübingen: Mohr, 1984); Italian trans., *Storia della ricerca sulla vita di Gesù* (Brescia: Paideia, 1986); English trans.: *The Quest of the Historical Jesus* (Minneapolis: Fortress, 2001).

10. See Ziegenaus, *Maria in der Heilsgeschichte*, 233.

11. See Pozo, "La consagración a los Corazones de Jesús y María en Juan Pablo II," 274f.; Pozo, *María, nueva Eva*, 290f.

12. DH 533.

man, and the being of the heroes who were half-god and half-man (that is, neither god nor man, but a mix).

(4) Since the theory of Hellenistic myth appeared too coarse, the *theory of Egyptian myth*, developed by Martin Dibelius (1932),[13] had a greater effect and still does today.[14] Dibelius argued that both Philo and Paul had recognized the influence of the Holy Spirit in the birth of a son without the involvement of the husband. The example of Sarah in the Letter to the Galatians (Gal 4:23–31) would be such a case, wherein the son of the slave woman is contrasted to the son of the free woman, and the physical paternity of Abraham would be almost denied. However, such a case would not be "myth," because it would not involve a physical mating.

Philo speaks of the "virginal" soul, one in which virtue is generated. He calls Sarah a "virgin" in an allegorical exegesis that affirms the importance of a conscience unhindered by sensual desires.[15] Dibelius thinks he has found the idea of the virgin birth here, but obviously this is only a moral allegory.

As the principal evidence for his theory, the author presents a text of Plutarch (Greek historian, †120 A.D.): according to an Egyptian doctrine, "It is not impossible that the spirit of a god may approach a woman to generate seeds of fecundity in her; but a man cannot have any carnal union or intercourse with a goddess."[16] According to Dibelius, here we can find the idea of a spiritual generation by means of the spirit (*pneûma*) of a god. This concept, he says, would have been able to influence the Jewish religion, as in Philo and Paul.

This interpretation clashes with the fact that Judaism has always held Abraham to be the bodily father of Isaac. This also applies to the Pauline passages questioned by Dibelius (Rm 4:18f and Gal 4:22). Yet the "Egyptian" idea mentioned by Plutarch does not seem to

13. Martin Dibelius, *Jungfrauensohn und Krippenkind* [Virgin's Son and Child in the Cradle] (Heidelberg; Carl Winter, 1932). See F. Hahn, "Dibelius," in *ML* 2:186f.; Pozo, "La consagración a los Corazones de Jesús y María en Juan Pablo II," 275–78; Pozo, *María, nueva Eva*, 291–94.

14. See, e.g., Wolfgang Pannenberg, *Systematische Theologie* (Göttingen: Vandenhoeck and Ruprecht, 1991), 2:358. English trans.: *Systematic Theology*, vol. 2 (Grand Rapids, Mich.: Eerdmans, 1994).

15. Especially Philo, *De Cherubim* 50.

16. Plutarch, *Numa* 4.6, cited in Pozo, "La consagración a los Corazones de Jesús y María en Juan Pablo II," 275f.; Pozo, *María, nueva Eva*, 291f.

show a real spiritual influence as such, but a bodily mating, as the second part of the quotation (goddess with man) and the technical term "approach" show.

(5) Hans von Campenhausen, author of a monograph devoted to the virgin birth in the early church (1962), examines specialized works on Egyptian theology, with the illuminating result that there is nothing in them to explain the virgin birth of Jesus. The theologian instead proposes the *theory of surpassing* (*Überbietungstopos*): it looks at the action of God in taking away the sterility of Old Testament women and of Elizabeth, mother of John the Baptist. In order to attribute more to Jesus, the virgin birth was invented so that the Old Testament example could be surpassed.[17]

This, however, faces the difficulty that Luke did not invent the "material" of the infancy narrative and that the same basic statements are also reported by Matthew.

(6) Ethelbert Stauffer (1957) proposes the *apologetical theory*: Christians could have invented the virgin birth to protect Jesus from the Jewish accusation of being an illegitimate son.[18]

On the contrary, the text of Mark 6:3 ("son of Mary") to which Stauffer points, assumes the death of Joseph (and probably constitutes an allusion to the virgin birth). The rabbinical texts cited by Stauffer do not seem to prove the thesis, even if we know from the testimony of Celsus (c. 180) that such Jewish claims circulated.

(7) A *biological objection* against the virgin birth is supported sometimes by the fact that a parthenogenesis (as happens in certain invertebrates and lower plants) would produce a daughter because Mary possesses the sexual chromosomes XX (and not XY like a male).

This alleged scientific argument forgets that the virgin birth of Jesus is not an event resulting from biology, but traces back to the intervention of God for whom "nothing is impossible" (Lk 1:37) as

17. Hans F. von Campenhausen, *Die Jungfrauengeburt in der Theologie der Alten Kirche* [The Virgin Birth in the Theology of the Early Church] (Heidelberg: Carl Winter, 1962), 20f. See Pozo, "La consagración a los Corazones de Jesús y María en Juan Pablo II," 278f.; Pozo, *María, nueva Eva*, 294f.; Ziegenaus, *Maria in der Heilsgeschichte*, 239.

18. Ethelbert Stauffer, *Jesus: Gestalt und Geschichte* (Bern: Francke, 1957), 22–24; English trans., *Jesus and His Story* (London: SCM, 1960). See Pozo, "La consagración a los Corazones de Jesús y María en Juan Pablo II," 279–82; Pozo, *María, nueva Eva*, 295–98.

long as it is not self-contradictory. The modality of the virgin birth we can calmly leave to the purposes of divine wisdom.[19]

These theories attempting to explain the New Testament message of the virgin birth of Jesus in a rationalist manner are so diverse that they cancel one another out. Various authors opposed to the doctrine of the church do not manage to explain away the origin of this message present in the Gospel (Wilhelm Bousset, Alfred Loisy).[20]

Nevertheless, since the 1960s rationalist theories have made inroads within the Catholic Church. The "Dutch Catechism" of 1966 avoided speaking of the "Virgin," and one of the authors of that book (Piet Schoonenberg) holds that the virginity of Mary (as distinguished from the Immaculate Conception and the Assumption) is not a dogma *de fide definita*.[21] Obviously, this is forgetting that dogma is usually proclaimed by the ordinary magisterium, especially in the creeds. Hans Urs von Balthasar was able to ask (in 1967), in the face of various attempts to "explain" the virginity of Mary from mythology:

> Are we dealing here with an event in the Egyptian and Hellenistic world, and not in the strict world of Judaism? Are we supposed to imagine ourselves back in an age when it was thought that the ancient Greek mysteries provided the model for the beliefs of the early Church—an age that is well and truly past? Are Catholic theologians becoming so blind that they can no longer see that the conception of Mary as a virgin mother is built into the very fabric of Christian dogma? Or are we to begin trying to distinguish between "theological" and "historical" truth in a religion that is concerned precisely with incarnation and therefore with the historical truth of its central content of belief?[22]

19. On this issue, see Pozo, "La consagración a los Corazones de Jesús y María en Juan Pablo II," 283f.; Pozo, *María, nueva Eva*, 299f.; Perrella, *Maria, Vergine e Madre*, 111–14; see also, analogously, Thomas Aquinas, *ST* III, q. 28, a. 1, ad 5.

20. See Köster, "Die Jungfrauengeburt," 46–48; Ziegenaus, "Jungfräulichkeitsgelübte" [Vow of Virginity], in *ML* 3:478.

21. See Pozo, "La consagración a los Corazones de Jesús y María en Juan Pablo II," 267; Pozo, *María, nueva Eva*, 284; Miguel Ponce Cuéllar, *María, Madre del Redentor y Madre de la Iglesia* [Mary, Mother of the Redeemer and Mother of the Church], 2nd ed. (Barcelona: Herder, 2001), 342f.; Perrella, *Maria, Vergine e Madre*, 10f.

22. Hans Urs von Balthasar, *The Moment of Christian Witness* (New York: Newman, 1969), 55.

The Dogmatic Character of the *Virginitas ante partum*

The dogmatic character of Mary's virginity before giving birth is already clear from the creeds, in which it is evidenced as early as the second century.[23] "From the first formulations of her faith, the church has confessed that Jesus was conceived solely by the power of the Holy Spirit in the womb of the Virgin Mary, affirming also the corporeal aspect of this event: Jesus was conceived 'by the Holy Spirit without human seed' [DH 503, Lateran Synod of 649]. The Fathers see in the virginal conception the sign that it truly was the Son of God who came in a humanity like our own."[24]

Without a doubt, the dogmatic status of this truth is *de fide divina et catholica*. Irenaeus, in the second century, affirms: those who hold Jesus to be the son of Joseph (and not of virginal conception) are excluding themselves from the kingdom of God.[25]

In our days, too, the church defends the truth of the virginal conception of Jesus; this is demonstrated by the Second Vatican Council,[26] the "Credo of the People of God" by Paul VI (1968),[27] the measures taken in regard to the Dutch Catechism,[28] and the Catechism of the Catholic Church, among others.

The Theological Significance of the Virginal Origin of Jesus

Particularly today, it is important to highlight the significance of the virgin birth.

(1) First it emphasizes that only *God takes the initiative* for the Incarnation. "Mary's virginity manifests God's absolute initiative in the Incarnation."[29]

23. See *CCC* 496.

24. *CCC* 496.

25. *Adversus haereses* III,21:1 and 21:9 (*SC* 211:398–400, 426).

26. *LG* 55f.

27. N. 14: Justo Collantes, ed., *La fede della Chiesa Cattolica: Le idee e gli uomini nei documenti dottrinali del Magistero* [The Faith of the Catholic Church: Ideas and Men in the Doctrinal Documents of the Magisterium] (Vatican City: Libreria Editrice Vaticana, 1993), 976f.

28. See Pozo, "La consagración a los Corazones de Jesús y María en Juan Pablo II," 271; Pozo, *María, nueva Eva*, 288f.

29. *CCC* 503.

(2) Moreover, the virgin birth points to a *new beginning* in salvation history. "Jesus is conceived by the Holy Spirit in the Virgin Mary's womb because he is the *New Adam*, who inaugurates the new creation."[30]

(3) The origin of Jesus as a *new birth* prepares the way for the gift of divine sonship in Baptism. If we read John 1:13 in the singular,[31] the virgin birth becomes a prototype for the coming of new life "from above"; but, even if it is read in the plural, the gift of new life is described along the lines of the virgin birth.[32] "By his virginal conception, Jesus, the New Adam, ushers in *the new birth* of children adopted in the Holy Spirit through faith.... Participation in the divine life arises 'not of blood nor of the will of the flesh nor of the will of man, but of God' (Jn 1:13). The acceptance of this life is virginal because it is entirely the Spirit's gift to man."[33] Tertullian affirms, "The author of the new birth had to be born in a new way."[34]

The idea of the new birth is tied to the elimination of original sin, which is absent in Jesus. Since the coming of Jesus takes us back to the grace of paradise, bringing it to fulfillment, the transmission of original sin stops. The idea that the virginal origin of Jesus checks the transmission of original sin is not well received in the thought of Origen and Augustine,[35] but in itself it is valid.

(4) The virginal conception underscores the *divinity of Jesus Christ.*[36] At times it is said that (theoretically), if he had been born of the marital union of Joseph and Mary, Jesus could have still been the eternal son of God.[37] This explanation fails to remember

30. *CCC* 504.

31. See "References to the Virgin Birth," in chapter 1.

32. See René Laurentin, *A Short Treatise on the Virgin Mary* (Washington, N.J.: Ave Maria Institute, 1991), 316.

33. *CCC* 505.

34. Tertullian, *De carne Christi* 17.2 (*SC* 216, 280).

35. See Manfred Hauke, *Heilsverlust in Adam: Stationen griechischer Erbsündenlehre; Irenäus—Origenes—Kappadozier* [Salvation Lost in Adam: Stages of Greek Teaching on Original Sin; Irenaeus, Origen, the Cappadocians] (Paderborn: Bonifatius, 1993), 28f., 407. Augustine holds that concupiscence present in the conjugal act would transmit original sin. In this a clear idea of the privative character of original sin is lacking (as a privation of original grace), something that has been highlighted since St. Anselm.

36. See *CCC*, n. 496.

37. For example, Joseph Ratzinger, *Introduction to Christianity*, 2nd ed. (San Francisco: Ignatius,

the inseparable nexus between the divine sonship of Jesus and the fact that his human nature came only from Mary. The virginity of Mary shows that "Jesus has only God as Father [see Lk 2:48–49]."[38] This tie is not of a metaphysical character in the strict sense, but "fitting," as Thomas affirms, so that the dignity of God the Father is not passed to Joseph.[39]

(5) While the first four reasons indicated highlight the significance of the divine part, we also need to emphasize the part of Mary. The virginity of Mary, besides the bodily constitutive element, implies *total giving to* God. "Mary is a virgin because her virginity is *the sign of her faith* 'unadulterated by any doubt,' and of her undivided gift of herself to God's will."[40]

With this perspective before us, the virginity of Mary also becomes an example for couples and for the whole church, which is described as "Virgin" in a figurative sense ever since the era of the fathers (see, even earlier, 2 Cor 11:2). Vatican II recalls this perspective: the church is "mother" and also "a virgin, who keeps the faith given to her by her Spouse whole and entire. Imitating the mother of her Lord, and by the power of the Holy Spirit, she keeps with virginal purity an entire faith, a firm hope and a sincere charity."[41]

VIRGINITAS IN PARTU

The First Patristic References

In the historical overview, we have already seen the belief that the birth of Jesus does not destroy the virginity of his mother.[42] This

2004), 274–75, states this, even if in this context he is defending the virgin birth. This passage was misused by a few opponents of the dogma, and Ratzinger himself (after a criticism from von Balthasar) made a certain retraction: there is a distinction between the ontological level and the biological. "This should not be used to deny that, despite the distinction of levels, a deep, even an indissoluble correspondence exists between the two levels, between Jesus' unity of person with the eternal Son of the eternal Father and the earthly fatherlessness of the man Jesus. Yet I admit that I did not make the point clearly enough"; Ratzinger, *Daughter Zion: Meditations on the Church's Marian Belief* (San Francisco: Ignatius Press, 1983), 51.

38. *CCC* 503.

39. *ST* III, q. 28, a. 1.

40. *CCC* 506.

41. *LG* 64.

42. See, with further bibliography, Salvatore M. Perrella, OSM, "Il parto verginale di Maria

conviction is evidenced widely in the second century in various apocryphal writings (such as the Protoevangelium of James). Labor pains are also excluded, because they are seen as consequences of original sin (at first in the NT apocryphal writing "The Odes of Solomon,"[43] and with reference to Genesis 3:16). We can probably find an allusion as early as Ignatius of Antioch, according to whom "the virginity of Mary and her giving birth" (and the death of the Lord) are "three mysteries shouting aloud, fulfilled in the silence of God."[44] "As for Mary's giving birth, this cannot be reduced to the virginal conception, given that Ignatius speaks of three mysteries. It is not said expressly that the birth is virginal, but that qualification is implicit inasmuch as the text speaks of a mysterious event."[45]

Irenaeus cites a prophecy that speaks of the "daughter of Zion": "Before she was in labor she gave birth; before her pain came upon

---

nel dibattito teologico contemporaneo (1962–1994): Magistero—Esegesi—Teologia" [The Virginal Delivery of Mary in Contemporary Theological Debate (1962–1994): Magisterium, Exegesis, Theology], *Marianum* 56 (1994): 95–213; Perrella, *Maria, Vergine e Madre: La verginità feconda di Maria tra fede, storia e teologia* [Mary, Virgin and Mother: The Fruitful Virginity of Mary, in the Faith, History, and Theology] (Cinisello Balsamo: San Paolo, 2003), 199–212; Peter Damian M. Fehlner, *La verginità nel parto* [Virginity in Childbirth] (Castelpetroso: Casa Mariana Editrice, 1995); Arthur B. Calkins, "Il concepimento e la nascita verginale di Gesù: Verità di fede ricevuta e trasmessa dalla Chiesa Cattolica" [The Virginal Conception and Birth of Jesus: Truths of Faith Received and Transmitted by the Church], *Immaculata Mediatrix* 4 (2004): 181–209; Hauke, "Die 'virginitas in partu': Akzentsetzungen in der Dogmengeschichte" ["Virginity in Childbirth": Emphases in the History of Dogmas], in *"Geboren aus der Jungfrau Maria": Klarstellungen*, ed. A. Ziegenaus, Mariologische Studien 19 (Regensburg: Friedrich Pustet, 2007), 88–131.

43. *Canto* 19, in *Gli Apocrifi del Nuovo Testamento* vol. 1, part 1, ed. Mario Erbetta (Casale Monferrato: Marietti, 1969), 636f. See Georg Söll, *Storia dei dogmi mariani* [History of Marian Dogmas] (Rome: Libreria Ateneo Salesiano, 1981), §2; Pozo, "La consagración a los Corazones de Jesús y María en Juan Pablo II," 256; Pozo, *María, nueva Eva*, 272f.; Edouard Cothenet, "La virginité de Marie dans les apocryphes" [The Virginity of Mary in the Apocrypha], *Études mariales* 53 (1998): 53–68; Ponce Cuéllar, *María*, 362; Hauke, "Die 'Virginitas in partu,'" 98–100.

44. *In Eph.* 19:1, in *Die Apostolischen Väter*, 7th ed., ed. J. A. Fischer (Darmstadt: Wissenschaftliche Buchgesellschaft, 1976), 157. See also "The First Mariological Witnesses of the Tradition," in chapter 2.

45. Stefano De Fiores, *Maria sintesi di valori: Storia culturale della mariologia* [Mary, Synthesis of Values: Cultural History of Mariology] (Cinisello Balsamo: San Paolo, 2005), 110. See also José A. de Aldama, *María en la Patrística de los siglos I y II* [Mary in in the Fathers of the First and Second Centuries] (Madrid: Editorial Católica, 1970), 198; Ferdinando Bergamelli, "La verginità di Maria nelle Lettere di Ignazio di Antiochia" [The Virginity of Mary in the Letters of Ignatius of Antioch], *Theotokos* 9 no. 2 (2001): 322f. The exegete Klaus Berger, *Theologiegeschichte des Urchristentums* [History of Early Christian Theology], 2nd ed. (Tübingen-Basel: Francke, 1995), 309f., holds that virginity during birth is clearly presupposed in this text, making it the oldest affirmation in tradition on this topic. Inasmuch as it deals with the "hiding" of the birth (from the view of the powers of the world), that tradition would be found in Luke and Matthew.

her she was delivered of a son" (Is 66:7). "These words," comments Irenaeus, "point to the delivery of the Virgin as an unexpected event."[46] Here, too, a reference to virginity during birth seems implicit. Immediately before, Irenaeus cites Isaiah 7:14 LXX, according to which "the virgin shall conceive and bear a son" (the Hebrew text, literally, states that the *alma* is "conceiving and giving birth"). The fact that both the conception and the birth are attributed to the "virgin" is often noted by the fathers and supports faith in the virginal birth. Irenaeus, in a passage already discussed,[47] compares the virgin birth with Baptism: Jesus "opens in a pure manner a pure womb, that womb that regenerates men in God and which He himself made pure."[48]

Besides Genesis 3:16 and Isaiah 7:14 (and the application of Isaiah 66:7), we can also pay attention to Luke 2:7: it is Mary herself who wraps Jesus in swaddling clothes and lays him in a manger.[49]

Biblical References?

Until about twenty years ago, in the writing of manuals no one thought that the New Testament contained direct attestation of Mary's virginity during birth. However, there are a few recent explanations that consider just this prospect possible.[50] Starting in 1978, Ignace de la Potterie considered it possible to recognize the virginal birth in the singular version of John 1:13 and in Luke 1:35.[51] The ex-

46. Irenaeus, *Demonstratio* 54 (*SC* 62:115).

47. Regarding the Marian analogy in Baptism, see p. 81.

48. *Adversus haereses* IV. 33.11 (*SC* 100:830). On Irenaeus, see de Aldama, *María en la patristica,* 216–24, 300–309, 318–29; Rodrigo Polanco, "La mariologia di Sant'Ireneo" [The Mariology of St. Irenaeus], *Theotokos* 9 (2001): 382f.; De Fiores, *Dizionario* 2:1786f.; Hauke, "Die 'Virginitas in partu,'" 100f.

49. The observation is based on Jerome, *Adv. Helvidium* 8 (PL 23:201B–C). See Aristide Serra, "... e lo avvolse in fasce ..." (Lk 2:7b). Un segno da decodificare," in *E c'era la Madre di Gesù: Saggi di esegesi biblico-mariana (1978–1988)* [And the Mother of Jesus Was There ... Essays in Biblical-Marian Exegesis] (Milan and Rome: CENS and Marianum, 1989), 253–57.

50. See Hauke, "Die 'Virginitas in partu,'" 90–98.

51. See "References to the Virgin Birth," in chapter 1; Ignace de la Potterie, "Il parto verginale del Verbo incarnato: 'Non ex sanguinibus ... sed ex Deo natus est'" [The Virginal Birth of the Incarnate Word: "Born not of Blood ... but of God"], *Marianum* 45, no. 130 (1983); de la Potterie, *Maria nel mistero dell'alleanza* [Mary in the Mystery of the Covenant] (Genoa: Marietti, 1988), 118–43; Serra, "Vergine: Testimonianza biblica," in *NDM*, 2:1431–33, 1445–49; Perrella, "Il parto verginale di Maria," 153–74; Perrella, *Maria, Vergine e Madre,* 101–5.

pression that Jesus Christ was born "not of bloods" (*ouk ex haimáton)* (Jn 1:13) would mean being born without the shedding of blood, considered a cause of ritual impurity (Lv 12:5, 12:7; Ez 16:6, 16:9). De la Potterie then adds his interpretation of Luke 1:35, which corresponds to an exegesis already present in the fathers.[52] He reads the verse as follows: "He who is to be born holy will be called Son of God" (*tò gennómenon hágion kletesetai huiòs theoû*) (while it is usually translated, e.g., in the RSV2CE, "the child to be born will be called holy, the Son of God"). Among the arguments presented is the text's rhythmic correspondence, which is also evident in the Vulgate.[53] The famous biblical scholar's interpretation of John 1:13 and Luke 1:35 can boast good arguments and, to our knowledge, has not been seriously contradicted.[54] Pointing to a lack of ritual impurity is no doubt foreign to the contemporary mentality of the Western world, but corresponds very well to the cultural environment of the Gospels and of the primitive church. If the indicated reading is right, then Mary's virginity during birth would find a basis immediately in the most central passages of the Gospels on the mystery of the Incarnation.

The Road to the Creed

At the end of the second century, conviction regarding Mary's virginal birth is already widespread, but not yet generally supported. Tertullian thinks that Mary lost her virginal integrity during the birth: "She was a virgin in regard to man, but not in regard to birth."[55] In this context, the theologian is confronting the Gnostics, according to whom Jesus had a heavenly body and only passed through Mary as

52. As in Cyril of Jerusalem, *Cat.* 12.32 (PG 33:765A). See Joseph M. Bover, "'Quod nascetur (ex te) sanctum vocabitur Filius Dei' (Lc 1,35)," *Biblica* 1 (1920): 92–94; *Estudios Eclesiásticos* 8 (1929): 318–92.

53. Bover, "'Quod nascetur (ex te) sanctum.'" See Ignace de la Potterie, SJ, "Il parto verginale del Verbo incarnato: 'Non ex sanguinibus ... sed ex Deo natus est'" [The Virginal Birth of the Incarnate Word: "Born not of Blood ... but of God"], *Marianum* 45, no. 130 (1983): 170–74.

54. His interpretation of Jn 1:13, in good harmony with ancient tradition, seems to have greater plausibility, while the position of de la Potterie in regard to Lk 1:35 was criticized by Silverio Zedda, "Lc. 1,35b, 'Colui che nascerà santo sarà chiamato Figlio di Dio'" [Lk 1:35b: "He Who Is to Be Born Will Be Called Son of God"], *Rivista Biblica* 33 no. 1 (1985): 29–43, 165–89.

55. *De carne Christi* 23:2 (*CChr. SL* 2.914).

through a channel. However, according to Exodus 13:2, it is birth that opens the maternal womb.

Clement of Alexandria (from 215 on) maintains that "the greater part" of the people, "as it seems," thinks that Mary endured labor, but that "some" (as in the Protoevangelium of James) state that she was found to be a virgin after the birth also; Clement himself accepts the message of the Protoevangelium.[56] Origen, too, while more skeptical toward the apocrypha, supports virginity during birth.[57]

In the fourth century we find faith in the virginity of Mary, including during birth, throughout the church.[58] In Epiphanius and Athanasius the term *aeiparthénos*, "ever Virgin," appears for the first time. There is only one clear difference: one school of thought held that the uterus remained closed during birth (e.g., Jerome and Augustine), while another school (older) presupposes the *apertio vulvae* (for this, some use the image of a pearl that comes from a shell without destroying it, e.g., Ephrem). The position of the church received its definitive form in the wake of a denial of the virginity *in partu*. Jovinian, an ex-monk, held that this truth was a Manichean doctrine and took up a formula similar to that of Tertullian: *virgo a viro, non virgo a partu*.[59] The motivation for this denial was in argument against the preference given in the church for the virginal life. According to Jovinian, there was no difference of spiritual degree between matrimony and consecrated virginity.[60]

The great theologians of the time took to the field against this denial (around 385), especially Ambrose, Jerome, and Augustine. A synod of Milan, in 393, organized by St. Ambrose and preceded by

56. *Stromata* VII 16:93 (*GCS* 17:66).

57. Even if the reference to *apertio vulvae* (Ex 13:2)—*In Lc. hom.* 14.7–8 (*SC* 87:226)—is seen by some interpreters as disputed by other texts that affirm the permanence of the virginity during birth: *In Lev. hom.* 8:2 (*SC* 287:12–14); *In Mt. comm. ser.* 25 (*GCS* 38, 42). See Georg Söll, *Storia dei dogmi mariani* [History of Marian Dogmas] (Rome: Libreria Ateneo Salesiano, 1981), 87; Hauke, "Die 'Virginitas in partu,'" 103f.

58. See de Aldama, *Virgo Mater: Estudios de teología patristica* [Virgin Mother: Studies in Patristic Theology] (Granada: Facultad de Teología, 1963), 19–49; Söll, *Storia dei dogmi mariani*, 97–108, 139, 142f.; Ziegenaus, "Jungfräulichkeitsgelübte" [Vow of Virginity], *ML* 3:471–75; Ponce Cuéllar, *María*, 362–68; Hauke, "Die 'Virginitas in partu,'" 104–11.

59. See Jerome, *Apologeticum ad Pammachium* 2 (PL 22:494A; *CSEL* 54:351).

60. See the sources reported in Jerome, *Contra Iovinianum* (PL 95:211–338; the fragments are collected suitably in *TU* 17/2:1–31).

a synod in Rome, rejected the doctrine of Jovinian, pointing to the Creed: the formulation *ex Maria Virgine* also implies the virginal birth;[61] this interpretation then becomes general. As biblical references Isaiah 7:14 (the Virgin shall give birth) and Luke 2:7 (Mary herself prepares the swaddling clothes for the child) are mentioned. Moreover, to illustrate the possibility of a virginal birth, various biblical analogies are mentioned: especially the glory of God that comes out of the temple through closed doors (Ez 44:2: Ambrose, Jerome) and the entrance of the risen Christ into the house of the apostles through closed doors (Jn 20:26: Augustine). A year earlier, in 392, a synod at Capua had confronted Bonosus, bishop of Serdica, who had denied Mary's virginity after the birth. The sixteenth centenary of this synod, in 1992, was the occasion of a major scholarly conference and a far-reaching intervention by John Paul II, which was also dedicated to the virginity *in partu*.[62] We will return to this later.

The Council of Chalcedon (451) is also named among subsequent interventions of the Magisterium; it explicitly recognized the letter of Pope Leo to Flavian, Patriarch of Constantinople, in which the supreme pontiff professes Mary's virginity, also during birth, with clarity.[63]

We find a solemn definition of the perpetual virginity of Mary, with particular reference to the *virginitas in partu*, at the *Lateran Synod of 649*, called by Pope Martin I against monothelitism:

If anyone does not, following the holy Fathers, confess properly and truly that holy Mary, ever virgin and immaculate, is Mother of God, since in this latter age she conceived really and truly, without human seed from the Holy

61. See Ambrose, Ep. 42 (PL 16:1124–29). Probably the error of Jovinian had already been rejected a little earlier by a synod at Rome in the same year (393): de Aldama, *Virgo Mater*, 52–57; Hauke, "Die 'Virginitas in partu,'" 106f.

62. Giovanni Liccardo, Franco Ruotolo, and Sergio Tanzarella, eds., *Atti del Convegno Internazionale di studi Mariologici, Capua 19–24 Maggio 1992* [Acts of the International Mariological Study Meeting, Capua, May 19–24, 1992], Torre del Greco (Naples): Istituto Superiore di Scienza Religiose, 1993.

63. Giuseppe Alberigo et al., eds., *Conciliorum Oecumenicorum Decreta* [*COD*], 3rd ed. (Bologna: Istituto per le Scienze Religiose, 1973), 85. See Hauke, "Die 'Virginitas in partu,'" 111. Leo I, 449, Letter to Flavian: Mary bore Jesus, "her virginity ... undiminished" (DH 291). See also the letter to Julian of Cos the same year: Jesus is born "of the inviolate Virgin, ... because he was brought forth from the womb of the Mother in such a way that her fertility gave birth while her virginity remained, nevertheless, his flesh was not of another nature than our own" (DH 299).

Spirit, God the Word himself, who before the ages was born of God the Father, and gave birth to him without corruption (*incorruptibiliter)*, her virginity remaining equally inviolate after his birth, let him be condemned.[64]

In this case we are not dealing with an ecumenical Council in the precise sense, even if its subsequent reception raises it nearly to that level. But if the supreme pontiff, during a synod, proposes a doctrine of faith subject to anathema, as well as a *conditio sine qua non* of communion with the Roman Church, it will be difficult to consider it other than a solemn *ex cathedra* definition.[65]

Martin I, in his allocution before the synod, speaks against Theodore of Pharan according to whom the Lord would have come out "in an incorporeal way" (*asomátos*) from his mother's womb or that he would have only appeared to walk on the waters. The pope thus rejects a Docetist interpretation of the virgin birth; it is a true bodily reality (thus a true birth), even if it takes place in a miraculous way beyond the capacity of nature (*hypèr fúsin*).[66] The dogmatic definition of 649 is notable because it affirms the miracle of the virgin birth against a Docetist devaluation of the humanity of Jesus. There is no way to deduce Mary's virginity during birth if one starts from an outlook hostile toward the bodily state.

64. DH 503. We also find various magisterial documents that mention the fact, such as the Synod of Orange in 529 (DH 368: Jesus "opening the Mother's womb by his birth and yet not damaging the virginity of the Mother by the power of the Godhead"); the *Second Council of Constantinople*, 553 (DH 422: "If anyone does not confess ... [that he] was made flesh from Mary, the holy and glorious Mother of God ever Virgin ... *anathema sit*"; see DH 437); Pope Pelagius I, 557 (DH 442: "I believe and profess ... [that Jesus was] born preserving the integrity of the Mother's virginity: since she bore him while remaining a Virgin just as she conceived him as a Virgin"). See also, afterward, the Sixteenth Synod of Toledo, 693 (DH 571).

65. See M. Hurley, "Born Incorruptly: The Third Canon of the Lateran Council (A.D. 649)," *Heythrop Journal* 2 (1961): 217–36; de Aldama, *Virgo Mater*, 101–27; Pozo, "La consagración a los Corazones de Jesús y María en Juan Pablo II," 259; Pozo, *María, nueva Eva*, 275f.; Perrella, *Maria, Vergine e Madre*, 201f.; De Fiores, *Dizionario* 2:1790; Hauke, "Die 'Virginitas in partu,'" 112–15. The fact of the dogmatic definition is left silent in Galot, *Maria, La donna*, 158f., while the erroneous interpretation of Karl Rahner only considers the event a provincial synod with no dogmatic decisions: Karl Rahner, "Virginitas in partu: Ein Beitrag zum Problem der Dogmenentwicklung und Überlieferung" [Virginity in Childbirth: A Contribution on the Problem of the Development and Transmission of Dogma], in *Schriften zur Theologie* (Einsiedeln, etc.: Benziger, 1960), 4:178f. English trans. "Virginitas in partu," in *Theological Investigations* (Baltimore: Helicon Press, 1966), 4:134–62.

66. Mansi 10:964–66.

The Debate in Modern Times

The Protestant Reformers themselves did not deny the perpetual virginity of Mary. Nevertheless, due to their principles (*solus Christus, sola Scriptura*), the figure of Mary shrank in importance; thus they led the way for the modern dispute that began with the sect of the Unitarians who denied the virginity of Mary along with the Trinity and the divinity of Jesus: Jesus was considered to be the natural son of Joseph. Against this sect, Pope Pius IV reaffirmed the denied doctrines, among which was that of Mary *semper Virgo*, as belonging to the foundations of the faith itself.[67]

Certainly the liturgical witness is important, such as, for example, that of the Roman Canon, cited in *Lumen gentium*: the faithful "must in the first place reverence the memory 'of the glorious ever Virgin Mary, Mother of our God and Lord Jesus Christ.'"[68] With his birth, the Council adds, Jesus "did not diminish His mother's virginal integrity but sanctified it."[69] The *CCC* also points explicitly to Mary's virginity during birth: "The deepening of faith in the virginal motherhood led the Church to confess Mary's real and perpetual virginity even in the act of giving birth to the Son of God made man."[70]

Despite the clear affirmations of the ecclesial Magisterium there is no lack of disputations or interpretations today that subtly deny the content of the dogma. These attempts within the Catholic environment began in 1952 with a book by the Viennese doctor Albert Mitterer, with the strange title *Dogma and Biology of the Holy Family*.[71] According to this author, we must maintain the dogma of the virginity in birth, but this truth has nothing to do with the perma-

67. DH 1880: Mary did "always persist in the integrity of virginity, namely, before giving birth, in giving birth, and perpetually after giving birth." See Pozo, "La consagración a los Corazones de Jesús y María en Juan Pablo II," 260; Pozo, *María, nueva Eva*, 277, with reference to the preceding text from "Denzinger" (ed. 31) n. 993, which presents the whole beginning of the decree: "*quidem non solum diversas haereses profiteri, sed etiam ipsius fidei fondamenta negare praesumant.*"

68. *LG* 52.

69. *LG* 57. On the Council's doctrine, see O'Carroll, *Theotokos*, 361; Juan Luis Bastero, *Virgen singular: La reflexión teológica mariana en el siglo XX* [Singular Virgin: Theological Reflection on Mary in the 20th Century] (Madrid: Rialp, 2001), 77f.; Hauke, "Die 'Virginitas in partu,'" 120–22.

70. *CCC* 499.

71. Albert Mitterer, *Dogma und Biologie der Heiligen Familie* [Dogma and Biology of the Holy Family] (Vienna: Herder, 1952). See Bastero, *Virgen singular*, 60–64.

nence of the hymen or with the lack of labor pains. The birth would have taken place like any other birth. The difference would consist only in the precondition: Mary conceived without the intervention of a human father. Virginity in birth is reduced to virginity before the birth. In 1960, the Holy Office deplored "the crudity of expression and, what is more serious, Mitterer's opening to disassociate himself from the ecclesiastical Tradition and the pious sentiments of the faithful."[72]

In 1960 various theologians took positions on the topic, among them Karl Rahner.[73] He criticized the thesis of Mitterer, inasmuch as it did not distinguish virginity in birth from virginity before the birth. For Rahner, it is necessary to maintain that not only the conception but also the birth corresponded to the virginal maternity of Mary. But it would not be necessary to maintain the permanence of the hymen or freedom from pain. One could say that Mary, free from concupiscence, had positively integrated the suffering of labor, since suffering had become part of her life.[74]

But it does not seem that this thesis reaches to the meaning of the dogma. René Laurentin, for example (from 1960 on), affirms Mary's physical integrity, the absence of pains, and the miraculous character of the event as central elements of the doctrine of the faith; yet he did not clarify the manner of the birth (whether *utero clauso* or *miracolosa dilatione*).[75] Nor does it seem that any really new el-

72. Holy Office, Monitum of July 27, 1960: *Ephemerides Mariologicae* 11 (1961): 138. See Gherardini, *La Madre*, 124; Bastero, *Virgen singular*, 76.

73. Rahner, "Virginitas in partu." A repetition of these theses is found, inter alia, in Gerhard L. Müller, *Nato dalla Vergine Maria* [Born of the Virgin Mary] (Brescia: Morcelliana, 1994), 99–117; also in Müller, *Maria: Die Frau im Heilsplan Gottes*, 197–212. See also Alessandro M. Apollonio, "Rilievi critici sulla mariologia di Rahner" [Critical Reviews of the Mariology of Rahner], *Fides catholica* 2 (2007): 438–57.

74. Similarly Jean Galot, from 1960 on, defends the thesis of a painful birth with tearing of the hymen. See Galot, "*La verginité de Marie et la naissance de Jésus*" [The Virginity of Mary and the Birth of Jesus], *Nouvelle Revue Théologique* 82 (1960): 449–69; Galot, *Maria, La donna*, 157–75; Hans Urs von Balthasar, *Theodramatik*, vol. 2, part 2 (Einsiedeln: Johannes Verlag, 1978), 304–6 (Italian trans., *Teodrammatica* (Milan: Jaca, 1983), 3:306–9) (which explains the birth with an "anticipated passion"). In this sense, along with Leonardo Boff and Gianni Colzani, *Maria: Mistero di grazia e di fede* [Mary: Mystery of Grace and Faith], 3rd ed. (Cinisello Balsamo: Ed. Paoline, 2006), 212; see also Perrella, *Maria, Vergine e Madre*, 207f.

75. René Laurentin, "Le mystère de la naissance verginale" [The Mystery of the Virgin Birth], *Ephemerides Mariologicae* 10 (1960): 345–74; *A Short Treatise on the Virgin Mary* (Washington, N.J.:

ements have come to the discussion since 1960. The documents of the magisterium do not lend themselves to a spiritualistic interpretation that eliminates the scandal of the physical concreteness of the salvific events. John Paul II, in an allocution given at Capua in 1992, strongly affirms the virginal integrity of Mary with particular clarity, comparing the birth of Christ *ex intacta Virgine* with the resurrection *ex intacto sepulcro.*[76]

The Connection with Mariology as a Whole

To understand the dogma, it is very important to connect it with the fundamental characteristic of Mary, in whom motherhood and virginity are closely united. It is not only a matter of physical facts, but of a bodily reality sustained by a spiritual attitude: to receive the divine Word in her mind (motherhood) and open herself to the creative initiative of God (virginity). Being Virgin was part of the personal character of the Madonna. Mary "realizes bodily what the Church realizes spiritually, namely, virginity in fecundity.... To deny her bodily integrity would be thus to lay hands on the faith of the Church in its sign, ... this *fides incorrupta* of which the *Virgo incorrupta* is the icon, the symbol revealed in the realities of the flesh."[77]

Summarizing the reflections of the fathers, Laurentin shows that the virgin birth of Jesus is connected with the eternal origin of the Son and with his temporal coming in the believing soul. Also interconnected are "the three births of the Word ... he is born of the Father from all eternity, born from the Virgin Mary in time, and born of every Christian soul by faith and baptism."[78]

Ave Maria Institute, 1991), 324–34. See also Pozo, "La consagración a los Corazones de Jesús y María en Juan Pablo II," 256–67; Pozo, *María, nueva Eva*, 272–81; Juan Luis Bastero de Eleizalde, *Mary, Mother of the Redeemer* (Dublin: Four Courts, 2006), 173–82.

76. John Paul II, Homily of May 24, 1992 (*AAS* 85 [1993]: 662–70). See Perrella, "Il parto verginale di Maria," 122–33; Salvatore M. Perrella, *Ecco tua Madre (Gv 19,27): La Madre di Gesù nel magistero di Giovanni Paolo II e nell'oggi della Chiesa e del mondo* [Behold Your Mother (Jn 19:27): The Mother of Jesus in the Magisterium of John Paul II and in the Church and the World Today] (Cinisello Balsamo: San Paolo, 2007), 197–230; Bastero, *Virgen singular,* 81f.; Hauke, "Die 'Virginitas in partu,'" 125–28.

77. Laurentin, *Short Treatise*, 332f.

78. Ibid., 331.

Moreover, the virgin birth shows a connection with the Immaculate Conception.

The preserving grace that exempted Mary from original sin freed her likewise from its principal personal consequences, not only in soul (*concupiscentia*), but in body as well. Mary, the new Eve, the point of departure for the new creation, incurred neither original sin nor the pains promised the sin of the first Eve (Gn 3): the servitude of libido (3:16b), the pains of labor (3:16a), the corruption of the tomb (3:19).... As to childbirth without pain, ... it is paradoxical that it should begin to be contested in the very day when scientific progress is beginning to speak of "painless childbirth" as available to all women. It is surprising that certain theologians and preachers should begin to praise the "crucifying" sufferings of Mary at the Lord's birth, just at the time when obstetrical clinics are most concerned with denouncing the pains of labor as an alienating and dehumanizing myth.[79]

The virginal birth of Jesus is a prelude of the future world, freed from every kind of suffering.

The connection of *virginitas in partu* with the bodily Assumption of Mary was affirmed by Pius XII in the Apostolic Constitution *Munificentissimus Deus* (1950) when the dogma was defined. The pope cites John Damascene: "It was fitting that she, who had kept her virginity intact in childbirth, should keep her own body free from all corruption even after death."[80] The reference to Mary "ever Virgin" also enters into the formula of the definition itself: "We pronounce, declare, and define it to be a divinely revealed dogma: that the Immaculate Mother of God, the ever Virgin Mary, having completed the course of her earthly life, was assumed body and soul into heavenly glory."[81]

In the definition by Martin I of the perpetual virginity of Mary, it was quite clear that he was not teaching a Docetism that eliminated the true motherhood of Mary. To the objection that the virginity *in partu* would suggest a body only in appearance, Thomas Aquinas responds, "To show that His body was real, He was born of a woman. But in order to manifest His Godhead, He was born of a virgin."[82]

79. Ibid., 334.
80. *EE* 6, n. 1951.
81. DH 3903.
82. *ST* III, q. 28, a. 2, ad 2.

VIRGINITAS POST PARTUM

Mary's virginity after giving birth is not found directly in the New Testament. It is rather "the result of a cognizance based on certain biblical indications, and especially of an overall view of the implications of the plan of salvation."[83]

The biblical debate arises from the fact that "brothers" and "sisters" of Jesus are mentioned more than once, for example in the following passage: "Is not this the carpenter's son? Is not his mother called Mary? And are not his brethren James and Joseph and Simon and Judas? And are not all his sisters with us?" (Mt 13:55f.)[84]

To identify the "brothers" of Jesus, three solutions have been proposed: (1) they refer to other children of Mary; (2) they are children of Joseph from a prior marriage; (3) they are cousins of Jesus.

Today's Protestant theology (unlike the Reformers) nearly always interprets the references to "brothers" of Jesus as references to other children of Mary.[85] As it happens, some exegetes who teach in Catholic faculties align themselves with such positions.[86] This explanation was proposed in antiquity (probably) by Tertullian[87] and (especially) by Helvidius (380), who provoked the church's definitive clarification on the topic.[88]

83. Laurentin, *Short Treatise*, 318.

84. See Mt 12:46; Mk 3:31, 6:3; Lk 8:19; Jn 2:12, 7:3, 7:5; Acts 1:14; 1 Cor 9:5; Gal 1:19.

85. See Achim Dittrich, *Protestantische Mariologie-Kritik: Historische Entwicklung bis 1997 und dogmatische Analyse* [Protestant Criticism of Mariology: Historical Development to 1997 and Dogmatic Analysis], Mariologische Studien 11 (Regensburg: Pustet, 1998), 308f. Max Thurian (1921–96) appears as an exception, the most important theologian of the Taizé Community, who became Catholic and was ordained a priest in 1987.

86. Such as Rudolf Pesch, *Das Markusevangelium* (Freiburg im Breisgau: Herder, 2000), 1:322f; Lorenz Oberlinner, *Historische Überlieferung und christologische Aussage: Zur Frage der "Brüder Jesu" in der Synopse* [Historical Tradition and Christological Expression] (Stuttgart: Verlag Katholisches Bibelwerk, 1975), in contrast to Josef Blinzler, *Die Brüder und Schwestern Jesu*, 2nd ed. (Stuttgart: Verlag Katholisches Bibelwerk, 1967). See Leo Scheffczyk, "Exegese und Dogmatik zur virginitas post partum," after *Münchner Theologische Zeitschrift* 28 (1977): 291–301; Ziegenaus, *Maria in der Heilsgeschichte*, 250–59.

87. See Albert Viciano, "Tertullian," in *ML* 6:374; Luigi Gambero, *Mary and the Fathers of the Church: The Blessed Virgin Mary in Patristic Thought*, trans. Thomas Buffer (San Francisco: Ignatius Press, 1999), 65f. The statements were made in an anti-Docetist context, but it is not said expressly that the "brethren" were other children of Mary. See Blinzler, *Die Brüder*, 139–41.

88. Other denials came at the same time from the Antidicomarianites, a sect in Arabia fought by Epiphanius, and from Bonosus of Serdica (= Sofia), refuted by Ambrose. See Galot, *Maria, La donna*, 181f. Jerome's writing against Helvidius is now available in Italian translation: Girolamo,

To evaluate the references to "brothers," one needs to know that Hebrew and Aramaic do not have a specific word to indicate "cousins." The word *ah* (Aramaic *aha*), "brother," is used to indicate generally all the members of the family group. The term *adelphoí* is therefore a translation from the Semitic. Some examples (in the *Nova Vulgata*):

- *"Fratres enim sumus,"* says Abram to Lot, his nephew (Gn 13:8; see Gn 14:14, 14:16).
- Jacob calls himself a *"frater"* of Laban, his uncle (Gn 29:12).
- In 1 Chronicles 23:21, the sons of Kish marry the daughters of Eleazar and are called their *"fratres"*; the text is referring to cousins.[89]

In the New Testament, the "brothers" of Jesus are never called sons of Mary (or of Joseph). The passage in Matthew, cited previously, speaks of "all his sisters" (Mt 13:56). Jerome notes, "No one says 'all' if not for a crowd."[90] Probably it refers to a more numerous group than a single nuclear family. Yet Jesus, in Mark 6:3, is described as *the* son of Mary, with the definite article.

The indication that Jesus is the "first-born" does not imply anything about other possible brothers.[91] But the reference is important because it casts doubt on the theory that the Gospels are talking about other children of Mary, because in Mark 3:21, 3:31–35 and John 7:2–5, the "brothers" act in a dominating manner, and this, in the ancient East, is unthinkable on the part of younger brothers addressing the first-born.

If Jesus had had actual brothers, properly speaking, it would be incomprehensible that he entrusted his mother under the Cross to the Apostle John (Jn 19:26f.) Even if this were a legend (as some lib-

---

La perenne verginità di Maria (contro Elvidio), 2nd ed., ed. Maria Ignazia Danieli, Collana di testi patristici 70 (Rome: Città Nuova, 1996). See also "On the Perpetual Virginity of the Blessed Mary against Helvidius," in St. Jerome, *Dogmatic and Polemical Works*, trans. John N. Hritzu, Fathers of the Church 53 (Washington, D.C.: The Catholic University of America Press, 1965). Giancarlo Rocca, *L'Adversus Helvidium di san Girolamo nel contesto della letteratura ascetico-mariana del secolo IV* (Bern: Peter Lang, 1998).

89. Other examples: Blinzler, *Die Brüder*, 42–44; Laurentin, *Short Treatise*, 322.

90. *Adv. Helvidium* (PL 23:200).

91. See "The Birth of Jesus" in chapter 1.

eral exegetes think), in any case this would represent the conviction of the primitive church that Mary had no other sons.

The names of four brothers are mentioned: James, Joses, Judah, and Simon (Mk 6:3; Mt 13:55: "Joseph," *Iosef* instead of Joses). James appears in the list of witnesses of the encounter with the risen Christ (1 Cor 15:7) and he figures later as head of the Church of Jerusalem (Gal 1:19, 2:9) According to Mark, a woman of the name "Mary, mother of James the younger and of Joses" stood under the Cross (Mk 15:40). This Mary cannot be the mother of Jesus, but is distinguished by means of her sons; she is also called "Mary, mother of Joses" (Mk 15:47) or "Mary, mother of James" (Mk 16:1). It seems that Mark is presupposing an awareness of these sons on the reader's part, and indeed the same names are mentioned already in Mark 6:3 in the same sequence: "James, Joses." In this case it is obvious that they are not other sons of Jesus' mother.

In the "Ecclesiastical History" of Eusebius we find citations drawn from the Palestinian writer Hegesippus (second century) with interesting notes on the primitive church. He recounts that after the death of James, "Simon (son of) Clopas was nominated bishop; everyone preferred him, since he was a second cousin of the Lord" (*Sumeòn ho toû Clopâ katístatai epíscopos, hon proétento pántes, ónta anépsion tou kyríou deúteron*).[92] Clopas (Cleofas) was a brother of Joseph, the husband of Mary.[93] On the other hand, it does not seem that Simon was a brother of James, since he is identified through his father, Clopas. And therefore, the hypothesis of considering James and Joses as sons of Mary, a relative of the mother of Jesus, and of seeing Simon (and Judah) instead as sons of Clopas, brother of Joseph, is well founded. It is not clear how to fit in the "sister" of Mary, present under the Cross together with (or identical to) "Mary of Clopas" (Jn 19:25).

In this setting we cannot develop the philological and historical debate with all its nuances. If we consider only the historical

92. *Hist. eccl.* IV,22:4 (*SC* 31:200). The suggestion from some (Protestant) scholars of connecting the adjective "second" with "bishop" is not very convincing. See Blinzler, *Die Brüder*, 104–7. It is undeniable that Simon is mentioned as a "cousin" of Jesus.

93. *Hist. eccl.* III,11:2 (*SC* 31:118).

data, it does not seem possible to reach any certainty as to whether there were other sons of Mary or not. But for the faith it is enough that the dogmatic fact does not contradict historical knowledge; besides, we find further historical signs that support the position of the church in affirming that Mary had no other sons.

As for the historical setting, the following explanation is offered: since Joseph, after the infancy narratives, does not appear any more as an active figure, it seems very probable that he died before the public activity of Jesus began. After the death of Joseph, Mary was near her relatives; so Jesus grew up together with his cousins, called "brothers" and "sisters" in Aramaic. As Mary, a woman, could not appear in public without a man accompanying her, she turned to her nearest male relatives for this purpose—that is, the "brothers" of Jesus (Mk 3:21, 3:31; see also Jn 2:12; Acts 1:14). The fact that the term "brothers" is used in Greek and not "cousins" is explained by the important position of the cousins of the Lord in the primitive community. Being a "brother" of the Lord himself was a particular honor.

To defend the virginity of Mary after the birth, the Protoevangelium of James presents the thesis that the "brothers" of Jesus are sons of Joseph from a first marriage. In that case they would be true brothers (or rather stepbrothers), since Joseph is the legal father of Jesus. This is the solution that prevails in the East. Nevertheless, we find the opinion of Theodoret of Cyrus and of John Chrysostom who (independently of Hegesippus) consider them cousins of the Lord and reject the theory of stepbrothers.[94]

Jerome prepared the way in the West for the prevailing thesis, that the "brothers" are not stepbrothers, but cousins of Jesus. This is the best solution.

In any case, the early church was convinced that Mary had no other children. Only Tertullian (?) and Helvidius (and companions) are exceptions. The position of the church is guided by a Christological and ascetical argument, as a reflection of Origen shows:

94. John Chrysostom, *In Gal.* 1:19 (PG 61:632); Theodoret of Cyrus, *In Gal.* 1:19 (PG 82:468C–D). See Viciano, "Antike versus zeitgenössische Exegese: Theodoret von Kyros' Kommentar zu Gal 1,19" [Ancient vs. Contemporary Exegesis: Theodoret of Cyrus' commentary on Gal. 1:19], *Forum Katholische Theologie* (hereinafter *FKTh*) 12 (1996): 285–89; Ziegenaus, *Maria in der Heilsgeschichte*, 256.

Those who speak thus mean to safeguard Mary's dignity in the virginity she conserved until the end, so that that body chosen to serve the Word, who said, "The Holy Spirit will come upon you and the power of the Most High will overshadow you," did not know any relations with a man, after the point the Holy Spirit came down upon her and the power of the Most High overshadowed her. I consider it to be conformity with reason that, with regard to the purity that consists in chastity, Jesus was the first among men, while Mary was the first among women. It is the act of a wicked man to attribute the first place in virginity to anyone else.[95]

Similarly Basil explains, "The lovers of Christ [i.e., the faithful] do not allow themselves to hear that the Mother of God (*Theotókos*) ceased at a given moment to be a virgin."[96]

Exegetical and historical references on their own are not enough to bring us fully to the dogma of the perpetual virginity of Mary. Instead, these important data are integrated in a broader vision that sees the entire figure of Mary, Virgin and Mother of God. As Mary meditated on the Word of God (Lk 2:19, 2:51), the church also has contemplated the history of salvation with the support of the Holy Spirit to reach a clarification of the doctrine.

A PLAN OF VIRGINITY

While the perpetual virginity of Mary is a dogma, theologians remain free to debate the thesis of a plan of virginity,[97] chosen by the mother of the Lord prior to the Annunciation. In the exegesis of Luke 1:34 we have already discussed the biblical source of the question.[98] A prior plan of virginity is mentioned for the first time by Gregory of Nyssa and Augustine; but it is implicit already in the legendary account of the Protoevangelium of James.

95. *Commentary on Matthew* 10:17 (PG 13:877A); English trans. in Gambero, *Mary and the Fathers*, 75f.

96. *On the Holy Generation of Christ* 5 (PG 31:1468B); English trans. in Gambero, *Mary and the Fathers*, 146.

97. See Serra, "Vergine," 2:1437–45; Gherardini, *La Madre*, 128–33; Anton Ziegenaus, "Jungfräulichkeitsgelübte" [Vow of Virginity], in *ML* 3:481–83; Michael O'Carroll, CSSp., *Theotokos: A Theological Encyclopedia of the Blessed Virgin Mary* (Eugene, Ore.: Wipf and Stock, 2000), 363–65; Frederick L. Miller, "Lk 1:34: Mary's Desire for Virginity?" *Angelicum* 75 (1998): 189–208; Galot, *Maria, La donna*, 143–56.

98. See "The Annunciation," in chapter 1.

The Middle Ages universally accepts the thesis that Mary had a plan of virginity. There was only debate on whether the vow was already absolute before the betrothal (the Franciscan view) or conditional before the betrothal and absolute only afterward (the Dominican view, following Aquinas). Thomas distinguishes between a conditional and an unconditional plan: before the betrothal Mary could have made a plan only in a conditional way ("if God wills it") but after the betrothal and before the Annunciation, she would have made an unconditional plan (together with Joseph).[99]

In addition, Thomas mentions the importance of the vow, pointing out Augustine's explanation. Augustine sees in the formulation "I do not know man" a vow made prior to the Annunciation. Mary's consecration to God was undertaken freely and not by a divine command "so that the imitation of a heavenly life in an earthly and mortal body should take place by vow, not by command; through a choice of love, not through the necessity of service."[100] Already in Mary, Augustine sees the consecration of virgins by free choice and by vow.

A contentious debate on the plan of virginity came in the sixteenth century, when Calvin denied such an intention on Mary's part.[101] The Protestant interpretation was determined by their rejection of consecrated virginity. In contemporary theology skepticism prevails regarding a plan for virginity by Mary, but the interpretation of Gregory of Nyssa and Augustine finds its supporters even today. Indeed the "classic" thesis seems, for its part, to bring the better arguments. A *via media is* the proposal of Romano Guardini, adopted among others by Anton Ziegenaus: "To interpret Mary exclusively according to expectations of a Jewish girl does not render justice to the uniqueness of the woman chosen as Mother of God: it seems appropriate to accept a hidden desire for virginity, interpreted by the Annunciation."[102]

99. *ST* III, q. 28, a. 4.

100. *De sancta Virginitate* 4 (PL 40:398). See English trans. in *Nicene and Post-Nicene Fathers*. First Series (hereinafter *NPNF1*), ed. Philip Schaff, 14 vols. (1886–89; repr. Peabody, Mass.: Hendrickson, 1994), 3, online at http://www.newadvent.org/fathers/1310.htm.

101. It does not seem that Cardinal Cajetan cast doubt on such a plan; e.g., Ziegenaus, *Maria in der Heilsgeschichte*, 270. See Galot, *Maria, La donna*, 153.

102. Ziegenaus, "Jungfräulichkeitsgelübte" [Vow of Virginity], in *ML* 3:483; see Ziegenaus, *Maria in der Heilsgeschichte*, 269–75; Romano Guardini, *La Madre del Signore* [Mother of the Lord] (Brescia: Morcelliana, 1989), 28–33.

The magisterium has not intervened to clarify the controversy among theologians definitively. But we need to value John Paul II's repeated affirmations of Mary's plan for virginity, a point underscored in the encyclical *Redemptoris Mater*,[103] in two apostolic letters,[104] and in various catecheses,[105] one of which was specially dedicated to the question. The pope reaffirms the connection between consecration to God and the divine maternity: "Mary consents to God's choice, in order to become through the power of the Holy Spirit the Mother of the Son of God. It can be said that a *consent to motherhood* is above all a result of her *total self-giving to God in virginity*."[106]

In his catechesis on the plan of virginity, John Paul II treats the question with a certain fullness. For the context in which the decision of Mary was able to mature, the supreme pontiff refers, among other things, to the example of the Essenes who "lived in celibacy or restricted the use of marriage because of community life and the search for greater intimacy with God.... It does not seem that Mary ever knew about these Jewish religious groups.... But the fact that John the Baptist probably lived a celibate life and that in the community of his disciples this was held in high esteem would support the supposition that Mary's choice of virginity belonged to this new cultural and religious context:

> The extraordinary case of the Virgin of Nazareth must not lead us into the error of tying her inner dispositions completely to the mentality of her surroundings, thereby eliminating the uniqueness of the mystery that came to pass in her. In particular, we must not forget that, from the very beginning of her life, Mary received a wondrous grace.... Thus, it should be maintained that Mary was guided to the ideal of virginity by an exceptional inspiration of that same Holy Spirit who, in the course of the Church's history, will spur many women to the way of virginal consecration.[107]

103. *RM* 39a.

104. John Paul II, *Mulieris dignitatem*, 20, and *RC* 18.

105. Among others, John Paul II, CM 25 (July 3, 1996), nn. 1, 3; CM 27 (July 24, 1996). See Miller, "Lk 1:34," 197f. See also the comment of Antoine Nachef, *Mary's Pope: John Paul II, Mary, and the Church since Vatican II* (Franklin, Wisc.: Sheed and Ward, 2000), 174: "Mediation is based on motherhood; motherhood takes place in the context of virginity; virginity strengthens the spousal character of union with God."

106. *RM* 39a.

107. John Paul II, CM 27 (July 24, 1996), nn. 3–4.

THE ROLE OF THE MARRIAGE OF MARY AND THE FIGURE OF JOSEPH

The virginity of Mary is concretely united with a true marriage. According to the Jewish customs of the time of Jesus, the conclusion of the matrimonial contract itself constituted the beginning of the marriage, even if the cohabitation only took place later. Matthew calls Joseph "husband" (*anḗr*, literally "man") of Mary (Mt 1:16, 1:19), who appears as the "wife" of Joseph (1:20, 1:24: *gunḗ*).[108] So Jesus, through the marriage and through Joseph as the legal father, becomes "son of David" (Mt 1:1).

Augustine understands the situation well when he declares: marriage is not established by carnal union, but by consent. Because of this consent to fidelity both Mary and Joseph deserved to be called "parents" of Jesus, and Joseph deserved to be called his "father" (Lk 2:33, 2:41, 2:48). The three specific elements of matrimony (*fides, proles, sacramentum*) are present, even if carnal union is lacking:

> The entire good ... of the nuptial institution was effected in the case of these parents of Christ: there was offspring, there was faithfulness, there was the bond. As offspring, we recognise the Lord Jesus Himself; the fidelity, in that there was no adultery; the bond, because there was no divorce.[109]

For this reason Joseph, Mary, and Jesus form a true family.

The marriage between Mary and Joseph is certainly unique and yet possesses a strong exemplary character for Christian marriage oriented toward Christ. Mary is the prototype of virgins, but with her maternity it becomes clear that virginity is not identified with the *single* life, through the fact that she is open to God for the "generation" of Christ in the church. At the same time, Mary is prototype of the mother whose maternity is not limited to the biological contribution, but has to transcend itself in openness to God. In this way, Mary, as virgin and mother, makes concrete the convergence of these

108. See also p. 423, regarding the marriage of Mary and Joseph.

109. Augustine, *De nuptiis et concupiscentia* 11.3 (PL 44:421); English trans. in *NPNF1*, 5, online at http://www.newadvent.org/fathers/15071.htm. See Ziegenaus, *Maria in der Heilsgeschichte*, 267f. Thomas Aquinas accepts the explanation of Augustine: *ST* III, q. 29, a. 2.

two states in the church, consecrated virginity and matrimony, even to the bodily dimension.

Or rather, as John Paul II formulates it: In Mary we find "two kinds of love ... both of which together represent the mystery of the Church—virgin and spouse—as symbolized in the marriage of Mary and Joseph. 'Virginity or celibacy for the sake of the Kingdom of God not only does not contradict the dignity of marriage but presupposes and confirms it. Marriage and virginity are two ways of expressing and living the one mystery of the Covenant of God with his people.'"[110]

To understand the role of Joseph better, it is worthwhile to study the apostolic letter of John Paul II, *Redemptoris Custos* (1989). It emphasizes the true marriage between Mary and Joseph.[111] The pope then cites the preface of the Solemnity of St. Joseph: "A wise and faithful servant in charge of your household to watch like a father over your Only Begotten Son (*paterna vice custodiret*), who was conceived by the overshadowing of the Holy Spirit, our Lord Jesus Christ."[112] Following Augustine, the pope attributes to Joseph a "true fatherhood." In the "human form of the family of the Son of God, ... Joseph is the father: his fatherhood is not one that derives from begetting offspring; but neither is it an 'apparent' or merely 'substitute' fatherhood. Rather, it is one that fully shares in authentic human fatherhood and the mission of a father in the family."[113]

Despite this, the pope also uses the formula "presumed father."[114] This tension finds resolution in the distinction of Estius (†1613), who affirms, "Joseph was a true father in the order of matrimony," but "only putative in the order of generation."[115] The adjective "putative" traces back to Luke 3:23: "Jesus ... being the son (as was supposed [Vulgate: *ut putabatur*]) of Joseph." We can also recall the distance

110. John Paul II, Apostolic Exhortation *Redemptoris Custos* (hereinafter *RC*), 20. The citation is from John Paul II, *Familiaris consortio* (1981), n. 16.

111. *RC* 7.

112. *RC* 8.

113. *RC* 21.

114. *RC* 15, 22, 27f.

115. Estius, IV Sent. d. 30 §11, cited in Tarcisio Stramare, *Gesù lo chiamò padre: Rassegna storico-dottrinale di san Giuseppe* [Jesus Called Him Father: Historical-Doctrinal Review of St. Joseph] (Vatican City: Libreria Editrice Vaticana, 1997), 48.

between the "fatherhood" of Joseph and that of God the Father, as is shown in Luke 2. At Mary's observation, "your father and I have been looking for you," Jesus responds, "Did you not know that I must be in *my Father's* house?" (Lk 2:48f).[116]

The solicitude of Joseph had to express, in some way, that of the heavenly Father (a task that, in an analogous way, applies to every parent). Joseph's role of representing the heavenly Father, even to the incarnate Son of God, presupposes particular gifts received from God: "It is inconceivable that such a sublime task would not be matched by the necessary qualities to adequately fulfill it." With "fatherly authority over Jesus, God also gave Joseph a share in the corresponding love, the love that has its origin in the Father 'from whom every family in heaven and on earth is named' (Eph 3:15)."[117]

REFERENCES

The Virginity of Mary

Ecclesiastical Texts

CCC 496–507.

Collantes, Justo, ed. *La fede della Chiesa Cattolica: Le idee e gli uomini nei documenti dottrinali del Magistero,* 301–14. Vatican City: Libreria Editrice Vaticana, 1993. Spanish: *La fe de la Iglesia Católica: Las ideas y los hombres en los documentos doctrinales del Magisterio.* Madrid: Biblioteca de Autores Cristianos, 1983.

The Creeds (DH 1–76).

John Paul II. Allocution for the Sixteenth Centenary of the Plenary Synod of Capua (392–1992) on the Perpetual Virginity of Mary: *AAS* 85 (1993): 662–70 (in Italian).

———. Marian Catecheses of July 10, July 24, July 31, Aug. 7, Aug. 21, Aug. 28, 1996; Aug. 20, 1997.

Lateran Synod (649). Can. 3 (DH 503).

Paul IV. Bull against the Unitarians, 1555 (DH 1880).

Second Council of Constantinople (553). Can. 2, 6, 14 (DH 422, 427, 437).

Other Sources

Auer, Johann. *Gesù il Salvatore: Soteriologia–Mariologia* [Jesus the Savior: Soteriology, Mariology]. Translated by Carlo Molari. Assisi: Cittadella, 1993. German original: *Jesus Christus—Heiland der Welt: Maria, Christi Mutter im Heilsplan Gottes,* §7. Regensburg: Friedrich Pustet, 1988.

Bastero, Juan Luis. *Mary, Mother of the Redeemer,* 166–82. Dublin: Four Courts, 2006.

116. See *RC* 15.

117. *RC* 8.

———. *Virgen singular: La reflexión teológica mariana en el siglo XX* [Singular Virgin: Theological Reflection on Mary in the 20th Century], 58–112. Madrid: Rialp, 2001.

Calero, Antonio Maria. *La Vergine Maria nel mistero di Cristo e della Chiesa: Saggio di mariologia* [The Virgin Mary in the Mystery of Christ and the Church: Essay in Mariology], 118–52. Leumann (Turin): Elle Di Ci, 1995. Spanish original: *María en el misterio de Cristo y de la Iglesia.* Madrid: CCS, 1990.

Calkins, Arthur B. *Il concepimento e la nascita verginale di Gesù: Verità di fede ricevuta e trasmessa dalla Chiesa Cattolica* [The Conception and Virginal Birth of Jesus: Truths of Faith Received and Transmitted by the Catholic Church]. *Immaculata Mediatrix* 4 (2004): 181–209.

———. "Our Lady's Perpetual Virginity." In *Mariology: A Guide*, edited by M. Miravalle, 277–315. Goleta, Calif.: Queenship, 2007.

Capizzi, Nunzio. "Vergine." In De Fiores, Schiefer, and Perrella, *DMar*, 1255–64.

Courth, Franz. "Jungfrauengeburt im exegetisch-dogmatischen Disput" [Virgin Birth in Exegetical-Dogmatic Debate]. In *De cultu mariano s. XX*, edited by PAMI, 4:293–314. Rome: PAMI, 1999.

de Aldama, José A. "La maternité verginale de Notre Dame" [The Virginal Maternity of Our Lady]. In *Maria*, edited by H. du Manoir, 7:117–54. Paris: Beauchesne, 1964.

———. *Virgo Mater: Estudios de teología patristica* [Virgin Mother: Studies of Patristic Theology]. Granada: Facultad de Teología, 1963.

De Fiores, Stefano. *Maria nella teologia contemporanea* [Mary in Contemporary Theology]. 3rd ed., 438–53. Rome: Centro di Cultura Mariana "Madre della Chiesa," 1991.

De Fiores, Stefano. "Vergine." In *Maria: Nuovissimo dizionario*, 2:1771–1814. Bologna: EDB, 2006.

———. "Vergine I. Problematica attuale; III. Tradizione ecclesiale; IV. Prospettive teologiche attuali" [Virgin: I: Current Issues; III: Ecclesial Tradition; IV: Theological Perspective]. In *NDM* 1418–24, 1454–76. In De Fiores and Meo, *NDM* 1418–24, 1454–76.

Dittrich, Achim. *Protestantische Mariologie-Kritik: Historische Entwicklung bis 1997 und dogmatische Analyse* [Protestant Critique of Mariology: Historical Development up to 1997 and Dogmatic Analysis], 308f. Mariologische Studien 11. Regensburg: Friedrich Pustet, 1998.

Donnelly, Philip J. "La virginidad perpetua de la Madre de Dios" [The Perpetual Virginity of the Mother of God]. In *Mariología*, edited by J. Carol, 619–83. Madrid: Biblioteca de autores cristianos, 1964. English original: "The Perpetual Virginity of the Mother of God." In *Mariology*, edited by J. Carol, 2:228–96. Milwaukee: Bruce, 1957.

Fehlner, Peter Damian M. *La verginità nel parto* [Virginity in Birth]. Castelpetroso: Casa Mariana Editrice, 1995.

Galot, Jean. *Maria, La donna nell'opera della salvezza* [Mary the Woman in the Work of Salvation]. 3rd ed., 113–83. Rome: Ed. Pontificia Università Gregoriana, 2005. 2nd ed. 1991.

Gherardini, Brunero. *La Madre: Maria in una sintesi storico-teologica* [The Mother:

Mary in a Historical-Theological Synthesis], 93–133. Frigento: Casa Mariana, 1989.

Haffner, Paul. *The Mystery of Mary*, 134–74. Leominster, UK: Gracewing; Mundelein, Ill.: Hillenbrand, 2004.

Hauke, Manfred. "Die 'virginitas in partu': Akzentsetzungen in der Dogmengeschichte" [Virginity in Childbirth: Emphases in the History of Dogma]. In "*Geboren aus der Jungfrau Maria*": *Klarstellungen* ["Born of the Virgin Mary": Elucidations], edited by A. Ziegenaus, 88–131. Mariologische Studien 19. Regensburg, 2007.

———. "Jungfrau und Mutter: Geboren von der Jungfrau Maria" [Virgin and Mother: Born of the Virgin Mary]. In *Maria: Mutter der Kirche*, edited by G. Stumpf, 43–70. Landsberg: Initiativkreis Kath. Laien und Priester in die Diözese Augsburg, 2004.

Laurentin, René. "Le mystère de la naissance verginale" [The Mystery of the Virgin Birth]. *Ephemerides Mariologicae* 10 (1960): 345–74.

———. *A Short Treatise on the Virgin Mary*, 284–301. Washington, N.J.: AMI, 1991.

Malnati, Ettore. *Maria nella fede della Chiesa* [Mary in the Faith of the Church], 27–77. Casale Monferrato: Piemme, 2001.

Masini, Mario. *Maria di Nazaret la Vergine*. Padua: Messaggero, 2008.

Menke, Karl-Heinz. *Incarnato nel seno della vergine Maria: Maria nella storia di Israele e nella Chiesa* [Incarnate in the Womb of the Virgin Mary: Mary in the History of Israel and of the Church], 81. Cinisello Balsamo: Paoline, 2002. German original: *Fleisch geworden aus Maria: Die Geschichte Israels und der Marienglaube der Kirche*. Regensburg: Friedrich Pustet, 1999.

Merkelbach, Benoît Henri. *Mariologia*, 216–63. Paris: Desclée, 1939.

Müller, Gerhard L. *Nato dalla Vergine Maria* [Born of the Virgin Mary]. Brescia: Morcelliana, 1994 (updated ed.) *Maria: Die Frau im Heilsplan Gottes*. Mariologische Studien 15. 116–225. Regensburg: Pustet, 2002.

Perrella, Salvatore M. "Il parto verginale di Maria nel dibattito teologico contemporaneo (1962–1994): Magistero—Esegesi—Teologia" [The Virginal Delivery of Mary in Contemporary Theological Debate (1962–1994): Magisterium, Exegesis, Theology]. *Marianum* 56 (1994): 95–213.

———. *Maria, Vergine e Madre: La verginità feconda di Maria tra fede, storia e teologia* [Mary, Virgin and Mother: The Fruitful Virginity of Mary between Faith, History and Theology]. Cinisello Balsamo: San Paolo, 2003.

Ponce Cuéllar, Miguel. *María: Madre del Redentor y Madre de la Iglesia* [Mary: Mother of the Redeemer and Mother of the Church]. 2nd ed., 323–82. Barcelona: Herder, 2001.

Pozo, Cándido, SJ. *María en la obra de la salvación* [Mary in the Work of Salvation]. 2nd ed., 250–84. Madrid: Biblioteca de Autores Cristianos, 1990.

———. *María, nueva Eva* [Mary, the New Eve], 265–300. Madrid: Biblioteca de Autores Cristianos, 2005.

Roschini, Gabriele M. *La Madonna: Secondo la fede e la teologia*, 3:163–88. Rome: Libreria Editrice Francesco Ferrari, 1953–54.

———. *Maria Santissima nella storia della salvezza: Trattato completo di mariologia alla luce del Concilio Vaticano II* [Mary Most Holy in the History of Salvation: Complete Treatise on Mariology in Light of the Second Vatican Council]. Vol. 3. Isola del Liri: Pisani, 1969.

Scheffczyk, Leo. *Maria, crocevia della fede cattolica* [Mary, Crossroads of the Catholic Faith], 81–92. CdM 1. Lugano: Eupress FTL, 2002.

Serra, Aristide. "Vergine. II. Testmonianza biblica" [Virgin. II. Biblical Witness]. In *NDM*, 1424–54.

Söll, Georg. *Storia dei dogmi mariani*, 81–88, 97–108, 131–41, 178–86. Rome: Libreria Ateneo Salesiano, 1981. German original: *Mariologie* [*Handbuch der Dogmengeschichte*, vol. 3, part 4. Freiburg i.Br.: Herder, 1978.

Ziegenaus, Anton. "Jungfräulichkeit II. Dogmatik." In *ML* 3:469–81.

———. *Maria in der Heilsgeschichte: Mariologie*, 232–87. Katholische Dogmatik 5. Aachen: MM-Verlag, 1998.

———. ed. *"Geboren aus der Jungfrau Maria": Klarstellungen* ["Born of the Virgin Mary": Elucidations]. Mariologische Studien 19. Regensburg: Friedrich Pustet, 2007.

The Role of the Marriage of Mary and the Figure of Joseph

The Marriage of Mary

Ecclesiastical Texts

John Paul II. Marian Catechesis of August 21, 1996 ("Mary and Joseph Lived the Gift of Virginity").

Other Sources

Aparicio Rodriguez, Angel. "María esposa de José" [Mary Spouse of Joseph]. *Ephemerides Mariologicae* 46 (1996): 293–317.

Cipriani, Nello. "Il vero matrimonio di Maria e Giuseppe in S. Agostino" [The True Marriage of Mary and Joseph in St. Augustine]. *Theotokos* 12 (2004): 169–82.

Llamas, Enrique. "El matrimonio de José y María, y su predestinación" [The Marriage of Joseph and Mary, and Its Predestination]. In *Die Bedeutung des hl. Josef in der Heilsgeschichte*, edited by J. Hattler and G. Rovira, 1:143–60. Kisslegg: Fe-Medienverlag, 2006.

O'Carroll, Michael, CSSp. *Theotokos: A Theological Encyclopedia of the Blessed Virgin Mary*, 234f. Eugene, Ore.: Wipf and Stock, 2000.

Perrella. *Maria, Vergine*, 218–22.

Stöhr, Johannes. "Maria in der christlichen Ehe nach päpstlichen Verlautbarungen" [Mary in Christian Marriage according to Papal Writings]. *Sedes Sapientiae: Mariologisches Jahrbuch* 11 (2007): 84–126.

Stramare, Tarcisio. "Il matrimonio della Madre di Dio" [The Marriage of the Mother of God]. *Divinitas* 46 (2003): 19–52.

———. *Il matrimonio della Madre di Dio: I santi sposi* [The Marriage of the Mother of God: The Holy Spouses]. Verona: Edizioni Stamattine, 2001.

———. "Josef, der 'Gerechte,' jungfräulich mit Maria im Ehebund vereint" [Joseph the "Just Man," Virginally United with Mary in the Bond of Marriage]. *Sedes Sapientiae: Mariologisches Jahrbuch* 5, no. 2(2001): 53–86.
Ziegenaus, Anton. "Ehe III. Dogmatik" [Marriage III. Dogmatics] In *ML* 2:284–86.

The Figure of Joseph

Ecclesiastical Texts

John Paul II. Apostolic Letter *Redemptoris Custos* (August 15, 1989).
Leo XIII, Encyclical *Quamquam pluries* (August 15, 1889) (*PE* 2:110; *EE* 3, nn. 706–31).

Other Sources

Candido, D. G. "Giuseppe di Nazaret." In *DMar*, 586–96.
Ferrer Arellano, Joaquín. *San José nuestro Padre y Señor: La trinidad de la tierra, teología y espiritualidad josefina* [St. Joseph, Our Father and Lord: The Earthly Trinity, Josephite Theology and Spirituality]. Madrid: Arca de la Alianza, 2007.
Hattler, Johannes, and German Rovira, eds. *Die Bedeutung des hl. Josef in der Heilsgeschichte* [The Meaning of St. Joseph in Salvation History]. Vols. 1–2. Kisslegg: Fe-Medienverlag, 2006 (multi-lingual contributions of the international symposium on St. Joseph at Kevelaer 2005).
O'Carroll. *Theotokos*, 206–9.
Royo Marin, Antonio. *La Virgen María: Teología y espiritualidad marianas* [The Virgin Mary: Marian Theology and Spirituality]. 2nd ed., 426–39. Madrid: Biblioteca de Autores Cristianos, 1997.
Stramare, Tarcisio. *Gesù lo chiamò padre: Rassegna storico-dottrinale di san Giuseppe* [Jesus Called Him Father: Historical-Doctrinal Review of St. Joseph]. Vatican City: Libreria Editrice Vaticana, 1997.
Stramare, Tarcisio, and Stefano De Fiores. "Giuseppe." In *NDM*, 633–55.
———. "Joseph." In *ML* 3:436.

Six

The Holiness of Mary

INTRODUCTION

Through being Mother of God, Mary was enriched with an immense holiness. The angel Gabriel greets her as "full of grace" (Lk 1:28). Such a spiritual richness implies freedom from any sin. Mary's preservation from original sin constitutes the doctrine of the "Immaculate Conception." This grace includes the absence of disordered inclination toward evil (concupiscence). We need to devote particular attention to the road that led to the dogmatic declaration of the Immaculate Conception, proclaimed by Pope Pius IX in 1854:

> The most Blessed Virgin Mary, at the first instant of her conception, by the singular grace and privilege of almighty God and in view of the merits of Jesus Christ, the Savior of the human race, was preserved immune from all stain of original sin.[1]

Yet the holiness of Mary is not limited to freedom from original sin. It also includes an abundance of graces with a special value for understanding the holiness of the church. Finally, we will study the expression of holiness in the Immaculate Heart of the blessed Virgin.

1. DH 2803.

FREEDOM FROM ALL PERSONAL SIN

The Relationship between the Universality of the Redemption and the Function of the New Eve: A Tension to Resolve

Even before the absence of original sin in Mary was clarified, the fact was already recognized that Mary is free from all personal sin. But reaching this awareness also required a certain journey.

Sacred Scripture is aware that all men are sinners (e.g., 1 Jn 1:8), a fact that Paul lays to the influence of Adam (Rom 5:19). For this reason, we need not be surprised that in the first centuries we still find statements about imperfections or outright sins on the part of Mary. On the other hand, we see a juxtaposition between Eve and Mary presented: the new Eve stands beside the new Adam, associated with him. Because of this, Mary's obedient response of faith opens the way of salvation, setting right what the disobedience of Eve had left us. With the parallelism Eve/Mary, we can perceive the particular role of the Mother of the Lord, the like of which is not found elsewhere among the descendants of Adam.

Patristic Development and the Importance of the Council of Ephesus

Starting in the second century,[2] the expression "holy Virgin" becomes current. It appears that the virginity of Mary comes to be seen as a bodily expression of holiness, as St. Ambrose teaches in exemplary fashion: Mary "was a virgin, not only in body but in her mind as well" (*virgo non solum corpore, sed etiam mente*).[3]

Origen is a typical example of this still immature stage of doctrine on the holiness of Mary. On one hand, the renowned theologian attributes the title "holy Virgin" only to Mary; on the other

2. At first in the *Epistula Apostolorum*, then repeatedly in Hippolytus (†235): Anton Ziegenaus, *Maria in der Heilsgeschichte: Mariologie* [Mary in Salvation History: Mariology], Katholische Dogmatik 5 (Aachen: MM-Verlag, 1998), 43–74, 288.

3. *De virginibus* 2.7 (PL 16:220). See Luigi Gambero, *Mary and the Fathers of the Church: The Blessed Virgin Mary in Patristic Thought*, trans. Thomas Buffer (San Francisco: Ignatius Press, 1999), 191.

hand, he feels constrained to find something sinful in her in order to be able to explain the universality of the redemption. He interprets the prophecy of Simeon (Lk 2:35: "a sword will pierce through your own soul also") as a sign of the scandal she experienced during the passion of Jesus. Otherwise (if this weakness had not existed), Jesus would not have died for Mary's sins. Origen explains the "sword" as incredulity and doubt in the face of the Cross. Nevertheless, like the apostles, Mary suddenly experienced a healing that strengthened her heart in faith.[4] Also, in Origen, the Virgin's question at the Annunciation is seen as a slight doubt.[5]

Origen's exegesis of the "sword" is transmitted (in a mitigated form) in Basil, Amphilochius of Iconium, and Cyril of Alexandria.[6] Other passages that provoked comment on presumed imperfections or sins in Mary (besides Luke 1:34, 2:35) were: Luke 2:49 ("Did you not know ... ?"); John 2:4 ("What have you to do with me?"); Luke 11:27f (true motherhood); Matthew 12:47–50 and others (true family); John 19:25–27 (standing under the Cross; Origen's exegesis of Luke 2:35).[7]

The most drastic statements are found in John Chrysostom: that Mary had doubted the message of the angel and, for this reason, Gabriel had spoken of the miracle of Elizabeth's motherhood.[8] While she expected to be able to give her son orders, she had to be educated by Jesus.[9] She would not have known the hidden aspect of Jesus, his divinity.[10] Chrysostom the preacher was guided by the need to educate his hearers: his homilies on Matthew and John correspond to a

4. *In Lc. hom.* 17:3–8 (*SC* 87:252–61); see. *TMPM* 1:222f.

5. *In Gen. hom.* 1:14 (*SC* 7 bis, 66).

6. On the Eastern interpretation, see Aristide Serra, "Una spada *trafiggerà la tua vita" (Lc 2,35a): Quale spada? Bibbia e tradizione giudaico-cristiana a confronto* ["A Sword Will Pierce Your Life" (Lk 2:35a): Which Sword? Bible and Jewish-Christian Tradition in Contrast] (Rome: Marianum, 2003), 98–170; Luigi Gambero, "La santità di Maria: Contesto in cui si sviluppa la dottrina dell'Immacolata Concezione: il contributo dei Padri della Chiesa" [The Holiness of Mary: Context in Which the Doctrine of the Immaculate Conception Developed; The Contribution of the Church Fathers], in *Il dogma dell'Immacolata Concezione di Maria: Problemi attuali e tentativi di ricomprensione* [The Dogma of the Immaculate Conception of Mary: Current Issues and Attempts at Reinterpretation], ed. E. Toniolo (Rome: Ed. Marianum, 2004), 285–90.

7. See the list in Anton Ziegenaus, "Unvollkommenheiten" [Imperfections], in *ML* 6:547. On these passages, see, for instance, Jean Galot, *Maria, La donna nell' opera della salvezza,* 2nd ed. (Rome: Gregoriana, 1991), 228–31 (and in the biblical section, earlier).

8. *In Gen.* 49:2 (PG 54:446).

9. *In Ioannem* 21:2 (PG 59:129f).

10. *In Ps.* 49:1 (PG 55:242).

schema, according to which Mary is by turns honored and reproved.[11]

It is no accident that these homilies arise from an Antiochian environment, while in the Alexandrian environment (where there is more awareness of the divine maternity of Mary) these themes have gentler shadings. Cyril of Alexandria mitigates Origen's exegesis of the "sword" in Luke 2:35, speaking instead of temptation and sorrow. Nonetheless, he still considers Mary's alleged doubts under the Cross "likely."[12] Subsequently, the Council of Ephesus will cause any assertion of imperfections or sins in Mary to disappear from later development.

The virginity and divine maternity of Mary, seen together with the task of the new Eve, are therefore determining factors for recognizing Mary's freedom from all sin. Already in the fourth century we find notable affirmations on the perfect holiness of Mary, a holiness that per se excludes sin. The Syrian Ephrem (fourth century) gives voice to the "sickly" church of Edessa: "Only you [Jesus] and your Mother are more beautiful than everything. For on you, O Lord, there is no mark: neither is there any stain in your Mother."[13]

A very important testimony in the West comes from Augustine, who debated with Pelagius on the possibility of men without sin. Pelagius presents a list of them (which includes Mary), while Augustine denies his presumption. The theologian makes an exception only for Mary: "With the exception of the holy Virgin Mary, in whose case, out of respect for the Lord (*propter honorem Domini*), I do not wish there to be any further question as sin is concerned, since how

11. Jesus, subject to Mary and Joseph (Lk 2:51), an honor; "What have you ..." (Jn 2:4), a reproof; "Fill the jars with water" (Jn 2:7), honor; "Who is my mother ..." (Mt 12:48), reproof; "Jesus went out of the house ..." (Mt 13:1), honor; "Blessed rather are those who hear ..." (Lk 11:28), reproof; "Behold your mother" (Jn 19:26), honor. See Giuseppe Maria Ellero, "Maternità e virtù di Maria in San Giovanni Crisostomo" [Motherhood and Virtue of Mary in St. John Chrysostom], *Marianum* 25 (1963): 405–46; Gambero, *Mary and the Fathers*, 172–74; Manfred Hauke, "Maria in alexandrinischer und antiochenischer Denkform [Mary in Alexandrian and Antiochian Forms of Thought]. In *De cultu mariano saeculo XX*, edited by PAMI, 2:222–24.

12. See *In Ioannem* 12 (PG 74:661A–65A); *In Zach.* 5.99 (PG 72:237); *Hom.* 12 (PG 77:1049C); George Jouassard, "L'interprétation par saint Cyrille d'Alexandrie de la scène de Marie au pied de la croix" [St. Cyril of Alexandria's Interpretation of the Scene of Mary at the Foot of the Cross], in *De immaculata conceptione apud SS. Patres et scriptores orientales,* ed. AMI, Virgo Immaculata 4 (Vatican City: AMI, 1955), 28–47; Hauke, "Maria in alexandrinischer und antiochenischer Denkform," 225–27.

13. *Carmi Nisibeni* 27.8 (*CSCO* 219:76). See Gambero, *Mary and the Fathers*, 109. The text is cited inter alia by Pius XII, *Fulgens corona* (*PE* 4:247, n. 10; *EE* 6, n. 953).

can we know what great abundance of grace was conferred on her to conquer sin in every way, seeing that she merited to conceive and bear him who certainly had no sin at all?"[14]

The Council of Trent as a Landmark

Awareness of Mary's absolute lack of personal sin is very clear in the Middle Ages, including in Thomas, despite the fact that the theologian presupposes she had original sin.[15] Only a few of the Reformers began to speak anew of imperfections and sins in Mary—for example, Brenz and Melanchthon, in contrast to Luther—in general—and Calvin.[16]

In 1439 the Council of Basel, which is not recognized as authentic, "defined" the perfect holiness of Mary, including freedom from all personal sin and therefore also from original sin. The argument of the theologians referred to the dignity of Mary as a temple in whom eternal truth lived, referring thus to the divine maternity.[17]

An authentic and proper dogmatic affirmation, on the other hand, is found in the decree on justification of the *Council of Trent*:

> If anyone says that a man once justified cannot sin again ... or, on the contrary, says that a man once justified can avoid all sins, even venial sins, throughout his entire life, unless it be by a special privilege of God as the Church holds of the Blessed Virgin, let him be anathema.[18]

This conviction is also expressed in Vatican II: "Embracing God's salvific will with a full heart and impeded by no sin, she devoted herself totally as a handmaid of the Lord to the person and work of her Son, ... by the grace of almighty God."[19] "But while in the most

14. *De natura et gratia* 36:42 (PL 44:267). English trans. from Gambero, *Mary and the Fathers*, 226.

15. *ST* III, q. 27, a. 4.

16. See Anton Ziegenaus, "Ohnmacht" [Helplessness], in *ML* 4:684.

17. The text of the definition is found in the introduction to DH 1400; also Mansi 29:182f; see Stefano M. Cecchin, *L'Immacolata Concezione: Breve storia del dogma* [The Immaculate Conception: A Short History of the Dogma] (Vatican City: PAMI, 2003), 93.

18. DH 1573. This statement is not formally a solemn definition, but no doubt constitutes "a firm doctrine of the church and not a mere pious opinion": Galot, *Maria, La donna*, 3rd ed., 226. See also, later, the condemnation of a contrary thesis of Michael Baius (DH 1973).

19. *LG* 56.

holy Virgin the church has already reached that perfection whereby she is without spot or wrinkle (cf. Eph 5:27), the followers of Christ still strive to increase in holiness by conquering sin. And so they turn their eyes to Mary who shines forth to the whole community of the elect as the model of virtues."[20] The *CCC* affirms that "by the grace of God Mary remained free of every personal sin her whole life long."[21]

The same faith is generally professed by the Orthodox Church, on the basis of the Eastern fathers. "The Fathers of the Eastern Tradition call the Mother of God 'the All-Holy' (*Panagia*),"[22] a title that has been attested since Eusebius of Caesarea (†339).[23] Nevertheless, we find Orthodox theologians who state that Mary was purified from (original and) personal sin only at the Annunciation.[24]

The Impeccability of Mary

According to Catholic theology, Mary was free from any personal sin not only in fact (*impeccantia*), but "in principle," due to the "impeccability" of Mary: she was unable to sin (*impeccabilitas*). Certainly we need to distinguish the absolute impeccability of Jesus, a divine person, from that of Mary, a human person subject to the trials of life in a journey of faith. While we need to recognize a "physical" impeccability in Jesus Christ, which results from the very constitution of his being, in Mary only a "moral" impeccability can be accepted, "in the sense that Mary received, in view of her mission, graces so powerful that her constant perseverance in the way of good was morally certain."[25] In regard to this, John Damascene compares the

20. *LG* 65.

21. *CCC* 493. See n. 411: "By a special grace of God [Mary] committed no sin of any kind during her whole earthly life."

22. *CCC* 493.

23. See Ziegenaus, *Maria in der Heilsgeschichte: Mariologie* [Mary in Salvation History: Mariology], Katholische Dogmatik 5 (Aachen: MM-Verlag, 1998), 290.

24. See T. Nikolaou, "Sündenlosigkeit II. Orthodoxe Theologie" [Sinlessness: II. Orthodox Theology], in *ML* 6:332f. See also David Stiernon, "Marie dans la théologie orthodoxe gréco-russe" [Mary in Greco-Russian Orthodox Theology], in *Maria: Études sur la Sainte Vierge*, ed. H. du Manoir (Paris: Beauchesne, 1964), 7:300f.

25. Galot, *Maria, La donna*, 3rd ed., 235.

firmness of Mary's will in goodness with the will of the saints in heaven who can no longer sin.[26] This observation does not claim that Mary enjoyed the beatific vision, but a degree of grace greater than that of her progenitors in paradise. The impeccability of our Lady, her confirmation in grace, corresponds to her personal character as Mother of God and cooperator with the new Adam. Scheeben explains Mary's impeccability by means of an analogy with the infallibility of the church, which is guaranteed by Christ.[27]

Nevertheless, impeccability does not mean the absence of external temptations, which were present in the life of Jesus Christ himself.[28] "These temptations were not able to cast any shadows on the perfection of Mary, because they found no consent in her. They served to stimulate the ardor of her sanctity."[29]

FREEDOM FROM ORIGINAL SIN (IMMACULATE CONCEPTION)

The Meaning of the Dogma

The Immaculate Conception signifies the preservation of Mary from original sin. Thus it refers to the passive conception of Mary in the womb of Anne and not (as is sometimes thought) to her active conception, which happened without the intervention of a human father. It is not a statement about the procreative activity of Joachim and Anne, but about the person of Mary, who is free from all sin from the beginning. The Immaculate Conception is the root of the perfect holiness of the Mother of God.

26. *Hom. I in dorm. BVM* (PG 96:718).

27. Matthias J. Scheeben, *Handbuch der katholischen Dogmatik* [Handbook of Catholic Dogmatic Theology], vol. 5 (Freiburg im Breisgau: Herder, 1954), n. 173; Scheeben, *Immakulata und päpstliche Unfehlbarkeit: Sedes Sapientiae und Cathedra Sapientiae* [The Immaculate and Papal Infallibility: Seat of Wisdom and Cathedra of Wisdom], ed. J. Schmitz (Paderborn: F. Schöningh, 1954). See on the whole question Ziegenaus, "Befestigung in der Gnade" [Firmness in Grace], in *ML* 1:399f; Ziegenaus, "Unsündlichkeit" [Impeccability], in *ML* 6:545f.

28. See Mk 1:13 and parallels; Heb 4:15.

29. Galot, *Maria, La donna*, 3rd ed., 236.

Biblical Foundation

The biblical foundation of the dogma is centered in the "Protoevangelium" (Gn 3:15) and in the angelic salutation (Lk 1:28).[30] The Protoevangelium describes the "enmity" between the "woman" and her offspring on one hand, and the "serpent" on the other hand. Since the "offspring" of the woman is the Messiah, the "woman" brings to mind the Marian dimension.[31] Mary is united to Jesus in opposition to Satan. Given the fact that every sin makes room for the devil, a total conflict against Satan also reminds us of the total absence of sin.[32]

Chaíre, kecharitoméne: "Hail, full of grace" (Lk 1:28), the angelic salutation, points to the fullness of grace in Mary, who receives this address as a title.[33] Mary is filled with grace and for this reason responds with generosity to Gabriel's message. The abundance of grace implies the exclusion of sin.

While the Protoevangelium and the angelic salutation constitute demonstrative arguments, used as well in the bull *Ineffabilis Deus* (1854),[34] other biblical signs have a somewhat indirect value. John Paul II also returns to chapter 12 of Revelation,

30. See inter alia, Domenico Bertetto, *Maria Immacolata: Il domma della concezione immacolata di Maria nel centenario della sua definizione 1854–8 Dicembre–1954* [Mary Immaculate: The Dogma of the Immaculate Conception of Mary at the Centenary of its Definition: 1854–December 8, 1954] (Rome: Edizioni Paoline, 1953), 125–60; Gabriele M. Roschini, *Maria Santissima nella storia della salvezza: Trattato completo di mariologia alla luce del Concilio Vaticano II* [Mary Most Holy, in the History of Salvation: Complete Treatise on Mariology in Light of the Second Vatican Council] (Isola del Liri: Pisani, 1969), 3:25–37; Michael Seybold, "Unbefleckte Empfängnis": I. "Dogmatik" [Immaculate Conception: I. Dogmatic Theology], in *ML* 6:520; Miguel Ponce Cuéllar, *María, Madre del Redentor y Madre de la Iglesia* [Mary, Mother of the Redeemer and Mother of the Church], 2nd ed. (Barcelona: Herder, 2001), 389f; Galot, *Maria, La donna*, 3rd ed., 189–95; more broadly Aristide Serra, "Immacolata II. Fondamenti biblici," in De Fiores and Meo, *NDM*, 688–95; Serra, "Immacolata e alleanza: Verso una verifica dei fondamenti biblici del dogma di Pio IX" [The Immaculate and the Covenant: Toward a Verification of the Biblical Basis of the Dogma of Pius IX], in Toniolo, *Il dogma dell'Immacolata Concezione*, 223–69; Luis Diez Merino, "Los textos biblicos y el dogma de la Inmaculada Concepción" [Biblical Texts and the Dogma of the Immaculate Conception], *Estudios Marianos* 71 (2005): 183–96.

31. See "The Protoevangelium," in chapter 1.

32. See Pius IX, *Ineffabilis Deus* (*EE* 7, n. 750).

33. Regarding the angelic salutation, see "The Annunciation," in chapter 1.

34. See Galot, *Maria, La donna*, 3rd ed., 189–95. The same references are also found in Pius XII, *Fulgens corona* (1953) (*PE* 4:247, n. 7–8; *EE* 6, n. 950f).

which speaks of the "woman clothed with the sun" (12:1).... The woman-community is actually described with the features of the woman-Mother of Jesus.... Despite her sufferings, she is "clothed with the sun"—that is, she reflects the divine splendor—and appears as a "great sign" of God's spousal relationship with his people. Although not directly indicating the privilege of the Immaculate Conception, these images can be interpreted as an expression of the Father's loving care which surrounds Mary with the grace of Christ and the splendor of the Spirit.... The woman clothed with the sun represents the Church's holiness, which is fully realized in the Holy Virgin by virtue of a singular grace.[35]

Basis for the Historical Development

Biblical perspectives are also open to the exclusion of original sin, which received its systematic formulation in the West from Augustine on. The Latin fathers prior to Augustine and the Eastern fathers did not yet possess such an explicit consciousness of original sin having originated as guilt, even if they described the spiritual consequences of Adam's fall fully: death as a privation of divine life, the lack of the original gift (in paradise) of the Holy Spirit, the loss of the supernatural element of the image of God. Because of this, the express question of whether Mary was free from original sin is posed only from Augustine onward.

In any case, the journey toward the definition of the Immaculate Conception begins with a look at the role of Mary in the history of salvation: as the new Eve, preparing for the arrival of the new Adam, Mary remedies the negative consequences of the first sin. While Eve refuses to believe, Mary opens herself with all her availability to the message of the Incarnation. The parallelism Eve/Mary integrates the perspective opened by the Protoevangelium and the angelic salutation in the scene of the Annunciation. The analogy between Eve and Mary is the decisive milestone that leads to the bull *Ineffabilis Deus* of Pius IX (1854).

35. John Paul II, CM 21 (May 29, 1996), n. 3. See also Galot, *Maria, La donna*, 3rd ed., 195–97.

Development in the East

The Observations of John Paul II

The first explicit traces of doctrine about the Immaculate Conception of Mary, about her holiness from the first moment of her existence, are found in the East.[36] John Paul II makes reference to them in his encyclical *Redemptoris Mater*[37] and above all in one of his Marian Catecheses.[38] As first witnesses of the dogma, the pope presents Theoteknos of Livias (ca. 600) in addition to Andrew of Crete, Germanus of Constantinople, and John Damascene (three holy fathers of the eighth century). The pope's references have a great importance for dialogue with the Orthodox churches, whose theologians today generally reject the doctrine of the Immaculate Conception.

Original Sin according to the Greek Fathers

To interpret the Eastern witnesses correctly, first of all we need to underscore the character of the doctrine of original sin, which was imprecise then.[39] The Orthodox are divided on the very existence of original sin because the systematic clarity that had come to the West ever since the contributions of Augustine was often lacking in

36. See Martin Jugie, *L'Immaculée Conception dans l'Écriture Sainte et dans la Tradition Orientale* [The Immaculate Conception in Holy Scripture and in Eastern Tradition] (Rome: Academia Mariana, 1952); Georg Söll, *Storia dei dogmi mariani* [History of Marian Dogmas]. Rome: Libreria Ateneo Salesiano, 1981, 217–25, 230–40; Manfred Hauke, "Die Unbefleckte Empfängnis Mariens bei den griechischen Vätern: Die Hinweise Johannes Pauls II. im ökumenischen Disput," *Sedes Sapientiae: Mariologisches Jahrbuch* 8, no. 2 (2004); Hauke, "Die Gottesmutter als irdisches Paradies bei Johannes von Euböa: Die erste Predigt zum Fest der makellosen Empfängnis Mariens" [The Mother of God as Earthly Paradise in John of Euböa: The First Sermon on the Feast of the Spotless Conception of Mary], *Klerusblatt* 84 (2004): 272–74; Hauke, *Urstand, Fall und Erbsünde: In der nachaugustinischen Ära bis zum Beginn der Scholastik; Die griechische Theologie* [Original State, Fall, and Original Sin: Greek Theology in the Post-Augustinian Era to the Beginning of Scholasticism], *Handbuch der Dogmengeschichte*, vol. 3, fascicle 3a, part 2 (Freiburg im Breisgau: Herder, 2007), 135–46; Galot, *Maria, La donna*, 3rd ed., 198–204.

37. *RM* 10, note 26.

38. John Paul II, CM 20 (May 15, 1996). The content of this catechesis depends on the contemporary work of Jean Galot; see in particular Galot, *Maria, La donna*, 3rd ed., 199–204.

39. On original sin in the Greek fathers, see Hauke, *Heilsverlust in Adam: Stationen griechischer Erbsündenlehre; Irenäus—Origenes—Kappadozier* [Salvation Lost in Adam: Stages of Greek Teaching on Original Sin; Irenaeus, Origen, the Cappadocians] (Paderborn: Bonifatius, 1993); Hauke, *Urstand, Fall und Erbsünde.*

the East. The Council of Trent describes original sin as the loss of righteousness and holiness present in the original paradise[40] and, following a treatise of Augustine, as *mors animae*—that is to say, as a privation of divine life, caused by the first sin.[41] The privation of divine life is also a fault for the descendants of Adam, because this situation contradicts the will of God, which was to initially share grace, his friendship, to all men by means of the obedience of our progenitors. Original (i.e., caused) sin is nothing but the privation of the grace of paradise, which placed man in need of spiritual rebirth by means of Baptism.

This basic content is also present in the Greek fathers, although it is less explicit that the privation of divine life has the character of guilt. In view of the Orthodox, we need to reaffirm that the ecumenical Council of Ephesus (431) condemned Pelagianism,[42] which denied original sin, and Messalianism,[43] which confused concupiscence with sin, as Luther did later in the West. The Second Synod of Trullo (691–92), recognized as an ecumenical council by the Orthodox (and not by the Catholic Church on account of certain anti-Roman contents), accepted and translated into Greek, among other things, the two most important canons of the Synod of Carthage (418) on original sin.[44] Among other things, they state that the Baptism of children is administered "for the remission of sins." Newborns somehow contract the sin of their progenitors (*progonikè hamartía*) in such a way that they must be purified by means of Baptism. Orthodox theologians who are acquainted with the texts of Trullo II (many, however, are not aware of them) also accept original (caused) sin.

40. DH 1511f.

41. DH 1512.

42. DH 267f.

43. See *COD* 66f; Hauke, "Die Taufgnade und die 'Wurzel des Bösen': Anmerkungen zur Verurteilung des Messalianismus auf dem Konzil von Ephesus" [Baptismal Grace and the "Problem of Evil": Remarks on the Judgment of Messelianism at the Council of Ephesus], *Archivum Historiae Conciliorum* 35 (2003): 307–21; also in *I Padri e le scuole teologiche nei concili*, ed. Johannes Grohe, Jerónimo Leal, and Vito Reale (Vatican City: Libreria Editrice Vaticana, 2006), 325–40; Hauke, *Urstand, Fall und Erbsünde*, 19–25.

44. DH 222f. See Perikles-Petros Joannou, *Discipline générale antique*, vol. 1, part 2 (Rome: S. Nilo, 1962), 377f. (or rather, inter alia, PG 138:368A–69A); Hauke, *Heilsverlust in Adam*, 47; Hauke, *Urstand, Fall und Erbsünde*, 117–19.

Original sin presupposes the original state, the first paradise. The most typical description of the situation of paradise in the Greek fathers places divine "life" in the foreground, going beyond the human structure. Other similar terms are "salvation" (*soteria*) and being "at home" with God (*oikeíosis*). Then the Greek fathers teach, with various terms, a gratuitous element in man created in the image of God, a grace present in Paradise, lost because of the first sin and reestablished in Jesus Christ. Furthermore, we find numerous references to a particular gift of the Holy Spirit and to freedom from the disorder of concupiscence.

The consequences of the Fall constitute, so to speak, Paradise upside down. The gravest fact is death, which not only means having to die, but above all the privation of divine life. Here we find the strongest systematic contact with the doctrine of Augustine. Privation of divine life corresponds to what medieval Latin theology calls *peccatum habituale*—that is, sin seen as a state (originating from a *peccatum actuale*, in this case the sin of Adam). In this perspective the "death of the soul" is not only a consequence of sin, but is sin itself as a state (*habitus*). Other consequences of the first sin, in the Greek fathers, are the loss of the gratuitous element in the image of God, the privation of the gift of the Holy Spirit, the disorder of concupiscence, and weakening of the intellect and of the will, as well as the tyranny of Satan. This situation is described, for example as early as in Melito (second century) as "perdition" (*apóleia*), transmitted as the "heredity of Adam." Many times, the nexus of the situation of Adam and of his descendants appears in terms such as "first sin" or "ancient sin." Or, rather, it is stated that "we" have sinned in Adam.

Also important is the reception of Job 14:4f LXX, according to which every man is rendered as "unclean" (*rúpos*) from the first day of his existence.[45] Origen, explaining this passage, wavers between an explanation based on his theory of preexistence and another that stresses the sin of Adam: in the perspective of preexistence, the *rúpos* appears as earthly corporeality (given as a punishment for sin committed by the soul in its preexistence); the way based on salvation

45. See ibid., 74–81.

history, in contrast, tends to present the "uncleanness" as sin in the proper sense, removed by Baptism. While in the West the reception of Job 14 decisively favors the development of the dogma of original sin, the interpretation in the East is hindered by Origen's preexistentialist explanation. Nonetheless we already find in the fourth century the first explicit witnesses for the transmission of a "sin," in particular in Didymus of Alexandria (following Origen), Apollinaris of Laodicea, and Gregory of Nyssa. Since the Greeks were not spurred by the Pelagian denial of original sin, their doctrine remains somewhat less clear and at times marked with some contradictions. Yet there is no doubt that the doctrine of the Greek fathers on Paradise and on original sin contain, at least implicitly, the faith of the church. For the Orthodox of today, it would be necessary in some way to explicitly accept the tradition proper and the explanation brought by the universal church under the guidance of the successor of Peter.

Mariological Assumptions

The terrain that provided the first explicit affirmations on Mary's original sanctity was prepared by three factors: the parallelism between Eve and Mary, praise of the Theotokos (especially after the Council of Ephesus in 431), and the feast of the Assumption of Mary, celebrated under the title of the "Dormition of Mary" in the whole Byzantine empire since the end of the sixth century. At the end of the patristic era we no longer find statements that attribute sinful shadows to the figure of Mary. The Mother of God appears with titles such as "All-Holy" (*panágia*) (first in Eusebius of Caesarea)[46] and "Immaculate" (in Gregory of Nyssa, fourth century).[47] Earlier still, the apocryphal tradition of the Protoevangelium of James is inclined to look to the conception of Mary in the womb of her mother.

46. *De ecclesiastica theologia* 3.16 (PG 24:1033B; *GCS* 14:174). Eusebius probably found the term already in the works of Origen: see Gambero, *Mary and the Fathers*, 77; Michael O'Carroll, CSSp, *Theotokos: A Theological Encyclopedia of the Blessed Virgin Mary* (Eugene, Ore.: Wipf and Stock, 2000), 138f.

47. *De virginitate* 2.2 (Gregorii Nysseni Opera VIII/1, 254): *en tê amiánto María.* See Hauke, *Heilsverlust in Adam*, 677; Giulio Maspero, "El misterio de la Virgen toda limpia en Gregorio de Nisa" [The Mystery of the All-Pure Virgin in Gregory of Nyssa], *Scripta de Maria* 2nd ser., 1 (2004): 183–203.

This tradition, starting from the second century, is historically problematic, but it turns attention to the holiness of Mary from the beginning and flows into two liturgical celebrations: the memorial of the Presentation of Mary at the temple (since the sixth century) and the feast of the Conception of Anne (since the eighth century). The first sign of this feast comes from St. Andrew of Crete.[48]

The original purity of Mary, of which the first testimonies will be described later, needs to take account of another thread of the Byzantine tradition, which may appear (in the eyes of many Orthodox theologians) as "competing" with it: the texts on the "purification" of Mary. Gregory of Nazianzus (fourth century) presents a first sign of the intervention of the Holy Spirit for the sanctification of Mary. Before the virginal conception, Mary was "pre-purified," or rather, "sanctified," so as to be able to receive the incarnate Son of God fittingly.[49] It is not said when this "purification" takes place, but probably the author is thinking of the descent of the Holy Spirit at the Annunciation. Since, under the influence of neo-Platonic philosophy, the purification can be understood as a greater sanctification (becoming "brighter"), the reference to *kátharsis* is open to an interpretation of this type, as happened in the Byzantine era.[50] But the concept of a true and proper purification would also not be abnormal at this stage of dogmatic development. Irenaeus speaks of a "purification" of the "maternal womb" (including the person of Mary); in his case too, the event of the Annunciation seems to be implicit:

> Those [of them] who proclaimed Him as Immanuel, born of the Virgin, manifested the union of the Word of God with His own workmanship, when the Word becomes flesh, and the Son of God the Son of man, the pure One opening purely that pure maternal womb which regenerates men unto God, and which He Himself made pure.[51]

48. See Cecchin, *L'Immacolata Concezione*, 18f.

49. *Or.* 38.13 (= 45.9) (PG 36:325B; 633D): *psuchèn kaì sárka prokathartheíses tô Pneúmati. Carm.* I.1.9, v. 67f (PG 37:462A): *hégnise prósthen. Carm.* I.1.10, v. 53 (PG 37:469A): *Tò Pneúma epêlthe parthéno kathársion.* See Hauke, *Heilsverlust in Adam*, 560.

50. See "The Divine Maternity Brings with It a Transforming Relationship," in chapter 4.

51. *Adversus haereses* IV.33.11 (*SC* 100:830f). See also p. 81.

The Pure Origin of Mary according to Theoteknos of Livias

The first clear testimony to the pure origin of Mary is found in a sermon by the bishop Theoteknos of Livias on the Assumption of Mary. It is one of the most ancient texts on the Assumption, only published in 1955.[52] Livias, a city on the left bank of the Jordan (the "Tell er-Ram" of modern Jordan), faded as an episcopal see toward the middle of the seventh century due to the invasion of the Muslim Arabs. As Bishop Theoteknos is not yet using the technical term *"koimesis"* (dormition), but rather that of "Assumption" (*análepsis*) of Mary into heavenly glory, the most probable origin of the sermon is around the middle of the sixth century. Pope John Paul II, following the recommendations of Galot (and of the editor Antoine Wenger), indicates the time between 550 and 650 as the origin of the sermon.[53]

The celebration of the heavenly fulfillment of the Mother of God also becomes the occasion to explain the start of Mary's earthly life. If Jesus Christ opened the heavenly kingdom to the saints and opened Paradise to the good thief, he did so with all the more reason "for her who offered him the dwelling place of her womb, for her whom He Himself created, whom He Himself formed."[54] Therefore Theoteknos affirms a special intervention of God at the origin of Mary's life. Hence it is not surprising to find a reference to the sanctity and purity that already surround her conception:

> She was born like the cherubim, she who was formed of a pure and immaculate clay. Indeed, when she was still in the loins of her father Joachim, her mother Anna received the message of a holy angel in the following words: "Your offspring will be renowned in all the world." And thus Anna presented her to the Lord in the temple.[55]

A comparison to the holy ground of Paradise, from which the first Adam was formed, appears as early as the second century in

52. Antoine Wenger, *L'Assomption de la Très Sainte Vierge dans la tradition byzantine du VI au X siècle: Études et documents* [The Assumption of the Most Holy Virgin in Byzantine Tradition of the Sixth to Tenth Centuries: Studies and Documents] (Paris: Institut français d'études byzantines, 1955), 271–91.

53. John Paul II, CM 20 (May 15, 1996), n. 3.

54. Theoteknos, *Laus in Assumptionem* 3, in Wenger, *L'Assomption*, 272.

55. Ibid., 6, in Wenger, *L'Assomption*, 274 and addendum.

Irenaeus: as Adam was formed from virgin earth (that had never yet been worked), so Jesus Christ comes as man from the Virgin Mary.[56] However, there is a new idea in Theoteknos, that the immaculate origin of Jesus from the Virgin Mary already includes the origin of Mary and even her conception. Starting from the origin of Mary, the bishop's strong statements on the Mother of God are better understood; she is called "holy," "all beautiful," "pure," and "without blemish."[57] The "immaculate body of the perfectly holy one (*panágia*)" experienced death (as did Christ himself), but in no way corruption.[58] Her immaculate origin and her assumption into heaven make possible Mary's mediating intervention on our behalf: she has become "ambassadrix of the human race before the immaculate king" and "mediatrix of all" (*présbis pánton*).[59]

Theoteknos does not provide any explicit statement on "original sin," but it is evident that the loss of the goods of paradise, of which we all have need in order to be saved, is replaced by the holiness of Mary: "She found as much as Eve lost. She found the goods of which Adam was deprived due to his disobedience." In Mary Paradise opens because the divine Word enters into her and dwells in her.[60]

The Conception of Mary as Reestablishment of Paradise according to Andrew of Crete

While Theoteknos describes the purity of the creation of Mary, St. Andrew of Crete presents the conception of Mary in the womb of her mother as a reestablishment of Paradise. Together with SS. Germanus of Constantinople and John Damascene, St. Andrew is one of the three great theologians singing of the Mother of God in the eighth century, the "golden age" of Byzantine Marian devotion.[61] For our presentation it suffices to report and comment on three passag-

56. Irenaeus, *Adversus haereses* III.18.7; 21.10 (*SC* 211:368–70; 428); *Demonstratio* 33f (*SC* 62:83–87). See Hauke, *Heilsverlust in Adam*, 263.

57. Theoteknos, *Laus*, 5, in Wenger, *L'Assomption*, 274.

58. Ibid., 15, in Wenger, *L'Assomption*, 278.

59. Ibid., 17, 31, in Wenger, *L'Assomption*, 280, 288.

60. Ibid., 25, in Wenger, *L'Assomption*, 284.

61. This is the opinion of Wenger, "Foi et piété mariales à Byzance" [Marian Faith and Piety in Byzantium], in *Maria*, ed. Hubert du Manoir (Paris: Beauchesne, 1958), 5:944.

es presented by the Holy Father. The first passage, only cited in the encyclical, comes from the canticle on the birth of Mary.[62] The birth of Mary is one of the most ancient Marian feasts, celebrated at Constantinople since the sixth century. Its date—September 8—later determined the date of the feast of the Conception of Anne, set nine months earlier at December 9. Andrew of Crete left not only an ode, but also the most ancient sermon handed down to us on the birth of Mary. Since (even today) the date falls at the start of the Byzantine liturgical year, the birth of the Theotokos is "the first of the feasts that look within to the laws and shadows (of the Old Covenant)" and at the same time "bring it to feasts that point to grace and truth."[63]

As the feast of the birth does not yet specifically distinguish the conception of Mary in the womb of Anne, it celebrates the whole earthly origin of Mary. It also takes account of the fact that the term used for "birth," *génnesis*, means not only birth in the narrow sense, but also involves the first origin, a fact very clear in the citation mentioned by Pope John Paul II:

> Undefiled is your birth, O undefiled Virgin Mary (*Áchrantos sou he génnesis, parthéne áchrante*); marvelous is both the conception [!] and the birth (*áfrastos kaì he súllepsis kaì he odís).*[64]

The second passage, cited in the encyclical in a footnote, is quoted explicitly in the Marian Catecheses and comes from the first sermon on the nativity of Mary:

> Today humanity, in all the radiance of her immaculate nobility, receives its ancient beauty. The shame of sin had darkened the splendor and attraction of human nature; but when the Mother of the Fair One *par excellence* is born, this nature regains in her person its ancient privileges and is fashioned according to a perfect model truly worthy of God.... The reform of our nature begins today and the aged world, subjected to a wholly divine transformation, receives the first fruits of the second creation.[65]

62. *Canon in B. Mariae Natalem* (PG 97:1321f). See *RM* 10, n. 25.
63. *In Nativitatem B. Mariae* I (PG 97:805A).
64. *Canon in B. Mariae Natalem* (PG 97:1321C).
65. *In Nativ. B. Mariae* I (PG 97:812A, 812C). See *RM* 10, n. 25; CM 20 (May 15, 1996), n. 4.

The pope himself emphasizes: Andrew of Crete "was the first theologian to see a new creation in Mary's birth."[66] The vocabulary related to "fashioning" (*plásis*) refers to the forming of the first man in the earthly paradise, a formation that is then compared with the origin of Mary: in the birth of Mary, humanity receives anew "the charism of the first forming on the part of God" (*tes prótes theoplastías apolambánei tò chárisma*).[67] In this context, the term "clay" (*pélos*) also appears, already used by Theoteknos of Livias: "You are blessed among women, you, truly desirable earth from which the potter took the clay of our land to renew the vessel broken by sin." Mary is therefore "the first reparation of the first fall of our progenitors."[68]

The motif of clay is also recalled by the pope with a quotation from a sermon on the Dormition: "The Virgin's body is ground which God has tilled, the first fruits of Adam's soil divinized by Christ, the image truly like the former beauty, the clay kneaded by the divine Artist."[69]

The first patristic references to the holy origin of Mary, in turn, impel us to a certain caution. Laurentin, for instance, notes, "These panegyrics [of the Greek preachers] are the first sketch of the dogma of the Immaculate Conception, a sketch still quite imprecise. On the one hand, Mary's initial purity had not yet been collated with the universality of Christ's redemption. On the other hand, the poetic language of the Byzantine homilists is so enthusiastic that oratorial overstatement is difficult to distinguish from dogmatic affirmation."[70]

It is true that the original holiness of Mary is not yet being brought together systematically with the universal necessity of the Redemption. It is somewhat evident, particularly in Andrew, that redemptive grace already reaches to the conception of Mary in the womb of her mother, even if the systematic problem will be formulated only some centuries later in the West. One cannot say, howev-

66. John Paul II, CM 20, n. 4.

67. *In Nativ. B. Mariae* I (PG 97:812A).

68. *In Nativ. B. Mariae* IV (PG 97:865C, 880C).

69. *Hom. in Dormitionem S. Mariae* 1 (PG 97:1068C). See John Paul II, CM 20, n. 4.

70. René Laurentin, *A Short Treatise on the Virgin Mary* (Washington, N.J.: Ave Maria Institute, 1991), 87.

er, at least by the evidence presented to us, that oratorical excesses could not be distinguished from doctrinal affirmations. We are not just finding some isolated quotation; rather, we see here the manifestation of a systematic vision that endows Mary from the beginning with divine grace, the fruit of an anticipated intervention by the Redeemer. Its connection with the fall of our progenitors, which deprived all humanity of the clothing of grace, is clear. The immaculate origin of Mary appears as a new beginning that reestablishes the purity of the original state in Paradise. Better still, Mary herself is the "Paradise" in which Christ, the new Adam, dwells.[71] Andrew praises her with the words of the Canticle of Canticles, as "all beautiful" and "without blemish" (Sg 4:7).[72] The Mother of God "is holier than all the Saints; she appears totally pure through Him who dwelt in her, body and soul."[73]

The Prevenient Action of Divine Grace in the Conception of Mary according to Germanus of Constantinople

Important testimony is also found in St. Germanus, Patriarch of Constantinople. John Paul II's encyclical *Redemptoris Mater* refers to Germanus's sermon on the Annunciation: Mary is already holy before the Annunciation, because the angel finds her "totally and in every respect pure and immaculate."[74] Mary is "without blemish" already in her childhood, having passed into the temple (according to the apocryphal tradition) starting at the age of three.[75] The sermon on the angel's Annunciation therefore reaffirms the perfect purity of Mary since infancy, but does not refer explicitly to her conception in the womb of Anne. That fact, however, is indicated by a sermon on the Presentation of Mary in the temple, a text cited by Jean Galot, but not appearing as such in the Marian Catecheses.[76] It deals with a very meaningful passage, set on the lips of Anne:

71. *In Nativ. B. Mariae* III (PG 97:868C); *In Annunt. B. Mariae* (PG 97:900B).
72. *In Nativ. B. Mariae* IV (PG 97:872A); *In Dorm. Mariae* III (PG 97:1097C).
73. *In Nativ. B. Mariae* II (PG 97:832B).
74. *In Annuntiationem SS. Deiparae Hom.* (PG 98:328A). See John Paul II, *RM* 10, n. 25.
75. Ibid. (PG 98:329C).
76. See Galot, *Maria, La donna*, 3rd ed., 203.

After (the Annunciation of the angel) my nature received the fetus, at the command of God: my nature had not dared to receive the fetus before the divine grace. But when grace arrived, the closed womb opened its gates. It received the deposit coming from God and preserved it to this day, when that seed sown in a mother's womb by the will of God came into the light.[77]

The grace of God points not only to the miraculous power of overcoming sterility, but also the power of sanctification. This fact is suggested by the context of the sermon that praises the presentation of Mary in the temple as a "prelude of divine grace" that will overshadow the holy Virgin again at the Annunciation.[78]

Mary Immaculate according to John Damascene

While *Redemptoris Mater* refers only to Andrew of Crete and Germanus, the Marian Catechesis also mentions (Theoteknos and) John Damascene, the most important "dogmatic theologian" of the Byzantine Church.[79] Orthodox theologians, in contrast, often cite the same holy doctor as a principal witness against the Immaculate Conception, pointing to a passage coming from the tradition of "pre-purification":

After the consent of the holy Virgin, the Holy Spirit descended on her ... and purified her.[80]

Jean Galot knows this text well, but gives more weight to another passage: "John Damascene takes up the prior opinion of a pre-purification of Mary at the moment of the Annunciation. But in a *homily on the Nativity of Mary*, he speaks of a "seed all immaculate," of a girl (in the sense of a fetus) all holy."[81] Indeed the text is clear:

Why was the Virgin Mother born of a sterile woman? ... Nature ... was conquered by grace. Trembling, nature was closed and dared not to proceed. As the virgin Mother of God had to be born of Anna, nature had not the courage to precede the bud of grace, but remained sterile until grace pro-

77. *In Praesentationem SS. Deiparae* II (PG 98:313D).

78. Ibid. (PG 98:309 B–C).

79. John Paul II, CM 20 (May 15, 1996), n. 4.

80. *De fide orthodoxa* III.2 (PG 94:985). See, for example, T. Nikolaou, "Sündenlosigkeit," 332f.

81. Galot, *Maria, La donna*, 3rd ed., 203, n. 48.

duced its fruit.... O happy the loins of Joachim from which came a seed totally immaculate! O marvelous womb of Anna in which grew a baby perfectly holy."[82]

Is there perhaps a contradiction between John Damascene's "dogmatics" (which teach the purification of sin at the Annunciation) and his "homiletics" (which press poetically toward the conception)? Or perhaps do we need to consider the homily an inauthentic work? But there are not sufficient reasons to eliminate this text from the works of the Damascene.[83] Besides, in the same "dogmatics" that contain the most famous statement on pre-purification, the theologian manifests his conviction that Mary is, as a girl, already a temple of the Holy Spirit and abode of every virtue.[84]

Further Developments in Byzantium

For the Eastern theologians, it is also plausible that Mary was born already holy, by way of analogy with the sanctification of John the Baptist in his mother's womb (Lk 1:15) and the consecration of the prophet Jeremiah before his birth (Jer 1:5).

After the eighth century, in the Byzantine church it becomes a general conviction that holiness came to Mary in the womb of her mother from her conception on. Photius, patriarch of Constantinople (†891), states that Mary was fully sanctified at her formation in her mother's womb, to become a living temple of God.[85] Indeed, John Geometres (tenth century) affirms, "Already before the angelic salutation, from her conception on, Mary was purified and made beautiful."[86] The liturgical feast, which arose in the sixth century, is called "Annunciation of the holy *Theotókos*" (or "of Joachim and

82. *In Nativ. S. Dei Gen. Mariae* 2 (PG 96:664A–B).

83. See Jugie, *L'Immaculée Conception*, 121; Johannes M. Hoeck, "Stand und Aufgaben der Damaskenosforschung" [Status and Tasks of Research on St. John of Damascus], *Orientalia Christiana Periodica* 17 (1951): 37.

84. *De fide orthodoxa* IV, 14 (PG 94:1156A).

85. See Alexis Stawrowsky, "La Sainte Vierge Marie: La doctrine de l'Immaculée Conception des Églises Catholique et Orthodoxe; Étude comparée par un Théologien Orthodoxe" [The Holy Virgin Mary: The Catholic and Orthodox Churches' Doctrine of the Immaculate Conception; Comparative Study by an Orthodox Theologian], *Marianum* 35 (1973): 52; Hauke, *Urstand, Fall und Erbsünde*, 157f.

86. *In Deiparae Ann.* (PG 106:825).

Anne"), "Conception of Anne," or "Conception of Mary." In the twelfth century, December 9 is celebrated as a solemnity of precept in the whole Byzantine empire.

Gregory Palamas and Nicholas Cabasilas (fourteenth century) are among the Byzantine authors closer to the idea of a conception without sin. The latter writes:

> Mary is the ideal type of humanity. Only she has fully realized the divine idea of man [the human person] *par excellence*.... Unique among all men who have lived or live now, the Virgin remained free of any iniquity, from the beginning to the end of her existence; only she rendered back to God in its integrity the beauty He gives us ... she held the human form in all its splendor, free from any extraneous form. No one else, says the prophet, is foreign to all uncleanness [this refers to Job 14:4 LXX: "Who can bring a clean thing out of an unclean? There is not one, though his life last only a day"]. No one was holy before the blessed Virgin; she was the first and is the only one to be absolutely void of sin.[87]

Thus we find in the East witnesses to Mary's freedom from sin from the beginning. Still, it does not seem appropriate to speak in a strict sense of "preservation" from original sin, because we owe that category to William of Ware and Duns Scotus. Many texts are close to the affirmation that Mary was never under the dominion of original sin. But inasmuch as thought regarding original sin was less developed, the description of complete holiness comes into the foreground. "The Eastern theologians are more concerned with highlighting the holiness of Mary than in specifying her situation in relation to the application of the law of original sin."[88]

The opinion that attributes to Mary a purification from original sin (*progonikòs rúpos*) at the Annunciation appears for the first time only in the fourteenth century in a Greek theologian (Nicephoros Callistos Xanthopoulos) who expresses his fear of committing an error: may the Theotokos pardon him if he should stray from the or-

87. *In Nativ.*, cited in ibid., 56f. See Christiaan Kappes, *The Immaculate Conception: Why Thomas Aquinas Denied, While John Duns Scotus, Gregory Palamas, and Mark Eugenicus Professed the Absolute Immaculate Existence of Mary* (New Bedford, Mass.: Academy of the Immaculate, 2014).

88. Galot, *Maria, La donna*, 3rd ed., 204.

thodox faith, in attributing the stain of original sin to the All-Holy.[89] A formal opposition to the doctrine of the Immaculate Conception appears among the Orthodox only since the sixteenth century and becomes more fixed after the dogmatic definition of 1854.[90]

Development in the West up to the Twelfth Century (Eadmer)

The parallelism Eve/Mary, in the West, led St. Ambrose to the conclusion that Mary is free of any blemish of sin.[91] One important event was the statement of St. Augustine, which declared, in regard to sins, "I do not want to include Mary, who overcame sin 'in every regard.'"[92] From that moment on (429), the way was open to debate whether Mary was or was not touched by original sin. After Augustine, there was a strong affirmation of the universality of original sin and of its absence in Jesus, due to his virginal conception, so it became difficult to exclude Mary from the sin of Adam. Otherwise, would we not run the risk of denying the universality of the Redemption? Because of this, the first explicit denial of the Immaculate Conception, made by Caesarius of Arles (sixth century), is explained with Augustinian categories: not even Mary, the Mother of the Redeemer, is free from the kind of sin that reaches into the mother's womb.[93]

The first traces of the Eastern feast of December 9 in the West are found in the ninth century, in a marble calendar in Naples. It

89. Cf. Jugie, *L'Immaculée Conception*, 211–307; Wenger, "Foi et piété mariales à Byzance," 5:951f; Luigi Gambero, *Fede e devozione mariana nell'impero bizantino* [Marian Faith and Devotion in the Byzantine Empire] (Cinisello Balsamo: San Paolo, 2012), 284.

90. See "The Ecumenical Debate," in this chapter.

91. *In Ps. 118, sermo* 22.30 (PL 15:1521): "Suscipe me non ex Sara, sed ex Maria; ut incorrupta sit virgo, sed virgo per gratiam ab omni integra labe peccati." See J. Huhn, "Ambrosius von Mailand" [Ambrose of Milan], in *ML* 1:129.

92. *De natura et gratia* 36.42 (PL 44:267). See also pp. 211–12. It does not seem that freedom from original sin follows from this, but the question is controversial: see, e.g., Gambero, *Mary and the Fathers*, 263f; Gambero, "La santità di Maria," 272–77 (with a wide-ranging bibliography); Daniel E. Doyle, OSA, "Mary, Mother of God," in *Augustine through the Ages: An Encyclopedia*, ed. A. D. Fitzgerald (Grand Rapids, Mich.: Eerdmans, 1999), 542–45.

93. See *Hom.* 2.4 (*CChr. SL* 101:26). Cándido Pozo, SJ, *María, nueva Eva* [Mary, the New Eve] (Madrid: Biblioteca de Autores Cristianos, 2005), 321, note 23.

was not attesting to a Western liturgical celebration yet, but presenting a reference to the Eastern practice, which was also followed by Byzantine monasteries in southern Italy.[94] The current liturgical celebration in the West, December 8, has been identified with certainty around 1060 in England. The feast was suppressed a little later because of the Norman conquest (1066) and revived from 1120 on, thanks to Benedictine spirituality and later the influence of St. Anselm's theology and that of his disciples.[95]

The introduction of the Feast of the Conception of Mary encountered some resistance. When the canons of the cathedral of Lyon introduced the new feast, a protest arrived from St. Bernard (1138). Certainly Mary was already holy before her birth, but the feast of her conception would be contrary to tradition, and it would need to be approved by the Apostolic See anyway. Even some errors of biology clashed with the feast: since "conception" appears to be the origin of the body prior to the infusion of the soul, Bernard states that it would not make sense to speak of sanctification prior to existence.[96]

A student of Anselm, the Benedictine monk Eadmer († 1141), is the first theologian to teach expressly the Immaculate Conception of Mary.[97] It is possible that he was responding to St. Bernard.[98] It

94. See Cecchin, *L'Immacolata Concezione*, 20.

95. See ibid., 21.

96. Ep. 174 (PL 182:332–36). See Gambero, *Maria nel pensiero dei teologi latini medievali* (Cinisello Balsamo: Ed. Paoline, 2000), 163–65; English trans. in Gambero, *Mary in the Middle Ages: The Blessed Virgin Mary in the Thought of Medieval Latin Theologians*, translated by Thomas Buffer (San Francisco: Ignatius, 2005), 137–38; Cecchin, *L'Immacolata Concezione*, 31–34.

97. Eadmer, *De conceptione sanctae Mariae* (PL 159:305–6A); see Gambero, *Maria nel pensiero*, 136–38 (English trans. in Gambero, *Mary in the Middle Ages*, 118–19); Barnaba Hechich, "La teologia dell'Immacolata Concezione in alcuni autori prescolastici" [The Theology of the Immaculate Conception in Several Pre-Scholastic Authors], in *La "Scuola Francescana e l'Immacolata Concezione*, ed. S. Cecchin (Vatican City: PAMI, 2005), 150–54; Pietro Maranesi, "Gli sviluppi della dottrina sull'Immacolata Concezione nei secoli XII–XV secolo" [Developments in the Doctrine of the Immaculate Conception in the 12th to 15th Centuries], in *Storia della Mariologia*, ed. E. Dal Covolo and A. Serra (Rome: Città Nuova, 2009), 1:846f. (Eadmer is not an isolated case but is present amid other contributions of the same period, some of them anonymous.)

98. This thesis is supported by Heinrich M. Köster, "Der Beitrag Eadmers OSB 1060/64–1141 zur theologischen Erkenntnis der Unbefleckten Empfängnis" [The Contribution of Eadmer, OSB, to the Theological Recognition of the Immaculate Conception], in *Im Gewande des Heils: Die Unbefleckte Empfängnis Mariens als Urbild der menschlichen Heiligkeit* [Clothed with Holiness: The Immaculate Conception of Mary as an Archetype of Human Holiness], ed. German Rovira (Essen: Ludgerus-Verlag, 1980), 61–70.

would not be acceptable that, at her conception, Mary had been under the dominion of sin, which had been brought into the world by the devil. If Jeremiah and John the Baptist were sanctified in their mother's wombs, how much more was Mary, the Mother of God? To counter the objection that Mary arose from sinful parents, Eadmer used the analogy of a chestnut that comes out of a spiny shell, but is without spines. The theologian formulated a principle summarized later in the words: *potuit, decuit, ergo fecit.* God was able to free Mary from original sin (*potuit*); it was fitting that he realize this possibility (*decuit*); therefore God did it (*fecit*).[99] This principle is an aid, but cannot prove a priori a thesis apart from Revelation.[100]

Anselm, Eadmer's teacher, does not yet teach the Immaculate Conception, but presents one of its presuppositions. Even those who lived before Christ were redeemed in view of his death; in this way Mary was purified by means of her faith (this is a sort of "pre-redemption," to accept the term used later by Scotus).[101] In addition, the theologian formulates a principle whose expression resembles the "ontological" proof of the existence of God: "It was fitting that this Virgin should shine with a purity so great that, except for God, no greater purity could be conceived!"[102] Furthermore, Anselm no longer connects the transmission of original sin to procreation as such (and to the concupiscence of the conjugal act, as did Augustine), but describes it as a privation of original justice (*absentia debitae iustitiae*).[103] This privation, caused by Adam, takes place when soul and body are united.

99. Eadmer, *De conceptione s. Mariae* (PL 159:305): "He certainly could do it. Therefore, if He willed to, He did it." This approach finds a precedent in the work of Pseudo-Augustine on the Assumption of Mary: Christ was able to preserve his Mother from the corruption of the tomb and He willed to do so because it was fitting: "Mariam sine corruptione servare potuit Christus. Voluit, quia et decuit" (*De Assumptione BMV* [PL 40:1147f]). The work is from the ninth or tenth century. See "Development in the West," in chapter 7.

100. Leo Scheffczyk, "Konvenienzgründe" [Grounds of Fittingness], in *ML* 3:637–39, speaks of an *a posteriori* auxiliary principle ("ein aposteriorischer Hilfsleitsatz") (638).

101. *Cur Deus homo* 2.16 (PL 158:419A); *De concept. Virg.* 18 (PL 158:451A–B).

102. *De concept. Virg.* 18 (PL 158:451); Gambero, *Maria nel pensiero*, 127f [*Mary in the Middle Ages*, III]. See "Nihil est aequale Mariae; nihil, nisi Deus, maius Maria" (*Oratio* 52 [PL 158:956A]).

103. *De concep. Virg.* 3 (PL 158:136A).

The Contributions of William of Ware and of Duns Scotus

Despite the approach of Eadmer, it was not yet clear how to put together Mary's need for redemption and her tremendous holiness. For this reason, most of the Scholastics speak of a purification from original sin "immediately after conception" (Bonaventure, Thomas).[104] Thomas explains the liturgical feast of the Conception of Mary by the tolerance of the Roman Church and maintains: this feast can be celebrated not because the Conception was holy, but because no one knows exactly when the sanctification in her mother's womb took place.[105]

The English Franciscan William of Ware (thirteenth century), who introduces the idea of preservation, made way for decisive progress: "All the cleanness of the Mother came from her Son. Consequently, she needed the Passion of Christ not for sin that she already had, but for sin that she would have had if that Son had not preserved her by means of faith."[106] Obviously the "by means of faith" does not refer to the faith of Mary, but to that of her parents, Joachim and Anne.

The definitive solution to the problem came from the student of William of Ware, John Duns Scotus, OFM (†1308).[107] In his expo-

104. See Cecchin, *L'Immacolata Concezione*, 39–54; Bogusław Kochaniewicz, "L'Immacolata Concezione e la dottrina di San Tommaso d'Aquino" [The Immaculate Conception and the Doctrine of St. Thomas Aquinas], in Cecchin, *La "Scuola Francescana,"* 87–140.

105. *ST* III, q. 27, a. 2.

106. *Quaestiones disputatae de Immaculata Conceptione BMV* 10, cited in Cecchin, *L'Immacolata Concezione*, 60f; see also the publication and Italian translation of the corresponding question of the Commentary of William of Ware on the Sentences of Peter Lombard, *Sent.* III q. 11 (d. 3 q. 1), in Cecchin, *La "Scuola Francescana,"* 769–90 (B. Hechich). See Söll, *Storia dei dogmi mariani*, §10c; Michael O'Carroll, CSSp, "Wilhelm von Ware" [William of Ware], in *ML* 6:738; see O'Carroll, *Theotokos*, 367. The initiator of the "immaculatist movement" in the Franciscan order was the English bishop of Lincoln, Robert Grosseteste (†1253). While not a Franciscan, he has the distinction of having instructed the first teachers of the Order at the university level at Oxford, starting in 1224. Grosseteste already allows for the possibility of the Immaculate Conception and seems also to teach the fact. The idea of preservation from original sin, the crucial systematic step, is found only (according to the sources at our disposal) in William of Ware and in Scotus. On Grosseteste, see Cecchin, *L'Immacolata Concezione*, 56–58.

107. John Duns Scotus, *Four Questions on Mary*, trans. and introduction Allan B. Wolter, OFM (St. Bonaventure, N.Y.: Franciscan Institute, 2012). The texts of Scotus are presented and translated in Italian in Cecchin, *La "Scuola Francescana,"* 802–68 (B. Hechich). On the doctrine

sition on the book of the Sentences (of Peter Lombard), the "Doctor of the Immaculata" treats the topic with particular accuracy.[108] At first the "doctor subtilis" lists ten voices (from John Damascene up to Bernard) against the Immaculate Conception and two favorable voices: Augustine ("If sin is the topic, I would not want Mary to be considered") and Anselm ("It was fitting that this Virgin should shine with a purity so great that, except for God, no greater purity could be conceived"). The Subtle Doctor indicates the three possibilities for distancing original sin from Mary: (1) that she was never found in original sin, (2) that she was found in original sin only for a moment, (3) that she was freed from it after a certain time. "God knows which of these three possibilities was realized, but if it is not against the authority of the Church or of Scripture, to me it appears probable to attribute the most noble one to Mary." The creation of Mary's soul could have taken place along with her conception. Mary "would have contracted original sin by reason of common propagation, had it not been prevented by the grace of the Mediator; and as others needed Christ, so that by his merit they were remitted of sin

of Scotus, see Roberto Zavalloni and Eliodoro Mariani, eds., *La dottrina mariologica di Giovanni Duns Scoto* [The Mariological Doctrine of John Duns Scotus] (Rome: PAA-Edizioni Antonianum, 1987); Ruggero Rosini, *Mariologia del beato Giovanni Duns Scoto* [Mariology of Blessed John Duns Scotus] (Castelpetroso: Casa Mariana Editrice, 1994), 74–100; Tobias Hoffmann, "Duns Scotus: Die Unbefleckte Empfängnis Mariens" [Duns Scotus: The Immaculate Conception of Mary], in *Im Ringen um die Wahrheit*, ed. Remigius Bäumer (Weilheim-Bierbronnen: Gustav-Siewerth-Akad., 1997), 711–34; Gambero, *Maria nel pensiero*, 303–8 (*Mary in the Middle Ages*, 243–54); Cecchin, *L'Immacolata Concezione*, 61–73; Cecchin, "Giovanni Duns Scoto Dottore dell'Immacolata Concezione: Alcune questioni" [John Duns Scotus, Doctor of the Immaculate Conception: Some Questions], in Cecchin, *La "Scuola Francescana,"* 219–71; Cecchin, "Giovanni Duns Scoto, martire dell'Immacolata" [John Duns Scotus, Martyr of the Immaculate], in *Religioni et Litteris: Miscellanea di studi dedicate a P. Barnaba Hechich OFM*, ed. Benedykt J. Huculak (Vatican City: PAMI, 2005), 165–96; Pietro Parrotta, "Father Roschini and the Contribution of Blessed John Duns Scotus to the Dogma of the Immaculate Conception," in *Mary at the Foot of the Cross* (New Bedford, Mass.: Academy of the Immaculate, 2004) 5:360–92; Axel Schmidt, "Johannes Duns Scotus über die Immaculata Conceptio" [John Duns Scotus on the Immaculate Conception], *Sedes Sapientiae: Mariologisches Jahrbuch* 8, no. 2 (2004): 55–78; Alfonso Pompei, "Giovanni Duns Scoto e la dottrina sull'Immacolata Concezione" [John Duns Scotus and the Doctrine of the Immaculate Conception], in Cecchin, *La "Scuola Francescana,"* 193–217; Leonardo Sileo, "Filosofia, medicina e teologia: Il concepimento di Maria nella svolta teoretica di Duns Scoto" [Philosophy, Medicine, and Theology: The Conception of Mary in the Theoretical Turn Wrought by Duns Scotus], in *Giovanni Duns Scoto: Studi e ricerche nel VII Centenario della sua morte*, ed. M. Carbajo Nuñez (Rome: Pontificio Ateneo Antonianum, 2008), 2:39–89.

108. The title is used by, among others, John Paul II, CM 22 (June 5, 1996), n. 3.

already contracted, so with all the more reason she needed a mediator who preceded sin, so that there was never a necessity on her part to contract it and because in fact she never did contract it."[109]

The idea that God preserved Mary from original sin in view of the merits of Christ is decisive. In this way the perfect sanctity of Mary is not detached from the Redemption, but grounded in it. After "the intervention of Scotus, the doctrine of the Immaculate Conception only needed to find consensus, because it was already formulated in its substance."[110]

Let us also note the importance of anthropology. Thomas Aquinas followed the biological doctrine of Aristotle that separates conception from the moment of the infusion of the soul into the embryo. Duns Scotus, on the other hand, basing himself on the teachings of Hippocrates, makes the moment of animation coincide with that of conception. This gives much more importance to conception, which includes the infusion of the soul.[111]

The Battle of the Maculists and Immaculists up to Alexander VII (1661)

There followed a long controversy between maculists (especially Dominicans) and immaculists (led by the Franciscans). The positions taken by the *universities* and by the Holy See became important. The Sorbonne at Paris at first tolerated both schools. But when a Spanish Dominican (in 1387) drastically attacked the Immaculate Conception (as *contra fidem*), the university condemned the theologian's theses. And when the Dominican rejected the criticism, the Archbishop of Paris threatened him with excommunication, if he should dare to publish his doctrine. So, in reality, the Sorbonne was closer to the immaculist position. In 1497 the Parisian university decided to re-

109. *Ord.* III d. 3 q. 1 n. 42, translated in Cecchin, *La "Scuola Francescana,"* 859.

110. Cecchin, *L'Immacolata Concezione*, 62.

111. See Kochaniewicz, "L'Immacolata Concezione," 140. The acceptance of the medical doctrine of Hippocrates and of Galen on conception, in place of the theory of Aristotle, also raises the importance of woman's active contribution by means of a feminine seed, which was denied by the Aristotelian school: see Sileo, "Filosofia, medicina, e teologia," 2:40–42.

quire that every aspirant to an academic degree make an oath to fervently spread the doctrine of the Immaculate Conception of Mary. Other universities followed, first of all at Cologne (1499), Mainz (1500), and Vienna (1501).[112]

A notable episode was the *Council of Basel*, which "defined" the perfect sanctity of Mary in 1439, lacking original or actual sin. The council is not legitimate, because it considered itself superior to the pope (conciliarism), for which reason it was not recognized. However, the assembly had a favorable impression of the Immaculate Conception:

> We define ... that the doctrine that maintains that the glorious Virgin and Mother of God, Mary, by the power of a singular prevenient grace and the working of the divine will, was never subject to original sin, but was always in a state immune from actual and original fault, holy and immaculate, is to be approved by all Catholics as pious and in conformity with ecclesiastical custom, the Catholic faith, right reason, and Sacred Scripture, ... and that henceforth it is not permitted for anyone to preach or teach to the contrary.[113]

Up to the fifteenth century, the *Holy See* did not intervene. Thereafter its intervention occurred in three ways: (1) to promote the feast of the Immaculate Conception more and more; (2) to clarify the object of the feast; and (3) to make magisterial decisions toward a real and proper definition.[114]

1. Sixtus IV (1471–84), coming from the Franciscan Order, officially recognized the Feast of the Immaculate Conception (to which the Roman curia attested from the fourteenth century on) and publicly celebrated it. The feast was given an octave and was outfitted with abundant opportunities for gaining indulgences.[115]

112. Söll, *Storia dei dogmi mariani*, 314f.

113. From the introduction to DH 1400. Mansi 29:183, translated to Italian in Antonio Maria Calero, *La Vergine Maria nel mistero di Cristo e della Chiesa: Saggio di mariologia* [The Virgin Mary in the Mystery of Christ and the Church: Essay in Mariology] (Leumann [Turin]: Elle Di Ci, 1995), 181f; see Cecchin, *L'Immacolata Concezione*, 93. On the Council of Basel, see Pietro Maranesi, "L'inizio delle dispute: Il concilio di Basilea e i documenti pontifici" [The Beginning of the Debates: The Council of Basel and Papal Documents], in Cecchin, *La "Scuola Francescana,"* 307–28.

114. See Söll, *Storia dei dogmi mariani*, 311–18.

115. See DH 1400; Maranesi, "L'inizio delle dispute," 328–34.

2. The object of the feast was not yet totally clear. The liturgical offices approved by Sixtus IV clearly expressed the Immaculate Conception, but the Dominican missal expressed with equal clarity a liberation from original sin after the infusion of the soul. And the feast supported by Sixtus IV was not yet prescribed for the entire church. This was established, however, in 1708 by Clement XI.

3. The measures taken in regard to theology are important: Sixtus IV condemned the statements that considered faith in the Immaculate Conception heretical (and gravely sinful). But at the same time he underscored that the problem "has not yet been decided by the Roman Church and by the Apostolic See."[116]

In the same sense, we can hear the Declaration of Trent (1546), which referred to Sixtus IV and was not willing to include Mary in the topic of original sin: "This holy synod declares ... that it is not its intention to comprehend in this decree, which deals with original sin, the blessed and immaculate Virgin Mary, Mother of God."[117]

In 1567, Pope St. Pius V, a Dominican, condemned the error of Michael Baius, according to which Mary died because of original sin,[118] and he introduced the feast of the Immaculate Conception into the Roman Breviary. Furthermore, the supreme pontiff forbade public debate on the immaculist theory outside academic settings.

In the Constitution *Sanctissimus* (1617), Pope Paul V extended the prohibition to preachers, who were forbidden to defend the thesis that Mary had been conceived with original sin or to attack the contrary proposition.[119]

The conduct of the great *religious orders* is also important. In the Counter-Reformation, the Jesuits committed themselves officially to profess this doctrine (1593). The Franciscans already supported it, and the Dominicans too followed the immaculist trend more and more (in 1605 the General Chapter of Valladolid committed the preachers to abstain from any statement that could diminish the belief of

116. DH 1425–26.
117. DH 1516.
118. DH 1973.
119. O'Carroll, *Theotokos*, 181.

the faithful in Mary's freedom from original sin).[120] At the end of the seventeenth century nearly all the university faculties of theology followed the example given by the Sorbonne. In the language of the Roman curia, however, a certain caution was maintained: they did not speak of the "Immaculate Conception" but of the "Conception of the Immaculate Virgin." Only in 1767 (with the feast of the "Immaculate Conception" in Spain) was the liturgical use of the title permitted; in 1834 this favor was also requested on part of the Dominicans.

Pope Alexander VII, in 1661, published a bull that already presented the most important points of the definition of 1854:

1. preservation from original sin;
2. "from the first instant of her creation and the infusion [of the soul] into the body";
3. the event happened "by a special grace and privilege of God";
4. "in consideration of the merits of her son Jesus Christ, Redeemer of the human race."

From the beginning Mary "was filled with the gift of the Holy Spirit and was preserved from original sin."[121]

The Definition of the Immaculate Conception by Pius IX (1854)

After a preparation lasting multiple centuries, Pope Pius IX considered that the time had matured for a solemn definition of the Immaculate Conception,[122] an act requested from various parts over a

120. On the debate in the Dominican order, see Ulrich Horst, *Die Diskussion um die Immaculata Conceptio im Dominikanerorden* [The Debate on the Immaculate Conception in the Dominican Order] (Paderborn: F. Schöningh, 1987); Horst, "Die Theologie des Dominikanerordens, illustriert an den Kontroversen um die Immaculata Conceptio" [The Theology of the Dominican Order, Illustrated by the Controversy over the Immaculate Conception], *RTLu* 5, no. 2 (2000): 301–8.

121. DH 2015–17.

122. See Juan Alfaro, SJ, "La formula definitoria de la Inmaculada Concepción" [The Definitory Formula of the Immaculate Conception], in *Acta magisterii ecclesiastici de immaculata B.V.M. conceptione*, ed. AMI, Virgo Immacolata 2 (Rome: AMI, 1956), 201–74; Cecchin, *L'Immacolata Concezione*, 179–200; Cecchin, "Pius IX e i francescani nella definizione dogmatica dell'Immacolata Concezione" [Pius IX and the Franciscans in the Dogmatic Definition of the Immaculate Conception], in Cecchin, *La "Scuola Francescana,"* 525–59; Michele G. Masciarelli, "Sviluppo sulla dottrina dell'Immacolata Concezione di Maria nel magistero dal 1854 al nostro tempo" [Development

long time. In 1849 the pope sent the encyclical *Ubi primum* to all the bishops to invite them to report their position, together with that of the Christian people.[123] In all, 603 bishops sent a response: 546 were favorable to the definition; a few others declared themselves to the contrary; a few abstained and others only expressed reserve for reasons of timing (in particular some of the German bishops). "Of those opposed, 24 were for reasons of opportunity; only four or five were opposed to the definability."[124]

As a subsequent stage, in 1852, the pope established a theological commission to formulate criteria to be respected and the doctrine to present in the definition. There was an open discussion with eight successive schemas. Liturgical practice (*lex orandi*), the *sensus fidelium* and the *factum Ecclesiae*—that is, the doctrine and practice of the present-day church, were reaffirmed.[125] The final redaction was carried out by a group of cardinals, and the solemn definition took place on December 8, 1854, with the bull *Ineffabilis Deus*.[126] We cite the decisive phrases:

To the honor of the holy and undivided Trinity, to the glory and distinction of the Virgin Mother of God, for the exaltation of the Catholic faith and for the increase of the Christian religion, by the authority of our Lord Jesus Christ, of the blessed Apostles Peter and Paul, and Our (own), We declare, pronounce, and define: that the doctrine that maintains that the Most Blessed Virgin *Mary, at the first instant of her conception, by the singular*

of the Doctrine of the Immaculate Conception of Mary in the Magisterium from 1854 to Our Time], in Toniolo, *Il dogma dell'Immacolata Concezione*, 58–74; Peter Vrankic, "Der selige Pius IX, der Papst der Immacolata" [Bl. Pius IX, Pope of the Immaculate], *Sedes Sapientiae: Mariologisches Jahrbuch* 8, no. 2 (2004): 79–99; Primitivo Tineo, "Pío IX y la definición de la Inmaculada" [Pius IX and the Definition of the Immaculate], *Scripta de Maria 2nd ser.*, no. 1 (2004): 205–36; Juan Luis Bastero, "La fundamentación patrística en la Bula Ineffabilis Deus" [Patristic Foundation in the Bull 'Ineffabilis Deus'], *Scripta de Maria 2nd ser.*, 1 (2004): 237–63.

123. The text is found (Latin-Italian) in *EE* 7, nn. 133–36; in English in *PE* 1:43.

124. Galot, *Maria, La donna*, 3rd ed., 216.

125. At the end of the debate a "Summary of the arguments" is assembled as a basis for drawing up the dogmatic bull. Five principal arguments are identified: fittingness, Scripture, Tradition, the liturgical feast, the *sensus fidei*. See Vincenzo Sardi, *La solenne definizione del Dogma dell'Immacolato Concepimento di Maria santissima: Atti e documenti* [The Solemn Definition of the Dogma of the Immaculate Conception of Mary Most Holy: Acts and Documents] (Rome: Tipografia Vaticana, 1905), 2:46–60; Cecchin, *L'Immacolata Concezione*, 191f.

126. *EE* 7, nn. 739–55; also in Cecchin, *L'Immacolata Concezione,* 211–28; Toniolo, *Il dogma dell'Immacolata Concezione*, 11–53.

grace and privilege of almighty God and in view of the merits of Jesus Christ, the Savior of the human race, was preserved immune from any stain of original sin, is revealed by God and, therefore, firmly and constantly to be believed by all the faithful.[127]

The preceding text affirms, first of all, the particular position of Mary in the plan of salvation: God has foreordained "with one and the same decree the origin of Mary and the Incarnation of the Divine Wisdom."[128] God "filled her, far more than all the angels and saints, with an abundance of all the heavenly gifts taken from the treasury of his divinity. In this way, she, being always and absolutely free from every stain of sin, completely beautiful and perfect, would possess such a plenitude of innocence and sanctity that, under God, none greater could be known and, apart from God, no mind could ever succeed in comprehending."[129]

The argument points first of all to the liturgy, because "the norm of faith" is "established in the norm of prayer."[130] Then, Pius IX recalls how his predecessors specified the object of the cultus and prohibited the contrary doctrine. The agreement of theologians and the bishops is indicated. For biblical references the Protoevangelium (Gn 3:15) and the angelic salutation (Lk 1:28) are presented. There follows a hint of the biblical images of Mary in Sacred Scripture (Noah's ark, Jacob's ladder, the burning bush, invincible tower, enclosed garden, splendid city of God)—all of this seen as "images" chosen by the fathers to illustrate the holiness of Mary. From Tradition, there is emphasis on the parallelism between Eve and Mary and on the praise of the Fathers: Mary as a "lily among thorns," the "Immaculate," the Paradise planted by God himself, the incorruptible wood immune from the worms of sin. Last, the pope indicates the assent of faith that led to the request to define the dogma.

Let us also point out a few particularly important elements of the

127. DH 2803.

128. *EE*, n. 740.

129. DH 2800; *EE*, n. 739.

130. The idea that the *lex supplicandi* (or *orandi*) constitutes the *lex credendi* was formulated by Prosper of Aquitaine (fifth century): *Legem credendi lex statuat supplicandi* (see *Indiculus*, chap. 8: DH 246; PL 51:209).

dogmatic definition. The expression "*at the first instant of her conception*" replaces the one employed by Pope Alexander VII, which in the bull *Sollicitudo* of 1661 had spoken of the preservation of Mary's soul "from the first instant of its creation and infusion into the body."[131] Pius IX does not maintain the theoretical distinction between conception and the infusion of the soul, but assumes that the soul is infused at the moment of conception. The subject of the definition is not only the soul of Mary, but her person, thereby conforming to the language of the liturgical feast.[132] The Marian dogma thus also provides clearer anthropological awareness that the human person exists starting from conception.[133]

The expression "*preserved immune from any stain of original sin*" does not refer to freedom from personal sin, a doctrine already established authoritatively (but not defined) at the Council of Trent,[134] nor to freedom from the disorder of concupiscence, a point no longer denied by anyone.[135] It only deals with preservation from original sin. If someone were to deny the existence of original sin, he would not grasp the content of the dogma of the Immaculate Conception either.[136]

The formula "*by the singular grace and privilege of almighty God*" is also emphasized. "The dogmatic definition does not say that this singular privilege is unique, but lets that be intuited. The affirmation of this uniqueness, however, is explicitly stated in the Encyclical *Fulgens corona* of 1953, where Pius XII speaks of 'the very singular privilege which was never granted to another person,' (*AAS* 45 [1953], 580; *PE* 4:247, n. 10), thus excluding the possibility, maintained by some but without foundation, of attributing this privilege also to St. Joseph."[137]

Another important point is the expression "*in view of the merits of*

131. DH 2015.

132. See Galot, *Maria, La donna*, 3rd ed., 186.

133. See (not in a Marian context) John Paul II, Encyclical *Evangelium vitae* (1995), n. 60.

134. DH 1573.

135. See "Freedom From Concupiscence," in this chapter.

136. See Alfaro, "La formula definitoria," 265f; Galot, *Maria, La donna*, 3rd ed., 186f; Hauke, "Maria 'scettro della vera fede': L'Immacolata Concezione e la discussione sul peccato originale" [Mary, "Scepter of the True Faith": The Immaculate Conception and the Debate on Original Sin], *RTLu* 8, no. 2 (2004): 318f.

137. John Paul II, CM 23 (June 12, 1996), n. 3. See Galot, *Maria, La donna*, 3rd ed., 187f.

Jesus Christ, the Savior of the human race." The Mother of God is not placed beyond the orbit of the Redemption, but constitutes the most perfect application of the saving work of Christ. The bull states this explicitly, outside the defining formula: "The most holy Virgin Mary, Mother of God, in foresight of the merits of the Redeemer Christ Jesus, was never subject to original sin and was thereby redeemed in a most sublime manner."[138]

The doctrine of the Immaculate Conception is "*revealed by God*" and must be believed by all the faithful. The pope was conscious of exercising his power of infallible teaching. Thus the definition of 1854 prepared for the dogma of infallibility proclaimed solemnly during the First Vatican Council (1870).[139]

The Theological Context of the Dogma

The Immaculate Conception of Mary is explained first of all in her relation to *Jesus Christ*.[140] "The blessed Virgin ... is Mother of God; by this fact she is so pure and so holy that no greater purity can be

138. *EE* 2, n. 748. This is affirmed also by Pius XII (*Fulgens corona*: *AAS* 45 (1953): 581 = *EE* 6, n. 955), Vatican II (*LG* 53), the *CCC* (492), and John Paul II, CM 23 (June 12, 1996), n. 3.

To speak of the "redemption" of Mary presupposes her need to be freed from original sin, if God had not made an exception for the future Mother of God. To express this need, the term "*debt* of original sin" has been used since the time of Cajetan (1515). This perspective corresponds particularly to the Thomist approach that sees in sin an occasion for the Incarnation. Franciscan Scotist theology, on the other hand, affirming the independence between Mary's predestination and sin, is led to deny any debt. On the question of "debt" there is a very nuanced debate that we cannot explore here. See, inter alia, Benoît-Henri Merkelbach, OP, *Mariologia* (Paris: Desclée, 1939), 131–42; *De officio immaculatae conceptionis nonnullisque aliis quaestionibus marialibus*, ed. AMI, Virgo Immaculata 11 (Rome: AMI, 1957); Johannes Brinktrine, *Die Lehre von der Mutter des Erlösers* [Doctrine of the Mother of the Redeemer] (Paderborn: F. Schöningh, 1959), 32f; Juniper B. Carol, OFM, "The Blessed Virgin and the 'Debitum Peccati': A Bibliographical Conspectus," *Marian Studies* 28 (1977): 181–256; O'Carroll, *Theotokos*, 118f; Cecchin, *Maria Signora Santa e Immacolata nel pensiero francescano: Per una storia del contributo francescano alla mariologia* [Mary, Holy and Immaculate Lady in Franciscan Thought: Towards a History of the Franciscan Contribution to Mariology] (Vatican City: PAMI, 2001), 233f; Galot, *Maria, La donna*, 3rd ed., 224f.

139. Pius XII, on the occasion of the anniversary of the dogma of the Immaculate Conception, recalls the role of the Marian apparitions at Lourdes in 1858: "It seems that the same Blessed Virgin Mary had wished to confirm, so to speak, the sentence pronounced by the vicar on earth of her divine Son, in a prodigious manner through the applause of all the church.... 'I am the Immaculate Conception'"; Pius XII, *Fulgens corona* (1953): *EE* 6, n. 946.

140. In greater depth, see Leo Scheffczyk, *Maria, crocevia della fede cattolica* [Mary, Crossroads of the Catholic Faith], CdM 1 (Lugano: Eupress FTL, 2002), 93–115 ("*L'Immacolata Concezione nel contesto integrale della fede*"); Hauke, "Maria, 'scettro della vera fede.'"

conceived, beneath the purity of God."[141] To be Mother of God is not a passing duty, but determines Mary in her whole existence from its beginning. As the new Eve, she is at the side of the new Adam to collaborate in restoring salvation. But this role arises from the work of Christ the Redeemer: Mary "was never subject to original sin and thereby was redeemed in a most sublime manner."[142] The Immaculate Conception is the most efficacious form of the Redemption.

In addition, the perfect holiness of Mary helps us to understand in its depth the holiness of the *church*, which is "holy and immaculate" (Ep 5:27). This purity does not find full expression in the other members of the church, who continually need to confess that they are sinners. Mary, free of any sin, is the type of the church and assurance of its unshakable holiness. The church as church ("bride" of the divine "bridegroom") is holy. Had there been no Immaculate Conception, the Redemption of Christ would not have been realized perfectly in anyone.[143]

In the *anthropological* context, Mary Immaculate strengthens man, who finds himself on a journey and in struggle. She shows that the new existence is not a dream, but finds its perfect realization in a human person, in Mary. Freedom from sin does not distance the Immaculate from spiritual struggles because the disastrous character of evil is felt more profoundly by the saints. Help to overcome sin does not come from us, but from a greater holiness. The sign raised up with the Immaculate Conception shows "that man as willed by God, the 'ideal' man, so to speak, is man without guilt. So sin is not part … of man's nature. The human journey in the world and in history does not necessarily pass through sin."[144]

141. Cornelius a Lapide, *In Matth.*, I.16, cited in Pius XII, *Fulgens corona* (*PE* 4:247, n. 12; *EE* 6, n. 953). The text is inspired by Saint Anselm: see p. 232.

142. Pius IX, *Ineffabilis Deus* (*EE* 2, n. 748).

143. On the holiness of the church, against the erroneous expression of a "sinful church," see Brunero Gherardini, *La Chiesa: Mistero e servizio* [The Church: Mystery and Service], 3rd ed. (Rome: Associazione Apollinare Studi, 1994), 130–35; Adriano Garuti, *Il mistero della Chiesa* [The Mystery of the Church] (Rome: Pontificio Ateneo Antonianum, 2004), 148–51; Johannes Stöhr, *"Er hat sich für uns hingegeben" (Tit 2,14): Die Erlösungstat Christi und seine Kirche* ["He Gave Himself Up for Us" (Ti 2:14): Christ's Act of Redemption and His Church] (Weilheim-Bierbronnen: Books on Demand, 2007), 131–74.

144. Scheffczyk, *Maria, crocevia*, 105.

Mary's conception, exempt from sin, also highlights the *gratuitous character of grace*: it is God who initiates sanctity, not man.

Seen from the *mariological context* itself, the Immaculate Conception, together with the holiness of the new Eve, is oriented toward cooperation in the Redemption that begins at the Annunciation, when the holy Virgin becomes Mother of God. "It was fitting that like Christ the new Adam, Mary the new Eve also would not know sin and thus would be more suited to cooperate in the redemption."[145] This cooperation, this mediation in Christ, then reaches all who are united to the Savior. The Assumption into heaven, body and soul, is a consequence of the Immaculate Conception and of Mary's salvific cooperation. It is no accident that the biblical argument for the dogmas of the Immaculate Conception and (as we shall see) for the Assumption rests on the same principal texts—that is, on the Protoevangelium and the angelic salutation.

The Ecumenical Debate

The dogma of the Immaculate Conception is also a topic for ecumenical dialogue, above all with regard to the Orthodox Church.[146] As was mentioned in the historical overview, Eastern theologians describe a perfect holiness of Mary and associate the origin of her personal purity with her conception in her mother's womb. The first denial of the Immaculate Conception by an Orthodox theologian only appeared in 1577 in a treatise published at Venice.[147] The first

145. John Paul II, CM 21 (May 29, 1996), n. 4.

146. See Constantine P. Charalampidis, "Culto e dottrina della Chiesa greco-ortodossa circa la Panaghia" [Cult and Doctrine of the Greek Orthodox Church Regarding the All-Holy Virgin], in *Maria Santa e Immacolata*, ed. Stefano De Fiores and Enrico Vidau (Rome: Edizioni Monfortane, 2000), 77–89; Demetrius Sizonenko, "Fede e tradizione teologica della Chiesa ortodossa russa circa la Tuttasanta" [Faith and Theological Tradition of the Russian Orthodox Church on the All-Holy Virgin], in De Fiores and Vidau, *Maria Santa e Immacolata*, 91–103; Hauke, "Die Unbefleckte Empfängnis bei den griechischen Vätern" [The Immaculate Conception among the Greek Fathers], *Sedes Sapientiae: Mariologisches Jahrbuch* 8, no. 2 (2004); Giuseppe Forlai, *L'irruzione della grazia: Per una rilettura ecumenica del dogma dell'Immacolata* [The Eruption of Grace: Toward an Ecumenical Re-Reading of the Dogma of the Immaculate] (Cinisello Balsamo: San Paolo, 2010), 298–305.

147. Damascenos the Studite, *Thesauros* (Venice, 1568). See Jugie, *L'Immaculée Conception*, 326–28; Stiernon, "Marie dans la théologie orthodoxe gréco-russe," 250, 278.

statement of the "maculist" position by a Greek patriarch appeared in 1626 by Metrophanes Kritopoulos, patriarch of Alexandria. Kritopoulos had spent more time in the Protestant West and in the region of Venice than in the East from which he had come. The profession of faith in which he rejects the Immaculate Conception was drafted at the request of the Lutheran university of Helmstedt and was subject to a discreet Protestant influence. His statement can be understood as a response to the Constitution *Sanctissimus* of Paul V (1617), which forbade preachers to defend the thesis that Mary had been conceived with original sin.[148] Resistance grew after the definition of the dogma by Pius IX. In any case, there is no definitive statement of the position;[149] for this reason, at times even Orthodox theologians speak in favor of the Immaculate Conception.[150] This willingness was particularly strong in the school of Kiev (seventeenth century: Peter Mogila). The so-called Old Believers (a group separate from the main current of Russian Orthodoxy) defend the conception of Mary without original sin to this day.[151] An obstacle to the acceptance of the Immaculate Conception today is still usually an unclear concept of original sin.[152] But inasmuch as the praise of the *Panágia* ("All-Holy") is particularly strong in the Orthodox Church, one cannot rule out a development of doctrine that leads to the acceptance of the dogma.

The difference is much greater with regard to Protestantism.[153]

148. See ibid., 278f.

149. See Stawrowsky, "La Sainte Vierge," 38–40.

150. E.g., ibid.

151. See ibid., 59.

152. See Hauke, *Heilsverlust in Adam*, 46–52; *Urstand, Fall und Erbsünde*, 161–74.

153. See Franz Courth, *Maria, die Mutter des Herrn* [Mary, the Mother of the Lord] (Vallendar: Theologische Hochschule der Pallotiner, 1991), 91–97; Courth, "Mariologie," in *Glaubenszugänge*, ed. W. Beinert (Paderborn: F. Schöningh, 1995), 2:368–72; Achim Dittrich, *Protestantische Mariologie-Kritik: Historische Entwicklung bis 1997 und dogmatische Analyse* [Protestant Criticism of Mariology: Historical Development to 1997 and Dogmatic Analysis], Mariologische Studien 11 (Regensburg: Pustet, 1998), 310–12; Dittrich, "'Die Erfindung des Scotus': Protestantische Kritik an der Immaculata-Definition nach 1854 und im 20. Jahrhundert" ["Scotus' Invention": Protestant Critique of the Definition of the Immaculate after 1854 and in the 20th Century], *RTLu* 9 (2004): 341–76; Gottfried Hammann, "Il punto di vista della Riforma circa l'Immacolata Concezione" [The Reformation Outlook on the Immaculate Conception], in De Fiores and Vidau, *Maria santa e immacolata*, 105–23; Bernard Sesboüé, SJ, "La doctrine de l'Immaculée Conception dans le dialogue oecuménique (Groupe de Dombes et accord luthéro-catholique de 1999)"

In Luther we still find affirmations of the Immaculate Conception: there can be no shadow of sin on the woman chosen by God as Mother. Yet other texts by Luther call Mary a "sinner," and Calvin does not acknowledge the Immaculate Conception. Zwingli speaks of a purification of Mary enabling her to become Mother of God. The principle of *sola scriptura* could not support the Immaculate Conception.

An objection that only arose after 1854 is that the Immaculate Conception of Mary represents the infallible sanctity of the church. In Mary, the Roman Church is said to have erroneously exalted herself. In this way the argument is indeed criticizing the connection between the unshakable sanctity of the church and that of Mary.

Broadly speaking, modern Protestantism does not accept the dogma. The dialectical theology of Barth almost makes created being into sinfulness, thus leading the opposition between God and man to an extreme. But we find in other authors a certain interest in recognizing in Mary that grace prevails in the face of sin. Also, for one German author (Ulrich Wickert), immaculate holiness appears as a gift of grace. In this one might find a starting point for ecumenical dialogue.[154]

Since the Anglican community has a stronger connection with

[The Doctrine of the Immaculate Conception in Ecumenical Dialog: The Dombes Group and the Lutheran-Catholic Agreement of 1999], in Toniolo, *Il dogma dell'Immacolata Concezione*, 406–14; Salvatore M. Perrella, OSM, *"Non temere di prendere con te Maria" (Matteo 1,20): Maria e l'ecumenismo nel postmoderno; Dalla "Mater divisionis" alla "Mater unitatis"* ["Fear Not to Take Mary with You" (Mt 1:20): Mary and Ecumenism in the Postmodern; From "Mother of Division" to "Mother of Unity"] (Milan: San Paolo, 2004), 136–50; Imre von Gaal, "Ein Weg von der Polemik zum Lobpreis: Die unbefleckte Empfängnis Mariens in der Sicht von Eduard Preuß (1834–1904)" [A Way from Polemics to Praise: The Immaculate Conception in the View of Eduard Preuss], *Sedes Sapientiae: Mariologisches Jahrbuch* 9, no. 1 (2005): 39–67; Giancarlo Bruni, *Mariologia ecumenica: Approcci, documenti, prospettive* (Bologna: EDB: 2009), 501–34.

154. See also Dombes Group, *Mary in the Plan of God and the Communion of Saints* (New York: Paulist Press, 2002), nn. 269–72; French original: *Marie dans le dessein de Dieu et la communion des saints*, 2 vols. (Paris: Bayard and Centurion, 1997–98). Bilaterale Arbeitsgruppe der Deutschen Bischofskonferenz und der Kirchenleitung der Vereinigten Evangelisch-Lutherischen Kirche Deutschlands, eds., *Communio Sanctorum: Die Kirche als Gemeinschaft der Heiligen* (Paderborn and Frankfurt am Main: Bonifatius, 2000), nn. 259, 267; English translation: Bilateral Working Group of the German Bishops Conference and the Leadership of the United Evangelical-Lutheran Church of Germany, ed., *Communio Sanctorum: The Church as the Communion of the Saints* (Collegeville, Minn.: Liturgical Press, 2005).

the tradition of the ancient church, it has been possible for us to draw near in the Joint Declaration of 2004 by the official commission for dialogue between Anglicans and Catholics:

> The Scriptures point to the efficacy of Christ's atoning sacrifice even for those who preceded him in time (cf. 1 Peter 3:19, John 8:56, 1 Corinthians 10:4). Here again the eschatological perspective illuminates our understanding of Mary's person and calling. In view of her vocation to be the mother of the Holy One (Luke 1:35), we can affirm together that Christ's redeeming work reached "back" in Mary to the depths of her being, and to her earliest beginnings.[155]

FREEDOM FROM CONCUPISCENCE

As a consequence of the first sin we find not only original guilt, but also death and the tendency toward evil, which is concupiscence.[156] Baptism removes original sin and personal sins, but not concupiscence, which remains "for the struggle" (*ad agonem*), as the Council of Trent teaches. Concupiscence, "which comes from sin and is inclined to it," is the human weakness connected to the disordered tendency of the senses.[157] Paul places this tendency under the title "sin" (Rom 7:23).

In contrast, a harmony between spirit, the sense faculties, and the gift of grace is presupposed as the original state of man. The description of Mary as the "new Eve" implies a certain renewal of this paradisiacal grace. A summary of patristic thought is found in John Damascene (†749): "Keeping her spirit far from every worldly and carnal concupiscence, she maintained virginity of the soul along with that of the body."[158] "All her desire is oriented toward Him who

155. Donald Bolen and Gregory K. Cameron, eds., *Mary: Grace and Hope in Christ; The Seattle Statement of the Anglican-Roman Catholic International Commission* (London and New York: Continuum: 2006), n. 59. See also "Ecumenical Aspects," in chapter 4.

156. See Aidan Carr, OFM Conv., and Germain Williams, OFM Conv., "Inmaculada concepción de María," in *Mariología*, ed. J. Carol (Madrid: BAC, 1964), 363–67; Roschini, *Maria Santissima* 3:287–94; Hauke, "Begierlichkeit" [Concupiscence], in *ML* 1:402–4; Alejandro Martinez Sierra, "El dogma de la Inmaculada Concepción y su relación con la concupiscencia" [The Dogma of the Immaculate Conception and Its Relation with Concupiscence], *Estudios Marianos* 71 (2005): 183–96.

157. DH 1515.

158. *De fide orthodoxa* 4.14 (PG 94:1160A).

alone is worthy to be desired and loved. She only feels anger toward sin and its author.... Her pure and immaculate heart contemplates and desires God, the Immaculate One."[159]

Scholasticism links the sanctification of Mary with liberation from the disordered appetite of the senses. Some theologians differentiate between the purification from original sin (in the womb of her mother) and liberation from the "incitement to sin" (*fomes peccati*) at the Annunciation (e.g., Alexander of Hales). Others distinguish a first restriction (a "binding") of concupiscence and an extinguishing of it at the Incarnation (Thomas and others); both of these events are caused by the abundance of grace, which finds increase at the Annunciation.

The victorious arrival of the Scotist explanation put together Mary's preservation from original sin and from concupiscence. "Pius IX's definition refers only to freedom from original sin and does not explicitly include freedom from concupiscence. Nevertheless, Mary's complete preservation from every stain of sin also has as a consequence her freedom from concupiscence."[160] Vatican II affirms that Mary embraced "God's salvific will with a full heart and impeded by no sin," devoting herself "totally."[161]

Concupiscence, by itself, is not sin. But, inasmuch as it constitutes a disorder of the inclinations, it does not correspond to the moral ideal. It is that consequence of sin that further damages the situation of man before God. In contrast, the other consequences of original sin, which are suffering and death, do not imply any moral disorder.

The lack of concupiscence derives from the Immaculate Conception and from the divine maternity. It is also connected with the virginity of Mary inasmuch as it expresses total donation to God. The same integration between sense powers and spirit is shown in the veneration of the Immaculate Heart of Mary.[162]

159. *In Nativ. B. Mariae* (PG 96:676A, C).

160. John Paul II, CM 23 (June 12, 1996), n. 2. See Bertetto, *Maria Immacolata*, 249–60; Galot, *Maria, La donna*, 3rd ed., 223f.

161. *LG* 56.

162. See "The Expression of Holiness in the Immaculate Heart of Mary," in this chapter, and "The Consecration of Others and of the Entire World to the Mother of God," in chapter 10.

FULLNESS OF GRACE

The Immaculate Conception, the absence of original sin and of concupiscence constitute the negative aspect of the holiness of Mary. But it is even more important to highlight the positive aspect, being "full of grace" (Lk 1:28). The Greek term *kecharitoméne* is used as a name, even before the angel pronounces the word "Mary," and it means "filled with grace."[163] "This term, in the form of a perfect participle, enhances the image of a perfect and lasting grace that implies fullness."[164] Furthermore, we can notice that the term *cháris*, "grace," also describes charm or graciousness. "This charm, which is essential, will be perceived better by Christian piety, more than a doctrinal analysis: it is felt in a person-to-person contact. This gives the holiness of Mary its true face: it is an attractive holiness, to the point that, in order to express it rightly, language not only needs doctrinal precision but poetry."[165]

Fullness of grace is fitting for the Mother of the Kyrios, whom Elizabeth called "blessed among women" (Lk 1:42f). The infancy narrative according to Luke particularly exalts the faith of Mary (Lk 1:38, 1:45), her humility (1:38, 1:48, 1:52),[166] and her obedience, her total readiness to accept the will of God (1:38: "Behold, I am the handmaid of the Lord; let it be done to me according to your word").

We have already hinted at the praises given throughout history

163. Regarding the angelic salutation, see "The Annunciation," in chapter 1.

164. John Paul II, CM (May 8, 1996), n. 2. See *RM* 8.

165. Galot, *Maria, La donna*, 3rd ed., 227. Here the opportunity to explore the aesthetic aspect opens up, and it is strongly affirmed in recent years: Alfonso Langella, ed., *Via pulchritudinis and Mariologia* [The Way of Beauty and Mariology] (Rome: AMII, 2003); Langella, "Bellezza" [Beauty], in De Fiores, Schiefer, and Perrella, *DMar*, 190–99; "Una bellezza chiamata Maria" [A Beauty Called Mary], *Theotokos* 13, no. 1 (2005); "Mariologia estetica per il nostro tempo" [Aesthetic Mariology for Our Time], *Theotokos* 14, no. 2 (2006); De Fiores, *Maria: Nuovissimo dizionario* [Mary: Newest Dictionary] (Bologna: EDB, 2006), 1:237–89; Michele G. Masciarelli, *La Bellissima: Maria sulla "Via Pulchritudinis"* (Vatican City: Libreria Editrice Vaticana, 2012). On the beauty attributed to Mary in general, see Ziegenaus, "Schönheit" [Beauty], in *ML* 6:51f. The beauty of grace is recognized also by the German dogmatic theologian Scheeben (eighteenth century): Hauke, "Das Faszinierende der göttlichen Gnade. Zur charitologischen Ästhetik bei M. J. Scheeben" [The Fascination of Divine Grace: The Charitological Aesthetic in M. J. Scheeben], *Forum Katholische Theologie* 9 (1993): 275–89.

166. On humility, see Ziegenaus, "Demut Marias I. Dogmatik" [Humility of Mary: I. Dogma], in *ML* 2:167–69.

to the holiness of Mary. It is not an "abstract" sanctity, comprising all the possible particular charisms, but corresponds to the permanent duty of Mary as the Mother of God and the new Eve.[167] The concrete setting of the grace of Mary is also respected in the meaning of the aphorism *De Maria nunquam satis*, a formula coined by Grignion de Montfort (1712), although it has roots as far back as the patristic age.[168] "The basic content of the saying, as interpreted by the tradition of the Church, is not related to generalized *talking* about Mary but to the prospect of *praising* her fittingly in her capacity as Theotokos and according to the demands of a love that is felt. In this sense the aphorism takes on a permanent value, inasmuch as it is a historical realization of the New Testament prophecy: 'From this day all generations will call me blessed' (Lk 1:48)."[169]

Clearly, the fullness of grace implies gifts in abundance that constitute the nucleus of holiness for everyone: sanctifying grace, the three theological virtues (faith, hope, charity), and the four cardinal virtues (prudence, justice, fortitude, temperance). Furthermore, it has to presuppose an abundance of gifts received for service to others: that is, the charisms. Let us recall the reference of Vatican II: Mary, being Mother of God, beloved daughter of the Father and temple of the Holy Spirit, because of "this gift of sublime grace, ... far surpasses all creatures, both in heaven and on earth."[170] God has endowed Mary "with the gifts which befit such a role."[171] Pius IX mentions fullness of grace directly at the start of his Bull *Ineffabilis Deus*, which defines the Immaculate Conception: God, in His eternal plan, chose Mary as Mother of his Son. "Therefore he miraculously filled her, more than all the angels and all the saints, with the abundance of all heavenly gifts.... Thus she ... possesses such a full-

167. See *ST* III, q. 7 a., 10 ad 3; III, q. 27, a. 5, ad 3; John Paul II, *RM* 9: "The 'fullness of grace' indicates all the supernatural munificence from which Mary benefits by being chosen and destined to be the Mother of Christ."

168. On the origin of the formula, see Heinrich M. Köster, "De Maria nunquam satis: Wer fand, was bedeutet diese Formel?" ["De Maria nunquam satis": Origin and Meaning of the Formula], *Marian Library Studies* 17–23 (1987–91): 617–32. On its correct interpretation, see Merkelbach, *Mariologia*, 72–74; De Fiores, *Dizionario*, 1:445–62.

169. De Fiores, *Dizionario* 1:457f.

170. *LG* 53.

171. *LG* 56.

ness of innocence and holiness that none greater can be conceived, excepting that of God; and no mind below that of God can attain to understanding its depth."[172]

The theological virtue of faith presents Mary as the first believer of the New Covenant:[173] "Blessed is she who believed that there would be a fulfillment of what was spoken to her from the Lord" (Lk 1:45). Consenting to the word of God, Mary becomes Mother of the Son of God with her free cooperation. "Hence not a few of the early Fathers gladly assert in their preaching, 'The knot of Eve's disobedience was untied by Mary's obedience; what the virgin Eve bound through her unbelief, the Virgin Mary loosened by her faith.'"[174] The Mother of God undergoes a "pilgrimage of faith" and remains true to her union of faith with the Son all the way to the foot of the Cross.[175] Mary is "the perfect icon of faith," as Pope Francis stated in his encyclical on faith.[176] The journey of faith is also accompanied by times of incomprehension, as when she met the twelve-year-old Jesus in the Temple (Lk 2:48–50), but without the shadow of doubt. The knowledge of faith became deeper as she went along, passing through joyful and sorrowful experiences, but it would be a mistake to raise doubts about the fact that Mary, already at the Annunciation, grasped the divinity of her Son.[177] Completing his

172. Pius IX, *Ineffabilis Deus* (*EE* 3, n. 739).

173. On the faith of Mary, see Merkelbach, *Mariologia*, 184f; Jean Galot, *La fede di Maria e la nostra* [Mary's Faith and Ours] (Assisi: Cittadella Editrice, 1973); Galot, *Maria, la donna*, 3rd ed., 50–72; Pierre M. Theas, *La fede di Maria* [The Faith of Mary] (Rome: Città Nuova, 1978); Settimo Cipriani, "Credente" [Believer], in De Fiores and Meo, *NDM*, 417–25; Alois Stöger, "Glaube Marias" [The Faith of Mary], in *ML* 2:646f; Alessandro M. Apollonio, *Maria, modello di fede?* [Mary, Model of Faith?] (Castelpetroso: Casa Mariana Editrice, 1995); José C. R. Garcia Paredes, *Maria nella comunità del regno: Sintesi di Mariologia* [Mary in the Community of the Kingdom: Synthesis of Mariology] (Vatican City: Libreria Editrice Vaticana, 1997), 97–124; Ziegenaus, *Maria in der Heilsgeschichte*, 281–83; O'Carroll, *Theotokos*, 142–44, 212–14; Roberto de Mattei, "Il sabato e la fede di Maria" [Saturday and the Faith of Mary], *Immaculata Mediatrix* 3 (2003): 271–83; Franco Manzi, "Credente" [Believer], in *DMar*, 349–56.

174. *LG* 56.

175. See *LG* 58. See also John Paul II, *RM* 12–19.

176. Francis, Encyclical *Lumen fidei* (2013), n. 58.

177. This position of doubt comes from Erasmus; it was later opposed by Suárez. On the historical development of the question of the knowledge of Mary, see Roschini, *Dizionario di mariologia* [Dictionary of Mariology] (Rome: Editrice Studium, 1961), 453–56; Roschini, *Maria Santissima*, 3:279–84; Francis J. Connell, C.Ss.R., "Our Lady's Knowledge," in Carol, *Mariology* (1957), 2:313–24; A. Bodem, "Wissen Marias" [The Knowledge of Mary], in *ML* 6:746–48;

praise of Mary's faith (Lk 1:45), Pius X observes, "Given that the Son of God is the 'author and finisher of our faith,' it is necessary that His Mother be known as a sharer in the divine mysteries and that in some way she protects them and that the faith of all the centuries rests upon her, as upon the most noble foundation, after Christ."[178]

The same pope also makes a good point about all three of the theological virtues in the life of Mary: "Faith, hope, and charity toward God and toward neighbor" are "like the nerves and joints of the Christian life.... All of Mary's life bears the radiant stamp of these virtues in all their phases; but they achieved the highest degree of splendor at the time when she stood by her dying Son. Jesus is crucified and is reproached and cursed for 'having made himself son of God' (Jn 19:7). Mary, with steadfastness, recognizes and adores the divinity in him. She lays him in the tomb after his death, never doubting his resurrection for a split second. Her burning charity toward God renders her a participant 'in the sufferings of Christ' and companion in His Passion; and with him, as though she were forgetful of her own sadness, begs pardon for the executioners, even when they stubbornly shout: 'His blood be upon us and our children' (Mt 27:25)."[179]

Absolute fullness of grace is found only in Jesus Christ, "the only-begotten Son from the Father," "full of grace and truth" (Jn 1:14). "And from His fulness have we all received, grace upon grace" (Jn 1:16). The

---

O'Carroll, *Theotokos*, 212–14. Thinking for the moment of the Annunciation, an explicit awareness of the divinity of Christ surpasses Old Testament expectations and presupposes an infused knowledge whose existence cannot be proved: thus, the objection of Michael Schmaus, *Katholische Dogmatik*, vol. 5, *Mariologie*, 2nd ed. (Munich: Hueber, 1961), 82–85. On the other hand, there is also no need to underestimate the degree of faith of the Blessed Virgin, who accepts the divine character of her Son, greater than all the prophets, as the account of Luke implies with clarity. This also applies to the Trinitarian dimension of the passage (see Alberto Valentini, *Maria secondo le Scritture: Figlia di Sion e Madre del Signore* [Mary according to the Scriptures: Daughter of Zion and Mother of the Lord]. [Bologna: EDB, 2007], 104). Hence the statement of Galot, *Maria, La donna*, 3rd ed., 69, cannot be accepted, according to which Mary "would be hindered in her maternal affection," "if at the moment of the Annunciation ... she had been made aware that her son was God." See, to the contrary, Dominic Unger, OP, "Utrum secundum Doctores Ecclesiae Virgo Maria Filium suum Dei Filium esse nuntio angelico cognoverit" [According to the Doctors of the Church, Did the Virgin Mary Know Her Son to Be the Son of God through the Message of the Angel?], in *Maria in Sacra Scriptura*, ed. C. Balić (Rome: PAMI, 1967), 4:347–420; Apollonio, *Maria, modello di fede*; O'Carroll, *Theotokos*, 212–14.

178. Pius X, Encyclical *Ad diem illum* (1904) (*PE* 3:165, n. 5; *EE* 4, n. 19).

179. Pius X, *Ad diem illum* (*PE* 3:165, n. 21; *EE* 4, n. 32).

grace of Mary also comes from this source: the Virgin is preserved from sin and filled with grace in view of the saving work of Jesus Christ.

Jesus Christ experienced the Beatific Vision already on earth, seeing God (Jn 1:18) and thereby reaching the limit of holiness (he is *viator et comprehensor*, as in the medieval theological formula: being on the way and already at the completion). Because of this, he was not able to grow in holiness; he possessed it in the greatest fullness from the beginning.[180] Mary, on the other hand, was able to grow in the fullness received at the beginning of her life.[181] In particular, there were times of growth in grace at the Annunciation, under the Cross, and on the day of Pentecost. In the earthly journey (*in statu viae*) everyone can grow in sanctifying grace and in merit. Among the charisms, theologians have emphasized that of wisdom (with reference to Lk 2:19, 2:51) and that of prophecy, proclaiming the wonders of God in the *Magnificat*.[182]

The abundance of heavenly glory corresponds to the richness of grace with which Mary left this earth in order to be transfigured and see God face to face. Inasmuch as glory depends on grace, the beatitude of Mary surpasses that of every other created person.[183]

THE EXPRESSION OF HOLINESS IN THE IMMACULATE HEART OF MARY

In biblical language, the heart is a central symbol to describe human love directed to God (Dt 6:46). The prophets promise a "new heart" in which the law of God is written (Ez 36:26; Jer 31:33f). Jesus de-

180. See Fernando Ocáriz, Lucas F. Mateo-Seco, and José A. Riestra, *Il mistero di Cristo: Manuale di Cristologia* [The Mystery of Christ: Manual of Christology], trans. Carla Rossi Espagnet (Rome: Apollinare Studi, 2000), 163–70, 194–96; Hauke, "La visione beatifica di Cristo durante la passione: La dottrina di san Tommaso d'Aquino e la teologia contemporanea" [The Beatific Vision of Christ during the Passion: The Doctrine of St. Thomas Aquinas and Contemporary Theology], *Annales theologici* 21 (2007): 381–98.

181. See *ST* III, q. 27, a. 5, ad 2.

182. See Johannes Stöhr, "Charismen" [Charisms], in *ML* 2:25–31; Stöhr, "Gnadenfülle" [Fullness of Grace], in *ML* 2:662–64.

183. See *ST* III, q. 27, a. 5, ad 2. On the heavenly glory of Mary, see (in addition to manuals on eschatology in general) Roschini, *Maria Santissima* 3:633–37.

clares, "Blessed are the pure of heart, for they shall see God" (Mt 5:8). The "heart" refers to the center of the person, without distinguishing between will and knowledge or mind and feeling.

The Son of God "has loved us all with a human heart. For this reason, the Sacred Heart of Jesus, pierced by our sins and for our salvation, 'is quite rightly considered the chief sign and symbol of that ... love with which the divine Redeemer continually loves the eternal Father and all human beings.'"[184] In Jesus Christ, human love is totally directed to God, and divine love pours itself into his human soul, influencing all his rational and emotional being. Since we have seen that in Christ God has loved us with a human heart, we have a new perspective in which we can also contemplate the Old Testament passages that describe God's love for us (such as Hos 11:1, 11:3f; Jer 31:3). Thus a double love, that of man for God, and that of God for us, is united in the same person, in the same heart. The adoration of the Sacred Heart, which developed from the Middle Ages onward, with reference points in Sacred Scripture (such as Mt 11:29; Jn 7:37f, 19:34), is focused on the love of Jesus Christ under the symbol of his heart. The heart is seen as a bodily organ, but in its union to the divine person of the Son and as an expression of the interior life of the Savior. Pius XII, in the encyclical cited earlier by the Catechism, calls the Sacred Heart of Jesus "as it were, the sum of the whole mystery of our redemption."[185]

The heart of Mary is also mentioned in the New Testament and, since the Middle Ages, has become an object of devotion. The evangelist Luke, beholding the wonderment of the Mother of God at the mystery of the Nativity and at finding the twelve-year-old Jesus in

184. *CCC* 478, with reference to Pius XII, Encyclical *Haurietis aquas* (DH 3924); see Encyclical *Mystici Corporis* (DH 3812). For a deeper examination of the Christological theme, see, e.g., Bertetto, *Gesù Redentore: Cristologia* (Firenze: Libreria Editrice Fiorentino, 1958), 466–537; Friedrich Schwendimann, *Herz-Jesu-Verehrung heute?* [Devotion to the Heart of Jesus Today?] (Regensburg: J. Habbel, 1974); Roger Vekemans, SJ, ed., *Cor Christi: Historia, teología, espiritualidad y pastoral* [Heart of Christ: History, Theology, Spirituality and Pastoral Care] (Bogotá: Instituto Internacional del Corazón de Jésus, 1980); Timothy T. O'Donnell, *Heart of the Redeemer: An Apologia for the Contemporary and Perennial Value of the Devotion to the Sacred Heart of Jesus* (San Francisco: Ignatius, 1992); Bertrand de Margerie, *Histoire doctrinale du culte envers le coeur de Jésus*, 2 vols. (Paris: Mame, 1992–95).

185. Pius XII, Encyclical *Haurietis aquas* 86, booklet. English translation from *The Pope Speaks: Church Documents Quarterly* (Boston: St. Paul Editions). Also in *PE* 4:253, n. 103.

the Temple, states that Mary kept these saving events, meditating on them in her heart (see Lk 2:19, 2:51). This devotion also integrates the prophecy of Simeon that Jesus is "a sign that is spoken against (and a sword will pierce through your own soul also), that thoughts out of many hearts may be revealed" (Lk 2:34f). In this way the veneration of the Heart of Mary associates the Mother of God with the saving work of Christ, especially with the Passion.

John Paul II contemplated its biblical basis: "We can say that the mystery of the Redemption took shape beneath the heart of the Virgin of Nazareth when she pronounced her 'fiat.' From then on, under the special influence of the Holy Spirit, this heart, the heart of both a virgin and a mother, has always followed the work of her Son and has gone out to all those whom Christ has embraced and continues to embrace with inexhaustible love. For that reason her heart must also have the inexhaustibility of a mother."[186]

With the words of Scripture as a basis, there is already in the fathers a modest attention to the heart of the Mother of God. Augustine affirms that Mary is blessed more for having conceived Christ in her heart than for having received him in her womb.[187] According to an emblematic saying of Richard of Saint-Laurent (thirteenth century), the faith and the consent by which the salvation of the world began arose from the heart of the Virgin.[188] Arnold of Chartres speaks of two altars at Calvary, united in the offering of the same holocaust: one in the body of Christ and the other in the heart of Mary.[189] Medieval reflection appears with vigor in the first written prayer to the Heart of Mary, by Eckbert of Schönau (1184), Benedictine abbot as well as brother and advisor of the holy mystic Elisabeth of Schönau. He already makes use of the expression "immaculate heart."[190]

186. John Paul II, Encyclical *Redemptor hominis* 22.

187. Augustine, *De sancta virginitate* 3 (PL 40:398): "Materna propinquitas nihil Mariae profuisset, nisi felicius Christus corde quam carne gestasset."

188. Richard of Saint-Laurent, *De laudibus b. Mariae Virginis* 2.2.2 (*Inter opera Alberti Magni*, ed. Borgnet, 36:82, cited in O'Carroll, *Theotokos*, 167.

189. Regarding Mary at Calvary, see also p. 314.

190. See Henri Barré, "Une prière d'Ekbert de Schönau au Coeur de Marie" [A Prayer of Ekbert of Schönau to the Heart of Mary], *Ephemerides Mariologicae* 2 (1952): 409–23. See O'Carroll, *Theotokos*, 130, 167; Otto Stegmüller and Heinrich M. Köster, "Ekbert von Schönau," in *ML* 2:312.

The influence of St. John Eudes (1601–80), who wrote the first theological work dedicated to the heart of Mary, has been particularly important in the history of theology.[191] He presents the heart of Mary as a fountain of all graces because of her relationship with the Most Holy Trinity.[192] The first liturgical feast also stems from Eudes, first celebrated only locally (1648), then permitted generally (1805, 1857) and finally prescribed by Pius XII for the entire church (1944).[193] John Eudes presents the hearts of Jesus and Mary with complete harmony between them; the first liturgical feast of the Sacred Heart (1672) is also due to the influence of this French saint.

Consecration to the Heart of Mary has appeared in approved formulas, endowed with indulgences, since 1807.[194] This entrustment was strongly supported in the wake of the apparitions to St. Catherine Labouré in the Rue du Bac (Paris, 1830).[195] The expression "Immaculate Heart" became habitual after the proclamation of the dogma of the Immaculate Conception in 1854 and impressed itself on ecclesiastical language, above all after the Marian apparitions connected with Fatima and by means of the solemn act of consecration pronounced by Pius XII in 1942.[196] The motivation for it is strongly accented in the second apparition (June 1917), with words addressed to Lucia: "Jesus wishes to make use of you so that I may be known and loved. He wants to establish devotion to my Immaculate Heart in the world. I promise salvation to anyone who practices it: these souls will be loved by God like flowers set by me to adorn His throne."[197] This prophetic message underscores a matter of importance that can also be reached, at least in principle, by dogmatic reflection on the basis of Scripture and Tradition.

191. Jean Eudes, *Le coeur admirable de la très Sacrée Mère de Dieu* (Caen, 1681); English translation: John Eudes, *The Admirable Heart of Mary* (New York : P. J. Kenedy, 1948; repr.: Fitzwilliam, N.H.: Loreto, 2004).

192. See Joaquín María Alonso and Danilo Sartor, "Cuore immacolato" [Immaculate Heart], in *NDM* 447; Karl Wittkemper, "Eudes," in *ML* 2:411f.

193. Regarding the liturgical observance for the Immaculate Heart of Mary, see "Mary in the Liturgical Calendar," in chapter 10.

194. See O'Carroll, *Theotokos*, 168.

195. See pp. 391–92.

196. See pp. 396–98.

197. Cited in Alonso and Sartor, "Cuore immacolato," 448.

The decree of the Congregation of Rites in 1944, instituting the liturgical celebration for all the church, provides an excellent description of the devotion to the Heart of Mary: "With this devotion the Church renders the honor due to the Immaculate Heart of the Blessed Virgin Mary, because under the symbol of this heart she venerates with reverence the eminent and singular holiness of the Mother of God and especially her most ardent love for God and for her Son Jesus and also her maternal compassion for all those redeemed by the divine Blood."[198] A marvelous liturgical synthesis of the entire devotion to the pure Heart of Mary is found in the preface of the corresponding formulary in the "Collection of Masses of the Blessed Virgin Mary" (1987; English 1992, 2012).[199]

The significance of the Heart of Mary obviously is different from that of the Sacred Heart of Jesus: the love of Mary is only that of a human person, but one sustained by the fullness of grace and by the theological virtue of charity. "The heart of Mary is ... a symbol ... of the spiritual and supernatural love with which She has been loved by God and with which She loves both God and men, but also of the natural and motherly love with which She has looked and continues to look both to her Son and to men. As the 'Heart of Jesus' is a synthesis of the whole mystery of Christ, so the whole Marian mystery is contained within the 'Heart of Mary.' Both mysteries form part of the order of the redemption. The second mystery is part of the first and is subordinate to it, as the love and suffering of Mary formed part, in a subordinate way, to the love and suffering of Christ."[200] By "*dedicating ourselves to the heart of Mary we discover a sure way to the Sacred Heart of Jesus, symbol of the merciful love of our Savior.*"[201]

There is a relationship more than merely etymological between

198. See Sacred Congregation of Rites, *AAS* 37 (1945): 50; see John Paul II, Address of September 22, 1986, quoted by Arthur B. Calkins, *Totus tuus: John Paul II's Program of Marian Consecration and Entrustment* (New Bedford, Mass.: Academy of the Immaculate, 1992), 253–54. The text of this address is available on the internet at http://www.vatican.va/holy_father/john_paul_ii/speeches/1986/september/documents/hf_jp-ii_spe_19860922_simposio-maria-gesu_en.html.

199. "Immaculate Heart of the Blessed Virgin Mary," n. 28, in *MBVM* (Collegeville, Minn., 2012), 113.

200. Scheffczyk, *Maria, Mutter und Gefährtin Christi* [Mary, Mother and Companion of Christ] (Augsburg: Sankt Ulrich, 2003), 339.

201. John Paul II, Address of September 22, 1986; in Calkins, *Totus tuus* (1992 ed.), 255.

the heart (*cor*) and mercy (*misericordia*): "*misericors dicitur aliquis quasi habens miserum cors*: a person is said to be merciful [*misericors*], who is, so to speak, sorrowful at heart [*miserum cors*], being affected with sorrow at the misery of another as though it were his own. Hence it follows that he endeavors to dispel the misery of this other, as if it were his; and this is the effect of mercy."[202] In compassion, the Mother of God has been associated with the Cross of Christ, and thus has become able to intervene effectively in situations of misery with her heavenly intercession. In the *Magnificat*, Mary praises the divine mercy (Lk 1:50).[203] The fathers of the church already emphasized the mercy of the *Theotókos*.[204] The most ancient Marian prayer transmitted to us by an inscription, the *Sub tuum praesidium* (third or fourth century) bears in the most ancient Greek text the invocation "Under the wing of your mercy we take refuge, Mother of God."[205] In the Middle Ages, since Odo, the second abbot of Cluny († 942), the title *Mater misericordiae* has spread, especially by means of the hymn *Salve Regina*.[206] Mary is "mother" and "queen" of mercy.[207] "The title of 'queen of mercy' also was dear to the faithful because it shaped the famous 'major' antiphon *Salve Regina misericordiae*, sung every day since 1218 by Cistercian monks, whose evening salute to their Lady swiftly became very popular."[208]

202. Thomas Aquinas, *ST* I, q. 21, a. 3.

203. See Alberto Valentini, "Maria canta la misericordia di Dio" [Mary Sings the Mercy of God], in *Maria Madre di misericordia: Mostra te esse Matrem* [Mary, Mother of Mercy: Show Thyself a Mother], ed. P. Di Domenico and E. Peretto (Padua: Messagero, 2003), 122–45.

204. See Johannes Stöhr, "Barmherzigkeit Mariens" [Mercy of Mary], in *ML* 1:365; Gambero, "Maria e il mistero della misericordia di Dio: Riflessioni nei Padri della Chiesa" [Mary and the Mystery of the Mercy of God: Reflections on the Fathers of the Church], in Di Domenico and Peretto, *Maria Madre di misericordia*, 158–85; De Fiores, *Dizionario*, 2:1172.

205. See De Fiores, *Maria sintesi di valori: Storia culturale della mariologia* [Mary, Synthesis of Values: Cultural History of Mariology] (Cinisello Balsamo: San Paolo, 2005), 138.

206. See Stöhr, "Barmherzigkeit Mariens," 365–69; Angelo M. Gila, "'Maria, Regina e Madre di misericordia': Un tema tipico dell'epoca medioevale" [Mary, Queen and Mother of Mercy: A Theme Typical of the Medieval Era], in Di Domenico and Peretto, *Maria Madre di misericordia*, 186–217 (on Odo: 189). See the first account, the *Vita sancti Odonis* (PL 133:47 B–C) by John of Salerno, in Gambero, *Maria nel pensiero*, 98. A few less influential appearances of the title are recorded even earlier (Jacob of Sarugh, Syria, 6th centuries; Paul the Deacon, eighth century) and are indicated in De Fiores, *Dizionario*, 2:1172f.

207. See *MBVM*, n. 39 ("Holy Mary, Queen and Mother of Mercy").

208. Ignazio Calabuig, "La Vergine, oggetto della misericordia di Dio: Riflessioni a partire dalla liturgia" [The Virgin, Object of God's Mercy: Reflections from the Liturgy], in Di Domenico and Peretto, *Maria Madre di misericordia*, 263.

The mercy of Mary is not opposed to the justice of Christ, as it took place in some homiletic exaggerations, but is derived from the merciful mediation of her Son. The mercy of God is conveyed into the order of our salvation by means of Mary, in the heart of a woman.[209]

No one has experienced, to the same degree as the Mother of the crucified One, the mystery of the cross, the overwhelming encounter of divine transcendent justice with love: that "kiss" given by mercy to justice (cf. Ps 85 [84]:11). No one has received into his heart, as much as Mary did, that mystery, that truly divine dimension of the redemption effected on Calvary by means of the death of the Son, together with the sacrifice of her maternal heart, together with her definitive "fiat."

The revelation of the merciful love of Christ in the Mother of God is based

upon the unique tact of her maternal heart, on her particular sensitivity, on her particular fitness to reach all those who most easily accept the merciful love of a mother. This is one of the great life-giving mysteries of Christianity, a mystery intimately connected with the mystery of the Incarnation.[210]

For our presentation, we have set the doctrine on the Heart of Mary at the end of the chapter on her holiness, because the Immaculate Heart symbolizes very well the abundance of graces received, since the beginning of her life, by the Blessed Virgin. In reference to the Assumption of Mary body and soul into heaven, it has been remarked that "her Immaculate Heart is the place in which the new creation is already realized."[211] Holiness becomes active in the motherly mediation of Mary. Because of this, the Immaculate Heart also enters into the supreme form of Marian devotion, which is consecration.[212]

209. See Stöhr, "Barmherzigkeit Mariens," 369; De Fiores, *Dizionario* 2:1177–85.

210. John Paul II, Encyclical *Dives in misericordia* (1980), 9 (*PE* 5:279, n. 97, 100; *EE* 8, nn. 160, 163).

211. Christoph Schönborn, OP, "Maria—Herz Der Theologie—Theologie Des Herzens" [Mary, Heart of Theology, Theology of the Heart], in *Weisheit Gottes—Weisheit der Welt: Festschrift für Joseph Kardinal Ratzinger zum 60. Geburtstag*, ed. W. Baier et al. (St. Ottilien: EOS Verlag, 1987), 1:588.

212. See "Consecration to Mary," in chapter 10.

REFERENCES

The Holiness of Mary

Ecclesiastical Texts

Alexander VII, Bull *Sollicitudo*: DH 2015f.
CCC 411, 490–93.
Collantes, Justo, ed. *La fede della Chiesa Cattolica: Le idee e gli uomini nei documenti dottrinali del Magistero* [The Faith of the Catholic Church: Ideas and Men in the Doctrinal Documents of the Magisterium], 314–24. Vatican City: Libreria Editrice Vaticana, 1993.
John Paul II. *RM* 7–11; CM 19–24 (May 8, May 15, May 29, June 5, June 12, June 19, 1996).
Pius V. Bull against Michael Baius: DH 1973.
Pius IX, Bull *Ineffabilis Deus* (Dogmatic Definition of the Immaculate Conception of Mary, 1854): DH 2800–2803 (in full: *EE* 2, nn. 739–65).
Pius XII. Encyclical *Fulgens corona: PE* 4:247.
Sixtus IV. Constitution *Cum praeexcelsa:* DH 1400.
———. Constitution *Grave nimis:* DH 1425f.
Trent, Council of. Decree on Original Sin, Can. 6: DH 1516.

Other Sources

La Inmaculada Concepción. Teología—Historia—Espiritualidad [The Immaculate Conception: Theology, History, Spirituality]. *Estudios Marianos* 71 (2005).
Mary at the Foot of the Cross. Vol. 5, *Redemption and Coredemption under the Sign of the Immaculate Conception.* New Bedford, Mass.: Academy of the Immaculate, 2005.
Virgo immaculata. 18 vols. Vatican City: AMI, 1955–58 (acts of the 1954 Rome Congress).
Auer, Johann. *Gesù il Salvatore: Soteriologia–Mariologia* [Jesus the Savior: Soteriology, Mariology], §§8–10. Translated by Carlo Molari. Assisi: Cittadella, 1993. German original: *Jesus Christus—Heiland der Welt: Maria, Christi Mutter im Heilsplan Gottes.* Regensburg: Friedrich Pustet, 1988.
Bastero, Juan Luis. *Mary, Mother of the Redeemer*, 183–96. Dublin: Four Courts: 2006.
———. *Virgen singular: La reflexión teológica mariana en el siglo XX* [Singular Virgin: Theological Reflection on Mary in the 20th Century], 113–70. Madrid: Rialp, 2001.
Bertetto, Domenico. *Maria Immacolata: Il domma della concezione immacolata di Maria nel centenario della sua definizione 1854—8 Dicembre—1954* [Mary Immaculate: The Dogma of the Immaculate Conception of Mary at the Centenary of Its Definition; December 8, 1954]. Rome: Edizioni Paoline, 1953.
Calero, Antonio Maria. *La Vergine Maria nel mistero di Cristo e della Chiesa: Saggio di mariologia* [The Virgin Mary in the Mystery of Christ and the Church: Essay in Mariology], 163–223. Leumann (Turin): Elle Di Ci, 1995. Spanish original: *María en el misterio de Cristo y de la Iglesia.* Madrid: CCS, 1990.
Carr, Aidan, OFM Conv., and Germain Williams, OFM Conv. "Inmaculada concep-

ción de María." In *Mariología*, edited by J. Carol, 307–70. Madrid: Biblioteca de Autores Cristianos, 1964. English original: "Mary's Immaculate Conception." In *Mariology*, edited by J. Carol, 1:328–94. Milwaukee: Bruce: 1954.

Cecchin, Stefano M., ed. *La "Scuola Francescana" e l'Immacolata Concezione* [The "Franciscan School" and the Immaculate Conception]. Vatican City: PAMI, 2005.

———. *L'Immacolata Concezione: Breve storia del dogma* [The Immaculate Conception: Brief History of the Dogma]. Vatican City: PAMI, 2003.

Colzani, Gianni. *Maria: Mistero di grazia e di fede* [Mary: Mystery of Grace and Faith], 218–24. Cinisello Balsamo (Milan): Ed. Paoline, 1996. 3rd ed., 2006.

De Fiores, Stefano. "Immacolata." In De Fiores and Meo, *NDM*, 679–88, 695–708.

———. *Maria nella teologia contemporanea* [Mary in Contemporary Theology]. 3rd ed., 454–49. Rome: Centro di Cultura Mariana "Madre della Chiesa," 1991.

———. *Maria: Nuovissimo dizionario*, 1:839–97. Bologna: EDB, 2006.

De Fiores, Stefano, and Enrico Vidau, eds. *Maria Santa e Immacolata segno dell'amore salvifico di Dio Trinità: Prospettive ecumeniche* [Mary, Holy and Immaculate, Sign of the Salvific Love of the Triune God: Ecumenical Perspectives]. Rome: Ed. Monfortane, 2000.

Galot, Jean, SJ. "La sainteté de Marie." In *Maria*, edited by H. du Manoir, 6:417–48. Paris: Beauchesne, 1961.

———. "L'Immaculée Conception." In *Maria*, edited by H. du Manoir, 7:9–116. Paris: Beauchesne, 1964.

———. *Maria, La donna nell'opera della salvezza* [Mary, the Woman in the Work of Salvation]. 3rd ed., 185–238. Rome: Ed. Pontificia Università Gregoriana, 2005. 2nd ed., 1991.

Gherardini, Brunero. *La Madre: Maria in una sintesi storico-teologica* [The Mother: Mary in a Historical-Theological Synthesis], 134–72. Frigento: Casa Mariana, 1989.

Haffner, Paul. *The Mystery of Mary*, 73–106. Leominster, UK: Gracewing; Mundelein, Ill.: Hillenbrand, 2004.

Hauke, Manfred. "Die Gottesmutter als irdisches Paradies bei Johannes von Euböa: Die erste Predigt zum Fest der makellosen Empfängnis Mariens" [The Mother of God as Earthly Paradise in John of Euböa: The First Sermon on the Feast of the Spotless Conception of Mary]. *Klerusblatt* 84 (2004): 272–74.

———. "Die Unbefleckte Empfängnis Mariens bei den griechischen Vätern: Die Hinweise Johannes Pauls II. im ökumenischen Disput." *Sedes Sapientiae: Mariologisches Jahrbuch* 8 (2004): 13–54 = "The Immaculate Conception of Mary in the Greek Fathers and in an Ecumenical Context." *Chicago Studies* 45 (2006): 327–46.

———. "Maria 'scettro della vera fede': L'Immacolata Concezione e la discussione sul peccato originale" [Mary, "Scepter of the True Faith": The Immaculate Conception and the Debate on Original Sin]. *RTLu* 8 (February 2004): 315–39.

Jugie, Martin. *L'Immaculée Conception dans l'Écriture Sainte et dans la Tradition Orientale* [The Immaculate Conception in Holy Scripture and in the Eastern Tradition]. Rome: Academia Mariana, 1952.

Lamy, Marielle. *Immacolata*. In De Fiores, Schiefer, and Perrella, *DMar*, 612–28.

———. *L'Immaculée Conception: Étapes et enjeux d'une controverse au Moyen-âge (XIIe–XVe siècles)* [The Immaculate Conception: Stages and Stakes of a Controversy in the Middle Ages (12th to 15th Centuries)]. Paris: Institut d'Études Augustiniennes, 2000.

Le Bachelet, Xavier-Marie, SJ, and Martin Jugie. "Immaculée Conception." In *DThC* 7:845–1218.

Maranesi, Pietro. "Gli sviluppi della dottrina sull'Immacolata Concezione dal XII al XV secolo" [Developments in the Doctrine of the Immaculate Conception in the 12th to 15th Centuries]. In *Storia della Mariologia*, edited by E. Dal Covolo and A. Serra, 1:843–72. Rome: Città Nuova, 2009.

Merkelbach, Benoît Henri. *Mariologia*, 157–213. Paris: Desclée, 1939.

O'Carroll, Michael, CSSp. *Theotokos: A Theological Encyclopedia of the Blessed Virgin Mary*, 179–82. Eugene, Ore.: Wipf and Stock, 2000.

Ponce Cuéllar, Miguel. *María: Madre del Redentor y Madre de la Iglesia* [Mary: Mother of the Redeemer and Mother of the Church]. 2nd ed., 387–413. Barcelona: Herder, 2001.

Pozo, Cándido, SJ. *María en la obra de la salvación* [Mary in the Work of Salvation]. 2nd ed., 296–313. Madrid: Biblioteca de Autores Cristianos, 1990.

———. *María, nueva Eva* [Mary, the New Eve], 315–33. Madrid: Biblioteca de Autores Cristianos, 2005.

Roschini, Gabriele Maria. *La Madonna: Secondo la fede e la teologia* [The Madonna, according to the Faith and Theology], 3:6–162. Rome: Libreria Editrice Francesco Ferrari, 1953–54.

———. *Maria Santissima nella storia della salvezza: Trattato completo di mariologia alla luce del Concilio Vaticano II* [Mary Most Holy in the History of Salvation: Complete Treatise on Mariology in Light of the Second Vatican Council], 3:9–36. Isola del Liri: Pisani, 1969.

Rovira, German, ed. *Im Gewande des Heils: Die Unbefleckte Empfängnis Mariens als Urbild der menschlichen Heiligkeit* [Clothed in Salvation: The Immaculate Conception of Mary as an Archetype of Human Holiness]. Essen: Ludgerus-Verlag, 1980.

Scheffczyk, Leo. *Maria, crocevia della fede cattolica* [Mary, Crossroads of the Catholic Faith], 93–115. CdM 1. Lugano: Eupress FTL, 2002.

———. *Maria, Mutter und Gefährtin Christi*, 128–45. Augsburg: Sankt Ulrich, 2003.

Serra, Aristide. "Immacolata II. Fondamenti biblici." In De Fiores and Meo, *NDM*, 688–95.

Seybold, Michael. "Unbefleckte Empfängnis. I. Dogmatik." In *ML* 6:519–25.

Söll, Georg. *Storia dei dogmi mariani* [History of Marian Dogmas]. Rome: Libreria Ateneo Salesiano, 1981. German original: *Mariologie* [*Handbuch der Dogmengeschichte*, vol. 3, part 4]. Freiburg im Breisgau: Herder, 1978.

Stöhr, Johannes. "Zur Bibliographie der Immakulata." *Sedes Sapientiae: Mariologisches Jahrbuch* 8, no. 1 (2004): 61–90.

Toniolo, Ermanno M., ed. *Il dogma dell'Immacolata Concezione di Maria: Problemi attuali e tentativi di ricomprensione* [The Dogma of the Immaculate Conception of Mary: Current Issues and Attempts at Reinterpretation]. Rome: Ed. Marianum, 2004.

Ziegenaus, Anton. *Maria in der Heilsgeschichte: Mariologie*, 287–309. Katholische Dogmatik 5. Aachen: MM-Verlag, 1998.

Fullness of Grace

Ecclesiastical Texts

John Paul II. CM 19 (May 8, 1996).
———. *RM* 8–9.
Pius IX. Bull *Ineffabilis Deus* (*EE* 3, n. 739).
Vatican II. *Lumen gentium* 53.

Other Sources

Calkins, Frank P., OSM. "Plenitud de gracia" [Fullness of Grace]. In *Mariología*, edited by J. Carol, 684–99. English original: "Mary's Fullness of Grace." In *Mariology*, edited by J. Carol, 2:297–312. Milwaukee: Bruce: 1957.
de Candido, Luigi M. "Santa Maria." In *NDM*, 1242–53.
De Fiores, Stefano. "Santa Maria." In De Fiores, *Maria. Nuovissimo dizionario*, 2:1451–89.
Galot, Jean, SJ. "La Sainteté de Marie." In *Maria*, edited by H. du Manoir, 6:417–48. 1961.
———. *Maria. La donna*, 231–38.
Merkelbach. *Mariologia*, 157–213.
O'Carroll. *Theotokos*, 172–74.
Roschini. *La Madonna secondo la fede* 3:91–110, 134–162.
———. *Maria Santissima* 3:269–84.
Royo Marin, Antonio. *La Virgen María: Teología y espiritualidad marianas* [The Virgin Mary: Marian Theology and Spirituality]. 2nd ed. 250–358. Madrid: Biblioteca de Autores Cristianos, 1997.
Stöhr, Johannes. "Charismen." In *ML* 2:25–31.
———. "Gnadenfülle" [Fullness of Grace]. In *ML* 2:662–64.

The Immaculate Heart of Mary

Ecclesiastical Texts

John Paul II. Consecration of the World to the Immaculate Heart of Mary, May 13, 1982 and March 25, 1984.
———. Discourse to Participants in the Symposium on Jesus and Mary, September 22, 1986.
———. Encyclical *Dives in Misericordia*, 9.
———. Encyclical *Redemptoris Mater*, 22 (see, along with other texts, Calkins' anthology in *Totus tuus*, 205–17 of the 1992 edition).
Pius XII. Consecration of the World to the Immaculate Heart of Mary, October 31, 1942, *AAS* 34 (1942): 345f. (Italian translation in *Atti e discorsi di Pius XII*, 4:263–72. Rome, 1943.)

Other Sources

Alonso, Joaquín María. *Doctrina y espiritualidad del mensaje de Fátima* [Doctrine and Spirituality of the Fatima Message], 167–201. Madrid: Arias Montana Editores, 1990.

Alonso, Joaquín María, and Danilo Sartor. "Cuore immacolato" [Immaculate Heart]. In De Fiores and Meo, *NDM*, 443–55.

Arragain, Jacques, CJM. "La Dévotion au Coeur de Marie" [Devotion to the Heart of Mary]. In *Maria*, edited by H. du Manoir, 5:1007–48. Paris: Beauchesne, 1958.

Augé, M. "Cuore Immacolato." In De Fiores, Schiefer, and Perrella, *DMar*, 370–76.

Brogeras Martinez, Pablo. "Introducción a la teología del Corazon de María" [Introduction to the Theology of the Heart of Mary]. *Ephemerides Mariologicae* 50 (2000): 441–54.

Calkins, Arthur B. "The Hearts of Jesus and Mary in the Magisterium of Pope John Paul II." In *De cultu mariano s. XX*, 4:147–67. Vatican City: PAMI, 1999.

———. *Totus tuus: John Paul II's Program of Marian Consecration and Entrustment*, 79–111, 248–56, 281f. New Bedford, Mass.: Academy of the Immaculate, 1997.

Canal, José María, and Joaquín María Alonso. *La consagración a la Virgen y a su Corazón* [Consecration to the Virgin and Her Heart]. 2 vols. Madrid: Co. Cul. S.A., 1960.

de Margerie, Bertrand. *Le coeur de Marie, coeur de l'Église: Essai de synthèse théologique* [The Heart of Mary, Heart of the Church: Essay in Theological Synthesis]. 2nd ed. Paris: P. Téqui, 1993.

Esquerda Bifet, Juan. "El Corazón de María, memoria contemplativa de la Iglesia" [The Heart of Mary, Contemplative Memory of the Church]. *Marianum* 66 (2004): 659–98.

Geenen, Godfried, OP. "Les antécédents doctrinaux et historiques de la consécration du monde au coeur immaculé de Marie" [Doctrinal and Historical Antecedents of the Consecration of the World to the Immaculate Heart of Mary]. In *Maria*, edited by H. du Manoir, 1:825–873. Paris: Beauchesne, 1949.

Hauke, Manfred, ed. *Die Herz-Mariä-Verehrung: Geschichtliche Entwicklung und theologischer Gehalt* [Veneration of the Heart of Mary: Historical Development and Theological Content]. Mariologische Studien 22. Regensburg: Pustet, 2011.

Köster, Heinrich M. "Herz Mariä I. Verehrung" [Heart of Mary. I. Veneration]. In *ML* 3:163f.

O'Carroll. *Theotokos*, 166–68.

Pozo, Cándido. "La consagración a los Corazones de Jesús y María en Juan Pablo II" [Consecration to the Hearts of Jesus and Mary in John Paul II]. In *El Corazón de Jesús en la ensenanza de Juan Pablo II*, 337–57. Madrid: Instituto Internacional del Corazón de Jesús, 1990.

Ruiz Tintoré, Miguel. "La devoción al Corazón de María, corazón de las devociones a María" [Devotion to the Heart of Mary, Heart of Devotions to Mary]. *Ephemerides mariologicae* 63 (2013): 467–88.

Scheffczyk. *Maria, Mutter und Gefährtin*, 337–43.

Schönborn, Christoph, OP. "Maria—Herz Der Theologie—Theologie Des Herzens" [Mary, Heart of Theology, Theology of the Heart]. In *Weisheit Gottes—Weisheit der Welt. Festschrift für Joseph Kardinal Ratzinger*, edited by W. Baier et al., 1:575–89. St. Ottilien: EOS Verlag, 1987.

Stimpfle, Josef. "Entschiedenheit für Gott: Begründung, Sinn, Ziel und Durchführung der Weihe an das Unbefleckte Herz Mariä" [Commitment for God: Basis, Meaning, Goal, and Implementation of Consecration to the Immaculate Heart of Mary]. In Stimpfle, *Im Dienst des Evangeliums*, 98–136. Donauwörth: Auer, 1988.

Stöhr, Johannes. "Corazón de Madre (Considerazziones teológicas sobre la Consagración a María)" [Heart of Mary (Theological Considerations on Consecration to Mary)]. *Scripta de Maria 2nd ser.* 1 (2004): 141–80.

———. "Herz Mariä III. Dogmatik." In *ML* 3:167–69.

———. "Neuere Impulse zur Theologie und Verehrung des Herzens Mariä" [Newer Impulses to the Theology and Devotion of the Heart of Mary]. In *De cultu mariano s. XX*, 2:397–427.

Ziegenaus. *Maria in der Heilsgeschichte*, 385–87.

Seven

The Assumption of Mary

INTRODUCTION

"We pronounce, declare, and define it to be a divinely revealed dogma: that the Immaculate Mother of God, the ever Virgin Mary, having completed the course of her earthly life, was assumed body and soul into heavenly glory."[1] With these words, in 1950, Pope Pius XII solemnly defined the Assumption of Mary both body and soul into heaven. The definition leaves open the question debated between mortalists and immortalists on whether the Mother of God, before being glorified, suffered death or not. Instead, the dogmatic explanation refers to the exposition preceding it in the same Apostolic Constitution *Munificentissimus Deus*, affirming the theological connection of the Assumption with the Immaculate Conception, the divine maternity, and the perpetual virginity of Mary.

In the following pages we will trace the historical path leading to the dogma, and we will discuss its theological significance and a few of the questions debated today. Given that Mary's entrance into heavenly glory renders the Mother of the Lord a partaker, gloriously, in the kingship of Christ, we shall add some observations about her role as Queen.

BIBLICAL FOUNDATIONS

Direct references to the Assumption of Mary body and soul into heaven are not found in Sacred Scripture. In this regard the dogma

1. DH 3903.

is comparable to the dogma of the Immaculate Conception. But in the Word of God we find the starting point that leads theological reflection to a knowledge of Mary's preservation from bodily corruption.

Some theologians (Martin Jugie, André Feuillet)[2] have wanted to find a hint of the Assumption already in Revelation 12:1: "A great sign appeared in heaven, a woman clothed with the sun, with the moon under her feet, and on her head a crown of twelve stars." However, we need to say here,[3] that the "woman clothed with the sun" is not simply Mary but rather the church, even if a certain Marian nuance is implicit. The "woman" is rather a symbolic figure. After she has appeared "in heaven," she is found on earth, suffers the pains of birth, and is forced to flee from the persecution of the "dragon." "Applied to Mary, this representation would signify a glory prior to the fulfillment of her messianic motherhood."[4]

At most we can say that in the victory of the "woman" over the forces of the devil, the fuller sense of the passage also implies victory over death, whose author is Satan (see Ws 2:24). So there is reason to use Revelation 12 in the liturgy of the feast of August 15. "(The) scholastic Doctors have recognized the Assumption of the Virgin Mother of God as something signified, not only in various figures of the Old Testament,[5] but also in that woman clothed with the

2. See Cándido Pozo, SJ, "La consagración a los Corazones de Jesús y María en Juan Pablo II" [Consecration to the Hearts of Jesus and Mary in John Paul II], in *El Corazón de Jesús en la enseñanza de Juan Pablo II: Antología de textos, Estudios* (Madrid: Instituto Internacional del Corazón de Jesús, 1990), 314f; Pozo, *María, nueva Eva*, 336, referring to Martin Jugie, "Assomption de la sainte Vierge," in *Maria: Études sur la Sainte Vierge*, ed. Hubert du Manoir (Paris: Beauchesne, 1949), 1:627–30; A. Feuillet, "Marie dans le Nouveau Testament," in du Manoir, *Maria* (1961), 6:64f.

3. See "The 'Woman' of the Apocalypse," in chapter 1.

4. Galot, *Maria, La donna nell'opera della salvezza* [Mary, Woman in the Work of Salvation]. 3rd ed. (Rome: Ed. Pontificia Università Gregoriana, 2005), 296.

5. Obviously, we are dealing here with the method of "accommodation," which does not pertain to the literal sense. Pius XII indicates this usage on the part of many theologians "to explain their belief in the Assumption." They "have been rather free in their use of events and expressions taken from Sacred Scripture. Thus, to mention only a few of the texts rather frequently cited in this fashion, some have employed the words of the psalmist: 'Arise, O Lord, into your resting place: you and the ark, that you have sanctified' (Ps 131:8); and have looked upon the *Ark of the Covenant*, built of incorruptible wood and placed in the Lord's temple, as a type of the most pure body of the Virgin Mary, preserved and exempt from all the corruption of the tomb and raised up to such glory in heaven. Treating of this subject, they also describe her as the Queen entering triumphantly into the royal halls of heaven and sitting at the right hand of the divine Redeemer (Ps 45:9–10,

sun whom John the Apostle contemplated on the island of Patmos (Rv 12:1f.)."[6]

Looking to Revelation 12, we are also close to the Protoevangelium as a starting point (Gn 3:15). The victory of the mother of the Messiah over the devil also includes the conquest of bodily death. This is implied in the description of Mary as "the new Eve, who, although subject to the new Adam, is most intimately associated with him in that struggle against the infernal foe that, as foretold in the Protoevangelium (Gn 3:15), would finally result in that most complete victory over the sin and death that are always mentioned together in the writings of the Apostle of the Gentiles (cf. Rom 5 and 6; 1 Cor 15:21–26, 54–57). Consequently, just as the glorious resurrection of Christ was an essential part and the final sign of this victory, so that struggle that was common to the Blessed Virgin and her divine Son should be brought to a close by the glorification of her virginal body, for the same Apostle says: 'When this mortal thing hath put on immortality, then shall come to pass the saying that is written: Death is swallowed up in victory' (1 Cor 15:54)."[7]

Together with the Protoevangelium, we can contemplate the angelic salutation: Mary "full of grace" (Lk 1:28). Many theologians "saw, in the mystery of the Assumption, the fulfillment of that most perfect grace granted to the Blessed Virgin and the special blessing that countered the curse of Eve."[8]

It is also good to consider Matthew 27:51–53, a scene presented immediately after the death of Jesus: "And behold, the curtain of the temple was torn in two, from top to bottom, and the earth shook, and the rocks were split; the tombs also were opened, and many bodies of the saints who had fallen asleep were raised, and coming out of the tombs after his resurrection they went into the holy city and appeared to many."

45:14–16). Likewise they mention the Spouse of the Canticles 'that goes up by the desert, as a pillar of smoke of aromatical spices, of myrrh and frankincense' to be crowned (Sg 3:6; see 4:8, 6:9). These are proposed as depicting that heavenly Queen and heavenly Spouse who has been lifted up to the courts of heaven with the divine Bridegroom" (*EE* 6, n. 1956).

6. Pius XII, *Munificentissimus Deus* (*EE* 6, n. 1957).

7. Ibid (*EE* 6, n. 1969).

8. Ibid (*EE* 6, n. 1957).

If we take this text literally, it is dealing with a certain group of saints of the old covenant who rise and appear (after the resurrection of Jesus) at Jerusalem. This is an exception to the rule that the bodily resurrection will take place only at the parousia.[9] If this was granted already to certain Old Testament saints, it would seem easier to include Mary also.

To summarize: there is no direct attestation of the Assumption in the New Testament; but the association of Mary with the destiny of Jesus and her participation in his victory over the devil imply, in view of the preceding development, that she overcame death.

DEVELOPMENT OF THE DOCTRINE IN THE EASTERN CHURCH

The Silence of the First Centuries

Epiphanius, bishop of Salamis († 403), toward the end of the fourth century, speaks of the silence of Sacred Scripture on the death of Mary in these terms: there is "no hint of the death of Mary, whether to say if she died or didn't, if she was buried or not.... Personally, I don't dare to speak of it; I prefer to impose an attitude of reflection and silence upon myself." Epiphanius does not uphold the immortality or the death of Mary. "Even if the holy Virgin died and was buried, her death is surrounded with great honor and her end came to pass in chastity; her crown was virginity. If she was killed, according to the Scripture: 'And a sword will pierce through your own soul' (Lk 2:35), her glory is among the martyrs and her holy body, from which the light of the world began, is among the blessed. But she really remained alive, since for God it is not impossible to do everything He wishes; in fact, no one knows her end exactly."[10] The

9. On the interpretation of the passage, see Rafael Aguirre-Monasterio, *Exégesis de Mateo 27:51b–53: Para una teología de la muerte de Jesús en el Evangelio de Mateo* [Exegesis of Mt 17:51b–53: Toward a Theology of the Death of Jesus in the Gospel of Matthew] (Vitoria: Editorial Eset, 1980); Ulrich Luz, *Das Evangelium nach Matthäus (Mt 26–28)* [The Gospel according to Matthew (Mt 26–28)], Evangelisch-katholischer Kommentar zum Neuen Testament, vol. 1, part 4. (Düsseldorf: Benziger-Neukirchener, 2002), 354–71.

10. *Panarion* 78.11.2 (PG 42.716B–37A), translated in Luigi Gambero, "Maria Assunta: Rilievi dell'escatologia patristica" [Mary Assumed: Review of Patristic Eschatology], in *Maria, icona viva*

testimony cited has a certain weight because Epiphanius comes from Palestine, and he maintained close contacts there.[11]

Also Modestus of Jerusalem, two hundred years after Epiphanius, observes in a sermon on the Assumption that the teachers of times past "strangely never declared a thing on the venerable passing" of the Mother of God.[12]

These texts seem to imply, according to the most widespread interpretation, that in the teaching of the church's faith there does not exist a historical transmission on the passing of Mary. Therefore, the dogma is formulated on the basis of theological reflection, joined to the historic fact that there is no tomb that contains the remains of Mary.

The Tradition of the Tomb of Mary at Gethsemane

On this subject we need to have a look at the archeological witnesses. The old tradition regarding the tomb of Mary appears in the oldest Marian church in Jerusalem, situated at Gethsemane.[13] The temple was erected during the fifth century, excavating an older necropolis. The tomb of Mary has characteristics typical of the first century, described for the first time in 1972, when a flood made the appropriate research possible. Three chambers in the tomb of the Virgin were discovered, a trait that corresponds to the description in the apocrypha according to which Mary was placed in a burial complex of three chambers.[14]

---

della Chiesa futura [Mary, Living Icon of the Future Church], ed. C. Carvello and S. De Fiores (Rome: Edizioni Monfortane, 1998), 127f.

11. See S. Heid, "Epiphanius von Salamis," in *ML* 2:375f.; Stephen J. Shoemaker, *Ancient Traditions of the Virgin Mary's Dormition and Assumption* (Oxford: Oxford University Press, 2002), 11f.

12. *Encomium in dormitionem SS: Deiparae* (PG 86:3280). See Georg Söll, *Storia dei dogmi mariani* [History of Marian Dogmas] (Rome: Libreria Ateneo Salesiano, 1981), 196–99; M. Lochbrunner, "Modestus von Jerusalem," in *ML* 4:495f.

13. We will also return to the old tradition of the tomb of Mary at Gethsemane later in this chapter: see "The Liturgical Witness" and "Theological Explanation."

14. See Frédéric Manns, "Scoperte archeologiche e tradizioni antiche sulla Dormizione e Assunzione di Maria" [Archaeological Discoveries and Ancient Traditions on the Dormition and Assumption of Mary], in *L'Assunzione di Maria Madre di Dio*, ed. Gaspar Calvo Moralejo and Stefano Cecchin (Vatican City: PAMI, 2001), 176; Shoemaker, *Ancient Traditions*, 98–107. It is also possible that the Marian church called the "Kathisma," discovered on the road between Bethle-

Interpretation of the Apocrypha

Some researchers assume the existence of an "underground tradition" on the passing of Mary. This tradition would explain the source of the apocryphal writings on the Assumption that appear (at the latest) at the fifth century. The advocates of this hypothesis are above all Martin Jugie, Assumptionist father and noted scholar on Eastern theology, and Bellarmino Bagatti, OFM, together with other theologians of the Studium Biblicum Franciscanum at Jerusalem (in particular Emmanuele Testa and currently Frédéric Manns).[15] Jugie goes back to the political situation of Palestine after the destruction of Jerusalem in 70. Referring to an ancient tradition according to which the Apostle John is said not to have left the Holy Land for Ephesus until after the Jewish War, the scholar hypothesizes that

---

hem and Jerusalem, had had iconography dedicated to the Dormition. The "Kathisma" (= "seat," resting place of Mary) was built around a rock on that Mary (according to the Protoevangelium of James, 17) is said to have rested before arriving in Jerusalem for the birth of the infant Jesus. Just as after the Council of Chalcedon the church of the Dormition at Gethsemane was in the hands of the opponents of the Council, the "Kathisma" probably was used by the orthodox (i.e., Catholic) Christians with reference to the final "resting place" of Mary. See Manns, "Scoperte archeologiche e tradizioni antiche," 170–75; Shoemaker, *Ancient Traditions*, 81–98.

There has also been debate about whether there is any value in mystical experiences about the place of Mary's passing. in particular in regard to the visions of Anne Catherine Emmerick, German seer (†1824), declared blessed in 2004. According to the visions of this seer (about the house of Mary) the ruin of a church was found near Ephesus, called "Gate of the All-Holy" by the populace. The building stems from the thirteenth century but was constructed in a place that seems to have had a religious importance already. According to Emmerick, a tomb was prepared for Mary at Jerusalem (mentioned in the apocryphal tradition), because she was ill during a visit to the holy city. But she supposedly returned to Ephesus, where she died. In the same night she is said to have been assumed into Heaven, and the Apostles found the tomb empty. Emmerick expresses the conviction that the tomb still exists on earth and will be discovered one day. In any case, there are ancient references about the dwelling place of Mary at Ephesus, near the Apostle John. A definitive evaluation on the visions of this seer requires, so it seems, a deeper investigation, and (if positive) could be convincing, if an archeological excavation were to confirm her description of the sepulchre. Otherwise the tradition of a death at Jerusalem seems more plausible. See J. J. Seller, OSA, and Ildefons M. Dietz, "Emmerick," in *ML* 2:335f; U. Bleyenberg, "Maria in den Visionen Anna Katharina Emmericks" [Mary in the Visions of Anna Katharina Emmerick], in *Volksfrömmigkeit und Theologie: Die eine Mariengestalt und die vielen Quellen* [Popular Piety and Theology: The One Figure of Mary and Its Many Sources], ed. Anton Ziegenaus (Regensburg: Friedrich Pustet, 1998), 137–61.

15. On the history of the research see, among others, Shoemaker, *Ancient Traditions*, 9–25; E. Norelli, "Maria nella letteratura apocrifa cristiana antica" [Mary in Ancient Christian Apocryphal Literature], in *Storia della Mariologia* [History of Mariology], ed. E. Dal Covolo and A. Serra (Rome: Città Nuova, 2009), 1:222–39.

Mary concluded her earthly existence in the period when Christians were staying at Pella (across the Jordan). This way it would have been difficult to communicate the mystery of the final glorification of Mary to successive generations. In any case, there would have been some ancient tradition in existence that would explain the explosion of apocryphal witnesses in the fifth century.[16]

Bagatti, in contrast, maintains that the first apocrypha, from which come the other texts of the fifth and sixth centuries, would itself be from the second or third century. In this source two points would have to appear—in particular, the natural death of Mary at Jerusalem in the presence of the apostles and her burial at Gethsemane, despite the difficulties presented by the Jews. However, it is not clear what would have happened afterward: the apocrypha affirm either that the body of Mary was borne to an earthly paradise to await the final resurrection or that she was assumed into Heaven. Referring to excavations made at Jerusalem, the Franciscan maintains that the initial silence regarding the tomb of Mary, as with other monuments, would have stemmed from the opposition between Jewish Christians (the custodians of the monuments) and those stemming from paganism. Inasmuch as the former were somewhat at the margins of the church (considered schismatics), the latter would have lain a veil of silence even over the documents that they preserved. By the time Christians of pagan origin took over precedence as custodians of the monuments (in the fourth century), a lot of information would have been lost.[17]

As support for his thesis, Bagatti notes a reference in the apocrypha of Pseudo-Melito to Leucio, who, it is said, wrote a work on the

16. See Jugie, *La mort et l'assomption de la Sainte Vierge: Étude historico-doctrinale* [The Death and Assumption of the Holy Virgin: Historical-Doctrinal Study] (Vatican City: Biblioteca Apostolica Vaticana, 1944); Jugie, "Assomption de la sainte Vierge."

17. See inter alia Bellarmino Bagatti, "Richerche sulle tradizioni della morte della Vergine" [Research on Traditions about the Death of the Virgin], *Sacra Doctrina* 18 (1973): 185–214. Other works by this scholar are listed by Elio Peretto, "Assunzione," in *Nuovo dizionario patristico e di antichità cristiane* [New Dictionary of the Fathers and Christian Antiquity], ed. Angelo Di Berardino (Genoa and Milan: Marietti, 2006), 1:608f. The argument is based, among other things, on the 1982 Vatican Greek manuscript studied by Frédéric Manns, *Le récit de la Dormition de Marie (Vatican grec 1982): Contribution à l'étude des origines de l'exégèse chrétienne* [The Narrative of the Dormition of Mary (Vatican, Greek, 1982): Contribution to the Study of the Origins of Christian Exegesis] (Jerusalem: Franciscan Printing Press, 1989), 201–24.

Transitus of Mary. Leucio supposedly had associated with the apostles but later had become a heretic.[18] If this information is correct, the writing would stem from the beginning of the second century. But obviously here we are wandering in the field of hypotheses.

The most recent historical-critical research is that of Stephen J. Shoemaker, who attempts a classification of the ancient sources known to date on the Dormition and Assumption of Mary. According to his research, we find a flourishing of corresponding apocrypha around 500. It does not seem possible to establish a "genealogy" to indicate one prime source from which the subsequent traditions arise.[19] Shoemaker identifies three major literary families as well as a couple of "atypical" narratives.[20] The first traces are visible in a family of texts that stem at least from the fourth century, probably as early as the second century.[21] Other traditions appear in the fifth century, without a dependence on the literary family attested earlier. Shoemaker does not agree with Simon Mimoumi (Paris, 1995), who contends that testimonies to the Assumption (the glorification of Mary, body and soul, in Heaven) would be assigned a place at the end of the development, whereas a Dormition would be earlier (in which the soul of Mary enters Heaven while the body is preserved in paradise).[22] These common themes are identified in (nearly) all the sources: the death of Mary at Jerusalem; the involvement of at least some of the apostles; the reception of Mary's soul by Jesus Christ;

18. See Pseudo-Melito, *De Transitu Virginis Mariae* 1 (PG 5:1231–32). On Leucio, see Roschini, *Maria Santissima nella storia della salvezza: Trattato completo di mariologia alla luce del Concilio Vaticano II* [Mary Most Holy, in the History of Salvation: Complete Treatise on Mariology in Light of the Second Vatican Council] (Isola del Liri: Pisani, 1969), 3:460–66; Angelo Di Berardino, "Leucio Carino," in DiBerardino, *Nuovo dizionario patristico*, ed. Di Berardino, 2:2811.

19. On this point, Shoemaker confirms the research of Antoine Wenger, *L'Assomption de la Très Sainte Vierge dans la tradition byzantine du VI au X siècle: Études et documents* [The Assumption of the Most Holy Virgin in Byzantine Tradition of the Sixth to Tenth Centuries: Studies and Documents] (Paris: Institut français d'études byzantines, 1955), 17.

20. Shoemaker, *Ancient Traditions*, 282.

21. Ibid., 285f. This tradition is called that of the "palm," conferred by an angel to Mary before her dormition. A typical text is presented in Shoemaker, 290–350 (*Liber Requiei*, taken from an Ethiopian source); an imprecise Italian version is in Mario Erbetta, *Gli apocrifi del Nuovo Testamento* [Apocrypha of the New Testament] (Casale Monferrato: Marietti, 1981), 1:421–56.

22. See Simon Claude Mimoumi, *Dormition et assomption de Marie: Histoire des traditions anciennes* [Dormition and Assumption of Mary: History of the Ancient Traditions], Théologie historique 98 (Paris: Beauchesne, 1995). Also see Shoemaker, *Ancient Traditions*, 20–25 (and passim).

the transfer of Mary with body and/or soul into Paradise; hostility of the Jews toward the Mother of God.[23]

According to Antoine Wenger,[24] the more widespread apocrypha on the Transitus of Mary stem from a single original source written in Greek, on which depend a Syriac fragment (fifth century) and a Latin translation (fifth–seventh centuries). According to this (hypothetical) text the apostles arrive on a cloud in order to come together at the death of Mary. At the passing of Mary her soul is received by Jesus, who then has the body of Mary brought to Paradise, where it is reunited with the soul. Her passing takes place at Jerusalem, despite the attempt of the high priests to burn the remains and kill the apostles. Instead the high priest, through a miracle, is depicted as finding the faith and professing it before a large crowd.

Such an account could not fail to cause some confusion and (at least in the West) was probably an obstacle in the historic road to the dogma. In any case, the apocrypha were accepted by the people, because their reference to the glorification of Mary, body and soul, corresponded to what, in their view, one could expect in regard to the earthly end of the Mother of God.

The Liturgical Witness

The apocrypha are not the only sources to bear witness to faith in the Assumption of Mary in the early church. First of all, we have the liturgy.[25] The first Marian feast, from the fourth century on, probably had a generic character. At Jerusalem it was set at August 15 and was called the "Day of Mary Theotokos." Probably around 500, this feast was transferred to the Marian shrine at Gethsemane where the tomb of the Virgin was venerated. For this reason the feast was transformed into a feast of the Dormition (*koímesis*), intended to specially commemorate the death of Mary. From Jerusalem the feast

23. See Shoemaker, *Ancient Traditions*, 2. On this author's study, see also the review by Luigi Gambero: *Marianum* 65 (2003): 261–77.

24. Wenger, *L'Assomption*, 66; see also Söll, *Storia dei dogmi mariani*, §8a; Shoemaker, *Ancient Traditions*, 33.

25. See Danilo Maria Sartor, "Assunta III: Celebrazione liturgica" [Mary Assumed. III. Liturgical Celebration], in De Fiores and Meo, *NDM*, 178–83.

spread so much that the Byzantine emperor Maurice († 602) introduced it for the whole empire. The feast of the *koímesis* (dormition) of Mary was interpreted also as *análepsis* (assumption) into Heaven, body and soul.[26]

Theological Explanation

Together with that formulation of the Feast of the Dormition come the first theological statements that, inasmuch as they are theology, are not necessarily connected to apocryphal writings. Among the first we should mention Theoteknos, bishop of Livias (a city on the west bank of the Jordan) and (geographically nearby) the patriarch Modestus of Jerusalem. In a sermon preached on August 15, around 550 (in any case before 649),[27] Theoteknos declares, "We are celebrating the feast of feasts, the Assumption of Mary ever-virgin." Several times, the preacher states that Mary was assumed into Heaven, body and soul. He makes reference to the apocryphal accounts without focusing on the details, but looks for a theological rationale, based on the dignity of Mary as Mother of God and ever virgin. "It was fitting that her most holy body, that body which bore God, a body divinized, incorruptible, illumined with divine light and full of glory, be transported by the Apostles, in the company of the angels, entrusted for a short time to the earth and elevated to Heaven in glory, with her soul welcomed by God."[28]

In the encyclical of Pius XII a sermon is cited, attributed to Modestus of Jerusalem († ca. 634):[29] "As the most glorious Mother

26. The homily of Theoteknos of Livias (a city on the left bank of the Jordan facing Jericho), given around 550, bears the title *Análepsis tes hagías Theotókou* (Assumption of the Holy Mother of God), while at the end of the sixth century, after the official introduction of the feast for the whole Byzantine empire, the solemnity receives the name "Dormition." See the critical text of Theoteknos in Wenger, *L'Assomption*, 271–91.

27. After the Muslim invasion of 649, the city of Livias was no longer named as an episcopal see.

28. *Panegyricus* 9, in Wenger, *L'Assomption*, 276, translated in Galot, *Maria, La donna*, 306.

29. The pope does not cite the name, because there is debate about whether the sermon truly comes from Modestus or another author toward the end of the same century (Jugie wanted to set the sermon in the context of the struggle against the Monothelites, a hypothesis not truly convincing). In the meantime, research is generally satisfied to attribute the homily to Modestus: Söll, *Storia dei dogmi mariani*, 196f; M. Lochbrunner, "Modestus von Jerusalem," in *ML* 4:495f. Also,

of Christ, our Savior and God, giver of life and immortality, she was given life by him, reclothed in the body with an eternal incorruptibility by him who raised her from the tomb and assumed her to Himself, in a manner known to him alone."[30]

As though there were not yet any homilies on the feast of the Dormition, Modestus wants to draw up his "little work." The central argument in favor of the Assumption is the mystery of the divine maternity and the perpetual virginity, seen as the basis of Mary's bond with Jesus Christ. He affirms the nexus between Incarnation and Assumption: "Christ God, who assumed flesh with soul and spirit from this perpetual Virgin, by the Holy Spirit, called her to Himself and reclothed her with incorruptibility joined to the body, and glorified her above every measure so that she would become an heir as his all-holy mother according to the word of the Psalmist: 'At your right hand stands the queen in gold'" (Ps 45:9).[31]

Modestus states that Mary died at Jerusalem on Mount Zion and was buried by the apostles on the Mount of Olives. But more often Modestus decisively distances himself from the curiosity of the apocrypha, repeating the formula "as God alone knows."[32]

The patriarch Germanus of Constantinople († 733), cited by Pius XII,[33] also bears important testimony. He underscores the idea of fittingness (or "necessity"): "It was in effect impossible that the dwelling place of God, the living temple of the most holy divinity of the Only-Begotten, would become the prey of death in the tomb." "It cannot be said truly that her body, the abode of God, had been the victim of deathly corruption."[34]

As a consequence of the Assumption into Heaven, Germanus affirms the heavenly mediation of the Mother of God. A person who is fully redeemed can develop her mediating activity to the full.

John Damascene († 749), "an outstanding herald of this tradi-

Vatican II, *LG* 59, note 184, mentions the *Encomium* under the name "Modestus." The text is found in PG 86:3277–3312.

30. *Encomium in Dormitionem* 14 (*EE* 6, n. 1952; PG 86:3312B).

31. Ibid., 5 (PG 86.3289C).

32. See, for instance, the citation in *Munificentissimus Deus* (*EE* 6, n. 1952).

33. *EE* 6, n. 1950; see Söll, *Storia dei dogmi mariani*, 212–14.

34. *In dorm.* I.II (PG 98:345; 357), translated in Söll, *Storia dei dogmi mariani*, 212.

tional truth, spoke out with powerful eloquence when he compared the bodily Assumption of the loving Mother of God with her other prerogatives and privileges," notes Pius XII, citing the following passage:

> It was fitting that she, who had kept her virginity intact in childbirth, should keep her own body free from all corruption even after death. It was fitting that she, who had carried the Creator as a child at her breast, should dwell in the divine tabernacles. It was fitting that the spouse, whom the Father had taken to himself, should live in the divine mansions. It was fitting that she, who had seen her Son upon the cross and who had thereby received into her heart the sword of sorrow which she had escaped in the act of giving birth to him, should look upon him as he sits with the Father. It was fitting that God's Mother should possess what belongs to her Son, and that she should be honored by every creature as the Mother and as the handmaid of God.[35]

The feast of the Assumption today is still the most solemn Marian feast of the Christian East.[36] The Byzantine empire introduced the usage (in the thirteenth–fourteenth centuries) of celebrating all of August as a month dedicated to our Lady; it is the final month of the Byzantine liturgical year, so affirming Mary as an eschatological icon of the church (to use a modern term).[37]

DEVELOPMENT IN THE WEST

The feast of August 15 has been celebrated at Rome since approximately 650 as the "Dormition" and since around 800 as the "Assumption." The oldest documentation of the church's faith is the Gregorian Sacramentary, which comes from the mid-seventh century at least: the texts clearly indicate the bodily Assumption of Mary. This Sacramentary, which came from Rome, also influenced the entire kingdom of the Franks. In the ninth century (Leo IV, 847) the Feast of the Assumption acquired an octave and afterward a vigil. In the

35. *Encomium in Dorm.* II.14 (*EE* 6, n. 1951; PG 96:741B).

36. This also applies somewhat for the West: The Assumption is the only Marian solemnity with two formularies for the Holy Mass (the vigil and the feast day itself).

37. See Sartor, "Assunta III," 179f.

Sacramentary of Pope Adrian, which he himself sent to Charlemagne and which consists of a developed edition of Gregorian chant, we find a notable prayer on August 15: "Worthy of our veneration, O Lord, is the feast of this day, in which the holy Mother of God underwent temporal death, though she who bore your Son, our Savior, incarnate of her, could not be humiliated by the chains of death."[38]

The first narrative testimony is that of Gregory of Tours (†594), who made himself the narrator of an apocryphal work on the Transitus of Mary.[39] But the West was more reticent, relative to the East, which considered the empty tomb of Mary at Jerusalem as a support for belief. The *Decretum Gelasianum*,[40] which consists of a list of canonical books (and apocrypha), notes a book "called the Transitus of St. Mary" among the apocryphal texts (obviously not accepted). In any case, the apocryphal stories spread. Opposing them was the Carolingian theologian Paschasius Radbertus (†859), writing under the pseudonym of "Jerome."[41] His effort was a great success: it was received into the Roman Breviary as a reading for the feast of August 15, remaining until Pius V removed the text in 1568.

"Jerome" cautions against reading an apocryphal work on the Transitus. Because God is omnipotent, it was possible that he assume the body of Mary into heavenly glory, but Sacred Scripture recounts nothing about it. Paschasius Radbertus thus affirms an agnostic position in regard to the fate of the body of Mary. But he too indicates a few reasons for a "pious desire" in favor of the Assumption, among which are the empty tomb and Mary's precedence among the saints participating in the Resurrection (according to Matthew 27:52).

The influence of "Jerome" was later neutralized by another pseudonymous publication under the name "Augustine" in the tenth or

38. Cited by Pius XII (*EE* 6, n. 1947). In the *Missale Romanum* of Pius V (1570) this prayer is removed; in the new prayer the death of Mary is not mentioned. See Söll, *Storia dei dogmi mariani*, 322.

39. Gregory of Tours, *De gloria beatorum martyrum* 4 (PL 71:708); see Gambero, *Mary and the Fathers*, 353f.

40. DH 354.

41. Pseudo-Jerome, *Ep. 9 ad Paulam et Eustochium* (PL 30:122–42); also in Albert Ripberger, *Der Pseudo-Hieronymus-Brief IX "Cogitis me"* (Fribourg: Universitätsverlag, 1962), 57–113. See Luigi Gambero, *Maria nel pensiero dei teologi latini medievali* (Cinisello Balsamo: Ed. Paoline, 2000), 82–84. English version in Gambero, *Mary in the Middle Ages*, 74–80.

early eleventh century: *De Assumptione Beatae Mariae Virginis.*[42] Together with the second homily of John Damascene on the Dormition, this text is the decisive literary factor for the Western reception of the doctrine of the Assumption.[43] It prescinds totally from any reference to apocrypha and only presents reasons of suitability. The author lists seven arguments:

1. A penal sentence that imposes corruption cannot apply to Mary (Gn 3:19). The flesh of Christ, assumed from the flesh of Mary, evaded any state of punishment. The body of Jesus is the flesh of Mary.

2. Mary did not share the fate of Eve, inasmuch as regards the pains of birth (Gn 3:16), but bore her Son while remaining a virgin and without pain. Therefore, Mary was able to undergo death, but could not be held by the chains of death.

3. If Jesus preserved Mary from the loss of her virginity, why could he not have also preserved her from corruption? If in him the flesh he assumed from his Mother has gone up to Heaven, it would also be fitting to honor his Mother likewise. If Jesus prayed for his disciples, that they be with him (Jn 17:24), how much more should the Mother of God be near her Son.

4. Mary must be in heaven not only in the soul, but also in the body.

5. The promise "Where I am, there also will my servant be" (Jn 12:26), applies most strongly to Mary, who received more grace than all other human beings.

6. As Christ has the power to not let a hair on our heads be lost, this power also extends to the safety of the body and soul of Mary.

7. Anyone who does not believe that Christ carried out the bodily Assumption of Mary needs to tell a reason this would not have been suitable.

42. The text can be found in PL 40:1141–48; in Italian: *TMPM* 3:827–38, and in Calvo Moralejo and Cecchin, *L'Assunzione*, 21–35. On the following, see G. Riedl, "Die pseudoaugustinische Schrift 'De assumptione beatae Mariae virginis': Theologische Argumentationskunst und dogmengeschichtlicher Kontext" [The Pseudo-Augustinian Document "De assumptione beatae Mariae virginis": The Theological Art of Its Argument; Context in the History of Dogma], in Ziegenaus, *Volksfrömmigkeit*, 75–103.

43. See Riedl, "Die pseudoaugustinische Schrift," 103.

Pseudo-Augustine shows that it is possible to resolve the problem without the support of the apocrypha, through reason illuminated by faith.

Scholasticism followed the line indicated by Pseudo-Augustine.[44] Thomas attests that the author ("Augustine") argues reasonably (*rationabiliter*).[45] Pope Alexander III (†1181) professes that Mary passed away "without corruption."[46] The words of Peter Damian (†1072) are typical of the time: he does not dare to define such a truth, but states that it is "pious" to believe in the Assumption of Mary into Heaven.[47] In the twelfth century we find no one who denied the bodily Assumption of Mary, only a few voices who express a doubt.

In the thirteenth century, on the other hand, the great theologians of Scholasticism all teach the truth of the bodily Assumption, without dealing with it in a separate *quaestio*, and did the same for the topic of the Immaculate Conception: in 1497 the University of Paris censured the opinion of a theologian who had affirmed that one could deny the Assumption, given that it was not a defined dogma. Melchior Cano (sixteenth century) made the point that it would not be heretical to deny the bodily Assumption, but opposed to the universal agreement of the church; for this reason it would be impertinent and temerarious.[48]

In the sixteenth century a more critical sense becomes apparent in regard to evaluating the historical sources. In 1568 Pius V eliminated the reading by Pseudo-Jerome from the Roman Breviary, since it had been recognized as false. Peter Canisius laid the foundations for work on the history of Marian dogma, including on the Assumption. The definition of the Immaculate Conception in 1854 awakened the desire to also define the Assumption. Already at the First Vatican Council about two hundred bishops made the request to define

44. See Söll, *Storia dei dogmi mariani*, 267–71; Bogusław Kochaniewicz, "L'Assunzione di Maria in cielo nella riflessione teologica dei domenicani del XIII secolo," in Calvo Moralejo and Cecchin, *L'Assunzione*, 529–83; Cecchin, "L'assunzione di Maria nella scuola mariologica francescana," in Calvo Moralejo and Cecchin, *L'Assunzione*, 585–629.

45. *ST* III, q. 27, a. 1.

46. *Instructio fidei catholicae* (PL 207:1077).

47. *De s. Joanne Apost.*, sermo 64 (PL 144.870).

48. *De locis theologicis* XII.10.

this doctrine, and only circumstances prevented the realization of the plan (the Franco-Prussian War, the shortening of the Council). A great number of petitions for this cause arrived at the Holy See, particularly between 1926 and 1946. The number of specialized studies on the question rose, and the groundwork for the definition was prepared.[49]

THE DEFINITION OF THE DOGMA

On May 1, 1946, Pius XII posed to all the Catholic bishops of the world the official question whether they favored a definition of the "bodily Assumption of the Most Blessed Virgin as a dogma of the faith." Of the 1191, 1169 agreed without reserve, while only 22 expressed doubts, of which 16 were for reasons of opportuneness. The greater part of the faculties of theology were in solidarity with the episcopate in support of the definition. The people were prepared for the millennial celebration of the Feast of the Assumption. In any case, the definition was preceded by lively debates on how to prove the doctrine by means of Tradition.

The definition itself took place on November 1, 1950, at St. Peter's Basilica. The Apostolic Constitution *Munificentissimus Deus* pronounced the dogma in the following words:

For this reason, after we have poured forth prayers of supplication again and again to God, and have invoked the light of the Spirit of Truth, for the glory of Almighty God who has lavished his special affection upon the Virgin Mary, for the honor of her Son, the immortal King of the Ages and the Victor over sin and death, for the increase of the glory of that same august Mother, and for the joy and exultation of the entire Church; by the authority of our Lord Jesus Christ, of the Blessed Apostles Peter and Paul, and by our own authority, we pronounce, declare, and define it to be a divinely revealed dogma: that the Immaculate Mother of God, the ever Virgin Mary,

49. See Söll, *Storia dei dogmi mariani*, 352–71. On the movement for the dogmatic proclamation, see also Angelo Amato, "Come la Chiesa cattolica è giunta alla definizione dogmatica dell'Assunzione di Maria" [How the Church Reached the Dogmatic Definition of the Assumption], in Calvo Moralejo and Cecchin, *L'Assunzione*, 43–70; Cecchin, "L'assunzione di Maria," 633–45; De Fiores, *Dizionario* 1:78–80.

having completed the course of her earthly life, was assumed body and soul into heavenly glory.[50]

The accent was placed on the Assumption of the body, since the glorification of the soul of Mary was never the object of any controversy.

The arguments contained in the Apostolic Constitution possess no guarantee of infallibility, but deserve attention as an authentic commentary on the definition. As a systematic argument for the Assumption, the dogma of the Immaculate Conception is highlighted first of all. Then the concrete details leading to the definition are listed: the petitions to the Holy See, the responses to the 1946 inquiry, and the manifest conviction of the church. Then the witness of the liturgy and the voices of the fathers follow, in particular John Damascene, Germanus of Constantinople, and (as described previously) Modestus of Jerusalem. The Scholastic contribution is composed of multiple authors: Amadeus of Lausanne, Anthony of Padua, "Albert the Great" (that is to say, the "Mariale" of Pseudo-Albert, as was discovered in 1954), Thomas Aquinas, Bonaventure, Bernardine of Siena, Robert Bellarmine, Francis de Sales, Peter Canisius, and Suárez. Then there is a statement that the meditations of the fathers and the theologians rest on Sacred Scripture as their ultimate foundation: the close union between mother and Son, the idea of the new Eve at the basis of the Protoevangelium. A real proof from Scripture is not given, but in the citations there are reminders of the Protoevangelium (Gn 3:15) and the angelic salutation (Lk 1:28). The pope does not refer to the resurrection of the just in Matthew 27:52f. It is left undecided whether Mary died prior to her glorification or not.

CONNECTION WITH OTHER MARIAN DOGMAS

For a systematic understanding we need to see the Assumption in the light of the other three (principal) Marian dogmas: the Immac-

50. *EE* 6, n. 1974; see DH 3903. The whole text can also be found in Calvo Moralejo and Cecchin, *L'Assunzione*, 1–20.

ulate Conception, the divine maternity, and the perpetual virginity.[51]

The Assumption appears as the ultimate consequence of the Immaculate Conception: in Mary God's original plan for man shines, the plan that man could attain from the gift of grace to the fullness of glory. The Protoevangelium and the angelic salutation are treated as a scriptural basis for the Immaculate Conception as for the Assumption. Mary's opposition to Satan also implies overcoming death, which came into the world "through the devil's envy" (Ws 2:24).

The divine maternity creates a spiritual and corporeal bond between Mary and Christ, a bond destined to be fulfilled in her final glorification with soul and body. Just from the "familial" point of view, we can wonder, along with Francis de Sales, "What son, if he could, would not call his own mother back to life and would not bring her after death with himself into paradise?"[52]

But this is not only to speak of a familial bond, but of the cooperation of the Mother of God in the plan of salvation, as, for example, Robert Bellarmine affirms: "And who, I ask you, could believe that the ark of holiness, the abode of the Word, the temple of the Holy Spirit were fallen? The very thought is abhorrent to my soul, that that virginal flesh which was mother to God, bore him, fed him, carried him, was either reduced to ashes or was given as food for worms."[53]

The divine maternity is closely tied to Mary's virginity. John Damascene, for example, underscores, "It was necessary that she who had preserved her virginity intact in birth, would see her body kept sheltered from any corruption, even after her death."[54]

Besides the Marian dogmas clearly established, we also need to think of their connection with the mediation of Mary in Christ, and therefore with her cooperation in salvation. Among others, John Paul II did this in his Marian Catecheses:

51. See, inter alia, Roschini, *Maria Santissima,* 3:597–614; Leo Scheffczyk, "Il dogma dell'Assunzione corporea di Maria nell'insieme della fede," in Scheffczyk, *Maria, crocevia,* 117–33.

52. Francis de Sales, *Sermon autographe pour la fête de l'Assomption*, cited by Pius XII (*EE* 6, n. 1965).

53. Robert Bellarmine, *Conciones habitae Lovanii*, concio 40: *De Assumptione B. Mariae Virginis*, cited by Pius XII (*EE* 6, n. 1964).

54. *Encomium in Dorm.* 2.14 (PG 96.741), translated in Galot, *Maria, La donna*, 319.

According to some of the Church Fathers, another argument for the privilege of the Assumption is taken from Mary's sharing in the work of Redemption. St. John Damascene underscores the relationship between her participation in the Passion and her glorious destiny: "It was right that she who had seen her Son on the Cross and received the sword of sorrow in the depths of her heart ... should behold this Son seated at the right hand of the Father" (Hom. 2, PG 96:741). In the light of the paschal mystery, it appears particularly clear that the Mother should also be glorified with her Son after death.[55]

ANTHROPOLOGICAL AND ESCHATOLOGICAL SIGNIFICANCE

The Assumption of Mary into Heaven leads to a transfiguration or (in the case of a death preceding) to the resurrection of the body. Thus the value of the human body is affirmed, as Pius XII states: "Thus, while the illusory teachings of materialism and the corruption of morals that follows from these teachings threaten to extinguish the light of virtue and to ruin the lives of men by exciting discord among them, in this magnificent way all may see clearly to what a lofty goal our bodies and souls are destined."[56]

The same observation, made in regard to the human body in general, also applies to the dignity of woman in particular. Being a woman (or being male) is destined to endure even in heavenly glory. As early as the 1400s Bernardine of Siena, cited by Pius XII, observes that "it is reasonable and fitting that not only the soul and body of a man, but also the soul and body of a woman should have obtained heavenly glory."[57] Such an appreciation of the body encourages Christians to be involved here on earth, that the dignity of the human body as a temple of God be respected.

The anthropological relevance of the Assumption was exalted after the definition of the dogma by, among others, the Swiss psychologist C. G. Jung (†1961), son of a Protestant pastor and one of

55. John Paul II, CM 55 (July 9, 1997), n. 3.
56. *EE* 6, n. 1972.
57. Bernardine of Siena, *In Assumptione B. M. Virginis*, sermo 2, translated in *EE* 6, n. 1963.

the principal founders of "depth psychology." His theories, with a strongly Gnostic imprint, contain many rather problematic elements. Notwithstanding that, it seems interesting to note his comment. Jung describes the dogma of the Assumption "in every respect conforming to the exigencies of the time." He said it was indeed "the most important religious event since the Reformation." The papal definition, he said, "would leave Protestantism in the milieu of an exclusively masculine religion that knows no metaphysical representation of woman." The Catholic Church, seeing the importance of masculine and feminine archetypes, would correspond to the greater importance of woman in modern times. In Jung's opinion, the new dogma would have to lead to a new "quaternity"—that is, to exalt Mary as a fourth person of the divinity, an inadequate observation: the Assumption does not regard Mary as a "goddess," but as the vanguard of humanity, as the prototype of the church.[58]

Materialism and moral decline, which were mentioned by Pius XII as contemporary factors opposed by the Assumption of Mary, have not diminished since 1950. In the years that immediately followed the Second World War with its terrible consequences, respect for life was surely stronger than it is today. Since then that respect for life and the human body has declined greatly, if we consider the almost ubiquitous practice of abortion, of pornography, and of certain uses of biotechnology.

The great relevance of the dogma has not been matched by an equal interest on the part of theology after 1950. To be sure, a great amount of work was concentrated in the period before the definition and came to a certain conclusion with it. But the lack of interest seems to have other reasons as well:[59] the denial in certain sectors of the bodily resurrection of Jesus, by which denial the basis of the Assumption is undermined; the fear of offending Protestants, and thus a poorly understood ecumenism; but, above all, the thesis of universal resurrection at the moment of death.

58. See A. Moreno and R. Schenk, "Jung," in *ML* 3:461–65.

59. See Anton Ziegenaus, *Maria in der Heilsgeschichte: Mariologie* [Mary in Salvation History: Mariology], Katholische Dogmatik 5 (Aachen: MM-Verlag, 1998), 318.

The latter topic is studied systematically in a course in eschatology. Here we can only dedicate a brief glance.[60] The New Testament presupposes an "eschatology in two phases"—that is, today, the situation after personal death and the situation after the Parousia. The resurrection of the body is connected to the Parousia and not to the hour of death. Otherwise Jesus would have also arisen directly from the Cross, leaving behind his remains, which would later be reduced to dust.

The theory of resurrection at the moment of death comes from twentieth-century Protestant theology. At first we find the theory of "total death" to underscore that man is nothing before God. In particular Karl Barth (holding this theory) adds that man, in the moment of death, reaches the time of eternity and thus immediately comes from death to resurrection. In this case we have an "eschatology in one phase." There is no intermediate state between death and resurrection. Eschatological events do not change this world, but take place above it.

These theses will also influence Catholic theology. Karl Rahner thought that all men would rise at the moment of death.[61] Because of this, the bodily Assumption of Mary is nothing special, but something open to everyone.[62] Therefore it would not cause any distress in the dialogue with Protestants.

60. The latest support for eschatology is Cándido Pozo, SJ, *Theology of the Beyond* (Staten Island, N.Y.: St. Paul's, 2009). For a review of the eschatological debate in the light of the dogma of the Assumption, see, among others, Ziegenaus, *Maria in der Heilsgeschichte*, 318–24; Pozo, "Maria Assunta partecipe alla risurrezione di Cristo: Dalla Kenosi alla gloria" [Mary, Assumed, Sharer in the Resurrection of Christ: From Kenosis to Glory], in Calvo Moralejo and Cecchin, *L'Assunzione*, 247–61; Salvatore M. Perrella, "L'Assunzione di Maria nella teologia post-conciliare," in Calvo Moralejo and Cecchin, *L'Assunzione*, 71–167; also in Salvatore M. Perrella, *Ecco tua Madre (Gv 19,27): La Madre di Gesù nel magistero di Giovanni Paolo II e nell'oggi della Chiesa e del mondo* [Behold Your Mother (Jn 19:27): The Mother of Jesus in the Magisterium of John Paul II and in the Church and the World Today] (Cinisello Balsamo: San Paolo, 2007), 297–406; Juan Luis Bastero, *Virgen singular: La reflexión teológica mariana en el siglo XX* [Singular Virgin: Theological Reflection on Mary in the 20th Century] (Madrid: Rialp, 2001), 179–205.

61. At the outset of his statements on this topic (in 1951), however, he stated only that many have been raised already, as demonstrated by Mt 27:52f: Karl Rahner, "Zum Sinn des Assumpta-Dogmas" [The Meaning of the Dogma of the Assumption], in *Schriften zur Theologie* (Einsiedeln: Benziger, 1962), 2:239–52 (initially in "Schweizer Rundschau," 1951); English translation: "The Interpretation of the Dogma of the Assumption," in *Theological Investigations* (London: Darton, Longman and Todd, 1961), 1:215–27. This argument was supported from 1951 on by Otto Karrer, according to whom a "vanguard of the saints" is already risen. This laid the groundwork for denying the Assumption of Mary as a privilege. See Ziegenaus, *Maria in der Heilsgeschichte*, 319–22.

62. Rahner, *Grundkurs des Glaubens: Einführung in den Begriff des Christentums* [Basic Course

Philosophically, the theory of resurrection at the moment of death is supported by the thesis of Durandus (thirteenth century), who held that a continuity between the earthly body and the risen body is not necessary at all, because the identity of the subject is given only by the soul as *forma corporis*. The soul can form itself a new body of whatever material.

The model of Durandus does not apply to the resurrection of Christ, but to the future resurrection of the faithful. It can explain the continuity between the earthly and the risen subject. But the model is limited by the conviction that the future resurrection will not happen at the site of mortal remains still in existence, in particular the relics of saints. Besides, it does not accord with dogma to think that the body of Mary had become prey to corruption. The Assumption of Mary is not described as part of the events that are accessible to all Christians, but as a privilege proper to her like the divine maternity, the virginity, and above all the Immaculate Conception. In the risen body of Mary hope also shines for us, but we do not find ourselves on the same level and we await resurrection when Christ will return.

Paul VI, in the 1968 "Credo of the People of God," states that Mary was "raised body and soul to heavenly glory and likened to her risen Son in anticipation of the future lot of all the just."[63] A document of the Congregation for the Doctrine of the Faith in 1979 on certain questions concerning eschatology emphasizes the faith of the church in the intermediate state between death and resurrection. In regard to the Assumption of Mary it affirms:

> In teaching her doctrine about man's destiny after death, the Church excludes any explanation that would deprive the Assumption of the Virgin Mary of its unique meaning, namely the fact that the bodily glorification of the Virgin is an anticipation of the glorification that is the destiny of all the other elect.[64]

---

in the Faith: Introduction to the Idea of Christianity] (Freiburg im Breisgau: Herder, 1976), 375: "something thoroughly obvious to all Christians" (Italian trans., *Corso fondamentale della fede* [Cinisello Balsamo 1990], 493: "un'evidenza comune a tutta la cristianità").

63. Paul VI, "Credo of the People of God" (1968), n. 15, in Justo Collantes, ed., *La fede della Chiesa Cattolica: Le idee e gli uomini nei documenti dottrinali del Magistero* [The Faith of the Catholic Church: Ideas and Men in the Doctrinal Documents of the Magisterium] (Vatican City: Libreria Editrice Vaticana, 1993), 0.535, 977.

64. DH 4656.

In the Assumption of Mary, even now, shines the glory that will be shared with all the redeemed faithful at the end of earthly time.[65]

DEBATE BETWEEN THE MORTALISTS AND THE IMMORTALISTS

The dogmatic definition of 1950 did not resolve the question of whether Mary died or not.[66] The debate about this topic is rather recent, dating only to the years prior to the definition of the Assumption. Before then, the death of Mary was usually taken for granted.[67] On the other hand, the "immortalists" (in particular Martin Jugie, G. M. Roschini, and Tibor Gallus) state: in Mary we can see what would have happened if Eve had had no sin: that is to say, a transfiguration ("re"-surrection without death). The Apostle Paul expected that destiny for those who will be alive at the coming of the last judgment (1 Cor 15:51f: "We shall not all sleep, but we shall all be changed, in a moment, in the twinkling of an eye, at the last trumpet"; see 1 Thes 4:17; 2 Cor 5:2–4). In this way Mary anticipates the immortality of the church. "In being clothed with immortality without being deprived of her mortal body, Mary would be more perfectly the eschatological image of the incorruptible Church."[68]

The first voice to formulate the question is Epiphanius (fourth

65. See also John Paul II, CM 54 (July 2, 1997), n. 1.

66. See Johannes Brinktrine, *Die Lehre von der Mutter des Erlösers* [Doctrine of the Mother of the Redeemer] (Paderborn: F. Schöningh, 1959), 72–75; Roschini, *La Madonna*, 3:253–95; *Maria Santissima* 3:624–32 (bibliography); René Laurentin, *A Short Treatise on the Virgin Mary* (Washington, N.J.: Ave Maria Institute, 1991), 112–23, 132–34; J. Finkenzeller, "Tod Mariens" [Death of Mary], in Bäumer and Scheffczyk, *ML* 6:436–38; O'Carroll, *Theotokos*, 117f; Galot, *Maria, La donna*, 324–36; Perrella, *Ecco tua Madre*, 376–82.

67. See Galot, *Maria, La donna*, 326f.

68. Laurentin, *Short Treatise*, 338. Among those who support a passing of the Blessed Virgin without death, see Jugie, "Assomption," 623–25, 652; Tiburzio Gallus, *La Vergine immortale* (Rome: Angelo Belardetti Editore, 1949); Gallus, "Perché la Madonna non poteva morire" [Why the Madonna Could Not Die], *Palestra del Clero* 34 (1955): 841–47; Roschini, *La Madonna*, 3:253–95; Roschini, *Maria Santissima* 3:453f (a more nuanced position: a passing in an ecstasy of love that resembles death without being a real death itself, a position perhaps influenced by the visions of Maria Valtorta: see Gabriele M. Roschini, *La Madonna negli scritti di Maria Valtorta* [Mary in the Writings of Maria Valtorta], 2nd ed. (Isola del Liri: Centro Editoriale Valtortiano, 1986), chap.3, section 3.3); Manfred Forderer, *Königin ohne Tod in den Himmel aufgenommen* [Queen Assumed into Heaven without Death] (Stein am Rhein, Switzerland: Christiana-Verlag, 1988).

century): no one knows whether Mary died or remains immortal.[69] The first witness in favor of immortality is Timothy of Jerusalem, probably from the seventh century (according to Jugie, the fourth century): reacting to the thesis that Mary had died as a martyr, following Simeon's prophecy of the sword (Lk 2:35), the homilist says that the "sword" passes through the body and does not divide the soul: "Thereby the Virgin remains immortal to this day, for He who dwelt in Her transported her to the place of his ascension," to the heavenly paradise.[70]

The apocrypha, on the other hand, speak in their accounts of Mary's death and burial before her glorification. Some liturgical witnesses also mention death, as do many theologians, though excluding any corruption of the body. Though they speak of death, Mary's parting is seen in fact as a "dormition" (*koímesis*).[71] In any case the traditions on the Assumption of Mary and on her death are not found at the same level: "Whereas all sorts of reasons of fittingness and implications converge unrestrictedly on the fact of the Blessed Virgin's bodily glorification, the reasons of fittingness in favor of her death are at once less numerous and contradicted by other reasons."[72]

The argument of the immortalists states (rightly) that bodily death was not necessary for Mary. Death, per se, is a fact of nature (see Gn 3:19: "You are dust and to dust you shall return"), but in the order of salvation it is a consequence of original sin, from which the Mother of the Lord was free, a fact not yet clarified for many centuries. "Mary suffered pains of external origin (persecutions, wickedness and perversity of men, trials linked to the complexity of the world as well as to its disorder), but not pains originating from within, that is, not those that for every man stem from the degradation

69. See "The Silence of the First Centuries," earlier in this chapter.

70. Timothy of Jerusalem, *In Symeonem* (PG 86:245B–C). On Timothy of Jerusalem, see Jugie, *La mort et l'assomption de la Sainte Vierge*, 70–76, 507–10; Roschini, *Maria Santissima* 3:470f; O'Carroll, *Theotokos*, 388; A. Di Berardino, ed., *Patrologia*, vol. 5, *Dal Concilio di Calcedonia (451) a Giovanni Damasceno (+750): I padri orientali* (Genoa: Marietti, 2000), 318f; Galot, *Maria, La donna*, 326; Georg Röwekamp, "Timoteo di Gerusalemme," in Döpp and Geerlings, *DLCA*, 831.

71. See the references to various ancient liturgies in Brinktrine, *Die Lehre von der Mutter*, 73f.

72. Laurentin, *Short Treatise*, 337.

of his own nature."[73] The mortalists, in contrast, indicate that the death of Mary implies imitation of Christ, who died and then was risen. Therefore, it would have been fitting for her to undergo death.

The immortalists respond that Mary was already bound with great suffering to the death of Christ, at the foot of the Cross; therefore, it was not fitting for her to be subject to death a second time (Tibor Gallus). Furthermore, Mary can be seen as an anticipation of the church that does not die at the moment of the Parousia; this event depends on the death of Christ, without requiring her own bodily death.

The first pope to take up the controversy was John Paul II, in a catechesis that forms part of the ordinary magisterium, without the intention of definitively ending the theological debate yet underway. In his discourse on "Mary and the Human Drama of Death" (June 25, 1997), the supreme pontiff says that the opinion of theologians who support Mary's exemption from death only appears in the seventeenth century, "while a common tradition actually exists which sees Mary's death as her entry into heavenly glory." "Since Christ died, it would be difficult to maintain the contrary for his Mother. The fathers of the church, who had no doubts in this regard, reasoned along these lines." Certainly, Mary is free from death as a punishment for original sin. "The Mother," however, "is not superior to the Son who underwent death, giving it a new meaning and changing it into a means of salvation."

As a reason for Mary's death, the pope highlights her cooperation in the Redemption. "Mary was able to share in his suffering and death for the sake of humanity's Redemption.... To share in Christ's Resurrection, Mary had first to share in his death." Another motivation, also taken from her motherly mediation, is the thought that thanks to the experience of death, Mary "can more effectively exercise her spiritual motherhood toward those approaching the last moment of their lives."

As to the modality of the Dormition, the pope quotes a suggestion of St. Francis de Sales,[74] who "maintains that Mary's death was

73. Ibid., 339.

74. Francis De Sales, *Treatise on the Love of God*, book VII, ch. 13f.

due to a transport of love. He speaks of a dying 'in love, from love and through love.'"[75]

Among mariologists, the "mortalists" are more prevalent, but the problem remains open. René Laurentin, while sympathizing somewhat with the immortalist position, concludes his exposition thus: "One has the right, with Epiphanius, to go on thinking that the end of Mary remains a mystery, hidden in God, and that here below we must resign ourselves in this matter simply to not knowing."[76]

THE DOGMA IN THE ECUMENICAL CONTEXT

In Dialogue with the Separated Eastern Churches

Our conviction of the bodily Assumption of Mary into Heaven is shared by the Orthodox Church.[77] In fact, this dogma of the faith

75. John Paul II, CM 53 (June 25, 1997), in *L'Osservatore Romano*, English edition, July 2, 1997, 11. See the strong resemblances to Galot, *Maria, La donna*, 324–35. Tracing back the origin of the immortalist thesis only to the seventeenth century seems to somewhat overlook the witness of Timothy of Jerusalem, quoted earlier, from the patristic era. On the pope's catecheses, see also Perrella, "L'Assunzione di Maria" (2001): 139–45, also published in Perrella, *La Madre di Gesù nella coscienza ecclesiale contemporanea* [The Mother of Jesus in Contemporary Ecclesial Consciousness] (Vatican City: Libreria Editrice Vaticana, 2005), 376–82; Salvatore M. Perrella, *Ecco tua Madre (Gv 19,27): La Madre di Gesù nel magistero di Giovanni Paolo II e nell'oggi della Chiesa e del mondo* [Behold Your Mother (Jn 19:27): The Mother of Jesus in the Magisterium of John Paul II and in the Church and the World Today] (Cinisello Balsamo: San Paolo, 2007), 257–60.

76. Laurentin, *Short Treatise*, 343. An intermediate position between the mortalists and immortalists, not unlike that mentioned in the words of Francis de Sales, appears in the visions of Maria Valtorta, whose publication was not approved by the Holy Office, and that led to even more hermeneutical problems than those of Anne Catherine Emmerick (mentioned in the notes of this chapter: see note 14). The seer speaks of a "death" of Mary, but of a death "not rightly called so," because "it was a rapture unto God" (*Poema dell'Uomo-Dio* X:352). That is, she writes that the soul of Mary had an ecstasy that separated it from the body for a certain time, but then she came back to herself and entered body and soul into the glory of God. Valtorta speaks of a "death" at Jerusalem. In any case, it is obvious that such visions are not historic records, even if they can contain historical references not derived from study. This leads to a field for research that really has not begun yet. See Roschini, *La Madonna negli scritti di Maria Valtorta*; Aloysius Winter, "Das Werk der Maria Valtorta: Ein beliebtes Skandalon?" [The Work of Valtorta: A Popular Scandal?], in Ziegenaus, *Volksfrömmigkeit*, 163–90; Emilio Pisani, *Pro e contro Maria Valtorta* [For and against Maria Valtorta], 4th ed. (Isola del Liri: Centro Editoriale Valtortiano, 2005). Another visionary testimony, in this case from a Venerable, is by Mary of Agreda: Gaspar Calvo Moralejo, OFM, "La morte della Vergine in M. Agreda (1602–1665)" [The Death of the Virgin in Mary of Agreda], in Calvo Moralejo and Cecchin, *L'Assunzione di Maria*, 647–65.

77. This applies also to the Eastern churches separated after the Council of Ephesus (Nestorians) and Chalcedon (Monophysites). See W. de Vries, "Die getrennten Kirchen des Ostens," in

appeared first in the East. Nonetheless, we also find critique from various Orthodox theologians in regard to the dogma of the Assumption proclaimed in 1950. In particular, the opposition is directed against the papal authority that defined the dogma. So they accept faith in the doctrine, but not the manner in which the doctrine was proposed.[78] At times, however, the critique goes further. There is no lack of interpretations emphasizing that one can see a poetic exaggeration characteristic of the Eastern liturgy in the doctrine of the bodily Assumption of Mary into Heaven.[79] In the Orthodox milieu after the proclamation of the dogma there were two positions: on one hand, opposition to the pope brought theologians closer to Protestantism (especially on the part of some Greek voices, such as J. N. Karmiris); on the other hand, there was no lack of voices who affirmed their agreement with the Catholic belief (e.g., J. Meyendorff). If we look at creedal writings of the Orthodox Church, the Assumption is listed among known facts (the "Orthodox Confession" of Peter Mogila, the "Confession" of Dositheus and even that of Cyril Lucaris, Patriarch of Constantinople, deposed under the accusation of being a Calvinist).[80] This conviction certainly corresponds with the faith of the people who participate in the Divine Liturgy, but perhaps not always with the doctrine of the theologians.

Konfessionskunde [The Study of Creeds], ed. Konrad Algermissen, 8th ed. (Paderborn: Bonifacius, 1966), 79–278, passim; Ermanno M. Toniolo, "Maria nelle chiese orientali" [Mary in the Eastern Churches], in *Dizionario enciclopedico dell'Oriente Cristiano*, ed. E. G. Farrugia (Rome: Pontifical Oriental Institute, 2000), 469–75. English translation in *Encyclopedic Dictionary of the Christian East* (Rome: Pontifical Oriental Institute, 2015).

78. The attitude of the Romanian theologian Ionascu seems typical in I. Ionascu, "L'assunzione nell'Oriente ortodosso" [The Assumption in the Orthodox Church], in Calvo Moralejo and Cecchin, *L'Assunzione*, 439–44. According to this author two difficulties exist: the dogmatic formulation by the pope without asking the consent of the Orthodox patriarchs and the establishment of the doctrine as dogma ("a truth to which the church has always testified but which cannot be considered a dogma," 443). A lack of clarity on this point appears in the suggestion of convoking "a mixed commission that would establish a definition of what represents a dogma in the church"; ibid.

79. See Karl Christian Felmy, *Einführung in die Orthodoxe Theologie der Gegenwart* (Darmstadt: Wiss. Buchges., 1990), 84, or the strict article by K. B. Kallinikos, "Koimesis," in *ML* 3:598f. According to this author the Catholic Church had, until 1950, considered the Assumption as mere symbolism (as did Orthodox theology), not to be interpreted literally; to take it as an event would correspond to the understanding of simple people and to popular piety.

80. See Algermissen, ed., *Konfessionskunde*, 7th ed. (Celle: 1957), 485f.

Ecumenical Dialogue with the Ecclesial Communities Arising from the Reformation

In contrast, a virtually complete divergence separates the Catholic dogma from Protestantism.[81] At the beginning, the reformers still, more or less, shared faith even in the bodily glorification of the Mother of God. Luther, for example, gave a sermon for the Feast of the Assumption in 1522, and Bullinger (1590) presents several theological reasons in favor of the bodily Assumption of Mary into heavenly glory.[82] But the principle *sola Scriptura* in this case also becomes like a pair of scissors that eliminate faith in the Assumption. Even in his own time Luther removed the feast of the Assumption, replacing it with the feast of the Visitation, with its explicitly biblical content.

On the occasion of the 1950 dogma we find numerous clearly negative statements. It was said that the doctrine does not exist in the Bible, but arose from problematic (apocryphal) traditions. According to the theological faculty at Heidelberg, the Catholic Church had dogmatized a myth lacking historical basis. For this reason the Protestant "bishops" of Germany declared that the prerequisites for continuing the ecumenical process had been destroyed. The Assumption of Mary was supposedly a garbled parallel with Christ that would place her outside the church.

Then we find the disapproving rebuke that the definition had

81. See Henry Chavannes, "Die Protestanten und die Lehre von Marias Aufnahme in den Himmel" [Protestants and the Doctrine of Mary's Assumption into Heaven], in *Die sonnenbekleidete Frau*, ed. G. Rovira (Kevelaer: Butzon and Bercker, 1986), 59–71; H. Bürkle, "Himmelfahrt Mariae II: Protestantische Theologie" [Assumption of Mary II: Protestant Theology], in *ML* 3:199–202; Achim Dittrich, *Protestantische Mariologie-Kritik: Historische Entwicklung bis 1997 und dogmatische Analyse* [Protestant Criticism of Mariology: Historical Development to 1997 and Dogmatic Analysis], Mariologische Studien 11 (Regensburg: Pustet, 1998), 312–14; Dombes Group, *Mary in the Plan of God and the Communion of Saints* (New York: Paulist Press, 2002), nn. 252–65, 325f; Bilaterale Arbeitsgruppe, *Communio sanctorum: Die Kirche als Gemeinschaft der Heiligen* (Paderborn and Frankfurt am Main: Bonifatius, 2000), nn. 260f, 265 (see "The Ecumenical Debate," in chapter 6); Renzo Bertalot, "Posizione del gruppo di Dombes riguardo al dogma dell'assunzione di Maria," in *L'Assunzione di Maria Madre di Dio*, ed. Gasper Calvo Moralejo and Stefano M. Cecchin, Vatican City: PAMI, 2001, 433–37; Perrella, "*Non temere*," 150–71; Giancarlo Bruni, *Mariologia ecumenica: Approcci, documenti, prospettive* (Bologna: EDB: 2009), 501–34 (on Dombes).

82. The successor of Zwingli at Zurich.

been a self-glorification of the Catholic Church in the person of Mary. It removed eschatological tension, bringing into the present a reality that is only to be hoped for in the future. A few voices spoke of outright idolatry, of a sin against the first Commandment. Catholics were making the same mistake as the Israelites, criticized by Jeremiah, who worshipped Astarte as a "Queen of heaven" (Jer 7:18, 44:17).

In any case, there were a few voices (perhaps not really representative) that called for an understanding of the dogma. It was observed by Stephen Benko (1968) that the term *assumptio* itself emphasizes an event of grace, in distinction to the term used with regard to Jesus Christ, *Ascensio*: The Son of God ascends by means of his own divine power, whereas Mary, being a creature, is assumed. The Assumption of Mary underscores the dignity of the human body and the importance of the resurrection to be hoped for at the end of time, a message most relevant in our secularized world. A few other Protestant theologians affirmed their outright agreement with belief in the bodily Assumption of Mary, such as Max Lackmann (1968), Ulrich Wickert (from 1979 on), and Henry Chavannes (a Romand Swiss, 1986) who emphasized: it is important to open the immense treasury of Marian doctrine and devotion, even to Protestants.[83]

Probably the most profound critique is that of the systematic theologian Gerhard Ebeling (1950).[84] According to this author, faith in the Assumption is already implicit in the definition of the *Theótokos* at the Council of Ephesus in 431, due to the fact that this title clearly indicates an exceptional role for Mary in the history of salvation. As the new Eve, beside the new Adam, Mary is the personification of the church, which understands itself as the mediatrix of all graces. Marian dogma establishes the basic structure of Catholicism—that is, the unity between nature and grace.

Indeed, in this case too, we come to the importance of human cooperation in the work of salvation, denied again by the Protestant

83. For references on these authors, see Horst Bürkle, "Himmelfahrt Mariae II. Protestantische Theologie," in *ML* 3:199–202.

84. Ibid.

principle of *sola gratia*. The Assumption is an event of grace, but corresponds to the dignity of the Mother of God, and that comes along with an active cooperation in salvation.

In regard to the Anglican Communion, the 2004 Joint Declaration on Mary between Anglican and Roman Catholic theologians is relevant: the Anglican representatives in that official commission recognized that God had assumed the person of Mary entirely into heavenly glory, although that statement was not of a binding character.[85]

THE QUEENSHIP OF MARY

Connection with the Assumption

The Assumption into heavenly glory places Mary at the side of Christ, King of the universe. To illustrate this fact, Psalm 45 (44) came to be used often, seen as a messianic psalm in the Jewish religion: at the right hand of the King "stands the queen in gold of Ophir" (Ps 45:9). Her full glorification qualifies her for the task of interceding for the entire world. For this reason Pius XII, four years after the definition of the Assumption, at the end of the Marian Year 1954 (at the centenary of the dogma of the Immaculate Conception), introduced the feast of "The Blessed Virgin Mary, Queen," placing it on May 31.[86] This new observance took the place of the Feast of Mary "Mediatrix of All Graces," introduced in 1921 in many dioceses at the urging of the Belgian Cardinal Mercier and later moved to other dates (May 8, but in Belgium August 31).[87] The new Feast of

85. See Seattle Declaration = Anglican-Roman Catholic International Commission, *Mary: Grace and Hope in Christ* (Harrisburg, Pa.: Morehouse, 2005), n. 58, online at https://iarccum.org/doc/?d=16, also mentioned at "Ecumenical Aspects" in chapter 4. See a few years earlier, Jonathan Boardman, "Prospettive anglicane sulla Madre di Gesù Assunta in cielo" [Anglican Perspectives on the Mother of God Assumed into Heaven], in Calvo Moralejo and Cecchin, *L'Assunzione*, 445–48.

86. A feast of Mary the Queen on the same date had already been celebrated in Spain and in many dioceses of Latin America since 1870: see Sergio Gaspari, "Maria Regina coronata di gloria. Significato teologico-liturgico" [Mary, Queen Crowned with Glory: Theological-Liturgical Significance], in Carvello and De Fiores, *Maria icona viva della Chiesa futura*, 254.

87. See Hauke, *Mary, "Mediatress of Grace": Mary's Universal Mediation of Grace in the Theological and Pastoral Works of Cardinal Mercier* (New Bedford, Mass.: Academy of the Immaculate, 2004), 54–60.

Mary the Queen was promoted by a movement launched at Rome in 1933 with numerous expressions of popular support.[88] (Note that in 1925 Pope Pius XI had instituted the Solemnity of Christ, King of the Universe.)[89] The new calendar introduced in 1969 by Pope Paul VI chose the octave day of the Assumption, August 22, to celebrate the Queenship of Mary. It also established that this annual observance would be celebrated with the rank of "memorial." The memorial is therefore recent, but its content is ancient.

Biblical Basis

First, the entire people of God is given a sharing in the kingly office of Christ (see "the royal priesthood" in 1 Pt 2:9 and Rv 5:9–10). The indelible character of Baptism and Confirmation conforms souls to Christ, the King of the universe, conqueror over the power of Satan, sin, and death. According to the "Shepherd of Hermas" (second century), a crown is placed on the head of the newly baptized.[90] This practice was adopted particularly in the Eastern liturgies. Even today various rituals of the East (except for the Byzantine rite) include placing a band on the forehead of the newly confirmed, in the form of an ornate crown.[91]

The crown, according to Biblical symbolism, possesses yet another meaning: the eschatological reward for faithful service rendered on earth (e.g., 2 Thes 2:19; 1 Cor 9:25). The queenship of Mary also therefore bears this double meaning: dignity and reward. These two elements shine in *Lumen gentium*, which declares that Mary "was taken up body and soul into heavenly glory, and exalted by the Lord as Queen of the universe, that she might be the more fully conformed to her Son, the Lord of lords (see Rv 19:16) and the conqueror of sin and death."[92]

88. See Roschini, *Maria Santissima* 2:482f, which sees the beginning of the "Marian queenship movement" already in the apparition of the Virgin to St. Catherine Labouré on November 27, 1830 (478).

89. See Danilo Sartor, Aristide Serra, and Stefano De Fiores. "Regina," in De Fiores and Meo, *NDM* 1202f.

90. *Para.* 8.2:1–2 (*SC* 53 *bis* 262–64).

91. See Gaspari, "Maria Regina coronata," 255.

92. *LG* 59.

The starting point in Scripture for the queenship of Mary consists of the texts that set the Mother of God in relation with the lordship of Jesus Christ. This happens particularly in the story of the nativity according to Matthew, where the role of the *gebirah*, the mother of the king in the Davidic dynasty, shines in the figure of Mary (for example, in the adoration of the Magi).[93] Her power consists, among other things, in intercession (see the appeal of Bathsheba in 1 Kgs 2:12–20). While this reminder of the Queen Mother seems implicit in the Gospel of Matthew, the figure of the Queen Bride for the veneration of Mary (as in Psalm 45, and in the personage of Esther) was accepted later in the liturgy.[94] Just as the Protoevangelium (Gn 3:15) associates the Mother of the Messiah with the Savior's victory over the serpent, this text is also a foundational reference for the queenship of Mary.[95]

In the Gospel according to Luke, Gabriel declares that the son of Mary will be "called the Son of the Most High; and the Lord God will give to him the throne of his father David, and he will reign over the house of Jacob for ever; and of his kingdom there will be no end" (Lk 1:32f). And Elizabeth calls Mary "blessed … among women," because she is the "mother of my Lord" (Lk 1:43), of the Kyrios.

Historical Development

Attributing the title of "queen" to Mary assumes an awareness on her part regarding her role of heavenly mediation. The first testimony to this is found, it seems, in the Syriac world, in the writings of St. Ephrem (fourth century):

Heaven upholds me with its arm, because I am more greatly honored than it is. Indeed, Heaven was only your throne, not your mother. Now, how much more is the mother of the King to be honored and revered than is his

93. See Sartor, Serra, and De Fiores, "Regina," 1191–93; Brunero Gherardini, *Sta la regina alla tua destra: Saggio storico-teologico sulla Regalità di Maria* [The Queen Stands at Your Right Hand: Historical-Theological Essay on the Queenship of Mary] (Rome: Vivere In, 2002), 47–66; see also "The Child and His Mother," in chapter 1.

94. See Roschini, *Maria Santissima* 2:360–69, 375–77.

95. See ibid., 2:370f; Pozo, *María, nueva Eva*, 393–95.

throne! … august virgin and patroness, queen, lady, protect me under your wings, guard me, so that Satan not exult over me, for he sows ruin; nor let the wicked adversary triumph against me.[96]

From this time on, it became frequent to call Mary queen, patroness, lady, ruler. A particularly meaningful synonym for the term "queen" is "Lady" (*domina* in Latin, *déspoina* and *kyria* in Greek).[97] Maria appears as the queen of all created things, queen of the world, lady of the universe. Among the many liturgical witnesses in the East and West we see a passage of the *Akáthistos* hymn as exemplary:

I shall sing a hymn of praise to the Mother and Queen; with great joy I shall celebrate and sing her praise.… O Lady, the most brilliant speakers fall short when they sing your praise, for you are set above the Seraphim for having given birth to Christ the King! … Hail, Queen of the universe! Hail, Mary, the Lady of us all!"[98]

For the Latin liturgy we can cite, among other things, the Marian hymns: *Salve Regina, Ave Regina coelorum, Regina coeli laetare.* The various titles contained in the Litany of Loreto are renowned (*Regina angelorum, patriarcharum, prophetarum, apostolorum, martyrum, confessorum, virginum, sanctorum omnium, sine labe originali concepta, in caelum assumpta, familiae, sacratissimi rosarii, pacis*). Since the fifteenth century, the fifth glorious mystery of the rosary has contemplated the crowning of Mary in Heaven.

Since the Council of Ephesus, Christian art too "portrayed Mary as Queen and Empress seated upon a royal throne adorned with roy-

96. Ephrem, *Hymni de B. Maria* 19, ed. T. J. Lamy (Malines 1886, 624). Cited in Pius XII, *Ad caeli Reginam* (*PE* 4:251, n. 10; *EE* 6, n. 1131). On the patristic witnesses, see Roschini, *Maria Santissima* 2:379–97; Luigi Gambero, "La regalità di Maria nel pensiero dei Padri" [The Queenship of Mary in the Thought of the Fathers], *Ephemerides Mariologicae* 46, no. 4 (1996): 433–52; Gherardini, *Sta la regina*, 67–79, in addition to N. Schmuck, "Katakombenmalerei" [Catacomb Painting], in *ML* 3:523–26 (on the first witnesses in the catacombs: Mary appears with regal or imperial traits; the most popular Marian scene is the Adoration of the Magi).

97. The use of the corresponding titles begins in the third century, with Origen among others, in his *Hom. 7 in Lc.* (*GCS* 9, 48) commenting on Lk 1:43 ("You are the mother of the Lord; you are my Lady," *kyria*): Roschini, *Maria Santissima* 2:380f; Karl Wittkemper, "Herrin" [Lady], in *ML* 3:161f.

98. Cited in Pius XII, *Ad caeli Reginam* (*PE* 4:251, n. 28; *EE* 6, n. 1148). English translation from Joseph Raya and José de Vinck, eds., *Byzantine Daily Worship* (Allendale, N.J.: Alleluia, 1969), 960, 965, 967.

al insignia, crowned with the royal diadem and surrounded by the host of angels and saints in heaven, and ruling not only over nature and its powers but also over the machinations of Satan."[99]

The motif of Mary's crowning by the Redeemer is also often present in iconography. In addition, we find the practice of crowning Marian images, since the eighth century,[100] and particularly since the sixteenth century in the West (especially at shrines). There is a proper rite for this custom, published again in 1981 during the pontificate of John Paul II,[101] who used it quite a few times.[102]

Since the start of the 1900s, the theology of the queenship of Mary has received a boost due to the Marian congresses, which called for the consecration of the world to Mary, "Queen of the Universe," and for a liturgical feast dedicated to the universal queenship of the Mother of God.[103] This vigorous movement found its greatest acceptance in the consecration of the world to the Immaculate Heart of Mary, Queen of the Universe, by Pius XII in 1942, and by the introduction of the corresponding feast in 1954, as explained in the encyclical *Ad caeli reginam*.[104]

Systematic Exposition

Next, in the systematic exposition, we will show the queenship of Mary connected with the kingship of Jesus and made an example

99. Pius XII (*PE* 4:251, n. 32; *EE* 6, n. 1152). On the history of art, see Friederike Tschochner, "Königtum Mariens II. Kunstgeschichte" II, in *ML* 3:593–96.

100. See N. Gussone, "Krönung von Marienbildern" [Crowning of Marian Images], in *ML* 3:683f.

101. See Ignazio Calabuig, "Significato e valore del nuovo Ordo Coronandi imaginem BMV" [Meaning and Value of the New Order of Crowning of an Image of the BVM], *Notitiae* 18 (1981): 268–324; Gaspari, "Maria Regina coronata," 254f.

102. For example, see the Address of June 19, 1983, at Jasna Gora, Poland; *Insegnamenti di Giovanni Paolo II*, vol 6, part 1 (Vatican City: Libreria Editrice Vaticana, 1984), 1579–82, reported also in Arthur B. Calkins, *Totus tuus: John Paul II's Program of Marian Consecration and Entrustment* (1992; repr. New Bedford, Mass.: Academy of the Immaculate, 2006), 195–97.

103. See Roschini, *Maria Santissima* 2:480f, which fully describes the theological development of the Middle Ages (395–479); various references (up to Suárez) also in Gherardini, *Sta la regina*, 93–116.

104. On the encyclical, see Roschini, "Breve commento all'enciclica 'Ad coeli reginam'" [Brief Comment on the Encyclical "Ad coeli reginam"], *Marianum* 16 (1954): 409–32; *Maria Santissima* 2:352–59, 506; Gaspari, "Maria Regina coronata," 258–61; Pozo, *María, nueva Eva*, 383–86.

for the royal dignity of all Christians. Also, a social reflection will be included that considers the meaning of "kingship": Thomas Aquinas describes "to govern" as to order the multitude of a complete society [that is, a society self-sufficient in the necessities of life] toward a common end.[105] To assume such a function, some eminent qualities are called for. Kingship is therefore a primacy of excellence and dominion.

To present Mary as queen, "the main principle on which the royal dignity of Mary rests is without doubt her Divine Motherhood."[106] But her qualification to be proclaimed Queen comes "also because God has willed her to have an exceptional role in the work of our eternal salvation." Just as Jesus Christ is not only our King by birthright (being the incarnate Son of God), but also by an acquired right (through the Redemption), Mary, analogously, is Queen by virtue of being Mother of God and by the work in which she was "most closely associated with Christ."[107]

A third reason for the queenship is the fullness of grace that exalts Mary above all creatures.

The queenship of Mary also relates to the angels, because the Mother of God participates in the universal dominion of Christ the King. Therefore, the regal invocations of the Litany of Loreto start with the title *Regina angelorum*. Jesus Christ did not die for the angels,[108] nor was the salvific compassion of Mary directed for the good of the heavenly spirits. Her eminence in grace, however, exalts her above all the angels who honor her with praise and obedience. Among the liturgical hymns, the antiphon *Ave Regina caelorum, ave domina angelorum* is particularly meaningful.[109] In addition, the

105. Thomas Aquinas, *De regimine principum* I.1–2, in *St. Thomas Aquinas: Political Writings*, ed. R. W. Dyson (Cambridge: Cambridge University Press, 2004), 5–10; see Roschini, *Maria Santissima* 2:345f. The qualities of a "complete society," with respect to the church, are briefly characterized by Leo XIII, Encyclical *Immortale Dei* (1885) (DH 3167; also, *PE* 2:91, n. 8f). The doctrine is taken for granted by Vatican II (e.g., *LG* 8), but without the adjective used by Aquinas.

106. Pius XII (*PE* 4:251, n. 34; *EE* 6, n. 1154).

107. Pius XII (*PE* 4:251, n. 35; *EE* 6, n. 1155f).

108. See Heb 2:16: "It is not with angels that he [Christ the High Priest] is concerned, but with the descendants of Abraham."

109. On the relation of Mary and the angels, see A. de Villalmonte, "María y los angeles" [Mary and the Angels], *Estudios Marianos* 20 (1962): 401–37; Anton Ziegenaus, "Engel II. Dogmatik," in *ML* 2:339.

Franciscan school, especially after St. Bernardine of Siena (fifteenth century), affirms a spiritual motherhood toward the angels.[110]

Being "queen of the world" does not stand in competition to Christ, but consists of a sharing in the kingship of the one King. It is a royalty in Christ that comes from him and leads to him. As Christ makes use of the sacraments as means of grace, Pius XII emphasizes, he similarly makes use of the office of his Mother to distribute the fruits of the Redemption to us.[111]

"The title of queen," John Paul II emphasizes, "does not of course replace that of Mother. Her queenship remains a corollary of her particular maternal mission and simply expresses the power conferred on her to carry out that mission."[112]

The royalty of Mary is greater than ours, but it is not detached from our situation. The "crown" is given to Mary after the travail of her earthly journey, and it is an invitation, given so that we may also reach that final destination.

In particular, those who open themselves to the mediation of the Mother of God "profit" from the queenship of Mary. Thus Pius XII stated:

We likewise ordain that on the same day [every May 31, the Feast of the Blessed Virgin Mary, Queen] the consecration of the human race to the Immaculate Heart of the Blessed Virgin Mary be renewed, cherishing the hope that through such consecration a new era may begin, joyous in Christian peace and in the triumph of religion.[113]

110. See Bernardo Aperribay, "María, Madre de los Angeles?" [Mary, Mother of the Angels?], *Verdad y vida* 18 (1960): 261–80; O'Carroll, CSSp, *Theotokos: A Theological Encyclopedia of the Blessed Virgin Mary* (Eugene, Ore.: Wipf and Stock, 2000), 27. The basis of this teaching of St. Bernardine is the idea that the division between the good and wicked angels depended on their acceptance or rejection of the Incarnation of the Word. According to Bernardine, the good angels were saved by means of their acceptance of the grace of Christ the Savior, shared in advance. Therefore, Christ would have also died for the angels, a problematic thought that is in tension with biblical soteriology (see in particular Heb. 2:16). See Renzo Lavatori, *Gli angeli: Storia e pensiero* [The Angels: History and Thought] (Genoa: Marietti, 1991), 47–50, 186–89.

111. Pius XII (*PE* 4:251, n. 42; *EE* 6, n. 1161).

112. John Paul II, CM 56 (July 23, 1997), n. 3. On the relation of the divine maternity and the Marian queenship in John Paul II, see Arthur B. Calkins, *Totus tuus: John Paul II's Program of Marian Consecration and Entrustment* (1992; New Bedford, Mass.: Academy of the Immaculate, 1997), 279f.

113. Pius XII (*PE* 4:251, n. 47; *EE* 6, n. 1166).

Twelve years before his first encyclical on Mary our Queen, Pius XII had solemnly consecrated the church and the whole human race to the Immaculate Heart of Mary, Queen of the Universe, on October 31, 1942, on the occasion of the twenty-fifth anniversary of the apparitions of Fatima.[114] "As the Kingship of Christ is the basis of the consecration of the world to the Sacred Heart of Jesus (made by Leo XIII with the encyclical *Annum sacrum* of 1899), in the same way—by an obvious analogy—the Queenship of Mary is the basis of the consecration of the church and the human race to her Immaculate Heart. Indeed, we all belong to Christ and to Mary the Queen. With this 'consecration' we are doing nothing but recognizing this, our belonging to the King and the Queen of the Universe."[115]

REFERENCES

The Assumption of Mary

Ecclesiastical Texts

CCC 966.
John Paul II. CM 53–56 (June 25, July 2, July 9, July 25, 1997).
———. *RM* 41.
Pius XII. Apostolic Constitution *Munificentissimus Deus*: *EE* 6, nn. 1931–64 (excerpt: DH 3900–3904).
Vatican II. *LG* 59.

Other Sources

Auer, Johann. *Gesù il Salvatore: Soteriologia–Mariologia* [Jesus the Savior: Soteriology, Mariology], §11. Translated by Carlo Molari. Assisi: Cittadella, 1993. German original: *Jesus Christus—Heiland der Welt: Maria, Christi Mutter im Heilsplan Gottes*. Regensburg: Friedrich Pustet, 1988.
Balić, Carolus. *Testimonia de assumptione B.V. Mariae ex omnibus saeculis* [Testimony of the Assumption of the BVM across the Centuries]. 2 vols. Rome, 1948–50.
Bastero, Juan Luis. *Mary, Mother of the Redeemer*, 197–217. Dublin: Four Courts, 2006.
———. *Virgen singular: La reflexión teológica mariana en el siglo XX* [Singular Virgin: Theological Reflection on Mary in the 20th Century], 171–205. Madrid: Rialp, 2001.
Beumer, Johannes, and Anton Ziegenaus. "Aufnahme" [Assumption]. In Bäumer and Scheffczyk, *ML* 1:276–86.
Calero, Antonio María. *La Vergine Maria nel mistero di Cristo e della Chiesa: Saggio di*

114. Regarding the act of consecration in 1942, see p. 256 and p. 399.
115. Roschini, *Maria Santissima* 2:485.

mariologia [The Virgin Mary in the Mystery of Christ and the Church: Essay in Mariology], 225–80. Leumann (Turin): Elle Di Ci, 1995. Spanish original: *María en el misterio de Cristo y de la Iglesia*. Madrid: CCS, 1990.

Calì, R. "La tradizione del Transitus negli apocrifi del IV e V secolo: Aspetti teologici" [The Tradition of the Transitus in 4th- and 5th-Century Apocrypha: Theological Aspects]. In *Maria, icona viva della Chiesa futura*, edited by Carmelo Carvello and Stefano De Fiores, 141–57. Rome: Edizioni Monfortane, 1998.

Calì, Rosa, Carmelo Carvello, and Domenico Marcucci, eds. *Maria assunta segno di speranza per l'umanità in cammino* [Mary Assumed, Sign of Hope for Humanity on the Way]. Rome, 2006.

Calvo Moralejo, Gaspar, OFM, and Stefano M. Cecchin, eds. *L'Assunzione di Maria Madre di Dio*. Vatican City, 2001.

Colzani, Gianni. *Maria: Mistero di grazia e di fede* [Mary: Mystery of Grace and Faith], 245–56. Cinisello Balsamo (Milan): Ed. Paoline, 1996. 3rd ed., 2006.

De Fiores, Stefano. "Assunta." In *Maria: Nuovissimo dizionario* 1:71–99. Bologna: EDB, 2006.

Dittrich, Achim. *Protestantische Mariologie-Kritik: Historische Entwicklung bis 1997 und dogmatische Analyse* [Protestant Critique of Mariology: Historical Development up to 1997 and Dogmatic Analysis], 312–15. Mariologische Studien 11. Regensburg: Friedrich Pustet, 1998.

Everett, Lawrence P., C.SS.R. "La muerte y asunción corporal de María." In *Mariología*, edited by J. Carol, 838–66. Madrid: Biblioteca de Autores Cristianos, 1964. English original: "Mary's Death and Bodily Assumption." In *Mariology*, edited by J. Carol, 2:461–92. Milwaukee: Bruce, 1957.

Galot, Jean, SJ. "Le mystère de l'assomption." In *Maria*, edited by H. du Manoir, 7:153–237. Paris: Beauchesne, 1964.

———. *Maria, La donna nell'opera della salvezza* [Mary, the Woman in the Work of Salvation]. 3rd ed., 293–334. Rome: Ed. Pontificia Università Gregoriana, 2005. 2nd ed., 1991.

Gambero, Luigi. "Maria Assunta: Rilievi dell'escatologia patristica" [Mary Assumed: Review of Patristic Eschatology]. In Carvello and De Fiores, *Maria, icona viva della Chiesa futura*, 119–40.

———. *Maria nel pensiero dei teologi latini medievali*. Cinisello Balsamo: Ed. Paoline, 2000. English translation: *Mary in the Middle Ages: The Blessed Virgin Mary in the Thought of Medieval Latin Theologians*. Translated by Thomas Buffer. San Francisco: Ignatius Press, 2005.

Gila, Angelo M. *Le più antiche testimonianze letterarie sulla morte e glorificazione della Madre di Dio: I racconti sul Transito di Maria tra fede e teologia* [The Oldest Literary Witnesses on the Death and Glorification of the Mother of God: Accounts of the Transitus of Mary in Faith and Theology]. Padua, Messaggero: 2010.

Haffner, Paul. *The Mystery of Mary*, 208–37. Leominster, UK: Gracewing; Mundelein, Ill.: Hillenbrand, 2004.

Jugie, Martin. "Assomption de la Sainte Vierge." In du Manoir, *Maria*, 1:619–58. Paris: Beauchesne, 1949.

———. *La mort et l'assomption de la Sainte Vierge; Étude historico-doctrinale* [The Death and Assumption of the Holy Virgin: Historical-Doctrinal Study]. Vatican City: Biblioteca Apostolica Vaticana, 1944.

Laurentin, René. *A Short Treatise on the Virgin Mary*, 86–89, 97f., 239–50. Washington, N.J.: Ave Maria Institute, 1991.

Levering, Matthew. *Mary's Bodily Assumption.* Notre Dame, Ind.: University of Notre Dame Press, 2015.

Meo, Salvatore, OSM. "Assunta: II: Dogma, storia e teologia" [Mary Assumed: II. Dogma, History and Theology]. In De Fiores and Meo, *NDM*, 167–78.

Merkelbach. *Mariologia*, 263–94.

Mimoumi, Simon Claude. *Dormition et assomption de Marie: Histoire des traditions anciennes* [Dormition and Assumption of Mary: History of the Ancient Traditions]. Théologie historique 98. Paris: Beauchesne, 1995.

O'Carroll. *Theotokos*, 55–58.

Perrella. *La Madre di Gesù*, 297–406, updated ed. of Calvo Moralejo and Cecchin, *L'Assunzione*, 71–167.

Perrella, Salvatore M., and Stefano De Fiores. "Assunta." In De Fiores, Schiefer, and Perrella, *DMar*, 175–89.

Ponce Cuéllar, Miguel. *María: Madre del Redentor y Madre de la Iglesia* [Mary, Mother of the Redeemer and Mother of the Church]. 2nd ed., 413–41. Barcelona: Herder, 2001.

Pozo, Cándido, SJ. *María en la obra de la salvación* [Mary in the Work of Salvation]. 2nd ed., 314–324. Madrid: Biblioteca de Autores Cristianos, 1990.

———. *María, nueva Eva* [Mary, the New Eve], 335–46. Madrid: Biblioteca de Autores Cristianos, 2005.

Riedl, G. "Die pseudoaugustinische Schrift 'De assumptione beatae Mariae virginis': Theologische Argumentationskunst und dogmengeschichtlicher Kontext" [The Pseudo-Augustinian Document "De assumptione beatae Mariae virginis": The Theological Art of Its Argument; Context in the History of Dogma]. In *Volksfrömmigkeit und Theologie: Die eine Mariengestalt und die vielen Quellen* [Popular Piety and Theology: The One Figure of Mary and Its Many Sources], edited by A. Ziegenaus. 75–103. Regensburg: Friedrich Pustet, 1998.

Roschini, Gabriele Maria. *La Madonna: Secondo la fede e la teologia* [The Madonna, according to the Faith and Theology], 3:196–295. Rome: Libreria Editrice Francesco Ferrari, 1953–54.

———, *Maria Santissima nella storia della salvezza: Trattato completo di mariologia alla luce del Concilio Vaticano II* [Mary Most Holy in the History of Salvation: Complete Treatise on Mariology in Light of the Second Vatican Council], 3:451–632. Isola del Liri: Pisani, 1969.

———. *Mariologia.* 3 vols. Milan: Belardetti, 1941–42.

Rovira, German, ed. *Die sonnenbekleidete Frau: Die leibliche Aufnahme Marias in den Himmel; Überwindung des Todes durch die Gnade* [The Woman Clothed with the Sun: The Bodily Assumption of Mary into Heaven; The Overcoming of Death by Grace]. Kevelaer: Butzon and Bercker, 1986.

Sartor, Danilo Maria. "Assunta: III. Celebrazione liturgica" [Mary Assumed: III. Liturgical Celebration]. In *NDM*, 178–83.

Scheffczyk, Leo. "Maria Assumpta—im Licht des Erlösungsgeheimnisses" [Mary Assumed, in the Light of the Mystery of Redemption]. *Sedes Sapientiae: Mariologisches Jahrbuch* 4, no. 1 (2000): 45–70.

———. *Maria, crocevia della fede cattolica* [Mary, Crossroads of the Catholic Faith], 117–33. CdM 1. Lugano: Eupress FTL, 2002.

Serra, Aristide. "Assunta: I. Fondamenti biblici dell'Assunzione" [Mary assumed: I. Biblical Foundations]. In *NDM*, 163–67.

Shoemaker, Stephen J. *Ancient Traditions of the Virgin Mary's Dormition and Assumption.* Oxford: Oxford University Press, 2002.

Söll, Georg. *Storia dei dogmi mariani*, 189–217, 240–44, 263–72, 321–25, 352–81. Rome: Libreria Ateneo Salesiano, 1981. German original: *Mariologie* [Handbuch der Dogmengeschichte, vol. 3, part 4]. Freiburg im Breisgau: Herder, 1978.

Toniolo, Ermanno M., ed. *Assunta al cielo perché Corredentrice sulla terra* [Assumed into Heaven Because She Was Coredemptrix on Earth]. Frigento: Casa Mariana Editrice, 2013.

———, ed. *Il dogma dell'Assunzione di Maria: Problemi attuali e tentativi di ricomprensione* [The Dogma of the Assumption: Current Issues and Attempts at Reinterpretation]. Rome: Centro di cultura Mariana "Madre della Chiesa," 2010.

Wenger, Antoine. *L'Assomption de la T. S.* [*Très Sainte*] *Vierge dans la tradition byzantine du VI au X siècle: Études et documents* [The Assumption of the Most Holy Virgin in Byzantine Tradition of the Sixth to Tenth Centuries: Studies and Documents]. Paris: Institut français d'études byzantines, 1955.

Ziegenaus, Anton. *Maria in der Heilsgeschichte: Mariologie*, 309–31. Katholische Dogmatik 5. Aachen: MM-Verlag, 1998.

The Queenship of Mary

Ecclesiastical Texts

John Paul II. CM (July 23, 1997) ("Christians look to Mary, Queen").

———. *RM* 41.

Pius XII. Encyclical *Ad caeli Reginam* (1954) (*PE* 4:251; *EE* 6, nn. 1122–71).

Other Sources

Auer. *Gesù*, §15.

Bastero. *Mary, Mother*, 211–17.

Cantera, Santiago. "Pio XI y la dimensión social de la realeza mariana" [Pius XI and the Social Dimension of the Queenship of Mary]. *Scripta de Maria, 2nd ser.* 6 (2009): 101–30.

De Fiores, Stefano, and Nereo Zamberlan. "Regina." In De Fiores, Schiefer, and Perrella, *DMar*, 1022–34.

du Manoir, Hubert. "La royauté de Marie: État de la question depuis l'encyclique 'Ad caeli Reginam'" [The Queenship of Mary: State of the Question after the Encyclical 'Ad caeli Reginam']. In *Mater et Ecclesia*, 5:1–37. Rome: PAMI, 1959.

Fastenrath, E. "Königtum Mariens." In *ML* 3:589–93.

Gaspari, Sergio. "Maria Regina coronata di gloria: Significato teologico-liturgico" [Mary, Queen, Crowned with Glory: Theological-Liturgical Significance]. In Carvello and De Fiores, *Maria, icona viva della Chiesa futura*, 251–92.
Gherardini, Brunero. *La Madre: Maria in una sintesi storico-teologica* [The Mother: Mary in a Historical-Theological Synthesis]. Frigento: Casa Mariana, 1989.
———. *Sta la regina alla tua destra: Saggio storico-teologico sulla Regalità di Maria* [The Queen Stands at Your Right Hand: Historical-Theological Essay on the Queenship of Mary]. Rome: Vivere In, 2002.
Haffner. *The Mystery of Mary*, 229–32.
La Realeza de María [The Queenship of Mary]. *Estudios Marianos* 17 (1956).
Malek, Paweł. *La regalità di Maria nelle odierne celebrazioni eucharistiche: Analisi dogmatico-liturgica degli appropriati formulari liturgici del Rito romano* [The Queenship of Mary in the Present-Day Celebration of the Eucharist: Dogmatic-Liturgical Analysis of the Proper Liturgical Formularies of the Roman Rite]. CdM 13. Lugano: Eupress FTL, 2015.
O'Carroll, Michael, CSSp. *Theotokos: A Theological Encyclopedia of the Blessed Virgin Mary*, 301f. Eugene, Ore.: Wipf and Stock, 2000.
Roschini, Gabriele M. "Breve commento all'enciclica 'Ad coeli reginam'" [Brief Comment on the Encyclical "Ad coeli reginam"]. *Marianum* 16 (1954): 409–32.
———. *La Madonna secondo la fede* 2:499–519.
———. *Dizionario di mariologia* [Dictionary of Mariology], 426–39. Rome: Editrice Studium, 1961.
———. *Maria Santissima* 2:345–515.
———. "Royauté de Marie." In du Manoir, *Maria* 1:603–18. 1949.
Sartor, Danilo, Aristide Serra, and Stefano De Fiores. "Regina." In *NDM*, 1189–1206.
Schmidt, Firmin M., OFM Cap. "La realeza universal de María." In Carol, *Mariología*, 867–920. English original: "The Universal Queenship of Mary." In Carol, *Mariology* 2:493–549. 1957.
Söll. *Storia dei dogmi mariani*, 383–86.

Eight

The Mediation of Mary

PRELIMINARY NOTE

The divine maternity of Mary implies a collaboration in the work of salvation: the *fiat* of the Virgin says yes so that the Word of God can enter into this world. This collaboration does not end at the moment of the Incarnation, but goes further:

> She conceived, brought forth and nourished Christ. She presented Him to the Father in the temple, and was united with Him by compassion as He died on the Cross. In this singular way she cooperated by her obedience, faith, hope and burning charity in the work of the Savior in giving back supernatural life to souls, wherefore she is our mother in the order of grace.[1]

In her task on earth, Mary found herself to be, in a way, "in the middle" between God and humanity. The same is true of her heavenly intercession. In a general sense, we can speak here about mediation that relates (1) to the work of redemption carried out by Christ on the earth (the objective redemption) and (2) to the distribution of the fruits of salvation to concrete subjects (subjective redemption). In addition to "objective" and "subjective redemption," we also find the terminology *redemptio in actu primo* and *redemptio in actu secundo*.

The terminology used by authors is not always well defined. The term "co-redemption," for example, generally indicates cooperation in the work of salvation, in the sense of the objective redemption, but at times it also indicates the role of intercession in subjective redemp-

1. *LG* 61.

tion. The word "mediation," on the other hand, is often used only in reference to cooperation in distributing graces, but, in itself, it is suited to a global meaning that extends to objective and subjective redemption. In the following we shall take "mediation" in a global sense, referring both to Mary's cooperation during the earthly journey of the Savior and also to her cooperation after Pentecost (and after the Assumption) for the good of the church. This global meaning appears, among other places, in the encyclical *Redemptoris Mater* (1987), whose third part is dedicated to the "motherly mediation" of Mary in Christ.[2]

A formal definition of mediation comes from St. Thomas: "The office of a mediator is to join together and unite those between whom he mediates: for extremes are united in the mean [*medio*]."[3] A mediator therefore is one who finds himself "in the middle" between two extremes with the task of uniting them. For this reason, Jesus Christ, as mediator, unites men with God.

Jesus Christ is the sole mediator (1 Tm 2:5); other persons can collaborate only *dispositive vel ministerialiter*[4]—that is, they can dispose (prepare) men for union with God, or rather, convey salvation as ministers in whom Christ himself acts.

To understand the mediation of Christ it is important to maintain that this includes and does not exclude cooperation by human persons. Vatican II affirms this with great intensity:

> There is but one Mediator as we know from the words of the apostle, "for there is one God and one mediator of God and men, the man Christ Jesus, who gave himself a redemption for all" (1 Tm 2:5–6). The maternal duty of Mary toward men in no wise obscures or diminishes this unique mediation of Christ, but rather shows his power, for all the salvific influence of the Blessed Virgin on men originates not from some inner necessity, but from the divine pleasure. It flows forth from the superabundance of the merits of Christ, rests on his mediation, depends entirely on it, and draws all its power from it. In no way does it impede, but rather does it foster the immediate union of the faithful with Christ.[5]

2. See Hauke, "La mediazione materna di Maria secondo Papa Giovanni Paolo II" [Mary's Maternal Mediation according to Pope John Paul II], *Maria Corredentrice* 7 (2005) 62f.

3. *ST* III, q. 26, a. 1.

4. Ibid.

5. *LG* 60.

Philosophically, the subordinate mediation of human persons in the economy of salvation is explained by analogy with being: the creature participates in some way in the perfections of the Creator and, if God so wills, in the work of redemption.

Vatican II indicates that Mary

> is invoked by the Church under the titles of Advocate, Auxiliatrix, Adjutrix, and Mediatrix. This, however, is to be so understood that it neither takes away from nor adds anything to the dignity and efficaciousness of Christ the one Mediator.
>
> For no creature could ever be counted as equal with the Incarnate Word and Redeemer. Just as the priesthood of Christ is shared in various ways both by the ministers and by the faithful, and as the one goodness of God is really communicated in different ways to his creatures, so also the unique mediation of the Redeemer does not exclude but rather gives rise to a manifold cooperation which is but a sharing in this one source.
>
> The Church does not hesitate to profess this subordinate role of Mary. It knows it through unfailing experience of it and commends it to the hearts of the faithful, so that encouraged by this maternal help they may the more intimately adhere to the Mediator and Redeemer.[6]

Mary's cooperation in the objective and subjective redemption is a topic greatly in need of further clarification. The titles "Co-redemptrix" and "Mediatrix of all graces" are objects of particular controversy. But before entering into the debate, it is important to see the common ground within Mariology. Then we can highlight the various positions discussed today and seek a proper solution.

The distinction between Mary's cooperation in the objective redemption and in subjective redemption can also be seen in two central moments of her task as the "new Eve." Eve, in Genesis, appears as a companion of Adam ("a helper fit for him" [Gn 2:18]) and as "mother of all the living" (Gn 3:20). The anthropological basis of these aspects consists in the central relationships of woman as wife and mother. Mary, the new Eve, is oriented toward Christ, the new Adam, and also toward all men called to become part of the church. "Mary is associated as a woman in the work of salvation. Having

6. *LG* 62.

created man 'male and female' (cf. Gn 1:27), the Lord also wants to place the New Eve beside the New Adam in the Redemption. Our first parents had chosen the way of sin as a couple; a new pair, the Son of God with his Mother's co-operation, would re-establish the human race in its original dignity."[7]

In our presentation we will follow the twofold structure of cooperation in the objective redemption, which is co-redemption (Mary as "companion of the Redeemer"), and in subjective redemption (Mary as "dispensatrix of graces"). The whole doctrine of mediation can also be taken under the title of "the new Eve." There are also other approaches that we shall add.[8] The basic approach is the analysis of the "mystery of the life of Jesus," which is the presentation of the saving events in which the Blessed Virgin is involved. Various soteriological terms also need to be applied; for example, "redemption," "ransom," "sacrifice," and "merit." A further possible way to present the mediation of Mary is the schema of sharing in the three ministries of Christ as king, priest, and prophet. Analogously, the Mother of God appears as queen,[9] prophetess,[10] and bearer of a maternal priesthood. We will make note of her spiritual motherhood, a term formally distinct from Mary's mediation but that de facto coincides with her cooperation in salvation (Mary as spiritual "mother," "companion," and "helper"). Her spiritual motherhood is expressed for the good of the church, as the title *Mater Ecclesiae* demonstrates (Mary as "Mother of the Church"). In order to unite all men to Christ and his church, including non-Catholics and non-Christians, Mary works as the "Mother of unity" (*Mater unitatis*).

7. John Paul II, CM 48 (April 9, 1997), n. 3.

8. See Hauke, "Maria, 'compagna del Redentore,'" 66–68; "La cooperazione attiva di Maria alla Redenzione: Prospettiva storica (patristica, medievale, moderna, contemporanea)" [The Active Cooperation of Mary in the Redemption: Historical (Patristic, Medieval, Modern, Contemporary) Perspective], in *Mary, "unique cooperator in the Redemption"* (New Bedford, Mass.: Academy of the Immaculate, 2005), 175–80; also in Immaculata Mediatrix 6 (2006): 157–89, passim.

9. See chap. 7, on "The Queenship of Mary."

10. See chap. 9, on Marian apparitions.

MARY AS "COMPANION OF THE REDEEMER" (*SOCIA REDEMPTORIS*)

The Starting Point

Lumen gentium offers a summary of the known facts of Mary's association with the work of salvation. The document recalls that "the holy Fathers see her as used by God not merely in a passive way, but as freely cooperating in the work of human salvation through faith and obedience."[11] It was a "singular" cooperation as the "associate" of the Redeemer (*socia Redemptoris*).[12]

Biblical Foundation

As a biblical basis for Mary's cooperation in the work of the Redeemer,[13] we can refer, first of all, to the role of Mary in the Incarnation and at the foot of the Cross. Also relevant are the presentation of Jesus at the Temple, Mary's intercession at the wedding of Cana, and her presence in the nascent church praying for the coming of the Holy Spirit. Let us also recall the *Protoevangelium*, which announces the participation of the "woman" in the victory over the "serpent" (Gn 3:15).

At the *Annunciation*, Mary "devoted herself totally as a handmaid of the Lord to the person and work of her Son, under Him and with Him, by the grace of almighty God, serving the mystery of redemption."[14] The Council cites Irenaeus: Mary, "being obedient, became the cause of salvation for herself and for the whole human race."[15]

11. *LG* 56.

12. See *LG* 61.

13. A systematic exposition of the biblical passages (cited in chapter 1) appears, among other places, in Galot, *Maria, La donna*, 3rd ed., 251–65; Brunero Gherardini, *La Corredentrice nel mistero di Cristo e della Chiesa* [The Coredemptrix in the Mystery of Christ and the Church] (Rome: Vivere In, 1998), 147–220; Stefano M. Manelli, "Maria Corredentrice nella Sacra Scrittura" [Mary Coredemptrix in Sacred Scripture], *Maria Corredentrice* 1 (1998)37–114; Heinz-Lothar Barth, *Ipsa conteret: Maria die Schlangenzertreterin; Philologische und theologische Überlegungen zum Protoevangelium* [She Herself Will Crush: Mary the Treader of the Serpent; Philological and Theological Considerations on the Protoevangelium] (Ruppichteroth: Canisius-Werk, 2000), 169–87.

14. *LG* 56.

15. *Adversus haereses* III.22.4 (*SC* 211:441). The usual version, given earlier, follows the old Latin translation. The original Greek text, which is lost, probably refers the "for herself" to Eve and not

The fathers, "comparing Mary with Eve, call her 'the Mother of the living,' and still more often they say: 'death through Eve, life through Mary.'"[16] We recall how St. Thomas mentions that the Annunciation demonstrates the existence of "a certain spiritual wedlock between the Son of God and human nature, wherefore in the Annunciation the Virgin's consent was besought in lieu of that of the entire human nature."[17] We find in Mary, under Christ and dependent on grace, a "true cooperation [in the work of salvation], because it is realized 'with him' and, beginning with the Annunciation, it involves active participation in the work of redemption."[18]

"This union of the Mother with the Son in the work of salvation is made manifest from the time of Christ's virginal conception up to His death."[19] In the story of the infancy, especially the *presentation of Jesus at the Temple* has attracted systematic attention (Lk 2:22–38). The "presentation to the Lord" (*parastésai to kurío*) (Lk 2:22) is not only a "showing," but an offering: Mary gives her Son, who is at the same time the Son of God and therefore the greatest offering man can present to God.[20] The presentation at the Temple already prepares Mary for her role below the Cross, at which the prophecy of Simeon hints (Lk 2:35: "A sword will pierce your soul.)"[21] The apostolic exhortation *Marialis cultus* of Paul VI (1974) cites a saying of St. Bernard:

to Mary. Therefore, we should render the expression *sibi causa facta est salutis* differently: "With her obedience Mary became for her (Eve) and for all the human race, a cause of salvation." Thus Galot, *Maria, La donna*, 88f, 266, with reference to José A. de Aldama, "'Sibi causa facta est salutis' (S. Ireneo, *Adv. Haereses* 3,22,4)" ["Became the Cause of Salvation for Herself" (St. Irenaeus, *Against the Heresies* III.22.4)], *Ephemerides Mariologicae* 16 (1966). See also pp. 80–81.

16. *LG* 61.

17. *ST* III, q. 30, a. 1.

18. John Paul II, CM 33 (Sept. 18, 1996), n. 4. See also Juan Carlos Loor Alarcon, *La cooperazione di Maria alla Redenzione, focalizzata nell'Annunciazione* [Mary's Cooperation in the Redemption, Focused upon the Annunciation], CdM 12 (Lugano: EuPress FTL, 2014).

19. *LG* 57.

20. See Anton Ziegenaus, "Darbringung Jesu im Tempel II. Dogmatik" [Presentation of Jesus in the Temple. II: Dogma], in *ML* 2:142f.

21. See Settimio M. Manelli, "'E una spada trapasserà anche la tua stessa anima' (Lc 2,35): Esegesi del versetto e il suo sviluppo dottrinale in riferimento alla cooperazione di Maria all'opera salvifica di Gesù" ["And a Sword Will Also Pierce Your Soul" (Lk 2:35): Exegesis of the Verse and Its Doctrinal Development in Reference to Mary's Cooperation with the Salvific Work of Jesus], *Maria Corredentrice* 6 (2003).

"Offer your Son, holy Virgin, and present to the Lord the blessed fruit of your womb. Offer for the reconciliation of us all the holy Victim which is pleasing to God."[22]

"The divine intention to call for the specific involvement of woman in the work of Redemption can be seen by the fact that Simeon's prophecy is addressed to Mary alone, although Joseph also took part in the offering rite."[23]

At the wedding of *Cana*, the intercession of Mary brings the first miracle in the life of Jesus (Jn 2:1–11). We saw in the biblical section that the word "woman" (Jn 2:4) seems to hint at the role of Mary as representative of Israel and as the new Eve. According to John Paul II, the event of Cana is "a sort of *first announcement of Mary's mediation*, wholly oriented towards Christ and tending to the revelation of his salvific power."[24] "By emphasizing Mary's initiative in the first miracle and then recalling her presence on Calvary at the foot of the Cross, the Evangelist helps us understand how Mary's co-operation is extended to the whole of Christ's work. The Blessed Virgin's request is placed within the divine plan of salvation."[25]

The central point for reflecting on the role of Mary in the redemption is no doubt her presence under the *Cross* (Jn 19:25–27). "The first explicit affirmation of Mary's cooperation in the redeeming sacrifice appears in Byzantine theology, from John Geometres, a monk at the end of the tenth century, author of a 'Life of Mary.'"[26] The observation by Jean Galot is also taken up by John Paul II: according to John Geometres, Mary is "united to Christ in the whole work of Redemption according to God's plan, sharing in the Cross and suffering for our salvation. She remained united to the Son 'in every deed, attitude and wish.' Mary's association with Jesus' saving work came about through her Mother's love, a love inspired by grace,

22. *In purificatione B. Mariae, Sermo* III.2 (PL 183:370). See Paul VI, *MCu*, n. 20; John Paul II, CM 3 (Oct. 25, 1995), n. 3.

23. John Paul II, CM 41 (Jan. 8, 1997), n. 3. See Galot, *Maria, La donna*, 3rd ed., 256.

24. *RM* 22.

25. John Paul II, CM 45 (March 5, 1997), n. 2.

26. Galot, *Maria, La donna*, 266; see Galot, "La plus ancienne affirmation de la Corédemption mariale: Le témoignage de Jean le Géomètre" [The Earliest Affirmation of Marian Coredemption: The Witness of John the Geometer], *Recherches de Science Religieuse* 45 (1957): 187–208.

which conferred a higher power on it: love freed of passion proves to be the most compassionate."[27]

In the Middle Ages, a process began of deepening the theological relevance of this presence and the central importance of the sacrifice of Jesus on the Cross. A particularly influential witness is that of Arnold of Chartres (also "of Bonneval"), a disciple and friend of St. Bernard. "He distinguished in the Cross 'two altars: one in Mary's heart, the other in Christ's body. Christ sacrificed his flesh, Mary her soul.' Mary sacrificed herself spiritually in deep communion with Christ, and implored the world's salvation: 'What the mother asks, the Son approves and the Father grants.'"[28] Vatican II, summarizing the preceding tradition, affirms: Mary "faithfully persevered in her union with her Son unto the cross, where she stood, in keeping with the divine plan, grieving exceedingly with her only begotten Son, uniting herself with a maternal heart with His sacrifice, and lovingly consenting to the immolation of this Victim which she herself had brought forth."[29]

The presence of Mary is therefore connected with consent to the sacrifice of Christ for the salvation of humanity. Here Paul VI sees the summit of union with Christ in the work of redemption. The pope cites Vatican II, adding that Mary also, for her part, offered the victim to the eternal Father.[30] This affirmation, stated repeatedly by the preceding popes, is also found in John Paul II: "The Council text also stresses that her consent to Jesus' immolation is not passive acceptance but a genuine act of love, by which she offered her Son as a 'victim' of expiation for the sins of all humanity."[31]

27. John Paul II, CM 3 (Oct. 25, 1995), n. 2. See Galot, *Maria, La donna*, 267–69. See also Erich Trapp, "Geometres Johannes" [John the Geometer], in Bäumer and Scheffczyk, *ML* 2:618; O'Carroll, *Theotokos*, 203f; Hauke, "La cooperazione attiva," 168.

28. John Paul II, CM 3 (Oct. 25, 1995), n. 3. See Arnold of Chartres ("of Bonneval"), *De septem verbis Domini in cruce* [The Seven Words of the Lord on the Cross] 3 (PL 189:1694); Juniper B. Carol, OFM, *De corredemptione Beatae Virginis Mariae: Disquisitio positiva* [The Coredemption of the BVM: Positive Inquiry] (Vatican City: Typis Polyglottis Vaticanis, 1950), 156–59; Galot, *Maria, la donna*, 2nd ed. (1991), 269f; Luigi Gambero, *Maria nel pensiero dei teologi latini medievali* [Mary in the Thought of the Medieval Latin Theologians] (Cinisello Balsamo: Ed. Paoline, 2000), 179f, 184; Otto Stegmüller and R. Schulte, "Arnald von Bonneval," in *ML* 1:243f.

29. *LG* 58.

30. Paul VI, *MCu*, 20, with reference to Pius XII, Encyclical *Mystici Corporis* (*PE* 4:225, n. 110; *EE* 6, n. 258).

31. John Paul II, CM 47 (April 2, 1997), n. 2. See Hauke, "La mediazione materna," 49f. See also the interventions of Benedict XVI, 2006 to 2010; see pp. 104–6.

Besides the salvific role of the Mother of God, we speak also of the *priesthood of Mary*, distinct from the hierarchical priesthood (in representation of Christ, head of the church), and distinct from the common priesthood of all the faithful (despite being the prototype of the faithful).[32] Mary was, as the *Mariale* of Pseudo-Albert formulates it, the "companion" of the Redeemer (*socia*), but not his *vicar*. Mary is not to carry out the sacrifice of the Cross, but her interior participation in it can also be called "sacrifice" (like the spiritual association of the faithful in the eucharistic sacrifice). The priesthood of Mary is found on the "spousal" line of the common priesthood of all the faithful, although it precedes the latter, inasmuch as she is Mother of God and the new Eve. Mary's participation in the sacrifice of the Cross can be compared to the participation of the faithful in the sacrifice of the Mass: it is Christ who works the sacrifice, made present on the altar by means of the priest as representative of Christ, head of the church; but Mary unites herself to the bloody sacrifice, as the faithful unite themselves to the sacrificial act of the Eucharist.

Vatican II, speaking of "the role of the Mother of the Saviour in the economy of salvation,"[33] concludes its description with the role of Mary after the Ascension of Jesus, "by her prayers imploring the gift of the Spirit, who had already overshadowed her in the Annunciation."[34] Paul VI underscores "the prayerful presence of Mary in the early Church and in the Church throughout all ages, for, having been assumed into heaven, she has not abandoned her mission of intercession and salvation."[35]

32. See René Laurentin, *Marie, l'Église et le Sacerdoce* [Mary, the Church, and the Priesthood], 2 vols. (Paris: Nouvelles éditions latines, 1952–53); Laurentin, *Marie Deluil-Martiny: Précurseur et martyre béatifiée par Jean Paul II* [Marie Deluil-Martiny: Precursor and Martyr Beatified by John Paul II] (Paris: Fayard, 2003); Hauke, "Priestertum I. Dogmatik" [Priesthood: I. Dogmatic Theology], in Bäumer and Scheffczyk, *ML* 5:314–17; De Fiores, *Dizionario*, 2:1271–1320; Serafino M. Lanzetta, *Il sacerdozio di Maria nella teologia cattolica del XX secolo: Analisi storico-teologica* [The Priesthood of Mary in 20th-Century Catholic Theology] (Rome and Frigento: Pontificia Universitas Sanctae Crucis and Casa Mariana Editrice, 2006); F. Ochayta Piñeiro, "El sacerdocio de María desde un punto de vista teológico" [The Priesthood of Mary from a Theological Viewpoint], *Estudios Marianos* 77 (2011): 37–57; J. Ibáñez, "María, Madre-Sacerdote" [Mary, Mother-Priest], *Scripta de Maria* 2nd ser., 10 (2013): 167–200.

33. *LG* 55–59.

34. *LG* 59.

35. *MCu* 18.

Mary as Spiritual "Mother," "Companion," and "Helper"

The systematic discussion of Mary's cooperation in the objective redemption unfolds under various titles. Vatican II states that Mary, by her cooperation in the work of salvation on the earth, became "our mother in the order of grace."[36] "Motherhood" means, above all, the generation of a child, but also includes care for its growth and education. The spiritual motherhood of Mary is, so to speak, the organic continuation of her motherhood to the Son of God: her motherhood looks toward our birth to divine life and toward its growth. Because of this, *spiritual motherhood* can be oriented to both the objective redemption and the subjective.[37] In this sense we can recount

36. *LG* 61.

37. On spiritual motherhood, see in particular Benoît-Henri Merkelbach, OP, *Mariologia* (Paris: Desclée, 1939), 295–306; Théodore Koehler, "Maternité spirituelle de Marie" [Spiritual Motherhood of Mary], in *Maria: Études sur la Sainte Vierge*, ed. Hubert du Manoir (Paris: Beauchesne, 1949) 1:573–600; Koehler, "Maternité spirituelle, maternité mystique" [Spiritual Motherhood, Mystical Motherhood], in *Maria*, ed. H. du Manoir (Paris: Beauchesne, 1961), 6:551–639; Koehler, "Mary's Spiritual Maternity after the Second Vatican Council," *Marian Studies* 23 (1972): 39–68; Koehler, "Mary, Mother and 'Mediatrix' in the Post-Vatican II Liturgy," in *De cultu mariano s. XX* (Vatican City: PAMI, 2000), 2:1–24; Roschini, *La Madonna*, 2:219–93; Gabriele M. Roschini, *Dizionario di mariologia* [Dictionary of Mariology] (Rome: Editrice Studium, 1961), 296–318; Roschini, *Maria Santissima nella storia della salvezza: Trattato completo di mariologia alla luce del Concilio Vaticano II* [Mary Most Holy, in the History of Salvation: Complete Treatise on Mariology in Light of the Second Vatican Council] (Isola del Liri: Pisani, 1969), 2:255–343; Wenceslao Sebastian, "Maternidad espiritual de María," in *Mariología*, ed. J. Carol (Milwaukee: Bruce, 1957), 711–59; Tullio Faustino Ossanna and S. Cipriani, "Madre nostra" [Our Mother], in De Fiores and Meo, *NDM*, 830–42; Jean-Marie Salgado, *La Maternité Spirituelle de la Très Sainte Vierge Marie* [The Spiritual Motherhood of the Most Holy Virgin Mary], Studi Tomistici 36 (Vatican City: Libreria Editrice Vaticana, 1990); Johannes Stöhr, "Mutterschaft, geistliche" [Spiritual Motherhood], in Bäumer and Scheffczyk, *ML* 4:560–63; Juan Luis Bastero de Eleizalde, *Mary, Mother of the Redeemer* (Dublin: Four Courts, 2006), 218–26; Bastero, *Virgen singular*, 206–31; Antonio Royo Marin, *La Virgen María: Teología y espiritualidad marianas* [The Virgin Mary: Marian Theology and Spirituality], 2nd ed. (Madrid: Biblioteca de Autores Cristianos, 1997), 116–40; Miguel Ponce Cuéllar, *Maria, Madre del Redentor y Madre de la Iglesia* [Mary, Mother of the Redeemer and Mother of the Church], 2nd ed. (Barcelona: Herder, 2001), 467–69; O'Carroll, *Theotokos*, 253–56; Roberto Coggi, *La Beata Vergine: Trattato di Mariologia* [The Blessed Virgin: Treatise on Mariology] (Bologna: Studio Domenicano, 2004), 218–36; Pietro Parrotta, "The Spiritual Maternity of Mary in G. M. Roschini: The Post-Conciliar Period," in *Mary at the Foot of the Cross* (New Bedford, Mass.: Academy of the Immaculate, 2004), 4:369–86; C. M. Mangan, "The Spiritual Maternity of the Blessed Virgin Mary," in *Mariology: A Guide*, ed. M. Miravalle (Goleta, Calif.: Queenship, 2007), 507–50; D. G. Candido, "Madre dei discepoli" [Mother of Disciples], in De Fiores, Schiefer, and Perrella, *DMar*, 765–73.

a thought of Augustine cited by Vatican II: Mary is "the mother of the members of Christ ... having cooperated by charity that faithful might be born in the Church, who are members of that Head."[38]

In addition to spanning the objective and subjective redemption, the spiritual motherhood of Mary can also be presented as the logical consequence of her mission as mother and companion of the Redeemer. Thus we read in another conciliar text, "She conceived ... Christ. She ... was united with Him by compassion as He died on the Cross. In this singular way she cooperated ... in the work of the Saviour ... *wherefore* she is our mother in the order of grace."[39]

The spiritual motherhood of Mary coincides de facto with the mediation of Mary toward us. For this reason there is thought of proposing a dogmatic definition on Mary's spiritual motherhood and also on her universal mediation.[40] Despite this, mediation and spiritual motherhood are formally distinct from each other: motherhood places Mary's action for our good in the foreground (thus "descending" mediation), while mediation points to being "in the middle" between Christ, the other members of the ecclesial community, and the Trinity, integrating the "descending" aspect (seeing that graces reach concrete subjects) with the "ascending" aspect (uniting oneself to the sacrifice of Christ, which "ascends" to God). For this reason, invoking the concept of mediation allows for a fuller perspective to present the salvific task of the Mother of God.[41]

From the Eve-Mary parallelism comes the title "companion" (*socia*) (Gn 3:12: "The woman whom you gave to be with me, she gave me fruit of the tree, and I ate"). The Marian application of Genesis 3:12

38. Augustine, *De sancta virginitate* 6 (PL 40:399), in *LG* 53.

39. *LG* 61 (emphasis ours).

40. Thus, for example, Carolus Balić, "De spiritualis B. V. Mariae maternitatis definibilitate," in *Acta et documenta Concilio Oecumenico Vaticano II Apparando*, Series 1 *(Antepraeparatoria)*, 4, nos. 1, 2 (Vatican City: Typis Polyglottis Vaticanis, 1961), 55–61; Bertrand de Margerie, "Can the Church Define Dogmatically the Spiritual Motherhood of Mary?" in *Mary Coredemptrix, Mediatrix, Advocate: Theological Foundations*, ed. M. Miravalle (Santa Barbara, Calif.: Queenship, 1995), 191–214; Jean Galot, "Maria: Mediatrice o Madre universale?" [Mary: Mediatrix or Universal Mother?], *La Civiltà Cattolica* 1, no. 147 (1996): 244.

41. See Joaquín Ferrer Arellano, *La Mediación Materna de la Inmaculada, esperanza ecuménica de la Iglesia, hacia el quinto dogma mariano: Razones teológicas* [The Maternal Mediation of the Immaculate, Ecumenical Hope of the Church, toward the Fifth Marian Dogma: Theological Reasoning] (Madrid: Arca de la Alianza, 2006), 186–93.

began in the Middle Ages and is found in the passage cited from the *Mariale* (thirteenth century), among other places, which speaks of a threefold association: *associatio in essendo* (in being, inasmuch as Christ's human nature comes from Mary), *in patiendo* (in the Passion: the compassion of the mother), and *in agendo* (in acting: the generation of the Son, help to humanity).[42] Pius XII prefers to use the title *socia*, in part to avoid the debated term of co-redemptrix.[43] The expression then appears, inter alia, in *Lumen gentium*[44] and in the preface of the Mass of the *Mater Boni Consilii* ("you poured out the gifts of your Holy Spirit upon the Blessed Virgin Mary to make her worthy to be the Mother and companion of the Redeemer").[45] The title expresses Mary's nearness to the work of the Redeemer, but at the same time her subordination and dependence.[46]

Eve is not only called the "companion" of Adam, but also "a *helper* (*adiutorium*) fit for him" (Gn 2:18,20). The fathers did not take the step of applying this element to Mariology. To the contrary: Ambrose declares (in regard to Mary's presence under the Cross), "Jesus had no need for a helper for the redemption of all.... He accepted the love of his mother, but sought no help from another."[47] Only with Richard of Saint-Laurent (thirteenth century) is Genesis 2:18 applied to Mariology, but with a change of meaning for Genesis: Mary does not help the Redeemer, but provides an additional help for afflicted humanity. Pseudo-Albert sees Mary as a "helper at the Redemption by means of her compassion"; thus she is (spiritual) mother of all.[48]

42. Pseudo-Albert, *Mariale*, q. 42; see O'Carroll, *Theotokos*, 53f.

43. See Hauke, "Maria, 'compagna del Redentore,'" 52.

44. *LG* 61.

45. *MBVM*, n. 33.

46. See Michael O'Carroll, "Socia: The Word and Idea in Regard to Mary," *Ephemerides Mariologicae* 25 (1975): 337–57; O'Carroll, "Maria Socia, Consors, Adjutrix Christi," in *De cultu mariano s. XII–XV* (Rome: PAMI, 1980), 4:27–51; O'Carroll, *Theotokos*, 53–55; Anton Ziegenaus, "Socia" [Associate], in *ML* 6:194f; Ziegenaus, *Maria in der Heilsgeschichte*, 336f.

47. Ambrose, *In Lucam* X.132 (PL 15:1837C). See *Ep.* 63.110 (PL 16:1218C); *De inst. virg.* 7.49 (PL 16:333).

48. See Pseudo-Albert (Richard of Saint-Laurent), *De laudibus sanctae Mariae* II.1.19; Pseudo-Albert, *Mariale*, q. 42; Ziegenaus, *Maria in der Heilsgeschichte*, 336f.

The Recurrence of the Title "Co-Redemptrix"

Meaning of the Term

The most debated term in modern theology relating to the cooperation of Mary is that of "co-redemption" and the noun "Co-redemptrix."[49] "Co-redemption" per se means nothing other than "cooperation in the Redemption." That was stated in the first systematic presentations, whereas a full debate developed after 1904.[50] The problem often raised is that the term could suggest placing Jesus and Mary on the same level. But this risk also exists to some extent with the word "cooperation," used by the Apostle Paul to indicate participation in the salvific work wrought by God: "We are God's fellow workers (*Theou sunergoi*)" (1 Cor 3:9). The "operation" in which Mary is associated with Christ is indeed the Redemption. No doubt the term "Co-redemptrix" is a strong expression for such involvement, indicating the "singular" cooperation of the Mother of God. This cooperation unfolds by means of the grace of Christ, conferred in advance, starting at the Immaculate Conception.

Before the Term First Appeared

In the early church, the participation of Mary in the Redemption appears primarily under the titles of "new Eve" and "Mother of God." We find strong expressions, such as those of Irenaeus who calls Mary *causa salutis* (commenting on the holy Virgin's *fiat* at the Annunciation).[51] The Akathist Hymn, typical of Eastern spirituality, calls

49. See René Laurentin, "Le titre de Corédemptrice: Étude historique" [The Title of Coredemptrix: Historical Study], *Marianum* 13 (1951): 396–452; Hauke, "Maria, 'compagna del Redentore,'" 50–53; "La cooperazione attiva," 171f, 175–79, 187f; Mark Miravalle, *"With Jesus": The Story of Mary Co-redemptrix* (Goleta, Calif.: Queenship, 2003).

50. See Hauke, *Mary, "Mediatress of Grace": Mary's Universal Mediation of Grace in the Theological and Pastoral Works of Cardinal Mercier* (New Bedford, Mass.: Academy of the Immaculate, 2004), 60–66, 121f.

51. See Irenaeus, *Adversus haereses* III.22.4 (*SC* 211:441); Hauke, "La cooperazione attiva," 165; Manfred Hauke, *Heilsverlust in Adam: Stationen griechischer Erbsündenlehre; Irenäus—Origenes—Kappadozier* [Salvation Lost in Adam: Stages of Greek Teaching on Original Sin; Irenaeus, Origen, the Cappadocians] (Paderborn: Bonifatius, 1993), 265–67. On the early church, see, from the chapter-end bibliography, Carol, *De corredemptione*, 125–50; Maria Francesca Perillo, *Maria nella Mistica: La mediazione mariana in santa Veronica Giuliani* [Mary in Mysticism: Marian Mediation

Mary the "restoration of the fallen Adam" and "redemption (*lútrosis*) of the tears of Eve."[52] St. Andrew of Crete (eighth century) speaks of the "Mother of the Redeemer" and says, "In you (Mary), we have been redeemed from corruption"; "we have all received salvation by means of her."[53] From the tenth century on, Mary occasionally receives the title of *redemptrix* in order to affirm her role as Mother of the Redeemer. Similar expressions accumulate, such as *salvatrix, reconciliatrix, reparatrix*, Mother of the restoration of all, Mother of justification, Gateway of life and salvation.[54]

With the twelfth century, in particular in St. Bernard, the role of Mary at the foot of the Cross was explored further in devout meditations. Through her compassion, Mary is the "mother of sorrows." According to the *Mariale* of Pseudo-Albert, Mary was the *adiutrix redemptionis per compassionem, ita mater fieret omnium per recreationem.*[55] In her heart, the Mother of God suffered the passion that her Son underwent in the body (Arnold of Chartres).[56] In this context "co-redemptive" expressions were born that prepared the ground for the term we are analyzing now. In the visions of St. Bridget of Sweden, Jesus says, "My mother and I saved man as one single heart, I suffering in my heart and in my flesh, she with the sorrow and love of her heart."[57]

The term "co-redemptrix" (*corredemptrix*) also enters the contemplation of the Passion for the first time in a hymn of the fifteenth century, found in a manuscript at Salzburg (Austria):

in St. Veronica Giuliani], CdM 5 (Lugano and Frigento: Eupress FTL, 2004), 135–43; Miravalle, *With Jesus*, 63–73; Hauke, "La cooperazione attiva," 165–67.

52. *Akathist Hymn*, First Chant; English trans. taken from *Byzantine Daily Worship*, ed. J. Raya and J. de Vinck, 968.

53. *Canon in Nativitatem* 4–5 (PG 97:1322B–C); *Canon in Beatae Annae Conceptionem* (PG 97:1307). See Miravalle, *With Jesus*, 79.

54. See Miravalle, *With Jesus*, 82–85.

55. *Mariale*, q. 150, cited in Carol, *De Corredemptione*, 165.

56. See Miravalle, *With Jesus*, 85–88.

57. *Revelationes extravagantes*, c. 3; see also *Revelationes* I.35: Luigi Gambero, *Maria nel pensiero*, 342. See U. Montag and T. Nyberg, "Birgitta von Schweden II. Werke," in *ML* 1:489–91. John Paul II summarizes the message, saying: the saint invokes Mary as "Co-redemptrix" (Address, October 6, 1991: *Insegnamenti di Giovanni Paolo II*, vol. 14, part 2 (Vatican City: Libreria Editrice Vaticana, 1984), 756).

Good, sweet and kind,
Absolutely worthy of no grief;
If you would root out mourning from here,
As one suffering with the redeemer,
For the captured transgressor
You would become co-redemptrix.[58]

From the Appearance of the Term to Its Papal Reception

In the following centuries, the title advanced but also met resistance, as in a work of the jurist Adam von Widenfeld (1673), spread particularly with the efforts of Jansenist circles (against the terms *salvatrix* and *coredemptrix*).[59] In the eighteenth century, the term "redemptrix" was replaced by that of "co-redemptrix" to underscore the role proper to Christ as Redeemer.[60] In 1870, a German bishop wrote a letter to Pius IX asking him to propose the doctrine of the Assumption authoritatively at the Vatican Council, something that a good two hundred bishops desired at the Council itself, and the doctrine of Co-redemption (Johann Theodor Laurent, formerly the ordinary of Luxembourg).[61] The situation of about a hundred years ago was well described in 1914 by B.-H. Merkelbach: "Today the term is used customarily in the French and Italian authors, while generally avoided in the heretical countries."[62] The Belgian Redemptorist François

58. G. M. Dreves and C. Blume, *Analecta hymnica medii aevi* (Leipzig, 1905), 46:126f., n. 79, cited and translated in Miravalle, *With Jesus*, 101–2: *"Pia, dulcis et benigna/Nullo prorsus luctu digna,/Si fletum hinc eligeris/Ut compassa redemptori/Captivato transgressori/Tu corredemptrix fieres."* In the next strophe Mary is also called *redemptrix.*

59. *Monita salutaria Beatae Mariae Virginis ad cultores suos indiscretos* [Salutary Warning from the Blessed Virgin Mary to her Imprudent Devotees] (Ghent, 1673), monitum 10: "Cavendum tamen, ne per hyperbolem vel immoderatum zelum, mihi quidquid tribuas quod soli Deo debetur. Ne itaque me vocaveris Salvatricem aut Corredemtricem." One thesis in this book appears among the errors of the Jansenists rejected by Pope Alexander VIII (1690) (DH 2326). With a span of just two years about forty publications appeared contrary to von Widenfeld (see Carol, *De corredemptione*, 302–21).

60. See Laurentin, "Le titre de Corédemptrice," 413.

61. See the text in Mansi 53, 619, proposed as a *votum dogmaticum.* See Carol, *De corredemptione*, 593.

62. Benoît-Henri Merkelbach, "Mater divinae gratiae" [Mother of Divine Grace], *Revue ecclésiastique de Liège* 10 (1914): 25f., quotation translated. For further witnesses see Carol, *De corredemptione*, 397–404. Initially, Merkelbach prefers to speak of "collaboration" with the Redemption. Later, the theologian changes his opinion and considers that the term, at first sight equivocal, had become

Xavier Godts, author of the first monograph on the Co-redemption (1920), synthesizes the meaning of the term in this way:

Through her close union with the Redeemer and through her continual sharing in all his sufferings, Mary has her part in the work of our Redemption and our salvation, a part secondary and totally subordinate to that of her Son, but no less universal; thus it can be affirmed that in every grace we receive there are the infinite merits of the blood of the Redeemer, to whose sufferings are added those of the Co-redemptrix.[63]

The International Mariological Congress at Rome, held in 1904, was of fundamental importance for the doctrine of Marian mediation, including the title of "co-redemptrix." The address by Alexis-Henri-Marie Lépicier, a Servite father and later cardinal, was decisive: "The Immaculate Virgin Mary, Co-redemptrix of the human race." The address, partly published in 1905, was translated into French and German. This publication was the spark for a controversial debate.[64] But beyond the controversy, the word "co-redemptrix" also appeared in the official language of the church. This happened for the first time during the pontificate of Pius X in documents of the Congregation of Rites[65] and documents of the Holy Office.[66] Pius XI is the first pope to use the title "Co-redemptrix"

commonplace by then, and was used in a correct manner—that is to say, as subordinate cooperation with the Redemption: Benoît-Henri Merkelbach, OP, *Mariologia* (Paris: Desclée, 1939), 333. See Hauke, *Mary, "Mediatress of Grace,"* 62–63.

63. F.-X. Godts, "La Corédemptrice," in *Mémoires et rapports du Congrès Marial tenu à Bruxelles, 8–11 septembre 1921* (Brussels: L'Action Catholique, 1922), 1:157. See also Godts, *La Corédemptrice* (Brussels: Libraire Albert de Wit, 1920).

64. See, particularly, Aléxis-Henri-Marie Lépicier, *L'Immaculée Mère de Dieu, corédemptrice du genre humain* [The Immaculate Mother of God, Coredemptrix of the Human Race] (Turnhout: Imprimerie de l'École Professionnelle, 1906). See Hauke, *Mary, "Mediatress of Grace,"* 12; Hauke, "Alexis-Henri-Marie Lépicier–Förderer der thomistischen Dogmatik und 'Kardinal Mariens'" [Alexis-Henri-Marie Lépicier, Promoter of Thomistic Dogmatic Theology and "Marian Cardinal"], *Doctor Angelicus* 7 (2007): 189–97.

65. See *Acta Sanctae Sedis* 41 (1908): 409.

66. See "Suprema S. Congregatio S. Officii, Decretum," *AAS* 5 (1913): 364; "Decretum," *AAS* 6 (1914): 108. A superb analysis of the use of the term in the official language of the church is by Arthur B. Calkins, "The Mystery of Mary Coredemptrix in the Papal Magisterium," in *Mary Co-redemptrix: Doctrinal Issues Today*, ed. M. Miravalle (Goleta, Calif.: Queenship, 2002), 25–92; earlier in Calkins, "Il mistero di Maria Corredentrice nel magistero pontificio" [The Mystery of Mary Coredemptrix in the Pontifical Magisterium], *Maria Corredentrice* 1 (1998), 141–220. See also Miravalle, *With Jesus*, 155f.

in various statements (1933–35).[67] According to Pius XI, Mary "as a co-sufferer and co-redemptrix" "assisted" her Son "who, on the altar of the Cross, completed the redemption of the human race."[68] Pius XII, on the other hand (at least as pope), consciously avoids the word, probably in order not to enter into the controversy by any action.[69] We find the title of "Co-redemptrix" anew in some speeches by John Paul II, but not in the most relevant documents (such as *Redemptoris Mater*).[70] This usage surely shows that we are not dealing with a forbidden term. It seems interesting to mention an official communiqué of the Commission for the Second Vatican Council (on the schema *De Beata*): "A few expressions and words used by the Supreme Pontiffs, which are most true in the themselves, but which can be very difficult to understand for our separated brethren (especially Protestants), have been omitted. The expression 'Co-redemptrix of the

67. See Miravalle, *With Jesus*, 158f (Allocution to pilgrims from Vicenza, November 30, 1933; Allocution to Spanish pilgrims, March 23, 1934; Radio message on the occasion of the conclusion of the Holy Year at Lourdes, April 28, 1935).

68. Radio message of April 28, 1935, cited in Antonio Maria Calero, *La Vergine Maria nel mistero di Cristo e della Chiesa: Saggio di mariologia* [The Virgin Mary in the Mystery of Christ and the Church: Essay in Mariology] (Leumann [Turin]: Elle Di Ci, 1995), 290; see *L'Osservatore Romano*, April 29–30, 1935, p. 1; *Discorsi di Pio XI*, vol. 3 (1934–1939) (Vatican City: Libreria Editrice Vaticana, 1985).

69. See Hauke, "Maria, 'compagna del Redentore,'" 52f; Miravalle, *With Jesus*, 159–62.

70. See Arthur B. Calkins, "Pope John Paul II's Teaching on Marian Coredemption," in *Mary Coredemptrix, Mediatrix, Advocate: Theological Foundations*, ed. M. Miravalle (Santa Barbara, Calif.: Queenship, 1996), 2:113–46; Hauke, "La mediazione materna," 52–54; Paolo M. Siano, FI, "Uno studio su Maria Santissima 'Mediatrice di tutte le grazie' nel magistero pontificio fino al pontificato di Giovanni Paolo II" [A Study of Mary Most Holy "Mediatrix of All Graces" in the Pontifical Magisterium up to the Pontificate of John Paul II], *Maria Corredentrice* 8 (2006)257f; Lázaro Ilzo Daniel, *La mediazione materna di Maria in Cristo negli insegnamenti di Giovanni Paolo II* [The Maternal Mediation of Mary in Christ in the Teachings of John Paul II], CdM 9 (Lugano and Gavirate [Varese]: Eupress FTL, 2011), 116–18. Addresses of St. John Paul II: "Co-redemptrix of Humanity": General Audience of September 8, 1982 (message to the sick); Angelus on the Feast of St. Charles, Arona, November 4, 1984 ("Co-redemptrix"); discourse at the Marian sanctuary of Guayaquil, Ecuador, January 31, 1985: "Mary's role as Co-redemptrix did not cease with the glorification of her Son" [obviously the term is also being applied to the subjective redemption]; Angelus, May 31, 1985 ("Co-redemptrix"); commemoration of the 600th anniversary of the canonization of St. Bridget of Sweden, October 6, 1991: the saint invokes Mary as (among other things) "Co-redemptrix, exalting Mary's singular role in the history of salvation and in the life of the Christian people." Gherardini, *La corredentrice*, 53f., then presents the densest catechesis on the topic, adding a detail from his own experience: "It is disconcerting, not that the Pope, during the catechesis of April 9, 1997, insists on the part reserved to Mary in the work of salvation, and faithfully completed by Her, but that the 'Osservatore Romano' of April 10 softened the papal catechesis, converting 'Co-redemptrix' into 'singular cooperator'"!

human race' (St. Pius X, Pius XI) can be counted among them."[71] John Paul II, evidently, held that a term "most true in itself" should not be suppressed for diplomatic reasons. Otherwise, would we not also have to sacrifice the title of "Mother of God" (*Theotókos*), which is not pleasing to Protestants?[72]

Beyond the appearance of the terms "co-redemption" and "co-redemptrix" we also need to remain attentive for equivalent expressions, quite present especially since the magisterium of Leo XIII: "Having become the servant (*administra*) of human redemption, she also became, by the virtually unlimited power conferred upon her, the dispensatrix (*administra*) of the grace that flows from that redemption in every age." "The immaculate Virgin, chosen to be the Mother of God, and thereby associated with him in the work of man's salvation, has a favour and power with her Son greater than any human or angelic creature has ever obtained, or ever can gain."[73]

Pius X, in regard to merit, uses the distinction between "merit *de condigno*" and "merit *de congruo*." The first merit (*de condigno*), that of Christ, corresponds exactly to all the requirements of justice, while the merit of Mary (*de congruo*) only indicates a fittingness. "Merit is called thusly when its reward corresponds *not to reasons of strict justice*, but through a benevolent and friendly consideration of the action realized."[74] Pius X affirms in the encyclical *Ad diem illum* (1904) that, since Mary stands "over all in holiness and union with Christ and has been associated with Christ in the work of redemption, she merits for us *de congruo* (in a congruous manner), in the language of theologians, what Christ merits for us *de condigno* (in a condign

71. *Acta Synodalia Sacrosancti Concilii Oecumenici Vaticani secondi*, vol 1, part 4 (Vatican City: Typis Polyglottis Vaticanis, 1971), 99.

72. Among others, Miravalle, *With Jesus*, 169–72, poses the question; see in gentler terms Miravalle, "'Con Gesù': La storia di Maria Corredentrice", *Maria Corredentrice* 8 (2006): 144f. About Protestant reticence regarding the title of "Mother of God," see Achim Dittrich, *Protestantische Mariologie-Kritik: Historische Entwicklung bis 1997 und dogmatische Analyse* [Protestant Criticism of Mariology: Historical Development to 1997 and Dogmatic Analysis], Mariologische Studien 11 (Regensburg: Pustet, 1998), 305–7.

73. See Carol, *De corredemptione*, 514–16; Encyclical *Adiutricem*, 1895 (*PE* 2:136, n. 7; *EE* 3, n. 1220); *Supremi apostolatus officio*, 1883 (*EE* 3, n. 346; *PE* 2:89, n. 2: "associated with him in the work of man's salvation" translates *servandi hominum generis consors facta*).

74. Calero, *La Vergine Maria*, 297.

manner), and she is the supreme minister of the distribution of graces."[75]

In Benedict XV we find this affirmation in 1918: Mary, "as far as it depended on her, offered her Son to placate divine justice; so we may well say that she with Christ redeemed mankind."[76]

In the magisterium of John Paul II, the Marian Catechesis given on April 9, 1997, stands out: it was originally titled (so it appears) "Mary Co-redemptrix" and was reported by the *Osservatore Romano* under the title "Mary's Co-operation Is Totally Unique" (English edition, April 16, 1997):

Down the centuries the Church has reflected on Mary's co-operation in the work of salvation, deepening the analysis of her association with Christ's redemptive sacrifice. St. Augustine already gave the Blessed Virgin the title "cooperator" in the Redemption (cf. *De Sancta Virginitate* 6; PL 40:399), a title which emphasizes Mary's joint but subordinate action with Christ the Redeemer.

Reflection has developed along these lines, particularly since the fifteenth century. Some feared there might be a desire to put Mary on the same level as Christ. Actually the church's teaching makes a clear distinction between the Mother and the Son in the work of salvation, explaining the Blessed Virgin's subordination, as cooperator, to the one Redeemer.

The real possibility for man appears in the statement of St. Paul: "For we are God's fellow workers" (1 Cor 3:9).

However, applied to Mary, the term "cooperator" acquires a specific meaning. The collaboration of Christians in salvation takes place after the Calvary event, whose fruits they endeavour to spread by prayer and sacrifice. Mary, instead, cooperated during the event itself and in the role of mother; thus her cooperation embraces the whole of Christ's saving work. She alone was associated in this way with the redemptive sacrifice that merited the

75. DH 3370.

76. Apostolic Letter *Inter sodalicia* (*AAS* 10 [1918]: 182), English translation in Arthur B. Calkins, "Mary's Presence in the Mass according to Pope John Paul II," in *Mary at the Foot of the Cross*, vol. 6, *Marian Coredemption in the Eucharist* (New Bedford, Mass.: Academy of the Immaculate, 2007), 19. See Miravalle, *With Jesus*, 157f.

salvation of all mankind. In union with Christ and in submission to him, she collaborated in obtaining the grace of salvation for all humanity....

Mary is associated as a woman in the work of salvation. Having created man "male and female" (cf. Gn 1:27), the Lord also wants to place the New Eve beside the New Adam in the Redemption....

Mary, the New Eve, thus becomes a perfect icon of the Church. In the divine plan, at the foot of the Cross, she represents redeemed humanity which, in need of salvation, is enabled to make a contribution to the unfolding of the saving work.[77]

The Theological Debate on Co-Redemption

Theological debate on the co-operation of Mary in the Redemption has been strongly stimulated by requests for a dogmatic definition of the "universal mediation" of Mary, which started in 1915 from the Belgian church, guided by its primate Désiré Cardinal Mercier.[78] The petitions reached what was considered an intermediate result with the pontifical approval of the Mass of "Mary, Mediatrix of all Graces" (1921) for Belgium and for all the other local churches and religious communities that desired this liturgical formulary. As a consequence, "the commemoration of our Lady as mediatrix became almost universal."[79] In the context of the theological debate, which grew vigorously after 1921, a controversy also arose about the title of "Co-redemptrix" and, moreover, on the exact significance of Marian cooperation. The first monograph on co-redemption, that of F.-X. Godts in 1920,[80] found favor with the Belgian primate.[81]

The first phase of the debate was marked by the recognition or

77. CM 48 (April 9, 1997), English translation in John Paul II, *Theotokos: Woman, Mother, Disciple; A Catechesis on Mary, Mother of God* (Boston: Pauline, 2000), 185–87. See Hauke, "Maria, 'compagna del Redentore,'" 58f.

78. See Hauke, *Mary, "Mediatress of Grace"*; Hauke, "Maria, 'Mediatrice di tutte le Grazie' nell'Archivio Segreto Vaticano del Pontificato di Pio XI: Rapporto intermedio sulle tracce trovate," *Immaculata Mediatrix* 7 (2007). See also Gloria Falcão Dodd, *The Virgin Mary, Mediatrix of All Grace: History and Theology of the Movement for a Dogmatic Definition from 1896 to 1964* (New Bedford, Mass.: Academy of the Immaculate, 2012), 65–235.

79. *MBVM*, introduction to formulary n. 30, "The Blessed Virgin Mary, Mother and Mediatrix of Grace."

80. Godts, *La Corédemptrice.*

81. See Hauke, *Mary, "Mediatress of Grace,"* 64.

rejection of Mary's cooperation in the Redemption, a cooperation questioned in 1916 by the report of the Dominican Alberto Lepidi, an adviser of the Holy Office.[82] An analogous opposition was found in some French and German theologians (Jean Rivière, Bernhard Poschmann, and Bernhard Bartmann, the last of whom, however, made a retraction in 1925, impressed by Mercier's movement and by the position of Pius XI).[83] The difficulties are visible in the positions of Cardinal Billot, SJ, very influential within the Holy Office until his dismissal in 1927, and in Maurice de la Taille, SJ, professor at the Gregoriana.[84] The principal objection appears in the reference to Jesus Christ as the one Redeemer: the Redemption has to be considered complete for Mary before she received her first grace. The Redemption as such therefore unfolds without the activity of Mary. The response to this difficulty was formulated by the Jesuit August Deneffe in an article that appeared in the journal "Gregorianum" in 1927: in the sacrifice of Christ two intentions are found, together but logically distinct. "In the first intention, Christ poured out all the fullness of redemption into the one Blessed Virgin Mary, the Woman, the new Eve, spouse of Christ, type of the Church; then, in the second, in union with the will of the Virgin, he obtained redemption for us."[85]

By this explanation it is evident that the redemptive act, in its

82. See Hauke, *Maria, "Mediatrice di tutte le grazie": La mediazione universale di Maria nell'opera teologica e pastorale del Cardinale Mercier*, Collana di Mariologia 6 (Lugano: Eupress FTL, 2005), 209–12; Hauke, "Maria, 'Mediatrice di tutte le Grazie' nell'Archivio Segreto Vaticano del Pontificato di Pio XI: Rapporto intermedio sulle tracce trovate," *Immaculata Mediatrix* 7 (2007)," 119f. See Andrea Villafiorita Monteleone, *Alma Redemptoris Socia: Maria e la Redenzione nella teologia contemporanea* [Beloved Companion of the Redeemer: Mary and the Redemption in Contemporary Theology], CdM 8 (Lugano and Gavirate [Varese]: Eupress FTL, 2010), 15–21 (petition by Lepidi: 447–54); the preceding position of the Belgian bishops from 1915 was published in Hauke, "Riscoperta: La petizione del Cardinale Mercier e dei Vescovi belgi a Papa Benedetto XV per la definizione dogmatica della Mediazione universale delle grazie da parte di Maria (1915): Introduzione teologica e testo originale francese," *Immaculata Mediatrix* 10, no. 3 (2010): 305–38.

83. See Hauke, *Mary, "Mediatress of Grace,"* 31, 62–63.

84. Ibid., 107–11.

85. August Deneffe, "De Mariae in ipso opere redemptionis cooperatione" [Mary in Her Cooperation with the Work of Redemption], *Gregorianum* 8 (1927): 19. See Hauke, *Mary, "Mediatress of Grace,"* 121–24: "In prima intentione Christus totam redemptionis plenitudinem effudit in unam Beatam Virginem Mariam, mulierem Evam novam, Sponsam Christi, typum Ecclesiae; in secunda dein unita cum Virginis voluntate nobis redemptionem acquisivit."

substance, is due uniquely to Christ. Notwithstanding this, it values the unique contribution of Mary in the unfolding of the Redemption itself. Here we can make a comparison with original sin: the responsible party was Adam, and because of this, the fathers speak of a sin "in Adam"; and yet, the very existence of the original sin depends on the co-operation of Eve. The sin of Eve is not an essential part, but an integral part in our downfall. Similarly, the co-operation of Mary presents itself not as an "essential part" but as an "integral part" of our Redemption.[86]

While Marian cooperation considered globally was in play in the first phase of the debate, a second phase looked at the particular role of the presence of Mary under the Cross. Starting in the 1930s, Heinrich Lennerz, SJ, professor of Christology and Mariology at the Gregorian, differentiated between what is called "remote" cooperation in the Redemption, realized in Mary's consent to the Incarnation, and "proximate" cooperation in the sacrifice of the Cross, denied to Mary by the German mariologist. Lennerz also applied to Mary's mediation the terms (from Scheeben) "objective" and "subjective redemption": Mary's mediation only regards subjective redemption (that is, the distribution of the fruits of the Redemption), but the objective redemption not at all.[87] Since Mary has been redeemed, she could not merit the Redemption in any way, not even with *meritum de congruo*. Lennerz was the principal exponent of this "minimalist" tendency.

The subsequent debate highlighted that the Redemption begins already at the Incarnation. This is seen, for example, in the Letter to the Hebrews, which has the redemptive sacrifice begin when the Word assumes human nature (Heb 10:5–10). The fact that Mary maintains her "yes" even under the Cross is thus a true and proper cooperation in the Redemption. The minimalist position has been

86. See Roschini, "Equivoci sulla Corredenzione" [Misunderstandings about Coredemption], *Marianum* 10 (1948): 280f.

87. See Manfred Hauke, "La questione del 'Primo principio,' e l'indole della cooperazione di Maria all'opera redentrice di Cristo: Due temi rilevanti nella mariologia di Gabriele M. Roschini" [The Question of the "First Principle" and the Contribution of Mary to Christ's Work of Redemption: Two Relevant Themes in the Mariology of Roschini], *Marianum* 64, no. 161–62 (2002): 591–97.

surpassed since the International Mariological Congress at Lourdes in 1958, where we find among the exponents of the various schools a unanimous conviction that there exists a true immediate cooperation by Mary in the objective redemption.[88]

The majority tendency is well presented in Gabriele Maria Roschini (†1977), the most famous mariologist of the twentieth century.[89] "Co-redemption" is nothing other than cooperation with the Redemption:

> To "cooperate" means to unite one's own action to that of another, so as to produce, with him, a common work which is the result of two causes, distinct in principle, but associated in their activity and in effect, the end of their action. The work in which the Virgin united her action to that of Christ is the Redemption of the human race. This cooperation can be collateral and independent (for example, two people who pull a cart, each with his own power) or subordinate (for example, two people, one of whom does not act directly by his own power, but by means of power received from the other).[90]

Mary's cooperation in the Incarnation with the *fiat* extends into the entire mystery of salvation. It is not an independent contribution, but subordinate and dependent on the action of Christ. Nonetheless, this is an immediate cooperation by Mary in the objective Redemption. Mary was pre-redeemed in view of the merits of Christ. With Christ and subordinate to him, the Mother of God offered her Son to the Eternal Father, especially on Calvary, for the reconciliation of humanity. First (in logical order) Mary was redeemed (preserved from original sin), and then Mary's cooperation took place: Redeemer → Mary → all redeemed men (and not Redeemer → church, among which was Mary).

An intermediate position is found in some German mariologists of the ecclesiotypical tendency. Its principal exponent is the Pallottine father Heinrich Maria Köster (†1993). Köster starts from the idea of the Covenant between Christ and the church: Mary represents

88. See ibid., 596.

89. See above all Roschini, *Maria Santissima*, vol. 2, and the summary by Parrotta, *La cooperazione di Maria*, 87–131.

90. Roschini, *Maria Santissima*, 2:120.

the church under the Cross, inasmuch as she accepts the sacrifice of Christ. Mary's acceptance is called "receptive co-redemption."[91] This theory has the merit of appreciating the femininity of Mary as type of the church, but does not take account sufficiently of the active contribution that is not only an acceptance of the sacrifice of Christ, but also an active offering directed to the Father, uniting itself profoundly with the expiatory self-giving of her Son.

Vatican II does not lend itself to the minimalist approach, because the conciliar texts confirm a co-operation by Mary in the whole work of salvation.[92] From the Annunciation to the Cross, Mary "in this singular way ... co-operated in the work of the Saviour."[93] The Council, in fact, teaches the doctrine of co-redemption without using the word, for ecumenical reasons. The same is true for the teaching of John Paul II, but with the recovery of the traditional vocabulary. Benedict XVI, without using the technical term, took up the same doctrine.[94] In distinction from the majority tendency before the Council, which was predominantly "Christotypical" (such as, for example, Roschini), *Lumen gentium* and the subsequent pontifical magisterium point more strongly to the "ecclesiotypical" aspect, thus integrating the teaching with some healthy elements of the intermediate position.

91. See Heinrich M. Köster, *Die Magd des Herrn* [The Handmaid of the Lord] (Limburg: Lahn-Verlag, 1947); 2nd ed., 1954; Guilherme Baraúna, *De natura corredemptionis marianae in theologia hodierna (1921–1958): Disquisitio expositivo-critica* [The Nature of Marian Coredemption in Today's Theology: Expository-Critical Inquiry] (Rome: Academia Mariana Internationalis, 1960), 93–164; Andrzej Kazimierz Zielinski, *Maria–Königin der Apostel: Die Bedeutung Mariens nach den Schriften des Palottiner-Theologen Heinrich Maria Köster für das Katholische Apostolat und die Neuevangelisierung in Lateinamerika* [Mary, Queen of Apostles: The Significance of Mary for the Catholic Apostolate and the New Evangelization in Latin America, according to the Pallottine Theologian H. M. Köster] (Frankfurt am Main: Peter Lang, 2000), 192–202; Gherardini, *La corredentrice*, 72f, 346f.

92. See Hauke, "La cooperazione attiva," 183–86.

93. *LG* 61. See Angelico Greco, *"Madre dei viventi": La cooperazione salvifica di Maria nella "Lumen gentium"; Una sfida per oggi* ["Mother of the Living": The Salvific Cooperation of Mary in "Lumen gentium"; A Challenge for Today], CdM 10 (Lugano and Gavirate (Varese): Eupress FTL, 2011).

94. See pp. 104–6.

The Call for a Dogma on the Title "Co-Redemptrix"

At the time of the Second Vatican Council, more than three hundred bishops desired a dogmatic definition on the universal mediation of Mary; about fifty were thinking of a definition of Mary as Co-redemptrix. Taking account of the fact that the universal mediation includes cooperation with salvation, we arrive at about four hundred bishops in favor of a dogmatic definition.[95] The pastoral character of the Council, however, did not allow for the proclamation of new dogmas. The absence of any use of the term "Co-redemptrix," considered "absolutely true in itself," was motivated, as we have seen, by ecumenical reasons, but it appears that there was no discussion on this point during the Council itself. Vatican II attentively describes Mary's cooperation in the (objective) Redemption, but avoids entering into disputed questions.[96]

Since then, a new element has entered, with the request from an international movement launched in 1993, to define a dogma with the three titles "Co-redemptrix, Mediatrix, Advocate."[97] The initiative boasts the written support of more than 550 cardinals and bishops and seven million of the faithful.[98] Among the forty-seven cardinals who have signed the petition are found, among others, Jean-Marie Lustiger (Paris), John O'Connor (New York), and Christoph von Schönborn (Vienna).[99]

The list of the three elements of the petition seems (at least

95. See Antonio Escudero Cabello, *La cuestión de la mediación mariana en la preparación del Vaticano II: Elementos para una evaluación de los trabajos preconciliares* [The Question of Marian Mediation in the Preparation for Vatican II: Elements toward an Evaluation of Preconciliar Works] (Rome: LAS, 1997), 86–92; Ignazio M. Calabuig, "Riflessione sulla richiesta della definizione dogmatica di 'Maria corredentrice, mediatrice, avvocata'" [Reflections on the Request for the Dogmatic definition of "Mary Coredemptrix, Mediatrix, Advocate"], *Marianum* 61 (1999): 139f.

96. See *LG* 54; Hauke, "La mediazione materna," 38–40; Miravalle, *With Jesus*, 167–81.

97. See Mark Miravalle, *Mary Coredemptrix, Mediatrix, Advocate* (Santa Barbara, Calif.: Queenship, 1993) and further works in 1995, 1996, 2000, 2002, 2003, and 2006, listed in the bibliography of this volume. See also the selected bibliography on the debate in Hauke, "La cooperazione attiva," 187f.

98. See Miravalle, *The Immaculate Conception and the Co-redemptrix* (Goleta, Calif.: Queenship, 2004), 36.

99. See the list reported by Paul Maria Sigl, *Die Frau aller Völker: Miterlöserin Mittlerin Fürsprecherin* [The Lady of All Nations: Co-Redemptrix, Mediatrix, Advocate] (Goldach, Switzerland: Familie Mariens der Miterlöserin, 1998), 90f.

at first glance) a bit surprising, referring to three distinct points. Among these three points the title "advocate" needs no definition, because it deals with Mary's involvement carried out through her intercession. The title "mediatrix" (to which we shall return) has appeared since the eighth century in Marian prayer and is seen also in *Lumen gentium*; the Council gives an explanation of the manner of this mediation. John Paul II underscores the maternal mediation of Mary in Christ and calls Mary "mediatrix."[100] In contrast, the title "Co-redemptrix" is less common.

The petition of the movement *Vox Populi Mariae Mediatrici*, under the guidance of the American theologian Mark Miravalle (Franciscan University of Steubenville), in its concrete form, is not explained by its doctrinal content alone. The request for the three Marian titles, it appears, comes from alleged apparitions of Mary to a Dutch seer (Ida Peerdeman, †1996), who claimed to have received messages on this point.[101] In 1951, half a year after the definition of the Assumption, the "Lady of All Nations" asked that the last Marian dogma be defined, although this fact is the object of dispute. She promises that the definition will take place despite the preceding theological controversy and will make the church stronger. The content of the dogma corresponds to the representation of the "Lady of All Nations" before the Cross, opening her hands for the transmission of grace. On May 31, 2002, the bishop of Amsterdam, Mons. Punt, recognized the supernatural character of the messages from 1945 to 1959, and therefore also recognized everything regarding the Marian dogma. Debate over the events, however, has not concluded yet and shows some elements that call for prudence.[102] The bishop

100. *LG* 62. See Hauke, "La mediazione materna"; Siano, "Uno studio su Maria Santissima." Among others, see CM 65 ("Mary's Mediation Derives from Christ's," October 1, 1997).

101. On the following, see Sigl, *Die Frau aller Völker*; Calkins, "The Theological Relevance of Our Lady of All Nations and the Amsterdam Apparitions," in *Mary Coredemptrix, Mediatrix, Advocate: Theological Foundations*, vol. 3, *Contemporary Insights on a Fifth Marian Dogma*, ed. M. Miravalle (Goleta, Calif.: Queenship, 2000), 217–24; P. Klos, "The Specific Message of the Lady of All Nations Regarding the Fifth Marian Dogma," in Miravalle, *Mary Coredemptrix*, 3:225–34. This leads us back also to the messages of the seer of Akita, recognized by the local bishop, in the course of which a statue representing the "Lady of All Nations" (Amsterdam) shed tears: Thomas T. Yasuda, "The Message of Mary Coredemptrix at Akita and Its Complementarity with the Dogma Movement," in Miravalle, *Mary Coredemptrix*, 3:235–49.

102. See, for example, Hildegard Alles, "'Amsterdam'—die Erscheinungen der 'Frau aller

has not respected the earlier negative decision by the Congregation for the Doctrine of the Faith in 1974;[103] a critical analysis reveals elements incompatible with an alleged supernatural origin.[104]

The evaluation of a supernatural origin (or lack thereof) of such a message does not bind theology. Miravalle himself underscores the methodological independence of the movement from the events of Amsterdam. The true and proper sources of theology are not private revelations ("private" in the sense that they do not form part of the public Revelation in Christ, which was completed with the end of the apostolic era). The work of theology, rather, consists in the study of Sacred Scripture and Tradition, to see whether or not there exists a solid foundation for such a doctrine. Prophetic messages (if they are authentic) do not bring doctrinal innovations, but reaffirm already existing realities of the deposit of faith and possibly add some point about action called for in the present time.[105]

The movement for the definition of the new dogma is centered in the United States where, among other things, four volumes have appeared with various articles, including some by noted authors (such as Bertrand de Margerie, Michael O'Carroll, Ignace de la Pot-

Völker'" ["Amsterdam": The Apparitions of the "Lady of All Nations"], *Theologisches* 35, no. 4 (2005): 411–34. Supportive voices are easily found in Sigl, *Die Frau aller Völker*, and on the internet at www.de-vrouwe.info ("The Lady of All Nations"); see also Patrick Sbalchiero, "Amsterdam," in *Dictionnaire des apparitions de la Vierge Marie* [Dictionary of Apparitions of the Virgin Mary], ed. René Laurentin and Patrick Sbalchiero (Paris: Fayard, 2007), 79–84. An intervention of the Congregation for the Doctrine of the Faith (A. Amato) prohibited the public use of the formula (recurring in a prayer "revealed" at Amsterdam) "the lady who once was Mary" (Letter of May 20, 2005, response to a question from the Catholic Bishops' Conference of the Philippines). Subsequently the bishop of Amsterdam published the prayer without that formula, on which the apparition received by the seer had insisted multiple times.

103. See Notification of May 25, 1974: *L'Osservatore Romano*, June 14–15, 1974, 2; republished by Congregation for the Doctrine of the Faith, ed., *Documenta inde a Concilio Vaticano Secondo expleto edita (1966–2005)* [Documents Issued Since the Completion of Vatican II] (Vatican City: Libreria Editrice Vaticana, 2006), 90; Charles J. Scicluna, "Orientamenti dottrinali e competenze del vescovo diocesano e della Congregazione per la Dottrina delle Fede nel discernimento delle apparizioni mariane" [Doctrinal Orientations and Competences of the Diocesan Bishop and of the Congregation for the Doctrine of the Faith], in *Apparitiones Beatae Mariae Virginis in Historia, Fide, Theologia: Acta Congressus mariologici-mariani internationalis in civitate Lourdes Anno 2008 celebrati* (Vatican City: PAMI, 2010), 1:355, note 3.

104. See Hauke, "Die Manifestationen der 'Frau aller Völker': Klärende Hinweise" [The Appearances of the "Lady of All Nations": Clarifying Indications], *Sedes Sapientiae: Mariologisches Jahrbuch* 36, no. 2 (2012): 60–87.

105. We will return to this point in chapter 9, on Marian apparitions.

terie).[106] The opposition of the majority of mariologists to this initiative has been shown in the following: the titles requested are said to be "ambiguous" and, at least for the moment, a definition does not seem opportune, especially for ecumenical reasons. That, in brief, is the statement of an ad hoc theological commission that met at the International Mariological Congress at Czestochowa in 1996.[107]

If we describe "Co-redemption" simply as "cooperation in the work of salvation," there would not have to be any theoretical difficulty about a dogmatic definition. Rather, the problems relate to more exact formulation of the doctrine's content, the atrophy in taking a systematic approach to Marian mediation in the post-conciliar era, and above all the fear of impeding ecumenical progress, especially with Protestants. For the rest, we need to take account of how much time was necessary to reach the definition of the Immaculate Conception and of the Assumption. The definition of a dogma cannot come as a thunderbolt from a serene sky without an adequate preparation on the part of theology and the *sensus fidelium*. Brunero Gherardini (most favorable to the title of Co-redemptrix) writes, "I

106. See these works edited by Miravalle: *Mary Coredemptrix, Mediatrix, Advocate: Theological Foundations* (Santa Barbara, Calif.: Queenship, 1995); *Mary Coredemptrix, Mediatrix, Advocate: Theological Foundations*, vol. 2 (Santa Barbara, Calif.: Queenship, 1996); *Mary Coredemptrix, Mediatrix, Advocate: Theological Foundations*, vol. 3, *Contemporary Insights on a Fifth Marian Dogma* (Goleta, Calif.: Queenship, 2000); *Mary Coredemptrix: Doctrinal Issues Today* (Goleta, Calif.: Queenship, 2002). Along the same lines are a good part of the contributions in *Mary at the Foot of the Cross*, vols. 1–6 (New Bedford, Mass.: Academy of the Immaculate, 2000–2007); *Maria Corredentrice*, vols. 1–8 (Frigento: Casa Mariana Editrice, 1998–2006).

107. Statement of the Theological Commission of the Congress of Czestochowa: *L'Osservatore Romano*, June 4, 1997, 10. See Angelo Amato, "Verso un altro dogma mariano?" *Marianum* 58 (1996): 229–32; Amato, *Gesù il Signore: Saggio di cristologia* [Jesus the Lord: Essay in Christology] (Bologna: EDB, 1999); Calkins, "'Towards Another Marian Dogma?' A Response to Father Angelo Amato, S.D.B.," *Marianum* 59 (1997): 159–67; Calkins, "Marian Co-Redemption and the Contemporary Papal Magisterium," *Immaculata Mediatrix* 6 (2006): 222–24; Calabuig, "Riflessione sulla richiesta"; Antonio Escudero Cabello, "Approcci attuali e proposte teologiche sul tema della cooperazione mariana" [Current Approaches and Theological Proposals on the Topic of Marian Coredemption], *Marianum* 61, no. 155–56 (1999): 177–211; various authors in Miravalle, *Mary Coredemptrix, Mediatrix, Advocate: Theological Foundations*, 3:109–66; Hauke, "Maria, 'compagna del Redentore,'" 56f.; Hauke, "La cooperazione attiva," 187–89; Salvatore M. Perrella, *Ecco tua Madre (Gv 19,27): La Madre di Gesù nel magistero di Giovanni Paolo II e nell'oggi della Chiesa e del mondo* [Behold Your Mother (Jn 19:27): The Mother of Jesus in the Magisterium of John Paul II and in the Church and the World Today] (Cinisello Balsamo: San Paolo, 2007), 409–88; Stefano De Fiores, *Maria sintesi di valori: Storia culturale della mariologia* [Mary, Synthesis of Values: Cultural History of Mariology] (Cinisello Balsamo: San Paolo, 2005), 515–24. It follows that that the statement cited earlier cannot be considered an intervention of the magisterium and that its genesis does provoke some critical questioning.

know well that the seasons of the Church do not always correspond to the accelerations of our times."[108] Moreover, for a dogmatic definition, there should always be some particular motive that makes the greatest commitment of the ecclesial magisterium useful.[109]

In the opinion of the author, it does not make sense to define a dogma with three diverse titles, mainly due to the unequal value among them. A single title would be better—for example, the "universal mediation of Mary," the "motherly mediation of Mary in Christ," or the "universal spiritual motherhood." Mediation is the fullest theme to join the various contents connected with Mary's cooperation in the objective and subjective Redemption. It is not precise, as one very recent and rather artificial systematic explanation proposes, to refer the title "Mediatrix" to the descending mediation (communication of grace to men) and that of "Advocate" to ascending mediation (supplication before God).[110] In fact, mediation com-

108. Gherardini, *La corredentrice*, 11.

109. Ten reasons in favor of the dogmatic definition have been formulated in Miravalle, "Mary Coredemptrix: A Response to 7 Common Objections," in Miravalle, *Mary Co-redemptrix: Doctrinal Issues Today*, 93–138: greater clarity in theological explanation; progress in ecumenism, which must face up to the entire deposit of faith; an adequate development of Marian doctrine; the affirmation of the dignity of the human person and its liberty (in view of Mary's "yes" at the Annunciation and under the Cross); the promotion of the dignity of woman; emphasis on the human cooperation owed to divine grace; the redemptive value of suffering; greater unity within the church by means of a pontifical definition; the promotion of the testimony of the Saints of the twentieth century; a new "effusion of grace" after the declaration. Ten contrary reasons, on the other hand, are listed in Hendro Munsterman, *Marie corédemptrice? Débat sur un titre marial controversé* (Paris: Cerf, 2006), 65–81. See also my critical review on Munsterman in *Revue d'Histoire Ecclésiastique* 101, no. 3–4 (2006): 1318–22.

110. This distinction entered into a petition addressed to the supreme pontiff by various bishops and cardinals who met in a symposium at Fatima (May 2005). The signers propose the following formulation of a dogmatic definition: *"Iesus Christus, hominis Redemptor in Cruce pendens, dedit hominibus Matrem suam tamquam omnium populorum Matrem spiritualem istam, videlicet Coredemptricem, quae et sub Filio suo et cum Eo in omnium populorum redemptione cooperata est, istam videlicet omnium gratiarum Mediatricem quae omnia dona aeternae vitae nobis portat, istam videlicet Advocatam quae preces nostras Filio suo facit praesentes."* The text was not reproduced in the acts of the symposium, which do not justify such a proposal: *Mary, "Unique Cooperator in the Redemption"*; but rather in Ferrer, *La Mediación Materna*, 311. With a letter on January 1, 2008, addressed to all the cardinals and bishops of the Catholic world, five of the cardinals present at the symposium at Fatima sent out this request at the worldwide level. See the petition on the site www.motherofallpeoples.com, which is edited by Miravalle. The distinction appears, for the first time, it seems, in Miravalle, *Mary Coredemptrix, Mediatrix, Advocate* (1993), 55f; see also Calkins, "Il dogma auspicato: Il come e il perché" [The Hoped-for Dogma: How and Why], *Immaculata Mediatrix* 1, no. 2 (2001): 43–64 (58f.). The novelty of the proposal, in turn, consists in putting the three titles requested under the term "spiritual motherhood."

prehends both the ascending and the descending aspects;[111] moreover, the communication of graces is carried out by means of the intercession of the Blessed Virgin, as John Paul II affirms.[112]

The title "Co-redemptrix," however, points rather to cooperation in the objective Redemption, culminating at the Cross. To place the title "Mediatrix" after that of "Co-redemptrix" suggests an explanation that reduces it to the distribution of graces, thus to the subjective Redemption. Still, supporting a Marian dogma that highlights the maternal task of Mary in relation to her children remains an interesting point, though probably requiring a long time yet. In this way we can be certain that the doctrinal content requested already forms part of the ordinary magisterium of the church.

MARY AS DISPENSATRIX OF GRACES

Introduction

This maternity of Mary in the order of grace began with the consent which she gave in faith at the Annunciation and which she sustained without wavering beneath the cross, and lasts until the eternal fulfillment of all the elect. Taken up to heaven she did not lay aside this salvific duty, but by her constant intercession continued to bring us the gifts of eternal salvation.... Therefore the Blessed Virgin is invoked by the Church under the titles of Advocate, Auxiliatrix, Adjutrix, and Mediatrix. This, however, is to be so

111. Regarding "ascending" and "descending" mediation, see "Mary as Spiritual 'Mother,' 'Companion,' and 'Helper'" in this chapter and the ongoing use of this schema (descending/ascending mediation) in Christology, for example, in Fernando Ocáriz, Lucas F. Mateo-Seco, and José A. Riestra, *Il mistero di Cristo: Manuale di Cristologia*, trans. from Spanish by Carla Rossi Espagnet (Rome: Apollinare Studi, 2000), 151: "The mediation of Christ has a double significance, *ascending*, inasmuch as He offers God adoration, gratitude, expiation for sins, and prayer in the name of men; and *descending*, inasmuch as Jesus causes all the divine gifts, all the graces of salvation, to reach men." In an analogous way, one could speak of two phases of mediation, the phase of coredemption and that of intercession, as does the manual by Benoît-Henri Merkelbach, OP, *Mariologia* (Paris: Desclée, 1939), 323, 345, which is the mature fruit of systematic discussions about the aforementioned initiative of Cardinal Mercier, and which distinguishes thus: *"Dei Mater mediatrix est primario ut adiutrix redemptionis"—"Dei Mater quoque est mediatrix ut perpetua pro nobis apud Deum advocata."*

112. See John Paul II, *RM* 21, 40; *Rosarium Virginis Mariae* (2002) 15; Hauke, "La mediazione materna," 61f. Separating mediation from intercession, one arrives at the much-discussed theory of a physical causality in the communication of graces: see "Is There a 'Physical' or 'Moral' Causality in Mary's Mediation?" in this chapter.

> understood that it neither takes away from nor adds anything to the dignity and efficaciousness of Christ the one Mediator ... the unique mediation of the Redeemer does not exclude but rather gives rise to a manifold cooperation which is but a sharing in this one source.
>
> The Church does not hesitate to profess this subordinate role of Mary. It knows it through unfailing experience of it and commends it to the hearts of the faithful, so that encouraged by this maternal help they may the more intimately adhere to the Mediator and Redeemer.[113]

This article of *Lumen gentium* offers a synthesis of the role of Mary as dispensatrix of graces. This function is rooted in the cooperation of Mary in the work of salvation on earth and consists essentially of intercession. It does not impede direct contact with Jesus (like a secretary in a boss's front office), but acts as a go-between for a direct meeting.[114] Mary's mediation makes the Christian able to unite himself more profoundly to Christ.

To understand how Mary's mediation does not prevent immediate contact with him, we can apply the example of the meeting of two people that happens by means of a third. Or rather, let us imagine a conversation between two people in which the presence of a third favors the hearing of one person's request by the other.

The Historical Trail of This Concept

Biblical Basis

The biblical approach presupposes what has been said earlier about Mary's cooperation in the work of salvation,[115] including her cooperation in bringing the Redemption to fulfillment in individual believers. The Johannine scene that presents Mary under the Cross is very significant: having united herself to the sacrifice of the Redeemer, the Mother of God receives John, who is a prototype of all

113. *LG* 62.

114. See *LG* 60.

115. See, among others, Commissio Belgica, "De definibilitate mediationis B. V. Mariae" [The Definability of Marian Mediation], *Marianum* 47 (1985): 100–147, originally published in 1923; see Hauke, *Mary, "Mediatress of Grace,"* 81–83); Roschini, *Maria Santissima*, 2:207–32; Gerhard L. Müller, "Mittlerin der Gnade," in *ML* 4:488f; O'Carroll, *Theotokos*, 238–45; Perillo, *Maria nella Mistica*, 193–207, 266–89; Siano, "Uno studio su Maria Santissima."

who belong to Christ (Jn 19: 25–27), as a spiritual son. This interpretation only begins to appear with clarity from the twelfth century on (Rupert of Deutz), but it is already based on the Johannine symbolism in which the beloved disciple (whose name is not given) brings an openness that goes beyond the literal sense.[116] The connection of the *testamentum crucis* with the universal spiritual motherhood of Mary is a common teaching of the modern pontifical magisterium, borne in mind by John Paul II, among others.[117]

> One can say that if Mary's motherhood of the human race had already been outlined, now it is clearly stated and established. It *emerges* from the definitive accomplishment *of the Redeemer's Paschal Mystery*. The Mother of Christ, who stands at the very center of this mystery—a mystery that embraces each individual and all humanity—is given as mother to every single individual and all mankind. The man at the foot of the Cross is John, "the disciple whom he loved." But it is not he alone. Following tradition, the Council does not hesitate to call Mary *"the Mother of Christ and mother of mankind"*: since she "belongs to the offspring of Adam she is one with all human beings.... Indeed she is 'clearly the mother of the members of Christ ... since she cooperated out of love so that there might be born in the Church the faithful.'"[118]

The universal role of Mary, the new Eve ("Woman") is already hinted at in the wedding at Cana, when the Mother of God obtains from her Son the first miracle, sign of the new covenant (Jn 2:1–11). The "episode at Cana in Galilee offers us a sort of *first announcement of Mary's mediation*, wholly oriented towards Christ and tending to the revelation of his salvific power."[119] The mystery of the Visitation points out how the sanctification of John the Baptist is connected with the arrival of the Mother of God (Lk 1:41–45).

116. See among others, Ignace de la Potterie, *Maria nel mistero dell'alleanza* [Mary in the Mystery of the Covenant] (Genoa: Marietti, 1988), 229–51; Stefano M. Manelli, *All Generations Shall Call Me Blessed: Biblical Mariology*, 2nd ed. (New Bedford, Mass.: Academy of the Immaculate, 2005), 371–90. See also p. 68.

117. See Arthur B. Calkins, *Totus tuus: John Paul II's Program of Marian Consecration and Entrustment*, 3rd ed. (1992; New Bedford, Mass.: Academy of the Immaculate, 1997), 205–17; Hauke, "La mediazione maternal," 67f.

118. *RM* 23b, with reference to *LG* 53f.

119. *RM* 22a.

The Era of the Fathers

According to the fathers, the mediating activity of Mary is realized in her role as new Eve and as Mother of God. We find very strong expressions in the most famous Marian homily of antiquity, attributed to Cyril of Alexandria at the Council of Ephesus:

> Through you ... the fallen creation is brought back to paradise, all creatures trapped in idolatry come to know of the truth. Through you, holy baptism and the oil of gladness are administered to believers; through you, churches are established throughout the world; the peoples are led to conversion.... Through you, the prophets made their predictions, and the apostles preached salvation to the nations; through you the dead rise, sovereigns reign, and through you the Holy Trinity reigns.[120]

In this passage, it appears that Mary is presented as a personal instrument of the action of the Trinity, in a manner corresponding to the trinitarian function of the church.

The terminology that corresponds to the title of "mediatrix," with various nuances, is presented with particular richness in the Greek milieu after the Council of Ephesus. Among others, see the expression *mesiteúousa*, evidenced for the first time in the fifth century, in Basil of Seleucia.[121] Romanos the Melodist (sixth century) uses the word *mesítes*, used in the New Testament for Jesus Christ himself.[122] The Latin title *mediatrix* for Mary's mediation in Christ has appeared since the sixth century, in a writing attributed to Origen,[123] then in Paul the Deacon, an author of the Carolingian era (eighth century): interceding for sinners, Mary is "mediatrix between the Son and men."[124]

120. Hom. 4 (PG 77:992–96). English trans. in Luigi Gambero, *Mary and the Fathers of the Church: The Blessed Virgin Mary in Patristic Thought*, trans. Thomas Buffer (San Francisco: Ignatius Press, 1999), 247–48.

121. Basil of Seleucia, *Oratio* 39.5 (PG 85:444A); see O'Carroll, *Theotokos*, 72, 240.

122. See O'Carroll, *Theotokos*, 240; Gambero, *Mary and the Fathers*, 327.

123. Pseudo-Origen, *Hom. in Mt* 12:38 (Florilegium Cassinense II.154B), mentioned in O'Carroll, *Theotokos*, 241.

124. Paul the Deacon, *Hom. 45 in Assump.* (PL 95:1496C). See Müller, *Mittlerin*, 488; Luigi Gambero, *Maria nel pensiero dei teologi latini medievali* [Mary in the Thought of the Medieval Latin Theologians] (Cinisello Balsamo: Ed. Paoline, 2000), 59. English trans. from Gambero, *Mary in the Middle Ages*, 57.

The dispensation of graces embraces the whole church. Augustine affirms: Mary is "the mother of the members of Christ … having cooperated by charity that faithful might be born in the Church, who are members of that Head."[125]

Mary's universal dispensation of graces is affirmed in the East, especially by Germanus of Constantinople (†733): "None receives salvation if not through Mary; grace is given to none if not through her."[126] The Akáthist hymn praises Mary as the "celestial ladder by whom God came down," as the "bridge leading earthly ones to heaven,"[127] and as the one "through whom creation is renewed."[128]

The Middle Ages

Thomas Aquinas explains, as noted earlier, the concept of mediation: the one mediator is Christ inasmuch as he brings about the union of God and man, but other persons become involved to prepare for this union (*dispositive*) or to help it be shared (*ministerialiter*).[129]

In the Middle Ages the question arose, whether all graces (after the Assumption of Mary into heaven) are given by Christ by means of Mary. This conviction is expressed with vigor in the West by Anselm (†1109): all the gifts of God in Jesus Christ (reconciliation of the sinner, new life, protection from the final judgment) have come to us also through Mary who bore Christ for us.[130] The intercession of the mother begs for reconciliation with the Son. Bernard of Clairvaux compares Mary to an "aqueduct" and emphasizes, "This is the will of him who wanted us to receive everything through Mary."[131]

125. *De sancta virg.* 6 (PL 40:399), quoted in *LG* 53.

126. *Orat. in zonam B. Mariae* (PG 98:280). On Germanus, see Erasmo Perniola, *La mariologia di san Germano patriarca di Costantinopoli* [The Mariology of St. Germanus, Patriarch of Constantinople] (Rome: Edizioni Padre Monti, 1954), 167–75; Roschini, *Maria Santissima*, 2:216–21.

127. Akathist Hymn, Third Chant (*Byzantine Daily Worship*, 969).

128. Ibid. See Ermanno M. Toniolo, OSM, *Akathistos: Saggi di critica e di teologia* [Akathistos: Critical and Theological Essays] (Rome: Centro di cultura mariana "Madre della Chiesa," 2000), 9f.

129. See "Preliminary Note" in this chapter.

130. *Oratio* 5–7 (e.g., Or. 7, vv. 102–4: "Palace of universal propitiation, cause of general reconciliation, vase and temple of life and universal salvation"; English trans. from Anselm of Canterbury, *The Prayers and Meditations of St. Anselm*, trans. Benedicta Ward (Harmondsworth: Penguin, 1979). See Inos Biffi and Costante Marabelli, eds., *Anselmo d'Aosta. Orazioni e meditazioni* (Milan: Jaca, 1997).

131. *Sermo in Nativ. BMV* 3.10 (PL 183:100), quoted by, among others, Pius XI, Enc. *Ingravescentibus malis* (1937) (*PE* 3:221, n. 8; *EE* 5, n. 1330). On Bernard, see Otto Stegmüller and

Bernardine of Siena uses the metaphor of a neck that joins the body with the head: She "is the neck of our head, by means of which he imparts all spiritual gifts to his mystical body."[132] Along the same line is a famous saying of Dante, quoted among others by Leo XIII, Pius XII, and John Paul II: "Lady, thou art so great and so powerful, that whoever desires grace yet does not turn to thee, would have his desire fly without wings."[133]

The Modern Era

In the magisterium of the popes of the modern age we find some very decisive affirmations on the mediation of all graces by Mary.[134] *Leo XIII*, in his 1891 encyclical on the rosary, refers to Thomas Aquinas according to whom Mary's consent at the Annunciation represents all human nature, as if the Word wished "to consummate thus a mystical union between Himself and all mankind." "With equal truth may it be also affirmed that, by the will of God, Mary is the intermediary through whom is distributed unto us this immense treasure of mercies gathered by God, for mercy and truth were created by Jesus Christ. Thus as no man goeth to the Father but by the Son, so no man goeth to Christ but by His Mother."[135]

The pope adds the idea that Jesus, "from the cross ... entrusted to her care and love the whole of the race of man in the person of His disciple John." And Mary, from that moment, begins "accepting the charge of her maternal duties towards us all"[136] (see Jn 19:26–27). Or again, in another encyclical, "'Behold thy son.' Now in John, as the Church has constantly taught, Christ designated the whole human race, and in the first rank are they who are joined with Him by faith."[137]

Helmut Riedlinger, "Bernhard von Clairvaux I. Leben und Werk" [Bernard of Clairvaux. I. Life and Work], in *ML* 1:445–47; Gambero, *Mary in the Middle Ages*, 135–36.

132. *Quadrag. de Evangelio aeterno* X.3.3, quoted in Pius X, Enc. *Ad diem illum* (*PE* 3:165, n. 13; *EE* 4, n. 26).

133. Divine Comedy, *Paradiso* 33.13–15. See Leo XIII, Enc. *Augustissimae Virginis* (1897) (*PE* 2:142, n. 9; *EE* 3, n. 1350); Pius XII (*AAS* 32 [1940]: 145); John Paul II, Apostolic Letter *Rosarium Virginis Mariae*, 16.

134. See Siano, "Uno studio su Maria Santissima."

135. Leo XIII, Encyclical *Octobri mense* (*PE* 2:118, n. 4; *EE* 3, n. 949).

136. Ibid. (*PE* 2:118, n. 5; *EE* 3, n. 950).

137. Enc. *Adiutricem populi*, 1895 (*PE* 2:136, n. 6; *EE* 3, n. 1219).

The idea of seeing the spiritual motherhood of Mary prefigured in the mission entrusted to her by Jesus is expressed for the first time, it seems, only in the Middle Ages by Anselm of Lucca (†1086) and Rupert of Deutz (†1129).[138] There is debate as to whether this interpretation corresponds in fact to the literal sense of the Johannine text.[139] In any case, there is a point of contact with the Gospel text. The theme has been deepened by John Paul II, as has already been indicated.

The exercise of Mary's spiritual motherhood begins fully with the Assumption into Heaven, as Leo XIII indicates. "From her heavenly abode she began ... to watch over the Church, to assist and befriend us as our Mother; so that she who was so intimately associated with the mystery of human salvation is just as closely associated with the distribution of the graces which for all time will flow from the Redemption."[140]

Like Leo XIII, Pius X also teaches Mary's distribution of all graces, in the encyclical *Ad diem illum*, published in 1904, upon the fiftieth anniversary of the dogmatic declaration of the Immaculate Conception:

When the supreme hour of the Son came, beside the Cross of Jesus there stood Mary His Mother, ... And from this community of will and suffering between Christ and Mary she merited to become most worthily the Repa-

138. See René Laurentin, *A Short Treatise on the Virgin Mary* (Washington, N.J.: Ave Maria Institute, 1991), 112. Still there are prefigurations. John Paul II, *RM* 23, n. 47, cites Origen: No one can perceive the importance of the Gospel according to St. John "if he has not put his head on the breast of Jesus and received Mary from Jesus, as a mother." (*In Ioan.* 1.6; see Ambrose, *Expos. Evang. sec. Luc.* X.129–31). On the meaning of this text, see Laurentin, *Short Treatise*, 72f., 112. It does not yet signify the universal spiritual maternity of Mary, but rather: "the disciples of Christ, inasmuch as they are identified with the Savior, are sons of Mary" (ibid., 105). It seems, though, that the testimony of George of Nicodemia (ninth century) goes a step further: the words "Behold your son" also signify the other disciples (on the other hand, it is not clear who are these "others": all Christians? see Laurentin, *Short Treatise*, 303).

139. See, for example, the commentary of Schnackenburg, *Il Vangelo di Giovanni*, vol. 3, comparing it with the work of de la Potterie, *Maria nel mistero dell'alleanza*, and Serra (see the bibliography). Because of the exegetical dispute, the interpretation was avoided in the text of *Lumen gentium*: Ziegenaus, *Maria in der Heilsgeschichte*, 225. The motivations chosen by Cardinal Bea, however, were not of a theological order but rather diplomatic, taking account of the difficulties of Protestants: see René Laurentin, *La Vierge au Concile* (Paris: P. Lethielleux, 1965), 107–9; Hauke, "La mediazione materna," 68.

140. Enc. *Adiutricem populi* (1895) (*PE* 2:136, n. 7; *EE* 3, n. 1220).

ratrix of the lost world (Eadmeri Mon. *De Excellentia Virg. Mariae*, c. 9) and Dispensatrix of all the gifts that Our Savior purchased for us by His Death and by His Blood.

It cannot, of course, be denied that the dispensation of these treasures is the particular and peculiar right of Jesus Christ, for they are the exclusive fruit of his Death, who by his nature is the mediator between God and man.... [Mary is] the most powerful mediatrix and advocate of the whole world with her Divine Son (Pius IX, *Ineffabilis*).... Mary, as St. Bernard justly remarks, is the channel (Serm. *De Aqueductu* n. 4), or ... the connecting portion the function of which is to join the body to the head.... We mean the neck. Yes, says St. Bernardine of Siena, "she is the neck of Our Head, by which He communicates to His mystical body all spiritual gifts".... She merits for us *de congruo*, in the language of theologians, what Jesus Christ merits for us *de condigno*.... Jesus "sitteth on the right hand of the majesty on high" (Heb 1:3). Mary [as Queen] "sitteth at the right hand of her Son."[141]

Benedict XV (1921) permitted all the ordinaries of the world who asked, following the example of Belgium, to celebrate the liturgical office and the Mass of Mary, Mediatrix of all Graces (May 31). On the other hand, the pope did not take a position on the request made by the Belgian bishops (with Cardinal Mercier, 1915) to make a dogma of the universal mediation of all graces by Mary. The Mass "Mary, Mediatrix of all Graces" became widespread.[142] Following the example of this text, a formulary was introduced in the Missal of the BVM (1986) with the more modest title of "Virgin Mary, mother and mediatrix of grace." This later formulary is, as it were, the "successor" of the prior one, and is set on May 8.[143]

The universal mediation of Mary is now a secure part of the ordinary magisterium, well visible in various interventions of John Paul II, which also use the formula "Mediatrix of all graces."[144] With

141. *Ad diem illum*, (1904) (*PE* 3:165, n. 12–14; *EE* 4, nn. 12–14).

142. See Hauke, *Mary, "Mediatress of Grace,"* 54–60.

143. The text was used from 1971 on; see the historical introduction on this Mass: *MBVM*, 216, n. 30: "the commemoration of our Lady as mediatrix became almost universal."

144. See Miravalle, *With Jesus*, 58–62; Hauke, "La mediazione materna," 82–90; Siano, "Uno studio," 248–53. For the universal character of Mary's mediation see, above all, *RM* 40a, 45c, 47b; CM 62 (September 24, 1997), n. 2. The formula "Mediatrix of all graces," as found in Calkins's research, appears seven times, in allocutions of Dec. 1, 1978, Aug. 30, 1980, Jan. 17, 1988, Apr. 10, 1988,

analogous terms, Benedict XVI also teaches the same doctrine: "There is no fruit of grace in the history of salvation that does not have as its necessary instrument the mediation of Our Lady.... Let us give thanks to God the Father, to God the Son, to God the Holy Spirit from whom, through the intercession of the Virgin Mary, we receive all the blessings of heaven."[145]

A Universal Mediation

The doctrine of the ordinary magisterium does not yet teach with full clarity, as a truth of the Faith, that Mary is the dispensatrix of *all* graces. Mary can be called "mediatrix of all graces," inasmuch as she bore the Redeemer to the world. We also find a consensus on the fact that the Mother of God, by her intercession in heaven, can communicate all salvific graces to all men. At the time of Cardinal Mercier, there was no concern about particular objections to the universal mediation of the Mother of God.[146]

On the other hand, there was discussion about the exact manner in which the spiritual maternity of Mary needs to be specified. Evidently Mary was not able to merit grace, properly speaking, as Fr. Godts thought (to note briefly a common criticism); for this reason, some theologians hesitated to call her "mediatrix of *all* graces." This "limitation" is, however, shared with the one mediator himself, Jesus Christ, who was not able to merit the grace communicated to his human nature at the moment of the Incarnation. Yet we do not stop calling the Lord the universal mediator of all graces.

Another objection relates to graces communicated before the Assumption of Mary into heaven, particularly the graces of the Old Testament, for which the Mother of God could not yet intervene with her intercession. This "limitation" is also shared by Jesus Christ—who is mediator, as he is man—who was not able to act in

Jul. 2, 1990, Sep. 18, 1994, Jun. 28, 1996 (*Insegnamenti di Giovanni Paolo II*, vol. 1, 250; vol. 3, part 2, 495; vol. 11, part 1, 119; vol. 11, part 1, 863; vol 13, part 2, 17; vol. 17, part 2, 344f; vol. 19, part 1, 1638).

145. Homily on the occasion of the canonization of Frei Galvão OFM (Brazil), May 11, 2007; Daniel, *La mediazione materna di Maria*, 190–97.

146. See Hauke, *Mary "Mediatress of Grace,"* 120–21.

the Old Testament era. The graces of the Old Testament were given, so to speak, in view of the Redemption by Christ on the Cross, and we can make the same affirmation in view of Mary's association with the redemptive sacrifice. So we need to distinguish between graces given "in view" of the salvific role of Mary as the new Eve and graces imparted as a consequence of her heavenly intercession, which could attain a universal range only when the Assumption into heaven took place (when Mary entered into the beatific vision, seeing God "face to face"). The reference of Vatican II to the "manifold intercessions" of Mary,[147] points, it seems, to the merit of the Mother of God: this merit, obtained in the grace of Christ, "appeals" to God to distribute grace to all men redeemed by the Savior. Thomas Aquinas calls the merits of the saints *oratio interpretativa*— that is, a de facto petition even without explicit intercession (*oratio expressa*).[148]

A third objection relates to sacramental graces, communicated *ex opere operato* by Christ by means of a human minister. What is their connection with the intervention of Mary? Some theologians have wanted to restrict Marian mediation to actual graces and exclude sacramental graces. This restriction forgets that the intervention of Mary takes place on a different level than that of sacramental actions. In any case, we can also connect baptismal graces to the merit of Mary, associated to the infinite merit of Christ. The Akathist Hymn, to bring only one example, lets the graces of the sacraments of initiation also depend on Mary's intervention.[149]

Let us also state that the universal intercession of Mary and the

147. *LG* 62.

148. See Thomas Aquinas, *ST* Suppl., q. 72, a. 3. See the authoritative voice of one of the two principal editors (even if the caution of the formulation is surprising): Gérard Philips, *La Chiesa e il suo mistero nel Concilio Vaticano II: Storia, testo e commento della Costituzione Lumen gentium* [The Church and Her Mystery in Vatican II: The Constitution "Lumen gentium"; History, Text, and Commentary] (1975; repr. Milan: Jaca, 1993), 560: "Perhaps in saying this the Council is alluding to the scholastic distinction between the formal request and the memory of acquired merits." In contrast, the proposal of Roschini, *Maria Santissima*, 2:202, that intercession "is vested with a double modality: that of the moral cause ... and that of the instrumental physical cause ...," seems less credible. It does not seem to us that scholastic or neoscholastic theology discussed an instrumental physical cause under the term of "intercession."

149. Akathist Hymn, Twenty-First Chant: "Hail, for you have raised the many-lighted Star; hail, for you have opened the many-coursed Stream! Hail, O you who traced the living Model of the Pool; hail, O you who erased the stain of sin!" (*Byzantine Daily Worship*, 978). See Toniolo, *Akathistos*, 143f.

more limited intercession of the saints do not exclude one another, as was determined by the debate occasioned by a healing at Lourdes: the Blessed Virgin was invoked through the intercession of Blessed Joan of Arc. Benedict XV recognized on this occasion that the Mother of God, quite on her own, is "Mediatrix of all graces."[150]

Is There a "Physical" or "Moral" Causality in Mary's Mediation?

Explicit or "accredited" intercession (*oratio espressa vel interpretativa*) possesses a moral causality in the sense that it makes appeal to the will of God, who grants his grace, which he connects with the cooperation of the saints. The adjective "moral" therefore refers to dependence on the will of God, conferred in a singular way for every case. Besides this, some mariologists propose a so-called "physical" efficacy, in which an instrumental cause acts under the power of a principal cause. The Mother of God's way of acting resembles the Thomist explanation of the humanity of Christ and of the sacraments: in Thomas Aquinas the operation of the humanity of Christ, under the power of his divinity, is compared to the operation of an arm, by means of which a person acts (the arm appears as an *instrumentum coniunctum*); in contrast, a staff moved by a human arm is compared to the sacraments (as *instrumenta separata*). In this way, salvific power is transmitted by the divinity of Christ, by means of his humanity, in the sacraments.[151] "Physical" causality thus constitutes a more immediate action, in comparison to the "moral" action in which explicit appeal is made in each case to the will of God.

At the philosophical level, there do not seem to be any obstacles in principle to attributing a "physical" causality to the Mother of God, but doubts remain in regard to the suitability of such a way of acting.[152] We need to take account of the specific efficacy of sac-

150. See Hauke, *Mary "Mediatress of Grace,"* 52, 110–11.

151. Thomas Aquinas, *ST* III, 62, a. 5.

152. The fullest statement on this theme, in favor of a physical causality, is that of Gabriele M. Roschini, "De natura influxus B. M. Virginis in applicatione Redemptionis" [The Nature of the Influence of the BVM in Application to the Redemption], in PAMI, *Maria et Ecclesia* (Vatican

ramental actions worked *ex opere operato* in the person of Christ, the head of the church. Mary does not participate in this headship. John Paul II affirms that the mediation of the Blessed Virgin has the "nature of intercession" and thus remains in the realm of moral causality.[153] Marian mediation is seen under the title of the priesthood of all the faithful in Christ, albeit in a most excellent manner as archetype and Mother of the church. This seems evident in a passage in the encyclical on the Eucharist: Mary's assent at the Annunciation is not compared to the words of consecration spoken by the consecrated priest, but with "the *Amen* which every believer says when receiving the body of the Lord."[154]

The Integrative Character of the Doctrine of the Universal Mediation of Mary

Cardinal Mercier's initiatives for a definition of the dogma of the universal mediation of Mary came to a halt after his passing in 1926. Of the three pontifical commissions instituted by Pius XI between 1922 and 1924, two gave a positive opinion: the Belgian commission (1923) and the Spanish (1925).[155] The results of the Roman commission (1925), on the other hand, were not published,[156] although one of the four expert reports, that of Garrigou-Lagrange, has been recovered.[157] From what is known to date, the obstacles to the defini-

City: AMI, 1959), 2:223–95. See also Alessandro M. Apollonio, "Maria Santissima Mediatrice di tutte le grazie: La natura dell'influsso della Beata Vergine nell'applicazione della Redenzione," *Immaculata Mediatrix* 7 (2007): 157–81. A contrary explanation is found, among others, in Merkelbach, *Mariologia*, 367–71.

153. See *RM* 21, 40, and others. See Hauke, "La mediazione materna di Maria secondo Papa Giovanni Paolo II" [Mary's Maternal Mediation according to Pope John Paul II], *Maria Corredentrice* 7 (2005)61f.

154. John Paul II, Encyclical Letter *Ecclesia de Eucharistia* (2003), 55.

155. See Hauke, *Mary "Mediatress of Grace,"* 75–88.

156. See ibid., 97–112; Hauke, "Maria, 'Mediatrice di tutte le Grazie' nell'Archivio Segreto Vaticano del Pontificato di Pio XI: Rapporto intermedio sulle tracce trovate," *Immaculata Mediatrix* 7 (2007).

157. Published in Hauke, *Mary, "Mediatress of Grace,"* 137–56; see also, with a fuller commentary, Hauke, "Das Gutachten von Garrigou-Lagrange zur dogmatischen Definition der universalen Mittlerschaft Mariens: Einführung, Text und Kommentar" [The Heritage of Garrigou-Lagrange on the Dogmatic Definition of the Universal Mediation of Mary; Introduction, Text, and Commentary], *Doctor Angelicus* 4 (2004): 37–90.

tion do not seem to have come very much from the aforementioned objections, but rather from issues about co-redemption, the likely motive for Cardinal Billot's resistance. Plans for Vatican II, already underway during the pontificate of Pius XI, did, however, anticipate the topic of the universal mediation of Mary and that of the Assumption.[158]

Both Pius XII and the Second Vatican Council avoided proceeding to the dogmatic proclamation of the universal mediation of Mary, leaving the discussion to theologians. For *Lumen gentium*, it sufficed to indicate that Mary "is our mother in the order of grace"[159] and that she is invoked with the title of "mediatrix," among others.[160] Moreover, it is a mediation in Christ and by means of him. In the conciliar texts the universal maternity of Mary in relation to men is clear (Mary "mother of Christ and mother of men, particularly of the faithful").[161]

To specify this role is a task left to the theologians, and it may also lead one day to a magisterial clarification. In any case, the texts cited by *Lumen gentium* in a footnote to the term "mediatrix" are noteworthy. Pope Leo XIII is cited; his encyclical *Adiutricem populi* says, among other things, that Mary, "who was so intimately associated [the *administra*] with the mystery of human salvation is just as closely associated with the distribution of the graces which for all time will flow from the Redemption.... Among her many other titles we find her hailed as 'our Lady, our Mediatrix,' 'the Reparatrix of the whole world,' 'the Dispenser of all heavenly gifts.'" The pope refers to St. Bernard in the West and to St. Tharasius and to the Byzantine liturgy of December 8 in the East. The pope then cites St. Germanus of Constantinople: "O Virgin most holy, none abounds in the knowledge of God except through thee; none, O Mother of God, attains salvation except through thee; none receives a gift from the throne of mercy except through thee."[162]

158. See Hauke, *Mary "Mediatress of Grace,"* 125–26.

159. *LG* 61.

160. *LG* 62.

161. See *LG* 54; Laurentin, *Breve trattato su la Vergine Maria* (Cinisello Balsamo: Paoline, 1987), 248.

162. *EE* 3, nn. 1220; also in *Aeta Sanctae Sedis* 15 (1895–96): 303.

The central passage of the encyclical *Ad diem illum* of Pius X is cited: Mary is "'most worthily the reparatrix of the lost world' and dispensatrix of all the gifts that our Savior purchased for us by his death and by his blood.... [By] this companionship in sorrow and suffering ... it has been allowed to the august Virgin to be 'the most powerful mediatrix and advocate of the whole world in the presence of her only begotten Son.'" Mary appears as "the aqueduct" (St. Bernard) and the "neck" by which Christ, the "fountain of grace," "communicates to his mystical Body all spiritual gifts" (St. Bernardine of Siena).[163]

The encyclical *Miserentissimus Redemptor* of Pius XI deals with the vicarious expiation of Christ in which the Mother of God is also involved. According to the document, Mary "offered Jesus as a victim by the Cross," thereby becoming "reparatrix." The pope trusts "in her intercession with Christ, who ... 'the one mediator of God and men' (1 Tm 2:5), chose to make His Mother the advocate of sinners, and the minister and mediatress of grace."[164]

Finally the Council cites a radio message of Pius XII from May 13, 1946 (to the faithful who were meeting at Fatima) in which the supreme pontiff states, "Associated as Mother and minister of the King of the Martyrs with the ineffable work of human redemption, she is always associated, with an immense power, as it were, in the distribution of graces that derive from the Redemption."[165]

If in the future the church should need to define the universal mediation of Mary in the distribution of graces, it would suffice to put the footnote from the Second Vatican Council into the principal text.

The apostolic exhortation *Signum magnum* of Paul VI (1967) affirms in very clear terms that Mary's universal spiritual motherhood is part of the deposit of faith:

> The blessed Virgin Mary, after participating in the redeeming sacrifice of the Son, and in such an intimate way as to deserve to be proclaimed by Him the Mother not only of His disciple John but—may we be allowed to affirm it—of mankind which he in some way represents, now continues to

163. *EE* 4, nn. 25f; also in Acts (of Pius X), 1:154; DH 3370.

164. *EE* 5, nn. 260; also in *AAS* 20 (1928): 178.

165. *AAS* 38 (1946): 266; Italian text in *L'Osservatore Romano*, May 19, 1946, cited in Roschini, *Maria Santissima*, 2:204.

fulfill from heaven her maternal function as the cooperator in the birth and development of divine life in the individual souls of redeemed men. This is a most consoling truth which, by the free consent of God the All-Wise, is an integrating part (*pars est expletiva*) of the mystery of human salvation; therefore it must be held as faith by all Christians (*ab omnibus christianis debet fide teneri*).[166]

MARY AS "MOTHER OF THE CHURCH"

Mary, "Image and Mother" of the Church

In the context of Marian mediation we can also discuss the title "Mother of the Church," proclaimed by Paul VI during the Second Vatican Council, at the end of the third session, on November 21, 1964. This title is used to affirm the role of Mary for the whole community of the faithful, not only for individual situations.

Mary's role as spiritual mother with regard to the church is contemplated along with her being a "type of the Church,"[167] a point already mentioned more than once.[168] Vatican II provides a good synthesis, pointing to the divine maternity and to the virginity of Mary, which are present analogously in the community of the church and in every believer.[169] The church, "by receiving the word of God in faith becomes herself a mother. By preaching and baptism she brings forth sons, who are conceived of the Holy Spirit and born of God, to a new and immortal life. She herself is a virgin, who keeps in its entirety and purity the faith she pledged to her Spouse. Imitating the mother of the Lord, and by the power of the Holy Spirit, she [*virginaliter*] keeps intact faith, firm hope and a sincere charity."[170]

166. *AAS* 59 (1967): 467f. See the references in de Margerie, "Can the Church Define," 196f.

167. See "Mary as Spiritual 'Mother,' 'Companion,' and 'Helper'" in this chapter.

168. In particular, see "Patristic Motifs Through the Sixth Century," in chapter 2; "The Contribution of Vatican II," in chapter 2; and chapter 3.

169. *LG* 63–65. See John Paul II, *RM* 43.

170. *LG* 64 (DH 4178). On Mary as "prototype" of the church, see Hugo Rahner, *Our Lady and the Church* (London: Darton, Longman and Todd, 1961); German original, *Maria und die Kirche* (Innsbruck: Marianischer Verlag, 1951); Roschini, *Maria Santissima*, 2:517–27; Brunero Gherardini, "Chiesa" [Church], De Fiores and Meo, in *NDM*, 350–68; Gherardini, *La Chiesa: Mistero e servizio*, 153–63; Calero, *La Vergine Maria*, 78–90; O'Carroll, *Theotokos*, 346–48; Paul Haffner, *The Mystery of Mary* (Leominster, UK: Gracewing; Mundelein, Ill.: Hillenbrand, 2004), 240–43.

The church, before appearing in her hierarchical and "Petrine" profile, is manifested in her Marian dimension, accepting divine grace and cooperating with the Lord.[171]

Mary is thus present in the mystery of the Church as a *model.* But the Church's mystery also consists in generating people to a new and immortal life: this is her motherhood in the Holy Spirit. And here Mary is not only the model and figure of the Church; she is much more. For, "with maternal love she cooperates in the birth and development" of the sons and daughters of Mother Church. The Church's motherhood is accomplished not only according to the model and figure of the Mother of God but also with her "cooperation."[172]

Precisely, the salvific cooperation of Mary surpasses the measure of every other member of the mystical body of Christ and assumes a universal role for all other men redeemed by her Son. Therefore, the relation of Mary with the church is grasped well in the title of three formularies of the Marian missal: she is "image and mother of the church."[173]

Biblical Foundations and Historical Development of the Title *Mater Ecclesiae*

At the basis of the title "Mother of the Church" is the maternal role of Mary, the new Eve, in regard to all those who belong (or are meant to belong) to Christ. Irenaeus brings together Mary and the church as the "maternal womb which causes men to be reborn in God."[174] References to Genesis 3:20 are also important: Mary, the new Eve, as "mother of all the living"—among others, in Athanasius, Ephrem, and Peter Chrysologus.[175] Another important trail is the Augustinian vision of the church as the total Christ (*Christus totus*); Augustine, cited by Vatican II, affirms: Mary is "the mother of the members of Christ ... since she has by her charity joined in bringing

171. See p. 135.
172. John Paul II, *RM* 44.
173. *MBVM*, nn. 25–27.
174. See p. 81.
175. See Ziegenaus, *Maria in der Heilsgeschichte*, 219f.

about the birth of believers in the Church, who are members of its head."[176]

The use of the title "mother of the Church" was debated at Vatican II. The objections took their starting point above all from the fact that Mary is part of the church, being the most excellent member. Is it possible to be mother of a reality to which one belongs?[177] But the term "church" here is obviously meant in the sense of the other members of the mystical body of Christ. The ecclesiotypical approach to mariology (Mary as type of the church) is not enough, for we also need to take account of the Christotypical question: Mary participates in the salvific influence that comes from the Savior, for the good of the church. While the ecclesiotypical tendency had triumphed (by only a few votes), in the integration of the Marian schema into the Dogmatic Constitution on the Church, Paul VI reestablished equilibrium, accepting the requests of the Christotypical tendency, solemnly proclaiming the title "Mother of the Church."

The most ancient testimony to the title originates in a medieval commentary on chapter 12 of the Apocalypse, written by Berengaudus (between the ninth and eleventh centuries): "In this passage, we can also understand the 'woman' as Mary: because she is the mother of the Church, because she generated him who is head of the Church." The theologian immediately adds, "She is daughter of the Church, for she is the most important member of the Church."[178] Rupert of Deutz († 1129), in a comment on the Canticle (4:13), calls Mary "the fountain of gardens, the spring of living waters; the fountain of gardens, that is, the mother of the churches."[179]

In the thirteenth century we rediscover the title under the pen of an English Cistercian, viewed from the same perspective: Mary is

176. *De virg.* 6, cited in *Lumen gentium* 53. For other patristic references, see Galot, *Maria, La donna*, 362–64; Achim Dittrich, *Mater Ecclesiae: Geschichte und Bedeutung eines umstrittenen Marientitels* [Mother of the Church: History and Meaning of a Disputed Marian Title] (Würzburg: Echter, 2009) 21–75.

177. One opponent of the title at the Council even maintained: if Mary is the mother of the church, our mother, then she would be our grandmother. See Pozo, "La consagración a los Corazones de Jesús y María en Juan Pablo II," 58; Pozo, *María, nueva Eva*, 34.

178. (Pseudo-) Ambrose, *In Apoc.* (PL 17:876C/D). See Otto Stegmüller, "Berengaudus," in *ML* 1:435.

179. *In Cant.* 4 (PL 168:898).

daughter of the universal church, but also mother of it: "Since she is surely mother of the head, she is understood in a not unsuitable way as mother also of the body."[180] The title *mater ecclesiae* then appears in liturgical texts starting from the thirteenth and fourteenth centuries.[181] We find it also in theological texts of the same time, though only in a scarce number. Then the title is used, among others, by Peter Canisius. The limited resonance it finds seems to trace back to a somewhat individualistic description of the role of Mary, neglecting the ecclesial perspective.[182]

As mentioned previously, starting from the eleventh century we encounter more frequently the interpretation of John 19:26–27 in the sense of the universal maternity of Mary.

Benedict XIV began the line of popes who speak of the maternity of Mary in relation to the church (1748). Leo XIII, for the first time among the pontiffs, formally uses the title *mater ecclesiae*, indicating John 19:26f. as its scriptural basis (John as representative of the human race) and Acts 1:14 (Mary in prayer in the midst of the church, as it is being born before Pentecost).[183] Subsequent popes speak of the maternity of Mary in relation to all the members of the body of Christ that is the church. John XXIII and Paul VI use the title anew in an explicit way.

Systematic Aspects

Paul VI, on the occasion of the solemn proclamation, based the title of Mother of the Church on the divine Maternity: as Christ assumed human nature from Mary, as head he united his mystical body that is the church to himself. As Mother of Christ, Mary is therefore also mother of the faithful and of the pastors—that is, of

180. See Walter Dürig, *Maria, Mutter der Kirche* [Mary, Mother of the Church] (St. Ottilien: EOS Verlag, 1979), 16f.; Galot, *Maria, La donna*, 362; Dittrich, *Mater Ecclesiae*, 90–129.

181. The most ancient text is a trope on the "Salve Regina" (Bibliothek St. Gall): *Virgo, mater ecclesiae, / Aeternae porta gloriae, / Ora pro nobis omnibus, / Qui tui memoriam agimus*; Dürig, *Maria, Mutter der Kirche*, 20.

182. See Ziegenaus, *Maria in der Heilsgeschichte*, 221f.

183. Enc. *Adiutricem populi*, 1895 (*PE* 2:136, n. 6; *EE* 3, n. 1219). Both references appear also in John Paul II, *RM* 24, on the maternity of Mary toward the church.

the church.[184] In 1968 the pope confirmed this affirmation in the "Credo of the People of God": "We believe that the Blessed Mother of God, the New Eve, Mother of the Church, continues in heaven her maternal role with regard to Christ's members, cooperating with the birth and growth of divine life in the souls of the redeemed."[185] John Paul II, in *Redemptoris Mater*, cites these points and adds, "Mary is present in the Church as the Mother of Christ, and at the same time as that Mother whom Christ, in the mystery of the Redemption, gave to humanity in the person of the Apostle John. Thus, in her new motherhood in the Spirit, Mary embraces each and every one *in* the Church, and embraces each and every one *through* the Church."[186]

On one hand, Mary is a member and type of the church (ecclesiotypical aspect). But, at the same time, she transcends the church by her maternal role toward all the other faithful, participating in the work of Christ (Christotypical aspect). This transcendence is expressed in the title "Mother of the Church," indicating the universal dispensation of graces in the ecclesial context.

MARY, *MATER UNITATIS*: THE MATERNAL MEDIATION OF THE MOTHER OF GOD IN ECUMENISM AND INTERRELIGIOUS DIALOGUE

Marian Mediation and Ecumenism

The Separated Eastern Christians

The topic of Marian mediation has also been debated in the realm of ecumenism. This, however, is not the case for the separated Christians of the East, in particular for the Orthodox: the Eastern Church, since ancient times, strongly affirms human cooperation (*sunergeía*) in the process of salvation. The "yes" of the Theotokos at the Annunciation appears on the center door of every iconostasis. Right

184. *AAS* 56 (1964): 1015.

185. *Credo of the People of God*, n. 15. English trans. from NC News Service.

186. *RM* 47. See also John Paul II, CM 63 ("The Blessed Virgin Is Mother of the Church," September 17, 1997).

at the end of the era of the Greek fathers are found the first witnesses for the universal mediation of the Mother of God. The technical terminology for this mediation (such as "mediatrix," *mesítes*, *mesiteúousa*) finds its first expression precisely in the ancient Greek milieu.[187] The Orthodox, being separated from union with Rome, only dislike its dogmatic definition (as they do on other topics). The term "co-redemptrix," of Western and medieval origin, also seems extraneous to them, but active cooperation in the Redemption, or respectively, Marian mediation, is quite present in their doctrine.[188] Metropolitan Damaskinos Papandreou, for example, very involved in ecumenical colloquy at the international level, took a position on Marian mediation on the occasion of the encyclical *Redemptoris Mater* (1987). Particularly valuable for him are three points "which derive their authenticity from the inexhaustible treasure of the common patristic tradition": (1) the involvement of the Mother of God in the mystery of the divine plan of salvation; (2) "the mediation of the Mother of God in the plan of the salvific work of Christ"; (3) the active and not merely passive (or even unconscious) motherhood of Mary.[189] Papandreou considers ecumenical relations irritated not by the statements of the pope on the universal mediation of Mary, but by the Marian dogmas of 1854 and 1950.[190]

Protestantism

The Heritage of Luther On the other hand, the situation is very different in the Protestant milieu. Already in the introduction we have been able to acknowledge the perplexities of Reformed theologians

187. See "The Era of the Fathers" in this chapter.

188. See O'Carroll, "Mary Coredemptress, Mediatress, Advocate: Instrument of Catholic-Orthodox Unity," in Miravalle, *Mary Coredemptrix*, 1:132–43; O'Carroll, "A Marian Dogma and Ecumenism," in Miravalle, *Mary Coredemptrix*, 2:229–36; Vladimir Zelinsky, "Mary in the Mystery of the Church: The Orthodox Search for Unity," in Miravalle, *Mary Coredemptrix*, 2:223f; Yannis Spiteris, *Salvezza e peccato nella tradizione orientale* [Salvation and Sin in Eastern tradition] (Bologna: EDB, 1999) 208f, 218–21. See also Bernhard Schultze, SJ, "Theologi palamitae saeculi XIV de mediatione B. M. Virginis" [The Palamite Theologians of the 14th Century on the Mediation of the Blessed Virgin Mary], in *Mariologia et oecumenismo* (Rome: PAMI, 1962), 355–422.

189. Damaskinos Papandreou, "Redemptoris Mater III. Orthodoxe Bemerkungen" [Mother of the Redeemer: III. Orthodox Observations], *Una Sancta* 42 (1987): 230.

190. Ibid., 231.

in the face of any human cooperation in the process of justification. Even contemporary ecumenical efforts have not been able to lead to a truly accepted agreement on this point.[191] The kernel is precisely Mary's cooperation in the Redemption, and the problematic aspect is already well explained by the Annunciation. The Dutch Calvinist theologian Cornelis A. de Ridder, in his monograph on Catholic debates about Mary Co-redemptrix (1965), applauds the interpretation (quite unique for a Catholic theologian) by the German Jesuit Heinrich Lennerz: the angel Gabriel communicates the divine decision on the Incarnation to Mary, but God does not make the Incarnation depend on the consent of the Blessed Virgin.[192] This reading completely overlooks the importance of free will (even though Lennerz, departing from Luther, does not deny the fact of free will itself in man's relationship with God). De Ridder tries to neutralize the Pauline passages that speak of a human cooperation with God (such as 1 Cor 3:9; 2 Cor 6:1). According to him, at the most one could speak of human cooperation in proclaiming the Gospel, but on no account in justification or in the realm of grace.[193] Luther's comment on the formulation *quem meruisti portare* in the *Regina coeli* is indicative: the "merit" of being Mother of God is the same as the "merit" of the wood of the Cross, for having borne the Savior.[194] In the process of salvation, God does everything, and Mary, the type of man justified *sola gratia*, does nothing.[195]

191. On Lutheran-Catholic ecumenical efforts, see also pp. 5–6.

192. Cornelis A. de Ridder, *Maria als Miterlöserin?* [Mary as Coredemptrix?] (Göttingen: Vandenhoeck and Ruprecht, 1965), 64f, with reference to Heinrich Lennerz, *De beata Virgine*, 2nd ed. (Rome: Pontificia Univ. Gregoriana, 1935), 164f. On Lennerz, see Hauke, "La questione del 'Primo principio,'" 591–97.

193. De Ridder, *Maria als Miterlöserin?*, 164.

194. Exposition of the Magnificat (1521): *WA* 7:573; on the context, see Dittrich, *Protestantische Mariologie-Kritik*, 29–37; Ziegenaus, *Maria in der Heilsgeschichte*, 52; Michael Kreuzer, *"Und das Wort ist Fleisch geworden": Zur Bedeutung des Menschseins Jesu bei Johannes Driedo und Martin Luther* ["And the Word Became Flesh": The Meaning of the Humanity of Jesus in Johannes Driedo and Martin Luther] (Paderborn: Bonifacius, 1998), 262–66; Gherardini, *La corredentrice*, 302–10; Gherardini, "Lutero e gli eredi della Riforma dinanzi al mistero di Maria Corredentrice" [Luther and the Heirs of the Reformation, Before the Mystery of Mary Coredemptrix], *Maria Corredentrice* 3 (2000): 54–65; Angelo Amato, *Gesù il Signore: Saggio di cristologia* [Jesus the Lord: Essay in Christology] (Bologna: EDB, 1999), 395–98; Wolfgang Layh, "Luthers Verständnis von Maria anhand seiner Magnificatauslegung von 1521" [Luther's Understanding of Mary, Based on His 1521 Exposition of the Magnificat], *Ephemerides Mariologicae* 50 (2000): 119.

195. See Horst Gorski, *Die Niedrigkeit seiner Magd: Darstellung und theologische Analyse der*

The Dombes Document The theme of Marian cooperation has been taken up recently, particularly in a document by the Dombes Group.[196] In it, the first ecumenical difficulty set forth is precisely "the 'cooperation' of Mary in salvation and the relation of grace with freedom." As an example of Protestant conviction Karl Barth is cited, taking a stand above all against Mary's "cooperation."[197] The Catholic interlocutors, as in the *Joint Declaration* on justification, always set the term "cooperation" between quotation marks. The theologians (Protestants, Catholics, and Orthodox) together cite Martin Luther: justification does not happen by means of works: works (only) reveal the salvation freely given as a gift by God.[198] In this view, Mary is an example of what happens in all the redeemed: man is passive before grace; his response to God, on the other hand, is the work of divine grace and human freedom.[199] When Paul speaks of cooperation in the ministry of God (1 Cor 3:9), God is the only "worker."[200] Mary does not cooperate in the sacrifice of the Cross, which is completed only by Christ.[201] Vatican II intentionally omitted the word "co-redemption," which would be "objectively erroneous, because it leads one to think that the role of Mary is of the same order as that of Christ." Therefore, the term must be avoided.[202]

Mariologie Martin Luthers als Beitrag zum gegenwärtigen lutherisch/römisch-katholischen Gespräch [The Lowliness of His Handmaid: Presentation and Theological Analysis of the Mariology of Martin Luther, as a Contribution to the Present Lutheran/Roman-Catholic Dialogue] (Frankfurt: Peter Lang, 1987), 64.

196. Dombes Group, *Mary in the Plan of God*. See Alfonso Langella, "La recezione critica del Documento di Dombes. Valori e limiti," *Marianum* 62 (2000): 319–45; Salvatore M. Perrella, "La recezione del Documento di Dombes su Maria: Ricognizione bibliografica," *Marianum* 62 (2000) 347–55; Perrella, "*Non temere*," 103–19; Perrella, *La Madre di Gesù nella coscienza ecclesiale contemporanea* [The Mother of Jesus in Contemporary Ecclesial Consciousness] (Vatican City: Libreria Editrice Vaticana, 2005), 569–83; Hauke, "Maria, 'compagna del Redentore,'" 62–64 (repeated here somewhat); Ismael Bengoechea, "La cooperación de María a la redención y el ecumenismo: El documento de 'Les Dombes'" [Mary's Cooperation in the Redemption and in Ecumenism: The Dombes Document], *Estudios Marianos* 70 (2004): 361–78; Giancarlo Bruni, *Mariologia ecumenica: Approcci, documenti, prospettive* (Bologna: EDB: 2009), 453–85.

197. Dombes Group, *Mary in the Plan of God*, n. 208.

198. Ibid., nn. 216–17.

199. Ibid., n. 219.

200. Ibid., n. 225.

201. Ibid., n. 218.

202. Ibid., n. 210. On the other hand, the Lutheran pastor Dickson holds another opinion: Charles Dickson, "Mary Mediatrix: A Protestant Response," in Miravalle, *Mary Coredemptrix*,

The Catholic interlocutors maintain that the question of Mary's "cooperation" (in quotation marks) is not entirely resolved, but the joint explanation permits one of speak of a communion of faith.[203] The Protestant theologians, on the other hand, refer to the possibility of seeing (like the Reformers) "in Mary, mother of the Lord, who, with her active response, 'cooperated' in salvation," on the condition that it be established unambiguously that grace is a work only of Christ. In this case Mary appears as an example of the faithful justified by means of faith and not by means of works.[204]

In the Dombes Group we need to recognize the virtue of having set the topic of Marian cooperation front and center on the ecumenical agenda, connecting it to the fundamental question of justification. It does not appear, however, that a real accord has been reached on the fact that God does not exclude but includes free human cooperation in the process of justification itself. In the document it is not clear how man, under the influence of grace, can prepare himself for friendship with God in justification. Man's cooperation in salvation is seen only as a response to the justification that has already taken place.

In the Dombes document, there is no lack of contradictions: how can one ever speak of a cooperation in salvation by means of active response while putting "cooperation" in quotation marks and maintaining that God is the only one acting? All things considered, this dialogue also "recognizes the difficulty of admitting, in a definitive way, an activity proper to creatures into the order of salvation."[205]

3:183: "Protestants need to understand that the words mediatrix and co-redemptrix do not mean equality."

203. Dickson, "Mary Mediatrix," n. 295. Regarding this unacceptable procedure, see the critique by Jean-Marie Hennaux, "Le Document du Groupe des Dombes sur la Vierge Marie" [The Dombes Group Document on the Virgin Mary], *Nouvelle Revue Théologique* 121 (1999): 54–58.

204. Hennaux, "Le Document du Groupe des Dombes," nn. 323–24.

205. Escudero Cabello, "Approcci attuali," 203, regarding a dialogue between Catholics and Evangelicals (*Enchiridion Oecumenicum* III, nn. 1132–48). See also Hennaux, "Le Document du Groupe des Dombes," 42–51. On the other hand, the problems on this point have been resolved according to Giancarlo Bruni, "Chiavi di lettura del documento su Maria del Gruppo di Dombes," *Marianum* 62, no. 157–58 (2000): 306–8.

The Inclusion of Christology In our opinion, it is necessary to deepen ecumenical dialogue by including Christology. A human cooperation in salvation is already found in Jesus Christ himself: according to the First Letter to Timothy (to cite an emblematic text), "the *man* Jesus Christ" is the one mediator between God and men (1 Tm 2:5). Therefore, the proper activity of the human freedom of Jesus Christ, sustained by the divine person of the Son, is indispensable for mediation between God and man. Instead Luther presents the humanity of Christ only as a "sign" of salvation; it is not a living instrument through which God acts.[206] The humanity of Jesus is seen as "bait" with which the divine fisherman "hooks" the devil: Satan "eats" the human "bait," "killing" God who is stronger than him. The "bait," the humanity of Jesus, is dead and cannot do anything but serve as a trap for the devil.[207]

Valuing the human cooperation of the Savior himself prepares the way to also overcome the *merely passive* attitude of man in justification. The active cooperation of Mary in the Redemption could gain a prominent role for arriving at a balanced doctrine in the area of justification: God does nothing by himself, but rather, with his grace, enables a creature to participate in the process of salvation.[208] While the Council of Trent describes with great fineness this involvement of man in the subjective Redemption (which is justification), Vatican II affirms (without quotation marks) the active cooperation of the Virgin Mary in the work of the Savior (and therefore in the objective Redemption). It would be desirable to advance this fact as well in ecumenical dialogue.

A Note about Language Protestant theology has difficulties in the face of the salvific cooperation of Mary, and not only about the term

206. See Peter Hünermann, *Jesus Christus: Gottes Wort in die Zeit* [Jesus Christ: God's Word in Time] (Münster: Aschendorff, 1994), 231, 234.

207. See Theobald Beer, *Der fröhliche Wechsel und Streit: Grundzüge der Theologie Martin Luthers* [Happy Exchange and Conflict: Principles of the Theology of Luther] (Einsiedeln: Johannes Verlag, 1980), 338–51; Kreuzer, *"Und das Wort ist Fleisch geworden."*

208. See Kreuzer, "Maria und die Gemeinsame Erklärung zur Rechtfertigungslehre" [Mary and the Common Declaration on the Doctrine of Justification], *Forum Katholische Theologie* 17 (2001): 47–58.

"co-redemptrix," avoided in the texts of Vatican II for ecumenical reasons.[209] This diplomacy (which at the same time holds the term to be "most true in itself") has not led to an agreement on the real kernel of the problem, Mary's cooperation in the process of salvation, but has compromised the use of technical terminology in the Catholic milieu, with the result that at times some Catholic theologians, for misunderstood ecumenical reasons, raise doubt about the active cooperation of Mary in the Incarnation itself.[210] Hiding the most specific expressions for speaking of the salvific cooperation of Mary does not lead to unity in the truth. "We may ask, now, if the anti-mariological fever of ecumenism itself has not made us lose, paradoxically and culpably, the direction to unity: Mary in Christ is his mother, not the stumbling block."[211]

Anglicanism

While the Protestant world remains somewhat difficult in regard to Marian mediation, we can find a greater openness in the realm of Anglicanism, notwithstanding its prohibition in principle against the invocation of saints.[212] The main reason for this is Anglicanism's greater closeness, at least on the part of Anglo-Catholics, to the spirituality of the fathers. This is seen quite well in the works of the theologian John Macquarrie, who even gives a positive assessment

209. On the use of the term "Coredemptrix" and the Second Vatican Council and the writings of Pope St. John Paul II, see pp. 323–24.

210. Thus Munsterman, *Marie corédemptrice?*, 77; see my review in *Revue d'Histoire Ecclésiastique* 101 (March–April 2006): 1318–22. See Apollonio, "Mary Coredemptress: Mother of Unity; A Probing Glance at the Hidden Face of Vatican Council II," in *Mary at the Foot of the Cross*, vol. 3, *Mater Unitatis* (New Bedford, Mass.: Academy of the Immaculate, 2003), 327: "The path from explicitly teaching the doctrine, to its *disguised and furtive* form, has produced a downward spiral which, by force of inertia (or perhaps gravity), has reached ground zero—that is, the denial of the doctrine itself."

211. Brunero Gherardini, "Ecumenismo e corredenzione mariana," *Maria Corredentrice* 8 (2006) 16.

212. See G. M. Corr, "La doctrine mariale et la pensée anglicane contemporaine," in du Manoir, *Maria*, 3:711–31; Konrad Algermissen and A. Radford, "Anglikanische Kirche," in Bäumer and Scheffczyk, *ML* 1:149–52; Galot, *Maria, La donna*, 412f., with reference to article 22 (of the Thirty-Nine Articles of 1562), according to which the invocation of saints and angels is "a fond thing vainly invented, and grounded upon no warranty of Scripture, but rather repugnant to the Word of God."

to the terms "co-redemptrix" "and mediatrix,"[213] and in the Seattle Declaration (2004) on "Mary: Grace and Hope in Christ."[214]

The Title *Mater unitatis*

Ecumenical dialogue should insist on the true cooperation of Christ's humanity in the Redemption and, dependent on him, the cooperation of the Mother of God. In particular, thanks to Mary's consent at the Annunciation and under the Cross, she has become *mater unitatis*, "mother of unity" for all her children, including those separated from full unity with the successor of Peter. The expression *mater unitatis* traces back to St. Augustine, though not with a specific application to ecumenism.[215] This beautiful title, for diplomatic reasons, was not incorporated into the texts of Vatican II,[216] but we can rejoice in its rediscovery by Paul VI[217] and in its use, even liturgical use, through the pontificate of John Paul II.[218] One cannot think it is a mistake to have recourse to the Mother of God in order to reestablish visible unity among all Christians. "Why should we not all together look to her as our common Mother, who prays for the unity of God's family?"[219] As there is no unity in a family without recognizing the mother, thus full communion among all Chris-

213. As noted perceptively by Amato, *Gesù il Signore*, 405–9, referring to John Macquarrie, *Mary for All Christians* (Grand Rapids, Mich.: Eerdmans, 1990; London: T. and T. Clark, 1991; 2nd ed., 2001), 98–115 ("Mary Coredemptrix"). See Macquarrie, "Mary Coredemptrix and Disputes over Justification and Grace: An Anglican View," in Miravalle, *Mary Coredemptrix*, 2:245–56; also in Miravalle, *Mary Co-redemptrix. Doctrinal Issues Today*, 139–50.

214. See Anglican-Roman Catholic International Commission (ARCIC), *Mary: Grace and Hope in Christ* (Harrisburg, Pa.: Morehouse, 2005), nn. 5, 16 (on the *fiat*), 44, 57, 67–72 (mediation), 78. See also Johannes Stöhr, "Neue Hoffnungen in der Mariologie für die Anglikaner" [New Hopes in Mariology for Anglicans], *Sedes Sapientiae: Mariologisches Jahrbuch* 9 no. 2 (2005): 91–98; ARCIC, *Mary: Grace and Hope in Christ; The Seattle Statement ... the Text with Commentaries and Study Guide*, ed. Donald Bohlen and Gregory Cameron (London and New York: Continuum, 2006); Bruni, *Mariologia ecumenica*, 243–96.

215. Augustine, *Sermo* 192:2. See Ignazio M. Calabuig, "Postfazione," in Perrella, "*Non temere*," 219–21.

216. As witness Apollonio, "Mary Coredemptress: Mother of Unity." *LG* 69, however, exhorts all Christians to invoke Mary for the cause of Christian unity.

217. See Calabuig, "Postfazione," 221–23.

218. *MBVM*, n. 38. This applies also to catechesis: see, above all, the last Marian Catechesis (n. 70), November 12, 1997. See Calabuig, "Postfazione," 223–31.

219. *RM* 30.

tians depends on the motherly mediation of Mary. Highlighting the salvific role of Mary is therefore an indispensable service toward attaining unity in the one church instituted by Christ.

Probably the most profound pages by the Magisterium on this topic comes from the encyclical *Adiutricem populi* by Pope Leo XIII, from 1895, entirely dedicated to Mary as "the foremost promoter of peace and unity" (*fautrix optima pacis et unitatis*) and to the prayer of the Rosary as the way to unity among all Christians.[220] The efficacy of Marian prayer is based on the spiritual motherhood of Mary. "For Mary has not brought forth—nor could she—those who are of Christ except in the one same Faith and in the one same love.... Every one of the multitudes, therefore, whom the mischief of calamitous events has stolen away from that unity, must be born again to Christ of that same Mother whom God has endowed with a never failing fertility to bring forth a holy people ... she will obtain by her entreaties help in abundance from the Spirit that quickeneth."[221]

Evidently, the intercession of the Mother of God also relates to the non-Christian world to draw all men nearer to the one Savior in the one church, as is shown in the Collect of the Mass "Mary, Virgin Mother of Unity": "Holy Father ... grant, by the intercession of the blessed Virgin Mary, mother of all mankind, that the various families of peoples be formed into the one people of the new covenant."[222]

The Figure of Mary in Relation to Other Religions

The liturgical formulary on the "Mother of Unity" seeks not only the unification of all Christians in the Catholic Church, but also the conversion of all those who have not yet accepted faith in Jesus Christ. The motherly mediation of Mary also works in missionary involvement, to which interreligious dialogue is related.[223] Mary was not a

220. Leo XIII, *Adiutricem populi* (*PE* 2:136, n. 24; *EE* 3, n. 1226).

221. Leo XIII, *Adiutricem populi* (*PE* 2:136, n. 27; *EE* 3, n. 1230).

222. *MBVM*, n. 38.

223. See John Paul II, Encyclical *Redemptoris Missio* (1990), 55: "Inter-religious dialogue is a part of the Church's evangelizing mission. Understood as a method and means of mutual knowledge and enrichment, dialogue is not in opposition to the mission *ad gentes*; indeed, it has special links with that mission and is one of its expressions"; *EE* 8, n. 1193.

missionary engaged in the type of public activity typical to the apostles, but her witness for Christ becomes an example for all Christians. Starting from her generous response in faith to the message of the angel, the blessed Virgin is the first believing person in the New Covenant and the perfect disciple. Her visit to Elizabeth, during which the Mother of God bears the Savior in the joy of the Holy Spirit to her relative and to John the Baptist (Lk 1:41–45), is an example for the missionary dynamic. Mary's "yes" at the Incarnation and her consent to the offering of Christ from the foot of the Cross participate in the foundation of salvation for all peoples. The intercession of the Mother of God prepares for the event of Pentecost (Acts 1:14). For this reason, the Council's Decree on the Missionary Activity of the Church was able to close with the exhortation to pray "that through the intercession of the Virgin Mary, Queen of the Apostles, the nations might soon be led to the knowledge of the truth and that the glory of God, which shines in the face of Jesus Christ, might shed its light on all men through the Holy Spirit."[224] The various missionary aspects of the figure of Mary are grasped in the liturgical formulary "Mary, Virgin and Queen of Apostles."[225] The existing approaches to a Marian missionary theology often start from her salvific cooperation and from the universal mediation of the blessed Virgin who prepares all peoples for the encounter with Jesus Christ.[226]

Mary's mediating preparation is particularly strong for the Jews, as one also concludes from a look at converts from Judaism who already find in the Old Testament many elements that reach their fulfillment in the Mother of the Messiah.[227] She appears as a "compendium" of Israel, especially in the figure of the "daughter of Zion."[228]

224. Vatican Council II, *Ad gentes*, 42.

225. *MBVM*, n. 18.

226. See the summary and bibliography in the works of Horst Rzepkowski, cited in the selected bibliography.

227. See Ferdinand Holböck, *"Wir haben den Messias gefunden": Die selige Edith Stein und andere jüdische Konvertiten vor und nach ihr* ["We Have Found the Messiah": Blessed Edith Stein and Other Jewish Converts Before and After Her], 2nd ed. (Stein am Rhein, Switzerland: Christiana-Verlag, 1987).

228. See S. Cavalletti, S. "Ebrei" [The Jews], in De Fiores and Meo, *NDM*, 514f; Stefano De Fiores, *Maria sintesi di valori: Storia culturale della mariologia* [Mary, Synthesis of Values: Cultural History of Mariology] (Cinisello Balsamo: San Paolo, 2005), 505–8.

Vatican II, in the Declaration on Non-Christian Religions, notes that Muslims, "though they do not acknowledge Jesus as God, … revere him as a prophet. They also honor Mary, His virgin Mother; at times they even call on her with devotion."[229] As regards the presence of Mary in the Quran, it is surprising to see its conviction on the virginity of the Mother of Christ[230] and a hint at the Immaculate Conception.[231] As Mohammed, considered the final prophet and superior to Christ by Muslims, did not come from a virgin mother, the figure of Mary constitutes a question to attentive readers: the virginity of Mary points to the divine character of Jesus, superior to Mohammed, and cannot be separated from her divine maternity. Being conceived without sin is only meaningful as a preparation for the Redeemer who is free from every moral fault, a fact that Islam does not proclaim of Mohammed. Mary appears as an example of those who believe in the word of God.[232] The testimony of the Quran is also accompanied by erroneous passages: it states that the Christian Trinity consists of God (the Father), Jesus, and Mary;[233] the mother of Jesus, it appears, is confused with Miriam, sister of Aaron and Moses;[234] in addition, there are traces of apocryphal traditions.[235] Since many Muslims also venerate the mother of the "prophet" Jesus, the "anonymous" presence of the Mother of *God* in their religion is an element that might, in the future, promote conversion to the Son of God.

229. Vatican II, *Nostra aetate*, 3. (Vatican translation.)

230. See Sura 3:45f; 4:171; 5:72; 19:20; 21:91; 66:12.

231. See Sura 3:42: "O Mary, God has chosen you, and has purified you. He has chosen you over all the women of the world." This hint of the Immaculate Conception, obviously of Christian origin, is notable (see Stefano M. Cecchin, *L'Immacolata Concezione: Breve storia del dogma* [The Immaculate Conception: A Short History of the Dogma] (Vatican City: PAMI, 2003), 103f.), even if Islam "does not know the significance of this grace or any notion of the transmission of an original sin." See also Georges Gharib, "Musulmani" [Muslims], in *NDM*, 1007.

232. See Sura 66:12.

233. See Sura 5:116. It is probably a misunderstanding of the title *Theotokos*: according to A. J. Wensinck and P. Johnstone, "Maryam," in *Encyclopédie de l'Islam*, ed. E. Van Donzel, (Leiden: Brill, 1996), 6:614.

234. See Sura 19:28; P. Antes, "Islam," in Bäumer and Scheffczyk, *ML* 3:325. Antes, "Koran," in *ML* 3:647; Gharib, "Musulmani," 1003.

235. See Gharib, "Musulmani," 1003–6; César Vidal Manzanares, "María en el Corán: Confluencia de los apócrifos cristianos con la polémica proselitista del Islam" [Mary in the Koran: Confluence of the Christian Apocrypha with the Proselytistic Polemics of Islam], *Ephemerides Mariologicae* 42 (1992): 295–309.

As regards the religions of pre-Christian origin such as Hinduism, let us consider the observations made earlier about feminine divinities: the desire to turn, in the religious sphere, to a feminine figure is accepted and transformed in the Mother of God.[236] A figure particularly close to the traits of Mary is Kuan-yin (Kannon), a mediating person (bodhisattva) in Buddhism, a "goddess" who represents divine mercy.[237]

REFERENCES

The Mediation of Mary

Ecclesiastical Texts

CCC 494, 501, 963–70.

Collantes, Justo, ed. *La fede della Chiesa Cattolica: Le idee e gli uomini nei documenti dottrinali del Magistero* [The Faith of the Catholic Church: Ideas and Men in the Doctrinal Documents of the Magisterium], 327–33. Vatican City: Libreria Editrice Vaticana, 1993.

John Paul II. CM 33 (Sept. 18, 1996): 39–41 (Dec. 11, 1996; Dec. 18, 1996; Jan. 8, 1997), 47–48 (Apr. 2, 1997; Apr. 9, 1997), 64–65 (Sept. 24, 1997, Oct. 1, 1997).

———. Encyclical *Redemptoris Mater*, part 3.

Leo XIII. Encyclical *Octobri mense* (DH 3274f).

———. Encyclical *Iucunda semper* (*PE* 2:132; *EE* 3, n. 1197).

———. Encyclical *Adiutricem populi* (*PE* 2:136; *EE* 3, nn. 1220f.).

Pius IX. Encyclical *Ubi primum* (*PE* 1:43; *EE* 2, n. 133).

Pius X. Encyclical *Ad diem illum* (DH 3370).

Pius XI. Encyclical *Ingravescentibus malis* (*PE* 3:221; *EE* 5, n. 1341).

Pius XII. Encyclical *Mediator Dei* (*PE* 4:233, n. 169–71; *EE* 6, n. 592).

———. Encyclical *Mystici Corporis* (*PE* 4:225, n. 110f; *EE* 6, nn. 258–59).

Vatican II. *LG* 60–62.

Other Sources

Amato, Angelo. "Gesù, Salvatore, definitivo, universale, e la cooperazione di Maria alla salvezza, problematiche nuove di una 'questione antica'" [Jesus, Definitive Universal Savior, and the Cooperation of Mary in Salvation]. In *Maria nel mistero di Cristo, pienezza del tempo e compimento del regno*, edited by E. Peretto, 387–427. Rome: Marianum, 1999.

Apollonio, Alessandro M. "Mary Mediatrix of All Graces." In Miravalle, *Mariology: A Guide*, 411–65. Goleta, Calif.: Queenship, 2007.

236. See "Mary the Woman, in the Context of Anthropology," in chapter 3. On the Marian apparitions of Guadalupe, see "Modern Apparitions Recognized by Ecclesiastical Authority," in chapter 9.

237. See Horst Rzepkowski, "Dialog," in *ML* 2:184; Rzepkowski, "Kuan-yin," in *ML* 3:692f.

Auer, Johann. *Gesù il Salvatore: Soteriologia—Mariologia* [Jesus the Savior: Soteriology, Mariology], §§13–14. Translated by Carlo Molari. Assisi: Cittadella, 1993. German original: *Jesus Christus—Heiland der Welt: Maria, Christi Mutter im Heilsplan Gottes*. Regensburg: Friedrich Pustet, 1988.

Bastero, Juan Luis. *Mary, Mother of the Redeemer*. 218–37. Dublin: Four Courts, 2006.

———. *Virgen singular: La reflexión teológica mariana en el siglo XX*, 206–59. Madrid: Rialp, 2001.

Bur, Jacques. "La Médiation de Marie: Essai de synthèse speculative" [The Mediation of Mary: Essay in Speculative Synthesis]. In du Manoir, *Maria*, 6:471–512. Paris: Beauchesne, 1961.

Calabuig, Ignazio M. "Riflessione sulla richiesta della definizione dogmatica di 'Maria corredentrice, mediatrice, avvocata'" [Reflections on the Petition for a Dogmatic Definition of "Mary Coredemptrix, Mediatrix, Advocate"]. *Marianum* 61 (1999): 129–75.

Calero, Antonio María. *La Vergine Maria nel mistero di Cristo e della Chiesa: Saggio di mariologia* [The Virgin Mary in the Mystery of Christ and the Church: Essay in Mariology], 281–343. Leumann (Turin): Elle Di Ci, 1995. Spanish original: *María en el misterio de Cristo y de la Iglesia*. Madrid: CCS, 1990.

Calkins, Arthur B. "Marian Co-redemption and the Contemporary Papal Magisterium." *Immaculata Mediatrix* 6 (2006): 191–227 Also in *Mary, "Unique Cooperator in the Redemption,"* 113–69. New Bedford, Mass.: Academy of the Immaculate, 2005.

———. "Mary Coredemptrix: The Beloved Associate of Christ." In Miravalle, *Mariology: A Guide*, 349–409.

Calkins, Arthur B., ed. *Totus tuus: Il magistero mariano di Giovanni Paolo II*, 29–33, 203–45, 271–325. Siena: Cantagalli, 2006.

Carol, Juniper B, OFM. "Corredención de Nuestra Senora." In Carol, *Mariología*, 760–804. Madrid: Biblioteca de Autores Cristianos, 1964. English original: "Our Lady's Coredemption," in Carol, *Mariology*, 2:377–425. Milwaukee: Bruce, 1957.

———. *De corredemptione Beatae Virginis Mariae: Disquisitio positiva* [The Coredemption of the Blessed Virgin Mary: Positive Inquiry]. Vatican City: Typis Polyglottis Vaticanis, 1950.

Ciappi, Luigi. "Dalla maternità di Dio alla maternità degli uomini" [From Motherhood of God to Motherhood of Men]. In *EMTheo*, 292–310.

Cumerlato, Guido. *"Ecce ancilla Domini": La mediazione materna come diakonia della Madre di Dio* ["Behold the Servant of the Lord": Maternal Mediation as the Diakonia of the Mother of God]. Naples: Pontificia Facoltà Teologica dell'Italia Meridionale, 2004.

De Fiores, Stefano. *Maria sintesi di valori: Storia culturale della mariologia* [Mary, Synthesis of Values: Cultural History of Mariology], 515–27. Cinisello Balsamo: San Paolo, 2005.

———. "Mediatrice." In *Maria: Nuovissimo dizionario* 2:1081–1141. Bologna: EDB, 2006.

de Menthière, Guillaume. *Marie Mère du Salut: Marie Corédemptrice? Essai de fondement théologique* [Mary, Mother of Salvation: Mary coredemptrix? Essay on Theological Foundations]. Paris: P. Téqui, 1999.

Dombes Group. *Mary in The Plan of God and the Communion of Saints*, nn. 207–26, 295, 323f. New York: Paulist Press, 2002. French original: *Marie dans le dessein de Dieu et la communion des saints*. 2 vols. Paris: Bayard/Centurion, 1997–98.

Druwé, Eugène, SJ. "La médiation universelle de Marie" [Mary's Universal Mediation]. In du Manoir, *Maria*, 1:417–572. Paris: Beauchesne, 1949.

Ducay, Antonio. "La cooperación de María en la obra de la salvación" [Mary's Cooperation in the Work of Salvation]. *Scripta de Maria* 2nd ser., 3 (2006): 201–25.

Escudero Cabello, Antonio. "Approcci attuali e proposte teologiche sul tema della cooperazione mariana" [Current Approaches and Theological Proposals on the Topic of Marian Cooperation]. *Marianum* 61 (1999): 177–211.

———. *La cuestión de la mediación mariana en la preparación del Vaticano II: Elementos para una evaluación de los trabajos preconciliares* [The Question of Marian Mediation in the Preparation of Vatican II: Elements for an Evaluation of the Pre-Conciliar Work]. Rome: LAS, 1997.

Dodd, Gloria Falcão. *The Virgin Mary, Mediatrix of All Grace: History and Theology of the Movement for a Dogmatic Definition from 1896 to 1964*. New Bedford, Mass.: Academy of the Immaculate, 2012.

Ferrer Arellano, Joaquín. *La Mediación Materna de la Inmaculada, esperanza ecuménica de la Iglesia, hacia el quinto dogma mariano: razones teológicas* [The Maternal Mediation of the Immaculate, Ecumenical Hope of the Church, towards the Fifth Marian Dogma: Theological Reasoning]. Madrid: Arca de la Alianza, 2006.

Finkenzeller, J. "Miterlöserin" [Coredemptrix]. In *ML* 4:484–86.

Galot, Jean. "L'Intercession de Marie." In du Manoir, *Maria*, 6:513–50. 1961.

———. *Maria, La donna nell'opera della salvezza* [Mary, the Woman in the Work of Salvation]. 3rd ed., 239–92. Rome: Ed. Pontificia Università Gregoriana, 2005. 2nd ed., 1991.

Gherardini, Brunero. *La Corredentrice nel mistero di Cristo e della Chiesa* [The Coredemptrix in the Mystery of Christ and the Church]. Rome: Vivere In, 1998.

Haffner, Paul. *The Mystery of Mary*, 187–207, 254–74. Leominster, UK: Gracewing; Mundelein, Ill.: Hillenbrand, 2004.

Hauke, Manfred. "Das Gutachten von Garrigou-Lagrange zur dogmatischen Definition der universalen Mittlerschaft Mariens. Einführung, Text und Kommentar" [The Assessment of Garrigou-Lagrange on the Dogmatic Definition of the Universal Mediation of Mary: Introduction, Text, and Commentary]. *Doctor Angelicus* 4 (2004): 37–90.

———. "Definición dogmática de la mediación universal de María: Iniciativas del cardenal Mercier y sus reflejos en España" [Dogmatic Definition of the Universal Mediation of Mary: Initiatives of Cardinal Mercier and Their Reflections in Spain]. *Scripta de Maria* 2nd ser., 2 (2005): 317–52.

———. "Die Lehre von der 'Miterlösung' im geschichtlichen Durchblick: Von den biblischen Ursprüngen bis zu Papst Benedikt XVI" [The Doctrine of "Coredemption" in Historical Overview: From the Biblical Sources to Pope Benedict XVI]. *Sedes Sapientiae: Mariologisches Jahrbuch* 11, no. 1 (2007): 17–64.

———. "La cooperazione attiva di Maria alla Redenzione: Prospettiva storica (patristica, medievale, moderna, contemporanea)" [The Active Cooperation of Mary in the Redemption: Historical (Patristic, Medieval, Modern, Contemporary) Perspective]. In *Mary, "unique cooperator in the Redemption,"* 171–219. New Bedford, Mass.: Academy of the Immaculate, 2005. Also in *Immaculata Mediatrix* 6 (2006): 157–89.

———. "La mediazione materna di Maria in Cristo: Una riflessione sistematica" [The Motherly Mediation of Mary in Christ: A Systematic Reflection]. *Maria Corredentrice* 13 (2011) 71–130.

———. "La mediazione materna di Maria secondo Papa Giovanni Paolo II" [The Maternal Mediation of Mary according to Pope John Paul II]. *Maria Corredentrice* 7 (2005) 35–91. German original: "Die mütterliche Vermittlung." In Ziegenaus, *Totus tuus*, 125–75.

———. "La questione del 'Primo principio' e l'indole della cooperazione di Maria all'opera redentrice di Cristo: Due temi rilevanti nella mariologia di Gabriele M. Roschini" [The Question of the "First Principle" and the Contribution of Mary to Christ's Work of Redemption: Two Relevant Themes in the Mariology of Roschini]. *Marianum* 64, no. 161–62 (2002): 569–97.

———. "Maria, 'compagna del Redentore': La cooperazione di Maria alla salvezza come pista di ricercar" [Mary, "Companion of the Redeemer": The Cooperation of Mary in Salvation as a Path of Research]. *RTLu* 7 (2002): 47–70. Reprinted as a monograph: *Quaderni mariani* 9. Frigento: Casa Mariana Editrice, 2002. Also in *Maria Corredentrice* 5 (2002)225–60. (There are also versions in German, English, and Romanian.)

———. "Maria, 'Mediatrice di tutte le Grazie' nell'Archivio Segreto Vaticano del Pontificato di Pio XI: Rapporto intermedio sulle tracce ritrovate" [Mary, "Mediatrix of All Graces," in the Vatican Secret Archives of the Pontificate of Pius XI; Intermediate Report on the Traces Found]. *Immaculata Mediatrix* 7 (2007): 118–29.

———. *Mary, "Mediatress of Grace": Mary's Universal Mediation of Grace in the Theological and Pastoral Works of Cardinal Mercier*. New Bedford, Mass.: Academy of the Immaculate, 2004.

Journet, Charles. *Maria Corredentrice* [Mary Coredemptrix]. Milan: Ares, 1989. French original: *Mater dolorosa: Notre Dame des Sept douleurs*. Stein am Rhein (CH): Christiana-Verlag, 1974.

"La colaboración de María a la Redención: Problema antiguo en proyección moderna" [Mary's Collaboration in the Redemption: An Ancient Problem in a Modern Projection]. *Estudios Marianos* 70 (2004).

Lacouture, Daniel. *Marie Médiatrice de toutes graces* [Mary, Mediatrix of All Graces]. Nouan le Fuzelier: Ed. des Béatitudes, 1995.

Laurentin, René. "Nuova Eva I: Il cammino storico del parallelismo Eva-Maria" [New Eve. I: The Historical Trail of the Parallelism Eve/Mary]. In De Fiores, Schiefer, and Perrella, *NDM*, 1017–21.

Maria Corredentrice. 21 vols. Frigento: Casa Mariana Editrice, 1998–2019.

Mary at the Foot of the Cross. Edited by Franciscans of the Immaculate. 9 vols. New Bedford, Mass.: Academy of the Immaculate, 2000–2009.

Mary, "Unique Cooperator in the Redemption." Acts of the Symposium on the Mystery of Marian Corredemption, Fatima, Portugal, May 3–7, 2005. New Bedford, Mass: Academy of the Immaculate, 2005.

Meo, Salvatore, OSM. "Mediatrice." In De Fiores, Schiefer, and Perrella, *NDM*, 920–35.

———. "Nuova Eva II: Lo sviluppo teologico della 'Nuova Eva'; La corredenzione" [New Eve II. Theological Development of the "New Eve": Coredemption]. In De Fiores, Schiefer, and Perrella, *NDM*, 1021–29.

Merkelbach, Benoît Henri. *Mariologia*, 295–381. Paris: Desclée, 1939.

Miravalle, Mark, ed. *Contemporary Insights on a Fifth Marian Dogma: Mary Coredemptrix, Mediatrix, Advocate; Theological Foundations*. Vol. 3. Goleta, Calif.: Queenship, 2000.

———. ed. *Mary Co-redemptrix: Doctrinal Issues Today*. Goleta, Calif.: Queenship, 2002.

———. *Mary: Coredemptrix, Mediatrix, Advocate.* Goleta, Calif.: Queenship, 1993.

———. ed. *Mary Coredemptrix, Mediatrix, Advocate: Theological Foundations*. Santa Barbara, Calif.: Queenship, 1995.

———. ed. *Mary Coredemptrix, Mediatrix, Advocate: Theological Foundations*. Vol. 2. Santa Barbara, Calif.: Queenship, 1996.

———. *"With Jesus": The Story of Mary Co-redemptrix.* Goleta, Calif.: Queenship, 2003.

Müller, Gerhard L. "Mittlerin der Gnade" [Mediatrix of Grace]. In Bäumer and Scheffczyk, *ML* 4:487–91.

Munsterman, Hendro. *Marie corédemptrice? Débat sur un titre marial controversé*. Paris: Cerf, 2006.

O'Carroll, Michael, CSSp. *Theotokos: A Theological Encyclopedia of the Blessed Virgin Mary*, 238–45. Eugene, Or.: Wipf and Stock, 2000.

Parrotta, Pietro. "Father Roschini and the Contribution of Blessed John Duns Scotus to the Dogma of the Immaculate Conception." In *Mary at the Foot of the Cross*, 5:360–92. New Bedford, Mass.: Academy of the Immaculate, 2004.

Pérez Toro, Carlos, and Salvatore M. Perrella. "Cooperatrice di salvezza mediatrice" [Mediating Cooperator in Salvation]. In De Fiores, Schiefer, and Perrella, *DMar*, 327–36.

Perrella, Salvatore M. *I "vota" e i "consilia" dei vescovi italiani sulla mariologia e sulla corredenzione nella fase antipreparatoria del Concilio Vaticano II* [The "Votes" and "Recommendations" of the Italian Bishops on Mariology and on Coredemption in the Preparatory Phase of Vatican II]. Rome: Marianum, 1994.

———. *La madre di Gesù*, 407–88.

Perillo, Maria Francesca. *Maria nella Mistica: La mediazione mariana in santa Veronica Giuliani* [Mary in Mysticism: Marian Mediation in St. Veronica Giuliani]. Collana di Mariologia 5. Lugano and Frigento: Eupress FTL, 2004.

Ponce Cuéllar, Miguel. *María: Madre del Redentor y Madre de la Iglesia* [Mary: Mother of the Redeemer and Mother of the Church]. 2nd ed., 442–500. Barcelona: Herder, 2001.

Pozo, Cándido, SJ. *María, nueva Eva* [Mary, the New Eve], 347–79. Madrid: Biblioteca de Autores Cristianos, 2005.

Robichaud, Armand J. "Maria, dispensadora de todas las gracias" [Mary, Dispensatrix of All Graces]. In Carol, *Mariología*, 805–37. English original: "Mary, Dispensatrix of All Graces." In Carol, *Mariology*, 2:426–60. 1957.

Roschini, Gabriele M. *Dizionario di mariologia* [Dictionary of Mariology], 323–54. Rome: Editrice Studium, 1961.

———. *La Madonna: Secondo la fede e la teologia* [The Madonna: According to the Faith and Theology], 2:219–498. Rome: Libreria Editrice Francesco Ferrari, 1953–54.

———. *La mediazione mariana oggi* [Marian Mediation Today]. Rome: Marianum, 1971.

———. *Maria Santissima nella storia della salvezza: Trattato completo di mariologia alla luce del Concilio Vaticano II* [Mary Most Holy in the History of Salvation: Complete Treatise on Mariology in Light of the Second Vatican Council], 2:111–343. Isola del Liri: Pisani, 1969.

———. *Problematica sulla corredenzione* [Issues in Coredemption]. Rome: Marianum, 1969.

Royo Marin, Antonio. *La Virgen María: Teología y espiritualidad marianas* [The Virgin Mary: Marian Theology and Spirituality]. 2nd ed., 116–203. Madrid: Biblioteca de Autores Cristianos, 1997.

Siano, Paolo M., FI. "Uno studio su Maria Santissima 'Mediatrice di tutte le grazie' nel magistero pontificio fino al pontificato di Giovanni Paolo II" [A Study on Mary Most Holy, "Mediatrix of All Graces" in the Pontifical Magisterium through the Pontificate of John Paul II]. *Maria Corredentrice* 8 (2006) 191–266.

Villafiorita Monteleone, Andrea. *Alma Redemptoris Socia: Maria e la Redenzione nella teologia contemporanea* [Beloved Companion of the Redeemer: Mary and the Redemption in Contemporary Theology]. CdM 8. Lugano and Gavirate (Varese): Eupress FTL, 2010.

Ziegenaus, Anton. *Maria in der Heilsgeschichte: Mariologie* [Mary in Salvation History: Mariology], 332–48. Katholische Dogmatik 5. Aachen: MM-Verlag, 1998.

Mary, Mother of the Church

Ecclesiastical Texts

John Paul II. CM 63 (September 17, 1997).

———. *RM* 43–47.

Paul VI. *Address at the Conclusion of the Third Session of the Second Vatican Council,* November 21, 1964. *AAS* 56 (1964): 1007–18.

Vatican II. *LG* 53–54, 61–63.

Other Sources

Bodem, A. "Mutter der Kirche" [Mother of the Church]. In *ML* 4:553–55.

Calero. *La Vergine Maria*, 152–62.

Colzani, Gianni. *Maria: Mistero di grazia e di fede* [Mary: Mystery of Grace and Faith], 271–74. Cinisello Balsamo: Ed. Paoline, 1996. 3rd ed., 2006.

Dittrich, Achim. *Mater Ecclesiae: Geschichte und Bedeutung eines umstrittenen Marientitels* [Mother of the Church: History and Significance of a Disputed Marian Title]. Würzburg: Echter, 2009.

Dürig, Walter. *Maria Mutter der Kirche* [Mary, Mother of the Church]. St. Ottilien: EOS Verlag, 1979.
Galot. *Maria: La donna*, 353–68.
Gherardini, Brunero. "Chiesa." In De Fiores, Schiefer, and Perrella, *NDM*, 350–68.
Ponce Cuéllar. *María, Madre*, 483–87.
Riestra, José Antonio. "El titulo 'Mater Ecclesiae' en los manuales recientes de mariología" [The Title "Mother of the Church" in Recent Manuals of Mariology]. *Annales theologici* 10 (1996): 449–69.
Rovira, German, ed. *Ungetrübter Spiegel: Maria, Mutter der Kirche* [Untroubled Mirror: Mary, Mother of the Church]. Essen: Ludgerus-Verlag, 1992.
Vollert, Cyril, SJ. "María y la Iglesia." In Carol, *Mariología*, 921–66. English original: "Mary and the Church." In Carol, *Mariology*, 2:550–96. 1957.
Ziegenaus. *Maria in der Heilsgeschichte: Mariologie*, 218–32.

Ecumenism and Interreligious Dialogue

Ecclesiastical Texts

John Paul II. CM (November 12, 1997) ("Our Separated Brethren Also Honor Mary").
———. *RM* (1987): 29–34.
Leo XIII. Encyclical *Adiutricem populi* (*PE* 2:136; *EE* 3, nn. 1217–32).
Paul VI. *Marialis cultus*, 32f.
Vatican II. *LG* 69.

Other Sources

Amato, Angelo. *Gesù il Signore: Saggio di cristologia*, 385–409. Bologna: EDB, 1999.
Apollonio, Alessandro M. "Mary Coredemptress: Mother of Unity; A Probing Glance at the Hidden Face of Vatican Council II." In *Mary at the Foot of the Cross*. Vol. 3, *Mater Unitatis*, 316–58. New Bedford, Mass.: Academy of the Immaculate, 2003.
Bengoechea, Ismael. "La cooperación de María a la redención y el ecumenismo: El documento de 'Les Dombes'" [Mary's Cooperation in the Redemption and in Ecumenism: The Dombes Document]. *Estudios Marianos* 70 (2004): 361–78.
Bruni, Giancarlo. "Ecumenismo." In De Fiores, Schiefer, and Perrella, *DMar*, 455–65.
———. *Mariologia ecumenica: Approcci, documenti, prospettive*. Bologna: EDB, 2009.
Calabuig, Ignazio. "Postfazione" [Afterword]. In "*Non temere di prendere con te Maria" (Matteo 1,20): Maria e l'ecumenismo nel postmoderno; Dalla "Mater divisionis" alla "Mater unitatis"* ["Fear Not to take Mary with You" (Mt 1:20): Mary and Ecumenism in the Postmodern; From "Mother of Division" to "Mother of Unity"], edited by S. Perrella, 213–39. Cinisello Balsamo: San Paolo, 2004.
De mariologia et oecumenismo [Mariology and Ecumenism]. Rome: PAMI, 1962.
de Ridder, Cornelis A. *Maria als Miterlöserin?* [Mary as Coredemptrix?] Göttingen: Vandenhoeck and Ruprecht, 1965.
Dickson, Charles. "Mary Mediatrix: A Protestant Response." In Miravalle, *Contemporary Insights*, 181–84.
Dittrich. *Protestantische Mariologie-Kritik: Historische Entwicklung bis 1997 und dog-*

matische Analyse [Protestant Critique of Mariology: Historical Development up to 1997 and Dogmatic Analysis], 281–92. Mariologische Studien 11. Regensburg: Friedrich Pustet, 1998.

Dombes Group. *Mary in the Plan of God*, nn. 207–27.

Galot. *Maria, La donna*, 407–12.

Gherardini. "Ecumenismo e corredenzione mariana." *Maria Corredentrice* 8 (2006) 5–16.

———. *La Corredentrice*, 302–18.

———. "Lutero e gli eredi della Riforma dinanzi al mistero di Maria Corredentrice" [Luther and the Heirs of the Reformation, before the Mystery of Mary Coredemptrix]. *Maria Corredentrice* 3 (2000) 53–74.

———. "Unity and Coredemption." In *Mary at the Foot of the Cross*. Vol. 3, *Maria, Mater Unitatis*, 54–69. New Bedford, Mass., 2004.

Hahn, Scott. "She Gave the Word Flesh." In Miravalle, *Contemporary Insights*, 169–80. Also as "Mary Coredemptrix: Doctrinal Development and Ecumenism." In Miravalle, *Mary Co-redemptrix: Doctrinal Issues Today*, 263–74.

Hauke. "La mediazione materna," 76–82.

———. "Maria, 'compagna del Redentore,'" 59–64.

Kreuzer, Michael. "Maria und die Gemeinsame Erklärung zur Rechtfertigungslehre" [Mary and the Common Declaration on the Doctrine of Justification]. *Forum Katholische Theologie* 17 (2001): 47–58.

Lutheran-Roman Catholic Dialogue Group, USA. *The One Mediator, the Saints and Mary* (1992). Minneapolis: Augsburg, 1992. Also in *Enchiridion Oecumenicum* 4, nn. 3083–360. Bologna: EDB, 1996.

Macquarrie, John. "Mary Coredemptrix and Disputes Over Justification and Grace: An Anglican View." In Miravalle, *Mary Coredemptrix, Mediatrix, Advocate: Theological Foundations*, 2:245–56. Also in Miravalle, *Mary Co-redemptrix. Doctrinal Issues Today*, 139–50.

Miravalle, Mark. "Mary Coredemptrix: A Response to 7 Common Arguments." In Miravalle, *Mary Co-redemptrix: Doctrinal Issues Today*, 93–138.

———. *With Jesus*, 167–72.

Munsterman, Hendro. *Marie coredemptrice?* 78–80.

O'Carroll, Michael, CSSp. "A Marian Dogma and Ecumenism." In Miravalle, *Mary Coredemptrix, Mediatrix, Advocate: Theological Foundations* 2:227–43.

———. "Mary Coredemptress, Mediatress, Advocate: Instrument of Catholic-Orthodox Unity." In Miravalle, *Mary Coredemptrix, Mediatrix, Advocate: Theological Foundations*, 119–43.

Perillo, Maria Francesca. "Maria SS. Corredentrice 'Mater unitatis.'" *Divinitas* 46 (2003): 320–50.

Perrella, ed. "Non temere," 103–19.

Scheffczyk, Leo. *Maria, crocevia della fede cattolica* [Mary, Crossroads of the Catholic Faith], 135–52. CdM 1. Lugano: Eupress FTL, 2002.

Söll, Georg. *Storia dei dogmi mariani* [History of Marian Dogmas], 409–16. Rome: Libreria Ateneo Salesiano, 1981. German original: *Mariologie* [Handbuch der Dogmengeschichte, vol. 3, part 4]. Freiburg im Breisgau: Herder, 1978.

Stöhr, Johannes. "Maria und die Einheit der Kirche" [Mary and Church Unity]. *Sedes Sapientiae: Mariologisches Jahrbuch* 4, no. 1 (2000): 71–99.
Zelinsky, Vladimir. "Mary in the Mystery of the Church: The Orthodox Search for Unity." In Miravalle, *Mary Coredemptrix, Mediatrix, Advocate: Theological Foundations*, 2:177–225.

Mary in Relation to Other Religions

Abd-El-Jalil, J.-M. "La vie de Marie selon le Coran e l'islam" [The Life of Mary according to the Quran and Islam]. In du Manoir, *Maria* 1:183–211. 1949.
Antes, P. "Islam." In Bäumer and Scheffczyk, *ML* 3:325.
———. "Koran." In Bäumer and Scheffczyk, *ML* 3:646f.
Ben-Chorin, S., and F. Hahn. "Judentum" [Judaism]. In Bäumer and Scheffczyk, *ML* 3:450f.
Buby, Bertrand A., SM. "Islam and Mary." In PAMI, *De cultu mariano s. XX*, 2:35–47. 2000.
Cavalletti, S. "Ebrei" [The Jews]. In De Fiores and Meo, *NDM*, 511–18.
Cerbelaud, Dominique. *Marie: Un parcours dogmatique* [Mary: A Dogmatic Survey], 243–68. Paris: Cerf, 2004.
Chappoulie, Henri. "Les missions et la spiritualité mariale." In du Manoir, *Maria*, 1:897–902. 1949.
De Fiores. *Maria: Nuovissimo dizionario*, 1:141f.
———. *Maria, sintesi*. 504–14.
Gharib, Georges. "Musulmani." In De Fiores and Meo, *NDM*, 1001–11.
Guemara, Raoudha. "Islam." In De Fiores, Schiefer, and Perrella, *DMar*, 657–67.
Hagemann, Ludwig. "Mariologische Aspekte im Koran: Forschungsergebnisse seit dem letzten Jahrhundert" [Mariological Aspects in the Quran: Research Results since the Last Century]. In PAMI, *De cultu mariano s. XIX et XX*, 2:605–35. Rome: PAMI, 1991.
Hauke, Manfred. "Maria als 'Mutter der Einheit' (Mater unitatis) als Beitrag zum authentischen interreligösen Dialog" [Mary as "Mother of Unity" as a Contribution to Authentic Interreligious Dialogue]. *Sedes Sapientiae: Mariologisches Jahrbuch* 15, no. 2 (2011): 8–26.
Maria nell'Ebraismo e nell'Islam oggi: Atti del 60 Simposio Internazionale Mariologico (Rome, 7–8–9 ottobre 1986) [Mary in Judaism and Islam Today: Proceedings of the 6th International Mariological Symposium, 7–9 October 1986]. Rome: Marianum, 1987.
O'Carroll. *Theotokos*, 192f. (Islam). 248f. (Missions).
Perrella, Salvatore M. *Virgo ecclesia facta: La Madre di Dio tra due millenni; Summula storico-teologica* [Virgo ecclesia facta: The Mother of God through Two Millennia; Historical-Theological Summary]. 67–76. Rome: Centro internazionale Milizia dell'Immacolata, 2002.
Perrella, Salvatore M., and Gian Matteo Roggio. "Dialogo interreligioso." In De Fiores, Schiefer, and Perrella, *DMar*, 384–96.
Risse, Günter. "Maria, die Gottesfürchtige: Das Marienbild im Koran" [Mary the

God-Fearer: The Image of Mary in the Quran]. *Sedes Sapientiae: Mariologisches Jahrbuch* 3, no. 1 (1999): 36–61.

Rzepkowski, Horst. "Dialog." In Bäumer and Scheffczyk, *ML* 2:184f.

———. *Lexikon der Mission* [Dictionary of Mission]. Graz: Verlag Styria, 1992, 283–85.

———. "Missiologie." In Bäumer and Scheffczyk, *ML* 4:472f.

Schumacher, Joseph. "Maria, die Mutter Jesu, im Islam" [Mary, the Mother of Jesus, in Islam]. *Sedes Sapientiae: Mariologisches Jahrbuch* 2, no. 1 (1998): 70–93.

———. "Maria im modernen Judentum" [Mary in Modern Judaism]. *Sedes Sapientiae: Mariologisches Jahrbuch* 2, no. 2 (1998): 102–19.

Seumois, André V. "Maria nei paesi di missione" [Mary in the Mission Countries]. In *EMTheo*, 212–20.

Stefani, Piero. "Ebrei" [The Jews]. In De Fiores, Schiefer, and Perrella, *DMar*, 447–55.

Vidal Manzanares, César. "María en el Corán: Confluencia de los apócrifos cristianos con la polémica proselitista del Islam" [Mary in the Koran: Confluence of the Christian Apocrypha with the Proselytizing Polemics of Islam]. *Ephemerides Mariologicae* 42 (1992): 295–309.

Wensinck, A. J., and P. Johnstone. "Maryam." In *Encyclopédie de l'Islam*, 6:613–17.

Nine

The Prophetic Role of Mary in Apparitions

THEOLOGICAL LOCUS OF THE PHENOMENON

We will now discuss apparitions of the Mother of God in close connection with the theme of mediation, studied in the previous chapter. Jesus Christ reveals his mission as mediator in the ministries of king, priest, and prophet. Mary also participates, in a manner consonant to her, in the prophetic function. The role of a prophet is that of communicating a divine message received by means of a revelation. The prophetic charism, carried out by men and women, is distinct from the sacrament of Orders and presupposes a special intervention of the Holy Spirit.[1] Such interventions of the Spirit call for our respect: "Do not quench the Spirit; do not despise prophesying" (1 Thes 5:19f). In the New Testament, the prophetic charism of Mary is manifested above all in the *Magnificat*, as Irenaeus of Lyons affirmed.[2] Ambrose, commenting on Mary's consciousness of her own salvific role, affirms that the Blessed Virgin "was not unaware of celestial mysteries."[3]

1. See Josef Scharbert, "Propheten," in Bäumer and Scheffczyk, *ML* 5:323f.

2. Irenaeus, *Adv. Haer.* III.10.2 (*SC* 211:122). On the patristic aspects of the title "prophetess" used for Mary, see Aloys Grillmeier, SJ, "Maria Prophetin: Eine Studie zur patristischen Mariologie" [Mary the Prophet: A Study in Patristic Mariology], *Geist und Leben* 30 (1957): 101–45.

3. Ambrose, *In Luc.* I.61 (*CSEL* 32:74). On the prophetic charism in Mary, see Leo Scheffczyk, "Prophetin" [Prophetess], in Bäumer and Scheffczyk, *ML* 5:324f.; Antonio Maria Calero, *La Vergine Maria nel mistero di Cristo e della Chiesa: Saggio di mariologia* [The Virgin Mary in the

Marian apparitions form part of the prophetic phenomena that have accompanied the journey of the people of God since the beginning of its history. The book of Proverbs puts it this way: "Where there is no prophecy, the people cast off restraint" (Prv 29:18). Prophecies do not end with the revelation of Jesus Christ, completed with the end of the apostolic era, but are a typical trait of the church that will remain until the Parousia.

The messages communicated, however, have a diverse locus: revelations called "private" run distinct from "public" revelation.[4] "Public revelation," or "Revelation" tout court, indicates a message destined to the entire church of all times; it is a content divinely revealed and proposed by the church to the faith of her members. (Revelation coincides therefore with the term "dogma," in which the *revelatio divina* and the *propositio ecclesiae*, the authoritative presentation mediated by the church, come together.) To explain the completeness of revelation, the *Catechism of the Catholic Church* (*CCC*) cites a text of St. John of the Cross: God "has now spoken all at once by giving us the All Who is His Son. Any person questioning God or desiring some vision or revelation would be guilty not only of foolish behavior but also of offending him, by not fixing his eyes entirely upon Christ, and by living with the desire for some other novelty."[5]

The term "private revelations," on the other hand, denotes messages destined for one person or for a group (or even the entire church) in a particular situation. The adjective "private" does not imply a purely personal interest that does not involve the ecclesial community, but only distinguishes these messages from general revelation. "Between the two realities there is a difference not only of degree but of essence."[6] Prophecies after the apostolic era are given "not to promote a new doctrine of the faith, but for the direction of human acts."[7]

Mystery of Christ and the Church: Essay in Mariology] (Leumann [Turin]: Elle Di Ci, 1995), 91–97; Gianni Colzani, *Maria: Mistero di grazia* [Mary, Mystery of Grace and Faith] (Cinisello Balsamo: Ed. Paoline, 1996), 240–42.

4. See Joseph Ratzinger, "Theological Commentary," in *The Message of Fatima*, ed. Congregation for the Doctrine of the Faith (Vatican City: Libreria Editrice Vaticana, 2000), 32–36.

5. John of the Cross, *Ascent to Mount Carmel* II.22: *CCC* 65.

6. Ratzinger. "Theological Commentary," 32.

7. Thomas Aquinas, *ST* II-II, q. 174, a. 6, ad 3; see *CCC* 67: "Through the ages there have

Private revelations recognized by the church are prophetic events that help us "to understand the signs of the times [Lk 12:56] and to find, by means of them, the right response in faith."[8]

Since the distinction between "public" and "private" does not appear to be very useful in respect to apparitions with an incisive message for the entire church (such as Guadalupe, Lourdes, and Fatima), more recently a distinction has been proposed "between *foundational* revelation and *particular* revelations, which continue according to the diversity of times and places."[9]

It is the task of ecclesiastical authority to evaluate the credibility of a prophecy, including that of a Marian apparition. The classic position of the church in this regard was expressed by Prospero Lambertini, later Benedict XIV (†1758), in his work on the processes of beatification (and canonization): "To such revelations, even if approved, we neither should nor could give an assent of catholic faith, but only of human faith, according to rules of prudence which discern if the aforesaid revelations are probable or worthy of pious belief."[10] Pius X also reminds us in his encyclical against Modernism, citing a decree from the Congregation of Rites: "These apparitions and revelations have neither been approved nor condemned by the Holy See, which has simply allowed that they be believed on purely human faith, on the tradition which they relate, corroborated by testimonies and documents worthy of credence."[11] "Ecclesial approbation of a private revelation contains three elements: the relevant message does not contain anything contrary to faith and good morals; it is licit to publish it, and the faithful are permitted to give adherence to it in a prudent manner."[12]

---

been so-called 'private' revelations, some of which have been recognized by the authority of the Church.... It is not their role to 'improve' or 'complete' Christ's definitive Revelation, but to help live us more fully by it in a certain period of history."

8. Ratzinger, "Theological Commentary," 36.

9. René Laurentin, "Apparizioni," in De Fiores and Meo, *NDM*, 129.

10. *De servorum Dei beatificatione* 2.32.11, cited in Stefano De Fiores, *Maria, Madre di Gesù: Sintesi storico-salvifica* [Mary, Mother of Jesus: Salvation-Historical Synthesis], Corso di teologia sistematica 6 (Bologna: EDB, 1992), 354. Also in this sense, Ratzinger, "Theological Commentary," 34f.

11. Pius X, *Pascendi* (1907) (*PE* 3:174, n. 55; *EE* 4, n. 244).

12. Ratzinger, "Theological Commentary," 35, with reference to Edouard Dhanis, SJ, "Sguardo su Fatima e bilancio di una discussione," *La Civiltà Cattolica* 2, no. 104 (1953): 397.

Nevertheless, it is plausible to speak not of "catholic faith," but of "divine faith" for the bearer of the prophetic charism, faith that clearly recognizes the authenticity of the revelation communicated (which may regard only an individual's destiny). For someone who is not himself a bearer of the charism, the act of assent appears as human faith, which may reach to a moral certainty.[13] According to a more daring position, the assent can become one of ecclesial faith, connected to a "dogmatic event," when a seer is canonized or when a Marian shrine arising from an apparition is involved, such as with certain obligatory observances in the universal liturgical calendar. "Dogmatic events" are realities connected to an infallible intervention of the magisterium, such as a canonization (which obliges the entire church to celebrate a saint) or the orthodoxy of a universal liturgical feast. For this reason some theologians even defend the possibility of a faith as a "theological virtue" for those who encounter a prophetic revelation.[14]

In the opinion of this author, it does not make sense to attribute theological faith in the strict sense to an event that does not form part of the Revelation completed with the apostolic era. Instead the question of "ecclesial faith" can be raised on the basis of the feast of Lourdes, present in the universal church with reference to the aforesaid apparitions (February 11), from the time of Pope Pius X (1907), until the liturgical reform of Paul VI (1969), in which the feast *In apparitione B. Mariae Virginis Immaculatae* became the optional memorial of Our Lady of Lourdes; in this memorial, the apparitions are mentioned only in the second reading of the Office of Readings.[15] Even in the case of Lourdes, as it were, the church does not formally propose the authenticity of the apparitions as "revealed by God." The

13. See Laurent Volken, *Le rivelazioni nella Chiesa* [Revelations in the Church] (Rome: Ed. Paoline, 1963), chap. 3, section 3. French original: *Les Révélations dans l'Église* (Tournai and Paris: Ed. Salvator, 1961).

14. In this sense, following Balić and Rahner: Laurentin, "Apparizioni," 132–34.

15. See Franz Courth, "Marienerscheinungen und kirchliches Amt" [Marian Apparitions and Church Office], in *Marienerscheinungen: Ihre Echtheit und Bedeutung im Leben der Kirche* [Marian Apparitions: Their Authenticity and Meaning in the Life of the Church], ed. Anton Ziegenaus, Mariologische Studien 10 (Regensburg: Friedrich Pustet, 1995), 187f.; François Reckinger, "Die Marienerscheinungen der Neuzeit" [Marian Apparitions of the Modern Era], in *Maria: Mutter der Kirche*, ed. Gerhard Stumpf (Landsberg: Initiativkreis Kath. Laien und Priester in die Diözese Augsburg, 2004), 209f.

true and proper object of the cultus *(obiectum cultus absolutum)* is the Immaculate Conception, while the apparition is considered an incidental object of devotion (*obiectum occasionale*).[16]

The charism of prophecy relates to the content of Marian manifestations. As regards their form, we must differentiate apparitions proper from visions. The term "apparition" points to the objectivity of the event in its visible manifestation (objective aspect), while "vision" describes the reality on the part of the seer (subjective aspect). "By apparition is meant the extranatural manifestation, perceptible either by the external senses or by the imagination, of an object that seems present."[17] "Vision," in contrast, in the sphere of the mystical, indicates the supernatural perception of an object that is naturally invisible to the eye. This perception may be a "corporeal vision" (that is, a perception in the visual sense), "imaginative" (sensible representations limited to the imagination), or "intellectual" (a perception by the understanding without sensible impressions or images).[18] An apparition is perceived by sight or at least by the imagination. In this way, therefore, "apparitions" and "visions" are realities that in part overlap.

The prophetic charism has an important role, but the exceptional character of apparitions is also underscored. "Christianity, like Judaism, presents itself as the religion of the heard word, not of vision: 'Blessed are they who will believe though they have not seen' (Jn 20:29f). For Jesus, eagerness for miracles (Jn 4:48) or the request for a sign from Heaven (Mk 8:11) are marks of an imperfect faith. So the Christian will avoid running after the sensational, in order to live in faith the condition of the Church as pilgrim."[19]

16. See Ziegenaus, *Maria in der Heilsgeschichte: Mariologie* [Mary in Salvation History: Mariology], Katholische Dogmatik 5 (Aachen: MM-Verlag, 1998), 370, with reference to C.V. (Karel Vladimir) Truhlar, SJ, "Principia theologica de habitudine Christiani erga Apparitiones" [Theological Principle of the Christian Attitude toward Apparitions], in *De apparitionibus virginis immaculatae*, edited by AMI, Virgo Immaculata XVI (Rome: AMI, 1956), 1–17. See also Pius X, *Pascendi* (1907) (*PE* 3:174, n. 55; *EE* 4, n. 244).

17. C. P. Paolucci, "Apparizioni," in *Dizionario di mistica*, ed. Luigi Borriello, OCD, Maria Rosaria Del Genio, and Edmondo Caruana (Vatican City: Libreria Editrice Vaticana, 1998), 146.

18. See V. Marcozzi, "Visioni," in Borriello, Del Genio, and Caruana, *Dizionario di mistica*, 1271. See also Ratzinger, "Theological Commentary," 36f.; Salvatore M. Perrella, OSM, *Le apparizioni mariane* (Cinisello Balsamo: San Paolo, 2007), 65–71.

19. De Fiores, *Dizionario* 1:34. See also Perrella, *Le apparizioni mariane*, 20, which speaks of the "primacy of the *heard* over *vision*."

CRITERIA FOR CREDIBILITY

Regarding criteria for the credibility of apparitions,[20] the rules formulated by Benedict XIV are important, as his quasi-official text has been used for about 250 years in the processes of beatification and canonization. There is no official procedure to regulate the discernment of alleged apparitions in detail, but a de facto procedure is followed. However, there is a 1978 note by CDF (Congregation for the Doctrine of the Faith), published in 2012, which establishes positive and negative criteria:

A. Positive criteria:
   a. Moral certitude, or at least great probability of the existence of the fact, acquired by means of a serious investigation;
   b. Particular circumstances relative to the existence and to the nature of the event, that is to say:

20. See Lambertini (Benedict XIV), book III, chap. 50–52, explored in Jean Stern, "L'examen canonique des apparitions mariales selon Benoît XIV" [The Canonical Examination of Marian Apparitions according to Benedict XIV], in *De cultu mariano s. XVII-XVIII*, ed. PAMI (Rome: PAMI, 1987), 5:341–63; Adolphe Tanquerey, *Compendio di teologia ascetica e mistica* (Rome and Paris: Desclée, 1930), nn. 1497–1508; Mario I. Castellano, "La prassi canonica circa le apparizioni mariane" [Canonical Practice Regarding Marian Apparitions], in *EMTheo* (1954), 468–74; (1958), 489–94; Volken, *Le rivelazioni*, chap. 3; Leo Scheffczyk, *Die theologischen Grundlagen von Erscheinungen und Prophezeiungen* [Theological Basis of Apparitions and Prophecies] (Leutesdorf: Johannes-Verlag, 1982), 17–24; Johannes B. Torelló, "Echte und falsche Erscheinungen: Besonnenheit und Offenheit vor den Marienerscheinungen" [Genuine and False Apparitions: Prudence and Openness in View of Marian Apparitions], in *Der Widerschein des ewigen Lichtes: Marienerscheinungen und Gnadenbilder als Zeichen der Gotteskraft* [Reflection of the Eternal Light: Marian Apparitions and Images of Grace as Signs of God's Power], ed. G. Rovira (Kevelaer: Butzon and Bercker, 1984), 89–107; Francisco de Paula Solá Carrió, "Verdaderas y falsas Apariciones: Criterios de discernimiento" [True and False Apparitions: Criteria of Discernment], *Estudios Marianos* 52 (1987): 115–34; Anton Ziegenaus, "Kriterien für die Glaubwürdigkeit: Zur Prüfung der Echtheit von Marienerscheinungen," in *Marienerscheinungen: Ihre Echtheit und Bedeutung im Leben der Kirche* [Marian Apparitions: Their Authenticity and Meaning in the Life of the Church], ed. Ziegenaus, Mariologische Studien 10 (Regensburg: Friedrich Pustet, 1995), 167–82; Augustinus Suh, *Le rivelazioni private nella vita della Chiesa* [Private Revelations in the Life of the Church] (Bologna: Edizioni Studio Domenicano, 2000), 254–64; François-Marie Dermine, *Mistici, veggenti e medium: Esperienze dell'aldilà a confronto* [Mystics, Seers, and Mediums: Confronting Experiences of the Beyond] (Vatican City: Libreria Editrice Vaticana, 2002), 66–77; Perrella, *Le apparizioni mariane*, 85–93, 99–115; Charles J. Scicluna, "Orientamenti dottrinali e competenze del vescovo diocesano e della Congregazione per la Dottrina della Fede" [Doctrinal Orientations and Competences of the Diocesan Bishop and CDF], in *Apparitiones Beatae Mariae Virginis in historia, fide, theologia*, ed. PAMI (Vatican City: PAMI, 2010), 1:329–56; Scicluna, "Criteri e norme della Congregazione per la Dottrina de la Fede nel discernimento delle apparizioni mariane" [Criteria and Norms of the Congregation for the Doctrine of the Faith in the Discernment of Marian Apparitions], *Marianum* 74 (2012): 229–81.

1. Personal qualities of the subject or of the subjects (in particular, psychological equilibrium, honesty, and rectitude of moral life, sincerity and habitual docility towards Ecclesiastical Authority, the capacity to return to a normal regimen of a life of faith, etc.)
2. As regards revelation, true theological and spiritual doctrine and immune from error.
3. Healthy devotion and abundant and constant spiritual fruit (for example, spirit of prayer, conversion, testimonies of charity, etc.)

B. Negative criteria:
   a. Manifest error concerning the fact.
   b. Doctrinal errors attributed to God himself, or to the Blessed Virgin Mary, or to some saint in their manifestations, taking into account however the possibility that the subject might have added, even unconsciously, purely human elements or some error of the natural order to an authentic supernatural revelation (see Saint Ignatius, *Exercises*, no. 336).
   c. Evidence of a search for profit or gain strictly connected to the fact.
   d. Gravely immoral acts committed by the subject or his or her followers when the fact occurred or in connection with it.
   e. Psychological disorder or psychopathic tendencies in the subject, that with certainty influenced on the presumed supernatural event, or psychosis, collective hysteria, or other things of this kind.

It is to be noted that these criteria, be they positive or negative, are not peremptory but rather indicative, and they should be applied cumulatively or with some mutual convergence.[21]

It seems useful to recall some fundamental points, taking account of what is cited earlier and also of other presentations, in particular

21. Congregation for the Doctrine of the Faith, *Norms Regarding the Manner of Proceeding in the Discernment of Presumed Apparitions or Revelations*, February 25, 1978 (published December 14, 2011); for a commentary, see Hauke, "Kurzer Kommentar zu den Normen der Glaubenskongregation über die Beurteilung mutmaßlicher Erscheinungen und Privatoffenbarungen" [Brief Commentary on the CDF Norms on the Evaluation of Alleged Apparitions and Private Revelations], *Sedes Sapientiae: Mariologisches Jahrbuch* 36, no. 2 (2012): 23–34; Scicluna, "Criteri e norme."

the important 1954 exposition by Mario Castellano OP,[22] a consultor of the Holy Office (the presentation was also expanded in 1958). The points enumerated by CDF predominantly relate to the internal criteria inherent in the apparition itself, while external criteria are also considered: spiritual fruits and, above all, miracles.[23] We can distinguish four fundamental points: rules regarding the seers, the content of the visions or apparitions (including the concrete modality of these perceptions), their effects, and miraculous signs supporting them. Discernment must take account of three possibilities: the event arises from natural forces, or from the intervention of the devil, or from the supernatural action of God. The event "is of supernatural character, *only when it can be absolutely excluded that the event was produced naturally or by demonic intervention.*"[24]

1. *The person of the seer* is examined from the moral and the psychophysical point of view. "It is not ... possible that the Madonna would appear to a person without any real virtues or, speaking hypothetically, if she were to appear to a sinner, that he would not radically change his life from one of vice to virtue: those greatly privileged by the Madonna are often raised to the honors of the altar." Prominent among the required virtues are humility and obedience to the legitimate representatives of the church.[25] The lack of humility is always a very bad sign.[26]

"Cases of imposture, illusion, or hallucination are not rare; however, it is certain that a person who is only pretending virtue will give himself away sooner or later."[27] We must take account of mental health and the risk of excessive sensitivity and impressionability: when the film "Bernadette" was shown in Italy, afterward various children "saw" the Madonna there, as at Lourdes.[28]

2. Regarding the *content of the apparition*, it is necessary to "con-

22. See De Fiores, *Dizionario* 1:50.

23. The distinction between internal and external criteria is found in Volken, *Le rivelazioni*, chap. 3.

24. Castellano, "La prassi canonica" (1958 ed.), 489.

25. Castellano, "La prassi canonica" (1954 ed.) 469; see 1958 ed., 490.

26. See Tanquerey, *Compendio*, n. 1499.

27. Castellano, "La prassi canonica" (1958 ed.), 490.

28. Ibid., 491.

sider *false* anything that contradicts reason, *false* and *evil* everything that contradicts morals; *false, evil,* and *wicked* everything that contradicts revealed truth."[29] The apostle Paul himself insists that not even an angel from heaven would be authorized to proclaim a different gospel (Gal 1:8). If we should find content that is "ridiculous or unworthy of God, we can dispense with any further examination: it is a diabolical intervention, or a pathological phenomenon, or a vile hoax."[30]

The form of the apparition must correspond to the work of God, which is always perfect. Any physical or moral defects in appearance, attitude, or movements of the Mother of God are to be excluded. It is a positive criterion when Mary reveals the secrets of the heart and shows a power greater than that of any created agent. The "only true and authentically supernatural prophecies are those related to future free events; all others may simply be preternatural" and thus also possible for demons.[31]

3. As for the effects of apparitions, the words of the Lord about the good tree that is known by its fruits (Mt 7:15–20) are valid. True prophets are recognizable by their fruits (see Mt 7:20). According to Ignatius of Loyola and Teresa of Avila, the vision of God first raises a feeling of awe and fear, but soon a feeling of peace, joy, and certainty follows. Diabolical visions, in contrast, unfold in the opposite way: at the beginning they can inspire joy, but confusion, sadness, and discouragement follow. Authentic revelations confirm the visionary in the virtues of humility, obedience, and patience. False revelations, however, create pride, presumption, and disobedience.[32]

4. The "decisive criterion" to certify the supernatural character of an apparition is a *miracle*, which must have "an *explicit or implicit but undeniable connection with the apparition*."[33] To recognize the supernatural character of a miracle and to distinguish it from preternatural interventions of evil spirits, a rigorous investigation is desired,

29. Ibid.
30. Ibid., 492.
31. Dermine, *Mistici*, 75. see Thomas Aquinas, *ST* II-II, q. 172, a. 5.
32. See Tanquerey, *Compendio*, nn. 1503–4.
33. Castellano, "La prassi canonica" (1958 ed.), 494.

as is carried out during the processes of beatification and canonization.[34] The "only decisive guarantees" for discerning a authentic prophecy "are a miracle prior to the prophecy, and/or the fulfillment of the prophecy."[35] "But miracles do *not always* accompany Marian apparitions: only when these have a social purpose, such as when they contain messages or warnings to the community of the faithful, must they be given the *signum comprobationis*, but not when it comes to apparitions given to comfort or console the seer, such as we read in the lives of many saints."[36]

Even when a prophetic revelation in itself proves authentic, it is possible that errors may creep in for two reasons: either because human imagination adds something to the divine manifestation, or because a revelation is interpreted in a confused way.[37]

For the *judgment of the church*, the diocesan bishop is responsible above all. His task is twofold: judging the fruits, he first gives permission for the *cultus* and then, subsequently, he gives a pronouncement on the authenticity of the apparitions. CDF can intervene when the phenomenon assumes vast proportions, or for other serious reasons, but still in consultation with the local bishop or possibly the episcopal conference.[38] The verdict can be *constat de supernaturalitate*, *constat de non supernaturalitate*, or *non constat de supernaturalitate*: the supernatural character of the event is confirmed, it is rejected, or the inability to affirm a divine origin is emphasized.

The question of the modality of apparitions is also connected with the criteria of authenticity. During an apparition, normally only the seers hear and see it. For this reason, some authors (foremost Karl Rahner) maintain that all apparitions consist of imaginative visions—that is, of impressions that are found only in the mind of

34. See Fabijan Veraja, *Le cause di canonizzazione dei santi: Commento alla legislazione e guida pratica* [Canonization Causes of Saints: Commentary on the Legislation and Practical Guide] (Vatican City: Libreria Editrice Vaticana, 1998), 81–88; Ulrike Marckhoff, *Das Selig- und Heiligsprechungsverfahren nach katholischem Kirchenrecht* [Procedures of Beatification and Canonization according to Catholic Church Law] (Münster: Lit.-Verlag, 2002), 154–70.

35. Dermine, *Mistici*, 77. See also Scheffczyk, *Die theologischen Grundlagen*, 24.

36. Dermine, *Mistici*, 77.

37. See Tanquerey, *Compendio*, nn. 1506–8.

38. See CDF, *Norms Regarding the Manner of Proceeding* (2012).

the seer (although they can be stimulated by the influence of God). Sometimes the theory is added that the human spirit could be driven by a divine impulse that is then transmitted into the linguistic and symbolic environment of the seer.[39]

These approaches may explain some phenomena, but not all. Some cases are obviously not dealing with an imaginative vision, but with the perception of an extramental object. At least that is the experience of the visionaries in most cases. One example that contradicts the aforementioned theory is the apparition at Cnoc Mhuire in 1879 in Ireland, an event hailed as authentic by church authority: fifteen people saw Mary with two other saints, Joseph and John the Evangelist, during an intermittent rain, and also saw an altar with a lamb and a cross. What is amazing was that the place where the saints were present remained dry, while the ground around it was wet. In this case, obviously this is not a subjective projection from a divine impulse, but the perception of celestial personages truly present.[40] It would be difficult to imagine that the visionaries would have knelt in front of something that had been only in their mind and not in external reality.

Furthermore, the site of the apparition is important; insistence on this cannot be explained by the imagination theory. On the other hand, the two approaches are not contradictory to one another: God not only stimulates the souls of seers, but also renders their senses capable to see and hear a supernatural reality that is revealed.[41]

39. See Karl Rahner, *Visions and Prophecies* (New York: Herder and Herder, 1964). The theory is accepted by, among others, De Fiores, *Dizionario* 1:28f, 38, along with another theory that hypothesizes "imaginative visions accompanied by a lively feeling of presence" (38). Ratzinger, "Theological Commentary," 37, also mentions only the interior perception of the imaginative vision. Interpreting in a sense contrary to Rahner are, for example, Torelló, "Echte und falsche Erscheinungen," 100; H. Lais, "Erscheinungen" [Apparitions], in *ML* 2:395–98; Anton Ziegenaus, *Marienerscheinungen*, 172–76; Thomas Müller, *Medjugorje: Ein Charisma und seine Bestätigung durch das Gottesvolk* [Medjugorje: A Charism and Its Affirmation by the People of God] (Vienna: Gebetsaktion Medjugorje, 2006), 103–13.

40. See Lais, "Erscheinungen," 395; Ziegenaus, *Marienerscheinungen*, 175; Müller, *Medjugorje*, 110. See also Laurentin and Sbalchiero, eds., *Dictionnaire des apparitions*, 493f.

41. See Ziegenaus, *Marienerscheinungen*, 169–76.

A HISTORICAL VIEW OF MARIAN APPARITIONS

Antiquity

Already in the patristic age we find accounts of Marian apparitions. The first was received by Gregory the Wonderworker († ca. 270), mentioned by Gregory of Nyssa.[42]

The Wonderworker, bishop of Neocaesarea (Pontus, Asia Minor), was a student of Origen. Under the guidance of the fervent bishop, the evangelization of Pontus made enormous progress. St. Gregory the Wonderworker was particularly venerated in Cappadocia, from which comes the famous discourse of Gregory of Nyssa. The latter recounts that the saintly bishop, shortly after his episcopal ordination, had had a celestial apparition. The Wonderworker was very concerned about heresies invading his young flock. John the Evangelist appeared to him to "reveal to him the truth of pious faith"; Mary also appeared to him. The two talked among themselves about the true faith, in this way instructing Gregory the Wonderworker. Then the bishop received a trinitarian creed that subsequently became of great help for maintaining faith in the one God, Father, Son, and Holy Spirit (*Expositio fidei*).[43]

42. See M. Lochbrunner, "Gregor der Wundertäter," in *ML* 3:19–21; Laurentin and Sbalchiero, *Dictionnaire des apparitions*, 398–400. The text is found in PG 10:984; PG 46:912f.; English trans. in Luigi Gambero, *Mary and the Fathers of the Church: The Blessed Virgin Mary in Patristic Thought*, trans. Thomas Buffer (San Francisco: Ignatius Press, 1999), 93f. See also M. J. Rouet de Journel, ed., *Enchiridion patristicum* [Patristic Handbook] (Freiburg im Breisgau, 1937), m. 611. For antiquity in general, see Alejandro Martinez Sierra, "De apparitionibus marianis in antiquitate christiana" [Marian Apparitions in Christian Antiquity], in *De primordiis cultus mariani*, ed. PAMI (Rome: PAMI, 1970), 5:195–211.

43. A Protestant researcher (L. Abramowski, 1976) denied the authenticity of the event, maintaining that the creed was a composition of ideas from Basil. But the opposite conclusion seems more convincing: that the trinitarian doctrine of the Cappadocian fathers also depends on the *Expositio fidei* handed on by Gregory the Wonderworker. We should note as well that Gregory of Nyssa mentions that the manuscript of the Wonderworker was still preserved at Neocaesarea. Even generally critical patrologists (Bardenhewer, Crouzel) have written in favor of the authenticity of the reported event. Methodologically one needs to distinguish between the writing of the creed on the part of the Wonderworker, its derivation from the apparition, and the formulation that seems to conform to Origen's trinitarian affirmations. See the account in M. Lochbrunner, "Gregor der Wundertäter" [Gregory the Wonderworker], in *ML* 3:19–21.

There are also numerous accounts of mariophanies in the Middle Ages. Historical inquiry, however, has to confront many difficulties tied to the particular character of the sources. See

Modern Apparitions Recognized by Ecclesiastical Authority

In regard to modern apparitions, we shall list those recognized by ecclesiastical authority.[44] Such recognition does not come easily. B. Billet lists 232 alleged apparitions or lacrimations in 32 countries from 1928 to 1975;[45] as we shall see, only a few of the phenomena have been tested seriously and then recognized credible as supernatural manifestations. Because the modality of recognition may appear in various forms (other than a single juridical act by the bishop), it is not easy to give an exact count.[46]

Let us begin with the apparitions at Guadalupe in Mexico.[47]

M. Martins, "Narrativas de aparicoes de Nossa Senhora (ate oa sec. XII)" [Accounts of Apparitions of Our Lady (up to the 12th Century)], *Salmanticensis* 5 (1958): 703–22, mentioned in Peter Dinzelbacher, "Erscheinung," in *Lexikon des Mittelalters* 3:2185f.; Sylvie Barnay, *Specchio del cielo: Le apparizioni della Madonna nel Medioevo* [Mirror of Heaven: Apparitions of the Madonna in the Middle Ages] (Genoa: Marietti, 1999); Gottfried Hierzenberger and Otto Nedomansky, *Dizionario cronologico delle apparizioni della Madonna* [Chronological Dictionary of Marian Apparitions] (Casale Monferrato: Piemme, 2004), passim; Laurentin and Sbalchiero, *Dictionnaire des apparitions*, passim.

44. See the review, with its additional bibliography, of Hauke, "Der prophetische Dienst Mariens: Inhaltliche Schwerpunkte der marianischen Botschaften seit 1830" [The Prophetic Service of Mary: Main Points of Content of the Marian Messages since 1830], in Ziegenaus, *Marienerscheinungen*, 29–62; Bäumer and Scheffczyk, *ML*, passim; Hierzenberger and Nedomansky, *Dizionario*, passim; Reckinger, "Die Marienerscheinungen der Neuzeit," 201–58; Laurentin and Sbalchiero, *Dictionnaire des apparitions*, passim; Yves Chiron, *Enquête sur les apparitions de la Vierge* [Inquiry into the Apparitions of the Virgin] (Paris: Perrin, 2007).

45. See Bernard Billet, "Le fait des apparitions non reconnues par l'Église" [Apparitions Not Recognized by the Church], in Billet et al., *Vraies et fausses apparitions dans l'Église: Société française d'études mariales, Session annuelle.* [True and False Apparitions in the Church: French Society of Marian Studies, Annual Session] (Paris: P. Lethielleux, 1973), 10–23.

46. Laurentin and Sbalchiero, *Dictionnaire des apparitions*, 96–98, report a list of only fourteen episcopally "recognized apparitions" (among the circa 2400 reports of alleged apparitions): Guadalupe (1531), Aparecida (1717, which is not an apparition but rather the inexplicable finding of an image), Alphonse Ratisbonne (1842, in turn linked to the apparitions of 1830 in the Rue du Bac), La Salette (1846), Lourdes (1858), Pontmain (1871), Gietrzwald (1877), Fatima (1917), Beauraing (1932), Banneux (1933), Amsterdam (1945), Betania (Venezuela, 1976); Akita (1973), and Kibeho (1981). De Fiores, *Dizionario* 1:53, counts eleven apparitions recognized since 1830, adding Zeitoun (Egypt, 1968) and omitting Betania. In what follows, we are describing the events indicated, plus a few other cases, although we cannot go into detail as regards the modality of their recognition (Rue du Bac 1830, Philippsdorf 1866, Pellevoisin 1876, Cnoc 1879), setting Amsterdam aside. If we also take account of other miraculous events, often regarding Marian statues and images, recognized by ecclesiastical authority: W. Pötzl, "Augenwende" [A Turn of the Eyes], in *ML* 1:286f; Reckinger, "Wunder," in *ML* 6:766–68; Laurentin and Sbalchiero, *Dictionnaire*, 899–930; Vittorio Messori and Rino Cammilleri, *Gli occhi di Maria* [The Eyes of Mary] (Rome, 1796; Milan: Rizzoli, 2001).

47. See Francis W. Johnston, *The Wonder of Guadalupe: The Origin and Cult of the Miraculous*

This event gained a worldwide resonance in 1990 when Pope John Paul II declared the seer of Guadalupe, Juan Diego, blessed; he was then canonized in 2002. The four Marian apparitions took place December 9–12, 1531—that is, ten years after the conquest of Tenochtitlán, the Aztec capital, in 1521 by the Spaniards, who had arrived in 1519. Until then, conversions to Christianity had been very few.

The principal historical source is an account written in the indigenous language Nahuatl by a friend of Juan Diego, based on his oral accounts between 1540 and 1550 (under the title *Nican Mopohua*, "You Told One Thing after Another"). The apparition took place on the hill called "Tepeyac," then north of the city of Mexico, but now integrated within the metropolis. Ruins of a temple of the goddess Tonantzin ("our venerable mother") are located on this hill.

On the morning of Saturday, December 9, 1531, the Indian Juan Diego wants to attend Holy Mass and catechism. That was the day when the Immaculate Conception was being celebrated. Passing by the foot of Tepeyac hill, the Indian hears a marvelous concert of birds, coming from the top of the mount. He is sent climbing. Mary presents herself as the Mother of God and asks that the bishop have a shrine built on the hill.

The bishop, the Franciscan Juan de Zumárraga, at first does not believe the message and asks the seer to come back another time.

Image of the Blessed Virgin in Mexico (Chulmleigh, UK: Augustine, 1981; repr. Charlotte, N.C.: TAN, 2011); Valerio Maccagnan, "Guadalupe," in De Fiores and Meo, *NDM*, 655–69; Maccagnan, *Guadalupe—Evangelio y cultura* (Guadalajara: Centro Mariano OSM, 2001); R. Nebel and H. Rzepkowski, "Guadalupe," in *ML* 3:38–42; Xavier Escalada, *Enciclopedia Guadalupana* [Encyclopedia of Our Lady of Guadalupe], 4 vols. (México, 1995); Escalada, *Enciclopedia Guadalupana: Apendice* (México, 1997); Manuela Testoni, *Le apparizioni della Madonna di Guadalupe: Storia e significato* [Apparitions of Our Lady of Guadalupe: History and Significance] (Cinisello Balsamo: San Paolo, 1998); Thomas M. Sennott, *Acheiropeta: Not Made by Hands; The Miraculous Images of Our Lady of Guadalupe and the Shroud of Turin* (New Bedford, Mass.: Academy of the Immaculate, 1999 (repr. San Francisco: Ignatius Press, 2011); Juan José Benitez, *El misterio de la Virgen de Guadalupe: Sensacionales descubrimientos en los ojos de la Virgen Mexicana* [The Mystery of the Virgin of Guadalupe: Sensational Discoveries in the Eyes of the Mexican Virgin], 2nd ed. (Barcelona: Planeta, 2004); Laurentin and Sbalchiero, *Dictionnaire*, 402–9; Clodovis M. Boff, *Mariologia sociale: Il significato della Vergine per la società* [Social Mariology: The Significance of the Virgin for Society]. BTC 136 (Brescia: Queriniana, 2007), 224–57;Eduardo Chávez Sanchez, "Guadalupe," in De Fiores, Schiefer, and Perrella, *DMar*, 596–602; Carl Anderson and Eduardo Chávez, *Nuestra Señora de Guadalupe: Madre de la civilización del amor* [Our Lady of Guadalupe: Mother of the Civilization of Love] (Mexico D. F.: Grijalbo; New York: Random House, 2010).

The same day, Juan Diego receives a second apparition on Tepeyac with the request to go to the bishop again. At this second meeting, the bishop asks for a sign that can testify to the truth of the events. In a third apparition, Mary promises the seer a sign, and in the fourth apparition, he is told to collect Castilian roses from the hilltop, which is covered in flowers in the middle of winter. The Indian collects the roses in his mantle and is given the order to take them to the bishop. When Juan Diego opens his mantle, the roses fall from it, and on the mantle the image of Mary is seen, as the seer saw her on the hill. With this the bishop is convinced: he recognizes the authenticity of the event and, that year, he places the image in a temporary chapel on Tepeyac. In 1566 a formal canonical process follows, which reaches a positive conclusion.

With regard to the image, the message reported is significant, as are its consequences for the Christianization of Mexico and modern research that confirms the supernatural origin of the icon. The name "Guadalupe" does not come from the eponymous Marian shrine in Spain, but probably consists of a "hispanicized" version of an indigenous word (Coatlaxopeuh), which means "she who crushes the serpent." The face of the woman represented is neither white nor Indian, but seems to be a mixture. She is not a goddess, because she does not wear a mask, and because she folds her hands in prayer. She stands in front of the sun, sets her feet upon the crescent moon (symbol of the serpent-god) and is clothed in a star-covered mantle; and thus she is more powerful than the gods indicated by those symbols. While in the Aztec mythology the gods oppose one another (the gods of the sun and the moon), the image unites the symbols around Mary. Both the sun-god and the moon-god were divinities to whom human victims were offered: in 1487, in a single day, at the dedication of a temple, 20,000 soldiers were sacrificed to placate the sun-god. In addition, 20,000 human victims were offered every year to the serpent god, the most terrible monster of the Aztec religion.

Her tunic is of a pale red, the color of the supreme god. The black bands that fall from Mary's hands are signs of motherhood. The color of the mantle, between blue and green, indicates the blue of the sky (seat of the supreme god) and the green of jade, considered more valuable than gold, silver, and the other precious stones. Blue and green were colors of divinity; only the king could wear such a garment. A little below the neck, Mary wears a Christian cross, which resembles an Aztec symbol that signifies the universe.

Along with the music heard by Juan Diego and the roses, which refer to a life beyond human suffering, the "tilma" (the mantle with the image) presents itself as an inculturation, manifested in the image, between the desires of paganism and their fulfillment in Christianity. After the apparition a mass conversion began, the greatest that ever took place in the history of the church. In the ten years between 1531 and 1541 about eight million conversions were counted in Mexico. The movement also spread beyond the Mexican environment to other countries of Latin America.

With regard to modern research on the "tilma," we can state that no one knows what the colors on the mantle consist of, since they are not from any material of a vegetable source, nor of animal or mineral origin. There is no trace of the use of a brush. It is also surprising how the image has remained on material that normally degrades into powder within twenty years. The image has remained intact and fresh despite the vapors to which it has been exposed and despite an attempted attack in 1921. Some surprising research has determined that the right eye of the Marian icon has the appearance of a human pupil and contains (as if in a photograph) the scene that took place at the opening of the "tilma" with its roses before Bishop Zumárraga. Not unreasonably, some see the "tilma" as the Marian counterpart of the Shroud of Turin. In 1999 the feast of Our Lady of Guadalupe, assigned to December 12, became a required observance for the entire American continent, and in 2002 it became an optional memorial for the whole Catholic world.

On May 4, 2008, the bishop of Gap and Embrun recognized "the supernatural character of the events seen and reported by Benoîte Rencurel, which took place from 1664 to 1718." He was referring to apparitions of Mary at *Le Laus*, in the Hautes-Alpes region of southeast France. The seer (1647–1718), a shepherd, had daily apparitions of the Blessed Virgin within the space of four months in 1664. The recognition also relates to mystical graces until the death of the seer in 1718, but it is not a case of daily apparitions for fifty years.

Mary asked that a church be built in honor of her Son and of her, "because many sinners will be converted here." She also asked for a house for priests, so that they could receive and hear the confessions of pilgrims. There were healings studied by an episcopal commission. There was no formal decree at all, but the vicar general, in 1665, named a rector for the shrine and ordered preparations for building a church. According to Mary's promise, the oil of the shrine's lamp was applied to the organs of the sick, and thereby many healings took place, to encourage the conversion of sinners. The seer, in 1673, received the stigmata. From 1692 on, Benoîte was subjected to persecutions by the Jansenists. The recent recognition found a basis in four accounts of eyewitnesses at the time of the events. The apparitions highlight divine mercy in the face of the rationalist rigorism of the Jansenists.[48]

For the Marian apparitions of recent times, those of 1830 at the *Rue du Bac* in Paris, which were expressed iconographically in the "Miraculous Medal," are noted as the beginning of a whole era. In it we find the basic program of subsequent apparitions. The three Marian apparitions (July 18; November 27; December 1830) were granted to Catherine Labouré, a young postulant of the Daughters of Charity of St. Vincent de Paul. On November 27 three images were shown to Catherine, according to which medals were to be struck:

1. Mary's feet rested on a sphere; under her feet was a serpent. The head of the Mother of God was surrounded with a crown of twelve stars. In the hands of the Virgin a golden orb appeared, a symbol of the earth that Mary offers to God; on the Madonna's fingers were many precious rings from which parted rays, a symbol of the graces bestowed by God through the intercession of Mary. The jewels without rays represented graces that were not requested.

48. See Chiron, *Enquête*, 149–57; Laurentin and Sbalchiero, *Dictionnaire*, 515–16; Bertrand Gournay, *Notre-Dame du Laus: L'espérance au cœur des Alpes* [Our Lady of Laus: Hope in the Heart of the Alps] (Paris: P. Téqui, 2008).

2. The little orb disappeared and Mary lowered her hands, so that the rays were directed downward. Around her appeared the inscription, "O Mary conceived without sin, pray for us who have recourse to you."

3. Last, the reverse of the medal was presented: the letter "M," with a cross above it, and below, the hearts of Jesus (with the crown of thorns) and of Mary (with the sword).

The bishop of Paris took the conversion of the former archbishop of Malines (Belgium) as a validation of the apparition's authenticity and of the efficacy of the medal. In 1832 he approved the minting of the medal, which spread rapidly, even through surprising events, such as the conversion of the Jew Alphonse Ratisbonne (1842, in the church of S. Andrea delle Fratte in Rome). The apparitions at the Rue du Bac, despite their de facto acceptance in various forms, never received formal recognition; on the other hand, such recognition was given to the mariophany to Ratisbonne.[49]

The design of the medal shows Mary between Christ and the church. The origin of grace in Christ is depicted in the cross and in the heart crowned with thorns. The church is represented in the orb that represents all of humanity and every man who is part of the church or is called to her. At the same time, Mary appears as a type of the church, in opposition to Satan: the crown with twelve stars recalls chapter 12 of the Book of Revelation, which is in turn a rereading of Genesis 3:15 (the Protoevangelium). The "great sign" of Revelation is thus shown in its Marian dimension.

Many authors interpret the relevance of Marian prophecy since 1830 with Grignion de Montfort's theology of history: the struggle of the church and Mary against Satan becomes stronger with the nearness of the Parousia. As Mary prepared the first coming of Jesus, she likewise prepares his second coming at the end of time. With consecration to Mary a stronger bond with Jesus is obtained.

The Most Sacred Heart of Jesus, wounded by the thorns of sin, shows the human love of Jesus for the Father and for men, a love

49. See Laurentin and Sbalchiero, *Dictionnaire*, 96, 824.

sustained by the infinite divine love of the Son of God. The human response to God's preceding love is revealed in the Immaculate Heart of Mary, pierced by the sword of sorrows, a sharer in the sufferings of Jesus. In this way, the heart is found in the center of the message as a sign of total love.

A Marian apparition took place on September 19, 1846, at *La Salette* in the French Alps, before two shepherd children: Mélanie and Maximin (illiterate and with almost no religious education at the ages of fourteen and eleven). The children saw a beautiful lady seated on a rock, her face covered by her hands, as if oppressed by a great suffering. The lady rises and calls to the children, "Come nearer, don't be afraid ... !" On her breast they see a large cross (Jesus, covered with blood, in agony) and the instruments of the Passion (hammer, pincers). A few roses form a crown on her head; others are on her shoulders and on her shoes. The lady weeps and says she can no longer stay the arm of her Son; she laments for the fact that Sunday is no longer kept holy; for the many blasphemies that are uttered, and because religion is mocked, we need to pray well morning and evening; and it is important to observe Lent. A spring that beforehand was only seen periodically wells up.

The apparition was recognized as authentic by the local ordinary in 1851. The seers were required to write down (separately) the "secrets" entrusted to them. The pages were sent to Rome, but their content was only published in 2000 (when the relevant archive of the Holy Office was opened to researchers).[50] In the past, the so-

50. See Michel Corteville, *La grande nouvelle des bergers de la Salette* [The Great News of the Shepherds of La Salette] (Paris: P. Téqui, 2001), partial publication of a doctoral thesis at the Angelicum, Rome 2000; Michel Corteville and René Laurentin, *Découverte du secret de la Salette* [Discovery of the Secret of La Salette] (Paris: Fayard, 2002), 46–49; Antonio Galli, *Scoperti in Vaticano: I segreti di La Salette* [Discoveries in the Vatican: The Secrets of La Salette] (Milan: Sugarco, 2007), 55f, 121 (texts by Maximin and Mélanie). The secret written by Maximin indicates great tribulations in the church and in the world. The faith will undergo a sharp drop, especially in France, but thanks to the conversion of a large country in northern Europe, "now Protestant," the whole world will be converted. There will be a great peace, but only for a brief time, because a monster will arrive to disturb it. The secret of Mélanie reports more details, among others that if conversions are lacking, there will be terrible punishments, including the destruction of Paris and Marseilles. The pope will be persecuted and there will be attempts to kill him, but he will triumph. After disorders that shake the world, there will be a new flowering of the Faith, but after some time, the disorder will begin again. The most terrible thing will be unrest between the ministers of God and the

called great secret revealed by Mélanie in a 1879 publication (with the bishop's imprimatur), was kept under lock and key by the Congregation. From 1915 to 1966 the circulation of the text published in 1879 was even barred with canonical penalties: suspension for priests and exclusion from the sacraments for lay Catholics.

The recognized part of the La Salette message underscores the importance of prayer and penance in the face of divine justice. In the tradition of La Salette, the Mass formulary on "The Blessed Virgin Mary, Mother of Reconciliation" was included in the Marian missal of 1986.[51]

The apparitions of *Lourdes* in 1858 have had a much greater importance for the whole church.[52] The seer, Bernadette Soubirous (age fourteen), came from the poorest family in the area, had a very modest education, and had not yet gone to her First Communion.

At the first apparition, February 11, 1858, Mary presents herself in the grotto of Massabielle as a girl, smiling, surrounded with light, with a white dress (and veil) and a blue belt, carrying a rosary. At the third apparition, Bernadette is asked to return to the grotto for fourteen days. The message consists of the invitation (1) to penance, (2) to prayer for the conversion of sinners, and (3) to atonement for sinners; also (4) in the request to wash in the spring that had arisen there (where the first healings occurred) and (5) to build a chapel. Other alleged "apparitions," which cannot claim any credibility, also took place there (but none before Bernadette).[53]

On March 25, the "Lady" reveals herself: "I am the Immaculate Conception," a message that Bernadette did not understand and that

---

religious sisters. The Antichrist will arrive, born of a religious sister. All this would happen within 100 years. For now, we cannot linger on the interpretation of these messages. See the bibliography in Laurentin and Sbalchiero, *Dictionnaire*, 511. The most noted historian of La Salette, Jean Stern, missionary of Our Lady of La Salette, reduces the secrets "to pious advice given to Maximin and Mélanie, and expanded by them and attributed to the Virgin later under the influence of unbalanced persons" (De Fiores, *Dizionario* 1:56); see Jean Stern, *La Salette: Documents authentiques*, 3 vols. (Paris: Cerf, 1984–91); Stern, "La Salette I. Geschichte," in Bäumer and Scheffczyk, *ML* 4:26; Stern, "La Salette: Une affaire de discernement" [La Salette: A Matter of Discernment], *Marianum* 72 (2010): 535–46.

51. *MBVM*, n. 14.

52. See Laurentin and Sbalchiero, *Dictionnaire*, 560–68.

53. See Laurentin and Sbalchiero, *Dictionnaire*, 564.

did not correspond to the local language. The final apparition occurred on the feast of Our Lady of Mount Carmel, July 16.

Recognition of the apparitions by the bishop came in 1862. The feast of the apparitions of Lourdes was permitted first at the regional level in 1891 (Leo XIII) and was extended to the entire church in 1907 (Pius X). Bernadette was beatified in 1925 and canonized in 1933. In 1969, the feast was converted into an optional memorial with the title of "Our Lady of Lourdes." The account of the apparitions is reported in the Liturgy of the Hours, in the second lesson of the Office of Readings.

In chronological order and a merely telegraphic style, let us mention the other apparitions received favorably by ecclesiastical authority:

- *Champion* (diocese of Green Bay, Wisconsin): three apparitions in October 1859 to Adèle Brise, a young immigrant woman from Belgium (1831–96); an invitation to conversion and to the task of gathering children for catechism; the miraculous protection of Sr. Adèle's foundation during a devastating fire in 1871; recognition of the supernatural character on December 8, 2010, by the bishop of Green Bay;[54]
- *Philippsdorf* (January 12–13, 1866, German-speaking northern Bohemia): apparition to Magdalena Kade and her miraculous healing recognized by a commission established by the bishop that year; however, there was no formal recognition on the part of the bishop;[55]
- *Pontmain* (January 17, 1871, France, during the war with Prussia): signs in the sky: Mary, particular stars; while sixty persons are praying at the site, Mary appears larger and more beautiful; inscription: "Pray, my children! God will answer you soon. My Son lets himself be moved." Mary shows the cross with the inscrip-

54. See Imre von Gaal, "Die Marienerscheinungen in Robinsonville/Champion im Bistum Green Bay (Wisconsin, USA)" [Marian Apparitions in Robinsonville/Champion in the Diocese of Green Bay], *Sedes Sapientiae: Mariologisches Jahrbuch* 16, no. 2 (2012): 35–59.

55. See Emil Valasek, "Philippsdorf," in Bäumer and Scheffczyk, *ML* 5:204; Laurentin and Sbalchiero, *Dictionnaire*, 726–29; Chiron, *Enquête*, 205–8.

tion "Jesus Christ"; shortly after the apparition, the advance of the Prussians stops; recognition in 1872;[56]

- *Pellevoisin* (twelve apparitions from February 15 to December 8, 1876 in central France): miraculous cure of the seer who was about to die; image similar to that of the Rue du Bac: from her hands, Mary pours out graces "taken" from the Heart of Jesus; scapular of the Sacred Heart of Jesus; recognition by the bishop of Bourges in 1983 [!], which did not explicitly confirm the supernatural character of the apparition, but speaks of the miraculous character of the healing that makes the message credible;[57]
- *Dietrichswalde* (1877, apparitions over the course of four months to two girls, twelve and thireen years old; Germany, East Prussia, diocese of Ermland [Warmia], its present-day Polish name is *Gietrzwald*); context: the *Kulturkampf*, the campaign of the German state against the Catholic Church; request to pray the Rosary; Mary as the Immaculate Conception; recognized by the Polish ordinary only in 1977;[58]
- *Cnoc (Knock) Mhuire* (August 21, 1879, Ireland, in the evening); the scene already described above;[59] recognition, at least de facto, 1879/80, reiterated in 1936; central Marian shrine of Ireland; focus on the eucharistic sacrifice.[60]

Besides the apparitions at the Rue du Bac (1830) and those of Lourdes (1858), the greatest importance among the Marian apparitions after Guadalupe undoubtedly belongs to those of *Fatima* in Portugal (1917).[61] The seers were three illiterate children (Lucia, ten

56. See Laurentin and Sbalchiero, *Dictionnaire*, 746–55.

57. See Laurentin and Sbalchiero, *Dictionnaire*, 713–15; Chiron, *Enquête*, 223–36.

58. See A. Poschmann and J. Schwalke, "Dietrichswalde," in Bäumer and Scheffczyk, *ML* 2:194f.; Laurentin and Sbalchiero, *Dictionnaire*, 389f.

59. Regarding Knock, see also p. 385.

60. See Laurentin and Sbalchiero, *Dictionnaire*, 493f; Chiron, *Enquête*, 240–44.

61. See the authoritative synthesis by the official responsible, for many years, for collecting historical material on Fatima, much of it still largely unpublished: Joaquín María Alonso, *Doctrina y espiritualidad del mensaje de Fátima* [Doctrine and Spirituality of the Message of Fatima] (Madrid: Arias Montana Editores, 1990). See also the classic by Luis Gonzaga da Fonseca, SJ, and J. M. Alonso, *Le meraviglie di Fatima* [The Miracles of Fatima], 31st ed. (Cinisello Balsamo: San Paolo, 1997). The most ample resource on the events, indispensable for a historical review, as well as on the reactions of ecclesiastics and of the world, is found in Michel de la Sainte Trinité, *Toute la vérité sur Fatima*, vol. 1, 5th ed.; vol. 2, 2nd ed.; vol. 3, 3rd ed. (Saint-Parres-lès-Vaudes: Maison

years old; Francisco, nine; Jacinta, seven). Six apparitions were said to have taken place in the "Cova da Iria" from May 13 to October 13, 1917, preceded by three angelic apparitions (1916), and followed by others to Lucia (Pontevedra, 1925—on the first five Saturdays of the month—and Tuy, 1929, on the consecration of Russia). For historical context the following are important: the First World War, the Russian Revolution, and the Masonic government in Portugal, with its strong opposition to the church.

The message can be summarized in five points:

1. pray the Rosary daily for world peace;
2. make sacrifices as atonement for sins;
3. veneration of the Immaculate Heart of Mary ("wounded" by sin) as a refuge and way that leads to God;
4. a secret in three parts, put in writing in 1943:

First part: a vision of hell;

Second part: the veneration of the Immaculate Heart of Mary; the impending end of the war, but the warning of another and more cruel war, if people do not convert; persecutions of the church and of the Holy Father; the consecration of Russia to the Immaculate Heart of Mary, and Communion of reparation on the first Saturday of the month; with the fulfillment of the requests, the conversion of Russia, peace; otherwise: the spread of Russia's errors in the world; wars and persecutions of the church; much suffering for the pope; the destruction of some nations; and finally the triumph of the Immaculate Heart; the pope consecrates Russia, which will be converted to the Immaculate Heart of Mary, and there will be a time of peace for the world; the true faith will be preserved in Portugal forever;

Third part ("third secret"): text only published June 26, 2000: a bishop dressed in white and other bishops, priests, and religious men

---

Saint-Joseph 1986); summarized and with additional material in François de Marie des Anges, *Fatima joie intime événement mondial*, 2nd ed. (Saint-Parres-lès-Vaudes: Editions de la contre-réforme catholique, 1993). For the debate among specialists see, as an exemplary case, *Actas do Congresso internacional de Fátima: Fenomenologia e teologia das apariçoes* (Fatima: Santuário de Fátima, 1998). A short recent summary: Laurentin and Sbalchiero, *Dictionnaire*, 316–46.

and women climb a mountain to a large cross and pass through a large city half destroyed, prayer for the souls of the dead; martyrdom of the pope and many others on the mountain top, the blood of martyrs flows from the cross and is collected by the angels who, with this blood, sprinkle souls so that they come closer to God. There has been controversy about the exact content of the third secret.[62]

5. the practice of the five first Saturdays of the month (Confession, Communion, Rosary, fifteen minutes contemplating the mysteries of the Rosary); given at Pontevedra, December 10, 1925: Lucia must "console" the heart of Mary, crowned with thorns that represent the sins of men.

From its trinitarian content to its eschatology,[63] the message traverses the entire traditional Catholic doctrine of the faith.[64]

As an "approval from Heaven," the "miracle of the sun" occurred October 13, 1917, before an immense crowd.

Official recognition of the apparitions of 1917 came on October 13, 1930, after eight years of work by the investigating commission; in 1939, the bishop also recognized the apparitions of Pontevedra (1925) and Tuy (1929), the latter bearing the message that the Holy Father must perform a consecration of Russia to the Immaculate Heart, together with all the bishops of the world; by this Russia will be saved.

62. See Congregation for the Doctrine of the Faith, *The Message of Fatima* (Vatican City: Libreria Editrice Vaticana, 2000); Luciano Guerra, *O "Segredo" de Fátima* [The "Secret" of Fatima] (Fatima: Reitoria do Santuario de Fátima, 2004); Solideo Paolini, *Fatima: Non disprezzate le profezie* [Fatima: Despise Not Prophecies] (Segno: Tavagnaco, 2005); Antonio Socci, *Il quarto segreto di Fatima* [The Fourth Secret of Fatima] (Milan: Rizzoli, 2006); Marco Tosatti, *La profezia di Fatima* (Casale Monferrato: Piemme, 2007); Tarcisio Bertone, *The Last Secret of Fatima* (New York: Image, 2013); Angelo Amato, "Giovanni Paolo II e il 'segreto' di Fatima," in *Maria la Theotokos* [Mary Theotokos: Consciousness and Experience] (Vatican City: Libreria Editrice Vaticana, 2011), 241–58; Salvatore M. Perrella, "Il 'messagio di Fatima' della Congregazione per la Dottrina della Fede (26 giugno 2000): Interpretazioni contemporanee" [CDF's "Message of Fatima" (June 26, 2000), Contemporary Interpretations], *Marianum* 74, no. 181–82 (2012): 283–356. The hypothesis of a "fourth mystery" of Fatima silenced by St. John Paul II is unfounded: see Antonio Borelli Machado, "Riflessioni amichevoli per chiarire una polemica" [Amicable Reflections to Clarify a Dispute], *Lepanto* 26, n. 174 (October 2007), 1–24; Hauke, "Die Diskussion um das dritte Geheimnis von Fatima" [The Debate on the Third Secret of Fatima], *Sedes Sapientiae: Mariologisches Jahrbuch* 14, no. 2 (2010): 92–109.

63. In the angelic prayer taught to the seers in 1916 (Author's note).

64. Stefano De Fiores, "Fatima," in *ML* 2:447.

The Portuguese bishops consecrated the country to the Immaculate Heart in 1931. In 1942 (October 31 and December 8) the consecration of mankind to the Immaculate Heart by Pius XII followed. Paul VI (1967) and John Paul II (1982, after the attack on May 13, 1981) renewed this consecration on the occasion of a pilgrimage to Fatima. The Feast of the Immaculate Heart of Mary was instituted in 1944, without reference to the apparitions of Fatima. It was first placed on August 22; then after 1969, on the Saturday following the second Sunday after Pentecost, as an optional memorial. There is a votive Mass in the Marian Missal of 1986: MBVM no. 28). The optional memorial of Our Lady of Fatima entered the general calendar in 2002, on May 13.

The doctrinal content inherent in the apparitions of Fatima is very rich and can be summarized with a few key words: the importance of penance, highlighted by temporal punishment for sins, especially war; the importance of prayer (the Rosary and its meditation), of the sacramental life (Confession, Eucharist) and Communion of reparation; the presence of the celestial world (Mary, angels), the reality of damnation and diligence about eternal salvation, the practice of Marian devotion (Immaculate Heart, Saturday, Rosary) and the theme of the heart (that is, of love). The core of these messages is devoted to adoration of the Most Sacred Heart of Jesus and veneration of the Immaculate Heart of Mary. These devotions are very important for the conversion of mankind. It underscores the importance of peace and presents concrete indications on the historical situation (the role of Russia, persecutions). The messages finish with assurance of the final triumph of the Immaculate Heart.[65]

In the 1930s apparitions took place in Belgium, at *Beauraing* (thirty-three appearances at a Lourdes grotto, November 29, 1932–January 3, 1933), witnessed by five seers, children from nine to fifteen years of age; its message: wisdom, prayer, especially the rosary, sacri-

65. Among the interpretations of the theological message, that of Cardinal Scheffczyk, *Maria, Mutter und Gefährtin Christi* [Mary, Mother and Companion of Christ] (Augsburg: Sankt Ulrich, 2003), 282–356 stands out; see also the synthesis by Stefano M. Manelli, "Fatima tra passato, presente e futuro" [Fatima between Past, Present, and Future], *Immaculata Mediatrix* 7 (2007): 299–431.

fice for sinners, veneration of the heart of Mary; recognized in 1943, miraculous healings;[66] and *Banneux* (eight appearances, January 15, 1932–March 2, 1933); the seer a girl, age twelve, from a religiously indifferent family; message: a strong connection with Lourdes, a spring for all nations to relieve the suffering of the sick; the title "Virgin of the poor," prayer; recognition in two stages: 1942 and 1949.[67]

Let us also mention, by way of example, a case in which the public cult has been permitted without yet reaching formal recognition of a supernatural origin. From December 8 to 14, 1947, ten apparitions took place at *L'Île-Bouchard* in the diocese of Tours (France) before four girls in the church of Saint-Gilles. The Marian manifestations were supported by miraculous events announced in advance: the healing of a severe myopia and a beam of light observed by the crowd present there for four minutes. Mary asked them to erect a grotto at the place of the apparitions and to pray for France, which found itself in great danger (in fact there was a risk of civil war because of the massive presence of the Communist Party). As early as December 20, 1947, the archbishop of Tours allowed the construction of the grotto. Archbishop André Vingt-Trois, on December 8, 2001, after studying the events, permitted the public cult and pilgrimages to the place of the apparitions.[68]

Lacrimations usually are not tied to apparitions, but tears themselves are already a message, a call to repentance. We already had cases in past centuries.[69] In modern times, the lacrimation at *Siracusa* in 1953 is particularly well documented. A portrait of the Madonna (with the Immaculate Heart) in the house of a young couple wept four days and three nights (from August 29 until September 1, 1953).

66. See Laurentin and Sbalchiero, *Dictionnaire*, 120–23.

67. See Reckinger, "Die Marienerschienungen der Neuzeit," 247–55; Laurentin and Sbalchiero, *Dictionnaire*, 111–15.

68. See Bernard Peyrous, *Les événements de l'Île-Bouchard: Une présence de Marie au milieu de nous* [The Events of Ile-Bouchard: A Presence of Mary in Our Midst] (Paray-le-Monial: Editions de l'Emmanuel, 2002); Laurentin and Sbalchiero, *Dictionnaire*, 529–35.

69. See Laurentin and Sbalchiero, *Dictionnaire*, 285 (announcing a dictionary on the subject); Rosaria Ricciardo, "Siracusa: Lacrime di Maria" [Syracuse: Tears of Mary], in De Fiores, Schiefer, and Perrella, *DMar*, 1104–13. In Ticino, for example, at the shrine of Castelletto sopra Melano a lacrimation occurred in 1633, recognized as miraculous by the diocese of Como: See Annibale Pagnamenta, *Storia del Castelletto* [History of Castelletto] (Lugano: Gaggini—Bizzozero, 1983).

The woman had first called on Mary because of the risk of a dangerous pregnancy; later came the announcement of a happy delivery, which occurred on Christmas day. There were thousands of witnesses and there was a scientific investigation of the portrait and the tears. Recognition by the Sicilian bishops took place on December 12, 1953. The message recalls the importance of penance and the help of Mary for human necessities.

The tears of Mary (La Salette, Siracusa) are a very impressive phenomenon. They show the maternal participation of Mary in the fate of her children; certainly, there is a connection with the tears shed by Mary on earth. But the tears cannot be interpreted as a description of the heavenly state, nor is this the case for the representation of Jesus' agony in La Salette and the vision of the infant Jesus in Fatima. One cannot maintain that the Mother of God in Heaven, who is in the Beatific Vision, is suffering and weeping: in Heaven, "God will wipe away every tear from their eyes" (Rv 7:17; see Rv 21:4; Is 25:5). The full beatitude of the saints is also the subject of the most important dogmatic decisions on eschatology.[70]

The tears do not describe the heavenly state of Mary, but highlight the situation of man in sin, exposed to eternal damnation. As Jesus (on earth) wept over Jerusalem, the tears of his mother reveal the seriousness of sin and the need for conversion.

An interesting bridge between the Muslim world and the Christian faith are the apparitions at *Zeitoun*, on the outskirts of Cairo, between 1968 and 1970 (from Easter Sunday, April 2, 1968, until September 1970).[71] There were hundreds of appearances at night above the Coptic church of Mary in front of some hundreds of thousands of witnesses. The first witnesses were two mechanics. There are even photographs.

Mary appears in a blue-white dress with a veil, always with the infant Jesus, and sometimes she moves her hand to bless or she shows an olive branch before the people. There is no verbal message.

As early as May 4, 1968, came the recognition of the Coptic pa-

70. DH 1000f.

71. See Hauke, "Der prophetische Dienst Mariens," 58f; Laurentin and Sbalchiero, *Dictionnaire*, 154–58.

triarch, followed by a positive position taken by the Catholic patriarch, the Archimandrite of the Greek-Catholic church, and the representative of the Protestant community (!) in Egypt. An additional confirmation exists by way of official documentation for the Egyptian government, written by the Department of Information.

Lacrimations, messages, and miraculous healings are connected to the phenomena that occurred at *Akita*, Japan (1973–82).[72] The seer is a retired catechist (born 1931), who was cured of deafness in 1982. There is a strong connection with the message of Fatima, particularly in the need for atonement for the sins of the world and to stop the impending universal chastisement. The apparitions ask for prayer, especially the Rosary, for the pope, the bishops, and priests; it speaks of wounds within the church and of mass desertion by priests and religious. More than a hundred times there were tears with blood on the statue. The Bishop of Niigata recognized the authenticity of the phenomena on April 22, 1984.

Marian apparitions have also been recognized in Venezuela, after they occurred on a farm two hours from Caracas: *Finca Betania* (1976–84).[73] The seer was the owner of the farm, Maria Esperanza Medrano de Bianchini (1928–2001). There were two main apparitions: March 25, 1976, at the foot of a grotto near a spring (Mary as refuge and as "reconciler of peoples"); March 25, 1984, in front of a waterfall after a Eucharistic celebration (over 1,000 witnesses: those attending the Mass, for others a surprise during their Sunday picnic; Mary was seen in several ways, recalling the apparitions of Lourdes, Rue du Bac, Mater Dolorosa, Our Lady of Mount Carmel, surrounded with light and the scent of roses).

The investigation was guided personally by the bishop (who had been a professor of psychology). Official recognition by the bishop of the supernatural character of the events took place in 1987.

A significant part of the apparitions at *Kibeho*, Rwanda (1981–89), was recognized by the local bishop, Mgr. Augustin Misago, with the tacit agreement of the Holy See and the Episcopal Conference of

72. See Laurentin and Sbalchiero, *Dictionnaire*, 1022–26.

73. See ibid., 1054–57; Antonio Larocca, "Las apariciones marianas en Betania (Cúa, Venezuela)" [Marian Apparitions in Betania (Cúa, Venezuela)], *Ephemerides mariologicae* 58 (2008): 509–16.

Rwanda, June 29, 2001 (approval of the public cult took place in 1988, with the invocation of Mary as "Mother of Sorrows" and "Mother of the Word"). There is an urgent call to prayer and conversion. *"Si vous ne vous repentez pas et ne convertissez pas vos coeurs vous allez tous tomber dans un gouffre."* "If you do not repent and convert your hearts you will all fall into a chasm." The prophetic vision of horrors that became reality later, in 1994–95, is impressive.[74]

On May 31, 2002, the bishop of *Amsterdam*, Bishop J. M. Punt, recognized the supernatural character of the messages received by Mrs. Ida Peerdeman (†1996) from 1945 to 1959. There are still problems: there is no tacit agreement (as in the case of Kibeho) with the bishops' conference (which is recommended, although not required by law); the negative decision of the Congregation for the Doctrine of the Faith in 1974 has not been revoked; this judgment of the Holy See prevails over the local bishop. In 2005, the CDF (through the secretary, Angelo Amato) released a document that prohibits the use of the formula (in a "revealed" prayer) "the woman who once [*sic*] was Mary." Since then, publications have appeared that show strong doubts with respect to the supernatural origin of the Amsterdam apparitions.[75]

This example also reminds us of the case of receiving a varied reception by ecclesiastical authority. A Marian prophecy reaches the highest degree of credibility when the recognized sanctity of the seers and the liturgical celebration of the events are united. For the liturgical aspect, the peak comes with a feast prescribed at the universal level. Saint Catherine Labouré (Rue du Bac), Saint Bernadette (Lourdes), and Saint Juan Diego (Guadalupe) were canonized; two of the seers of Fatima have been canonized. There is an optional liturgical memorial for the entire church in regard to Lourdes, Fatima, and Guadalupe, while the feast of Our Lady of Guadalupe was introduced for an entire continent (the Americas).

74. See Gianni Sgreva, *Le apparizioni della Madonna in Africa: Kibeho* [Apparitions of Our Lady in Africa: Kibeho], 2nd ed. (Camerata Picena: Shalom, 2004); Laurentin and Sbalchiero, *Dictionnaire*, 1162–64.

75. Regarding Amsterdam, see also "The Call for a Dogma on the Title 'Co-Redemptrix,'" in chapter 8.

Unrecognized Phenomena

A great number of phenomena that are not recognized or that are outright rejected by church authority are reported in Joachim Bouflet's essay on the "falsifiers of God" (2000). As a first case let us cite the Canadian visionary Marie-Paule *Giguère* (1921–2005), foundress of the "Army of Mary" (not to be confused with the "Blue Army" that is inspired by Fatima.)[76] The seer wrote 6,000 pages of alleged "revelations" in fifteen volumes, of which thirteen were published under the title "Vie d'amour." The group she founded in 1971, the Army of Mary, was recognized in 1975 by the Archbishop of Quebec, Mgr. Maurice Roy. Twelve years later, Cardinal Vachon, the successor to Archbishop Roy, withdrew the ecclesiastical approval of the "Army," in spite of numerous vocations inspired in Mrs. Giguère's organization. The reason lies in messages contrary to human common sense and the doctrine of the church: the defense of women priests, including the "mystical ordination" of Marie-Paule; the fact that the seer is considered a reincarnation of the Virgin Mary as well as the Coredemptrix who crushes the serpent's head, the announcement that the seer would receive the title "*doctor Ecclesiae*," would be already canonized during her life, and would perform miracles everywhere (it would be enough to embrace a photo of her), while her son Pierre would become "the great Pope of Peace." The true origin of these phenomena, of a spiritualist-magical type, is displayed in the seer's use of a crystal ball. It is not enough to look at the positive fruits (numerous vocations to the priesthood and to consecrated life) to assess the alleged apparitions to Marie-Paule that certainly cannot be accepted as authentic.[77]

A similar phenomenon, widely promoted and supported even by noted mariologists (such as Rene Laurentin and Michael O'Carroll), are the "dictations" given by "spirits" to Vassula Ryden, a member of

76. See Joachim Bouflet, *Faussaires de Dieu* [Forgers of God], 2nd ed. (Paris: Presses de la renaissance, 2007), 560–70.

77. In 2006, the Army of Mary formed a schismatic group, "L'Église de Jean"; its members were excommunicated in 2007 when a priest of this new "church" began to carry out diaconal and then priestly ordinations. See Robert Fastiggi, "The Rise and Fall of the Army of Mary (L'Armée de Marie)," *Marian Studies* 63 (2012): 124–55.

the Orthodox Church.[78] The events began when Ryden (in 1985) was forced (!) by her "guardian angel" to write certain messages.[79] The greater part of the messages is "orthodox," but several disturbing factors and doctrines are clearly present. Suffice it to quote the invitation of the "Eternal Father": "Peace be with you. Any word that you feel is not right and that bothers you, feel free to correct it. I, God, give you that feeling. Vassula, are you happy?" This message (October 12, 1986) is not only totally misleading, but also in open contradiction with other messages, including, "Repeat only the words that I myself have given you, do not add or subtract anything; be dedicated to Me" (July 14, 1992).[80] The spiritualistic provenance of the messages, which are identical to automatic writing, is evident. A Communique from the Congregation for the Doctrine of the Faith (October 6, 1995) somewhat put the brakes on Ryden's promotional activity within church circles: bishops were urged not to give room for the lady to spread her ideas, and the faithful were urged not to believe in the alleged supernatural origin of her messages. CDF warns, among other things, against confusion of the trinitarian persons and about misleading elements concerning ecumenism, including Ryden's habitual participation in the sacraments of the Catholic Church, despite her membership in the Greek Orthodox Church [and her being divorced and remarried].

While the cases of Ryden and Giguère are phenomena clearly to be rejected, there is a lively debate for and against the supernatural character of the events of *Medjugorje* that have taken place since June 24, 1981.[81] There is not adequate space in this book to present

78. See François-Marie Dermine, *Vassula Ryden: Indagine critica* [Vassula Ryden: Critical Inquiry] (Leumann (Turin): Editrice Elle Di Ci, 1995). In Laurentin and Sbalchiero, *Dictionnaire*, 1296, Laurentin speaks of a "rehabilitation" of Ryden in 2002 by then-Cardinal Ratzinger. The erroneous interpretation of a "rehabilitation" was denied by Cardinal William Levada, prefect of the CDF, in a letter to Catholic bishops, January 25, 2007, available on the internet at http://www.vatican.va/roman_curia/congregations/cfaith/doc_dottrinali_index.htm. The most recent published collection of CDF documents shows only the critical note of 1995, *Documenta inde a Concilio Vaticano secundo expleto edita (1966–2005)* (Vatican City: Libreria Editrice Vaticana, 2006), 455f = *AAS* 88 (1996) 956f.

79. See Dermine, *Vassula Ryden*, 25–27.

80. Quoted in ibid., 72, which adds, "Such management is sufficient by itself to reject the phenomenon en bloc."

81. See the bibliography given in Hauke, "Psychotrip, Teufelsspuk oder Werk des Heiligen

the debate here. The church's official position at present is "non constat de supernaturalitate" (Declaration of the Commission of the Yugoslav Bishops, April 10, 1991).[82] The CDF, with a letter from Archbishop Tarcisio Bertone to the bishop of Réunion (Indian Ocean), May 26, 1998, refers to this evaluation and indicates the possibility that the Episcopal Conference of Bosnia-Herzegovina could take up the question again. In turn, the assessment by the local bishop, Mgr. Perić ("constat de non supernaturalitate"), should be considered as "a personal opinion."[83] "Finally, as regards pilgrimages to Medjugorje which take place in a private [!] manner, this Congregation believes that they are allowed, on the condition that they not be considered as an authentication of events in progress that still require an examination by the Church."[84] From 2010 to 2014, an international commission acting in the name of the Holy See examined the presumed apparitions; their examinations are being continued in the Congre-

Geistes? Die Ereignisse von Medjugorje in neueren Veröffentlichungen" [Psycho-Trip, Devilish Ghost, or Work of the Holy Spirit? The Events of Medjugorje in New Publications], *Theologisches* 35, no. 9 (2005): 613–22 (the text can be downloaded gratis from the website www.theologisches.net); first published in *Sedes Sapientiae: Mariologisches Jahrbuch* 9, no. 1 (2005): 159–174; Hauke, "'Die Anhänger nicht ins Leere fallen lassen': Das Phänomen Medjugorje; Hilfen zur Unterscheidung der Geister" ["Don't Let the Followers Fall into the Void": The Medjugorje Phenomenon; Aids in the Discernment of Spirits], in Rudo Franken, *Eine Reise nach Medjugorje*, 2nd ed. (Augsburg: Dominus-Verlag, 2011), 204–30 (see also the remarks on 240–49, 257–66). See also Yves Chiron, *Medjugorje demasqué (1981–2010): "Constat de non supernaturalitate"* [Medjugorje Unmasked (1981–2010): "Confirmed Not Supernatural"], 2nd ed. (Versailles: Via romana, 2010); Joachim Bouflet, *Ces dix jours qui ont fait Medjugorje: Aux sources des apparitions de Medjugorje* [The Ten Days That Made Medjugorje: To the Sources of the Medjugorje Apparitions] (Tours: CLD, 2007); Donal A. Foley, *Medjugorje Revisited: 30 Years of Visions or Religious Fraud?* (Nottingham, UK: Theotokos, 2011); James Mulligan, *Medjugorje: The First Days* (Medjugorje: n.p., 2013).

82. See Ivan Zeljko, *Marienerscheinungen—Schein und Sein aus theologischer und psychologischer Sicht: Dargestellt am Beispiel der Privatoffenbarungen in Medjugorje* [Marian Apparitions: Appearance and Reality from Theological and Psychological Viewpoints, Illustrated by the Example of Private Revelations at Medjugorje] (Hamburg: Dr. Kovač, 2004), 338–41; Thomas Müller, *Medjugorje: Ein Charisma und seine Bestätigung durch das Gottesvolk* [Medjugorje: A Charism and Its Affirmation by the People of God] (Vienna: Gebetsaktion Medjugorje, 2006), 72–75.

83. Mgr. Perić stated in his homily at Medjugorje on June 14, 2001, "I think and I say what the Catholic Church, on the basis of investigations by experts and responsible authorities, believes officially: that there has not been, in all this period, for all twenty years, a single authentic, recognized, supernatural apparition, not one recognized supernatural message, not one recognized supernatural revelation. This is what I publicly think and clearly say, so there is absolutely no misunderstanding." Quoted in Riccardo Caniato and Vincenzo Sansonetti, *Maria, alba del terzo millennio: Il dono di Medjugorje* [Mary, Dawn of the Third Millennium: The Gift of Medjugorje] (Milan: Ares, 2001), 351.

84. Quoted in Caniato and Sansonetti, *Maria, alba*, 343f.

gation for the Doctrine of the Faith. After the conclusion of these efforts a decision of the Holy See may come.

ASSESSING THE CONTENT OF THE MARIAN APPARITIONS AFTER 1830

In the apparitions recognized by church authority, we find a strong Christological and ecclesiological orientation.[85] There is a call to repentance and encouragement to prayer. A particular role (in modern times) has appeared for children and women. In woman we see the importance of prophecy not tied to a hierarchical ministry. Often (but not always) an "option for the poor" can be observed in the choice of the seers. All these moments underscore the accent on divine initiative not arising from human powers (see 1 Cor 1:27b–29.) Often support for the sick appears in healings that become a sign to rekindle faith. In Marian shrines connected with apparitions there is an increase in sacramental life (renewal of baptismal graces, Confession, Eucharist). When there is reference to the "great sign" of Revelation 12, the eschatological dimension is more than evident.

Apparitions, as it were, draw a portrait of Mary under specific titles and with reminders of various dogmatic aspects. Preeminent among the titles are those of the Immaculate Conception (Lourdes), Queen of the Rosary (Fatima), Virgin of the Poor (Banneux), Reconciler of Peoples (Finca Betania), Mother of Sorrows, and Mother of the Word (Kibeho). Among the dogmatic aspects, those connected with the Immaculate Conception and with Marian mediation are particularly emphasized. With Mary Immaculate, the request for consecration to her Immaculate Heart is also added. The fullness of grace and of glory is made manifest: the color white refers to purity and to the transfiguration of the body of Mary in Heaven; the blue is the color of Heaven; gold indicates royal dignity. The symbolism of light and of the spring evokes the intercession of Mary to spread the graces of Christ. The increase in mariophanies since 1830 is "a cry of

85. See more fully, Hauke, "Der prophetische Dienst Mariens," 29–47. See also De Fiores, *Dizionario*, 1:53–57.

a Mother who assume the tones of prophecy and of the apocalyptic in order to stop the foolish steps of so much of the world"[86] and to cooperate, as the new Eve and motherly mediatrix, in the merciful plan of God.

REFERENCES

Ecclesiastical Texts

CCC 65–67.

Lambertini, Prospero. (Benedict XIV). *De servorum Dei beatificatione et beatorum canonizatione* [Beatification of Servants of God, and Canonization of Beati] I–IV; especially book III, ch. 50–52. Rome, 1748.

Other Sources

Balić, Carolus. "Apparizioni mariane dei sec. XIX–XX" [Marian Apparitions of the 19th and 20th centuries]. In *EMTheo*, 234–54.

Billet, Bernard, et al. *Vraies et fausses apparitions dans l'Église* [True and False Apparitions in the Church]. Paris: P. Lethiellieux, 1973. 2nd ed., 1976.

Bouflet, Joachim. *Faussaires de Dieu* [Forgers of God]. 2nd ed. Paris: Presses de la renaissance, 2007.

———. "Las apariciones marianas y su recepción actual" [Marian Apparitions and Their Current Reception]. *Ephemerides Mariologicae* 58 (2008): 399–535.

Bouflet, Joachim, and Philippe Boutry. *Un segno nel cielo: Le apparizioni della Vergine* [A Sign in the Heavens: Apparitions of the Virgin]. Genoa: Marietti, 1999. French original: *Un signe dans le ciel: Les apparitions de la Vierge*. Paris: B. Grasset, 1997.

Castellano, Mario. "La prassi canonica circa le apparizioni mariane" [Canonical Practice Regarding Marian Apparitions]. In *EMTheo* (1954): 465–86; (1958): 486–505.

Cecchin, Stefano M., and Antonio Ligotti, ed. *Apparitiones Beatae Mariae Virginis in historia, fide, theologia: Acta congressus mariologici-mariani internationalis in civitate Lourdes anno 2008 celebrati* [Marian Apparitions in History, Faith, Theology: Acts of the Marian-Mariological International Congress at Lourdes in 2008]. Vol. 1. Vatican City: PAMI, 2010.

Chiron, Yves. *Enquête sur les apparitions de la Vierge* [Inquiry on the Apparitions of the Virgin]. 2nd ed. Paris: Perrin, 2007.

Coggi, Roberto. *La Beata Vergine: Trattato di Mariologia* [The Blessed Virgin: Treatise on Mariology], 252–61. Bologna: Studio Domenicano, 2004.

Colzani, Gianni. "Apparizioni." In De Fiores, Schiefer, and Perrella, *DMar*, 136–44.

———. *Maria: Mistero di grazia e di fede* [Mary: Mystery of Grace and Faith], 300–303. Cinisello Balsamo: Ed. Paoline, 1996. 3rd ed., 2006.

86. De Fiores, *Dizionario*, 1:59.

Congregation for the Doctrine of the Faith. *Norms Regarding the Manner of Proceeding in the Discernment of Presumed Apparitions or Revelations.* Vatican City, 2012.

De Fiores, Stefano. *Maria, Madre di Gesù: Sintesi storico-salvifica* [Mary, Mother of Jesus: Salvation-Historical Synthesis], 347–60. Corso di teologia sistematica 6. Bologna: EDB, 1992.

———. *Maria: Nuovissimo dizionario* [Mary: Newest Dictionary], 1:21–69. Bologna: EDB, 2006.

Hierzenberger, Gottfried, and Otto Nedomansky. *Dizionario cronologico delle apparizioni della Madonna* [Chronological Dictionary of Marian Apparitions]. Casale Monferrato: Piemme, 2004.

Holstein, Henri, SJ. "Les apparitions mariales" [Marian Apparitions]. In du Manoir, *Maria*, 5:755–78. Paris: Beauchesne, 1958.

Lais, H. "Erscheinungen" [Apparitions]. In *ML* 2:395–98.

Laurentin, René. "Apparizioni." In *NDM*, 125–37.

———. *Le apparizioni della Vergine e i più grandi miracoli della Madonna* [The Apparitions of the Virgin and the Greatest Miracles of the Madonna]. Casale Monferrato: Piemme, 2001.

Laurentin, René, and Patrick Sbalchiero, ed. *Dictionnaire des apparitions de la Vierge Marie* [Dictionary of Apparitions of the Virgin Mary]. Paris: Fayard, 2007.

Llamas, Enrique, ed. *Las apariciones marianas en la vida de la iglesia* [Marian Apparitions in the Life of the Church]. *Estudios Marianos* 52 (1987).

O'Carroll, Michael, CSSp. *Theotokos: A Theological Encyclopedia of the Blessed Virgin Mary*, 47–49. Eugene, Ore.: Wipf and Stock, 2000.

O'Connor, E. "The Theologian and Apparitions." In *De cultu mariano s. XX*, edited by PAMI, 4:21–50. Vatican City: PAMI, 1999.

PAMI, ed. *Maria et Ecclesia*. Vol. 12. Vatican City: PAMI, 1962.

Perrella, Salvatore M. *Le apparizioni mariane* [Marian Apparitions]. Cinisello Balsamo: San Paolo, 2007.

Petri, Heinrich. "Marienerscheinungen" [Marian Apparitions]. In Beinert and Petri, *Handbuch der Marienkunde*, 2:31–59.

Piacentini, Ernesto. *Nuovo corso sistematico di Mariologia sub luce Immaculatae* [New Systematic Course of Mariology in Light of the Immaculate], 189–218. Frascati (Rome): Bannò, 2002.

Rahner, Karl. *Visioni e profezie* [Visions and Prophecies]. Milan: Vita e Pensiero, 1995. German original: *Visionen und Prophezeiungen.* 2nd ed. Freiburg im Breisgau: Herder, 1958; reprint 1989. English translation: *Visions and Prophecies.* New York: Herder and Herder, 1964.

Ratzinger, Joseph. "Theological commentary." In Congregation for the Doctrine of the Faith, *The Message of Fatima*, 32–44.

Reckinger, F. "Die Marienerscheinungen der Neuzeit" [Marian Apparitions of the Modern Age]. In *Maria Mutter der Kirche*, edited by G. Stumpf, 201–58. Landsberg: Initiativkreis Kath. Laien und Priester in die Diözese Augsburg, 2004.

Rovira, German, ed. *Der Widerschein des ewigen Lichtes: Marienerscheinungen und Gnadenbilder als Zeichen der Gotteskraft* [Reflection of the Eternal Light: Marian

Apparitions and Images of Grace as Signs of the Power of God]. Kevelaer: Butzon and Bercker, 1984.

Scheffczyk, Leo. *Die theologischen Grundlagen von Erscheinungen und Prophezeiungen* [Theological Principles of Apparitions and Prophecies]. Leutesdorf: Johannes-Verlag, 1982.

———. *Maria, Mutter und Gefährtin Christi* [Mary, Mother and Companion of Christ], 349–56. Augsburg: Sankt Ulrich, 2003.

———. "Privatoffenbarungen" [Private Revelations]. In *ML* 5:318–20.

Suh, Augustinus. *Le rivelazioni private nella vita della Chiesa* [Private Revelations in the Life of the Church]. Bologna: Edizioni Studio Domenicano, 2000.

Volken, Laurent. *Le rivelazioni nella Chiesa* [Revelations in the Church]. Rome: Ed. Paoline, 1963. French original: *Les Révélations dans l'Église*. Tournai and Paris: Ed. Salvator, 1961.

Ziegenaus, Anton. *Maria in der Heilsgeschichte. Mariologie*, 369–76. Katholische Dogmatik 5. Aachen: MM-Verlag, 1998.

———, ed. *Marienerscheinungen: Ihre Echtheit und Bedeutung im Leben der Kirche* [Marian Apparitions: Their Authenticity and Meaning in the Life of the Church]. Mariologische Studien 10. Regensburg: Friedrich Pustet, 1995.

Ten

Marian Veneration and Devotion

THE PRINCIPLES OF MARIAN *CULTUS*

The word "worship" (*cultus*), in its generic meaning, refers to honor directed to a person because of his or her excellence. In the religious realm it refers to the reverence expressed toward God and to the creatures united with him. First of all, worship is owed to God as Lord and End of every creature; we speak of adoration or latreutic worship (*cultus latriae*; the Greek word *latreía* refers to service of God). Honor directed to saints is motivated by their union with God; such veneration is called dulia (*cultus duliae; douleía* in Greek refers to service or slavery in general). Given that Mary is the Mother of God and surpasses all other creatures in dignity, an "altogether singular" *cultus is* appropriate for her;[1] this *cultus* has been called *cultus hyperduliae* [hyperdulia] since the thirteenth century (in the West) (that is, "above" simple dulia).[2]

The distinction among the various forms of devotion traces back to antiquity, when the veneration of sacred images was defended. The Second Council of Nicea (787) affirmed that "actual worship (*latreía)*," "according to our faith, is reserved to the divine nature alone," while veneration (*proskúnesis*) is also right for sacred images

1. *LG* 66: "*singularis omnino.*"

2. See Luigi Ciappi, OP, "Fondamenti e principi del culto a Maria" [Foundations and Principles of the Cult of Mary], in *EMTheo* (1958): 351–63; A. Bodem, "Hyperdulie," in Bäumer and Scheffczyk, *ML* 3:277.

because "he who venerates an image venerates in it the person whom the image represents."[3]

The cult of devotion expressed to the saints was rejected by the Reformers. According to Luther, the saints in heaven pray for us (including Mary), but it would a mistake to invoke their intercession. In any case, the German reformer was able to affirm that Mary could not be exalted highly enough.[4] In Protestantism we have some forms of veneration for the Mother of the Lord, but it is almost always forbidden to address a prayer to her.[5] Sometimes every kind of veneration is rejected, as is the case in Karl Barth: "Where Mary is 'venerated' [*verehrt*], where this whole doctrine [Mariology] with its corresponding devotions is current, there the Church of Christ is not."[6] Because they lack the distinction between veneration and adoration, Protestants at times accuse Catholics of "adoring" Mary.

To respond to the Protestant critique, the Council of Trent published a decree "on the Invocation, Veneration, and Relics of the Saints and on Sacred Images."[7] The faithful should be taught "that the saints, reigning together with Christ, pray to God for men; that it is good and useful to invoke them humbly and to have recourse to their prayers, to their help and assistance, in order to obtain favors from God through his Son, our Lord Jesus Christ, who alone is our Redeemer and Savior. Those, however, think in an impious way who deny that the saints enjoying eternal happiness in heaven are to be invoked; or who claim that the saints do not pray for men."[8]

The Mother of God is also implicit in this declaration. Moreover,

3. DH 601; see Fourth Council of Constantinople (870): DH 653; DH 1269 (Council of Constance, 1418).

4. *Tischreden* I, n. 494, cited in Leo Scheffczyk, *Maria, Mutter der Kirche* [Mary, Mother of the Church] (St. Ottilien: EOS Verlag, 1979), 275.

5. See Achim Dittrich, *Protestantische Mariologie-Kritik: Historische Entwicklung bis 1997 und dogmatische Analyse* [Protestant Criticism of Mariology: Historical Development to 1997 and Dogmatic Analysis], Mariologische Studien 11 (Regensburg: Pustet, 1998), 289f. Nor is there an exception in the Dombes Group, *Mary in the Plan of God and the Communion of Saints* (New York: Paulist Press, 2002), n. 333. For Protestants, at most, it is possible to pray to God together with Mary, but not to ask directly for the intercession of the Mother of God. Despite this, there are some Protestant theologians who are willing to recite the Rosary.

6. Barth, *Church Dogmatics*, vol. 1, part 2, 143.

7. DH 1821–25.

8. DH 1821.

the role of Mary in the history of salvation surpasses that of every other created person and is part of the deposit of faith. Here it also seems important to reaffirm that every mystery of the faith is also an object of veneration and liturgical worship.

The biblical foundations of Marian devotion can be seen with particular force in the Gospel according to Luke: the angelic salutation (Lk 1:28), the blessing given by Elizabeth (Lk 1:42) and the affirmation of the Magnificat: "From this day all generations will call me blessed" (Lk 1:48).

In the chapter on history, we already saw the development of Marian devotion in the early church. In the third and fourth centuries, we find the first traces of the invocation of Mary in prayer (*Sub tuum praesidium*, Gregory of Nazianzus).[9] After the Council of Ephesus (431) the number of churches dedicated to Mary grows sharply, as does the entire devotion to the *Theotókos*. At the same time the development of Marian feasts begins, whereas at first the Marian aspect was present, above all, in the liturgical commemorations of the Nativity and the Epiphany.

Already in the early church it was necessary to combat some deviations regarding the cult of Mary. Epiphanius takes a stand against the sect of the Kollyridians, in which women offered cakes as a sacrifice to Mary.[10] The same author speaks of the opposite extreme, of the Antidicomarianites, who denied the perpetual virginity of Mary and refused all *cultus* to her.[11]

In the constitution *Lumen gentium*, Vatican II affirms the principal notes of veneration directed to the blessed Virgin (nn. 66–67). The Council recommends "that the cult, especially the liturgical cult, of the Blessed Virgin, be generously fostered" and that "the practices

9. On the oldest Marian prayer, see "Patristic Motifs through the Sixth Century," in chapter 2.

10. See Epiphanius, *Haer.* 78.13; 79 (PG 42:736; 741–53); L. Barbian, "Kollyridianer" [The Collyridians], in Bäumer and Scheffczyk, *ML* 3:601; Luigi Gambero, *Mary and the Fathers of the Church: The Blessed Virgin Mary in Patristic Thought*, trans. Thomas Buffer (San Francisco: Ignatius Press, 1999), 122f; Manfred Hauke, *Die Problematik um das Frauenpriestertum vor dem Hindergrund der Schöpfungs- und Erlösungsordnung*, 4th ed. (Paderborn: Bonifatius, 1995), 411–413, 513; English translation: *Women in the Priesthood?* (San Francisco: Ignatius Press, 1988), 416–18].

11. See Epiphanius, *Haer.* 78 (PG 42:700–740); Konrad Algermissen, "Antidokimarianiten," in Bäumer and Scheffczyk, *ML* 1:172f.

and exercises of devotion towards her, recommended by the teaching authority of the Church in the course of centuries be highly esteemed." Theologians and preachers need to "refrain as much from all false exaggeration as from too summary an attitude in considering the special dignity of the Mother of God." Taking account of the fact that "the duties and privileges of the Blessed Virgin ... always refer to Christ," "let them carefully refrain from whatever might by word or deed lead separated brethren or any others whatsoever into error about the true doctrine of the Church." True Marian devotion does not consist of sentimentalism or credulity, "but proceeds from true faith, by which we are led to recognize the excellence of the Mother of God, and we are moved to a filial love towards our mother and to the imitation of her virtues."[12] Marian cultus therefore implies (1) recollection and (2) invocation of Mary, and also (3) a filial love toward her and (4) imitation of her holiness.

The fullest magisterial exposition on Marian devotion is found in the apostolic exhortation *Marialis cultus* by Paul VI (1974).[13] The first part of the document is dedicated to Marian cultus in the liturgy, called "the golden norm for Christian piety."[14] Then, in the second part, the pope indicates important references for the renewal of Marian devotion. The third part describes the importance of the Angelus and the Rosary.

In the second part we find directives of general importance for all of Marian cultus. The ultimate aim of this cultus is to glorify God and invite Christians to a life conformed to the divine will.[15] For theological context, the pope affirms the connection of Marian

12. *LG* 67.

13. See Scheffczyk, *Neue Impulse zur Marienverehrung* [New Impulses to Marian Devotion] (St. Ottilien: EOS, 1974), 5–121; Stefano De Fiores, *Maria nella teologia contemporanea* [Mary in Contemporary Theology], 3rd ed. (Rome: Centro di Cultura Mariana "Madre della Chiesa," 1991), 221–31; Michael O'Carroll, CSSp, *Theotokos: A Theological Encyclopedia of the Blessed Virgin Mary* (Eugene, Ore.: Wipf and Stock, 2000), 231, 382; Miguel Ponce Cuéllar, *Maria, Madre del Redentor y Madre de la Iglesia* [Mary, Mother of the Redeemer and Mother of the Church], 2nd ed. (Barcelona: Herder, 2001), 522–26; Salvatore M. Perrella, OSM, *Ecco tua Madre (Gv 19,27): La Madre di Gesù nel magistero di Giovanni Paolo II e nell'oggi della Chiesa e del mondo* [Behold Your Mother (Jn 19:27): The Mother of Jesus in the Magisterium of John Paul II and in the Church and the World Today] (Cinisello Balsamo: San Paolo, 2007), 119–25.

14. *MCu* 23.

15. Ibid., 39.

devotion with trinitarian doctrine, with Christology and ecclesiology.[16] Everything in Mary is oriented toward Christ and depends on him. Veneration dedicated to the mother redounds to the Son.[17] A point of particular attention regards the relation between Mary and the Holy Spirit: Mary has become the perennial dwelling of the Holy Spirit; with Mary's intercession, we ask the Holy Spirit for the ability to receive into our own souls Jesus, who was received by Mary in the Incarnation.

For ecclesial context, Paul VI refers to Vatican II, but also illustrates the relation between Mary and the church by pointing to the churches of the Byzantine rite: in the central door of the iconostasis is the image of the Annunciation, and in the apse, that of the *Theotókos* in glory. "In this way one perceives how through the assent of the humble handmaid of the Lord mankind begins its return to God and sees in the glory of the all-holy Virgin the goal towards which it is journeying."[18]

For the renewal of Marian devotion, Paul VI underscores four aspects:

1. The *biblical* aspect: devotion must be nourished from Sacred Scripture, and also draw its language from it.[19]

2. The *liturgical* aspect: nonliturgical forms of devotion should emanate from the liturgy and lead back to it (with reference to Vatican II, *Sacrosanctum concilium* 13). This does not mean to reject or abandon forms of Marian devotion practiced by the people of God and frequently commended by the Magisterium.[20]

3. The *ecumenical* aspect: the Pope points to common elements with Orthodox, Anglicans, and Protestants. It is important to invoke Mary for the unity of all the baptized in the one people of God. As Mary, by means of her mediation, stimulated the first miracle in the life of Jesus at the wedding of Cana, she will likewise promote full communion in the faith in our era.[21]

16. Ibid., 25–28.
17. Ibid., 25; See Ildefonso of Toledo, *De virginitate perpetua sanctae Mariae* 12 (PL 96:108).
18. *MCu* 28.
19. Ibid., 30.
20. Ibid., 31.
21. Ibid., 32–33.

4. The *anthropological* aspect: Marian devotion needs to be realized in the world of today, which finds itself in different social conditions from those at the time of Jesus. In particular the figure of Mary is exemplary for the active contribution of woman in modern society.[22]

MARY IN THE LITURGY

Introduction

Paul VI calls the liturgy a "golden norm for Christian piety"[23] and applies this principle to Marian cultus. *Marialis cultus* concentrates on the new Roman liturgy, but states that it was also his desire to contemplate the various liturgies of the West and East.[24] In the following we shall seek to draw at least a little closer to this desire.

The Role of Mary in the Eucharistic Celebration

Let us begin our study with the Eucharist,[25] the "source and summit of the entire Christian life."[26] The Eucharistic prayers, in the East

22. Ibid., 34–37. On this topic, which was particularly explored by John Paul II, *Mulieris dignitatem*, see "Mary the Woman, in the Context of Anthropology," in chapter 3.

23. *MCu* 23.

24. Ibid., 1.

25. See Pius XII, Encyclical Letter *Le pélerinage de Lourdes* (1957) (*PE* 4:259, n. 19; *EE* 6, n. 1376); Paul VI, *MCu*, 10–11, 20; John Paul II, *RM* 44; John Paul II, *Mulieris dignitatem*, 26–27; *Ecclesia de Eucharistia*, chap. VI; Amato, "Eucaristia," in De Fiores and Meo, *NDM*, 527–41; Ferdinand Holböck, *Das Allerheiligste und die Heiligen* [The Most Holy and the Saints], 2nd ed. (Stein am Rhein, Switzerland: Christiana, 1986), 420–28; Johannes Stöhr, "Eucharistie und Maria," in Bäumer and Scheffczyk, *ML* 2:406–9; Ermanno M. Toniolo, ed., *Maria e l'Eucaristia* (Rome: Centro di cultura Mariana "Madre della Chiesa," 2000); Hauke, "L'eucaristia: Fonte e culmine della vita cristiana; L'enciclica Ecclesia de Eucaristia" [The Eucharist: Source and Summit of Christian Life; The Encyclical Ecclesia de Eucharistia], in *Il papa teologo: Nel segno delle encicliche*, ed. G. Borgonovo and A. Cattaneo, 269f; Paul Haffner, *The Mystery of Mary* (Leominster, UK: Gracewing; Mundelein, Ill.: Hillenbrand, 2004), 249–54; Fernando Ocáriz, "María y la Eucaristía," *Scripta de Maria*, 2nd ser., 1 (2004): 33–44; De Fiores, *Dizionario* 1:669–94; Arthur B. Calkins, "La presenza di Maria nella Santa Messa nel Magistero di papa Giovanni Paolo II" [The Presence of Mary in the Holy Mass in the Magisterium of Pope John Paul II], *Immaculata Mediatrix* 6 (2006): 357–76; "María y la Eucaristia: María y dolor en el camino de la vida," *Estudios Marianos* 72 (2006); *Mary at the Foot of the Cross*, vol. 4, *Marian Coredemption in the Eucharistic Mystery* (New Bedford, Mass.: Academy of the Immaculate, 2007); Giuseppe Crocetti, "Eucaristia," in De Fiores, Schiefer, and Perrella, *DMar*, 482–89; Antonio Escudero Cabello, "La comprensión eucaristica de María: La Eucaristía como acceso a la mariologia" [The Eucharistic Comprehension of Mary: The Eucharist as a Way into Mariology], *Ephemerides mariologicae* 59 (2009): 375–92; Dominique Le Tourneau Barbé, "María, 'mujer eucaristica'" [Mary, "Eucharistic Mother"], *Scripta de Maria*, 2nd ser., 9 (2012): 67–97.

26. *LG* 11.

as in the West, recall the holy Virgin. Even the most ancient formulary in the "Apostolic Tradition" of Hippolytus mentions Mary in the anamnesis that precedes the institution narrative: "We give thee thanks, O God, through thy beloved Servant Jesus Christ ... who is thy Word inseparable from thee; through whom thou didst make all things and in whom thou are well pleased. Whom thou didst send from heaven into the womb of the Virgin, and who, dwelling within her, was made flesh, and was manifested as thy Son, being born of the Holy Spirit and the Virgin."[27]

The Roman Canon, the First Eucharistic Prayer, took its form (excepting a few small details) in the age of Pope Gregory the Great between the third and sixth centuries.[28] Mary appears in the first place of the first commemoration of the saints, followed by the twelve Apostles and by twelve Roman martyrs: "In communion with those whose memory we venerate, especially the glorious ever-Virgin Mary, Mother of our God and Lord, Jesus Christ." The Third Eucharistic Prayer of recent origin (1966), adds to the memory of Mary a petition to share her eternal inheritance: "May he make of us an eternal offering to you, so that we may obtain an inheritance with your elect, especially with the most blessed Virgin Mary, Mother of God, with your blessed Apostles and glorious Martyrs ... and with all the Saints, on whose constant intercession in your presence we rely for unfailing help." The Second Eucharistic Prayer (inspired by the eucharistic prayer of Hippolytus) has similar features, as does the Fourth Eucharistic Prayer, which is also recent and redacted with particular attention to the Eastern liturgy (of the Antiochene type); immediately before the final doxology, there is a petition "that we may enter into a heavenly inheritance with the Blessed Virgin Mary, Mother of God, and with your Apostles and Saints in your kingdom."[29]

27. *Apostolic Tradition* 4 (Fontes christiani 1:422–24). English translation from *The Apostolic Tradition of Hippolytus*, trans. Burton Scott Easton (Cambridge: Cambridge University Press, 1934).

28. See Hans Bernhard Meyer, *Eucharistie* (Regensburg: Friedrich Pustet, 1989), 179.

29. See Jesús Castellano, OCD, "Beata Vergine Maria," in *Liturgia*, ed. Domenico Sartore, Achille M. Triacca, and Carlo Cibien (Cinisello Balsamo: San Paolo, 2001), 213f. Quotations from ICEL, *The Roman Missal* (Washington, D.C.: USCCB, 2010).

In the Roman liturgy, in the fixed parts of the Holy Mass, Mary always appears in the eucharistic prayers and, on Sundays and solemnities, also in the Credo (or the Apostles' Creed). Yet the *Ordo Missae* is much richer in the Eastern liturgies.[30] As a well-known example, let us take the "Liturgy of St. John Chrysostom"; the anaphora appears to have come from the era when the saint was bishop of Constantinople.[31] Except for ten occasions in the year when the liturgy of St. Basil is used, the liturgy of John Chrysostom is the one universally followed in the Eastern churches arising from Byzantium.[32]

In the preparation rite of both liturgies, the priest and the deacon salute an icon of Christ and another of the Mother of God. In the *proskomedia*, the preparation of the gifts (before the beginning of the liturgy itself), the loaf is prepared on the *diskos* (paten). The order of the portions of bread on the diskos represents the whole church: in the center is the "lamb" (with the inscription "Jesus Christ conquers") and then to the right the portion that represents the Mother of God; to the left are the portions that refer to other saints, and, below, the portions offered for the living and the dead. When the priest cuts the portion for Mary from the loaf, he prays: "In honor and memory of our ... Lady, the Mother of God and ever-virgin Mary, through whose prayers do You, Lord, receive this sacrifice upon your altar in heaven." Placing a particle on the diskos, the priest cites Psalm 45: "At your right stood the Queen, clothed in an embroidered mantle of gold."

The anamnesis of Mary recurs multiple times in the liturgy itself:

1. The liturgy of the catechumens (which corresponds, generally, to the "liturgy of the word" in the modern Latin rite): in the great "Ektenia" (litany) for peace ("Let us remember our all-holy, spotless, most highly blessed and glorious Lady the Mother of God and ever-

30. See Office of Liturgical Celebrations of the Supreme Pontiff, ed., *Liturgie dell'Oriente cristiano a Roma nell'Anno Mariano 1987–88* [Eastern Christian Liturgy at Rome in the Marian Year 1987–88] (Vatican City: Libreria Editrice Vaticana, 1990).

31. See Hans-Joachim Schulz, *Die byzantinische Liturgie: Glaubenszeugnis und Symbolgestalt*, 2nd ed. (Trier: Paulinus-Verlag, 1980), 26*–33*. English translation: *The Byzantine Liturgy: Symbolic Structure and Faith Expression*, trans. Matthew J. O'Connell (New York: Pueblo 1986).

32. For the following quotations, see *Byzantine Daily Worship*, ed. Joseph Raya and José de Vinck (Allendale, N.J.: Alleluia Press, 1969), 256, 262–65, 269, 285.

virgin Mary with all the saints, and commend ourselves and one another and our whole life to Christ God"); in the first antiphon ("Through the prayers of the Mother of God, O Saviour, save us!"); in the second antiphon (the Word became flesh "from the Holy Mother of God and ever-virgin Mary"); in the priest's prayer at the Trisagion ("through the prayers of the holy Mother of God and of all the saints").

2. The liturgy of the faithful: in the recitation of the Creed; in the anaphora there is a prayer during the mention of the saints: "especially for our all-holy, spotless, most highly blessed and glorious Lady the Mother of God and ever-virgin Mary." The people respond, singing, "It is fitting and right to call you blessed, O Theotokos: you are ever-blessed and all-blameless and the Mother of our God. Higher in honor than the Cherubim and more glorious without compare than the Seraphim, you gave birth to God the Word in virginity. You are truly Mother of God: you do we exalt."

Finally, at the moment of the dismissal, there is again an invocation of Mary, with the reprise of the second part of the Marian chant sung during the anaphora.

In sum, the "hyperdulia" of Mary is clearly visible in the eucharistic liturgy, above all in the East, but in a more rudimentary form also in the West. The entire worship of the church is sustained by the intercession of the Mother of God.

"Mary guides the faithful to the Eucharist."[33] In his encyclical *Ecclesia de Eucharistia* (2003), John Paul II dedicated an entire chapter to Mary as the "Woman of the Eucharist."[34] The Pope compares Mary's "*fiat*" in response to the words of the Angel with the "Amen" that every believer says when approaching communion in the Eucharist. Making a visit to Elizabeth, Mary bears in her womb the Word made flesh and became, in a sense, "the first 'tabernacle' in history."[35] Mary orients us to the real presence of the Lord in the Eucharist, and also to union with Christ's sacrifice. The presence of

33. John Paul II, *RM* 44. See also Pius XII, Enc. *Le pélerinage de Lourdes.*

34. *Ecclesia de Eucharistia*, VI:53–58.

35. Ibid., VI:55.

Mary on Calvary includes "a kind of … 'spiritual communion'—of desire and of oblation," already foreshadowed in the events of Jesus' infancy: Mary brings the infant to the Temple "to present him to the Lord" (Lk 2:22) and receives the prophecy of the "sword" that will pierce her heart (Lk 2:34–35).[36] The pope also notes, without specifying the particulars, that "Mary is present, with the Church and as the Mother of the Church, at each of our celebrations of the Eucharist. If the Church and the Eucharist are inseparably united, the same ought to be said of Mary and the Eucharist."[37]

Mary in the Celebration of the Other Sacraments

Baptism

Since the earliest times Mary appears in the baptismal liturgy.[38] We see this first of all in the second question of the creed in the rite of Baptism, as Hippolytus testifies to us: we profess faith in Christ "born by the Holy Spirit, of the Virgin Mary."[39] For the era of the fathers, Jesus' birth from the Virgin Mary is a fundamental type for the new birth of Baptism.[40] Paul VI takes up this thread already strongly advanced by Vatican II:[41]

> The ancient Fathers rightly taught that the Church prolongs in the sacrament of Baptism the virginal motherhood of Mary.… "The origin which (Christ) took in the womb of the Virgin He has given to the baptismal font: He has given to water what He had given to His Mother—the power of the Most High and the overshadowing of the Holy Spirit (cf. Lk 1:35),

36. Ibid., VI:56.

37. Ibid., VI:57. On the presence of Mary, see A. Pizzarelli, "Presenza" [Presence], in De Fiores and Meo, *NDM*, 1161–69; Stöhr, "Eucharistie und Maria," 408f.; De Fiores, *Dizionario* 1:681–86.

38. See Armando Bandera, *La Virgen María y los Sacramentos* (Madrid: Rialp, 1978); Hauke, "Sakramente I. Kath. Theologie," in *ML* 5:632–35; J. Madey, "Sakramente II. Liturgie-Ost" [Sacraments. II. Liturgy, East], in *ML* 5:635–37; Castellano, "Beata Virgine Maria," 212–14; Angelo M. Gila, "Spunti della letteratura del primo millennio sulla presenza della Vergine Maria nel dinamismo dei sacramenti" [Starting Points in First-Millennium Literature on the Presence of the Virgin Mary in the Dynamism of the Sacraments], in *Fons lucis. Miscellanea di studi in onore di Ermanno M. Toniolo*, ed. R. Barbieri, I. M. Calabuig, and O. Di Angelo (Rome: Marianum, 2004), 287–332; De Fiores, *Dizionario* 1:203–36.

39. *Apostolic Tradition* 21 (*Fontes christiani* 1:262).

40. On Mary and baptism, see, for example, Irenaeus, at p. 000.

41. See *LG* 64.

which was responsible for Mary's bringing forth the Savior, has the same effect, so that water may regenerate the believer." [Saint Leo the Great][42]

The intercession of Mary is invoked in the Byzantine liturgy, a usage also accepted (after the liturgical reform) into the Roman liturgy: Mary appears in the litany of the saints. Consecration to Mary takes its decisive starting point from baptismal spirituality.[43] Already at the start of the Middle Ages the custom appears of bringing the newly baptized infant before an image of our Lady (a practice recommended in the new rite of Baptism of children). The old Roman liturgy also provides for the Magnificat as an expression of thanks for the newly baptized.

The reference to Mary in the creed, her invocation, and the recommendation for consecration to the Mother of God bear witness to the church's faith that Mary cooperates "with motherly love" in the "birth" of the faithful in Baptism.[44] For this reason John Paul II recalls the spirituality of Grignion de Montfort, "who proposes consecration to Christ through the hands of Mary, as an effective means for Christians to live faithfully their baptismal commitments."[45]

Confirmation

The sacrament of Confirmation, in a certain sense, revives the grace of Pentecost. As Mary prayed for the Pentecostal descent of the Holy Spirit (Acts 1:14), she is also involved with the liturgical realization of this event. Already at the Incarnation the descent of the Holy Spirit depended on the consent of Mary (Lk 1:26–38). We can also establish a certain analogy between the education of Jesus by Mary, her motherly support of the education of the baptized,[46] and the effect of Confirmation that strengthens baptismal grace and brings it to completion.[47]

42. *MCu* 19.

43. See "Consecration to Mary" in this chapter.

44. *LG* 63; see *RM* 44.

45. *RM* 48.

46. See *LG* 63.

47. See Bandera, *La Virgen María y los sacramentos*, 111–37; Hauke, *Die Firmung: Geschichtliche Entfaltung und theologischer Sinn* [Confirmation: Historical Development and Theological Interpretation] (Paderborn: Bonifatius, 1999), 467f.

The Sacrament of Penance

As Mary was associated with the Redeemer in the work of salvation on this earth, so "this motherhood of Mary in the order of grace continues uninterruptedly."[48] Because of this, the motherly love of Mary is also involved in a certain way in the actualization of the pardon of sins in the sacrament of reconciliation. In the Roman rite, Mary is mentioned in an optional manner, particularly in the prayer of the priest after the absolution: "May the Passion of our Lord Jesus Christ, the intercession of the Blessed Virgin Mary, and of all the saints, whatever good you do and suffering you endure, heal your sins, help you to grow in holiness, and reward you with eternal life."[49]

The Anointing of the Sick

With this sacrament, according to the summarizing description by Vatican II, the church "commends the sick to the suffering and glorified Lord, asking that He may lighten their suffering and save them (cf. Jas 5:14, 16) she exhorts them, moreover, to contribute to the welfare of the whole people of God by associating themselves freely with the passion and death of Christ. (cf. Rm 8:17; Col 1:24; 2 Tm 2:11–12; 1 Pt 4:13)."[50] The litany's invocation that defines Mary as "health of the sick" (*salus infirmorum*) shows the maternal care of the Blessed Virgin for all the sick in an exemplary way.[51] The Lady of Sorrows, below the Cross, was associated with the suffering of Christ, thus becoming our spiritual mother. Because of this, she is concerned for all the suffering and helps them to offer their own life for the good of the mystical body of Christ that is the church.[52]

The Mother of God also appears in prayers for the dying (that they can join in the sacraments intended for them—that is, Penance, Anointing of the sick, and Eucharistic viaticum). Thus she is present

48. *LG* 62.

49. Rite of Penance in ICEL, *The Rites* (N.Y.: Pueblo, 1976), 363.

50. *LG* 11.

51. See F. Angelini, "Infermi" [The Sick], in De Fiores and Meo, *NDM*, 712f.; De Fiores, *Dizionario* 1:563f.

52. See Gila, "Spunti," 318–22.

with particular attention at the hour of death, according to the insistent petition of the "Ave Maria."[53]

Marriage

Christian marriage brings those who receive the sacrament to participate in the covenant between Christ and his church. Inasmuch as Mary is the type and mother of the church, she is inseparably connected with spousal life. The intercession of Mary is seen, for example, when the Gospel of the Wedding at Cana (Jn 2:1–11) is chosen. In the Byzantine rite, this reading is always specified. The example of Mary is particularly meaningful for the dedication of her love as a wife and mother of a family. As the marriage of Mary and Joseph was oriented toward the birth of Jesus Christ, so also sacramental marriage is aimed toward the birth of children who in Baptism become partakers of divine life.[54]

The Sacrament of Orders

The ministerial priesthood represents Jesus Christ as head of the church,[55] but presupposes the common priesthood of all the faithful, with a Marian nuance.[56] The analogies between the role of Mary and that of the priest (specific vocation, nearness to the work of salvation, mediation) need to be included more fully in this overview.

The maternal care of Mary for priests has been illustrated, since the Middle Ages, by her dedication to the good of the apostle John. Conversely, there is Jesus' request for John to receive Mary into his personal life (Jn 19:26f). According to Vatican II, priests find an example of docility to the Holy Spirit "in the Blessed Virgin Mary who under the guidance of the Holy Spirit made a total dedication of herself for the mystery of the redemption of men. Priests should

53. See M. D. Klersy, "Sterbeliturgie" [Liturgy of the Dead], in *ML* 6:298; A. Bodem, "Todesstunde" [Hour of Death], in *ML* 6:442f.

54. See Gabriele M. Roschini, *Dizionario di Mariologia* [Dictionary of Mariology] (Rome: Editrice Studium, 1961), 318–22; Anton Ziegenaus, "Ehe III. Dogmatik" [Marriage. III. Dogmatics], in *ML* 2:284–86. See also chapter 5, in the section "The Role of the Marriage of Mary and the Figure of Joseph," 6.

55. See Hauke, "Priestertum I. Dogmatik," in *ML* 5:316.

56. See "The Contribution of *Mulieris dignitatem*," in chapter 3.

always venerate and love her, with a filial devotion and worship, as the mother of the Supreme and Eternal Priest, as Queen of Apostles and as protectress of their ministry."[57]

The Congregation for Catholic Education published a letter on the introduction of seminarians to the spiritual life in 1980. It affirms that Marian devotion is not "a personal and entirely optional matter" but leads to the economy of salvation with which Mary is inseparably associated. Contact with Mary, which has nothing to do with superficial sentimentalism, "can only lead to greater contact with Christ and his cross." As an example, there is a reference to the spirituality of Grignion de Montfort, which is also affirmed (for all Christians) by the supreme pontiff in *Redemptoris Mater*.[58]

Mary in the Liturgical Calendar

Earlier, in the historical overview (chapter 2), we looked at the beginnings of the Marian calendar[59] within the liturgical year:[60] the first Marian feast comes from the anamnesis of the mystery of the Nativity, inspired by, among other things, the definition of the title *Theotókos* at the Council of Ephesus (431); soon thereafter were added the feasts of the Annunciation (March 25), the Nativity of Mary (September 8), the *Hypapante* (February 2), and the Dormition (August 15).

57. Second Vatican Council, Decree *Presbyterorum ordinis*, December 7, 1965, 18.

58. John Paul II, *RM* 48. See also Congregation for the Clergy, *Directory on the Ministry and Life of Priests*, March 31, 1994, n. 68; Congregation for the Clergy, Instruction "The Priest, Pastor and Leader of the Parish Community," August 4, 2002, n. 13 (with selected quotations from John Paul II).

59. See Roschini, *La Madonna*, 4:352–404; *Maria Santissima nella storia della salvezza: Trattato completo di mariologia alla luce del Concilio Vaticano II* [Mary Most Holy, in the History of Salvation: Complete Treatise on Mariology in Light of the Second Vatican Council], vol. 4 (Isola del Liri: Pisani, 1969), passim; José Aldazabal, ed., *Celebrar las fiestas de María* [Celebrating the Feasts of Mary] (Barcelona: Centre de Pastoral Liturgica, 1985); Stefano Rosso, SDB, "Anno liturgico" [Liturgical Year], in De Fiores and Meo, *NDM*, 50–78; Wolfgang Beinert, ed., *Maria heute ehren: Eine theologisch-pastorale Handreichung* [To Honor Mary Today: A Theological-Pastoral Handbook] (Freiburg im Breisgau: Herder, 1977); Hansjörg Auf der Maur, "Feste und Gedenktage der Heiligen" [Feasts and Memorials of the Saints], in *Feiern im Rhythmus der Zeit* [Celebrations in the Rhythm of Time], vol. 2, pt. 1, edited by H. Auf der Maur and Philipp Harnancourt, Gottesdienst der Kirche 6, pt. 1 (Regensburg: Friedrich Pustet, 1994); Castellano, "Beata Vergine Maria," 216–26; Neil J. Roy, "Mary and the Liturgical Year," in *Mariology: A Guide for Priests, Deacons, Seminarians, and Consecrated Persons*, ed. Mark Miravalle (Goleta, Calif.: Queenship, 2007), 607–65.

60. On the earliest Marian feasts, see "Patristic Motifs through the Sixth Century," in chapter 2.

Paul VI's magisterial description is dedicated first of all to the seasons of Advent and the Nativity. Beyond the feast of the Immaculate Conception (December 8), which points to a fundamental preparation for the arrival of the Savior, the liturgy of Advent often recalls the blessed Virgin, in particular in the days from December 17 to 24 and on the Sunday immediately preceding Christmas. With Mary's love the faithful prepare to go out to meet the Lord.[61]

The season of Christmas is a prolonged recollection of the virginal motherhood of Mary. On "the Solemnity of the Birth of Christ the Church both adores the Savior and venerates His glorious Mother. On the Epiphany, when she celebrates the universal call to salvation, the Church contemplates the Blessed Virgin, the true Seat of Wisdom and true Mother of the King, who presents to the Wise Men, for their adoration, the Redeemer of all peoples.... On the Feast of the Holy Family ... the Church meditates with profound reverence upon the holy life led in the house at Nazareth by Jesus ..., Mary ..., and Joseph."[62]

Then the pope turns his attention to the festivity of Mary Mother of God (January 1), then recently introduced (1969).[63] In addition to highlighting the role of the *Theotókos*, the first of January is also "a fitting occasion for renewing adoration of the newborn Prince of Peace ..., and for imploring from God, through the Queen of Peace, the supreme gift of peace." For this reason, Paul VI has connected January 1 with the World Day of Peace, which he instituted.[64]

We have four Marian "solemnities": December 8, January 1, March 25, and August 15.[65] The "Annunciation of the Lord," March 25, is a Christological feast (nine months prior to Christmas), but also recalls the consent of the Virgin to the Incarnation: thus in the Byz-

61. *MCu* 3–4.

62. Ibid., 5.

63. The feast existed prior to the seventh century in Rome (as *Natale S. Mariae*), but was replaced later by the octave day of Christmas. The Byzantine calendar, since primordial times, has referred to a memorial of the Mother of God for December 26. Starting in 1931, the Roman calendar recognized a feast of the maternity of Mary set on October 11. In 1969, it was transferred to January 1.

64. *MCu* 5.

65. Ibid., 6.

antine world the solemnity bears the title "Annunciation of the *Theotókos*" (until the liturgical reform of Paul VI, the Roman liturgy reported the analogous title of "Annunciation of the BVM," excepting for the solemnity's first appearances in the seventh century).

The solemnity of the Assumption of Mary on August 15 recalls the entrance of Mary, body and soul, into heavenly glory.

Along with the *four Marian solemnities*, the universal calendar of the church indicates *two feasts*: the Birth of Mary (September 8; originating in Jerusalem) and the Visitation (May 31; originally on July 2, starting in the twelfth century, as it still is observed today in Germany). A strongly Marian character is also typical of the feast of February 2, which has received the new Christological title "Presentation of the Lord" with the liturgical reform (the earlier name was "Purification of the BVM").

Furthermore, we have *eleven memorials* in the universal calendar (six optional and five obligatory):

- the optional memorial of "Our Lady of Lourdes," February 12; introduced in 1907 by Pius X.
- the optional memorial of "Our Lady of Fatima," May 13, inserted into the universal calendar in the third typical edition of the Roman Missal, in 2002.
- the obligatory memorial of the "Immaculate Heart of Mary"; the Saturday after the solemnity of the Most Sacred Heart of Jesus (that is, the Saturday after the second Sunday after Pentecost); introduced by Pius XII on August 22 as a feast in 1944, inspired by the message of Fatima; reduced to an optional memorial in 1969 by Paul VI but made obligatory by John Paul II in 1998.
- "Our Lady of Mount Carmel," an optional memorial, July 16, introduced in 1726; connected with the use of the scapular[66] and the Carmelite tradition, which emphasizes Mary's help in the experience of prayer.
- the optional memorial of the "Dedication of the Basilica of St. Mary Major," August 5; this refers to the most important

66. See also the discussion of the Carmelite scapular in "The Historical Path of Consecration to Mary up to the 17th Century," in this chapter.

Marian church in the West (in Rome, on the Esquiline hill), dedicated shortly after the Council of Ephesus.

- the "Queenship of Mary," an obligatory memorial, August 22, a week after the solemnity of the Assumption; introduced in 1954 by Pius XII, and originally set at May 31.
- "Holy Name of Mary," an optional memorial, September 12, introduced in thanksgiving for the victory over the Turks on September 12, 1683, at Vienna; eliminated from the general calendar during the liturgical reform after Vatican II and revived in the third edition of the Roman Missal (2002), along with the optional memorial of the Holy Name of Jesus (January 3).
- "Our Lady of Sorrows," an obligatory memorial, September 15. Immediately after the "Exaltation of the Holy Cross," September 14; first celebrated by the Servites of Mary in the seventeenth century, extended to the entire church by Pius VII after his return from Napoleonic imprisonment. There already existed a feast of the "Seven Sorrows of the Blessed Virgin Mary," introduced in 1727 for the whole church and placed on the Thursday preceding Holy Thursday; the first traces of this feast lead back to the fifteenth century and are based on the medieval contemplation of the sorrows of Mary; the commemoration of the "Seven Sorrows" was removed in 1969 as a "duplication" of the September 15 observance.
- "Our Lady of the Rosary," an obligatory memorial, October 7; introduced by Pius V after the victory of the Christian fleet against the Turks at Lepanto (1571; originally under the title "Our Lady of Victory"), extended to the whole church after another victory in 1716.
- "Presentation of the Blessed Virgin Mary," an obligatory memorial, November 21; the title refers to the apocryphal tradition of the Protoevangelium of James, but the texts do not contain the particularities of that tradition; instead it affirms the total self-giving that Mary presented to God from her childhood on.
- "Our Lady of Guadalupe," an optional memorial for the universal church (made obligatory since 2002 as the feast of the Pa-

troness of the Americas). It recalls the Marian apparitions of 1531 in Mexico.[67]

Along with the four solemnities, the two (or three) feasts, and the ten memorials in the general calendar, the calendars of a particular church can provide for proper celebrations. Furthermore, it is possible to celebrate a votive Marian Mass, especially on Saturdays.[68] In 1986, on the occasion of the Marian Year 1987–88, a broader choice of "Marian Masses" was introduced with special editions of the Missal and the Lectionary (the "Collection of Masses of the Blessed Virgin Mary," containing forty-six formularies).[69]

Mary, Model of the Worshipping Church

"The Blessed Virgin as the Model of the Church in Divine Worship": under this title, *Marialis cultus* deals with the spiritual attitude of Mary as an exemplar for the church in worship.[70] The supreme pontiff traces five fundamental attitudes:

1. The *attentive Virgin*. Mary listens to the divine message and receives it in faith.

2. The *Virgin in prayer*. Paul VI refers to the Magnificat (Lk 1:46–55), to Mary's intercession at the wedding in Cana (Jn 2:1–11), and to the first prayer of Pentecost (Acts 1:14). The praying presence of Mary in the newborn church corresponds to her intercession for the church of all times.

3. The *Virgin-Mother*—model of the church that brings forth new children by the work of the Holy Spirit.

4. The *Virgin presenting offerings*. Pope Paul affirms the offering

67. Regarding the apparition at Guadalupe, see pp. 387–91.

68. *MCu* 9. On Saturday Masses of the Blessed Virgin Mary, see "Recurring Observances in the Weekly, Monthly, and Annual Cycles" in this chapter.

69. See Nereo Zamberlan, "La Collectio Missarum *de B. Maria Virgine: Bibliografia ragionata (1986–2001)*" [The "Collection of Masses of the BVM": A Critical Bibliography], *Marianum* 65, no. 163–64 (2003)"; A. Catella, "La Collectio Missarum *de Beata Maria Virgine: Analisi della eucologia*" [The Collection of Masses of the BVM: Analysis of Euchology], in Hauke, *La donna e la salvezza*"; also see "The Post-Conciliar Period," in chapter 2.

70. *MCu* 16–22.

that Mary made at the presentation of Jesus in the Temple (Lk 2:22–35) and her association with the sacrifice of the Cross.

5. A *teacher of spiritual life*. May everyone glorify God, as Mary did. Mary's "yes" (Lk 1:38) is an example for all Christians.

MARY IN POPULAR PIETY

Introduction

"The Second Vatican Council also exhorts us to promote other forms of piety side by side with liturgical worship, especially those recommended by the magisterium."[71] "The term 'popular piety' designates those diverse cultic expressions of a private or community nature which, in the context of the Christian faith, are inspired predominantly not by the Sacred Liturgy but by forms deriving from a particular nation or people or from their culture."[72] This realm is of great importance.[73] The "principles" indicated earlier by Paul VI in *Marialis cultus* 30–33 refer particularly to nonliturgical piety and are expressed in greater detail in the "Directory on Popular Piety and the Liturgy," published by the Congregation for Divine Worship and the Discipline of the Sacraments (2002).[74]

Prayers

The Ave Maria

The *Catechism of the Catholic Church* (*CCC*) dedicates a section to prayer "in communion with the holy Mother of God" (nn. 2673–79).

71. Ibid., 24; see *LG* 67.

72. *DPPL*, n. 9.

73. See Apostolic Penitentiary, *Manual of Indulgences: Norms and Grants*, 3rd ed. (Washington, D.D.: USCCB, 2006) (English edition of *Enchiridion indulgentiarum*, 4th ed., 1999); Congregation for Divine Worship and the Discipline of the Sacraments, *Directory on Popular Piety and the Liturgy* (2002) (hereafter *DPPL*), nn. 183–207 and passim; G. Agostino, "Pietà popolare" [Popular Piety], in De Fiores and Meo, *NDM*, 1111–22; Stefano De Fiores, *Maria, Madre di Gesù: Sintesi storico-salvifica* [Mary, Mother of Jesus: Salvation-Historical Synthesis], Corso di teologia sistematica 6 (Bologna: EDB, 1992), 269–87; Maria Marcellina Pedico, *La Vergine Maria nella pietà popolare* [The Virgin Mary in Popular Piety] (Rome: Monfortane, 1993); Toniolo, ed., *La Vergine Maria nel cammino orante della Chiesa: Liturgia e pietà popolare* [The Virgin Mary in the Praying Pilgrimage of the Church: Liturgy and Popular Piety] (Rome: Centro di cultura Mariana "Madre della Chiesa," 2003); Danilo M. Sartor, "Pietà popolare" [Popular Piety], in De Fiores, Schiefer, and Perrella, *DMar*, 944–53.

74. *DPPL*, nn. 183–86; see nn. 60–92.

"Mary is the perfect Orans (prayer), a figure of the Church. When we pray to her, we are adhering with her to the plan of the Father, who sends his Son to save all men. Like the beloved disciple we welcome Jesus' mother into our homes, for she has become the mother of all the living. We can pray with and to her. The prayer of the Church is sustained by the prayer of Mary and united with it in hope."[75]

"Two movements" in Marian prayer are highlighted: "The first 'magnifies' the Lord for the 'great things' he did for his lowly servant and through her for all human beings. The second entrusts the supplications and praises of the children of God to the Mother of Jesus, because she now knows the humanity which, in her, the Son of God espoused."[76]

"This twofold movement of prayer to Mary has found a privileged expression in the *Ave Maria*," which is composed of praise and intercession.[77] The first part of the Ave Maria comes from the Gospel according to Luke (the greetings of the angel and of Elizabeth), while the second part, in its current form, stems from Pius V who inserted it into the Roman Catechism (1566) and the Roman Breviary (1568).[78] However, similar forms have been joined to the prayer since the thirteenth century.

The angelic salutation[79] includes three parts: the greeting, which implies an invitation to joy (*chaire*, "Ave," "Rejoice"); the designation of Mary (*kecharitoméne,* "full of grace"); the reference to God's assistance ("the Lord is with you"). The prayer adds the name of "Mary."

The *CCC* comments:

Hail Mary [or *Rejoice, Mary*]: the greeting of the angel Gabriel opens this prayer. It is God himself who, through his angel as intermediary, greets

75. *CCC* 2679.

76. *CCC* 2675.

77. *CCC* 2676. See Roschini, *Maria Santissima*, 4:285–93; "Ave Maria," in *ML* 1:309–17; René Laurentin, *The Hail Mary: Its Meaning and Origin* (Milford, Ohio: Faith, 1991); Pedico, *La Vergine Maria*, 69–74; Tullio Faustino Ossanna, *L'Ave Maria. Storia, contenuti, problemi* [The Ave Maria: History, Content, Issues] (Cinisello Balsamo: San Paolo, 2002).

78. With the recommendation to recite (in silence) the Our Father and the Hail Mary before each Hour of the breviary and at the end of the Office.

79. See also "The Annunciation," in chapter 1.

Mary. Our prayer dares to take up this greeting to Mary with the regard God had for the lowliness of his humble servant and to exult in the joy he finds in her.

Full of grace, the Lord is with thee: These two phrases of the angel's greeting shed light on one another. Mary is full of grace because the Lord is with her. The grace with which she is filled is the presence of him who is the source of all grace. "Rejoice, ... O Daughter of Jerusalem, ... the Lord your God is in your midst" (Zep 3:14, 3:17a). Mary, in whom the Lord himself has just made his dwelling, is the daughter of Zion in person, the ark of the covenant, the place where the glory of the Lord dwells. She is "the dwelling of God ... with men" (Rv 21:3). Full of grace, Mary is wholly given over to him who has come to dwell in her and whom she is about to give to the world.[80]

The angelic salutation is joined to Elizabeth's prophetic blessing, inspired by the Holy Spirit: "Blessed are you among women, and blessed is the fruit of your womb." By these words, Mary is blessed, and above all, the child is the incarnate Son of God.

The addition of the name "Jesus" at the end of the first part of the Ave is like the highest point of a scale: the praise of Mary always leads to glorifying her Son. At the same time, "Jesus" is like a hinge that connects the two parts of the prayer.

The recitation of the first part of the "Ave" originated in the Eastern liturgy (sixth/seventh centuries), and it was already a very well-known prayer in the Middle Ages. The name "Jesus" as the end of the "Ave" seems to trace back to the twelfth century (it was still the habitual form in the sixteenth century). Around 1300, various particular synods prescribed that all the faithful should know and pray together the Credo and the Pater noster as well as the "Ave Maria." Subsequently the Ave (together with the Pater noster, the Credo and the Ten Commandments) formed an integral part of the "iron core" that every Christian needed to know.

Because, in the sixteenth century, the "Ave Maria" usually finished with the name "Jesus" without adding any petition expressly, Luther maintained the invocation with the argument that it did not

80. *CCC* 2676.

constitute a prayer, but only a greeting. To this day we find Protestant theologians who recommend reciting the biblical portion of the "Ave." But usually the "Ave Maria" is rejected because praise is implicitly united with a prayer that addresses the intercession of Mary. In any case, the Protestant controversy encouraged the addition of the second part, expressly defended in the Roman Catechism.[81]

Holy Mary, Mother of God.... The *CCC* comments, "Because she gives us Jesus, her son, Mary is Mother of God and our mother; we can entrust all our cares and petitions to her: she prays for us as she prayed for herself: 'Let it be to me according to your word' (Lk 1:38)."[82]

Pray for us sinners, now and at the hour of our death. "By asking Mary to pray for us, we acknowledge ourselves to be poor sinners and we address ourselves to the 'Mother of Mercy,' the All-Holy One. We give ourselves over to her now, in the Today of our lives. And our trust broadens further, already at the present moment, to surrender 'the hour of our death' wholly to her care. May she be there as she was at her son's death on the cross. May she welcome us as our mother at the hour of our passing to lead us to her son, Jesus, in paradise."[83]

The Angelus

The "Angelus,"[84] the "angelic salutation," is intended to sanctify the day with the recollection of the Incarnation, the Passion, and the Resurrection of Jesus. The prayer is recited in the morning, at midday, and in the evening.

The Angelus took its current form in the sixteenth century.[85] But already in the thirteenth century there was the practice of reciting three Hail Marys at the sound of the evening bells; later the practice was extended to morning and midday.

The three verses that precede the Hail Marys refer to the event of

81. Roman Catechism IV.5.8.

82. *CCC* 2677.

83. Ibid.

84. See Roschini, *La Madonna*, 4:304–8; Silvano Maggiani, "Angelus," in De Fiores and Meo, *NDM*, 25–39; Franz Courth, "Engel des Herrn" [Angels of the Lord], in *ML* 2:341; Pedico, *La Vergine Maria*, 85–90; *DPPL*, n. 195.

85. The first source is a Venetian catechism of 1560. Pius V, in 1571, added the Angelus to the "Little Office of the Blessed Virgin Mary," recommended as a daily prayer.

the Incarnation ("The Angel of the Lord declared unto Mary / And she conceived by the Holy Spirit." "Behold the handmaid of the Lord. / Be it done unto me according to your word." "And the Word was made flesh. / And dwelt among us.")[86] The verses affirm the message coming from God, Mary's promptness in consenting to the will of the Lord, and the coming of the Lord in our midst—events that can easily be connected to daily life.[87]

After the three "Aves" comes a verse that implores the intercession of Mary: "Pray for us, O holy Mother of God, / That we may be made worthy of the promises of Christ." The oration that follows points to the central events of the Redemption:

> Let us pray. Pour forth, we beseech you, O Lord, your grace into our hearts, that we, to whom the incarnation of Christ, your Son, was made known by the message of an angel, may by his passion and cross be brought to the glory of his resurrection, through the same Christ our Lord. Amen.

Paul VI urges us insistently to continue to pray the Angelus, "wherever and whenever possible. The Angelus does not need to be revised, because of its simple structure, its biblical character, its historical origin, which links it to the prayer for peace and safety,[88] and its quasi-liturgical rhythm, which sanctifies different moments during the day, and because it reminds us of the Paschal Mystery.... These factors ensure that the Angelus, despite the passing of centuries, retains an unaltered value and an intact freshness."[89] The practice of the popes of praying the Angelus together with pilgrims at midday (since Pius XI) has contributed in no small way to the current spread of the prayer.

Benedict XIV, in 1742, established that in the Easter season the Angelus was to be replaced by the *Regina coeli*.[90] In addition he decreed that on Sundays, after first Vespers (thus on Saturday eve-

86. English version from James Socias, ed., *Daily Roman Missal* (Woodridge, Ill.: Midwest Theological, 2011), 2299.

87. See John Paul II, CM 69 (November 5, 1997), n. 2.

88. Note (by Hauke): this has applied to the Angelus at midday since the fifteenth century; the historical occasion was above all the Turkish menace. See Maggiani, "Angelus," 30.

89. *MCu* 41.

90. See Pedico, *La Vergine Maria*, 90–94; "Regina caeli," in *ML* 5:435–37; *DPPL*, n. 196.

nings), the angelic salutation was to be recited standing (whereas on the other days, kneeling for the recitation was prescribed). This distinction shows the Paschal character of Sunday. The practice (particularly widespread in Italy) of adding three Glory Be's to the Angelus started with Pope Pius VII, who expressed his gratitude in 1815 for the "graces extended by the Most Holy Trinity to the Most Holy Virgin."[91]

The Rosary

The Church's Exhortations and the Obstacles to Overcome The profound exhortations of Paul VI and John Paul II to pray the Rosary were additions to a long chain:[92] one recent author counts forty-eight popes in 287 encyclicals and other documents that have praised this prayer; ten encyclicals were the work of Leo XIII.[93] The Marian apparitions of Lourdes and Fatima (to mention only the greatest ones accepted in the church) have spread the Rosary even more effectively.[94] John Paul II calls the Rosary his "favorite pray-

91. Roschini, *La Madonna*, 4:308.

92. See Paul VI, *MCu* 42–55; John Paul II, Apostolic Letter *Rosarium Virginis Mariae* (2002) (hereinafter *RVM*); *DPPL*, nn. 197–202; Franz Michel Willam, *Storia del rosario* [History of the Rosary] (Rome: Orbis catholicus, 1951); Roschini, *La Madonna*, 4:313–22; Roschini, *Maria Santissima*, 4:248f; Benoit Thierry d'Argenlieu, OP, "Théologie du Rosaire," in *Maria*, ed. Hubert du Manoir (Paris: Beauchesne, 1958), 5:721–55; Alfons Hiemer, *Der Rosenkranz, das wunderbare Gebet* [The Rosary, the Wonderful Prayer] (St. Ottilien; EOS, 1979); Karl Joseph Klinkhammer, *Adolf von Essen und seine Werke: Der Rosenkranz in der geschichtlichen Situation seiner Entstehung und in seinem bleibenden Anliegen* [Adolf von Essen and His Works: The Rosary in the Historical Situation of Its Development and Its Enduring Appeal] (Frankfurt: J. Knecht, 1972); Klinkhammer, *Ein wunderbares Beten: So entstand der Rosenkranz*, 2nd ed. (Leutesdorf: Johannes-Verlag, 1981); Klinkhammer, "Adolf von Essen," in *ML* 1:34–39; Ennio D. Staid, "Rosario" [Rosary], in De Fiores and Meo, *NDM*, 1207–15; "Rosenkranz," in *ML* 5:553–59; Pedico, *La Vergine Maria*, 75–83; "Rosenkranz," *Lexikon für Theologie und Kirche* 8 (1999): 1302–6; U.-B. Frei and Fredy Bühler, *Der Rosenkranz: Andacht-Geschichte -Kunst* [The Rosary: Devotion, History, Art] (Bern: Benteli; Sachseln: Museum Bruder Klaus, 2003); Stefano M. Cecchin, ed., *Contemplare Cristo con Maria: Atti della Giornata di studio sulla Lettera apostolica Rosarium Virginis Mariae di Giovanni Paolo II: Roma, 3 maggio 2003* [Contemplating Christ with Mary: Acts of the Study Day on the Apostolic Letter *Rosarium Virginis Mariae* by John Paul II: Rome, May 3, 2003] (Vatican City: PAMI, 2003); Krzysztof (Christoforo) Charamsa, *Il Rosario: Riflessioni sulla Lettera Apostolica Rosarium Virginis Mariae* [The Rosary: Reflections on the Apostolic Letter Rosarium Virginis Mariae] (Vatican City: Libreria Editrice Vaticana, 2003); Perrella, *La madre di Gesù nella coscienza ecclesiale contemporanea* [The Mother of Jesus in Contemporary Ecclesial Consciousness] (Vatican City: Libreria Editrice Vaticana, 2005), 227–38; Perrella, *Ecco tua Madre*, 380–401; De Fiores, *Dizionario* 2:1401–49; Riccardo Barile, "Rosario" [Rosary], in De Fiores, Schiefer, and Perrella, *DMar*, 1034–41.

93. See Hiemer, *Der Rosenkranz*, 20; *Enchiridion delle encicliche* 3.

94. See John Paul II, *RVM* 7.

er."[95] Pius XII and Paul VI speak of it as "the compendium of the entire Gospel."[96]

And yet the Rosary also encounters misunderstanding and opposition. It will suffice to cite the historical witness of St. Louis-Marie Grignion de Montfort. He targets the fearful theology that devotion to the Mother of God could distract attention from Christ. "If they come across one who loves our Lady, ... they soon move him to a change of mind and heart. They advise him to say the seven penitential psalms instead of the Rosary, and to show devotion to Jesus instead of to Mary."[97]

The saint speaks out in very strong tones:

> It has always been common knowledge that those who bear the sign of reprobation, as all formal heretics, evil-doers, the proud and the worldly, hate and spurn the Hail Mary and the Rosary. True, heretics learn to say the Our Father but they will not countenance the Hail Mary and the Rosary and they would rather carry a snake around with them than a rosary. And there are even Catholics who, sharing the proud tendencies of their father Lucifer, despise the Hail Mary or look upon it with indifference. The Rosary, they say, is a devotion suitable only for ignorant and illiterate people. On the other hand, we know from experience that those who show positive signs of being among the elect, appreciate and love the Hail Mary and are always glad to say it. The closer they are to God, the more they love this prayer.[98]

Sometimes in the Catholic world one sees disparagement of the Rosary on the ground that its recitation is not a part of the liturgy, in a strict sense. Its character as a substitute is criticized: in place of the 150 psalms, regularly recited by the clergy, the Christian people like to recite at least 150 Ave Marias. This criticism was already displayed by Grignion's opponents, the Jansenists: instead of praying the Rosary, they exhorted the faithful to recite the seven penitential psalms. "There are some who think that the centrality of the Liturgy, rightly stressed by the Second Vatican Ecumenical Council, necessarily

95. Ibid., 2.
96. *MCu* 42.
97. *TD* 64.
98. Ibid., n. 250.

entails giving lesser importance to the Rosary. Yet, as Pope Paul VI made clear, not only does this prayer not conflict with the Liturgy, *it sustains it*, since it serves as an excellent introduction and a faithful echo of the Liturgy, enabling people to participate fully and interiorly in it and to reap its fruits in their daily lives."[99]

There is also the objection that the Rosary is a monotonous prayer, and Protestants especially recall a line from the Sermon on the Mount: "Do not heap up empty phrases as the Gentiles do; for they think that they will be heard for their many words" (Mt 6:7). "If this repetition is considered superficially, there could be a temptation to see the Rosary as a dry and boring exercise. It is quite another thing, however, when the Rosary is thought of as an outpouring of that love which tirelessly returns to the person loved with expressions similar in their content but ever fresh in terms of the feeling pervading them."

For a biblical example, the pope recalls the threefold repetition of the Lord's question: "Simon, son of John, do you love me?," a question that calls for an answer each time. "To understand the Rosary, one has to enter into the psychological dynamic proper to love."[100] The repetition opens up space to contemplate the mysteries, to involve the emotions, and to call to mind the intentions for which one is praying.

History of the Rosary To understand the value of the Rosary, we should first look into its history. In order to identify the real starting point, it is necessary to see the characteristic connection between repeated recitation of the Ave Maria and contemplation of the life of Jesus. The decisive step took place in the contemplative orders (Cistercians and Carthusians) that developed the Marian Psalter, in which the recitation of the Angelic Salutation is combined with *clausulae* regarding various events in the life of Jesus. The first such Marian Psalter, according to recent research, is preserved in a manuscript of the Cistercian nuns of the Monastery of St. Thomas on

99. *RVM* 4.
100. Ibid., 26.

the Kyll (Germany), a text copied in 1300, containing ninety-eight *clausulae*.[101]

In this document we find the practice of repeating the Ave Maria 150 times. In Eastern monasticism and in early medieval monasticism in the West, monks sought to deepen their meditation by repeating a biblical passage, usually a verse of the Psalms. In that way one could approach the ideal of praying "without ceasing" (see 1 Thes 5:17). The number of repetitions was usually based on the number of the Psalms (150). In Irish monasticism particularly, the ideal was to recite all 150 Psalms daily (from memory), or at least one-third or two-thirds of them. We also find the Our Father among the repeated prayers counted on a cord. In penitential practice, the recitation of the psalms could be replaced by Our Fathers, for illiterate faithful.

Starting in the twelfth century, the Ave Maria was added to the repetition of the Our Father. An uninterrupted chain of 150 Ave Marias, the "Marian Psalter," was practiced. Like the scriptural psalter, the 150 Ave Marias were also divided into three groups of fifty. The rule of the Beguines at Ghent (Belgium), in 1242, for example, called on members of the community to recite at least fifty Ave Marias each day. The Cistercians, in the concern that prayer might degenerate into a "heap of words" as among the pagans (Mt 6:7), often recommended that fifty Aves would suffice.

The name "rosary" comes from the Cistercian milieu (thirteenth century): a legend recalls that a new monk was accustomed to decorating a statue of the Madonna with roses; but Mary revealed to him that she preferred a crown composed of fifty Aves.

At the same time, an intensive form of meditation on the life of Jesus developed that began by joining in the repetition of the Ave Maria. One of the first influential people who prayed the Rosary was Adolf of Essen, prior of the Charterhouse at Trier († 1439).[102] Around 1400, Adolf repeated fifty Ave Marias every day and simultaneously meditated on the life of Jesus. As a spiritual father,

101. See Bogusław Kochaniewicz, "Origine e storia del Rosario," in Cecchin, *Contemplare Cristo con Maria*, 23–26.

102. See Klinkhammer, *Adolf von Essen und seine Werke*; Klinkhammer, *Ein wunderbares Beten*; Klinkhammer, "Adolf von Essen."

he shared this method with others, including a duchess (Margaret of the Palatinate) who was in serious family difficulties. The prior taught her to contemplate the Sacred Scriptures with the heart of Mary (see Lk 2:19, 2:51) and so draw near to our Lord, thanking him and orienting her life toward him. When the duke of Lorraine won two victories over enemies with much greater forces, the victories were attributed to the prayers of the duchess. Margaret dedicated herself tirelessly to serving the poor and the sick, and many surprising cures due to her prayer are recalled. She felt strongly that the Rosary improved her Christian life, and so she did everything she could to spread the prayer. The experience was summarized in a saying of the prior Adolf: "A person must be extraordinarily bad if he doesn't experience a noticeable improvement in his life after praying the rosary well for a year."[103]

Another advance came with the arrival of Dominic of Prussia, a young university student († 1460), to the Charterhouse at Trier. He knocked at the monastery door and gave every appearance of being a vagrant, since he was so physically and mentally ruined by his dissolute life (1409). Adolf also wanted to teach him his method of prayer, but Dominic was incapable of concentrating on the meditations. So the idea came to him of dividing the life of Jesus into fifty phrases ("clauses") and adding an Ave Maria to each "clause."[104] These "clauses" spread rapidly. Later Dominic also published a series of 150 clauses for the entire Marian psalter.

Thereafter, the Rosary was spread in particular by the Dominicans, at first through the work, particularly, of Blessed Alain de la Roche († 1475), who erroneously held that St. Dominic had been the inventor of the Rosary.[105] The Dominicans were already praying the Rosary in common. Around 1460, Alain took up the method of Dominic of Prussia in regard to the entire Marian psalter; in addi-

103. See Klinkhammer, *Ein wunderbares Beten*, 30.

104. See Kochaniewicz, "Origine e storia del Rosario," 34–36.

105. See M. Lohrum, "Dominikus," in *ML* 2:210: St. Dominic (1170–1221), along with his confreres, prayed the Ave Maria with the aid of a cord; he "is not the author of the Rosary because there is no evidence for this thesis either in the process of his canonization (1233) or in the oldest biographies." The first sign of that attribution is in Alain de la Roche, who probably confused St. Dominic with the Carthusian Dominic of Prussia.

tion, he divided the psalter into portions of ten Ave Marias, adding a Pater noster each time. This division of the Marian psalter was already known in Alain's homeland of Brittany, among other places. He had his listeners pray the psalter, before or after his sermons.

Because the 150 "mysteries" were so numerous, their number was shortly reduced to fifteen. Evidence of this first appears in 1483 in southern Germany (Ulm). An engraving from Barcelona in 1488 shows the fifteen mysteries for the first time in the order known today.

What was lacking was only the addition of "Holy Mary" and of the trinitarian doxology (as at the end of every psalm). The first completion spread thanks to the intervention of Pius V. The "definitive" form of the Rosary was fixed in the eighteenth century in order to exactly specify the conditions for gaining the Dominican indulgence. The normal amount is one-third of the Marian psalter—that is, five decades of Ave Marias (joyful, sorrowful, or glorious mysteries).

Starting after the First World War (roughly) various modifications of the Rosary appear, with the addition of other mysteries. Moreover, there are presentations of biblical thoughts on each Ave Maria, as in the beginnings of the Rosary. And it is also possible to extend the meditation on the mysteries (as Vatican Radio does, for example). In general, according to the old tradition, the mysteries recited are joyful (Monday, Thursday), sorrowful (Tuesday, Friday), and glorious (Wednesday, Saturday, Sunday). With the apostolic letter *Rosarium Virginis Mariae* (2002), five "luminous mysteries" were introduced, with the effect that the distribution changed: the joyful mysteries are recited on Monday and Saturday, the sorrowful on Tuesday and Friday, the glorious on Wednesday and Sunday; and the luminous mysteries in turn are recited on Thursday. So one day in seven is dedicated to the luminous mysteries, while Saturday, dedicated to the joyful mysteries, underscores the Marian character of the day before Sunday, inasmuch as the joyful mysteries contemplate Mary's involvement most directly.[106]

106. See *RVM* 38.

The Theological and Pastoral Dimensions of the Rosary according to Paul VI The 1974 apostolic exhortation *Marialis cultus* presents a robust theological and pastoral evaluation of the Rosary. Its argument can be summarized in five points:

1. The Rosary is *a biblical prayer*. The formulas and the mysteries contemplated are inspired by the Gospel.[107]

2. The Rosary *presents the principal facts of salvation history*. "The Rosary considers in harmonious succession the principal salvific events accomplished in Christ, from his virginal conception and the mysteries of his childhood to the culminating moments of the Passover—the blessed passion and the glorious resurrection—and to the effects of this on the infant church on the day of Pentecost, and on the Virgin Mary when at the end of her earthly life she was assumed body and soul into her heavenly home." The threefold division of the mysteries does not just follow the chronological order, but also corresponds to the schema of the original Christian proclamation, described by St. Paul in the Letter to the Philippians: descent, death, glorification (Phil 2:6–11).[108]

3. The Rosary is *a Christocentric prayer*. The repetition of the Ave Maria becomes a persistent praise of Christ, the final object of the angel's announcement and of Elizabeth's greeting: "Blessed is the fruit of your womb" (Lk 1:42). The "succession of Hail Marys constitutes the warp on which is woven the contemplation of the mysteries." The pope also mentions the old practice of indicating a mystery after the name "Jesus" in each Ave Maria.[109]

4. The Rosary is *a meditative prayer*. Beside the element of praise and that of intercession, contemplation is also essential. "Without this the Rosary is a body without a soul, and its recitation is in danger of becoming a mechanical repetition of formulas and of going counter to the warning of Christ: 'And in praying do not heap up empty phrases as the Gentiles do; for they think that they will be heard for their many words' (Mt 6:7). By its nature the recitation

107. *MCu* 44.
108. Ibid., 45.
109. Ibid., 46.

of the Rosary calls for a quiet rhythm and a lingering pace, helping the individual to meditate on the mysteries of the Lord's life as seen through the eyes of her who was closest to the Lord. In this way the unfathomable riches of these mysteries are unfolded."[110]

5. There is a fruitful relationship between *the liturgy and the Rosary*. On one hand, the Rosary stems from the ancient trunk of the Christian liturgy: a "psalter of the Virgin" with which the simple faithful unite in the praise and universal intercession of the church. On the other hand, this process came about in a period when the liturgical spirit was in decadence: a certain alienation of the faithful from the liturgy developed, in favor of an emotional veneration of the humanity of Jesus and of the Blessed Virgin Mary. But we need not place the celebration of the liturgy in opposition to the recitation of the Rosary. The Rosary can be harmonized with the liturgy easily. "Like the liturgy," the Rosary "is of a community nature, draws its inspiration from Sacred Scripture and is oriented towards the mystery of Christ. The liturgical commemoration 'presents new, under the veil of signs and operative in a hidden way, the great mysteries of our Redemption.'" The contemplation evoked in the Rosary, on the other hand, "recalls these same mysteries to the mind of the person praying and stimulates the will to draw from them the norms of living." Rightly prayed, the Rosary guides us to the liturgy and makes the mysteries resound after their celebration in the spirit of the one who prays. But it is a mistake to recite the Rosary during the liturgical rite itself.[111]

Pope Paul VI indicates the *various methods* in which the Rosary is prayed: individually, in groups of faithful (with the promise of Matthew 18:20: "Where two or three are gathered in my name, there am I in the midst of them"), or publicly in assemblies of the church community.[112] The recitation of the Rosary *in families*, in the domestic church, is particularly recommended.[113] If the element of common prayer were missing "the family would lack its very charac-

110. Ibid., 47.
111. Ibid., 48.
112. Ibid., 50.
113. See Vatican II, *Apostolicam actuositatem*, 11.

ter as a domestic Church. Thus there must logically follow a concrete effort to reinstate communal prayer in family life if there is to be a restoration of the theological concept of the family as the domestic Church."[114] It would also be beneficial at times to pray some portion of the Liturgy of the Hours together in the family,[115] the highest point that family prayer can reach. But, along with this, the Rosary is no doubt the most efficacious common prayer. The pope hopes earnestly that common prayer can find its frequent and favored expression in the Rosary. This is a challenging undertaking today, because so many factors make family gatherings difficult, and many circumstances make it difficult to make such a gathering into an opportunity for prayer. But we need to apply all the effort possible to promote the family and common prayer.[116]

The Specific Contribution of Rosarium Virginis Mariae

It is not possible here to present all the richness of the apostolic letter *Rosarium Virginis Mariae* (2002), published for the Year of the Rosary (2002–3).[117] One specific point, obvious to all, is the introduction of five new mysteries, called the "mysteries of light": the Baptism of Jesus at the Jordan, the Lord's self-revelation at the wedding of Cana, the proclamation of the Kingdom of God with the call to conversion, the Transfiguration, and the institution of the Eucharist. "I believe," observes the pope, "that to bring out fully the Christological depth of the Rosary it would be suitable to make an addition to the traditional pattern which, while left to the freedom of individuals and communities, could broaden it to include *the mysteries of Christ's public ministry between his Baptism and his Passion*.... It is during the years of his public ministry that *the mystery of Christ is most evidently a mystery of light*: 'While I am in the world, I am the light of the world' (Jn 9:5)." Hence it is fitting to insert, between the

114. *MCu* 52.

115. Ibid., 53.

116. Ibid., 54.

117. Among others, see Charamsa, *Il Rosario*; Salvatore M. Perrella, "Il Rosario nel magistero dei Papi" [The Rosary in the Magisterium of the Popes], in Cecchin, *Contemplare Cristo con Maria*, 156–68; Perrella, *La Madre di Gesù*, 227–38; Perrella, *Ecco tua Madre*, 380–401; De Fiores, *Dizionario* 2:1402–13.

joyful and sorrowful mysteries, "certain particularly significant moments in his public ministry (*the mysteries of light*)" so that the Rosary may become "more fully a 'compendium of the Gospel.'"[118] This "innovation" actually returns to the original experience of the Rosary, which aims to contemplate Christ with the eyes and the heart of Mary. The Christological dimension is accompanied by an anthropological one: the Rosary "'marks the rhythm of human life' ... bringing it into harmony with the 'rhythm' of God's own life."[119]

Litanies

The Akathist Hymn The Marian litanies are composed of two elements: praise and supplication (*litaneía*, Greek, means "prayer of supplication").[120] We find their origin in the East; the best known Byzantine Marian litanies are those of the *Akâthistos hymn* (literally: to be sung "not seated," with great respect, as one hears the Gospel).[121] The text consists of an introduction and twenty-four strophes; the hymn is recited in full on the fifth Saturday of Lent, and also partially on other occasions. It arose around 500 and seems to

118. *RVM* 19.

119. Ibid. 25.

120. See Carl Kammer, *Die Lauretanische Litanei* [Litany of Loreto] (Innsbruck: Rauch, 1960); John Henry Newman, *Meditations and Devotions*, part 1, *The Month of May* (London: Longmans, 1929); Roschini, *La Madonna*, 4:308–13; *Maria Santissima*, 4:167–69; Giuseppe Maria Besutti, "Litanie," in De Fiores and Meo, *NDM*, 759–67; Walter Dürig, "Lauretanische Litanei," in *ML* 4:33–42; Pedico, *La Vergine Maria*, 94–100; Giorgio Basadonna and Giuseppe Santarelli, *Litanie lauretane* [Litany of Loreto] (Vatican City: Libreria Editrice Vaticana, 1997); Juan Luis Bastero, "Sinopsís histórica de las Letanias Lauretanas" [Historical Synopsis of the Litany of Loreto], in *Dar razón de la esperanza: Homenaje al Prof. Dr. J. L. Illanes*, ed. T. Trigo (Pamplona: Servicio de Publicaciones de la Universidad de Navarra, 2004), 1339–62; *DPPL*, n. 203; Ignazio M. Calabuig and Salvatore M. Perrella, "Litanie," in De Fiores, Schiefer, and Perrella, *DMar*, 719–26; Hauke, "Die Lauretanische Litanei: Systematische Aspekte marianischer Volksfrömmigkeit" [Litany of Loreto: Systematic Aspects of Marian Popular Piety], *Sedes Sapientiae: Mariologisches Jahrbuch* 15, no. 2 (2011): 56–88.

121. See Toniolo, "Akáthistos" [Akathist Hymn], in De Fiores and Meo, *NDM*, 16–25; Toniolo, *Akáthistos: Saggi di critica e di teologia* [Akáthistos: Critical and Theological Essays] (Rome: Centro di cultura mariana "Madre della Chiesa," 2000); Toniolo, "Maria 'donna nuova nella testimonianza liturgica: Maria nella liturgia orientale" [Mary, "New Woman" in the Liturgical Witness: Mary in the Eastern Liturgy], in *La donna e la salvezza: Maria e la vocazione femminile* [Woman and Salvation: Mary and the Feminine Vocation], ed. Manfred Hauke, in Scheffczyk, CdM 7 (2006): 100–11; T. Nikolaou, "Akáthistos Hymnos" [The Akathist Hymn], in *ML* 1:66f. Italian edition with Greek text and musical appendix: Rosa Calzecchi Onesti, ed., *Inno Akathistos alla Madre di Dio* [Akathist Hymn to the Mother of God], ed. R. Calzecchi Onesti (Rimini: Guaraldi, 1995). *DPPL*, n. 207.

precede Romanos the Melodist (early sixth century), to whom it is often attributed. The second part of the introduction (added later) makes reference to the liberation of Constantinople in 626, attributed to the invocation of the Virgin. The people gave thanks to Mary, standing the whole night: hence the name "not seated."[122]

As an example, let us cite a part of the twenty-third strophe:

Hail, O Tabernacle of God the Word;
hail, Holy One, more holy than the saints!
Hail, O Ark that the Spirit has gilded;
hail, inexhaustible Treasure of life!
Hail, precious Crown of rightful authorities;
hail, sacred Glory of reverent priests!
Hail, unshakable Tower of the Church;
hail, unbreachable Wall of the kingdom!
Hail, O you through whom the trophies are raised;
hail, O you through whom the enemies are routed!
Hail, O Healing of my body;
hail, O Salvation of my soul![123]

The *Akáthistos* is shared by our Orthodox brethren and Catholics of the Byzantine rite: it is an ancient and solemn bridge toward full communion of faith with the Churches of the East. But also for our Protestant brothers of the West, for whom the cultus of Mary is still a stumbling block, it may constitute an authentic value and a basis for dialogue: for its antiquity; for its form as praise, which redounds—as is easily seen—to the glory of the Lord; for its underlying christological-ecclesial basis; for its rich and sober doctrine, devoid of exaltations, which is florid with the mystery of the Incarnation itself, that is, with the first article of the christological faith professed by all the Churches.[124]

The Litany of Loreto Around 800, the *Akáthistos* hymn was translated into Latin and began to influence the countries of the West. The oldest Latin litany is that of the saints (seventh century), which serves as a model for later litanies. The invocation *Sancta Maria* was

122. See Toniolo, *Akáthistos: Saggi di critica*, 4.
123. See ibid., 21. (English from Raya and de Vinck, *Byzantine Daily Worship*, 978.)
124. Ibid., 24f.

complemented with other titles, such as (in the eighth century, for example) *Sancta Dei genitrix* and *Sancta Virgo virginum*. Among the various Marian litanies, only the litany of pilgrims at Loreto in the sixteenth century, called the Litany of Loreto, was approved for public use; but its texts go back to 1200 at least.[125] Today the litany is structured as follows: three initial invocations, twelve invocations under the title "Mother," six under the title of "Virgin," thirteen symbolic invocations (with a strong old Testament connection), four invocations of Mary as Helper (of the sick, of sinners, of the afflicted, of Christians), thirteen invocations of Mary as Queen.

After its official approval (in 1587 by Sixtus V; in 1601 by Clement VIII) new titles were added, in which various important invocations resound: "Queen of the Most Holy Rosary" (1675), "Queen conceived without original sin" (1846/1884), "Mother of good counsel" (1903), "Queen of peace" (1917, the first world war), "Queen assumed into Heaven" (1950), "Mother of the Church" (1980), "Queen of the family" (1995). The litany printed in 1572 contains forty-three invocations, whereas today we have fifty-one. Among the favorite titles in the Litany are those shaped by the invocations "Mother," "Virgin," and "Queen." The others, according to Roschini, could be summarized under the term "universal mediation." Thus we arrive at four fundamental ideas for a dogmatic analysis: the divine maternity, the perpetual virginity, the universal mediation, and the queenship. The fifty-one invocations are, as it were, "brilliant stars" that illuminate "the unique greatness of the Mother of God, the dazzling virginal purity of her body and her soul, the strong and powerful arm of the universal Mediatrix, the generous and tender heart of the Queen of earth and Heaven."[126]

Other Important Prayers

An outstanding criterion for evaluating the role of a prayer (including as a source of doctrine) is its recognition by church authority and the granting of indulgences. According to the new Manual of

125. The author was probably a professor at Paris, Magister Simon: Dürig, "Lauretanische Litanei," 34.

126. Roschini, *La Madonna*, 4:313.

Indulgences (1999), all approved Marian prayers are enriched with a partial indulgence.[127] Since the episcopal conferences are invited to publish a specific Manual for their regions, the general Manual contains only a few prayers of universal value. Mentioned are the Rosary, the *Magnificat*,[128] the Angelus (and the *Regina coeli*), "Mary, Mother of grace,"[129] the *Memorare* (which is inspired by St. Bernard),[130] the *Salve Regina*,[131] "Holy Mary, succor the miserable, help the fainthearted,"[132] the *Sub tuum praesidium* (the oldest Marian prayer),[133] the novena before the solemnity of the Immaculate Conception, the Little Office of the Blessed Virgin Mary,[134] or of the Immaculate Conception, and the Litany of Loreto. The *Akâthistos* hymn and the Office of the Paraclisis, a handbook of supplicatory hymns particularly used during the two weeks before August 15, bear witness to Eastern traditions, along with a Coptic prayer.[135]

127. Apostolic Penitentiary, *Manual of Indulgences*, 59.

128. See "The Magnificat" in chap. 1.

129. The invocation "Mother of grace," alongside that of "Mother of mercy," appears more or less at the time when the *Salve Regina was* born. Around 110 A.D. we find an entire litany dedicated to Mary as mother of grace: O'Carroll, *Theotokos*, 255.

130. See Roschini, *La Madonna*, 4:407; T. Maas-Ewerd, "Memorare," in *ML* 4:411. The entire text is attested for the first time in the fifteenth century. The prayer is impressive for the immense trust demonstrated in regard to the intercession of the Blessed Virgin.

131. See Roschini, *La Madonna*, 4:293–304; *Maria Santissima*, 4:143; "Salve Regina," in *ML* 5:648–50; O'Carroll, *Theotokos*, 317f. The most famous final Marian antiphon was already sung at the time of St. Bernard. "After the Ave Maria, the most beautiful and most universal Marian prayer is undoubtedly the 'Salve Regina'": Roschini, *La Madonna*, 4:294.

132. See Roschini, *La Madonna* 4:406: a prayer stemming from Carolingian times, attributed erroneously to St. Augustine.

133. Regarding *Sub tuum praesidium*, see "Patristic Motifs through the Sixth Century," in chapter 2; also Maria Francesca Perillo, "Sub tuum praesidium: Incomparable Marian Praeconium," in *Mary at the Foot of the Cross* (New Bedford, Mass.: Academy of the Immaculate, 2004), 4:138–69; Perillo, "Il 'Sub tuum praesidium': Singolare preconio di misteri mariani," *Immaculata Mediatrix* 8 (2008): 41–67.

134. The "little office" of Our Lady is of monastic origin and was originally placed on Saturdays (in the eighth century). It is composed of prayers that complement the Divine Office (the Liturgy of the Hours), which is fuller. Today this devotion is found in various religious families, in particular the Cistercians. In addition, the "Little Office of the BVM" serves as a shorter breviary for laity and for nonclerical religious. Before the liturgical reform of Pius V, the "little office" formed part of the daily breviary; the pope abolished this practice and, in place of it, introduced the Office of the Blessed Virgin Mary on Saturday, which still exists today. See Roschini, *La Madonna*, 4:323–26; *Maria Santissima*, 4:97, 123f, 137f, 166f; F. Baumeister and D. V. Hübner, "Offizium marianum" [Marian Office], in *ML* 4:681f; O'Carroll, *Theotokos*, 219f.

135. Apostolic Penitentiary, *Manual of Indulgences* (Washington, D.C.: USCCB, 2006), 82f. Nearly all the indulgenced prayers of the 1968 edition are published (in Latin/Italian) in *Preghiere*

Recurring Observances in the Weekly, Monthly, and Annual Cycles

The custom of dedicating Saturday to Mary comes from the Carolingian era (around 800).[136] Among various explanations, the most common reference is the fact that Mary, "in the 'great Sabbath' when Christ lay in the tomb, strong only in faith and hope, alone among all the disciples, kept vigil for the resurrection of the Lord."[137]

The first Saturday of the month has gained a particular importance from the message of Fatima: the graces necessary to die in peace with God are promised to all who, for five consecutive months, confess on the first Saturday (or shortly before), receive Communion, and contemplate the mysteries of the Rosary for fifteen minutes.[138] There is also an older custom (little observed today) of fifteen Saturdays in preparation for the feast of the Holy Rosary.

The practice of dedicating an entire month to Mary appears in the West in the Baroque era. Already in the Middle Ages we find a connection between the vernal symbolism of the month of May and Marian devotion; but the entire month of May was dedicated to Mary starting only in the eighteenth and nineteenth centuries. Some countries in the southern half of the globe prefer their own spring month for this devotion, such as the month of November in some countries of Latin America (Argentina, Chile, Paraguay) and in South Africa. Since the liturgical reform, it has become important to connect Marian devotion with the dominant theme of the Easter season, which includes a large part of the month of May.[139] Paul VI ded-

---

& canti liturgici, 7th ed. (Milan: Ares, 2003). See also, with a more reduced selection, *Lodate Dio: Guida alla preghiera e al canto* (Lugano: Centro di liturgia, 1985), nn. 84–95.

136. Cf. See Roschini, *La Madonna*, 4:337–44; Stefano Rosso, "Sabato" [Saturday], in De Fiores and Meo, *NDM*, 1216–28; De Fiores, *Maria, Madre di Gesù*, 272; *DPPL*, n. 188.

137. Congregation for Divine Worship, *Collection of Masses of the Blessed Virgin Mary* (New York: Catholic Book Pub., 1992); 2nd ed. (Collegeville, Minn.: Liturgical Press, 2012), introduction, 36; *Enchiridion Vaticanum* 10, n. 771.

138. Regarding the message of Fatima, see p. 396–98. A prefiguration of this custom existed already in consecration of the first Saturday of the month to Our Lady, recommended by St. John Eudes and J. J. Olier (seventeenth century).

139. See *DPPL*, n. 191; Rosso, "Mese mariano," in De Fiores and Meo, *NDM*, 935–45; K. Küppers, "Mai" [May], in *ML* 4:242f; K. Küppers and H. Rzepkowski, "Maiandacht" [May Devotion],

icated an entire encyclical to the month of May (*Mense maio*, 1965).[140]

Leo XIII, in 1898, directed that the whole month of October be consecrated to the prayer of the Rosary.[141]

The Marian month for Eastern Christians of the Byzantine rite (both Catholics and Orthodox) is (since the Middle Ages), the month of August, concentrating on the solemnity of the Assumption of Mary into heaven. In the two weeks before this feast, the faithful prepare with fasting, while the two subsequent weeks are regarded as an "afterfeast."

In the Coptic Church in Egypt, which recalls the sojourn of the Holy Family in its territory with particular tenderness, there is also a whole month dedicated to Mary: the fourth month of the Coptic calendar, from December 10 to January 8, which culminates with the feast of Christmas. Beforehand there is a fast of forty-six days, also called the "fast of Mary," which the Mother of God is said to have observed before the birth of the infant Jesus. During the Marian month there is a vigil every night, with prayers containing a rich Marian content, particularly in the chants called "theotokia."[142]

Consecration to Mary

The Meaning of "Consecration"

The term "consecration" (an act or rite by which a person or thing is made sacred) comes from the verb "consecrate" and means "to render sacred," or rather, to render a person or thing from the secular milieu sacred, dedicating it stably for God and divine worship.... Consecration is not only a giving into custody, but is a gift in property; it is not a gift in property for some time, but forever.[143]

Consecration to the Mother of God is, without doubt, the summit of Marian devotion.[144] "Consecration" means, in brief, that an ob-

in *ML* 4:244–48; De Fiores, *Maria, Madre di Gesú*, 271f; Pedico, *La Vergine Maria*, 113–25; C. Maggioni, "Mese mariano" [Marian Month], in De Fiores, Schiefer, and Perrella, *DMar*, 836–44.

140. *EE* 7, nn. 831–44.

141. Leo XIII, Encyclical *Diuturni temporis*, Sept. 5, 1898: *EE* 3, n. 1420.

142. See *TMPM* 4:802–21.

143. Roschini, *La Madonna*, 4:493f.

144. See Roschini, *La Madonna* 4:490–502; José María Canal, "La consagración a la Virgen

ject, a person, or a community is entrusted to the Mother of God. Such a consecration happens through a prayer that expresses dedication to Mary and the request to obtain her protection. Pius XII defines consecration as a "*total giving of the self*,"[145] while John Paul II can also speak of a filial "acceptance" of Mary.[146] There is no essential difference between the terms "entrustment" and "consecration," both used by John Paul II.[147] In the term "entrustment," which appears

---

y a su Corazón Inmaculada" [Consecration to the Virgin and to Her Immaculate Heart], in *Alma Socia Christi* (Rome: PAMI, 1956), 12:221–348; *Teologia e pastorale della consacrazione a Maria* [Theology and Pastoral Ministry of Consecration to Mary] (Padova: Messaggero, 1969); "La consagración a Maria," *Estudios Marianos* 51 (1986); Scheffczyk, "Weihe" [Consecration], in *ML* 6:696–98; Scheffczyk, *Maria, Mutter und Gefährtin Christi* [Mary, Mother and Companion of Christ] (Augsburg: Sankt Ulrich, 2003), 251–63; Scheffczyk, "Die 'Marienweihe' in Leben und Lehre Johannes Pauls II: unter systematischem Aspekt" [Marian Consecration" in the Life and Teaching of John Paul II, in a Systematic View], in Ziegenaus, *Totus tuus*, 109–24, Mariologische Studien 1 (Regensburg: Friedrich Pustet, 2004); Stefano De Fiores, "Consacrazione," in De Fiores and Meo, *NDM*, 394–417; De Fiores, *Maria, Madre di Gesú*, 292–95; De Fiores, *Dizionario* 1:1–20 (*affidamento*), 359–413 (*consacrazione*); Arthur B. Calkins, *Totus tuus: John Paul II's Program of Marian Consecration and Entrustment* (1992; New Bedford, Mass.: Academy of the Immaculate, 1997); (2006), 26–29, 352–58; Calkins, "Marian Consecration and Entrustment," in Miravalle, *Mariology: A Guide*, 725–66; Ziegenaus, *Maria in der Heilsgeschichte: Mariologie* [Mary in Salvation History: Mariology], Katholische Dogmatik 5 (Aachen: MM-Verlag, 1998), 387–90; O'Carroll, *Theotokos*, 107–09; Alessandro M. Apollonio, "La consacrazione a Maria," *Immaculata Mediatrix* 1, no. 3 (2001): 49–101; Brunero Gherardini, "Sta la regina *alla tua destra: Saggio storico-teologico sulla Regalità di Maria* [The Queen Stands at Your Right Hand: Historical-Theological Essay on the Queenship of Mary] (Rome: Vivere In, 2002)," 169–90; Toniolo, "La forma impegnativa di culto mariano: La consacrazione personale a Maria" [The Commitment Form of the Cult of Mary: Personal Consecration to Mary], in Toniolo, *La Vergine Maria nel cammino orante della Chiesa*, 237–50; Hauke, "Totus tuus—Theologische Grundlagen der Marienweihe" [Totally Yours: Theological Bases of Marian Consecration], in *Im Dienste der Inkarnierten Wahrheit: Festschrift zum 25jährigen Pontifikat Seiner Heiligkeit Papst Johannes Pauls II*, ed. A. von Brandenstein-Zeppelin, A. von Stockhausen, L. Roos, and J. H. Benirschke (Weilheim-Bierbronnen: Gustav-Siewerth-Akademie, 2003) 127–48; Hauke, "Die Weihe der Welt an die Gottesmutter Maria" [Consecration of the World to Mary, the Mother of God], *Sedes Sapientiae: Mariologisches Jahrbuch* 14, no. 2 (2010): 67–91; Hauke, "La consacrazione alla Vergine Maria nella teologia tedesca del XX secolo" [Consecration to the Virgin Mary in 20th-Century German Theology], in *La Consacrazione alla Vergine Maria nel 50° della Consacrazione dell'Italia al Cuore Immacolato di Maria: Atti del simposio Mariologico Internationale sulla Consacrazione alla Vergine Maria, Frigento, 5–7 luglio 2010* [Acts of the International Mariological Symposium at Frigento, July 5–7, 2010, on the 50th Anniversary of the Consecration of Italy to the Virgin Mary] (Frigento: Casa Mariana Editrice, 2011), 269–320; Perrella, *Ecco tua Madre*, 477–515; Perrella, "Affidamento consacrazione" [Entrustment, Consecration], in De Fiores, Schiefer, and Perrella, *DMar*, 16–24.

145. Pius XII, Allocution of January 21, 1945, in *Discorsi e radiomessaggi* (Vatican City: Tipografia Poliglotta Vaticana, 1961), 6:281.

146. Letter to Mons. Lorenzo Bellomi, August 15, 1984, cited in De Fiores, *Maria, Madre di Gesú*, 294.

147. A clarifying and precise discussion on this point is found in Calkins, *Totus tuus* (1997), 143–52.

multiple times in the language of the pope, there is an accent on filial abandonment, while "consecration" implies a "putting oneself at the disposition of" another.[148] The term "consecration" "is without a doubt vaster and more comprehensive than other terms noted in the same *Directory* [*DPPL*, 2002, n. 204], which have been observed by historical experience in direct relationship with Mary: *oblatio, servitus, commendatio, dedicatio* (offering, service, entrustment, dedication)." The term "entrustment" "lacks an inherent connection with the sacred, which the term 'consecration' includes."[149] For the sake of systematic clarity it seems more suitable to give preference to the term "consecration."[150]

Biblical Foundation

Is consecration to Mary, as a "total giving of the self," already present in Sacred Scripture?[151] According to John Paul II, entrustment to the Mother of God is based on her spiritual maternity, which is made manifest in the words of our Savior on the Cross (Jn 19:26f). In John, every man is entrusted to the maternal concern of Mary. At the same time, John appears as a first witness of entrustment to Mary, inasmuch as he receives the Mother of God "to his own home" (*eis ta idia*). The words of the Crucified establish a communion of life between Mary and John.[152] This symbolic interpretation of the Johannine text is reinforced by the title "woman" by which Mary is addressed, as happened at the wedding of Cana (Jn 2:4). Mary thus appears as the new Eve, "the woman" par excellence (Gn 3:15), and thus also as "mother of all the living" (Gn 3:20). the Johannine passage is read in light of the tradition that marks out more clearly the lines already present in the text itself. The explanation of John 19, as

148. See Gherardini, *Sta la Regina*, 170–72.

149. Toniolo, "La forma impegnativa," 240f, on the reserve expressed by the *DPPL*, n. 204, about the term "consecration," even though it appears in the title of that section ("Consecration and Entrustment to Mary").

150. See also Apollonio, "La consacrazione a Maria," 96–98; Calkins, *Totus tuus* (1997), 277f; 2006 ed., 26–29.

151. For the biblical foundation, see Apollonio, "La consacrazione a Maria," 60–71; Hauke, "Totus tuus," 135–39.

152. See John Paul II, *RM* 45. Other similar texts are mentioned in Calkins, *Totus tuus* (1997), 222–47; 2006 ed., 352–58.

the foundation of Mary's spiritual motherhood, has been seen with clarity since the twelfth century (Rupert of Deutz), but is already suggested in the patristic era.[153]

This reference to the spiritual motherhood of Mary in the words of Jesus crucified is a first starting point for consecration to the Mother of God. Another biblical motif is the example of Jesus Christ himself, who made himself dependent on the cooperation of Mary through the Incarnation. Entrustment to Mary is based on the gift of himself, which the Son of God made to his Mother. This idea, indicated by John Paul II,[154] is developed particularly by Grignion de Montfort: the Son of God "glorified his independence and his majesty in depending on this lovable virgin in his conception, his birth, his presentation in the temple, and in the thirty years of his hidden life. Even at his death she had to be present so that he might be united with her in one sacrifice and be immolated with her consent to the eternal Father, just as formerly Isaac was offered in sacrifice by Abraham, when he accepted the will of God. It was Mary who nursed him, fed him, cared for him, reared him, and sacrificed him for us."[155]

A third biblical approach is shown in Mary's *fiat* at the Annunciation (Lk 1:38). The Gospel of Luke presents Mary in a way that recalls the Old Testament figure of the "daughter of Zion," symbol of the "spousal" giving of the people to God and of motherly care for the children of Israel. With this symbolic reference, also emphasized by Vatican II,[156] Mary appears as the exemplary realization of the church. Just as the scene of the Annunciation points to the Incarnation as a work of the Trinity, Mary's response to God is shown to be an exemplary realization of self-gift on the part of every Christian, to the trinitarian God.

153. John Paul II, *RM* 23, cites Origen here, *Comm. in Ioan.* 1.6 (*SC* 120:71, 73). On Jn 19 see "Mary at the Foot of the Cross," in chapter 1.

154. *RM* 46.

155. *TD* 18.

156. *LG* 55.

The Historical Path of Consecration to Mary up to the Seventeenth Century

This intense Marian devotion began after the Council of Ephesus (431), when churches and shrines began to be dedicated to the Mother of God. Already this form of consecration indicates that it is not just a matter of a simple petitioning. An objective effect is implied, one that remains as a relationship of blessing and protection. This relationship becomes more intense when a person or community consecrates itself to Mary.[157]

In the early church, consecration to Mary is prepared by trusting recourse to the Mother of God in prayer, but also by looking at Mary, consecrated to God as a model of virgins.[158] Even the first Marian prayer, the *Sub tuum praesidium,* from the third century, is very close to an act of consecration. Saint Idelfonso of Toledo (seventh century) proclaims himself a *servus Mariae.*[159] The first total offering of self to Mary, formulated in terms of a consecration, is found in a homily of St. John Damascene († 749) in which the mariological teaching of the fathers is summarized: "We too present ourselves to you today, O Sovereign, O Virgin Mother of God our souls cling to you, our hope, as to an anchor, utterly firm and unbreakable, consecrating to you mind, soul, body, all our being."[160] "A true Marian spirituality in the Damascene already has the characteristics of totality and permanence, even though it does not yet have a systematic structure."[161]

In the Middle Ages, individual persons and various religious orders consecrated themselves to Mary. It also happened that children

157. See, for the whole historical path, De Fiores, "Consacrazione," 398–406; *Dizionario*, 361–78; Calkins, Totus tuus (1997 ed.), 41–156; Apollonio, "La consacrazione a Maria," 72–91; Hauke, "Totus tuus," 139–43.

158. See Hauke, "Jungfrauen (Maria als Vorbild der Jungfrauen)" [Virgins (Mary as Model of Virgins], in *ML* 3:484–87.

159. Ildefonso, *De virginitate perpetua s. Mariae* 12 (PL 96:105–8). See Luigi Gambero, *Maria nel pensiero dei teologi latini medievali* [Mary in the Thought of the Medieval Latin Theologians] (Cinisello Balsamo: Ed. Paoline, 2000), 24f. English trans. in Gambero, *Mary in the Middle Ages*, 31f.

160. *Hom. in Dorm.* I.14 (PG 96:720), translated to Italian in De Fiores, "Consacrazione," 400. English version by translator.

161. Ibid., 400.

were entrusted solemnly to the protection of Mary and to her service. In the thirteenth century, the Order of Servites of St. Mary, established at Florence, proposed to serve the Lord by means of dedication to the Virgin.

A particular nuance came with the influence of chivalric love: "A knight renders homage to a married lady with whom he has fallen in love, even if it is a platonic love in which she remains an unattainable ideal. In the field of religion, courtly love influenced the relationship with Mary, the Lady par excellence: that is, the 'Madonna.'" The Teutonic Knights promised in their vows, "I promise to be pure in body, without personal goods, and obedient to God, to Holy Mary, and to you, Master of the Order."[162]

The use of the scapular is connected with Carmelite spirituality. At first it was part of the monastic habit, a band of fabric with an opening for the head, hung on the chest and the back. The same garment, "in miniature," then came to be used by the laity and became a scapular as we know it: two small pieces of fabric with a sacred image joined by ribbons that hang over the shoulders. Carmelite tradition tells of an apparition of Mary on July 16, 1251, to Simon Stock, an English Carmelite (called the "general" of the order, because he held that post during his religious life). Holding the scapular in her hand, Mary is reported to have said, "This will be a privilege for you and yours. Whoever dies clothed in it will be saved."

In the so-called Sabbatine Bull Pope John XXII (1322) allegedly referred to a vision he had, according to which the Virgin assured him that all the Carmelites (and their tertiaries) who would observe chastity according to their state of life, who would pray and wear the habit of Carmel, were to be freed from purgatory on the first Saturday after death.[163]

Irrespective of the historical value of the aforementioned, the use of the scapular by tertiaries of the Carmelite order is a visible expression of dedication to Mary and of her protection (as a "mantle"). The

162. Ibid., 401.

163. The authenticity of this Bull was challenged in the seventeenth century by Jean de Launoy (1603–78) and more recently by Ludovico Saggi, in *La Bolla Sabatina* (Rome: Institutum carmelitanum, 1967). Some, though, continue to defend the authenticity of the bull.

idea of a "garment" allows us to evoke the baptismal garment, sign of the dignity of the adoptive sons of God, entrusted to the Mother of God. The habit of a monk recalls the commitments of Baptism, to observe them with care in the religious life. The *Manual of Indulgences* promises a partial indulgence to all the faithful who use a duly blessed devotional object, and the scapular is mentioned: ("a crucifix or cross, rosary, scapular, or medal").[164] The religious function of the scapular is similar to that of the "Miraculous Medal," which today is much more widespread.[165]

From the sixteenth century on, consecration to Mary was accepted by the Marian Congregations, associations of the faithful devoted to our Lady, guided by the Jesuits. Their members promised a total offering to Mary, a perpetual servitude.[166] In a 1622 formula of admission to the Marian Congregation we find the word "consecrate" for the first time, to manifest the specific will to place oneself under the patronage of Mary.

Marian Consecration as Proposed by Grignion de Montfort

The most profound and widespread teaching on consecration to Mary is that of St. Louis-Marie Grignion de Montfort († 1716)[167] in his celebrated "Treatise on True Devotion to Mary" (*TD*). The treatise remained hidden and unknown for a long time, but gained notable success after its publication in 1843. Grignion affirmed that dedication to Mary corresponds to the work of salvation itself: God

164. Apostolic Penitentiary, *Manual of Indulgences*, 16, n. 15.

165. Regarding the apparition in the *Rue du Bac*, see pp. 391–93.

166. A radical change and then a sharp decline came in 1968, when the Jesuits abandoned the name of "Marian Congregations," replacing it with "Christian Life Communities," the expression "consecration to Mary" was also eliminated. On Marian devotion in the Jesuits, see J. Stierli, "Jesuiten," in *ML* 3:373–75.

167. See De Fiores, "Consacrazione," 404f.; De Fiores, "Presentazione," in San Luigi M. Grignion da Montfort, *Trattato della vera devozione alla santa Vergine e Il segreto di Maria*, ed. S. De Fiores, 11th ed. (Cinisello Balsamo: San Paolo, 2000), 5–17; De Fiores, *Dizionario* 1:372–74; Ziegenaus, "Die vollkommene Hingabe an Jesus durch Maria nach Ludwig-Maria Grignion von Montfort" [Total Consecration to Jesus through Mary according to Louis Marie Grignion de Montfort], in *Totus tuus: Maria in Leben und Lehre Johannes Pauls II* [Totally Yours: Mary in the Life and Teaching of John Paul II], ed. Anton Ziegenaus, 31–45. Mariologische Studien 1. Regensburg: Friedrich Pustet, 2004; Battista Cortinovis, Stefano De Fiores, and Enrico Vidau, eds., *Spiritualità trinitaria in comunione con Maria secondo Montfort* [Trinitarian Spirituality in Communion with Mary, according to Montfort] (Rome: Edizioni Monfortane, 2002).

entrusted the Incarnation to her consent; thus it is fitting for us to entrust oneself to her, so that she can form the life of Christ in us. The Son of God desires to be formed anew every day in the members of his mystical body, through his Mother. Mary is the most efficacious and swiftest way to find Christ and to grow in sanctity.[168] Perfect consecration to Jesus takes place by means of total consecration to Mary. Inasmuch as Mary is the creature most similar to Christ, dedication to her conforms the soul to the Savior in the highest degree. Grignion emphasizes that this consecration is a perfect renewal of baptismal vows.[169] "Total" offering means offering to Mary our body and our soul, our goods both present and future, including spiritual goods (merits, virtues, and good works).[170] With this consecration one seeks to do everything through Mary, with Mary, in Mary, and for Mary so that everything is done perfectly through Jesus, with Jesus, in Jesus, and for Jesus.[171] As the first coming of Christ was prepared through Mary, so his second coming at the end of time will be prepared in the same way. But while at the first coming of Christ Mary remained hidden, as it were (so as not to obscure contact with Jesus), at the second coming she must be known, so that men will appreciate and love the Savior all the more.[172] The spirituality of Grignion profoundly influenced John Paul II.[173] In addition, we have the earlier example of St. Maximilian Kolbe, who appreciated de Montfort's teaching very much, adding to it the mystery of the Immaculata. The motto *Totus tuus* on the pontifical arms of John Paul II appears already in the "Treatise on True Devotion," in a quotation from Bonaventure,[174] and in a Latin prayer composed by the Saint: *tuus totus ego sum, et omnia mea tua sunt, o virgo super omnia*

168. *TD* 152–68.

169. Ibid., 120.

170. Ibid., 121.

171. Ibid., 257.

172. Ibid., 49–50.

173. See Calkins, *Totus tuus* (1997), 62–66; G. Riedl, "Der Einfluss Louis-Marie Grignions de Montfort (1673–1716) auf die Mariologie Papst Johannes Pauls II." [The Influence of de Montfort on the Mariology of Pope John Paul II], in Ziegenaus, *Totus tuus*, 47–69.

174. *TD* 216. See Cecchin, "'Totus tuus ego sum': La 'consacrazione a Maria' nella tradizione francescana," in *La Vergine Maria nella teologia e nella spiritualità francescana: Incontro di spiritualità francescana, Santuario della Verna, 17–23 agosto 2004*, ed. Pietro Messa, Quaderni di Spiritualità Francescana 26 (Santa Maria degli Angeli [Perugia]: Porziuncola, 2005), 139–85.

benedicta.[175] In *Redemptoris Mater*, John Paul II mentions the precious witness of individual persons and whole communities to Marian devotion. "In this regard, I would like to recall, among the many witnesses and teachers of this spirituality, the figure of Saint Louis Marie Grignion de Montfort, who proposes consecration to Christ through the hands of Mary, as an effective means for Christians to live faithfully their baptismal commitments."[176]

Total consecration to Mary according to Grignion implies a total commitment on the part of the person being consecrated. The effect of such a consecration is more intense than what can be verified in consecrations by which other persons or entire peoples are entrusted to Mary. Such a consecration can take place, for example, on the occasion of baptism or at the renewal of baptismal promises.

The Consecration of Others and of the Whole World to the Mother of God

The first consecration of an entire country is that of Hungary, entrusted to our Lady by the king St. Stephen I (†1038).[177] A dedication of this type is inspired by the idea of patronage: a patron has the duty to defend and protect the person who entrust himself to him: and this protection corresponds to the special duties of the person protected.

The most important example of the consecration of others is the entrustment of the world to the Immaculate Heart of Mary undertaken by Pius XII in 1942 on the occasion of the twenty-fifth anniversary of the Marian apparitions at Fatima, during the Second World War. The pope prayed as follows:[178]

175. Louis-Marie Grignion de Montfort, *Oeuvres complètes* (Paris: Seuil, 1982), 839. See Calkins, *Totus tuus* (1997), 27; De Fiores, *Trattato della vera devozione*, 150; Perrella, *Ecco tua Madre*, 19f, note 19.

176. *RM* 48.

177. See Scheffczyk, "Weihe," 698; Gábor Tüskes and Éva Knapp, "Stephan der Heilige" [St. Stephen], in Bäumer and Scheffczyk, *ML* 6:294f.

178. Pius XII, Radio address to the faithful of Portugal on October 31, 1942. See *AAS* 34 (1942): 345f. Italian trans. in *Atti e discorsi di Pio XII*, Gennaio-Dicembre 1942 (Rome: San Paolo, 1943), 4:263–72. The text in Portuguese is on the internet at https://w2.vatican.va/content/pius-xii/pt/speeches/1942/documents/hf_p-xii_spe_19421031_immaculata.html.

To you, to your Immaculate Heart, We, as the common Father of the great Christian family, as Vicar of Him to whom all power in heaven and on earth has been given (Mt 28:18), and from whom We have received the care of so many souls redeemed by his blood, inhabiting the whole world, to You, to your Immaculate Heart, in this tragic hour of human history, we entrust, render, consecrate not only the Holy Church, mystical body of your Jesus, which suffers and bleeds in so many places, and under tribulation in so many ways, but also the entire world tormented by fierce discords, parched in a fire of hatred, victim of its own iniquities.

Be moved by such great material and moral ruin; so many sorrows, so much anguish of fathers and mothers, of spouses, of brethren, of innocent children: so many lives cut short in their flowering; so many bodies wounded in horrible slaughter; so many souls tortured and agonizing, so many in danger of being eternally lost!

You, O Mother of Mercy, beseech God to bring peace for us! And above all those graces that can convert human hearts in an instant, those graces that prepare, reconcile, and assure peace! Queen of peace, pray for us and give to the world at war the peace for which the people are sighing, peace in truth, in justice, in the charity of Christ. Give them peace from arms and peace of souls, so that in the tranquility of order the Kingdom of God may spread forth.

Accord your protection to unbelievers and to those who still lie in the shadows of death: grant them peace and make the Sun of truth to rise for them, and may they, together with us, repeat for the one Savior of the world: Glory to God in the highest heavens and peace on earth to men of good will (Lk 2:14)!

To the peoples separated by error or discord, and particularly to those who profess especial devotion for You, and among whom there is not a house where your venerated icon is not held in honor (though perhaps hidden now, awaiting better days), give them peace, and lead them back to the one flock of Christ, under the one and true Shepherd.

Obtain full peace and liberty for the holy Church of God: bring an end to the overflowing flood of neo-paganism, all of it; enkindle the hearts of the faithful to purity, to practice of the Christian life and apostolic zeal, so that the people of those who serve God may grow in merit and in number.

Finally, as the Church and the whole human race were consecrated to the Heart of your Jesus, so that, resting every hope in Him, He may be for them the sign and pledge of victory and salvation (cf. encyclical Letter *Annum Sacrum*: Acta Leonis XIII, vol. 19, p. 79), may they be likewise consecrated perpetually, starting today, also to You and to your Immaculate Heart, O our Mother and Queen of the world: so that your love and patronage may hasten the triumph of the Kingdom of God, and that all the peoples, at peace with one another and with God, may proclaim you blessed, and intone with You, from one corner of the world to another, the eternal Magnificat of glory, love, and gratitude to the Heart of Jesus, in which only are found Truth, Life, and Peace.

Consecration to Mary in John Paul II

"Consecration to Mary reached a high point of official standing with John Paul II."[179] Among the various consecrations of nations, continents, and of the entire world, particular attention goes to his "entrustment and consecration" of the world and of "those nations particularly in need of this entrustment and this consecration" to the Heart of the Mother of God (March 25, 1984). "The power of this consecration lasts for all time and embraces all individuals, peoples and nations.... May your Immaculate Heart reveal for all the light of Hope!"[180]

Systematic Exploration

John Paul II takes his starting point from the consecration of Christ, completed by the Father, and directed to the Father. The biblical passage most cited in this context is that of the priestly prayer in John: "For their sake I consecrate (*hagiázo*) myself, that they also may be consecrated in truth" (Jn 17:19). Mary was perfectly consecrated by the Holy Spirit from the first moment of her existence (Immaculate Conception). For this reason, the Mother of God is totally united to the redemptive consecration of her Son. For a scriptural foundation,

179. De Fiores, "Consacrazione," 406. See Calkins, *Totus tuus* (1997); (2006), 26–29, 352–58; Apollonio, "La consacrazione a Maria," 86–91; Perrella, *Ecco tua Madre*, 279–96, 477–515; Bogusław Kochaniewicz, "La via mariana polacca e la mariologia di Giovanni Paolo II" [The Polish Marian Way and the Mariology of John Paul II], in *La Vergine Maria nel magistero di Giovanni Paolo II*, ed. T. Siudy (Vatican City: PAMI, 2007), 13–20; J. Krolikowski, "Consacrazione e affidamento a Maria nell'esperienza e nella teologia di papa Giovanni Paolo II" [Consecration and Entrustment to Mary in the Experience and the Theology of Pope John Paul II], in Siudy, *La Vergine Maria nel magistero di Giovanni Paolo II*, 179–201.

180. *Insegnamenti di Giovanni Paolo II*, vol. 7, part 1, 774–77.

the pope affirms the reciprocal entrustment between Mary and John mandated by Christ as he was dying on the Cross (Jn 19:25–27).[181] This idea has resonance in the *CCC* as well: "Like the beloved disciple we welcome Jesus' mother into our homes [see Jn 19:27], for she has become the mother of all the living."[182] Jesus Christ entrusted the human race to Mary (descending consecration), a reality to be accepted in the personal entrustment of every human person to Mary (ascending consecration),[183] accepting the Mother of God into our life.

The more general systematic foundation for consecration to Mary is the mediation exercised by Mary in Christ. John Paul II places a strong accent on the link between the universal motherhood of Mary and consecration to her. Following in the footsteps of Leo XIII, Pius XI, and Pius XII, we also need to affirm in a particular way the relation between consecration to the Most Sacred Heart of Jesus and his kingship, as well as the relationship between consecration to the Immaculate Heart of Mary and her queenship.[184] This connection is already present in St. Ildefonso of Toledo and John Damascene (and thus at the beginning of the theology of Marian consecration). A "slavery" of love, according to Grignion, is started by the encounter with the "Queen."[185]

The theology of the queenship also helps us understand the theological basis of consecration better, including the distinction between entrustment of oneself and that of whole world (which always includes people not wishing to be "consecrated"). Leo XIII, in the encyclical *Annum sacrum*, explains the consecration of the whole world to the Most Sacred Heart of Jesus, a theme that was fittingly studied by a commission before proceeding to this act. Universal kingship belongs to Christ under three titles: by natural right, by acquisi-

181. *RM* 45–46.

182. *CCC* 2679. "Mother of all the living" recalls Gn 3:20.

183. See Calkins, *Totus tuus* (1997), 222–48.

184. This dimension is also present in the Mariology of John Paul II, but not accented as in the documents of the popes mentioned. Thus also Calkins, *Totus tuus* (1997), 279f.

185. See the observations of Calkins, *Totus tuus* (1997), 279f. Gherardini, *Sta la Regina*, places the theme of consecration to Mary as an implication of the topic of the queenship of the Mother of God.

tion, and by free choice. As the eternal Son of God, Jesus Christ is the King of all the universe (natural right). Inasmuch as he merited salvation, offered now to all, through the redemptive sacrifice, the whole of humanity and every individual human being has become the people he has won (acquired right). That is to say, all are subjects to Christ "as to a sovereign." The kingship of Christ [and the objective redemption] takes effect only when it is also personally accepted [in the subjective redemption], in the voluntary consecration of individual subjects.[186]

The three titles for belonging to Christ the King can be applied analogously to Mary the Queen. Pius XII makes reference to this in his encyclical *Ad caeli Reginam.*[187] In his systematic exposition, "the main principle on which the royal dignity of Mary rests is without doubt her Divine Motherhood."[188] But the queenship of Mary is also due "because God has willed her to have an exceptional role in the work of our eternal salvation." As Jesus Christ is our King not only by native right (being the incarnate Son of God), but also by acquired right (through the Redemption), analogously Mary is likewise queen by being Mother of God and for the work in which She was "closely associated with Christ."[189]

The spiritual motherhood of Mary derives from her cooperation in the Redemption, a cooperation that began with the Annunciation and culminated at the foot of the Cross. The spiritual motherhood of Mary displays the social reflection of the fullness of grace based upon the Immaculate Conception. As the kingship of Christ becomes fully operative only when personally accepted, so also the queenship of Mary calls for personal consecration. Only then can the maternal mediation of grace be fully actualized.

In consecration to the immaculate Heart of Mary we draw nearer to the Mother of God who, for her part, draws us to Jesus Christ and to the Most Holy Trinity. Thus entrustment to the Virgin is the perfect acceptance of consecration to God, the origin and final aim

186. See *EE* 3, nn. 1424–41.
187. Ibid. 6, nn. 1122–71. See also "The Queenship of Mary," in chapter 7.
188. *EE* 6, n. 1154.
189. Ibid. 6, n. 1155f.

of every devotion. Jesus himself, beginning with the Incarnation, entrusted himself to Mary and has entrusted us to her in his last will, spoken on the Cross. The universal motherhood of the heavenly Queen is therefore the foundation of our response of accepting Mary "into our home" and letting ourselves be guided to Christ, Alpha and Omega of our existence.

REFERENCES

The Cult of Mary

Ecclesiastical Texts

CCC 971, 2673–79.

Congregatio Pro Cultu Divino. *Collection of Masses of the Blessed Virgin Mary* (*MBVM*) (2 vols., formulary and lectionary: *Collectio Missarum de beata Maria Virgine*. Vatican City, 1987. *Lectionarium pro missis de beata Maria Virgine*. Vatican City, 1987. English translation, *Collection of Masses of the Blessed Virgin Mary*. Collegeville, Minn.: Liturgical Press, 2012.

John Paul II. Apostolic Letter *Rosarium Virginis Mariae* (2002).

———. CM 66–69 (October 8, October 15, October 29, November 5, 1997).

Paul VI. Apostolic Exhortation *Marialis cultus*.

Vatican II. *LG* 66–67.

———. *Sacrosanctum concilium* 103.

Other Sources

De cultu mariano saeculis VI–XI [The Cult of Mary in the 6th to 11th Centuries]. 5 vols. Rome: PAMI, 1972.

De cultu mariano saeculis XII–XV. 6 vols. Rome: PAMI, 1979–81.

De cultu mariano saeculo XVI. 6 vols. Rome: PAMI, 1983–86.

De cultu mariano saeculis XVII–XVIII. 7 vols. Rome: PAMI, 1987.

De cultu mariano saeculis XIX–XX. 7 vols. Rome: PAMI, 1988–91.

De cultu mariano saeculo XX: A concilio Vaticano II usque ad nostros dies [The Cult of Mary in the 20th Century from Vatican II to the Present Day]. 4 vols. Vatican City: PAMI, 1999.

De cultu mariano saeculo XX: Maria, Mater Domini, in mysterio salutis quod ab Orientis et Occidentis Ecclesiis in Spiritu Sancto hodie celebratur [The cult of Mary in the 20th Century: Mary, Mother of the Lord, in the Mystery of Salvation as Celebrated Today in the Holy Spirit, in the Eastern and Western Churches]. 5 vols. Vatican City: PAMI, 1999–2000.

De primordiis cultus mariani [Origins of the Cult of Mary]. 6 vols. Rome: PAMI, 1970.

EMTheo, 351–485.

La Consacrazione alla Vergine Maria nel 50° della Consacrazione alla Vergine Maria, Frigento, 5–7 luglio 2010. Frigento: Casa Mariana Editrice, 2011.

Auer, Johann. *Gesù il Salvatore: Soteriologia—Mariologia* [Jesus the Savior: Soteriology, Mariology], §§17–18. Translated by Carlo Molari. Assisi: Cittadella, 1993. German original: *Jesus Christus—Heiland der Welt: Maria, Christi Mutter im Heilsplan Gottes*. Regensburg: Friedrich Pustet, 1988.

Bastero, Juan Luis. *Mary, Mother of the Redeemer*, 238–50. Dublin: Four Courts, 2006.

Beinert, Wolfgang, ed. *Il culto di Maria oggi: Teologia, liturgia, pastorale* [The Cult of Mary Today: Theology, Liturgy, Pastoral]. 3rd ed. Translated by Carlo Danna. Cinisello Balsamo (Milan): Ed. Paoline, 1987. German original: *Maria heute ehren: Eine theologisch-pastorale Handreichung*. Freiburg im Breisgau: Herder, 1977.

Beinert, Wolfgang, and Heinrich Petri, ed. *Handbuch der Marienkunde* [Handbook of Mariology], 1:469–632. Regensburg: Friedrich Pustet, 1996–97.

Calabuig, Ignazio. "Liturgia." In De Fiores and Meo, *NDM*, 767–87.

Calkins, Arthur B. "Marian Consecration and Entrustment." In *Mariology: A Guide*, edited by M. Miravalle, 725–66. Goleta, Calif.: Queenship, 2007.

———. *Totus tuus: John Paul II's Program of Marian Consecration and Entrustment*. 3rd ed. New Bedford, Mass.: Academy of the Immaculate, 1997. 2nd ed. 2017.

Campana, Emilio. *Maria nel culto cattolico* [Mary in Catholic Worship]. Vols. 1–2. 2nd ed. Torino: Casa Editrice Marietti, 1944.

Carol, Juniper B., ed. *Mariology*. Vol. 3. Milwaukee: Bruce, 1961.

Castellano, Jesús, OCD. "Beata Vergine Maria." In *Liturgia*, edited by D. Sartore et al., 201–35. Cinisello Balsamo (Milan): San Paolo, 2001.

Colzani, Gianni. *Maria: Mistero di grazia e di fede* [Mary, Mystery of Grace and Faith], 291–305. Cinisello Balsamo (Milan): Ed. Paoline, 1996. 3rd ed. 2006.

David, Alphonse. "La dévotion à la Sainte Vierge." In *Maria*, edited by H. du Manoir, 5:689–720. Paris: Beauchesne, 1958.

De Fiores, Stefano. "Consacrazione." In *Maria: Nuovissimo dizionario*, 1:359–413. Bologna: EDB, 2006.

———. "Consacrazione." In De Fiores and Meo, *NDM*, 394–417.

———. *Maria, Madre di Gesù: Sintesi storico-salvifica* [Mary, Mother of Jesus: Salvation-Historical Synthesis], 235–303. Corso di teologia sistematica 6. Bologna: EDB, 1992.

———. *Maria nella teologia contemporanea* [Mary in Contemporary Theology]. 3rd ed., 201–31. Rome: Centro di Cultura Mariana "Madre della Chiesa," 1991.

———. "Preghiera." In *Maria: Nuovissimo dizionario*, 2:1321–63.

Delius, Walter. *Geschichte der Marienverehrung* [History of Marian Devotion]. Munich and Basel: E. Reinhardt, 1963.

Di Domenico, Pier Giorgio M. "Preghiera" [Prayer]. In De Fiores, Schiefer, and Perrella, *DMar*, 975–86.

du Manoir, H., ed. *Maria: Études sur la sainte vierge*, 1:213–413. Paris: Beauchesne, 1949.

Gambero, Luigi. "Culto." In De Fiores and Meo, *NDM*, 425–43.

Gherardini, Brunero. *La Madre: Maria in una sintesi storico-teologica* [The Mother: Mary in a Historical-Theological Synthesis], 377–457. Frigento: Casa Mariana, 1989.

Hauke, Manfred. "Totus tuus: Theologische Grundlagen der Marienweihe" [Totus tuus: Theological Principles of Marian Consecration]. In *Im Dienste der Inkarni-*

erten Wahrheit: Festschrift zum 25jährigen Pontifikat Seiner Heiligkeit Papst Johannes Pauls II, edited by A. von Brandenstein-Zeppelin et al., 127–48. Weilheim-Bierbronnen: Gustav-Siewerth-Akademie, 2003.

Maggioni, C. "Liturgia." In De Fiores, Schiefer, and Perrella, *DMar*, 726–37.

Maggiani, Silvano M. "Culto." In De Fiores, Schiefer, and Perrella, *DMar*, 356–70.

Merkelbach, Benoît Henri. *Mariologia*, 391–413. Paris: Desclée, 1939.

O'Carroll, Michael, CSSp. *Theotokos: A Theological Encyclopedia of the Blessed Virgin Mary*, 220–24. Eugene, Ore.: Wipf and Stock, 2000.

Pedico, Maria Marcellina. *La Vergine Maria nella pietà popolare* [The Virgin Mary in Popular Piety]. Rome: Monfortane, 1993.

Perrella, Salvatore M., OSM. "Affidamento consacrazione" [Entrustment, Consecration]. In De Fiores, Schiefer, and Perrella, *DMar*, 16–24.

———. *La Madre di Gesù nella coscienza ecclesiale contemporanea* [The Mother of Jesus in Contemporary Ecclesial Consciousness], 489–542. Vatican City: Libreria Editrice Vaticana, 2005.

Ponce Cuéllar, Miguel. *María: Madre del Redentor y Madre de la Iglesia* [Mary, Mother of the Redeemer and Mother of the Church]. 2nd ed., 501–35. Barcelona: Herder, 2001.

Pozo, Cándido, SJ. *María en la obra de la salvación* [Mary in the Work of Salvation]. 2nd ed., 327–48. Madrid: Biblioteca de Autores Cristianos, 1990.

Righetti, Mario. "Il culto mariano attraverso i secoli" [The Cult of Mary through the Centuries]. In *EMTheo*, 364–71.

———. *Storia liturgica* [Liturgical History]. Vol. 2. 2nd ed. Milan: Ancora, 1955.

Roschini, Gabriele Maria. *La Madonna: Secondo la fede e la teologia* [The Madonna, according to the Faith and Theology]. Vol. 4. Rome: Libreria Editrice Francesco Ferrari, 1953–54.

———. *Maria Santissima nella storia della salvezza: Trattato completo di mariologia alla luce del Concilio Vaticano II* [Mary Most Holy in the History of Salvation: Complete Treatise on Mariology in Light of the Second Vatican Council]. Vol. 4. Isola del Liri: Pisani, 1969.

Royo Marin, Antonio. *La Virgen María: Teología y espiritualidad marianas* [The Virgin Mary: Marian Theology and Spirituality]. 2nd ed., 359–428. Madrid: Biblioteca de Autores Cristianos, 1997.

Scheffczyk, Leo. *Maria, Mutter und Gefährtin Christi* [Mary, Mother and Companion of Christ], 194–286. Augsburg: Sankt Ulrich, 2003.

Söll, Georg. "Verehrung Mariens." In *ML* 4:596–99.

Toniolo, Ermanno M., ed. *La Vergine Maria nel cammino orante della Chiesa: Liturgia e pietà popolare* [The Virgin Mary in the Praying Journey of the Church: Liturgy and Popular Piety]. Rome: Centro di cultura Mariana "Madre della Chiesa," 2003.

Ziegenaus, Anton. *Maria in der Heilsgeschichte: Mariologie* [Mary in Salvation History: Mariology], 377–90. Katholische Dogmatik 5. Aachen: MM-Verlag, 1998.

Appendix

Mariology on the Internet

The information offered on the internet is growing daily and changing continually. Nonetheless, it seems helpful to suggest some addresses useful for the study of Mariology.

MARIOLOGICAL ASSOCIATIONS

Academia Marial, Santuário Nacional de Nossa Senhora Aparecida (Brazil) (founded 1985)
http://www.a12.com/academia

Associazione Mariologica Interdisciplinare Italiana (AMII) (founded 1990)
http://www.amiroma.it/

Deutsche Arbeitsgemeinschaft für Mariologie (DAM) (founded 1951)
http://www.people.usi.ch/haukem

Ecumenical Society of the Blessed Virgin Mary (ESBVM) (founded 1967)
http://www.esbvm.com/

Internationaler Mariologischer Arbeitskreis Kevelaer (IMAK) (founded 1978)
http://www.imak-kevelaer.de

Mariological Society of America (founded 1949)
http://www.mariologicalsociety.com/

Polskie Towarzystwo Mariologiczne (founded 1999)
http://ptm.rel.pl/

Pontificia Academia Mariana Internationalis (since 1959, founded as an Academy in 1947)
http://www.pami.info/

Société Française d'Études Mariales (SFEM) (founded 1934)
http://www.sfem.free.fr/

INSTITUTES OF RESEARCH AND STUDY WITH ACADEMIC DEGREE PROGRAMS IN MARIOLOGY

Duns Scotus Chair of Mariological Studies, of the Faculty of Theology of the Pontificia Università Antonianum (Rome) (within the licentiate program in Dogmatic Theology or Spirituality)
https://www.pami.info/cattedra-duns-scoto
International Marian Research Institute, University of Dayton (Ohio)
http://www.udayton.edu/imri/
Pontifical Theological Faculty of the Servites of Mary, "Marianum" (Rome)
http://www.marianum.it

OTHER MARIAN CENTERS, USUALLY WITH SCHOLARLY LIBRARIES

Centre for Marian Studies, University of Roehampton
http://marianstudies.ac.uk/
Centro di Cultura Mariana, Roma
http://www.culturamariana.com
ESBVM (see "Mariological Associations")
Institutum Marianum, Regensburg
http://www.institutum-marianum-regensburg.de/
Instituto Mariológico Torreciudad (and the journal *Scripta de Maria*)
https://www.torreciudad.org/participa/instituto-mariologico/

JOURNALS AND BOOK SERIES

Biblioteca di Theotokos, directed for the AMII by Stefano De Fiores
http://www.amiroma.it/index.php?option=com_content&view=article&id=38&Itemid=123
Collana di Mariologia, under the direction of Manfred Hauke (Facoltà Teologica di Lugano)
http://www.teologialugano.ch/eupress.html
Ephemerides Mariologicae, Madrid, published by the Claretians
https://dialnet.unirioja.es/servlet/revista?codigo=8504
Madre di Dio, Marian monthly
http://www.madredidio.it/
Marian Studies, published by the Mariological Society of America
http://www.mariologicalsociety.com/
Marianum, Rome, published by the "Marianum" Pontifical Faculty
http://www.marianum.it/Rivmar.html
Mariologische Studien, published by the chairman of the DAM (Deutsche Arbeitsgemeinschaft für Mariologie)
https://www.verlag-pustet.de/shop/reihen/mariologische-studien?rkz=RO367

Sedes Sapientiae: Mariologisches Jahrbuch, published on behalf of the IMAK
http://www.teol.de/MarJb.htm
Theotokos, published by the AMII
http://www.amiroma.it/index.php?option=com_content&view=article&id=43&Itemid=132

OTHER RESOURCES

Bibliografia Mariana, 13 volumes from 1948 to 2008: http://www.culturamariana.com/
Franciscan Friars of the Immaculate, United States
http://www.marymediatrix.com
Marian texts (Scripture, the fathers, Vatican II, John Paul II, Servites)
http://www.testimariani.net

WEBSITES AND BIBLIOGRAPHIES OF INDIVIDUAL MARIOLOGISTS

Calkins, Arthur Burton (Rome)
http://www.christendom-awake.org/pages/calkins/calkins.html
Cecchin, Stefano, OFM, president of PAMI
http://www.pami.info/
Grasso, Antonino, Istituto Superiore di Scienze Religiose (Catania)
http://www.latheotokos.it
Hauke, Manfred, Facoltà di Teologia di Lugano (Switzerland)
http://www.manfred-hauke.de
Miravalle, Mark, Franciscan University of Steubenville (Ohio)
http://www.markmiravalle.com/
Perrella, Salvatore M., Pontifical Theological Faculty "Marianum" (Rome)
http://salvatoreperrella.it
Scheffczyk, Leo Cardinal (1920–2005)
http://www.leo-cardinal-scheffczyk.org/
Stöhr, Johannes (Cologne)
http://www.teol.de/bi-stoe.htm
(see also the links available at PAMI)

Bibliography

N.B.: Some titles of frequently cited works are abbreviated; see the list of abbreviations in the frontmatter.

UNATTRIBUTED WORKS

Works without a named author or editors—compilations of societies without named editors, unsigned encyclopedia entries, and complete themed issues of certain journals.

Acta Apostolicae Sedis. Vatican City: Typis Polyglottis Vaticanis (1909–91). Typis Vaticanis (1992–) (*AAS*).

Assunta al cielo perché Corredentrice sulla terra: Atti del Simposio internazionale sull'Assunzione della Beata Vergine Maria al Cielo [Assumed to Heaven Because She Was Coredemptrix on Earth: Proceedings of the International Symposium on the Assumption of the Blessed Virgin Mary into Heaven]. Frigento: Casa Mariana Editrice, 2013.

"Atto accademico nel venticinquesimo della morte di fra Gabriele M. Roschini, OSM" [Symposium on the Twenty-Fifth Anniversary of the Death of Friar Gabriele M. Roschini, OSM]. *Marianum* 64, no. 161–62 (2002): 549–606.

"Aufklärung" [Enlightenment]. In Bäumer and Scheffczyk, *ML* 1:270–76.

"Ave Maria." In Bäumer and Scheffczyk, *ML* 1:309–17.

Catechism of the Catholic Church (CCC). 2nd ed. Vatican City: Libreria Editrice Vaticana, 2000.

Catechismus Romanus (*CR*). 1566.

Collana di Mariologia (CdM). Lugano: EU Press FTL, 2002–.

Compendium of the Catechism of the Catholic Church. Vatican City: Libreria Editrice Vaticana. Washington, D.C.: U.S. Conference of Catholic Bishops, 2005.

Corpus Christianorum, Series Latin (*CChr. SL*). Turnhout and Paris: Brepols, 1953–.

Corpus Scriptorum Ecclesiasticorum Latinorum (*CSEL*). Vienna: 1866–.

Dictionnaire de Théologie catholique (*DThC*). 15 vols. Paris: Letouzey et Ané, 1903–50.

Die Griechischen Christlichen Schriftsteller der ersten drei Jahrhunderte (*GCS*). Leipzig: Hinrichs, 1897–.

"El misterio de María y la mujer (En torno a la 'Mulieris dignitatem')" [The Mystery of Mary and of Woman (in "*Mulieris dignitatem*")]. *Estudios Marianos* 62.

Enchiridion delle encicliche (*EE*). 8 vols. Bologna: EDB, 1994–98.

Enchiridion Vaticanum: Documenti ufficiali della Santa Sede (*EV*). Bologna: EDB, 1966–.

Enciclopedia mariana "Theotokos" (*EMTheo*). Genoa: Bevilacqua and Solari; Milan: Editrice Massimo, 1954. 2nd ed. 1958.

Fenomenologia e teologia das apariçoes: Actas do Congresso internacional de Fátima (9–12 de outubro de 1997). [Phenomenology and Theology of Apparitions: Acts of the International Congress of Fatima, 9–12 October 1997]. Fatima: Santuário de Fátima, 1998.

Forum Katholische Theologie (*FKTh*). 1985–.

Giornale di Teologia (*GdT*). Brescia.

The Holy Bible. Rev. Standard Version. 2nd Catholic ed. (*RSV2CE*) San Francisco: Ignatius Press, 2006.

The Jerusalem Bible (*JB*). New York: Doubleday, 1966.

"Joseph." In Bäumer and Scheffczyk, *ML* 3:436–36.

La Consacrazione alla Vergine Maria nel 50° della Consacrazione dell'Italia al Cuore Immacolato di Maria: Atti del simposio Mariologico Internationale sulla Consacrazione alla Vergine Maria, Frigento, 5–7 luglio 2010 [Acts of the International Mariological Symposium at Frigento, July 5–7, 2010, on the 50th Anniversary of the Consecration of Italy to the Virgin Mary]. Frigento: Casa Mariana Editrice, 2011.

La consagración a Maria. Estudios Marianos 51. Salamanca: Sociedad Mariológica Española, 1986.

La Inmaculada Concepción: Teología—Historia—Espiritualidad [The Immaculate Conception: Theology, History, Spirituality]. Estudios Marianos 71. Salamanca: Casa Mariana Editrice, 2005.

"La Madre di Gesù presso la Croce" [The Mother of Jesus at the Foot of the Cross]. *Theotokos* 7, no. 2 (1999).

La Maternidad divina de María [The Divine Maternity of Mary]. Estudios Marianos 68. Salamanca: Sociedad Mariológica Española, 2002.

La Realeza de María [The Queenship of Mary]. Estudios Marianos 17. Valencia: Sociedad Mariológica Española, 1956.

"Maria in scrittori del II secolo" [Mary in Writers of the 2nd Century]. *Theotokos* 10, no. 1 (2002).

"Maria in scrittori del V–VIII secolo" [Mary in Writers of the 5th–8th Centuries]. Part 1. *Theotokos* 14, no. 1 (2006).

"Maria in scrittori orientali del IV secolo" [Mary in Eastern Writers of the 4th Century]. *Theotokos* 10, no. 2 (2002) and 11, no. 1 (2003).

"Maria nei Concili ecumenici e in scrittori dei secoli IV–V" [Mary in the Ecumenical Councils and Writers of the 4th and 5th Centuries]. *Theotokos* 12, no. 1 and 2 (2004).

Maria nell'Ebraismo e nell'Islam oggi: Atti del 60 Simposio Internazionale Mariologico (Roma, 7–8–9 ottobre 1986) [Mary in Judaism and Islam today: Proceedings of the 6th International Mariological Symposium, 7–9 October 1986]. Rome: Marianum, 1987.

"Maria secondo le Scritture" [Mary according to the Scriptures]. *Theotokos* 8, no. 2 (2000): 377–905.

Maria, "Unica Cooperatrice alla Redenzione"/ Mary, "Unique Cooperator in the Redemption." New Bedford, Mass.: Academy of the Immaculate, 2005.

María y la Eucaristia: María y dolor en el camino de la vida [Mary and the Eucharist: Mary and Suffering in the Journey of Life]. Estudios Marianos 72. Salamanca: Sociedad Mariológica Española, 2006.

"Mariologia estetica per il nostro tempo" [Aesthetic Mariology for Our Time]. *Theotokos* 14, no. 2 (2006).

Mary at the Foot of the Cross. 8 vols. New Bedford, Mass.: Academy of the Immaculate, 2000–2007.

"Mirjam." In Bäumer and Scheffczyk, *ML* 4:467–69.

"Regina caeli." In Bäumer and Scheffczyk, *ML* 5:435–37.

Rivista Teologica di Lugano (*RTLu*). Lugano, Switzerland: Facolta di Teologia 1996–.

"Rosenkranz" [Rosary]. In Bäumer and Scheffczyk, *ML* 5:553–59.

"Rosenkranz." In *Lexikon für Theologie und Kirche* 8, 1302–6.

"Salve Regina." In Bäumer and Scheffczyk, *ML* 5:648–50.

Sources chrétiennes (*SC*). Paris: Éditions du Cerf, 1941–.

Teologia e pastorale della consacrazione a Maria [Theology and Pastoral Ministry of Consecration to Mary]. Padua: Messaggero, 1969.

Texte und Untersuchungen zur Geschichte der altchristlichen Literatur (*TU*). Leipzig and Berlin: 1882–.

"Una bellezza chiamata Maria" [A Beauty Called Mary]. *Theotokos* 13, no. 1–2 (2005).

Works with Author(s), Editor(s) Listed

Abd-El-Jalil, J.-M. "La vie de Marie selon le Coran e l'islam" [The Life of Mary according to the Koran and Islam]. In du Manoir, *Maria: Études sur la Sainte Vierge*, 1:183–211. 1949.

Academia Mariana Internationalis (hereafter AMI), ed. *Alma Socia Christi* [Beloved Companion of Christ]. 13 vols. Rome: AMI, 1951–58.

———, ed. *Alma Socia Christi.* Vol. 3, *De praedestinatione et regalitate B. Virginis Mariae.* Rome: AMI, 1952.

———. *Virgo Immaculata.* 18 vols. Vatican City: AMI, 1955–58.

Ago, Lorenzo M. *La "Salutatio Beatae Mariae Virginis" di san Francesco di Assisi* [St. Francis' "Salutation to the Blessed Virgin Mary"]. Rome: Edizioni Monfortane, 1998.

Agostino, G. "Pietà popolare" [Popular Piety]. In De Fiores and Meo, *NDM*, 1111–22.

Aguirre-Monasterio, Rafael. *Exégesis de Mateo 27,51b–53: Para una teología de la muerte de Jesús en el Evangelio de Mateo* [Exegesis of Matthew 27:51b–53: Toward a Theology of the Death of Jesus in the Gospels of Matthew]. Vitoria: Editorial Eset, 1980.

Alameda, S. "El primer principio mariologico segun los padres" [The First Mariological Principle according to the Fathers]. *Estudios Marianos* 3 (1944): 163–86.

Alastruey, Gregorio. *Tratado de la Virgen Santisima* [Treatise on the Most Holy

Virgin]. 3rd ed. Madrid: Editorial catolica, 1952. English translation: *The Blessed Virgin Mary*. Translated by M. Janet La Giglia. St. Louis: Herder, 1963.

Alberigo, Giuseppe et al., eds. *Conciliorum Oecumenicorum Decreta* [Decrees of the Ecumenical Councils] (*COD*). 3rd ed. Bologna: Istituto per le Scienze Religiose, 1973.

Aldazabal, Jose, ed. *Celebrar las fiestas de María* [Celebrating the Feasts of Mary]. Barcelona: Centre de Pastoral Liturgica, 1985.

Alfaro, Juan, SJ. "La formula definitoria de la Inmaculada Concepción" [The Definitory Formula of the Immaculate Conception]. In *Acta magisterii ecclesiastici de immaculata B.V.M. conceptione*, edited by AMI. Virgo Immaculata 2:201–74. Rome: AMI, 1956.

Algermissen, Konrad. "Antidokimarianiten." In Bäumer and Scheffczyk, *ML* 1:172f.

———. "Bekenntnisse und Bekenntnisschriften" [Confessions and Confessional Writings]. In Bäumer and Scheffczyk, *ML* 1:407–14.

———. *Konfessionskunde* [The Study of Creeds]. 7th ed. Celle: Giesel, 1957.

———. *Konfessionskunde*. 8th ed. Paderborn: Bonifacius, 1966 (collective work bearing only Algermissen's name).

Algermissen, Konrad, and A. Radford. "Anglikanische Kirche." In Bäumer and Scheffczyk, *ML* 1:149–52.

Alles, Hildegard. "'Amsterdam'—die Erscheinungen der 'Frau aller Völker'" ["Amsterdam": The Apparitions of the "Lady of All Nations"]. *Theologisches* 35, no. 4 (2005): 411–34.

Alonso, Joaquín María. *Doctrina y espiritualidad del mensaje de Fátima* [Doctrine and Spirituality of the Message of Fatima]. Madrid: Arias Montana Editores, 1990.

———. "Trinità." In De Fiores and Meo, *NDM*, 1406–17.

Alonso, Joaquín María, and D. Sartor. "Cuore immacolato" [Immaculate Heart]. In De Fiores and Meo, *NDM*, 443–55.

Alvarez Campos, Sergio, OFM. *Corpus marianum patristicum*. 6 vols. Burgos: Ediciones Aldecoa, 1970–85.

Amato, Angelo. "Come la Chiesa cattolica è giunta alla definizione dogmatica dell'Assunzione di Maria" [How the Church Reached the Dogmatic Definition of the Assumption]. In Calvo Moralejo and Cecchin, *L'Assunzione*, 43–70.

———. "L'Enciclica mariana 'Redemptoris Mater' di Giovanni Paolo II: Problemi e interpretazioni" [John Paul II's Marian Encyclical "Redemptoris Mater": Problems and Interpretations]. *Salesianum* 49 (1987): 813–33.

———. "Eucaristia." In De Fiores and Meo, *NDM*, 527–41.

———. *Gesù il Signore: Saggio di cristologia* [Jesus the Lord: Essay in Christology]. Bologna: EDB, 1999.

———. "Gesù, Salvatore, definitivo, universale, e la cooperazione di Maria alla salvezza, problematiche nuove di una 'questione antica'" [Jesus, Definitive Universal Savior, and the Cooperation of Mary in Salvation: New Issues of an "Old Question"]. In *Maria nel mistero di Cristo, pienezza del tempo e compimento del regno: Atti del XI Simposio Internazionale Mariologico (1997)* [Mary in the Mystery of Christ, the Fullness of Time, and the Fulfillment of the Kingdom: Acts of the Eleventh International Mariological Symposium], edited by Elio Peretto, 387–427. Rome: Marianum, 1999.

———. *Maria e la Trinità.* Cinisello Balsamo: San Paolo, 2000.
———. *Maria la Theotokos: Conoscenza ed esperienza* [Mary Theotokos: Consciousness and Experience]. Vatican City: Libreria Editrice Vaticana, 2011.
———. "Maria nell'insegnamento del magistero dal Concilio Vaticano II a oggi" [Mary in the Teaching of the Magisterium from Vatican II to Today]. In *Fons lucis: Miscellanea di studi in onore di Ermanno M. Toniolo*, edited by Rosella Barbieri, Ignazio M. Calabuig, and Ornella Di Angelo, 437–72. Rome: Marianum, 2004.
———. "Verso un altro dogma mariano?" *Marianum* 58 (1996): 229–32.
Amato, Angelo, E. Dal Covolo, and A. M. Triacca, eds. *Testi mariani del secondo millennio (TMSM)*. 8 vols. Rome: Città Nuova, 2000–2012.
Anderson, Carl, and Eduardo Chávez. *Nuestra Señora de Guadalupe: Madre de la civilización del amor* [Our Lady of Guadalupe: Mother of the Civilization of Love]. Mexico D.F.: Grijalbo; New York: Random House, 2010.
Angelini, F. "Infermi" [The Sick]. In De Fiores and Meo, *NDM*, 708–15.
Anglican-Roman Catholic International Commission. *Mary: Grace and Hope in Christ.* Harrisburg, Pa.: Morehouse, 2005. Available on the internet at https://ecumenism.net/archive/arcic/mary_en.php.
Anselm of Canterbury. *The Prayers and Meditations of St. Anselm.* Translated by Benedicta Ward. Harmondsworth: Penguin, 1979. Original: *Anselmo d'Aosta: Orazioni e meditazioni.* Edited by Inos Biffi and Costante Marabelli. Milan: Jaca, 1997.
Antes, P. "Islam." In Bäumer and Scheffczyk, *ML* 3:325.
———. "Koran." In Bäumer and Scheffczyk, *ML* 3:646f.
Antonelli, Cesare. *Il dibattito su Maria nel Concilio Vaticano II: Percorso redazionale sulla base di nuovi documenti di archivio* [The Debate on Mary at Vatican II: Redactional Survey on the Basis of New Archival Documents]. Padua: Messaggero, 2009.
Aparicio Rodriguez, Angel. "María esposa de José" [Mary Spouse of Joseph]. *Ephemerides Mariologicae* 46 (1996): 293–317.
Aperribay, Bernardo. "María, Madre de los Angeles?" [Mary, Mother of the Angels?]. *Verdad y vida* 18 (1960): 261–80.
Apollonio, Alessandro M. "La consacrazione a Maria." *Immaculata Mediatrix* 1, no. 3 (2001): 49–101.
———. *Maria, modello di fede?* [Mary, Model of Faith?]. Castelpetroso: Casa Mariana Editrice, 1995.
———. "Maria Santissima Mediatrice di tutte le grazie: La natura dell'influsso della Beata Vergine nell'applicazione della Redenzione." *Immaculata Mediatrix* 7 (2007): 157–81.
———. "Mary Coredemptress: Mother of Unity; A Probing Glance at the Hidden Face of Vatican Council II." In *Mary at the Foot of the Cross.* Vol. 3, *Mater Unitatis*, 316–58. 2003.
———. "Mary Mediatrix of All Graces." In Miravalle, *Mariology: A Guide for Priests, Deacons, Seminarians, and Consecrated Persons*, 411–465.
———. "Rilievi critici sulla mariologia di Rahner" [Critical Reviews of the Mariology of Rahner]. *Fides catholica* 2 (2007): 423–58. Reprinted in *Karl Rahner: Un'analisi critica; La figura, l'opera e la recezione teologica de Karl Rahner (1904–1984)*, edited by Serafino M. Lanzetta, 223–52. Siena: Cantagalli, 2009.

Apostolic Penitentiary. *Manual of Indulgences: Norms and Grants*. Washington, D.C.: USCCB, 2006. (English edition of *Enchiridion indulgentiarum.*)

Apostolic Tradition 4 (Fontes christiani 1:422–24). English translation from *The Apostolic Tradition of Hippolytus*, translated by Burton Scott Easton. Cambridge: Cambridge University Press, 1934.

Arragain, Jacques, CJM. "La Dévotion au Coeur de Marie." In du Manoir, *Maria*, 5:1007–48. Paris: Beauchesne, 1958.

Auer, Johann. *Gesù il Salvatore: Soteriologia—Mariologia* [Jesus the Savior: Soteriology, Mariology]. Translated by Carlo Molari. Assisi: Cittadella, 1993. German original: *Jesus Christus—Heiland der Welt: Maria, Christi Mutter im Heilsplan Gottes*. Regensburg: Friedrich Pustet, 1988.

Auf der Maur, Hansjörg. "Feste und Gedenktage der Heiligen" [Feasts and Memorials of the Saints]. In *Feiern im Rhythmus der Zeit* [Celebrations in the Rhythm of Time], II/1, edited by H. Auf der Maur and Philipp Harnancourt, 64–357. Gottesdienst der Kirche 6/1. Regensburg: Friedrich Pustet, 1994.

Bagatti, Bellarmino. "Ricerche sulle tradizioni della morte della Vergine" [Research on Traditions about the Death of the Virgin]. *Sacra Doctrina* 18 (1973): 185–214.

Baldini, Antonio. *Principio petrino e principio mariano ne "Il complesso antiromano" di Hans Urs von Balthasar* [Petrine Principle and Marian Principle in von Balthasar's "The Anti-Roman Attitude"]. Collana di Mariologia (CdM) 4. Lugano: Eupress FTL, 2003.

Balić, Carolus. "Apparizioni mariane dei sec. XIX–XX." In *EMTheo* (1954): 245–67; (1958): 234–54.

———. "De spiritualis B. V. Mariae maternitatis definibilitate" [On the Definability of the Spiritual Maternity of the Blessed Virgin Mary]. In *Acta et documenta Concilio Oecumenico Vaticano II Apparando, Series I (Antepraeparatoria)* [Acts and Documents Preparatory to the Second Vatican Ecumenical Council], vol. 4, part 1, book 2, 55–61. Vatican City: Typis Polyglottis Vaticanis, 1961.

———. "De titulo 'Mediatrix' B: Virgini Mariae adscripto" [The Title "Mediatrix" Ascribed to the Blessed Virgin Mary]. In *De cultu mariano saeculis VI–XI* [The Cult of Mary in the Sixth to Eleventh centuries], edited by PAMI, 4:269–83. Rome: PAMI, 1972.

———. "El capitolo VIII de la constitución "Lumen gentium" comparado con el primer esquema de la Virgen Madre de la Iglesia" [Chapter 8 of the Constitution "Lumen gentium," Compared with the First Schema on the Virgin, Mother of the Church]. *Estudios Marianos* 27 (1966): 135–83.

———. *Testimonia de assumptione Beatae Virginis Mariae ex omnibus saeculis* [Testimonies on the Assumption of the B.V.M. from All Centuries]. 2 vols. Rome: Academia Mariana, 1948–50.

Bandera, Armando. *La Virgen María y los Sacramentos*. Madrid: Rialp, 1978.

Baraúna, Guilherme. *De natura corredemptionis marianae in theologia hodierna (1921–1958): Disquisitio expositivo-critica* [The Nature of Marian Coredemption in Today's Theology: Expository-Critical Inquiry]. Rome: PAMI, 1960.

Barbagli, P. "Joseph, noli timere accipere Mariam coniugem tuam" ["Joseph, Fear Not to Accept Mary as Your Wife"]. In *Maria in Sacra Scriptura*, edited by Carolus Balić, 4:445–63. Rome: PAMI, 1967.

Barbian, L. "Kollyridianer" [The Collyridians]. In Bäumer and Scheffczyk, *ML* 3:601.

Barile, Riccardo. "Rosario" [Rosary]. In De Fiores, Schiefer, and Perrella, *DMar*, 1034–41.

Barnay, Sylvie. *Specchio del cielo: Le apparizioni della Madonna nel Medioevo* [Mirror of Heaven: Apparitions of the Madonna in the Middle Ages]. Genoa: Marietti, 1999. French original: *Le ciel sur la terre: Les apparitions de la Vierge au Moyen Age*. Paris: Éditions du Cerf, 1999.

Barré, Henri. "Une prière d'Ekbert de Schönau au Coeur de Marie" [A Prayer of Ekbert of Schönau to the Heart of Mary]. *Ephemerides Mariologicae* 2 (1952): 409–23.

Barth, Heinz-Lothar. *Ipsa conteret: Maria die Schlangenzertreterin; Philologische und theologische Überlegungen zum Protoevangelium* [She Herself Will Crush: Mary the Treader of the Serpent; Philological and Theological Considerations on the Protoevangelium]. Ruppichteroth: Canisius-Werk, 2000.

Barth, Karl. *Church Dogmatics*. Vol. 1, part 2. *The Doctrine of the Word of God*. Edinburgh, London, and New York: T. and T. Clark, 1956. Reprints 1970, 2004. German original *Die kirchliche Dogmatik*. Vol. 1, part 2. 4th ed. Zürich: 1948. Reprint 1983.

Bartolini, Elena L. "Figlia di Sion" [Daughter of Zion]. In De Fiores, Schiefer, and Perrella, *DMar*, 551–56.

Basadonna, Giorgio, and Giuseppe Santarelli, OFM. *Litanie lauretane* [Litany of Loreto]. Vatican City: Libreria Editrice Vaticana, 1997.

Bastero de Eleizalde, Juan Luis. "El Padre y María en el magisterio postconciliar" [The Father and Mary in the Post-Conciliar Magisterium]. *Estudios Marianos* 66 (2000): 343–65.

———. "El Espiritu Sancto y María en el Concilio Vaticano II y en Pablo VI" [The Holy Spirit and Mary in Vatican II and in Paul VI]. *Scripta teologica* 38, no. 2 (2006): 701–35.

———. "La fundamentación patrística en la Bula Ineffabilis Deus" [Patristic Foundation in the Bull "Ineffabilis Deus"]. *Scripta de Maria* 2nd ser., no. 1 (2004): 237–63.

———. *Mary, Mother of the Redeemer*. Dublin: Four Courts, 2006. Original *María, Madre del Redentor*. Pamplona: EUSNA, 1995. 2nd ed., 2004.

———. "Sinopsís histórica de las Letanias Lauretanas" [Historical Synopsis of the Litany of Loreto]. In *Dar razón de la esperanza: Homenaje al Prof. Dr. José Luis Illanes,* edited by Tomás Trigo, 1339–62. Pamplona: Servicio de Publicaciones de la Universidad de Navarra, 2004.

———. *Virgen singular: La reflexión teológica mariana en el siglo XX* [Singular Virgin: Theological Reflection on Mary in the 20th Century]. Madrid: Rialp, 2001.

Baumeister, F., and D. V. Hübner. "Offizium marianum" [Marian Office]. In Bäumer and Scheffczyk, *ML* 4:681f.

Bäumer, Remigius, and Leo Scheffczyk, eds. *Marienlexikon* (*ML*) [Dictionary of Mary]. 6 vols. St. Ottilien: EOS Verlag, 1988–94.

Bea, A. "Das Marienbild des Alten Bundes" [The Image of Mary in the Old Covenant]. In *Katholische Marienkunde*, edited by Paul Sträter, 1:23–43. Paderborn: F. Schöningh, 1947. 3rd ed. 1962. Italian translation: *Mariologia*, edited by P. Sträter, 21–40. Turin: Marietti Editori Pontifici, 1952.

Beer, Theobald. *Der fröhliche Wechsel und Streit: Grundzüge der Theologie Martin Luthers*

[Happy Exchange and Conflict: Principles of the Ttheology of Luther]. Einsiedeln: Johannes Verlag, 1980.

Beinert, Wolfgang. "Die mariologischen Dogmen und ihre Entfaltung" [Mariological Dogmas and Their Evolution]. In *Handbuch der Marienkunde*, 2nd ed., ed. W. Beinert and H. Petri, 299–305. Regensburg: F. Pustet, 1996.

———, ed. *Il culto di Maria oggi: Teologia, liturgia, pastorale* [The Cult of Mary Today: Theology, Liturgy, Pastoral]. 3rd ed. Translated by Carlo Danna. Cinisello Balsamo: Ed. Paoline, 1987. German original: *Maria heute ehren: Eine theologisch-pastorale Handreichung*. Freiburg im Breisgau: Herder, 1977.

———, ed. *Maria heute ehren: Eine theologisch-pastorale Handreichung* [To Honor Mary Today: A Theological-Pastoral Handbook]. Freiburg im Breisgau: Herder, 1977.

———. "Maria in Leben und Lehre der römisch-katholischen Kirche" [Mary in the Life and Teaching of the Roman Catholic Church]. In *Maria, die Mutter unseres Herrn: Eine evangelische Handreichung*, edited by Manfred Kiessig, 99–108. Lahr: Verlag Ernst Kaufmann, 1991.

Beinert, Wolfgang, and Heinrich Petri, eds. *Handbuch der Marienkunde* [Handbook of Mariology]. 2 vols. Regensburg: Friedrich Pustet, 1996–97.

Ben-Chorin, S., and F. Hahn. "Judentum" [Judaism]. In Bäumer and Scheffczyk, *ML* 3:450f.

Benedict XIV (Lambertini, Prospero). *De servorum Dei beatificatione et beatorum canonizatione* [The Beatification of the Servants of God and Canonization of the Blessed]. 4 vols. Rome, 1748.

Benedict XVI. *Christmas Address to the Roman Curia,* December 22, 2005, Italian text in *Insegnamenti di Benedetto XVI*, 1:1018–32. Vatican City: Libreria Editrice Vaticana, 2006.

———. Homily at the Marian shrine of Meryem Ana Evì, Nov. 29, 2006. *Insegnamenti di Benedetto XVI,* vol. 2, part 2. 710–14. Vatican City, Libreria Editrice Vaticana, 2007.

Bengoechea, Ismael. "La cooperación de María a la redención y el ecumenismo: El documento de 'Les Dombes'" [Mary's Cooperation in the Redemption and in Ecumenism: The Dombes Document]. *Estudios Marianos* 70 (2004): 361–78.

Benitez, Juan José. *El misterio de la Virgen de Guadalupe: Sensacionales descubrimientos en los ojos de la Virgen Mexicana* [The Mystery of the Virgin of Guadalupe: Sensational Discoveries in the Eyes of the Mexican Virgin]. 2nd ed. Barcelona: Planeta, 2004.

Bergamelli, Ferdinando. "La verginità di Maria nelle Lettere di Ignazio di Antiochia" [The Virginity of Mary in the Letters of Ignatius of Antioch]. *Theotokos* 9, no. 2 (2001): 311–27.

Berger, Klaus. *Theologiegeschichte des Urchristentums* [History of Early Christian Theology]. 2nd ed. Tübingen-Basel: Francke, 1995.

Bernard of Clairvaux. *St. Bernard's Sermons,* Westminster, Md.: Newman [Carroll], 1921.

Bertalot, Renzo. "Posizione del gruppo di Dombes riguardo al dogma dell'assunzione di Maria" [Position of the Dombes Group on the dogma of the Assumption of Mary].

In *L'Assunzione di Maria Madre di Dio*, edited by Gasper Calvo Moralejo, OFM, and Stefano M. Cecchin, 433–37. Vatican City: PAMI, 2001.

Bertetto, Domenico. *Gesù Redentore: Cristologia*. Firenze: Libreria Editrice Fiorentino, 1958.

———. *Maria Immacolata: Il domma della concezione immacolata di Maria nel centenario della sua definizione 1854–8 Dicembre–1954* [Mary Immaculate: The Dogma of the Immaculate Conception of Mary at the Centenary of its 1854 definition—December 8, 1954]. Rome: Edizioni Paoline, 1953.

———. *Maria la serva del Signore: Trattato di mariologia* [Mary the Servant of the Lord: Treatise on Mariology]. Naples: Edizioni Dehoniane, 1988.

Bertone, Tarcisio. *The Last Secret of Fatima*. New York: Image, 2013. Original: *L'ultima veggente di Fatima: I miei colloqui con Suor Lucia*. Milan, 2007.

Besutti, Giuseppe Maria, OSM, ed. *Bibliografia mariana*. 8 vols. Rome: Marianum, 1950–93; continuation: see Ermanno M. Toniolo, OSM, ed. *Bibliografia mariana*. Vol. 9. Rome: Marianum, 1998; Silvano M. Danieli, ed. *Bibliografia mariana*. Vols. 10–13. Rome: Marianum, 2005–10.

———. "Litanie." In De Fiores and Meo, *NDM*, 759–67.

———. *Lo schema mariano al Concilio Vaticano II: Documentazione e note di cronaca* [The Marian Schema at the Second Vatican Council: Documentation and Notes]. Rome: Marianum, 1966.

Beumer, Johannes, and Anton Ziegenaus. "Aufnahme" [Assumption]. In Bäumer and Scheffczyk, *ML* 1:276–86.

Biguzzi, Giancarlo. "La donna, il drago e il Messia in Ap 12" [The Woman, the Dragon, and the Messiah in Rv 12]. *Theotokos* 8, no. 1 (2000): 17–66.

Bilaterale Arbeitsgruppe der Deutschen Bischofskonferenz und der Kirchenleitung der Vereinigten Evangelisch-Lutherischen Kirche Deutschlands, ed. *Communio Sanctorum: Die Kirche als Gemeinschaft der Heiligen*. Paderborn and Frankfurt am Main: Bonifacius, 2000. English translation: Bilateral Working Group of the German Bishops Conference and the Leadership of the United Evangelical-Lutheran Church of Germany, ed. *Communio Sanctorum: The Church as the Communion of the Saints*. Translated by Mark W. Jeske, Michael Root, and Daniel R. Smith. Collegeville, Minn.: Liturgical Press, 2005.

Billet, Bernard, et al. *Vraies et fausses apparitions dans l'Église:* Société française d'études mariales, Session annuelle. [True and False Apparitions in the Church]. Paris: P. Lethielleux, 1973.

Bittremieux, Jacques. "De principio supremo Mariologiae" [The Supreme Principle of Mariology]. *Ephemerides Theologiae Lovanienses* 8 (1931): 249–51.

Bleyenberg, U. "Maria in den Visionen Anna Katharina Emmericks" [Mary in the Visions of Anna Katherina Emmerick]. In Ziegenaus, *Volksfrömmigkeit und Theologie*, 137–61.

Blinzler, Josef. *Die Brüder und Schwestern Jesu* [The Brothers and Sisters of Jesus]. 2nd ed. Stuttgart: Verlag Katholisches Bibelwerk, 1967. Italian translation: *I fratelli e sorelle di Gesù*. Translated by Gianfranco Forza. Brescia: Paideia, 1974.

Boaga, Emanuele, and Luigi Gambero, eds. *Storia della mariologia* [History of Mariology]. Vol. 2. Rome: Città Nuova, 2012.

Boardman, Jonathan. "Prospettive anglicane sulla Madre di Gesù Assunta in cielo" [Anglican Perspectives on the Mother of God Assumed into Heaven]. In Calvo Moralejo and Cecchin, *L'Assunzione di Maria*, 445–48.

Bodem, A. "Hyperdulie." In Bäumer and Scheffczyk, *ML* 3:277.

———. "Mutter der Kirche." In Bäumer and Scheffczyk, *ML* 4:553–55.

———. "Todesstunde" [Hour of Death]. In Bäumer and Scheffczyk, *ML* 6:442.

———. "Wissen Marias" [The Knowledge of Mary]. In Bäumer and Scheffczyk, *ML* 6:746–48.

Boff, Clodovis M. *Mariologia sociale: Il significato della Vergine per la società* [Social Mariology: The Significance of the Virgin for Society]. *BTC* 136. Brescia: Queriniana, 2007. Portuguese original: *Mariologia social.* São Paulo: Paulus, 2006.

Bolen, Donald, and Gregory K. Cameron, eds. *Mary: Grace and Hope in Christ; The Seattle Statement of the Anglican/Roman Catholic International Commission; The Text with Commentaries and Study Guide.* London and New York: Continuum, 2006.

Bonetti, Renzo, ed. *La reciprocità uomo-donna, via di spiritualità coniugale e familiare* [Reciprocity between Man and Woman, Way of Conjugal and Familial Spirituality]. Rome: Città Nuova, 2001.

Bonnefoy, John F., OFM. "The Predestination of Our Blessed Lady." In *Mariology*, edited by J. Carol, 2:154–56. Milwaukee: Bruce, 1957. Spanish translation: "La predestinación de Nuestra Señora." In Carol, *Mariología*, 548–69. 1964.

Borelli Machado, Antonio. "Riflessioni amichevoli per chiarire una polemica" [Amicable Reflections to Clarify a Dispute]. *Lepanto* 26, no. 174 (October 2007):1–24.

Borgonovo, Graziano, and Arturo Cattaneo, eds. *Il papa teologo: Nel segno delle encicliche* [The Theologian Pope: In the Sign of the Encyclicals]. Milan: Mondadori, 2003.

———. *Prendere il largo con Cristo: Esortazioni e lettere di Giovanni Paolo II* [Putting Out into the Deep with Christ: Exhortations and Letters of John Paul II]. Siena: Cantagalli, 2005.

Borriello, Luigi, OCD, Maria Rosaria Del Genio, and Edmondo Caruana, OC, eds. *Dizionario di mistica* [Dictionary of Mysticism]. Vatican City: Libreria Editrice Vaticana, 1998.

Bouflet, Joachim. *Ces dix jours qui ont fait Medj: Aux sources des apparitions de Medjugorje* [The Ten Days That Made Medjugorje: To the Sources of the Medjugorje Apparitions]. Tours: CLD éd., 2007.

———. *Faussaires de Dieu* [Forgers of God]. 2nd ed. Paris: Presses de la renaissance, 2007.

Bouflet, Joachim, and Philippe Boutry. *Un signe dans le ciel: Les apparitions de la Vierge* [A Sign in the Heavens: The Apparitions of the Virgin]. Paris: B. Grasset, 1997. Italian: *Un segno nel cielo: Le apparizioni della Vergine.* Genoa: Marietti, 1999.

Bouyer, Louis. *Le Trône de la Sagesse: Essai sur la signification du culte marial.* Paris: Éditions du Cerf, 1957. English translation: *The Seat of Wisdom: An Essay on the Place of the Virgin Mary in Christian Theology.* London: Darton, Longman and Todd, 1960.

Bover, Joseph M. "'Quod nascetur (ex te) sanctum, vocabitur Filius Dei' (Lc 1,35)" ["'He Who Will Be Born Holy of You Is Holy; He Will Be Called Son of God' (Lk 1:35)"]. *Biblica* 1, no. 1 (1920): 92–94; *Estudios Ecclesiasticos* 8, no. 31 (1929): 381–92.

Breid, Franz, ed. *Maria in Leben und Lehre der Kirche* [Mary in the Life and Teaching of the Church]. Steyr: Ennsthaler Verlag, 1995.

Brinktrine, Johannes. *Die Lehre von der Mutter des Erlösers* [Doctrine of the Mother of the Redeemer]. Paderborn: F. Schöningh, 1959.

Brogeras Martinez, P. "Introducción a la teología del Corazon de María" [Introduction to the Theology of the Heart of Mary.] *Ephemerides Mariologicae* 50 (2000): 441–54.

Brosch, Hermann Josef, and Josef Hasenfuss, eds. *Jungfrauengeburt gestern und heute* [Virgin Birth Yesterday and Today]. Mariologische Studien 4. Essen: Driewer, 1969.

Brown, Raymond E., et al. *Mary in the New Testament*. Philadelphia: Fortress; New York: Paulist Press; London: Geoffrey Chapman, 1978.

Bruni, Giancarlo. "Chiavi di lettura del documento su Maria del Gruppo di Dombes" [Keys to Reading the Dombes Group Document on Mary]. *Marianum* 62, no. 157–58 (2000): 289–317.

———. "Ecumenismo." In De Fiores, Schiefer, and Perrella, *DMar*, 455–65.

———. "Genesi, approdo e metodo della Dichiarazione anglicana-cattolica su Maria" [Genesis, Approach, and Method of the Anglican-Catholic Declaration on Mary]. *Marianum* 69, no. 171–72 (2007): 423–53.

———. *Mariologia ecumenica: Approcci, documenti, prospettive*. Bologna: EDB, 2009.

Bruni, Giancarlo, and M. Wirz. "Maria nella teologia di Martin Lutero [Mary in the Theology of Martin Luther]." In Boaga and Gambero, *Storia della mariologia*, 2:215–29.

Buby, Bertrand A., SM. "Islam and Mary." In PAMI, *De cultu mariano saeculo XX*, 2:35–47. PAMI, 2000.

Bueno de la Fuente, Eloy. *A mensagem de Fátima*. 2nd ed. Fatima: Santuário de Fátima, 2014.

———. "La revelación entre la Trinidad y la Virgen María desde la perspectiva de Lumen gentium" [Revelation between the Trinity and the Virgin Mary, from the Perspective of *Lumen gentium*]. *Ephemerides Mariologicae* 64, no. 4 (2014): 403–26.

Bürkle, H. "Himmelfahrt Mariae II: Protestantische Theologie" [Assumption of Mary II: Protestant Theology]. In Bäumer and Scheffczyk, *ML* 3:199–202.

Bur, Jacques. "La Médiation de Marie: Essai de synthèse speculative" [The Mediation of Mary: Essay in Speculative Synthesis]. In du Manoir, *Maria*, 6:471–512. 1961.

Burghardt, Walter J., SI. "María en el pensamiento de los Padres orientales" [Mary in the Thought of the Eastern Fathers]. In Carol, *Mariología*, 488–547. English original: In Carol, *Mariology*, 2:88–153.

———. "María en la patristica occidental." In Carol, *Mariología*, 111–55. English original: "Mary in Western Patristic Thought." In Carol, *Mariology*, 1:109–55. Milwaukee: Bruce: 1954.

Calabuig, Ignazio, OSM. "La Vergine, oggetto della misericordia di Dio: Riflessioni a partire dalla liturgia" [The Virgin, Object of God's Mercy: Reflections from the Liturgy]. In Di Domenico and Peretto, *Maria Madre di misericordia*, 244–65.

———. "L'insegnamento della mariologia nei documenti ecclesiali dal decreto conciliare 'Optatam totius' alla lettera circolare (25–III–1988) della Congregazione per l'Educazione Cattolica" [The Teaching of Mariology in Church Documents, from the Conciliar Decree *Optatam totius* to the Circular Letter (March 25, 1988) of the Congregation for Catholic Education]. In *La Mariologia nell'organizzazione delle discipline teologiche: Collocazione e metodo* [Mariology in the Organization of the Theological Disciplines: Locus and Method], edited by E. Peretto, 141–256. Rome: Marianum, 1992.

———. "Liturgia." In De Fiores and Meo, *NDM*, 767–87.

———. "Postfazione" [Afterword]. In Perrella, *"Non temere di prendere con te Maria" (Matteo 1,20): Maria e l'ecumenismo nel postmoderno; Dalla "Mater divisionis" alla "Mater unitatis"* ["Fear Not to Take Mary with You" (Mt 1:20): Mary and Ecumenism in the Postmodern; From "Mother of Division" to "Mother of Unity"], 213–39. Cinisello Balsamo: San Paolo, 2004.

———. "Riflessione sulla richiesta della definizione dogmatica di 'Maria corredentrice, mediatrice, avvocata'" [Reflections on the Request for the Dogmatic definition of "Mary Coredemptrix, Mediatrix, Advocate"]. *Marianum* 61, no. 155–56 (1999): 129–75.

———. "Significato e valore del nuovo Ordo Coronandi imaginem BMV" [Meaning and Value of the New Order of Crowning of an Image of the BVM]. *Notitiae* 18 (1981): 268–324.

Calabuig, Ignazio M., OSM, and Salvatore M. Perrella, OSM. "Litanie." In De Fiores, Schiefer, and Perrella, *DMar*, 719–26.

Calduch-Benages, Nuria. "Sapienza" [Wisdom]. In De Fiores, Schiefer, and Perrella, *DMar*, 1059–72.

Calero, Antonio Maria. *La Vergine Maria nel mistero di Cristo e della Chiesa: Saggio di mariologia* [The Virgin Mary in the Mystery of Christ and the Church: Essay in Mariology]. Leumann (Turin): Elle Di Ci, 1995. Spanish original: *María en el misterio de Cristo y de la Iglesia*. Madrid: CCS, 1990.

Calì, Rosa. "La tradizione del Transitus negli apocrifi del IV e V secolo: Aspetti teologici" [The Tradition of the Transitus in Apocrypha of the 4th and 5th Centuries: Theological aspects]. In Carvello and De Fiores, *Maria, icona viva della Chiesa futura*, 141–57.

Calì, Rosa, Carmelo Carvello, and Domenico Marcucci, eds. *Maria assunta segno di speranza per l'umanità in cammino* [Mary Assumed, Sign of Hope for Humanity on the Way]. Rome: AMII, 2007.

Calkins, Arthur B. "The Hearts of Jesus and Mary in the Magisterium of Pope John Paul II." In PAMI, *De cultu mariano saeculo XX*, 4:147–67. 1999.

———. "Il concepimento e la nascita verginale di Gesù: Verità di fede ricevuta e trasmessa dalla Chiesa Cattolica" [The Virginal Conception and Bbirth of Jesus: Truths of Faith Received and Transmitted by the Church]. *Immaculata Mediatrix* 4 (2004): 181–209.

———. "Il dogma auspicato: Il come e il perché" [The Hoped-for Dogma: How and Why]. *Immaculata Mediatrix* 1, no. 2 (2001): 43–64.

———. "Il mistero di Maria Corredentrice nel magistero pontificio" [The Mystery of Mary Coredemptrix in the Pontifical Magisterium]. *Maria Corredentrice* 1 (1998): 141–220.

———. "La presenza di Maria nella Santa Messa nel Magistero di papa Giovanni Paolo II" [The Presence of Mary in the Holy Mass in the Magisterium of Pope John Paul II]. *Immaculata Mediatrix* 6 (2006): 357–76.

———. "Marian Consecration and Entrustment." In Miravalle, *Mariology: A Guide*, 725–66.

———. "Marian Co-Redemption and the Contemporary Papal Magisterium." *Immaculata Mediatrix* 6 (2006): 191–227. Also in *Mary, "Unique Cooperator in the Redemption,"* 113–69.

———. "Mary Coredemptrix: The Beloved Associate of Christ." In Miravalle, *Mariology: A Guide*, 349–409.

———. "Mary's Presence in the Mass according to Pope John Paul II." In *Mary at the Foot of the Cross*. Vol. 6, *Marian Coredemption in the Eucharist*. New Bedford, Mass.: Academy of the Immaculate, 2007.

———. "The Mystery of Mary Coredemptrix in the Papal Magisterium." In *Mary Coredemptrix: Doctrinal Issues Today*, edited by M. Miravalle, 25–92. Goleta, Calif.: Queenship, 2002.

———. "Our Lady's Perpetual Virginity." In Miravalle, *Mariology: A Guide*, 277–315.

———. "Pope John Paul II's Teaching on Marian Coredemption." In *Mary Coredemptrix, Mediatrix, Advocate: Theological Foundations*, edited by Mark Miravalle, 2:113–46. Santa Barbara, Calif.: Queenship, 1996.

———. "The Theological Relevance of Our Lady of All Nations and the Amsterdam Apparitions." In *Mary Coredemptrix, Mediatrix, Advocate: Theological Foundations*. Vol. 3, *Contemporary Insights on a Fifth Marian Dogma*, edited by M. Miravalle, 217–24. Goleta, Calif.: Queenship, 2000.

———. *Totus tuus: John Paul II's Program of Marian Consecration and Entrustment*. New Bedford, Mass.: Academy of the Immaculate, 1997. 2nd ed. 2017. Anthology: *Totus tuus: Il magistero mariano di Giovanni Paolo II*. Siena: Cantagalli, 2006.

———. "'Towards Another Marian Dogma?' A Response to Father Angelo Amato, S.D.B." *Marianum* 59 (1997): 159–67.

Calkins, Frank P., OSM. "Plenitud de gracia." In Carol, *Mariología*, 684–99. English original: "Mary's Fullness of Grace." In Carol, *Mariology*, 2:297–312.

Calvo Moralejo, Gaspar, OFM. "La morte della Vergine in M. Agreda (1602–1665)" [The death of the Virgin in Mary of Agreda]. In Calvo Moralejo and Cecchin, *L'Assunzione di Maria*, 647–65.

Calvo Moralejo, Gaspar, and Stefano M. Cecchin, eds. *L'Assunzione di Maria Madre di Dio* [The Assumption of Mary, Mother of God]. Vatican City: PAMI, 2001.

Calzecchi Onesti, Rosa, ed. *Inno Akathistos alla Madre di Dio* [Akathist Hymn to the Mother of God]. Rimini: Guaraldi, 1995.

Campana, Emilio. *Maria nel culto cattolico*. 2 vols. [Mary in Catholic Worship]. 2nd ed. Turin: Casa Editrice Marietti, 1944.

Canal, José Maria. "La consagración a la Virgen y a su Corazón Inmaculada" [Consecration to the Virgin and to Her Immaculate Heart]. In AMI, *Alma Socia Christi*, 12:221–348. 1956.

Canal, José Maria, and Joaquín María Alonso. *La consagración a la Virgen y a su Corazón* [Consecration to the Virgin and to Her Heart]. 2 vols. Madrid: Co. Cul. S.A., 1960.

Candido, D. G. "Giuseppe di Nazaret" [Joseph of Nazareth]. In De Fiores, Schiefer, and Perrella, *DMar*, 586–96.

———. "Madre dei discepoli" [Mother of Disciples]. In De Fiores, Schiefer, and Perrella, *DMar*, 765–73.

Caniato, Riccardo, and Vincenzo Sansonetti. *Maria, alba del terzo millennio: Il dono di Medjugorje* [Mary, Dawn of the Third Millennium: The Gift of Medjugorje]. Milan: Ares, 2001.

Cantera, S. "Pio XI y la dimensión social de la realeza mariana" [Pius XI and the Social Dimension of the Queenship of Mary]. *Scripta de Maria* 2nd ser., 6 (2009): 101–30.

Cantinat, Jean. *La Madonna nella Bibbia* [The Madonna in the Bible]. 3rd ed. Cinisello Balsamo: San Paolo, 1987. French original: *Marie dans la Bible*. Paris: Éditions Xavier Mappus, 1964.

Capizzi, Nunzio "Vergine." In De Fiores, Schiefer, and Perrella, *DMar*, 1255–64.

Carelli, Roberto. *L'uomo e la donna nella teologia di Hans Urs von Balthasar* [Man and Woman in the Theology of Hans Urs von Balthasar]. Collana Balthasariana 2. Lugano: Eupress FTL, 2007.

Carlen, Claudia, ed. *The Papal Encyclicals* (*PE*). 4 vols. Raleigh, N.C.: Pierian, 1990.

Carol, Juniper B., OFM. "The Blessed Virgin and the 'Debitum Peccati': A Bibliographical Conspectus." *Marian Studies* 28 (1977): 181–256.

———. "Corredención de Nuestra Senora." In Carol, *Mariología*, 760–804. English original: "Our Lady's Coredemption." In Carol, *Mariology*, 2:377–425.

———. *De corredemptione Beatae Virginis Mariae: Disquisitio positiva* [The Coredemption of the BVM: Positive Inquiry]. Vatican City: Typis Polyglottis Vaticanis, 1950.

———, ed. *Mariology*. 2 vols. Milwaukee: Bruce, 1954–57. Spanish translation: *Mariología*. Madrid: Biblioteca de Autores Cristianos, 1964. (*Note:* A new English edition of the three-volume set has appeared: Carol, *Mariology*. 3 vols. Post Falls, Idaho: Mediatrix, 2018–19.)

———, ed. *Mariology*. Vol. 3. Milwaukee: Bruce, 1961.

Carr, Aidan, OFM Conv., and Germain Williams, OFM Conv. "Inmaculada concepción de María." In Carol, *Mariología*, 307–70. English original: "Mary's Immaculate Conception." In Carol, *Mariology* 2:328–94.

Carvello, Carmelo, and Stefano De Fiores, eds. *Maria, icona viva della Chiesa futura* [Mary, Living Icon of the Future Church]. Rome: Edizioni Monfortane, 1998.

Casagrande, Domenico. *Enchiridion marianum biblicum patristicum* [Biblical and Patristic Handbook of Mary]. Rome: Cor unum, 1974.

Castellano, Jesús, OCD. "Beata Vergine Maria." In *Liturgia*, edited by Domenico Sartore, Achille M. Triacca, and Carlo Cibien, 201–35. Cinisello Balsamo: San Paolo, 2001.

Castellano, Mario I. "La prassi canonica circa le apparizioni mariane" [Canonical Practice Regarding Marian Apparitions]. In *EMTheo* (1954): 465–86; (1958): 486–505.

Castelli, Ferdinando. ed. *Testi mariani del secondo millennio*. Vol. 8, *Poesia e prosa letteraria* [Marian Texts of the Second Millennium. Vol. 8, Poetry and Literary Prose]. Rome: Città Nuova, 2002.

Catella, A. "La *Collectio Missarum de Beata Maria Virgine: Analisi della eucologia*" [The Collection of Masses of the BVM: Analysis of Euchology]. In Hauke, *La donna e la salvezza*, 43–73.

Cavalletti, S. "Ebrei" [The Jews]. In De Fiores and Meo, *NDM*, 511–18.

Cecchin, Stefano M., ed. *Contemplare Cristo con Maria: Atti della Giornata di studio sulla Lettera apostolica Rosarium Virginis Mariae di Giovanni Paolo II: Roma, 3 maggio 2003* [Contemplating Christ with Mary: Acts of the Study Day on the Apostolic Letter *Rosarium Virginis Mariae* by John Paul II: Rome, May 3, 2003]. Vatican City: PAMI, 2003.

———. "Giovanni Duns Scoto Dottore dell'Immacolata Concezione: Alcune questioni" [John Duns Scotus, Doctor of the Immaculate Conception: Some Questions]. In *La "Scuola Francescana" e l'Immacolata Concezione* [The "Franciscan School" and the Immaculate Conception], edited by Stefano M. Cecchin, 219–71. Vatican City: PAMI, 2005.

———. "Giovanni Duns Scoto, martire dell'Immacolata" [John Duns Scotus, Martyr of the Immaculate]. In *Religioni et Litteris: Miscellanea di studi dedicate a P. Barnaba Hechich OFM*, edited by Benedykt J. Huculak, 165–96. Vatican City: PAMI, 2005.

———, ed. *La "Scuola Francescana" e l'Immacolata Concezione* [The "Franciscan School" and the Immaculate Conception]. Vatican City: PAMI, 2005.

———. "L'assunzione di Maria nella scuola mariologica francescana" [The Assumption of Mary in the Franciscan school of Mariology]. In Calvo Moralejo and Cecchin, *L'Assunzione di Maria*, 585–646.

———. *L'Immacolata Concezione: Breve storia del dogma* [Immaculate Conception: A Short History of the Dogma]. Vatican City: PAMI, 2003.

———. *Maria Signora Santa e Immacolata nel pensiero francescano: Per una storia del contributo francescano alla mariologia* [Mary, Holy and Immaculate Lady in Franciscan Thought: Towards a History of the Franciscan Contribution to Mariology]. Vatican City: PAMI, 2001.

———. "Pius IX e i francescani nella definizione dogmatica dell'Immacolata Concezione" [Pius IX and the Franciscans in the Dogmatic Definition of the Immaculate Conception]. In Cecchin, *La "Scuola Francescana,"* 525–59.

———. "'Totus tuus ego sum': La 'consacrazione a Maria' nella tradizione francescana" ["I Am Totally Yours": "Consecration to Mary" in the Franciscan Tradition]. In *La Vergine Maria nella teologia e nella spiritualità francescana: Incontro di spiritualità francescana, Santuario della Verna, 17–23 agosto* 2004, edited by Pietro Messa, 139–85. Quaderni di Spiritualità Francescana 26. Santa Maria degli Angeli (Perugia): Porziuncola, 2005.

Cecchin, Stefano M., and Jean-Pierre Sieme Lasoul. "Centri mariologici" [Mariological Centers]. In De Fiores, Schiefer, and Perrella, *DMar*, 244–56.

Cerbelaud, Dominique. *Marie: Un parcours dogmatique* [Mary: A Dogmatic Survey]. Paris: Cerf, 2004.

Chappoulie, Henri. "Les missions et la spiritualité mariale" [The Missions and Marian Spirituality]. In du Manoir, *Maria*, 1:897–902. 1949.

Charalampidis, Constantine P. "Culto e dottrina della Chiesa greco-ortodossa circa la

Panaghia" [Worship and Doctrine of the Greek Orthodox Church about Mary All-Holy]. In *Maria Santa e Immacolata*, edited by Stefano De Fiores and Enrico Vidau, 77–89. Rome: Edizioni Monfortane, 2000.

Charamsa, Krzysztof (Cristoforo). *Il Rosario: Riflessioni sulla Lettera Apostolica Rosarium Virginis Mariae* [The Rosary: Reflections on the Apostolic Letter Rosarium Virginis Mariae]. Vatican City: Libreria Editrice Vaticana, 2003.

Chavannes, Henry. "Die Protestanten und die Lehre von Marias Aufnahme in den Himmel" [Protestants and the Teaching of Mary's Assumption into Heaven]. In *Die sonnenbekleidete Frau*, edited by G. Rovira, 59–71. Kevelaer: Butzon and Bercker, 1986.

Chávez Sanchez, Eduardo. "Guadalupe." In De Fiores, Schiefer, and Perrella, *DMar*, 596–602.

Chiron, Yves. *Enquête sur les apparitions de la Vierge* [Inquiry into the Apparitions of the Virgin]. Paris: Perrin, 2007.

———. *Medjugorje demasqué (1981–2010): "Constat de non supernaturalitate"* [Medjugorje Unmasked (1981–2010): "Confirmed Not Supernatural"]. 2nd ed. Versailles: Via romana, 2010.

Ciappi, Luigi, OP. "Fondamenti e principi del culto di Maria" [Foundations and Principles of the Cult of Mary]. In *EMTheo* (1958): 351–63.

Cimosa, Mario. "Il senso del titolo kecharitoméne" [The Meaning of the Title *Kecharitoméne*]. *Theotokos* 4, no. 2 (1996): 589–97.

Cipriani, Nello. "Il vero matrimonio di Maria e Giuseppe in S. Agostino" [The True Marriage of Mary and Joseph in St. Augustine]. *Theotokos* 12, no. 1–2 (2004): 169–82.

Cipriani, Settimio. "Credente" [Believer]. In De Fiores and Meo, *NDM*, 417–25.

Coggi, Roberto. *La Beata Vergine: Trattato di Mariologia* [The Blessed Virgin: Treatise on Mariology]. Bologna: Studio Domenicano, 2004.

Collantes, Justo, ed. *La fede della Chiesa cattolica: Le idee e gli uomini nei documenti dottrinali del Magistero* [The Faith of the Catholic Church: Ideas and Men in the Doctrinal Documents of the Magisterium]. Vatican City: Libreria Editrice Vaticana, 1993. Spanish: *La fe de la Iglesia Católica: Las ideas y los hombres en los documentos doctrinales del Magisterio*. Madrid: Biblioteca de Autores Cristianos, 1983.

Colzani, Gianni. "Apparizioni." In De Fiores, Schiefer, and Perrella, *DMar*, 136–44.

———. "Dichiarazione di Seattle su 'Maria: Grazia e speranza in Cristo': Chiarimenti e problemi" [The Seattle Declaration on "Mary: Grace and Hope in Christ": Clarifications and Problems]. *Marianum* 69, no. 171–72 (2007): 454–80.

———. *Maria: Mistero di grazia e di fede* [Mary, Mystery of Grace and Faith]. Cinisello Balsamo: Ed. Paoline, 1996. 3rd ed. 2006.

———. "Mariologia." In *Teologia*, edited by Giuseppe Barbaglio, Giampiero Bof, and Severino Dianich, 934–53. Cinisello Balsamo: San Paolo, 2002.

Congar, Yves. *Je crois en l'Esprit Saint*. Paris: Éditions du Cerf, 1995 (Originally published in 1979–80). English translation: *I Believe in the Holy Spirit*. New York: Seabury, 1983 (reprint New York: Crossroad, 1997).

Congregation for Catholic Education. Letter, "The Virgin Mary in Intellectual and Spiritual Formation." March 25, 1988. In *The Message of Fatima*, ed. Congregation for the Doctrine of the Faith, June 26, 2000. Vatican City: Libreria Editrice Vaticana, 2000. http://www.vatican.va/roman_curia/congregations/cfaith/doc_doc_index.htm.

Congregation for Divine Worship. *Collectio Missarum de beata Maria Virgine* (*MBVM*). Vatican City: Libreria Editrice Vaticana, 1987. *Lectionarium pro missis de beata Maria Virgine*. Vatican City: Libreria Editrice Vaticana, 1987. English edition: *Collection of Masses of the Blessed Virgin Mary*. 2 vols. New York: Catholic Book Pub., 1992. 2 vols. Collegeville, Minn.: Liturgical Press, 2012. https://udayton.edu/imri/mary/c/collection-of-masses-of-the-blessed-virgin-mary.php.

Congregation for Divine Worship and the Discipline of the Sacraments. *Directory on Popular Piety and the Liturgy* (*DPPL*). 2002.

Congregation for the Doctrine of the Faith. *Documenta inde a Concilio Vaticano secundo expleto edita (1966–2005)* [Documents Issued Since the Completion of Vatican II]. Vatican City: Libreria Editrice Vaticana, 2006.

Connell, Francis J., C.Ss.R. "Our Lady's Knowledge." In Carol, *Mariology* 2:313–24. Spanish translation: "La ciencia de Nuestra Senora." In Carol, *Mariología*, 700–10.

Corr, Gérard M. "La doctrine mariale et la pensée anglicane contemporaine" [Marian Doctrine and Contemporary Anglican Thought]. In du Manoir, *Maria*, 3:711–31.

Corteville, Michel. *La grande nouvelle des bergers de la Salette* [The Great News of the Shepherds of La Salette]. Paris: P. Téqui, 2001.

Corteville, Michel, and René Laurentin. *Découverte du secret de la Salette* [Discovery of the Secret of La Salette]. Paris: Fayard, 2002.

Cortinovis, Battista, Stefano De Fiores, and Enrico Vidau, eds. *Spiritualità trinitaria in comunione con Maria secondo Montfort* [Trinitarian Spirituality in Communion with Mary, according to Montfort]. Rome: Edizioni Monfortane, 2002.

Cothenet, Edouard. "La virginité de Marie dans les apocryphes" [The Virginity of Mary in the Apocrypha]. Études mariales 53 (1998): 53–68.

———. "Marie dans les Apocryphes" [Mary in the Apocrypha]. In *Maria:* Études sur la sainte vierge, edited by H. du Manoir, 6:71–156. Paris: Beauchesne, 1961.

Courth, Franz. "Engel des Herrn" [Angels of the Lord]. In Bäumer and Scheffczyk, *ML* 2:341.

———. "Heinrich Maria Köster (1911–1993): Forscher und Künder Mariens." *Marianum* 55, no. 145 (1993) 429–59.

———. "Kongresse" [Congresses]. In Bäumer and Scheffczyk, *ML* 3:629f.

———. *Maria, die Mutter des Herrn* [Mary, the Mother of the Lord]. Vallendar: Theologische Hochschule der Pallottiner, 1991. (Lecture notes).

———. "Marienerscheinungen und kirchliches Amt" [Marian Apparitions and Church Office]. In *Marienerscheinungen: Ihre Echtheit und Bedeutung im Leben der Kirche.* [Marian Apparitions: Their Authenticity and Meaning in the Life of the Church], edited by Anton Ziegenaus, 183–98. Mariologische Studien 10. Regensburg: Friedrich Pustet, 1995.

———. "Mariologie." In *Glaubenszugänge*, edited by Wolfgang Beinert, 2:301–98. Paderborn: F. Schöningh, 1995.

Crocetti, Giuseppe. "Eucaristia." In De Fiores, Schiefer, and Perrella, *DMar*, 482–89.

Cumerlato, Guido. *"Ecce ancilla Domini": La mediazione materna come diakonia della Madre di Dio* ["Behold the Servant of the Lord": Marian Mediation as Diakonia of the Mother of God]. Naples: Pontificia Facolta Teologica dell'Italia Meridionale, 2004.

da Castelplanio, Ludovico. *Maria nel consiglio dell'Eterno, ovvero la Vergine predestinata alla missione medesima con Gesù Cristo* [Mary in the Counsels of Eternity, or the Virgin Predestined to Share the Mission of Jesus Christ]. 4 vols. Naples: Tipografia editrice degli accattoncelli, 1872–73.

Da Fonseca, Luis Gonzaga, SJ, and Joaquín María Alonso. *Le meraviglie di Fatima* [The Miracles of Fatima]. 31st ed. Cinisello Balsamo: San Paolo, 1997 (originally 1959).

Dal Covolo, Enrico. "Maria 'associata' a Gesù: La catechesi mariologica del *CCC*" [Mary "Associated" with Jesus: The Mariological Ccatechesis of the *CCC*]. In *La catechesi al traguardo: Studi sul Catechismo della Chiesa Cattolica*, edited by Angelo Amato, Enrico Dal Covolo and Achille M. Triacca, 283–300. Rome: LAS, 1997.

Dal Covolo, Enrico, and Aristide Serra, eds. *Storia della mariologia* [History of Mariology]. Vol. 1. Rome: Città Nuova, 2009.

Daniel, Lázaro Ilzo. *La mediazione materna di Maria in Cristo negli insegnamenti di Giovanni Paolo II* [The Maternal Mediation of Mary in Christ in the Teachings of John Paul II]. CdM 9. Lugano and Gavirate (Varese): Eupress FTL, 2011.

Danieli, Silvano M.. *Bibliografia mariana*. Vols. 10–13 (1994–2008). Rome: Ed. Marianum, 2005–2010; see the entry for Besutti, *Bibliografia mariana* for information on the series.

Daniélou, Jean. "Le culte marial et le paganisme" [The Cult of Mary and Paganism]. In *Maria Études sur la sainte vierge*, edited by H. du Manoir, 1:159–81 (Paris: Beauchesne, 1952.

d'Argenlieu, Benoit Thierry, OP. "Théologie du Rosaire." In du Manoir, *Maria*, 5:721–55. 1958.

da Spinetoli, Ortensio. *Maria nella Bibbia*. 2nd ed. Bologna: EDB, 1988.

David, Alphonse. "La dévotion à la Sainte Vierge." In du Manoir, *Maria* 5:689–720. 1958.

de Aldama, José A. "La maternité verginale de Notre Dame" [The Virginal Maternity of Our Lady]. In du Manoir, *Maria*, 7:117–54. 1964.

———. *María en la Patrística de los siglos I y II* [Mary in the Fathers of the First and Second Centuries]. Madrid: Editorial Católica, 1970.

———. "'Sibi causa facta est salutis' (S. Ireneo, Adv. Haereses 3,22,4)" ["Became the Cause of Salvation for Herself" (St. Irenaeus, Against the Heresies III.22.4)]. *Ephemerides Mariologicae* 16 (1966): 291–321.

———. *Virgo Mater: Estudios de teología patrística* [Virgin Mother: Studies in Patristic Theology]. Granada: Facultad de Teología, 1963.

de Beauvoir, Simone. *Le deuxième sexe*. 2 vols. Paris: Gallimard, 1949. English translation: *The Second Sex*. Translated and edited by H. M. Parshley. London: Knopf, 1953.

de Broglie, G. "Le 'principe fondamental' de la théologie mariale" [The "Fundamental principle" of Marian Theology]. In du Manoir, *Maria*, 6:297–365. 1961.

de Candido, Luigi M. "Fatima." In De Fiores, Schiefer, and Perrella, *DMar*, 540–51.

———. “Santa Maria.” In De Fiores and Meo, *NDM*, 1242–53.

De Fiores, Stefano. “Consacrazione.” In De Fiores and Meo, *NDM*, 394–417.

———. “Criticismo e movimiento illuministico” [Enlightenment: Critique and Movement]. In Boaga and Gambero, *Storia della mariologia*, 2:561–87.

———. “Fatima.” in Bäumer and Scheffczyk, *ML* 2:444–50.

———. “La nascita della mariologia come trattazione sistematica” [The Birth of Mariology as a Systematic Treatment]. In Boaga and Gambero, *Storia della mariologia*, 2:351–67.

———. *Maria, Madre di Gesù: Sintesi storico-salvifica* [Mary, Mother of Jesus: Salvation-Historical Synthesis]. Corso di teologia sistematica 6. Bologna: EDB, 1992.

———. *Maria nella teologia contemporanea* [Mary in Contemporary Theology]. 3rd ed. Rome: Centro di Cultura Mariana “Madre della Chiesa,” 1991.

———. *Maria: Nuovissimo dizionario*. Vols. 1–3. [Mary: Newest Dictionary. Vols. 1 and 2]. Bologna: EDB, 2006.

———. *Maria: Nuovissimo dizionario*. Vol. 3, *Testimoni e maestri*. [Vol. 3, Witnesses and Teachers]. Bologna: EDB, 2008.

———. *Maria sintesi di valori: Storia culturale della mariologia* [Mary, Synthesis of Values: Cultural History of Mariology]. Cinisello Balsamo: San Paolo, 2005.

———. “Microstoria della salvezza” [Micro-History of Salvation]. In *Maria: Nuovissimo dizionario*, 2:1143–69. Bologna: EDB, 2006.

———. “Presentazione.” In San Luigi M. Grignion da Montfort, *Trattato della vera devozione alla santa Vergine e Il segreto di Maria*, 11th ed., edited by Stefano De Fiores, 5–17. Cinisello Balsamo: San Paolo, 2000.

———. “Storia della mariologia.” In De Fiores, Schiefer, and Perrella, *DMar*, 1162–77.

———. “Trinità.” In De Fiores, Schiefer, and Perrella, *DMar*, 1219–32.

———. “Vergine I. Problematica attuale” [Virgin: I. Current Issues]. In De Fiores and Meo, *NDM*, 1418–24.

———. “Vergine III. Tradizione ecclesiale” [Virgin: III. Ecclesial Tradition]. In De Fiores and Meo, *NDM*, 1454–57.

———. “Vergine IV. Prospettive teologiche attuali” [Virgin: IV. Current Theological Perspectives]. In De Fiores and Meo, *NDM*, 1457–76.

De Fiores, Stefano, Valeria Ferrari Schieffer, and Salvatore M. Perrella, OSM, eds. *Mariologia* (*DMar*). Dizionari San Paolo. Cinisello Balsamo: San Paolo, 2009.

De Fiores, Stefano, and Salvatore Meo, OSM, eds. *Nuovo dizionario di mariologia* (*NDM*). Cinisello Balsamo: San Paolo, 1985. 4th ed. 1996. Spanish version: *Nuevo diccionario de Mariología*. Madrid: Ediciones Paulinas, 1988. 2nd ed. 1993.

De Fiores, Stefano, and Enrico Vidau, eds. *Maria Santa e Immacolata segno dell'amore salvifico di Dio Trinità: Prospettive ecumeniche* [Holy and Immaculate Mary, Sign of the Saving Love of the Triune God: Ecumenical Perspectives]. Rome: Ed. Monfortane, 2000.

De Fiores, Stefano, and Nereo Zamberlan. “Regina.” In De Fiores, Schiefer, and Perrella, *DMar*, 1022–34.

de la Potterie, Ignace, SJ. “Il parto verginale del Verbo incarnato: ‘Non ex sanguinibus … sed ex Deo natus est’” [The Virginal Birth of the Incarnate Word: ‘Born Not of Blood … but of God’]. *Marianum* 45, no. 130 (1983): 127–74.

———. "Kecharitomene en Lc. 1,28: Étude exégétique et théologique" [Kecharitomene in Lk 1:28. Exegetical and Theological Study]. *Biblica* 68, no. 4 (1987): 480–508.

———. "Kecharitomene en Lc. 1,28: Étude philologique" [Kecharitomene in Lk 1:28. Philological Study]. *Biblica* 68, no. 3 (1987): 357–82.

———. "La Madre de Jesús en el misterio de Caná" [The Mother of Jesus in the Mystery of Cana]. *Scripta de Maria* 1st ser., 4 (1981): 13.

———. *Maria nel mistero dell'alleanza* [Mary in the Mystery of the Covenant]. Genoa: Marietti, 1988.

De Liguori, Alfonso M. *Le glorie di Maria: Presentazione di Giovanni Velocci.* 2nd ed. Cinisello Balsamo: San Paolo, 2002.

Delius, Walter. *Geschichte der Marienverehrung* [History of Marian Devotion]. Munich and Basel: E. Reinhardt, 1963.

Delpero, Claudio. *La Chiesa del Concilio: L'ecclesiologia del Vaticano II* [The Church of the Council: The Ecclesiology of Vatican II]. Florence: Libreria Editrice Fiorentina, 2004.

de Margerie, Bertrand. "Can the Church Define Dogmatically the Spiritual Motherhood of Mary?" In Miravalle, *Mary Coredemptrix, Mediatrix, Advocate: Spiritual Foundations*, 191–214. French original: "L'Église peut-elle définir dogmatiquement la Maternité spirituelle de Marie? Objections et réponses." *Marianum* 43, no. 127 (1981): 394–418.

———. *Histoire doctrinale du culte envers le coeur de Jésus* [Doctrinal History of the Cult Directed to the Heart of Jesus]. 2 vols. Paris: Mame, 1992–95.

———. *Le coeur de Marie, coeur de l'Église: Essai de synthèse théologique* [Heart of Mary, Heart of the Church: Essay in Theological Synthesis]. 2nd ed. Paris: P. Téqui, 1993.

———. "Mary in Latin American Liberation Theologies." In *Kecharitoméne: Mélanges René Laurentin*, edited by Charles Augrain, 365–76. Paris: Desclée, 1990.

de Mattei, Roberto. "Il sabato e la fede di Maria" [Saturday and the Faith of Mary]. *Immaculata Mediatrix* 3 (2003): 271–83.

de Menthière, Guillaume. *Marie Mère du Salut: Marie Corédemptrice? Essai de fondement théologique* [Mary, Mother of Salvation: Mary Coredemptrix? Essay in Theological Foundations]. Paris: P. Téqui, 1999.

De Montfort, Louis-M. Grignion. *True Devotion to the Blessed Virgin.* Bay Shore, N.Y.: Montfort, 1980 (*TD*); Rockford, Ill.: TAN, 1985. Another edition: *God Alone: The Collected Writings of St. Louis Marie de Montfort.* Bay Shore, N.Y.: Montfort, 1995 (2010). French original: *Traité de la vrai dévotion à la Sainte Vierge; Le secret de Marie.* 1712.

Deneffe, August. "De Mariae in ipso opere redemptionis cooperatione" [Mary in Her Cooperation with the Work of Redemption]. *Gregorianum* 8 (1927): 3–22.

Denzinger, Heinrich, and Peter Hünermann (DH). *Enchiridion Symbolorum, definitionum et declarationum de rebus fidei et morum.* Bilingual Latin-Italian ed. Bologna: EDB, 1995. Bilingual Latin-English edition, *Compendium of Creeds, Definitions, and Declarations on Matters of Faith and Morals.* San Francisco: Ignatius Press, 2012.

de Ridder, Cornelis A. *Maria als Miterlöserin?* [Mary as Coredemptrix?] Göttingen: Vandenhoeck and Ruprecht, 1965.

Dermine, François-Marie. *Mistici, veggenti e medium: Esperienze dell'aldilà a confronto* [Mystics, Seers, and Mediums: Facing Experiences of the Beyond]. Vatican City: Libreria Editrice Vaticana, 2002.

———. *Vassula Ryden: Indagine critica* [Vassula Ryden: Critical Inquiry]. Leumann (Turin): Editrice Elle Di Ci, 1995.

de Roover, Emile, O.Praem. "La maternité virginale de Marie dans l'interprétation de Gal 4,4" [The Virginal Motherhood of Mary in the Interpretation of Gal 4:4]. In *Studiorum Paulinorum Congressus Internationalis Catholicus II* [Second International Catholic Congress in Pauline Studies], 17–37. Analecta Biblica 18. Rome: Pontificio Instituto Biblico, 1963.

de Villalmonte, A. "María y los angeles" [Mary and the Angels]. *Estudios Marianos* 20 (1959): 401–37.

de Vries, W. "Die getrennten Kirchen des Ostens" [The Separated Churches of the East]. In Algermissen, *Konfessionskunde*, 8th ed., 79–278.

Dhanis, Edouard, SJ. "Sguardo su Fatima e bilancio di una discussion." *La Civiltà Cattolica* 2, no. 104 (1953): 392–406.

Dibelius, Martin. *Jungfrauensohn und Krippenkind* [Virgin's Son and Child in the Cradle]. Heidelberg: Carl Winter, 1932.

Di Berardino, Angelo. "Leucio Carino." In Di Berardino, *Nuovo dizionario patristico e di antichità cristiane*, 2:2811. 2007.

———, ed. *Nuovo dizionario patristico e di antichità cristiane* [New Dictionary of Patristics and Christian Antiquity]. Vols. 1–3. Genoa and Milan: Marietti, 2006–8.

———, ed. *Patrologia*. Vol. 5, *Dal Concilio di Calcedonia (451) a Giovanni Damasceno (+750) - I padri orientali*. Genoa: Marietti, 2000. English translation: *Patrology*. Vol. 5, *The Eastern Fathers from the Council of Chalcedon (451) to John of Damascus (750)*. Translated by Adrian Walford. Cambridge: J. Clarke, 2008.

Dickson, Charles. "Mary Mediatrix: A Protestant Response." In Miravalle, *Mary Coredemptrix*, 3:181–84.

Di Domenico, Pier Giorgio M. "Preghiera" [Prayer]. In De Fiores, Schiefer, and Perrella, *DMar*, 975–86.

Di Domenico, Pier Giorgio M., and Elio Peretto, eds. *Maria Madre di misericordia: Monstra te esse Matrem* [Mary, Mother of Mercy: Show Thyself a Mother]. Padua: Messaggero, 2003.

Diez Merino, Luis. "Los textos biblicos y el dogma de la Inmaculada Concepción" [Biblical Texts and the Dogma of the Immaculate Conception]. *Estudios Marianos* 71 (2005): 183–96.

Dillenschneider, Clement. *Le principe premier d'une théologie mariale organique* [First Principle of an Organic Marian Theology]. Paris: Éditions Alsatia, 1955. Italian translation: *Il principio primo della teologia mariana*. Rome: Ares, 1957.

Dinzelbacher, Peter. "Erscheinung" [Apparition]. In *Lexikon des Mittelalters*, 3:2185f. Munich: Artemis, 1980.

Di Nola, Gerardo, Luigi Gambero, Georges Gharib, and Ermanno M. Toniolo, eds. *Testi mariani del primo millennio* [Marian Texts of the First Millennium]. Vol. 1, *Padri ed altri autori greci*. [Greek Fathers and Other Authors]. Rome: Città Nuova, 1988; 2nd ed. 2001. Vol. 2, *Padri ed altri autori bizantini (VI–XI sec.)* [Byzantine

Fathers and Other Authors]. Rome: Città Nuova, 1989. Vol. 4, *Padri e altri autori orientali* [Eastern Fathers and Other Authors]. Rome: Città Nuova, 1991.

Di Segni, Riccardo. "'Colei che non ha mai visto il sangue': Alla ricerca delle radici ebraiche dell'idea della concezione verginale di Maria" ["She Who Never Saw Blood": In Search of the Hebrew Roots of the Idea of Mary's Virginal Conception]. *Quaderni Storici* 75, no. 3 (1990): 757–89.

Dittrich, Achim. "'Die Erfindung des Scotus': Protestantische Kritik an der Immaculata-Definition nach 1854 und im 20. Jahrhundert" ["Scotus' Invention": Protestant Critique of the Definition of the Immaculate after 1854 and in the 20th Century]. *RTLu* 9, no. 2 (2004): 341–76.

———. *Mater Ecclesiae: Geschichte und Bedeutung eines umstrittenen Marientitels* [Mother of the Church: History and Meaning of a Disputed Marian Title]. Würzburg: Echter, 2009.

———. *Protestantische Mariologie-Kritik: Historische Entwicklung bis 1997 und dogmatische Analyse* [Protestant Criticism of Mariology: Historical Development to 1997 and Dogmatic Analysis]. Mariologische Studien 11. Regensburg: Pustet, 1998.

Dodd, Gloria Falcão. *The Virgin Mary, Mediatrix of All Grace: History and Theology of the Movement for a Dogmatic Definition from 1896 to 1964.* New Bedford, Mass.: Academy of the Immaculate, 2012.

Dombes Group. *Mary in the Plan of God and the Communion of Saints.* New York: Paulist Press, 2002. French original: *Marie dans le dessein de Dieu et la communion des saints.* 2 vols. Paris: Bayard and Centurion, 1997–98.

Donnelly, Philip J., SI. "La virginidad perpetua de la Madre de Dios" In Carol, *Mariología*, 619–83. English original: "The Perpetual Virginity of the Mother of God." In Carol, *Mariology*, 228–96.

Döpp, Siegmar, and Wilhelm Geerlings, eds. *Dizionario di letteratura cristiana antica* (*DLCA*). Rome: Città Nuova, 2006. German original: *Lexikon der antiken christlichen Literatur.* 3rd ed. Freiburg im Breisgau: Herder, 2002. English translation: *Dictionary of Early Christian Literature.* New York: Crossroad, 2011.

Dotolo, Carmelo. "Pensiero debole kenosi" [Weak Thought/Kenosis]. In De Fiores, Schiefer, and Perrella, *DMar*, 927–34.

Doyle, Daniel E., OSA. "Mary, Mother of God," in *Augustine through the Ages: An Encyclopedia*, ed. A. D. Fitzgerald. Grand Rapids, Mich.: Eerdmans, 1999. Italian translation: "Maria, madre di Dio." In *Agostino: Dizionario enciclopedico*, edited by Allan D. Fitzgerald, 907–12. Rome: Città Nuova, 2007.

Druwé, Eugène, SJ. "La médiation universelle de Marie" [The Universal Mediation of Mary]. In du Manoir, *Maria*, 417–572. 1949.

Ducay, Antonio. "La cooperación de María en la obra de la salvación" [Mary's Cooperation in the Work of Salvation]. *Scripta de Maria* 2nd ser., 3 (2006): 201–25.

du Manoir, Hubert. "Cyrill." In Bäumer and Scheffczyk, *ML* 2:114–19.

———, ed. *Maria: Études sur la Sainte Vierge.* Vols. 1–8. Paris: Beauchesne, 1949–71.

Duns Scotus, John. *Four Questions on Mary.* Translated by Allan B. Wolter, OFM. St. Bonaventure, N.Y.: Franciscan Institute, 2012.

Düren, Sabine. *Die Frau im Spannungsfeld von Emanzipation und Glaube* [Woman in the Voltage Field of Emancipation and Faith]. Regensburg: Roderer, 1998.

Dürig, Walter. "Lauretanische Litanei" [Litany of Loreto]. In Bäumer and Scheffczyk, *ML* 4: 33–42.

———. *Maria, Mutter der Kirche* [Mary, Mother of the Church]. St. Ottilien: EOS Verlag, 1979.

Durst, Michael. "Justin der Martyrer" [Justin the Martyr]. In Bäumer and Scheffczyk, *ML* 3:489–91.

Ellero, Giuseppe Maria. "Maternità e virtù di Maria in San Giovanni Crisostomo" [Motherhood and Virtue of Mary in St. John Chrysostom]. *Marianum* 25 (1963): 405–46.

Erbetta, Mario. *Gli apocrifi del Nuovo Testamento* [Apocrypha of the New Testament], vol. I/2. Casale Monferrato: Marietti, 1981.

Ernst, Josef. *Il Vangelo secondo Luca* [The Gospel according to Luke]. Vol. 1. 2nd ed. Brescia: Morcelliana, 1990.

Escalada, Xavier. *Enciclopedia Guadalupana* [Encyclopedia of Our Lady of Guadalupe]. 4 vols. México: s.n., 1995.

———. *Enciclopedia Guadalupana. Apendice*. México: s.n., 1997.

Escudero Cabello, Antonio. "Approcci attuali e proposte teologiche sul tema della cooperazione mariana" [Current Approaches and Theological Proposals on the Topic of Marian Coredemption]. *Marianum* 61, no. 155–56 (1999): 177–211.

———. "La comprensión eucaristica de María: La Eucaristía como acceso a la mariologia" [The Eucharistic Comprehension of Mary: The Eucharist as a Way into Mariology]. *Ephemerides Mariologicae* 59, no. 3–4 (2009): 375–92.

———. *La cuestión de la mediación mariana en la preparación del Vaticano II: Elementos para una evaluación de los trabajos preconciliares* [The Question of Marian Mediation in the Preparation for Vatican II: Elements toward an Evaluation of Preconciliar Works]. Rome: LAS, 1997.

Esquerda Bifet, Juan. "El Corazón de María, memoria contemplativa de la Iglesia" [Heart of Mary, Contemplative Memory of the Church]. *Marianum* 66, no. 165–66 (2004): 659–98.

———. *Spiritualità mariana della Chiesa: Esposizione sistematica* [Marian Spirituality of the Church]. Rome: Centro di Cultura Mariana "Madre della Chiesa," 1994.

Eudes, Jean. *Le coeur admirable de la très Sacrée Mère de Dieu* [The Admirable Heart of the Most Holy Mother of God]. Caen, 1681. Italian translation: G. Eudes, *Il Cuore Ammirabile della SS. Madre di Dio*. Casale Monferrato: Propaganda mariana, 1960 (reprint Castelpetroso: Casa Mariana Editrice, 2000; abridged edition); complete edition, Frigento, 2007. Spanish translation: *El Corazón admirable de la Madre de Dios. Introducción, traducción y notas* [The Admirable Heart of the Mother of God. Introduction, translation, and notes]. Edited by Joaquín María Alonso. Madrid: Editorial y Libreria Co. Cul. S.A., 1959. English translation: John Eudes. *The Admirable Heart of Mary*. Translated by Charles di Targiani and Ruth Hauser. New York: P. J. Kenedy, 1948. Repr. Fitzwilliam, N.H.: Loreto, 2004.

Everett, Lawrence P., CSSR. "La muerte y asunción corporal de María." In Carol, *Mariología*, 838–66. English original: "Mary's Death and Bodily Assumption." In Carol, *Mariology*, 2:461–92.

Farkaš, Pavol. *La "Donna" di Apocalisse 12: Storia, bilancio, nuove prospettive* [The

"Woman" of Revelation 12: History, Summary, New Perspectives]. Rome: Pontificia Università Gregoriana, 1997.

Farrugia, Edward G., SJ, ed. *Dizionario enciclopedico dell'Oriente Cristiano.* Rome: Pontifical Oriental Institute, 2000. English translation: *Encyclopedic Dictionary of the Christian East.* Rome: Pontifical Oriental Institute, 2015.

Fastenrath, E. "Königtum Mariens" [Royalty of Mary]. In Bäumer and Scheffczyk, *ML* 3:589–93.

Feckes, Carl. "Das Fundamentalprinzip der Mariologie: Ein Beitrag zu ihrem organischen Aufbau" [The Fundamental Principle of Mariology: A Contribution toward Its Organic Growth]. In *Scientia sacra, theologische Festgabe für Kardinal Schulte,* 252–76. Cologne and Düsseldorf: Bachem, 1935.

Fehlner, Peter Damian M. *La verginità nel parto* [Virginity in Childbirth]. Castelpetroso: Casa Mariana Editrice, 1995.

Felici, Sergio, ed. *La mariologia nella catechesi dei Padri (età postnicena)* [Mariology in the Catechesis of the Fathers (Post-Nicene Era)]. Rome: LAS, 1991.

———, ed. *La mariologia nella catechesi dei Padri (età prenicena)* [Mariology in the Catechesis of the Fathers (Pre-Nicene Era)]. Rome, LAS, 1989.

Felmy, Karl Christian. *Einführung in die orthodoxe Theologie der Gegenwart.* Darmstadt: Wiss. Buchges., 1990.

Ferrario, Fulvio, and Paolo Ricca, eds. *Il Consenso cattolico-luterano sulla dottrina della giustificazione* [The Catholic-Lutheran Agreement on the Doctrine of Justification]. Turin: Claudiana, 1999.

Ferrer Arellano, Joaquín. *La Mediación Materna de la Inmaculada, esperanza ecuménica de la Iglesia, hacia el quinto dogma mariano: Razones teológicas* [The Maternal Mediation of the Immaculate, Ecumenical Hope of the Church, Toward the Fifth Marian Dogma: Theological Reasoning]. Madrid: Arca de la Alianza, 2006.

———. *San José nuestro Padre y Señor: La trinidad de la tierra, teología y espiritualidad josefina* [St. Joseph, Our Father and Lord: The Josephite Trinity of Earth, Theology, and Spirituality]. Madrid: Arca de la Alianza, 2007.

Feuillet, A. "Marie dans le Nouveau Testament" [Mary in the New Testament]. In du Manoir, *Maria,* 6:15–69. 1961.

Finkenzeller, J. "Miterlöserin" [Coredemptrix]. In Bäumer and Scheffczyk, *ML* 4:484–86.

———. "Tod Mariens" [Death of Mary]. In Bäumer and Scheffczyk, *ML* 6:436–38.

Foley, Donal A. *Medjugorje Revisited: 30 Years of Visions or Religious Fraud?* Nottingham, UK: Theotokos, 2011.

Forderer, Manfred. *Königin ohne Tod in den Himmel aufgenommen* [Queen Assumed into Heaven without Death]. Stein am Rhein (Switzerland): Christiana-Verlag, 1988.

Forlai, Giuseppe. *L'irruzione della grazia: Per una rilettura ecumenica del dogma dell'Immacolata* [The Eruption of Grace: Toward an Ecumenical Re-Reading of the Dogma of the Immaculate]. Cinisello Balsamo: San Paolo, 2010.

Forte, Bruno. *Maria, la donna icona del Mistero: Saggio di mariologia simbolico-narrativa* [Mary the Woman, Icon of the Mystery: Essay in Symbolic-Narrative Mariology]. 3rd ed. Cinisello Balsamo: Ed. Paoline, 1996.

François de Marie des Anges. *Fatima joie intime événement mondial.* 2nd ed. Saint-Parres-lès-Vaudes: Editions de la contre-réforme catholique, 1993. English trans-

lation: *Fatima, Intimate Joy, World Event*. New York: Immaculate Heart Publications, 1993.
Frei, U.-B., and Fredy Bühler. *Der Rosenkranz: Andacht—Geschichte—Kunst* [The Rosary: Devotion, History, Art]. Bern: Benteli; Sachseln: Museum Bruder Klaus, 2003.
Fusi, Aurelio. *Ha creduto meglio degli altri: Maria modello della Chiesa nell'insegnamento di Giovanni Paolo II* [She Believed Better Than Others: Mary, Model of the Church in the Teaching of John Paul II]. Milan: Ed. Paoline, 1999.
Gächter, Paul, SJ. *Maria im Erdenleben: Neutestamentliche Marienstudien* [Mary in Earthly Life: New Testament Marian Studies]. 3rd ed. Innsbruck: Tyrolia, 1955.
———. *Marjam, die Mutter Jesu* [Mariam, the Mother of Jesus]. 2nd ed. Einsiedeln: Johannes Verlag, 1981.
Galli, Antonio. *Scoperti in Vaticano: I segreti di La Salette* [Discoveries in the Vatican: The Secrets of La Salette]. Milan: Sugarco, 2007.
Gallus, Tiburzio. *La Vergine immortale*. Rome: Angelo Belardetti Editore, 1949.
———. "Perché la Madonna non poteva morire" [Why the Madonna Could Not Die]. *Palestra del Clero* 34 (1955): 841–47.
Galot, Jean, SJ. *Être né de Dieu: Jean 1,13* [Being Born of God: John 1:13]. Analecta biblica 37. Rome: Pontifical Biblical Institute, 1969.
———. *Gesù Liberatore: Cristologia*. Vol. 2. 2nd ed. Firenze: Fiorentina, 1983. English translation: *Jesus Our Liberator: A Theology of Redemption*. Chicago: Franciscan Herald Press, 1982.
———. *La fede di Maria e la nostra* [Mary's Faith and Ours]. Assisi: Cittadella Editrice, 1973.
———. "La plus ancienne affirmation de la Corédemption mariale: Le témoignage de Jean le Géomètre" [The Earliest Affirmation of Marian Coredemption: The Witness of John the Geometer]. *Recherches de Science Religieuse* 45, no. 1 (1957): 187–208.
———. "La Sainteté de Marie" [The Holiness of Mary]. In du Manoir, *Maria*, 6:417–48. 1961.
———. "La verginité de Marie et la naissance de Jésus" [The Virginity of Mary and the Birth of Jesus]. *Nouvelle Revue Théologique* 82 (1960): 449–69.
———. "Le mystère de l'assomption" [The Mystery of the Assumption]. In du Manoir, *Maria*, 7:153–237. 1964.
———. "L'Immaculée Conception." In du Manoir, *Maria*, 7:9–116. 1964.
———. *Maria, La donna nell'opera della salvezza* [Mary, Woman in the Work of Salvation]. 3rd ed. Rome: Ed. Pontificia Università Gregoriana, 2005. 2nd ed. 1991.
———. "Maria: Mediatrice o Madre universale?" [Mary: Mediatrix or Universal Mother?]. *La Civiltà Cattolica*, year 147, vol. 1 (1996): 232–44.
Gambero, Luigi. "Culto." In De Fiores and Meo, *NDM* (1985), 425–43.
———. *Fede e devozione mariana nell'impero bizantino* [Marian Faith and Devotion in the Byzantine Empire]. Cinisello Balsamo: San Paolo, 2012.
———. "La regalità di Maria nel pensiero dei Padri" [The Queenship of Mary in the Thought of the Fathers]. *Ephemerides Mariologicae* 46, no. 4 (1996): 433–52.
———. "La riflessione mariologica post-tridentina in area italo-germanica" [Mariological Reflection after Trent in the Italo-Germanic Area]. In Boaga and Gambero, *Storia della mariologia*, 2:322–47.

———. “Maria Assunta: Rilievi dell’escatologia patristica” [Mary Assumed: Review of Patristic Eschatology]. In Carvello and De Fiores, *Maria, icona viva della Chiesa futura*, 119–40.

———. “Maria e il mistero della misericordia di Dio: Riflessioni nei Padri della Chiesa” [Mary and the Mystery of the Mercy of God: Reflections on the Fathers of the Church]. In Di Domenico and E. Peretto, *Maria Madre di misericordia*, 158–85.

———. “Maria negli antichi concili” [Mary in the Ancient Councils]. In Dal Covolo and Serra, *Storia della mariologia*, 1:451–502.

———. *Maria nel pensiero dei teologi latini medievali*. Cinisello Balsamo: Ed. Paoline, 2000. English translation: *Mary in the Middle Ages: The Blessed Virgin Mary in the Thought of Medieval Latin Theologians*. Translated by Thomas Buffer. San Francisco: Ignatius Press, 2005.

———. “La santità di Maria: Contesto in cui si sviluppa la dottrina dell’Immacolata Concezione; Il contributo dei Padri della Chiesa” [The Holiness of Mary: Context in Which the Doctrine of the Immaculate Conception Developed; The Contribution of the Church Fathers]. In Toniolo, *Il dogma dell’Immacolata Concezione di Maria*, 271–307.

———. *Mary and the Fathers of the Church: The Blessed Virgin Mary in Patristic Thought*. Translated by Thomas Buffer. San Francisco: Ignatius Press, 1999. Italian original *Maria nel pensiero dei padri della Chiesa*. Cinisello Balsamo: Ed. Paoline, 1991.

———, ed. *Testi mariani del primo millennio*. Vol. 3, *Padri e altri autori latini* [Marian Texts of the First Millennium. Vol. 3, Latin Fathers and Other Authors]. Rome: Città Nuova, 1990.

———, ed. *Testi mariani del secondo millennio*. Vol. 3, *Autori medievali dell’Occidente: Sec. XI–XII* [Marian Texts of the Second Millennium. Vol. 3, Medieval Western Authors, 11th–12th Centuries]. Rome: Città Nuova, 1996.

———, ed. *Testi mariani del secondo millennio*. Vol. 4, *Autori medievali dell’Occidente: Sec. XIII–XV* [… Vol. 4, 13th–14th Centuries]. Rome: Città Nuova, 1996.

Gambero, Luigi, and Stefano De Fiores, eds. *Testi mariani del secondo millennio*. Vol. 5, *Autori moderni dell’Occidente: Sec. XVI–XVII* [Marian Texts of the Second Millennium. Vol. 5, Modern Western Authors: 16th–17th centuries]. Rome: Città Nuova, 2003.

———, eds. *Testi mariani del secondo millennio*. Vol. 6, *Autori moderni dell’Occidente: Sec. XVIII–XIX* [… 18th–19th Centuries]. Rome: Città Nuova, 2005.

García Moreno, Antonio. “María en el Calvario (Jn 19,25–27)” [Mary at Calvary (Jn 19:25–27)]. *Scripta de Maria* 2nd ser., 2 (2005): 189–221.

García Paredes, José C. R. *Maria nella comunità del regno: Sintesi di Mariologia* [Mary in the Community of the Kingdom: Synthesis of Mariology]. Vatican City: Libreria Editrice Vaticana, 1997. Spanish original: *Maria en la comunidad del Reino*. Madrid: Publicaciones Claretianas, 1988.

———. *Mariología*. Madrid: Biblioteca de Autores Cristianos, 1995.

Garuti, Adriano. *Il mistero della Chiesa* [The Mystery of the Church]. Rome: Pontificio Ateneo Antonianum, 2004.

Gaspari, Sergio. “Maria Regina coronata di gloria: Significato teologico-liturgico” [Mary, Queen crowned with glory: Theological-Liturgical Significance]. In Carvello and De Fiores, *Maria icona viva della Chiesa futura*, 251–92.

Geenen, Godfried, OP. "Les antécédents doctrinaux et historiques de la consécration du monde au coeur immaculé de Marie" [Doctrinal and Historical Antecedents of the Consecration of the World to the Immaculate Heart of Mary]. In du Manoir, *Maria* 1:825–73. 1949.

Gessel, W. "Ephesos." In Bäumer and Scheffczyk, *ML* 2:367–70.

Gharib, Georges. "Musulmani" [Muslims]. In *NDM*, 1001–11.

Gharib, Georges, and Ermanno M. Toniolo, eds. *Testi mariani del secondo millennio.* Vol. 1, *Autori orientali (XI–XX sec.)* [Marian Texts of the Second Millennium. Vol. 1, Eastern Authors (11th–20th Centuries)]. Rome: Città Nuova, 2008.

Gharib, Georges, et al., eds. *Testi mariani del primo millennio* (*TMPM*). 4 vols. Rome: Città Nuova, 1988–91.

Gherardini, Brunero. "Chiesa" [Church]. In De Fiores and Meo, *NDM*, 350–68.

———. *La Chiesa: Mistero e servizio* [The Church: Mystery and Service]. 3rd ed. Rome: Associazione Apollinare Studi, 1994.

———. *La Corredentrice nel mistero di Cristo e della Chiesa* [The Coredemptrix in the Mystery of Christ and the Church]. Rome: Vivere In, 1998.

———. "Ecumenismo e corredenzione mariana" [Ecumenism and Marian Coredemption]. *Maria Corredentrice*, 8 (2006): 5–16.

———. "Lutero e gli eredi della Riforma dinanzi al mistero di Maria Corredentrice" [Luther and the Heirs of the Reformation, Before the Mystery of Mary Coredemptrix]. *Maria Corredentrice* 3 (2000): 53–74.

———. *Lutero—Maria. Pro o contro?* [Luther-Mary: For or Against?] Pisa: Giardini, 1985.

———. *La Madonna in Lutero* [The Madonna in Luther]. Rome: Città Nuova, 1967.

———. *La Madre: Maria in una sintesi storico-teologica* [The Mother: Mary in a Historical-Theological Synthesis]. Frigento: Casa Mariana, 1989.

———. *Sta la regina alla tua destra: Saggio storico-teologico sulla Regalità di Maria* [The Queen Stands at Your Right Hand: Historical-Theological Essay on the Queenship of Mary]. Rome: Vivere In, 2002.

———. "Unity and Coredemption." In *Mary at the Foot of the Cross*. Vol. 3, *Mater Unitatis*, 54–69. 2003.

Gila, Angelo M. "Apocrifi" [Apocrypha]. In De Fiores, Schiefer, and Perrella, *DMar*, 128–35.

———. "'Maria, Regina e Madre di misericordia': Un tema tipico dell'epoca medioevale" [Mary, Queen and Mother of Mercy: A Theme Typical of the Medieval Era]. In Di Domenico and Peretto, *Maria Madre di misericordia*, 186–217.

———. *Le più antiche testimonianze letterarie sulla morte e glorificazione della Madre di Dio: I racconti sul Transito di Maria tra fede e teologia* [The Most Ancient Literary Witnesses on the Death and Glorification of the Mother of God: Accounts of the Transitus of Mary, between Faith and Theology]. Padua: Messaggero, 2010.

———. "Spunti della letteratura del primo millennio sulla presenza della Vergine Maria nel dinamismo dei sacramenti" [Starting Points in First-Millennium Literature on the Presence of the Virgin Mary in the Dynamism of the Sacraments]. In *Fons lucis. Miscellanea di studi in onore di Ermanno M. Toniolo*, edited by Rosella Barbieri, Ignazio M. Calabuig, and Ornella Di Angelo, 287–332. Rome: Marianum, 2004.

Gnilka, Joachim. *Das Matthäusevangelium* [The Gospel of Matthew]. Vol. 1. Freiburg im Breisgau: Herder, 1986. Italian translation: *Il Vangelo di Matteo*. Vol. 1. Translated by Vincenzo Gatti. Brescia: Paideia, 1990.

Godts, F.-X. *La Corédemptrice*. Brussels: Libraire Albert de Wit, 1920.

———. "La Corédemptrice." In *Mémoires et rapports du Congrès Marial tenu à Bruxelles, 8–11 septembre 1921*, 1:154–70. Brussels: L'Action Catholique, 1922.

Görg, Peter H. *"Sagt an, wer ist doch diese": Inhalt, Rang und Entwicklung der Mariologie in dogmatischen Lehrbüchern und Publikationen deutschsprachiger Dogmatiker des 19. und 20. Jahrhunderts* ["Say Then, Who Is She": Content, Rank, and Development of Mariology in Dogmatic Manuals and Publications of German-Speaking Dogmatic Theologians of the 19th and 20th Centuries]. Bonn: Nova et Vetera, 2007.

Goodspeed, Edgar J., ed. *Die ältesten Apologeten* [The Earliest Apologists]. Göttingen: Vanderboeck and Ruprecht, 1914. Reprint 1984.

Gorski, Horst. *Die Niedrigkeit seiner Magd: Darstellung und theologische Analyse der Mariologie Martin Luthers als Beitrag zum gegenwärtigen lutherisch/römisch-katholischen Gespräch* [The Lowliness of His Handmaid: Presentation and Theological Analysis of the Mariology of Martin Luther, as a Contribution to the Present Lutheran/Roman-Catholic Dialogue]. Frankfurt: Peter Lang, 1987.

Gournay, Bertrand. *Notre-Dame du Laus: L'espérance au coeur des Alpes* [Our Lady of Laus: Hope in the Heart of the Alps]. Paris: P. Téqui, 2008.

Govaert, Lutgart. "Die Mariologie John Henry Newmans (1801–1890): Eine Antwort auf die Problematik der Reformation" [The Mariology of John Henry Newman: An Answer to the Issues of the Reformation]. *Sedes Sapientiae: Mariologisches Jahrbuch* 10, no. 2 (2006): 57–72.

———. *Kardinal Newmans Mariologie und sein persönlicher Werdegang* [Cardinal Newman's Mariology and His Personal Intellectual Development]. Salzburg: Pustet, 1975.

———. "Newman." In Bäumer and Scheffczyk, *ML* 4:608–10.

Graber, Rudolf, and Anton Ziegenaus, eds. *Die Marianischen Weltrundschreiben der Päpste von Pius IX: Bis Johannes Paul II (1849–1988)* [The Marian Encyclicals of the Popes: From Pius IX to John Paul II]. Regensburg: Institutum Marianum Regensburg, 1997.

Graef, Hilda: *Maria: Eine Geschichte der Lehre und Verehrung* [Mary: A History of Doctrine and Devotion]. Freiburg im Breisgau: Herder, 1964.

Greco, Angelico. *"Madre dei viventi": La cooperazione salvifica di Maria nella "Lumen gentium"; Una sfida per oggi* ["Mother of the Living": The Salvific Cooperation of Mary in "Lumen gentium"; A Challenge for Today]. CdM 10. Lugano and Gavirate (Varese): Eupress FTL, 2011.

Greshake, Gisbert. *Maria–Ecclesia: Perspektiven einer marianisch grundierten Theologie und Kirchenpraxis* [Mary—Church: Perspectives of a Marian-Based Theology and Church Praxis]. Regensburg: Friedrich Pustet, 2014.

Grillmeier, Aloys, SJ. "Maria Prophetin: Eine Studie zur patristischen Mariologie" [Mary the Prophet: A Study in Patristic Mariology]. *Geist und Leben* 30 (1957): 101–45.

Gruenthaner, Michael J., SJ. "María en el Nuevo Testamento." In Carol, *Mariología*, 83–110. English original: "Mary in the New Testament." In Carol, *Mariology*, 80–108.

Guardini, Romano. *La Madre del Signore* [Mother of the Lord: A Letter, and Therein a Sketch]. 2nd ed. Brescia: Morcelliana, 1997. German translation: *Die Mutter des Herrn: Ein Brief und darin ein Entwurf.* 2nd ed. Würzburg: Werkbund-Verlag, 1956.

Guerra, Luciano. *O "Segredo" de Fátima* [The "Secret" of Fatima]. Fatima: Reitoria do Santuário de Fátima, 2004.

Guemara, Raoudha. "Islam." In De Fiores, Schiefer, and Perrella, *DMar*, 657–67.

Gussone, N. "Krönung von Marienbildern" [Crowning of Marian Images]. In Bäumer and Scheffczyk, *ML* 3:683f.

Haffner, Paul. *The Mystery of Mary*. Leominster, UK: Gracewing; Mundelein, Ill.: Hillenbrand, 2004.

Hagemann, Ludwig. "Mariologische Aspekte im Koran: Forschungsergebnisse seit dem letzten Jahrhundert" [Mariological Aspects in the Koran: Research Findings since the Last Century]. In PAMI, *De cultu mariano saeculis XIX et XX*, 2:605–35. Rome: PAMI, 1991.

Hahn, F. "Dibelius." In Bäumer and Scheffczyk, *ML* 2:186f.

Hahn, Scott. "Mary Coredemptrix: Doctrinal Development and Ecumenism." In Miravalle, *Mary Co-Redemptrix: Doctrinal Issues Today*, 263–74.

———. "She Gave the Word Flesh." In Miravalle, *Mary Co-redemptrix*, 3:169–80.

Hammann, Gottfried. "Il punto di vista della Riforma circa l'Immacolata Concezione" [The Reformation Outlook on the Immaculate Conception]. In De Fiores and Vidau, *Maria Santa e Immacolata*, 105–23.

Hauke, Manfred. "Aléxis-Henri-Marie Lépicier–Förderer der thomistichen Dogmatik und 'Kardinal Mariens'" [Aléxis-Henri-Marie Lépicier, Promoter of Thomistic Dogmatic Theology and "Marian Cardinal"]. *Doctor Angelicus* 7 (2007): 189–97.

———. "Anthropologie und Mariologie in der zeitgenossischen theologischen Diskussion: Gemeinsame Perspektiven und Probleme" [Anthropology and Mariology in Contemporary Theological Debate: Common Perspectives and Problems]. *Forum Katholische Theologie* 29 (2013): 1–21; also in *Mariologia a tempore Concilii Vaticani II*, edited by PAMI, 241–70. Vatican City: PAMI, 2013. Italian version: "Antropologia e mariologia nel dibattito teologico contemporaneo: Temi condividi e nodi problematici." *RTLu* 19 (2014): 233–55.

———. "Begierlichkeit" [Concupiscence]. In Bäumer and Scheffczyk, *ML* 1:403.

———. "Das Faszinierende der göttlichen Gnade: Zur charitologischen Ästhetik bei M. J. Scheeben" [The Fascination of Divine Grace: The Charitological Aesthetic in M. J. Scheeben]. *Forum Katholische Theologie* 9, no. 4 (1993): 275–89.

———. "Das Gutachten von Garrigou-Lagrange zur dogmatischen Definition der universalen Mittlerschaft Mariens: Einführung, Text und Kommentar" [The Heritage of Garrigou-Lagrange on the Dogmatic Definition of the Universal Mediation of Mary: Introduction, Text, and Commentary]. *Doctor Angelicus* 4 (2004): 37–90.

———. *Das Weihesakrament für die Frau—eine Forderung der Zeit? Zehn Jahre nach der päpstlichen Erklärung "Ordinatio Sacerdotalis"* [The Ordination of Women: A Demand of the times?]. Respondeo 17. Siegburg: F. Schmitt, 2004.

———. "Das Zweite Vatikanum und die Überlieferung: Eine wichtige Wegweisung von Papst Benedikt XVI." [The Second Vatican Council and Tradition: An Important signpost from Pope Benedict XVI]. *Theologisches* 36, no. 3–4 (2006): 90–94.

———. "Definición dogmática de la mediación universal de María: Iniciativas del cardenal Mercier y sus reflejos en Espana" [Dogmatic Definition of the Universal Mediation of Mary: Cardinal Mercier's Initiatives and Their Reflections in Spain]. *Scripta de Maria* 2nd ser., no. 2 (2005): 317–52.

———. "Deliramenta apocryphorum: Die theologischen Klarstellungen des Hieronymus zu den Maria betreffenden Apokryphen" [Apocalyptic Folly: Jerome's Theological Elucidations on the Apocrypha with Reference to Mary]. In Ziegenaus, *Volksfrömmigkeit und Theologie*, 57–73.

———. "Der prophetische Dienst Mariens: Inhaltliche Schwerpunkte der marianischen Botschaften seit 1830" [The Prophetic Service of Mary: Main Points of Content in the Marian Messages since 1830]. In Ziegenaus, *Marienerscheinungen*, 29–62.

———. "'Die Anhänger niche ins Leere fallen lassen': Das Phänomen Medjugorje; Hilfen zur Unterschiedung der Geister" ["Don't Let the Followers Fall into the Void": The Medjugorje Phenomenon; Aids in the Discernment of Spirits]. In Rudo Franken, *Eine Reise nach Medjugorje*, 2nd ed. 204–30. Augsburg: Dominus-Verlag, 2011. (See also the remarks at 240–49, 257–66).

———. "Die Antwort des Konzils von Trient auf die Reformatoren" [The Council of Trent's Response to the Reformers]. In *Der Mensch zwischen Sünde und Gnade* [Man between Sin and Grace], edited by Anton Ziegenaus, 75–109. Buttenwiesen: Stella-Maris-Verlag, 2000.

———. "Die Bittschrift von Kardinal Mercier für die dogmatische Definition der universellen Gnadenmittlerschaft Mariens (1915)" [Cardinal Mercier's Petition for the Dogmatic Definition of the Universal Mediation of Mary (1915)]. *Sedes Sapientiae: Mariologisches Jahrbuch* 14, no. 2 (2010): 128–68; Italian version: "Riscoperta: La petizione del Cardinale Mercier e dei Vescovi belgi a Papa Benedetto XV per la definizione dogmatica della Mediazione universale delle grazie da parte di Maria (1915). Introduzione teologica e testo orignale francese." *Immaculata Mediatrix* 10, no. 3 (2010): 305–38; with an Italian translation of the French petition of 1915: *Maria Corredentrice: Storia e teologia,* 13:183–244. 2011.

———. "Die Diskussion um das dritte Geheimnis von Fatima" [The Debate on the Third Secret of Fatima]. *Sedes Sapientiae: Mariologisches Jahrbuch* 14, no. 2 (2010): 92–109.

———. *Die Firmung: Geschichtliche Entfaltung und theologischer Sinn* [Confirmation: Historical Development and Theological Interpretation]. Paderborn: Bonifacius, 1999.

———, ed. *Die Herz-Mariä-Verehrung: Geschichtliche Entwicklung und theologischer Gehalt* [Devotion to the Heart of Mary: Historical Evolution and Theological Content]. Mariologische Studien 22. Regensburg: Friedrich Pustet, 2011.

———. "Die 'Gemeinsame Erklärung' zur Rechtfertigung und die Norm des

Glaubens" [The "Common Declaration" on Justification and the Norm of Faith]. *FKTh* 22, no. 2 (2006): 127–34.

———. "Die Gottesmutter als irdisches Paradies bei Johannes von Euböa: Die erste Predigt zum Fest der makellosen Empfängnis Mariens" [The Mother of God as Earthly Paradise in John of Euböa: The First Sermon on the Feast of the Spotless Conception of Mary]. *Klerusblatt* 84 (2004): 272–74.

———. "Die Lauretanische Litanei: Systematische Aspekte marianischer Volksfrömmigkeit" [Litany of Loreto: Systematic Aspects of Marian Popular Piety]. *Sedes Sapientiae: Mariologisches Jahrbuch* 15, no. 2 (2011): 56–88.

———. "Die Lehre von der 'Miterlösung' im geschichtlichen Durchblick: Von den biblischen Ursprüngen bis zu Papst Benedikt XVI" [The Theory of "Coredemption" in Historical Perspective: From the Biblical Sources to Benedict XVI]. *Sedes Sapientiae: Mariologisches Jahrbuch* 11 (2007): 17–64.

———. "Die Manifestationen der 'Frau aller Völker': Klärende Hinweise" [The Appearances of the "Lady of All Nations": Clarifying Indications]. *Sedes Sapientiae: Mariologisches Jahrbuch* 16, no. 2 (2012): 60–87.

———. "Die marianischen Aussagen des Zweiten Vatikanischen Konzils und ihre Interpretation durch Johannes Paul II" [The Marian Statements of Vatican II and Their Interpretation by John Paul II]. *Sedes Sapientiae: Mariologisches Jahrbuch* 16, no. 1 (2012): 58–88.

———. "Die Mariologie Scheebens: Ein zukunftsträchtiges Vermächtnis" [Scheeben's Mariology: A Seminal Legacy]. In *Donum Veritatis: Theologie im Dienst der Kirche; Festschrift ... Anton Ziegenaus*, edited by Manfred Hauke and Michael Stickelbroeck, 255–74. Regensburg: Friedrich Pustet, 2006.

———. *Die Problematik um das Frauenpriestertum vor dem Hindergrund der Schöpfungs- und Erlösungsordnung*. 4th ed. Paderborn: Bonifatius, 1995. English: *Women in the Priesthood?* San Francisco: Ignatius Press, 1988.

———. "Die Taufgnade und die 'Wurzel des Bösen': Anmerkungen zur Verurteilung des Messalianismus auf dem Konzil von Ephesus" [Baptismal Grace and the "Problem of Evil": Remarks on the Judgment of Messalianism on the Council of Ephesus]. *Archivum Historiae Conciliorum* 35 (2003): 307–21. Also in *I Padri e le scuole teologiche nei concili*, edited by Johannes Grohe, Jerónimo Leal, and Vito Reale, 325–40. Vatican City: Libreria Editrice Vaticana, 2006.

———. "Die trinitarischen Beziehungen Mariens als Urbild der Kirche auf dem Zweiten Vatikanischen Konzil" [The Trinitarian Relations of Mary as a Model of the Church at the Second Vatican Council]. *Sedes Sapientiae: Mariologisches Jahrbuch* 4, no. 2 (2000): 78–114.

———. "Die Unbefleckte Empfängnis bei den griechischen Vätern: Die Hinweise Johannes Pauls II. im ökumenischen Disput." *Sedes Sapientiae: Mariologisches Jahrbuch* 8, no. 2 (2004): 13–54; English version, "The Immaculate Conception of Mary in the Greek Fathers and in an Ecumenical Context." *Chicago Studies* 45, no. 3 (2006): 327–46.

———. "Die 'virginitas in partu': Akzentsetzungen in der Dogmengeschichte" ["Virginity in Childbirth": Emphases in the History of Dogmas]. In "*Geboren aus der Jungfrau Maria*": *Klarstellungen*, edited by A. Ziegenaus, 88–131. Mariologische Studien 19. Regensburg: Friedrich Pustet, 2007.

———. "Die Weihe an das Unbefleckte Herz Mariens nach Leo Scheffczyk" [Consecration to the Immaculate Heart of Mary in Leo Scheffczyk]. *Theologisches* 41, no. 1–2 (2011): 17–30.

———. "Die Weihe der Welt an die Gottesmutter Maria" [Consecration of the World to Mary, the Mother of God]. *Sedes Sapientiae: Mariologisches Jahrbuch* 14, no. 2 (2010): 67–91.

———. *Essere cattolico? Un primo sguardo all'opera teologica del Cardinale Leo Scheffczyk* [To Be a Catholic? A First Look at the Theological Work of Cardinal Leo Scheffczyk]. Mane nobiscum 10. Vatican City: Lateran University Press, 2007.

———. "L'eucaristia: Fonte e culmine della vita cristiana; L'enciclica Ecclesia de Eucaristia" [The Eucharist: Source and Summit of Christian Life; The Encyclical Ecclesia de Eucharistia]. In Graziano Borgonovo and A. Cattaneo, *Il papa teologo: Nel segno delle encicliche*, 253–70. Milan: Mondadori, 2003.

———. "Frau" [Woman]. In Bäumer and Scheffczyk, *ML* 2:520–24.

———. "Geschichtliche und systematische Grundlinien der Herz-Mariä-Verehrung" [Historical and Systematic Principles of Devotion to the Heart of Mary]. In Hauke, *Die Herz-Mariä-Verehrung*, 7–34.

———. *Gott oder Göttin? Feministische Theologie auf dem Prüfstand.* Aachen: MM Verlag, 1993. English translation: *God or Goddess? Feminist Theology: What Is It? Where Does It Lead?* San Francisco: Ignatius Press, 1995.

———. *Heilsverlust in Adam: Stationen griechischer Erbsündenlehre; Irenäus—Origenes—Kappadozier* [Salvation Lost in Adam: Stages of Greek Teaching on Original Sin; Irenaeus, Origen, the Cappadocians]. Paderborn: Bonifatius, 1993.

———. "Il sacerdozio femminile nel recente dibattito teologico" [The Priesthood of Women in Recent Theological Debate]. *RTLu* 1, no. 2 (1996): 257–81.

———. "The Immaculate Conception of Mary in the Greek Fathers and in an Ecumenical Context." *Chicago Studies* 45, no. 3 (2006): 327–46.

———. "Introduzione all'opera teologica e alla mariologia del cardinale Leo Scheffczyk" [Introduction to the Theological Work and the Mariology of Leo Cardinal Scheffczyk]. In Scheffczyk, *Maria, crocevia della fede cattolica*, CdM 1, 11–39.

———. "Jungfrau und Mutter: Geboren von der Jungfrau Maria" [Virgin and Mother: Born of the Virgin Mary]. In Stumpf, *Maria: Mutter der Kirche*, 43–70.

———. "Jungfrauen (Maria als Vorbild der Jungfrauen)" [Virgins (Mary as Model of Virgins)]. In *ML* 3:484–487.

———. "Kurzer Kommentar zu den Normen der Glaubenskongregation über die Beurteilung mutmaßlicher Erscheinungen und Privatoffenbarungen" [Brief Commentary on the CDF Norms on the Evaluation of Alleged Apparitions and Private Revelations]. *Sedes Sapientiae: Mariologisches Jahrbuch* 36, no. 2 (2012): 23–34.

———. "La Chiesa ha demonizzato il sesso e disprezzato la donna? La questione femminile e l'amore matrimoniale nel Codice da Vinci alla luce della fede Cattolica" [Has the Church Demonized Sex and Despised Woman? The Question of Woman and Matrimonial Love in "The Da Vinci Code" in Light of the Catholic Faith]. In *La frode del Codice da Vinci: Giochi di prestigio ai danni del Cristianesimo*, edited by Arturo Cattaneo, 121–50. Leumann (Turin): Elledici, 2006.

———. "La consacrazione alla Vergine Maria nella teologia tedesca del XX secolo." In

La Consacrazione alla Vergine Maria nel 50° della Consacrazione dell'Italia al Cuore Immacolato di Maria: Atti del Simposio Mariologico Internazionale sulla Consacrazione alla Vergine Maria, Frigento, 5–7 luglio 2010, 269–320. 2011. Original "Die Marienweihe in der deutschsprachigen Theologie (20. Jh.)" [Marian Consecration in German-Language Theology (20th Century)]. *Sedes Sapientiae: Mariologisches Jahrbuch* 14 (2–2010): 5–66.

———. "La cooperazione attiva di Maria alla Redenzione: Prospettiva storica (patristica, medievale, moderna, contemporanea)" [The Active Cooperation of Mary in the Redemption: Historical (Patristic, Medieval, Modern, Contemporary) Perspective]. In *Mary, "Unique Cooperator in the Redemption,"* 171–219. New Bedford, Mass.: Academy of the Immaculate, 2005. Also in *Immaculata Mediatrix* 6 (2006) 157–89.

———, ed. *La donna e la salvezza: Maria e la vocazione femminile* [Woman and Salvation: Mary and the Feminine Vocation]. CdM 7. Lugano: Eupress FTL, 2006.

———. "La mariologia di Leo Scheffczyk." *Scripta de Maria* 2nd ser., 8 (2011): 65–91.

———. "La mediazione materna di Maria secondo Papa Giovanni Paolo II" [Mary's Maternal Mediation according to Pope John Paul II]. *Maria Corredentrice* 7 (2005): 35–91. German original: "Die mütterliche Vermittlung." In Ziegenaus, ed., *Totus tuus*, 125–75.

———. "La questione del 'Primo principio' e l'indole della cooperazione di Maria all'opera redentrice di Cristo: Due temi rilevanti nella mariologia di Gabriele M. Roschini" [The Question of the "First Principle" and the Contribution of Mary to Christ's Work of Redemption: Two Relevant Themes in the Mariology of Roschini]. *Marianum* 64, no. 161–62 (2002): 569–97.

———. "La visione beatifica di Cristo durante la passione: La dottrina di san Tommaso d'Aquino e la teologia contemporanea" [The Beatific Vision of Christ during the Passion: The Doctrine of St. Thomas Aquinas and Contemporary Theology]. *Annales theologici* 21 (2007): 381–98.

———. "Maria als 'Mutter der Einheit' (Mater unitatis) als Beitrag zum authentischen interreligösen Dialog" [Mary as "Mother of Unity" as a Contribution to Authentic Inter-Religious Dialogue]. *Sedes Sapientiae: Mariologisches Jahrbuch* 15, no. 2 (2011): 8–26.

———. "Maria als mütterliche Mittlerin in Christus: Ein systematischer Durchblick." *Sedes Sapientiae: Mariologisches Jahrbuch* 12, no. 2 (2008): 13–53; English translation: "Mary's Motherly Mediation in Christ: A Systematic Reflection." *Nova et Vetera*, English edition 7, no. 4 (2009): 941–72.

———, ed. *Maria als Patronin Europas: Geschichtliche Besinnung und Vorschläge für die Zukunft* [Mary as Patroness of Europe: Historical Consciousness and Suggestions for the Future]. Mariologische Studien 20. Regensburg: Friedrich Pustet, 2009.

———. "Maria, 'compagna del Redentore': La cooperazione di Maria alla salvezza come pista di ricercar" [Mary, "Companion of the Redeemer": The Cooperation of Mary in Salvation as a Path of Research]. *RTLu* 7 (2002): 47–70. Reprinted as a monograph: Quaderni mariani 9. Frigento: Casa Mariana Editrice, 2002. Also in *Maria Corredentrice* 5 (2002), 225–60. (There are also versions in German, English, and Romanian.)

———. "Maria im modernen Feminismus" [Mary in Modern Feminism]. In Breid, *Maria in Leben und Lehre der Kirche*, 165–202.

———. "Maria in alexandrinischer und antiochenischer Denkform" [Mary in Alexandrian and Antiochian Forms of Thought]. In PAMI, *De cultu mariano saeculo XX*, 2:203–31.

———. "Maria, 'Mediatrice di tutte le Grazie' nell'Archivio Segreto Vaticano del Pontificato di Pio XI: Rapporto intermedio sulle tracce ritrovate" [Mary, "Mediatrix of All Graces." In the Secret Archive of the Pontificate of Pius XI: Intermediate Report on the Indications Found]. *Immaculata Mediatrix* 7 (2007): 118–29. German original: "Maria, 'Mittlerin aller Gnaden,' im Vatikanischen Geheimarchiv aus der Zeit Pius IX. Zwischenbericht einer Spurensicherung." *Theologisches* 36, no. 11–12 (2006): 381–92.

———. "Maria: Mutter Gottes oder domestizierte Göttin? Zum Marienbild der Feministischen Theologie" [Mary: Mother of God or Domesticated Goddess? The Image of Mary in Feminist Theology]. In PAMI, *De cultu mariano saeculo XX*, 4:429–58.

———. "Maria 'scettro della vera fede': L'Immacolata Concezione e la discussione sul peccato originale" [Mary, "Scepter of the True Faith": The Immaculate Conception and the Debate on Original Sin]. *RTLu* 8, no. 2 (2004): 315–39.

———, ed. *Maria und das Alte Testament*. Regensburg: Friedrich Pustet, 2015.

———. "Maria: Urbild und Fülle des Katholischen" [Mary: Archetype and Fullness of Catholicism]. In *Das eigentlich Katholische: Profil und Identität, Grenzen des Pluralismus,* edited by Walter Brandmüller, 205–28. Aachen: MM Verlag, 1997.

———. "Marienlehre und Marienfrömmigkeit bei den Heiligen der Väterzeit" [Marian Doctrine and Piety in the Saints of the Patristic Era]. *Sedes Sapientiae: Mariologisches Jahrbuch* 6, no. 1–2 (2002): 49–68.

———. "Mariologie und Frauenbild: Wachstumskräfte für einen neuen Aufbruch" [Mariology and the Image of Woman: Forces of Growth toward a New Starting Point]. In Ziegenaus, *Das Marianische Zeitalter: Entstehung—Gehalt—bleibende Bedeutung*, 229–54.

———. *Mary, "Mediatress of Grace": Mary's Universal Mediation of Grace in the Theological and Pastoral Works of Cardinal Mercier.* New Bedford, Mass.: Academy of the Immaculate, 2004. Italian version: *Maria, "Mediatrice di tutte le grazie": La mediazione universale di Maria nell'opera teologica e pastorale del Cardinale Mercier.* Collana di Mariologia, 6. Lugano: Eupress FTL, 2005. German original: *Maria, "Mittlerin aller Gnaden": Die universale Gnadenmittlerschaft Mariens im theologischen und seelsorglichen Schaffen von Kardinal Mercier.* Mariologische Studien 17. Regensburg: Friedrich Pustet, 2004.

———. "Matthias Joseph Scheeben (†1888) nella mariologia tedesca del XIX secolo" [Scheeben in the German Mariology of the 19th Century]. In Boaga and Gambero, *Storia della mariologia*, 2:696–714.

———. "Merkelbach, Benoît Henri." In *Thomistenlexikon*, edited by David Berger and Jörgen Vijgen, 58–463. Bonn: Nova et Vetera, 2006.

———. "The Mother of God." In Miravelle, *Mariology: A Guide*, 167–212.

———. "Opfer" [Victim]. In Bäumer and Scheffczyk, *ML* 4:695–97.

———. "Pontificia Accademia Mariana Internationalis, La Madre del Signore. Memoria Presenza Speranza" (review). *RTLu* 9, no. 2 (2004): 500–504.

———. "Priestertum I. Dogmatik" [Priesthood: I. Dogmatic Theology]. In Bäumer and Scheffczyk, *ML* 5:314–17.

———. "Psychotrip, Teufelsspuk oder Werk des Heiligen Geistes? Die Ereignisse von Medjugorje in neueren Veröffentlichungen" [Psycho-Trip, Devilish Ghost, or Work of the Holy Spirit? The Events of Medjugorje in New Publications]. *Theologisches* 35, no. 9 (2005): 613–22; first published in *Sedes Sapientiae: Mariologisches Jahrbuch* 9, no. 1 (2005): 159–74.

———. "Sakramente I. Kath. Theologie." In Bäumer and Scheffczyk, *ML* 5:632–35.

———. "Solidarität Mariens mit der Menschheit" [Mary's Solidarity with Humanity]. In Bäumer and Scheffczyk, *ML* 6:198f.

———. "Totus tuus—Theologische Grundlagen der Marienweihe" [Totally Yours: Theological Bases of Marian Consecration]. In *Im Dienste der Inkarnierten Wahrheit: Festschrift zum 25jährigen Pontifikat Seiner Heiligkeit Papst Johannes Pauls II*, edited by Albrecht von Brandenstein-Zeppelin, Alma von Stockhausen, Lothar Roos, and J. Hans Benirschke, 127–48. Weilheim-Bierbronnen: Gustav-Siewerth-Akademie, 2003.

———. *Urstand, Fall und Erbsünde: In der nachaugustinischen Ära bis zum Beginn der Scholastik; Die griechische Theologie* (*Handbuch der Dogmengeschichte*, Vol. 2, Fascicle 3a, Part 2). [Original State, Fall, and Original Sin: Greek Theology in the Post-Augustinian Era to the Beginning of Scholasticism]. Freiburg im Breisgau: Herder, 2007.

Hechich, Barnaba. "La teologia dell'Immacolata Concezione in alcuni autori prescolastici" [The Theology of the Immaculate Conception in Several Pre-Scholastic Authors]. In Cecchin, *La "Scuola Francescana,"* 141–58.

Heid, S. "Epiphanius von Salamis." In Bäumer and Scheffczyk, *ML* 2:375f.

Heine, Susanne. *Wiederbelebung der Göttinnen? Zur systematischen Kritik einer feministischen Theologie* [Revival of the Goddesses? Toward a Systematic Critique of a Feminist Theology]. Göttingen: Vandenhoeck and Ruprecht, 1987.

Hennaux, Jean-Marie. "Le Document du Groupe des Dombes sur la Vierge Marie" [The Dombes Group Document on the Virgin Mary]. *Nouvelle Revue Théologique* 121, no. 1 (1999): 41–58.

Hiemer, Alfons. *Der Rosenkranz, das wunderbare Gebet* [The Rosary, the Wonderful Prayer]. St. Ottilien: EOS Verlag, 1979.

Hierzenberger, Gottfried, and Otto Nedomansky. *Dizionario cronologico delle apparizioni della Madonna* [Chronological Dictionary of Marian Apparitions]. Casale Monferrato: Piemme, 2004. See also *Tutte le apparizioni della Madonna in 2000 anni di storia.* Casale Monferrato: Piemme, 1996. German original: *Erscheinungen und Botschaften der Gottesmutter Maria: Vollständige Dokumentation durch zwei Jahrtausende.* Augsburg: Pattloch, 1993.

Hilion, Gustave. "La Sainte Vierge dans le Nouveau Testament" [The Holy Virgin in the New Testament]. In du Manoir, *Maria*, 1:43–68. 1949.

Hoeck, Johannes M. "Stand und Aufgaben der Damaskenosforschung" [Status and Tasks of Research on St. John of Damascus]. *Orientalia Christiana Periodica* 17 (1951): 5–60.

Hoffmann, Tobias. "Duns Scotus: Die Unbefleckte Empfängnis Mariens" [Duns Scotus: The Immaculate Conception of Mary]. In *Im Ringen um die Wahrheit*, edited by Remigius Bäumer, 711–34. Weilheim-Bierbronnen: Gustav-Siewerth-Akad., 1997.

Hofrichter, Peter. "Hochzeit zu Kana" [Wedding at Cana]. In Bäumer and Scheffczyk, *ML* 3:218f.

———. "Jungfräulichkeit I.4" [Jn]. [Virginity: Jn 1:4]. In Bäumer and Scheffczyk, *ML* 3:468f.

———. *Nicht aus Blut, sondern monogen aus Gott geboren: Textkritische, dogmengeschichtliche und exegetische Untersuchung zu Joh 1,13–14* [Born Not of Blood, but Only-Begotten of God: Text-Critical, Dogmatic-Historical, and Exegetical Investigation on Jn 1:13–14]. Würzburg: Echter, 1978.

Holböck, Ferdinand. *Das Allerheiligste und die Heiligen* [The Most Holy and the Saints]. 2nd ed. Stein am Rhein, Switzerland: Christiana-Verlag, 1986.

———. *Geführt von Maria: Marianische Heilige aus allen Jahrhunderten der Kirchengeschichte* [Led by Mary: Marian Saints from All Centuries of Church History]. Stein am Rhein (Switzerland): Christiana-Verlag, 1987.

———. *"Wir haben den Messias gefunden": Die selige Edith Stein und andere jüdische Konvertiten vor und nach ihr* ["We Have Found the Messiah": Blessed Edith Stein and Other Jewish Converts Before and After Her]. 2nd ed. Stein am Rhein (Switzerland): Christiana-Verlag, 1987.

Holstein, Henri, SJ. "Les apparitions mariales" [Marian Apparitions]. In du Manoir, *Maria*, 5:755–90. 1958.

———. "Le développement du Dogme Marial" [The Development of Marian Dogma]. In du Manoir, *Maria*, 6:241–93. 1961.

Horst, Ulrich. *Die Diskussion um die Immaculata Conceptio im Dominikanerorden* [The Debate on the Immaculate Conception in the Dominican Order]. Paderborn: F. Schöningh. 1987.

———. "Die Theologie des Dominikanerordens, illustriert an den Kontroversen um die Immaculata Conceptio" [The Theology of the Dominican Order, Illustrated by the Controversy over the Immaculate Conception]. *RTLu* 5, no. 2 (2000): 301–8.

Hünermann, Peter. *Jesus Christus: Gottes Wort in der Zeit* [Jesus Christ: God's Word in Time]. Münster: Aschendorff, 1994.

Huhn, J. "Ambrosius von Mailand" [Ambrose of Milan]. In Bäumer and Scheffczyk, *ML* 1:126–29.

Hurley, M. "Born Incorruptly: The Third Canon of the Lateran Council (A.D. 649)." *Heythrop Journal* 2 (1961): 217–36.

Ibáñez, J. "María, Madre-Sacerdote" [Mary, Mother-Priest]. *Scripta de Maria* 2nd ser., 10 (2013): 167–200.

Ibáñez, J., and F. Mendoza. "La Santísima Virgen en el Catecismo Romano y en el Nuevo Catecismo de la Iglesia Católica" [The Most Holy Virgin in the Roman Catechism and in the New Catechism of the Catholic Church]. *Estudios Marianos* 59 (1994): 213–28.

Ionascu, I. "L'assunzione nell'Oriente ortodosso" [The Assumption in the Orthodox Church]. In Calvo Moralejo and Cecchin, *L'Assunzione di Maria*, 439–44.

Ignatius of Antioch. *In Eph.* In *Die Apostolischen Väter*, 7th ed. Edited by J. A. Fischer. Darmstadt: Wissenschaftliche Buchgesellschaft, 1976.

Irenaeus. "The Demonstration of the Apostolic Preaching." Translated by J. Armitage Robinson. In Iain MacKenzie, *Irenaeus's Demonstration of the Apostolic Preaching: A Theological Commentary and Translation*, 11. Burlington, Vt.: Ashgate, 2002.

Jerome. "On the Perpetual Virginity of the Blessed Mary against Helvidius." In St. Jerome, *Dogmatic and Polemical Works*. Fathers of the Church 53. Translated by John N. Hritzu. Washington, D.C.: The Catholic University of America Press, 1965. Italian trans.: Girolamo, *La perenne verginità di Maria: Contro Elvidio* [Jerome: The Perpetual Virginity of Mary]. Edited by Maria Ignazia Danieli. Collana di testi patristici 70. Rome: Città nuova, 1988.

Joannou, Perikles-Petros. *Discipline générale antique*, vol. 1, part 2, 377f. Rome: S. Nilo, 1962.

John XXIII. Encyclical *Pacem in terris*. April 11, 1963.

John Paul II. Apostolic Exhortation *Redemptoris Custos* (*RC*). August 15, 1989.

———. Apostolic Letter *A Concilio Constantinopolitano I* (March 25, 1981).

———. Apostolic Letter *Mulieris Dignitate* (*MD*). August 15, 1988.

———. Apostolic Letter *Rosarium Virginis Mariae* (*RVM*). October 16, 2002.

———. Common Christological Declaration of the Catholic Church and the Assyrian Church of the East, Nov. 11, 1994. In *Insegnamenti di Giovanni Paolo II*, vol. 17, part 2. Vatican City: Libreria Editrice Vaticana, 1996. 745.

———. Encyclical *Redemptoris Mater* (*RM*). March 25, 1987. Also available in *Mother of the Redeemer*. Anniversary ed. Boston: Pauline Books and Media, 2012.

———. General audience, "Le definizioni cristologiche dei concili e la fede della Chiesa oggi." April 13, 1988. In *Insegnamenti di Giovanni Paolo II*, vol. 11, part 1. Vatican City: Libreria Editrice Vaticana, 1989, 878f.

———. *Maria Madre di Cristo e della Chiesa: Catechesi mariane* [Mary Mother of Christ and of the Church: Marian Catechesis], edited by Vincenzo Fagiolo. Casale Monferrato: Piemme, 1998.

———. Homily at Ephesus, Nov. 30, 1979. In *Insegnamenti di Giovanni Paolo II*, vol. 2, part 2, 1287–92. Vatican City, Libreria Editrice Vaticana, 1980.

———. Marian Catecheses (Catechesi Mariane) (CM). Seventy talks given at general audiences from 1995 to 1997. Published (among other places) in John Paul II, *Theotokos: Woman, Mother, Disciple: A Catechesis on Mary, Mother of God*. Boston: Pauline, 2000.

Johnson, Elizabeth A. *Truly Our Sister: A Theology of Mary in the Communion of Saints*. New York and London: Continuum, 2003. Italian translation: *Vera nostra sorella: Teologia di Maria nella comunione dei santi* [GdT 313]. Brescia: Queriniana, 2005.

Johnston, Francis W. *The Wonder of Guadalupe: The Origin and Cult of the Miraculous Image of the Blessed Virgin in Mexico*. Chulmleigh, UK: Augustine, 1981. Reprint: Charlotte, N.C.: TAN, 2011.

Jouassard, George. "L'interprétation par saint Cyrille d'Alexandrie de la scène de Marie au pied de la croix" [St. Cyril of Alexandria's Interpretation of the Scene of Mary at the Foot of the Cross]. In *De immaculata conceptione apud SS: Patres et scriptores orientales*, edited by AMI. Virgo Immaculata 4, 28–47. Rome: AMI, 1956.

Journet, Charles. *Maria Corredentrice* [Mary Coredemptrix]. Milan: Ares, 1989. French original: *Mater dolorosa: Notre Dame des Sept douleurs.* Stein am Rhein (CH): Christiana-Verlag, 1974.

Jugie, Martin. "Assomption de la sainte Vierge." In du Manoir, *Maria*, 1:619–58. 1949.

———. *L'Immaculée Conception dans l'Écriture Sainte et dans la Tradition Orientale* [The Immaculate Conception in Holy Scripture and in Eastern Tradition]. Rome: Academia Mariana, 1952.

———. *La mort et l'assomption de la Sainte Vierge: Étude historico-doctrinale* [The Death and Assumption of the Holy Virgin: Historical-Doctrinal Study]. Vatican City: Biblioteca Apostolica Vaticana, 1944.

Kallinikos, K. B. "Koimesis." In Bäumer and Scheffczyk, *ML* 3:598f.

Kallis, Anastasios. *Liturgie: Die Göttliche Liturgie der Orthodoxen Kirche; Deutsch—Griechisch—Kirchenslawisch* [Liturgy: The Divine Liturgy of the Orthodox Church; German-Greek-Church Slavonic]. 3rd ed. Mainz: Matthias-Grünewald-Verlag, 1997.

Kammer, Carl. *Die Lauretanische Litanei* [The Litany of Loreto]. Innsbruck: Rauch, 1960.

Kappes, Christiaan. *The Immaculate Conception: Why Thomas Aquinas Denied, While John Duns Scotus, Gregory Palamas, and Mark Eugenicus Professed the Absolute Immaculate Existence of Mary.* New Bedford, Mass.: Academy of the Immaculate, 2014.

Keller, A. "Über die Bedeutung der Apokryphen und der Transituslegenden" [On the Meaning of the Apocrypha and the Transitus Legends]. In *Volksfrömmigkeit und Theologie*, edited by A. Ziegenaus, 57–73. Regensburg: Friedrich Pustet, 1998.

Kijas, Z. J. "L'apostolo dell'Immacolata: Massimiliano Kolbe" [Apostle of the Immaculate: Maxmilian Kolbe]. In *La "Scuola Francescana,"* edited by S. Cecchin, 561–84. Vatican City: PAMI, 2005.

Kilian, R. "Die Geburt des Immanuel aus der Jungfrau: Jes 7,14" [The Birth of Emmanuel from the Virgin: Is. 7:14]. In *Zum Thema Jungfrauengeburt* [On the Topic of the Virgin Birth], edited by Karl Suso Frank. Stuttgart: Verlag Katholisches Bibelwerk, 1970.

Klersy, M. D. "Sterbeliturgie" [Liturgy of the Dying]. In Bäumer and Scheffczyk, *ML* 6:298.

Klinkhammer, Karl Joseph. "Adolf von Essen." In Bäumer and Scheffczyk, *ML* 1:34–39.

———. *Adolf von Essen und seine Werke: Der Rosenkranz in der geschichtlichen Situation seiner Entstehung und in seinem bleibenden Anliegen* [Adolf von Essen and His Works: The Rosary in the Historical Situation of Its Development and Its Enduring Appeal]. Frankfurt: J. Knecht, 1972.

———. *Ein wunderbares Beten: So entstand der Rosenkranz* [A Wonderful Prayer: How the Rosary Came to Be]. 2nd ed. Leutesdorf: Johannes-Verlag, 1981.

Klos, P. "The Specific Message of the Lady of All Nations Regarding the Fifth Marian Dogma." In Miravalle, *Mary Coredemptrix*, 3:225–34.

Knoch, O., and F. Mussner. "Maria in der Heiligen Schrift" [Mary in Sacred Scripture]. In Beinert and Petri, *Handbuch der Marienkunde*, 1:15–98.

Kochaniewicz, Bogusław. "L'Assunzione di Maria in cielo nella riflessione teologica dei domenicani del XIII secolo" [The Assumption of Mary into Heaven in the Theological Reflection of 13th-Century Dominicans]. In Calvo Moralejo and Cecchin, *L'Assunzione di Maria*, 529–83.

———. "La via mariana polacca e la mariologia di Giovanni Paolo II" [The Polish Marian Way and the Mariology of John Paul II]. In *La Vergine Maria nel magistero di Giovanni Paolo II*, edited by Teofil Siudy, 1–36. Vatican City: PAMI, 2007.

———. "L'Immacolata Concezione e la dottrina di san Tommaso d'Aquino" [The Immaculate Conception and the Doctrine of St. Thomas Aquinas]. In Cecchin, *La "Scuola Francescana,"* 87–140.

———. "Origine e storia del Rosario" [Origin and history of the Rosary]. In Cecchin, *Contemplare Cristo con Maria*, 1–60.

Koehler, Théodore, SM. "Mary, Mother and 'Mediatrix' in the Post-Vatican II Liturgy." In PAMI, *De cultu mariano saeculo XX*, 2:1–24.

———. "Mary's Spiritual Maternity after the Second Vatican Council." *Marian Studies* 23 (1972): 39–68.

———. "Maternité spirituelle de Marie" [Spiritual Motherhood of Mary]. In du Manoir, *Maria*, 1:575–600.

———. "Maternité spirituelle, maternité mystique" [Spiritual Motherhood, Mystical Motherhood]. In du Manoir, *Maria*, 6:551–639. 1961.

———. "Storia della mariologia" [History of Mariology]. In De Fiores and Meo, *NDM*, 1385–1405.

Köster, Heinrich M. "De Maria nunquam satis: Wer fand, was bedeutet diese Formel?" ["De Maria nunquam satis": Origin and Meaning of the Formula]. *Marian Library Studies* 17–23 (1987–91): 617–32.

———. "Der Beitrag Eadmers OSB 1060/64–1141 zur theologischen Erkenntnis der Unbefleckten Empfängnis" [The Contribution of Eadmer, OSB to the Theological Recognition of the Immaculate Conception]. In Rovira, *Im Gewande des Heils*, 61–70.

———. "Die Jungfrauengeburt als theologisches Problem seit D. F. Strauß" [The Virgin Birth as a Theological Problem since D. F. Strauss." In Brosch and Hasenfuss, *Jungfrauengeburt gestern und heute*, 35–87.

———. *Die Magd des Herrn* [The Handmaid of the Lord]. Limburg: Lahn-Verlag 1947; 2nd ed., 1954.

———. "Herz Mariä I. Verehrung" [Heart of Mary. I. Devotion]. In Bäumer and Scheffczyk, *ML* 3:163f.

Kolbe, Maximilian. *Scritti* [Writings], new ed. Translated by Cristoforo Zambelli. Rome: Assoc. Rel. Centro Nazionale Milizia dell'Immacolata, 1997.

Kreuzer, Michael. "Maria und die Gemeinsame Erklärung zur Rechtfertigungslehre" [Mary and the Common Declaration on the Doctrine of Justification]. *Forum Katholische Theologie* 17 (2001): 47–58.

———. *"Und das Wort ist Fleisch geworden": Zur Bedeutung des Menschseins Jesu bei Johannes Driedo und Martin Luther* ["And the Word Became Flesh": The Meaning of the Humanity of Jesus in Johannes Driedo and Martin Luther]. Paderborn: Bonifacius, 1998.

Krolikowski, J. "Consacrazione e affidamento a Maria nell'esperienza e nella teologia di papa Giovanni Paolo II" [Consecration and Entrustment to Mary in the Experience and the Theology of Pope John Paul II]. In Siudy, *La Vergine Maria nel magistero di Giovanni Paolo II*, 179–201.

Küppers, K. "Mai" [May]. In Bäumer and Scheffczyk, *ML* 4:242f.

Küppers, K., and H. Rzepkowski. "Maiandacht" [May Devotion]. In Bäumer and Scheffczyk, *ML* 4:244–48.

Kugelman, Richard, CP. "El santo nombre de María." In Carol, *Mariología*, 386–98. English original: "The Holy Name of Mary." In Carol, *Mariology*, 1:411–24.

Laconi, M. "Maria nel Nuovo Testamento." In *EMTheo* (1954): 33–47; (1958): 30–43.

Lacouture, Daniel. *Marie Médiatrice de toutes graces* [Mary, Mediatrix of All Graces]. Nouan le Fuzelier: Ed. des Béatitudes, 1995.

Lais, H. "Erscheinungen" [Apparitions]. In Bäumer and Scheffczyk, *ML* 2:395–98.

Lamy, Marielle. "Immacolata." In De Fiores, Schiefer, and Perrella, *DMar*, 612–28.

———. *L'Immaculée Conception: Étapes et enjeux d'une controverse au Moyen-âge (XIIe–XVe siècles)* [The Immaculate Conception: Stages and Stakes in a Medieval Controversy (13th–14th Centuries)]. Paris: Institut d'Études Augustiniennes, 2000.

Langella, Alfonso. "Bellezza" [Beauty]. In De Fiores, Schiefer, and Perrella, *DMar*, 190–99.

———. "La figura de Maria nel XIV secolo (con bibliografia)" [The Figure of Mary in the 14th Century (with Bibliography)]. *Theotokos* 20, no. 1 (2012): 7–32.

———. "La recezione critica del Documento di Dombes. Valori e limiti." *Marianum* 62 (2000): 319–45.

———. "Maria nella teologia del XIII secolo (con bibliografia)" [Mary in Theology of the 13th Century (with Bibliography)]. *Theotokos* 19, no. 1 (2001): 3–48.

———, ed. *Via pulchritudinis et Mariologia* [The Way of Beauty and Mariology]. Rome: AMII, 2003.

Lanzetta, Serafino M. *Il sacerdozio di Maria nella teologia cattolica del XX secolo: Analisi storico-teologica* [The Priesthood of Mary in 20th-Century Catholic Theology: Historical-Theological Analysis]. Rome: Pontificia Universitas Sanctae Crucis; Frigento: Casa Mariana Editrice, 2006.

———. *Il Vaticano II, un Concilio pastorale: Ermeneutica delle dottrine conciliari*. Siena: Cantagalli, 2014. English translation: *Vatican II, A Pastoral Council: Hermeneutics of Council Teaching*. Leominster, UK: Gracewing, 2016.

Larocca, Antonio. "Las apariciones marianas en Betania (Cúa, Venezuela)" [Marian Apparitions in Betania (Cúa, Venezuela)]. *Ephemerides Mariologicae* 58, no. 4 (2008): 509–16.

Laurentin, René. "Apparizioni." In De Fiores and Meo, *NDM*, 125–37.

———. "Die Marienerscheinungen: Ihre Bedeutung, ihr Wert, ihre wesentliche Botschaft" [Marian Apparitions: Meaning, Value, and Relevant Message]. In Breid, *Maria in Leben und Lehre der Kirche*, 9–31.

———. *The Hail Mary: Its Meaning and Origin*. Milford, Ohio: Faith, 1991. Italian translation: *L'Ave Maria*. Brescia: Queriniana, 1990. French original: *Je vous salue Marie*. Paris: Desclée de Brouwer, 1989.

———. *I Vangeli dell'infanzia di Cristo* [The Gospels of the Infancy of Christ]. Turin: Paoline, 1985. French original: *Les Évangiles de l'Enfance du Christ: Vérité de Noël au-delà des mythes; Exégèse et sémiotique, historicité et théologie.* 2nd ed. Tournai-Paris: Desclée de Brouwer, 1982.

———. *La Madonna del Vaticano II: Storia, esegesi e testo del capitolo ottavo della costituzione "De Ecclesia."* Bergamo: Priorato di Sant'Egidio, 1965. French original: *La Vierge au concile* [The Virgin at the Council]. Paris: P. Lethielleux, 1965.

———. *Le apparizioni della Vergine e i più grandi miracoli della Madonna* [Apparitions of the Virgin and the Madonna's Greatest Miracles]. Casale Monferrato: Piemme, 2001. French original: *Multiplication des apparitions de la Vierge aujourd'hui: Est-ce elle? Que veut-elle dire?* 5th ed. Paris: Fayard, 1995.

———. *Le apparizioni della Vergine si moltiplicano: e lei? Cosa vuol dirci?* [The Apparitions of the Virgin Multiply: What Does She Want to Say?] Casale Monferrato: Piemme, 1989. French original: *Multiplication des apparitions de la Vierge aujourd'hui: Est-ce elle? Que veut-elle dire?* Paris: Fayard, 1988.

———. "Le mystère de la naissance verginale" [The Mystery of the Virgin Birth]. *Ephemerides Mariologicae* 10 (1960): 345–74.

———. *Le titre de Corédemptrice: Étude historique* [The Title of Coredemptrix: Historical Study]. *Marianum* 13 (1951): 396–452.

———. "L'interprétation de Genèse 3,15 dans la tradition jusqu'au début du XIII siècle" [The Interpretation of Gen 3:15 in Tradition, up to the Beginning of the 13th Century]. *Études Mariales* 12 (1954): 79–156.

———. *A Short Treatise on the Virgin Mary.* Washington, N.J.: Ave Maria Institute, 1991. Original *Court traité sur la Vierge Marie.* 5th ed. Paris: P. Lethielleux, 1988. Italian translation: *Breve trattato su la Vergine Maria.* Cinisello Balsamo: Paoline, 1987.

———. *Marie, clé du mystère chrétien* [Mary, Key of the Christian Mystery]. Paris: Fayard, 1994. Italian translation: *Maria chiave del mistero Cristiano.* Cinisello Balsamo: Ed. Paoline, 1996.

———. *Marie Deluil-Martiny: Précurseur et martyre béatifiée par Jean Paul II* [Marie Deluil-Martiny: Precursor and Martyr Beatified by John Paul II]. Paris: Fayard, 2003.

———. *Marie, l'Église et le Sacerdoce* [Mary, the Church, and the Priesthood], I–II. Paris: Nouvelles éditions latines, 1952–53.

———. "Nuova Eva I. Il cammino storico del parallelismo Eva-Maria" [New Eve. I. The Historical Trail of the Eve-Mary Parallelism]. In De Fiores and Meo, *NDM*, 1017–21.

———. *Structure et théologie de Luc I-II* [Structure and Theology of Luke 1–2]. Paris: Gabalda, 1957.

Laurentin, René, and Patrick Sbalchiero, eds. *Dictionnaire des "apparitions" de la Vierge Marie* [Dictionary of Apparitions of the Virgin Mary]. Paris: Fayard, 2007.

Lavatori, Renzo. *Gli angeli: Storia e pensiero* [The Angels: History and Thought]. Genoa: Marietta, 1991.

Layh, Wolfgang. "Luthers Verständnis von Maria anhand seiner Magnificatauslegung von 1521" [Luther's Understanding of Mary, Based on His 1521 Exposition of the Magnificat]. *Ephemerides Mariologicae* 50, no. 1–2 (2000): 107–40.

Le Bachelet, Xavier-Marie, SJ, and Martin Jugie. "Immaculée Conception." In *DThC*, 7:845–1218. 1927.

Lefebvre, Philippe. *La Vierge au Livre: Marie et l'Ancien Testament* [The Virgin of the Book: Mary and the Old Testament]. Paris: Les Éditions du Cerf, 2004.

Lemmo, Nunzio. "Maria, 'Figlia di Sion,' a partire da Lc 1,26–38: Bilancio esegetico dal 1939 al 1982" [Mary, "Daughter of Zion," Starting from Lk 1:26–38: Exegetical Assessment from 1939 to 1982]. *Marianum* 45, no. 130 (1983): 175–258.

Lennerz, Heinrich. *De beata Virgine.* 2nd ed. Rome: Pontificia Univ. Gregoriana, 1935.

Lépicier, Aléxis-Henri-Marie. *L'Immaculée Mère de Dieu, corédemptrice du genre humain* [The Immaculate Mother of God, Coredemptrix of the Human Race]. Turnhout: Imprimerie de l'Ecole Professionnelle, 1906.

Le Tourneau Barbé, Dominique. "Maria, 'mujer eucaristica'" [Mary, "Eucharistic Mother"]. *Scripta de Maria* 2nd ser., no. 9 (2012): 67–97.

Levering, Matthew. *Mary's Bodily Assumption.* Notre Dame, Ind.: University of Notre Dame Press, 2015.

Liccardo, Giovani, Franco Ruotolo, and Sergio Tanzarella, eds. *Atti del Convegno Internazionale di studi Mariologico, Capua 19–24 Maggio 1992* [Acts of the International Mariological Study Meeting, Capua, May 19–24, 1992]. 2 vols. Torre del Greco (Naples): Istituto Superiore di Scienza Religiose, 1993.

Llamas, Enrique. "El matrimonio de José y María, y su predestinación" [The Marriage of Joseph and Mary and Its Predestination]. In *Die Bedeutung des hl. Josef in der Heilsgeschichte*, edited by Johannes Hattler and German Rovira, 1:143–60. Kisslegg: Fe-Medienverlag, 2006.

———. "Il Concilio de Trento e la mariologia spagnola nel XVI e XVII secolo" [The Council of Trent and Spanish Mariology in the 16th and 17th Centuries]. In Boaga and Gambero, *Storia della mariologia*, 2:275–321.

———, ed. *Las apariciones marianas en la vida de la iglesia* [Marian Apparitions in the Life of the Church]. *Estudios Marianos* 52. Salamanca: Sociedad Mariológica Española, 1987.

Lochbrunner, M. "Gregor der Wundertäter" [Gregory the Wonderworker]. In Bäumer and Scheffczyk, *ML* 3:19–21.

———. "Modestus von Jerusalem." In Bäumer and Scheffczyk, *ML* 4:495f.

Lohrum, M. "Dominikus" [Dominic]. In Bäumer and Scheffczyk, *ML* 2, 210.

Lombardi, Rosa. *Maria icona della Trinità* [Mary, Icon of the Trinity]. Rome: Edizioni Pro sanctitate, 2003.

Longenecker, Dwight, and David Gustafson. *Mary: A Catholic-Evangelical Debate.* Grand Rapids, Mich.: Brazos Press, 2003.

Loor Alarcon, Juan Carlos. *La cooperazione di Maria alla Redenzione, focalizzata nell'Annunciazione* [Mary's Cooperation in the Redemption, Focused on the Annunciation]. CdM 12. Lugano: Eupress FTL, 2014.

Losano Barragan, Javier. "La figura de María en la teología de la liberación" [The Figure of Mary in Liberation Theology]. *Ephemerides Mariologicae* 42, no. 3–4 (1992): 317–41.

Lutherans and Catholics in Dialogue. *The One Mediator, the Saints, and Mary*, nn. 3083–60. Minneapolis: Augsburg, 1992.

Luz, Ulrich. *Das Evangelium nach Matthäus (Mt 26–28)* [The Gospel according to Matthew (Mt 26–28)]. Evangelisch-katholischer Kommentar zum Neuen Testament I/4. Düsseldorf: Benziger-Neukirchener, 2002.

Lyonnet, Stanislas, SJ. "Chaíre, Kecharitoméne" [Hail, Full of Grace]. *Biblica* 20, no. 2 (1939): 131–41.

Maas-Ewerd, T. "Memorare." In Bäumer and Scheffczyk, *ML* 4:411.

———. "Sub tuum praesidium" [Under Your Protection]. In Bäumer and Scheffczyk, *ML* 6:327f.

Maccagnan, Valerio. "Guadalupe." In De Fiores and Meo, *NDM*, 655–69.

———. *Guadalupe—Evangelio y cultura* [Guadalupe, Gospel and Culture]. Guadalajara: Centro Mariano OSM, 2001.

Macquarrie, John. "Mary Coredemptrix and Disputes Over Justification and Grace: An Anglican View." In Miravalle, *Mary Coredemptrix*, 2:245–56. Also in Miravalle, *Mary Co-redemptrix: Doctrinal Issues Today*, 139–50.

———. *Mary for all Christians.* Grand Rapids: Eerdmans, 1990; London: T. and T. Clark, 1991; 2nd ed., 2001.

Madey, J. "Sakramente II. Liturgie-Ost" [Sacraments. II. Liturgy, East]. In Bäumer and Scheffczyk, *ML* 5:635–37.

Maffeis, Angelo. *Dossier sulla giustificazione: La Dichiarazione congiunta cattolico-luterana, commento e dibattito teologico* [Dossier on Justification. The Joint Catholic-Lutheran Declaration, Commentary and Theological Debate]. Brescia: Queriniana, 2000.

Maggiani, Silvano M., OSM. "Angelus." In De Fiores and Meo, *NDM*, 25–39.

———. "Culto." In De Fiores, Schiefer, and Perrella, *DMar*, 356–70.

Maggiolini, Sandro, ed. *Profezia della donna: Lettera apostolica "Mulieris dignitatem": Testo e commenti* [Prophecy of the Woman: Apostolic Letter "Mulieris dignitatem": Text and Commentary]. Rome: Città Nuova, 1988.

Maggioni, C. "Liturgia." In De Fiores, Schiefer, and Perrella, *DMar*, 726–37.

———. "Mese mariano" [Marian Month]. In De Fiores, Schiefer, and Perrella, *DMar*, 836–44.

Malek, Paweł. *La regalità di Maria nelle odierne celebrazioni eucharistiche: Analisi dogmatico-liturgica degli appropriati formulari liturgici del Rito romano* [The Queenship of Mary in Present-Day Eucharistic Celebrations: Dogmatic-Liturgical Analysis of the Proper Liturgical Formularies of the Roman Rite]. CdM 13. Lugano and Gavirate (Varese): Eupress FTL, 2015.

Malloy, Christopher J. *Engrafted into Christ: A Critique of the Joint Declaration.* New York: Peter Lang, 2005.

———. "Marian Coredemption and the Joint Declaration on the Doctrine of Justification." In *Mary at the Foot of the Cross.* Vol. 8, *Coredemption as Key to a Correct Understanding of Redemption*, 351–409. 2008.

Malnati, Ettore. *Maria nella fede della Chiesa* [Mary in the Faith of the Church]. Casale Monferrato: Piemme, 2001.

Manelli, Settimio M. "E una spada trapasserà anche la tua stessa anima" (Lc 2,35): Esegesi del versetto e il suo sviluppo dottrinale in riferimento alla cooperazione di Maria all'opera salvifica di Gesù ["And a Sword Will Also Pierce Your Soul"

(Lk 2:35): Exegesis of the Verse and Its Doctrinal Development in Reference to Mary's Cooperation with the Salvific Work of God]. *Maria Corredentrice* 6 (2003). 303 pp.

———. "Gen 3,15 e l'Immacolata Corredentrice" [Gen 3:15 and the Immaculate Coredemptrix]. *Immaculata Mediatrix* 5 (2005): 17–63.

Manelli, Stefano M., FI. *All Generations Shall Call Me Blessed: Biblical Mariology*. 2nd ed. New Bedford, Mass.: Academy of the Immaculate, 2005. Original: *Mariologia biblica*. 2nd ed. Frigento: Casa Mariana Editrice, 2005.

———. "Fatima tra passato, presente e futuro" [Fatima between Past, Present, and Future]. *Immaculata Mediatrix* 7 (2007): 299–431.

———. "La Mariologia nella storia della salvezza" [Mariology in Salvation History]. *Immaculata Mediatrix* 2 (2002): 43–78, 139–76, 285–322; 3 (2003): 19–57; 6 (2006): 17–62; 7 (2007): 13–62.

———. "Maria Corredentrice nella Sacra Scrittura" [Mary Coredemptrix in Sacred Scripture]. In *Maria Corredentrice: Storia e teologia* 1:37–114. Frigento: Casa Mariana Editrice, 1998.

Mangan, C. M. "The Spiritual Maternity of the Blessed Virgin Mary." In Miravalle, *Mariology: A Guide*, 507–50.

Manicardi, Ermenegildo. "La madre di Gesù nel Vangelo secondo Marco" [The Mother of Jesus in the Gospel according to Mark]. *Theotokos* 8, no. 2 (2000): 691–707.

Manicardi, L. "Il Salmo 45 (44) e il Cantico dei Cantici" [Psalm 45 (44) and the Song of Songs]. *Theotokos* 8, no. 2 (2000): 569–600.

Manns, Frédéric. "Esegesi di Gv 19,25–27" [Exegesis of Jn 19:25–27]. *Theotokos* 7, no. 2 (1999): 325–38.

———. *Le récit de la Dormition de Marie (Vatican grec 1982): Contribution à l'étude des origines de l'exégèse chrétienne* [The Narrative of the Dormition of Mary (Vatican, Greek, 1982): Contribution to the Study of the Origins of Christian Exegesis]. Jerusalem: Franciscan Printing Press, 1989.

———. "Scoperte archeologiche e tradizioni antiche sulla Dormizione e Assunzione di Maria" [Archeological Discoveries and Ancient Traditions on the Dormition and Assumption of Mary]. In Moralejo and Cecchin, *L'Assunzione di Maria*, 169–82.

Mansi, J. D. *Sacrorum conciliorum nova et amplissima collectio* (Mansi). 53 vols. Florence and Venice, 1759–1827. Reprint and continuation. 60 vols. Paris: Welter, 1899–1927.

Manzi, Franco. "Credente" [Believer]. In De Fiores, Schiefer, and Perrella, *DMar*, 349–56.

———. "Tratti mariologici del 'vangelo' di Paolo" [Mariological Traits of the "Gospel" of Paul]. *Theotokos* 8, no. 2 (2000): 649–89.

Maranesi, Pietro. "Gli sviluppi della dottrina sull'Immacolata Concezione dal XII al XV secolo" [Development of the Doctrine of the Immaculate Conception in the 12th to 14th Centuries]. In Covolo and Serra, *Storia della mariologia*, 1:843–72.

———. "L'inizio delle dispute: Il concilio di Basilea e i documenti pontifici" [The Beginning of the Debates: The Council of Basel and Pontifical Documents]. In Cecchin, *La "Scuola Francescana,"* 303–40.

Marckhoff, Ulrike. *Das Selig- und Heiligsprechungsverfahren nach katholischem Kirchenrecht* [Procedures of Beatification and Canonization according to Catholic Church Law]. Münster: Lit.-Verlag, 2002.

Marcozzi, V. "Visioni." In Borriello, Del Genio, and Caruana, *Dizionario di mistica*, 1271.

Marini, Vittoria. *Maria e il Mistero di Cristo nella teologia di Hans Urs von Balthasar* [Mary and the Mystery of Christ in the Theology of Hans Urs von Balthasar]. Vatican City: PAMI, 2005.

Maritano, Mario. "Maria nei Padri della Chiesa" [Mary in the Fathers of the Church]. In *Letteratura patristica*, edited by Angelo Di Bernardino, Giorgio Fedalto and Manlio Simonetti, 838–46. Cinisello Balsamo: San Paolo, 2007.

———. "Maria nell'area culturale latina: da Tertulliano († 240 ca.) a sant'Ildefonso di Toledo († 667)" [Mary in the Latin Cultural Area: From Tertullian to St. Ildefonso of Toledo]. In Dal Covolo and Serra, *Storia della mariologia* 1:306–27.

———. "Padri della Chiesa" [Fathers of the Church]. In De Fiores, Schiefer, and Perrella, *DMar*, 917–27.

Martinez Sierra, Alejandro. "De apparitionibus marianis in antiquitate christiana" [Marian Apparitions in Christian Antiquity]. In PAMI, *De primordiis cultus mariani*, 5:195–211. 1970.

———. "El dogma de la Inmaculada Concepción y su relación con la concupiscencia" [The Dogma of the Immaculate Conception and Its Relation with Concupiscence]. *Estudios Marianos* 71 (2005): 183–96.

Martins, M. "Narrativas de aparicoes de Nossa Senhora (ate oa sec. XII)" [Accounts of Apparitions of Our Lady (up to the 12th Century)]. *Salmanticensis* (1958): 5:703–22.

Masciarelli, Michele G. *Il segno della donna: Maria nella teologia di Joseph Ratzinger* [The Sign of the Woman: Mary in the Theology of Joseph Ratzinger]. Cinisello Balsamo: San Paolo, 2007.

———. *La Bellissima: Maria sulla "Via Pulchritudinis"* [The Most Beautiful: Mary on the "Way of Beauty"]. Vatican City: Libreria Editrice Vaticana, 2012.

———. "Sviluppo sulla dottrina dell'Immacolata Concezione di Maria nel magistero dal 1854 al nostro tempo" [Development of the Doctrine of the Immaculate Conception of Mary in the Magisterium from 1854 to Our Time]. In Toniolo, *Il dogma dell'Immacolata Concezione*, 55–168.

Masini, Mario. *Maria di Nazaret la Vergine* [Mary of Nazareth, the Virgin]. Padua: Messaggero, 2008.

Maspero, Giulio. "El misterio de la Virgen toda limpia en Gregorio de Nisa" [The Mystery of the All-Pure Virgin in Gregory of Nyssa]. *Scripta de Maria* 2nd ser., 1 (2004): 183–203.

Mateo-Seco, L. F. "Dimension mariana de la Exhortacion apostólica Verbum Domini." *Scripta de Maria* 2nd ser., no. 8 (2011): 183–204.

———. "La Maternidad divina de María: La lección de Efeso" [The Divine Maternity of Mary: The Lesson of Ephesus]. *Estudios Marianos* 64 (1998): 269–92.

———. "Der Titel 'Gottesmutter' in der Theologie der Kirchenväter vor dem Konzil von Ephesus" [The Title "Mother of God" in Patristic Theology before Ephesus].

Sedes Sapientiae: Mariologisches Jahrbuch 8 (1/2004): 5–36; Spanish original: "El titulo de 'Madre de Dios' en la teología de los Padres anteriores a Efeso." *Estudios Marianos* 68 (2002): 47–68.

May, Eric, OFM. "María en el Antiguo Testamento." In Carol, *Mariología*, 54–81. English original: "Mary in the Old Testament." In Carol, *Mariology*, 1:51 79.

Menke, Karl-Heinz. *Fleisch geworden aus Maria: Die Geschichte Israels und der Marienglaube der Kirche* [Became Incarnate of Mary: The History of Israel and the Marian Belief of the Church]. Regensburg: Friedrich Pustet, 1999. Italian translation: *Incarnato nel seno della vergine Maria: Maria nella storia di Israele e nella Chiesa.* Cinisello Balsamo: Ed. Paoline, 2002.

Meo, Salvatore, OSM. "Assunta II. Dogma, storia e teologia" [Assumed. II. Dogma, History, and Theology]. In De Fiores and Meo, *NDM*, 167–78.

———. "Concilio Vaticano II." In De Fiores and Meo, *NDM*, 379–94.

———. "Madre di Dio." Part 2, "Dogma, storia e teologia" [Mother of God. Part 2, Dogma, History, and Theology]. In De Fiores and Meo, *NDM*, 812–25.

———. "Mediatrice." In De Fiores and Meo, *NDM*, 920–35.

———. "Nuova Eva II. Lo sviluppo teologico della 'Nuova Eva': La corredenzione" [New Eve. II. The Theological Development of "New Eve": Co-Redemption]. In De Fiores and Meo, *NDM*, 1021–29.

Merk, A. "Das Marienbild des Neuen Bundes" [The Marian Image of the New Covenant]. In Sträter, *Katholische Marienkunde*. 3rd ed., 1:44–84.

Merkelbach, Benoît Henri, OP. *Mariologia*. Paris: Desclée, 1939.

———. "Mater divinae gratiae" [Mother of Divine Grace]. *Revue ecclésiastique de Liège* 10 (1914): 23–35.

Messori, Vittorio, and Rino Cammilleri. *Gli occhi di Maria* [The Eyes of Mary]. Rome, 1796; Milan: Rizzoli, 2001.

Meyer, Hans Bernhard. *Eucharistie: Geschichte, theologie, pastoral.* Regensburg: Friedrich Pustet, 1989.

Michel de La Sainte Trinité. Vol. 1, 5th ed.; vol. 2, 2nd ed.; vol. 3, 3rd ed. *Toute la vérité sur Fatima.* Saint-Parres-lès-Vaudes: Maison Saint-Joseph, 1986. English translation: *The Whole Truth about Fatima*. Buffalo, N.Y.: Immaculate Heart Publications, 1989.

Michl, J. "Frau" [Woman]. In Bäumer and Scheffczyk, *ML* 2:520.

Migne, J.-P. Patrologiae cursus completus. Series graeca (PG). Paris: 1857–66.

———. Patrologiae cursus completus. Series Latina (PL). Paris, 1841–64.

Miller, Frederick L. "Lk 1:34: Mary's Desire for Virginity?" *Angelicum* 75, no. 2 (1998): 189–208.

Mimoumi, Simon Claude. *Dormition et assomption de Marie: Histoire des traditions anciennes* [Dormition and Assumption of Mary: History of the Ancient Traditions]. Théologie historique 98. Paris: Beauchesne, 1995.

Miravalle, Mark. *The Immaculate Conception and the Co-redemptrix*. Goleta, Calif.: Queenship, 2004.

———, ed. *Mariology: A Guide for Priests, Deacons, Seminarians, and Consecrated Persons*. Goleta, Calif.: Queenship, 2007.

———. *Mary Co-redemptrix, Mediatrix, Advocate.* Santa Barbara, Calif.: Queenship,

1993. Italian translation: *Maria Corredentrice, Mediatrice, Avvocata*. Santa Barbara, Calif.: Queenship, 1993.
———, ed. *Mary Co-redemptrix: Doctrinal Issues Today*. Goleta, Calif.: Queenship, 2002.
———, ed. *Mary Coredemptrix, Mediatrix, Advocate: Theological Foundations*. Santa Barbara, Calif.: Queenship, 1995.
———, ed. *Mary Coredemptrix, Mediatrix, Advocate: Theological Foundations*. Vol. 2. Santa Barbara, Calif.: Queenship, 1996.
———, ed. *Mary Coredemptrix, Mediatrix, Advocate: Theological Foundations*. Vol. 3, *Contemporary Insights on a Fifth Marian Dogma*. Goleta, Calif.: Queenship, 2000.
———. *"With Jesus": The Story of Mary Co-redemptrix*. Goleta, Calif.: Queenship, 2003. Italian translation: *"Con Gesù": La storia di Maria Corredentrice*. In *Maria Corredentrice*, 8:17–190. 2006.
Mitterer, Albert. *Dogma und Biologie der Heiligen Familie* [Dogma and Biology of the Holy Family]. Vienna: Herder, 1952.
Montag, U. and T. Nyberg. "Birgitta von Schweden II. Werke" [Birgitta of Sweden. II. Works]. In *ML* 1:489–91.
Montanari, A. "San Bernardo di Clairvaux e la sua scuola" [St. Bernard of Clairvaux and His School]. In Dal Covolo and Serra, *Storia della mariologia*, 1:637–61.
Morales, J. "Il movimento di Oxford e John Henry Newman" [The Oxford Movement and John Henry Newman]. In Boaga and Gambero, *Storia della mariologia*, 2:715–27.
Moreno, A., and R. Schenk. "Jung." In Bäumer and Scheffczyk, *ML* 3:461–65.
Mori, E. G. "Figlia di Sion" [Daughter of Zion]. In De Fiores and Meo, *NDM*, 580–89.
Müller, Alois. "La posizione e la cooperazione di Maria nell'evento di Cristo" [Mary's Position and Her Cooperation in the Christ Event]. *Mysterium salutis* 6 (1971): 495–641. German original: "Marias Stellung und Mitwirkung im Christusereignis." *Mysterium salutis* 3, no. 2 [1969]: 393–510.
Müller, Gerhard L. "Gottesmutter" [Mother of God]. In Bäumer and Scheffczyk, *ML* 2:684–92.
———. *Maria: Die Frau im Heilsplan Gottes* [Mary: The Woman in God's Plan of Salvation]. Mariologische Studien 15. Regensburg: Friedrich Pustet, 2002.
———. "Mittlerin der Gnade" [Mediatrix of Grace]. In Bäumer and Scheffczyk, *ML* 4:487–91.
———. *Nato dalla Vergine Maria* [Born of the Virgin Mary]. Brescia: Morcelliana, 1994. German original: *Was heißt: Geboren von der Jungfrau Maria? Eine theologische Deutung*. Quaestiones disputatae 119. Freiburg im Breisgau: Herder, 1989.
Müller, M. "Maria: Ihre geistige Gestalt und Persönlichkeit in der Theologie des Mittelalters" [Mary: Her Spiritual Profile and Personality in Medieval Theology]. In Sträter, *Katholische Marienkunde* 1:268–316.
Müller, Thomas. *Medjugorje: Ein Charisma und seine Bestätigung durch das Gottesvolk* [Medjugorje: A Charism and Its Affirmation by the People of God]. Vienna: Gebetsaktion Medjugorje, 2006.
Mulligan, James. *Medjugorje: The First Days*. Medjugorje: n.p., 2013.

Muñoz Iglesias, Salvador. "Lo histórico en los Evangelios de la infancia" [The Historical Component in the Infancy Gospels]. *Estudios Marianos* 64 (1998): 3–36.

———. *Los evangelios de la infancia* [The Infancy Gospels]. 4 vols. Madrid: Biblioteca de Autores Cristianos, 1986–90.

Munsterman, Hendro. *Marie corédemptrice? Débat sur un titre marial controversé*. Paris: Cerf, 2006.

Mussner, Franz. *La lettera ai Galati* [The Letter to the Galatians]. Brescia: Paideia, 1987. German original: *Der Galaterbrief*. Freiburg im Breisgau: Herder, 1974; 5th ed. 1988; reprinted 2002.

———. *Maria, die Mutter Jesu im Neuen Testament* [Mary, the Mother of Jesus in the New Testament]. St. Ottilien: EOS Verlag, 1993.

Nachef, Antoine. *Mary's Pope: John Paul II, Mary, and the Church since Vatican II*. Franklin, Wisc.: Sheed and Ward, 2000.

Nebel, R., and H. Rzepkowski. "Guadalupe." In Bäumer and Scheffczyk, *ML* 3:38–42.

Nellessen, Ernst. *Das Kind und seine Mutter: Struktur und Verkündigung des 2. Kapitels im Matthäusevangelium* [The Child and His Mother: Structure and Proclamation of Matthew 2]. Stuttgart: Verlag Katholisches Bibelwerk, 1969.

Newman, John Henry. *Mary: The Virgin Mary in the Life and Writings of John Henry Newman*. Edited with an Introduction and Notes. Edited by Philip Boyce. Leominster, UK: Gracewing; Grand Rapids, Mich.: Eerdmans, 2001. Italian original: *Maria: pagine scelte*. Milan: Ed. Paoline, 1999.

———. *Meditations and Devotions*. Part 1, *The Month of May*. London: Longmans, 1929. Italian translation: *Litanie lauretane*. Casale Monferrato: Piemme, 1985.

Nichols, Aidan. "Von Balthasar and the Coredemption." In *Mary at the Foot of the Cross*, 1:301–15. 2000.

Nicolas, Jean-Hervé. *Sintesi dogmatica* [Dogmatic Synthesis]. Vol. 1. Vatican City: Libreria Editrice Vaticana, 1991. French original: *Synthèse dogmatique*. Fribourg and Paris: Beauchesne, 1985.

Nicolas, M.-J. "Marie et la Trinité." In du Manoir, *Maria*, 7:421–30.

Nikolaou, T. "Akáthistos Hymnos" [The Akathist Hymn]. In Bäumer and Scheffczyk, *ML* 1:66f.

———. "Sündenlosigkeit II. Orthodoxe Theologie" [Sinlessness II. Orthodox Theology]. In Bäumer and Scheffczyk, *ML* 6:332f.

Noll, Raymund. *Die mariologischen Grundlinien im exegetischen Werk des Cornelius a Lapide (1567–1637)* [Mariological Outlines in the Exegetical Work of Cornelius a Lapide, SJ]. Mariologische Studien 16. Regensburg: Friedrich Pustet, 2003.

Norelli, E. "Maria nella letteratura apocrifa cristiana antica" [Mary in Ancient Christian Apocryphal Literature]. In Dal Covolo and Serra, *Storia della mariologia*, 1:143–254, 2009.

Oberlinner, Lorenz. *Historische Überlieferung und christologische Aussage: Zur Frage der "Brüder Jesu" in der Synopse* [Historical Tradition and Christological Expression: On the Question of the "Brothers of Jesus" in the Synoptics]. Stuttgart: Verlag Katholisches Bibelwerk, 1975.

Ocáriz, Fernando. "María y la Eucaristía." *Scripta de Maria* 2nd ser., 1 (2004): 33–44.

Ocáriz, Fernando, Lucas F. Mateo-Seco, and José A. Riestra. *Il mistero di Cristo: Man-*

uale di Cristologia [The Mystery of Christ: Manual of Christology]. Translated by Carla Rossi Espagnet. Rome: Apollinare Studi, 2000. Spanish original: *El misterio de Jesucristo.* Pamplona: Ediciones Universidad de Navarra, 1991. 4th ed., 2010.

Ochayta Piñeiro, F. "El sacerdocio de María desde un punto de vista teológico" [The Priesthood of Mary from a Theological Viewpoint]. *Estudios Marianos* 77 (2011): 37–57.

O'Carroll, Michael, CSSp. "A Marian Dogma and Ecumenism." In Miravalle, *Mary Coredemptrix*, 2:227–43.

———. "Maria Socia, Consors, Adjutrix Christi" [Mary: Associate, Partner, Helper of Christ]. In PAMI, *De cultu mariano saeculis XII-XV*, 4:27–51. 1980.

———. "Mary Coredemptress, Mediatress, Advocate: Instrument of Catholic-Orthodox Unity." In Miravalle, *Mary Coredemptrix*, 1:119–43.

———. "Socia: The Word and Idea in Regard to Mary." *Ephemerides Mariologicae* 25 (1975): 337–57.

———. *Theotokos: A Theological Encyclopedia of the Blessed Virgin Mary*. Eugene, Ore.: Wipf and Stock, 2000.

———. "Wilhelm von Ware" [William of Ware]. In Bäumer and Scheffczyk, *ML* 6:738.

O'Connor, E. "The Theologian and Apparitions." In PAMI, *De cultu mariano saeculo XX*, 4:21–50.

Odasso, Giovanni. "Il segno dell'Emmanuele nella tradizione dell'Antico Testamento" [The Sign of Emmanuel in the Tradition of the Old Testament]. *Theotokos* 4, no. 1 (1996): 151–88.

O'Donnell, Timothy T. *Heart of the Redeemer: An Apologia for the Contemporary and Perennial Value of the Devotion to the Sacred Heart of Jesus.* San Francisco: Ignatius Press, 1992.

Office for The Liturgical Celebrations of The Supreme Pontiff, ed. *Liturgie dell'Oriente cristiano a Roma nell'Anno Mariano 1987–88* [Eastern Christian Liturgy at Rome in the Marian Year 1987–88]. Vatican City: Libreria Editrice Vaticana, 1990.

Orbe, Antonio, and Manlio Simonetti, eds. *Il Cristo.* Vol. 1, *Testi teologici e spirituali dal I al IV secolo* [The Christ. Vol. 1, Theological and Spiritual Texts of the First to Fourth Centuries]. 6th ed. Milan: A. Mondadori, 2005.

Orsatti, Mauro. "Storicità e vangeli dell'infanzia" [Historicity and the Infancy Gospels]. *RTLu* 9, no. 3 (2004): 603–22.

Ossanna, Tullio Faustino. *L'Ave Maria: Storia, contenuti, problemi* [The Ave Maria: History, Content, Issues]. Cinisello Balsamo: San Paolo, 2002.

Ossanna, Tullio Faustino, and S. Cipriani. "Madre nostra" [Our Mother]. In De Fiores and Meo, *NDM*, 830–42.

Pagnamenta, Annibale. *Storia del Castelletto* [History of Castelletto]. Lugano: Gaggini-Bizzozero, 1983.

PAMI (Pontificia Academia Mariana Internationalis), ed. *De cultu mariano saeculis VI–XI* [The Cult of Mary in the Sixth to Eleventh Centuries]. 5 vols. Rome: PAMI, 1972.

———, ed. *De cultu mariano saeculis XII–XV.* 6 vols. Rome: PAMI, 1979–81.

———, ed. *De cultu mariano saeculo XVI.* 6 vols. Rome: PAMI, 1983–86.

———, ed. *De cultu mariano saeculis XVII–XVIII.* 7 vols. Rome: PAMI, 1987.

———, ed. *De cultu mariano saeculis XIX–XX.* 7 vols. Rome: PAMI, 1988–91.

———, ed. *De cultu mariano saeculo XX: A concilio Vaticano II usque ad nostros dies* [The Cult of Mary in the 20th Century, from Vatican II to Our Day]. 4 vols. Vatican City: PAMI, 1998–99.

———, ed. *De cultu mariano saeculo XX: Maria, Mater Domini, in mysterio salutis quod ab Orientis et Occidentis Ecclesiis in Spiritu Sancto hodie celebratur* [The Cult of Mary in the 20th Century: Mary, Mother of God, in the Mystery of Salvation Celebrated Today by the Eastern and Western Churches in the Holy Spirit]. 5 vols. Vatican City: PAMI, 1999–2000.

———, ed. *De mariologia et oecumenismo.* Rome: PAMI, 1962.

———, ed. *De primordiis cultus mariani* [Origins of the Cult of Mary]. 6 vols. Rome: PAMI, 1970.

———, ed. *La Madre del Signore: Memoria presenza speranza; Alcune questioni attuali sulla figura e la missione della beata Vergine Maria.* Vatican City: PAMI, 2000. English translation: PAMI, *The Mother of the Lord: Memory, Presence, Hope.* Staten Island, N.Y.: St. Paul, 2007.

———, ed. *Maria et Ecclesia.* 16 vols. Vatican City: PAMI, 1959–62.

———, ed. *Mariologia a tempore Concilii Vaticani II: Receptio, ratio et prospectus; Acta Congressus Mariologici-mariani Internationalis in civitate Romae anno 2012 celebrati. Studia in sessionibus plenariis exhibita.* [Mariology during the Second Vatican Council] Vatican City: PAMI, 2013.

Panimolle, Salvatore A. *Lettura pastorale del vangelo di Giovanni* [Pastoral Reading of the Gospel of John]. Vol. 1. 3rd ed. Bologna: EDB, 1988.

Pannenberg, Wolfgang. *Systematische Theologie.* Vol. 2. Göttingen: Vandenhoeck and Ruprecht, 1991. Italian translation: *Teologia sistematica.* Vol. 2. Brescia: Queriniana, 1994. English translation: *Systematic Theology.* Vol. 2. Grand Rapids, Mich.: Eerdmans, 1994.

Paolini, Solideo. *Fatima: Non disprezzate le profezie* [Fatima: Despise Not Prophecies]. Tavagnaco: Edizioni Segno, 2005.

Paolucci, C.P. "Apparizioni." In Borriello, Del Genio, and Caruana, *Dizionario di mistica*, 146f.

Papandreou, Damaskinos. "Redemptoris Mater III. Orthodoxe Bemerkungen" [Mother of the Redeemer. III. Orthodox Observations]. *Una Sancta* 42, no. 3 (1987): 230f.

Parrotta, Pietro. "Father Roschini and the Contribution of Blessed John Duns Scotus to the Dogma of the Immaculate Conception." In *Mary at the Foot of the Cross*, 5:360–92. 2004.

———. *La cooperazione di Maria alla Redenzione in Gabriele Maria Roschini* [Mary's Cooperation in the Redemption, in Gabriele Maria Roschini]. CdM 3. Lugano: Eupress FTL, 2002.

———. "The Spiritual Maternity of Mary in G. M. Roschini: The Post-Conciliar Period." In *Mary at the Foot of the Cross*, 4:369–86. 2004.

Paul VI. Allocution *Post duos menses* [After Two Months]. *AAS* 56 (1964): 1014.

———. Apostolic Exhortation *Marialis cultus* (*MCu*), 1974 (in *EV* 5:13–97).

Paximadi, Giorgio. "L'importanza salvifica della donna nell'Antico Testamento" [The

Salvific Importance of Woman in the Old Testament]. In Hauke, *La donna e la salvezza*, 11–27.

Pedico, Maria Marcellina. "Centri mariani di studio" [Marian Study Centers]. In De Fiores and Meo, *NDM*, 332–50.

———. *La Vergine Maria nella pietà popolare* [The Virgin Mary in Popular Piety]. Rome: Monfortane, 1993.

Pelikan, Jaroslav. *Maria nei secoli*. Translated by Nerina Rodino. Rome: Città Nuova, 1999. English original: *Mary Through the Centuries: Her Place in the History of Culture*. New Haven and London: Yale University Press, 1996.

Peretto, Elio. "Apocrifi" [Apocrypha]. In De Fiores and Meo, *NDM*, 106–25.

———. "Assunzione." In *Nuovo dizionario patristico e di antichità cristiane*, edited by A. Di Berardino, 1:608f. Genoa and Milan: Marietti, 2006.

———, ed. *La Mariologia nell'organizzazione delle discipline teologiche: Collocazione e metodo* [Mariology in the Organization of the Theological Disciplines: Placement and Method]. Rome: Marianum, 1992.

———, ed. *La Spiritualità Mariana: Legittimità, natura, articolazione* [Marian Spirituality: Legitimacy, Nature, Articulation]. Rome: Marianum, 1994.

———. "Magnificat." In De Fiores and Meo, *NDM*, 853–65.

———. "Maria nell'area culturale greca: Da San Giustino (†165 ca.) a san Giovanni Damasceno (†749)" [Mary in the Greek Cultural Area, from St. Justin to St. John Damascene]. In Dal Covolo and Serra, *Storia della mariologia*, 1:263–305.

———, ed. *Maria nel mistero di Cristo, pienezza del tempo e compimento del regno: Atti del XI Simposio Internazionale Mariologico (1997)* [Mary in the Mystery of Christ, the Fullness of Time, and Fulfillment of the Kingdom: Acts of the Eleventh International Mariological Symposium]. Rome: Marianum, 1999.

———. *Percorsi mariologici nell'antica letteratura Cristiana* [Mariological Pathways in Ancient Christian Literature]. Vatican City: Libreria Editrice Vaticana, 2001.

Pérez Toro, Carlos, and Salvatore M. Perrella, OSM. "Cooperatrice di salvezza/Mediatrice" [Cooperator in Salvation/Mediatrix]. In De Fiores, Schiefer, and Perrella, *DMar*, 327–36.

Perillo, Maria Francesca. *Maria nella Mistica: La mediazione mariana in santa Veronica Giuliani* [Mary in Mysticism: Marian Mediation in St. Veronica Giuliani]. CdM 5. Lugano-Frigento: Eupress FTL, 2004.

———. "Maria SS. Corredentrice 'Mater unitatis.'" *Divinitas* 46, no. 3 (2003): 320–50.

———. "Sub tuum praesidium: Incomparable Marian Praeconium." In *Mary at the Foot of the Cross*, 4:138–69.

Perniola, Erasmo. *La mariologia di san Germano patriarca di Costantinopoli* [The Mariology of St. Germanus, Patriarch of Constantinople]. Rome: Edizioni Padre Monti, 1954.

Perrella, Salvatore M., OSM. "Affidamento consacrazione" [Entrustment, Consecration]. In De Fiores, Schiefer, and Perrella, *DMar*, 16–24.

———. *Ecco tua Madre (Gv 19,27): La Madre di Gesù nel magistero di Giovanni Paolo II e nell'oggi della Chiesa e del mondo* [Behold Your Mother (Jn 19:27): The Mother of Jesus in the Magisterium of John Paul II and in the Church and the World Today]. Cinisello Balsamo: San Paolo, 2007.

———. "Il 'Messaggio di Fatima' della Congregazione per la Dottrina della Fede (26 giugno 2000), Interpretazioni contemporanee" [CDF's "Message of Fatima" (June 26, 2000), Contemporary Interpretations]. *Marianum* 74, no. 181–82 (2012): 283–356.

———. "Il parto verginale di Maria nel dibattito teologico contemporaneo (1962–1994): Magistero—Esegesi—Teologia" [The Virginal Delivery of Mary in Contemporary Theological Debate (1962–1994): Magisterium, Exegesis, Theology]. *Marianum* 56 (1994): 95–213.

———. "Il Rosario nel magistero dei Papi" [The Rosary in the Magisterium of the Popes]. In Cecchin, *Contemplare Cristo con Maria*, 61–173.

———. *I "vota" e i "consilia" dei vescovi italiani sulla mariologia e sulla corredenzione nella fase antipreparatoria del Concilio Vaticano II* [The "Votes" and "Recommendations" of the Italian Bishops on Mariology and Coredemption in the Preparatory Phase of Vatican II]. Rome: Marianum, 1994.

———. *La Madre di Gesù nella coscienza ecclesiale contemporanea* [The Mother of Jesus in Contemporary Ecclesial Consciousness]. Vatican City: Libreria Editrice Vaticana, 2005.

———. "La recezione del Documento di Dombes su Maria: Ricognizione bibliografica." *Marianum* 62 (2000) 347–55.

———. "La ricezione e l'approfondimento del capitolo VIII della 'Lumen gentium' nel Magistero di Paolo VI, Giovanni Paolo II e Benedetto XVI" [The Reception and Deepening of Chapter Eight of "Lumen gentium" in the Magisterium of Paul VI, John Paul II, and Benedict XVI]. In PAMI, *Mariologia a tempore Concilii Vaticani II*, 1–146. 2013.

———. "L'Assunzione di Maria nella teologia post-conciliare" [The Assumption in Post-Conciliar Theology]. In Calvo Moralejo and Cecchin, *L'Assunzione di Maria*, 71–167.

———. *Le apparizioni mariane.* Cinisello Balsamo: San Paolo, 2007.

———. *L'insegnamento della mariologia ieri e oggi* [The Teaching of Mariology Yesterday and Today]. 142–75. Padua: Messaggero, 2012.

———. *Maria, Vergine e Madre: La verginità feconda di Maria tra fede, storia e teologia* [Mary, Virgin and Mother: The Fruitful Virginity of Mary in the Faith, History and Theology]. Cinisello Balsamo: San Paolo, 2003.

———. *"Non temere di prendere con te Maria" (Matteo 1,20): Maria e l'ecumenismo nel postmoderno; Dalla "Mater divisionis" alla "Mater unitatis"* ["Fear Not to Take Mary with You" (Mt 1:20): Mary and Ecumenism in the Postmodern; From "Mother of Division" to "Mother of Unity"]. Milan: San Paolo, 2004.

———. *Virgo ecclesia facta: La Madre di Dio tra due millenni; Summula storico-teologica* [Virgo Ecclesia Facta: The Mother of God through Two Millennia; Historical-Theological Summary]. Rome: Centro internazionale Milizia dell'Immacolata, 2002.

Perrella, Salvatore M., OSM, and Stefano De Fiores. "Assunta." In De Fiores, Schiefer, and Perrella, *DMar*, 175–89.

Perrella, Salvatore M., OSM, and Gian Matteo Roggio. "Dialogo interreligioso." In De Fiores, Schiefer, and Perrella, *DMar*, 384–96.

Pesch, Rudolf. *Das Markusevangelium.* Vol. 1. Freiburg im Breisgau: Herder, 2000 (1st

ed., 1976). Italian translation: *Il Vangelo di Marco*. Vol. 1. Brescia: Paideia, 1980.
Petri, Heinrich, ed. *Divergenzen in der Mariologie: Zur ökumenischen Diskussion um die Mutter Jesu* [Divergences in Mariology: Ecumenical Debate on the Mother of Jesus]. Mariologische Studien 7. Regensburg: Friedrich Pustet, 1989.
———. "Marienerscheinungen" [Marian Apparitions]. In Beinert and Petri, *Handbuch der Marienkunde*, 2:31–59. 1997.
Petrillo, Francisco. "Theotokos/Madre di Dio." In De Fiores, Schiefer, and Perrella, *DMar*, 1211–19.
Peyrous, Bernard. *Les évènements de l'Île-Bouchard: Une présence de Marie au milieu de nous* [The Events of the *Île-Bouchard*: A Presence of Mary in Our Midst]. Paray-le-Monial: Ed. de l'Emmanuel, 2002.
Philippe, M. D. "Le mystère de la Maternité Divine de Marie" [The Mystery of the Divine Maternity of Mary]. In du Manoir, *Maria*, 6:367–416. 1961.
Philips, Gérard. *La Chiesa e il suo mistero nel Concilio Vaticano II: Storia, testo e commento della Costituzione Lumen gentium* [The Church and Her Mystery in Vatican II: The Constitution "Lumen gentium"; History, Text, and Commentary]. Milan: Jaca, 1975 (reprint 1993). French original: *L'Église et son mystère au IIe Concile du Vatican: Histoire, texte et commentaire de la constitution Lumen gentium*. Paris: Desclée, 1967.
———. "La Vierge au IIe Concile du Vatican et l'avenir de la mariologie" [The Virgin at Vatican II and the Future of Mariology]. In du Manoir, *Maria*, 8:41–88. Paris: Beauchesne, 1971.
Piacentini, Ernesto. *Nuovo corso sistematico di Mariologia sub luce Immaculatae* [New Systematic Course of Mariology in Light of the Immaculate]. Frascati (Rome): Bannò, 2002.
Piazza, A. "Maria nell'Antico Testamento" [Mary in the Old Testament]. In *EMTheo* (1954): 15–32; (1958): 14–29.
Piepke, J. G. "*Befreiungstheologie*" [Liberation Theology]. In Bäumer and Scheffczyk, *ML* 1:400f.
Pisani, Emilio. *Pro e contro Maria Valtorta* [For and against Maria Valtorta]. 4th ed. Isola del Liri: Centro Editoriale Valtortiano, 2005.
Pius XI. Radio message of April 28, 1935. *L'Osservatore Romano*, April 29–30, 1935, p. 1; *Discorsi di Pio XI*, vol. 3 (1934–1939) (Vatican City: Libreria Editrice Vaticana, 1985).
Pius XII. Encyclical *Haurietis aquas*. English translation originally from *The Pope Speaks: Church Documents Quarterly*. Boston: St. Paul Editions. Also in PE 4:253, n. 103.
———. *Ruf an die Frau* [Appeal to Women]. 2nd ed. Edited by Käthe Seibel-Royer. Graz: Verlag Styria, 1956.
Pizzarelli, A. "Presenza" [Presence]. In De Fiores and Meo, *NDM*, 1161–69.
Pötzl, W. "Augenwende" [A Turn of the Eyes]. In Bäumer and Scheffczyk, *ML* 1:286f.
Polanco Fermandois, Rodrigo. "La mariologia di Sant'Ireneo" [The Mariology of St. Irenaeus]. *Theotokos* 9, no. 2 (2001): 359–400.
Pompei, Alfonso. "Giovanni Duns Scoto e la dottrina sull'Immacolata Concezione" [John Duns Scotus and the Doctrine of the Immaculate Conception]. In Cecchin, *La "Scuola Francescana,"* 193–217.

Ponce Cuéllar, Miguel. *María, Madre del Redentor y Madre de la Iglesia* [Mary, Mother of the Redeemer and Mother of the Church]. 2nd ed. Barcelona: Herder, 2001.

Pons Pons, Guillermo. *Textos marianos de los primeros siglos* [Marian Texts of the First Centuries]. Madrid: Ciudad Nueva, 1994.

Pontifical Biblical Commission. *The Interpretation of the Bible in the Church.* Vatican City: Libreria Editrice Vaticana, 1993.

Poschmann, A., and J. Schwalke. "Dietrichswalde." In Bäumer and Scheffczyk, *ML* 2:194f.

Pozo, Cándido, SJ. "La consagración a los Corazones de Jesús y María en Juan Pablo II" [Consecration to the Hearts of Jesus and Mary in John Paul II]. In *El Corazón de Jesús en la enseñanza de Juan Pablo II: Antología de textos, Estudios*, 337–57. Madrid: Instituto Internacional del Corazón de Jesús, 1990.

———. "Maria Assunta partecipe alla risurrezione di Cristo: Dalla Kenosi alla Gloria" [Mary, Assumed, Sharer in the Resurrection of Christ: From Kenosis to Glory]. In Calvo Moralejo and Cecchin, *L'Assunzione di Maria*, 247–61.

———. "María en la encrucijada de la Teología católica" [Mary at the Crossroads of Catholic Theology]. In *María en los Caminos de la Iglesia* [Mary on the Roads of the Church], edited by Centro de Estudios de Teología Espiritual, 31–53. Madrid: Centro de Estudios de Teologia Espiritual, 1982.

———. *María en la obra de la salvación* [Mary in the Work of Salvation]. 2nd ed. Madrid: Biblioteca de Autores Cristianos, 1990.

———. *María, nueva Eva* [Mary, the New Eve]. Madrid: Biblioteca de Autores Cristianos, 2005.

———. *Theology of the Beyond.* Staten Island, N.Y.: St. Pauls, 2009. Italian translation: *Teologia dell'aldilà* [Theology of the Beyond]. 5th ed. Translated by Luigi Rolfo. Cinisello Balsamo: Edizioni Paoline, 1990. Spanish original: *Teología del más allá.* 2nd ed. Madrid: Biblioteca de Autores Cristianos, 1981.

Ragazzini, Severino M., OFM, Conv. *La Divina Maternità di Maria nel suo concetto teologico integrale* [The Divine Maternity of Mary in Its Integral Theological Concept]. Frigento: Casa Mariana Editrice, 1986.

Rahner, Hugo. *Our Lady and the Church.* Translated by Sebastian Bullough. London: Darton, Longman and Todd, 1961. Italian: *Maria e la Chiesa.* Milan: Jaca Book, 1991. German original: *Maria und die Kirche.* Innsbruck: Marianischer Verlag, 1951.

———. *Symbole der Kirche: Die Ekklesiologie der Väter* [Creeds of the Church: The Ecclesiology of the Fathers]. Salzburg: Müller, 1964. Italian trans.: *Simboli della Chiesa: L'ecclesiologia dei Padri.* 2nd ed. Cinisello Balsamo: San Paolo, 1995.

Rahner, Karl. *Grundkurs des Glaubens: Einführung in den Begriff des Christentums.* Freiburg im Breisgau: Herder, 1976. Italian trans.: *Corso fondamentale sulla fede: Introduzione al concetto di cristianesimo.* Cinisello Balsamo: San Paolo, 1990. English translation: *Foundations of Christian Faith: An Introduction to the Idea of Christianity.* Translated by William V. Dych. New York: Crossroad, 1978, reprint 2013.

———. "Le principe fondamental de la théologie mariale" [The Fundamental Principle of Marian Theology]. *Recherches de science religieuse* 42, no. 4 (1954): 481–522.

———. "Virginitas in partu: Ein Beitrag zum Problem der Dogmenentwicklung und Überlieferung" [Virginity in Childbirth: A Contribution to the Problem of the Development of Dogma and Tradition]. In *Schriften zur Theologie*, 4:173–205. Einsiedeln: Benziger, 1960. Italian translation: "Virginitas in partu." In *Saggi di cristologia e mariologia*, 361–411. Rome: Edizioni Paoline, 1965. English translation: In *Theological Investigations*, 4:134–62. Baltimore: Helicon Press, 1966.

———. *Visions and Prophecies.* New York: Herder and Herder, 1964. Italian translation: *Visioni e profezie* [Visions and Prophecies]. Milan: Vita e Pensiero, 1995. German original: *Visionen und Prophezeiungen.* 2nd ed. Freiburg im Breisgau: Herder, 1958; reprint 1989. English translation:

———. "Zum Sinn des Assumpta-Dogmas" [The Meaning of the Dogma of the Assumption]. In *Schriften zur Theologie*, 2:239–52. Einsiedeln: Benziger, 1962. Italian translation: "Sul significato del dogma dell'assunzione." In *Saggi di cristologia e di mariologia*, 457–78. Rome: Edizioni Paoline, 1965. English translation: "The Interpretation of the Dogma of the Assumption." In *Theological Investigations*, 1:215–27. London: Darton, Longman and Todd, 1961.

Ratzinger, Joseph. *Daughter Zion: Meditations on the Church's Marian Belief.* San Francisco: Ignatius Press, 1983. German original: *Die Tochter Zion: Betrachtungen über den Marienglauben der Kirche*. Einsiedeln: Johannes Verlag, 1977; 4th ed., 1990.

———. *Introduction to Christianity.* 2nd ed. San Francisco: Ignatius Press, 2004. Italian: *Introduzione al cristianesimo.* Brescia: Queriniana, 1969. German original: *Einführung in das Christentum.* München: Kösel, 1968.

———. "Theological Commentary." In Congregation for the Doctrine of the Faith, *The Message of Fatima*, 32–44.

———. *Truth and Tolerance: Christian Belief and World Religions.* Translated by Henry Taylor. San Francisco: Ignatius Press, 2004. Original *Fede, verità e tolleranza: Il cristianesimo e le religioni del mondo* ["Faith, Truth, and Tolerance: Christianity and the World Religions]. Siena: Edizioni Cantagalli, 2003.

———. "Un'interpretazione dei segni dei tempi per il cammino della Chiesa e dell'umanità" [An Interpretation of the Signs of the Times for the Journey of the Church and of Humanity]. In *Una luce sul cammino dell'uomo: Per una lettura della "Redemptoris Mater."* Quaderni de "L'Osservatore Romano" 6. Vatican City: Libreria Editrice Vaticana, 1988.

Ratzinger, Joseph, and Vittorio Messori. *The Ratzinger Report: An Exclusive Interview on the State of the Church.* Translated by Graham Harrison. San Francisco: Ignatius Press, 1985. Italian original: *Rapporto sulla fede*. Cinisello Balsamo: Edizioni Paoline, 1985.

Raya, Joseph, and José de Vinck, eds. *Byzantine Daily Worship.* Allendale, N.J.: Alleluia Press, 1969.

Reckinger, François. "Die Marienerscheinungen der Neuzeit" [Marian Apparitions of the Modern Era]. In Stumpf, *Maria: Mutter der Kirche*, 201–58.

———. "Wunder" [Miracles]. In Bäumer and Scheffczyk, *ML* 6:766–68.

Rehm, M., and J. Scharbert. "David." In Bäumer and Scheffczyk, *ML* 2:150.

Reynolds, Bryan. *Porta Paradisi: Marian Doctrine and Devotion, Image and Typology in the Patristic and Medieval Period.* Taipei: Fu Jen University Press, 2009. New edition, with the title *Gateway to Heaven: Marian Doctrine and Devotion, Image and Typology in the Patristic and Medieval Periods.* New York: New City Press, 2012.

Ricciardo, Rosaria. "Siracusa: Lacrime di Maria" [Syracuse: Tears of Mary]. In De Fiores, Schiefer, and Perrella, *DMar*, 1104–13.

Richer, Étienne. "Marie, Epouse du Saint-Esprit? Le point de vue de la mariologie des saints et des papes" [Mary, Spouse of the Holy Spirit? The Mariological Viewpoint of the Saints and the Popes]. *RTLu* 12, no. 2 (2007): 257–77.

Riedl, G. "Der Einfluss Louis-Marie Grignions de Montfort (1673–1716) auf die Mariologie Papst Johannes Pauls II" [The Influence of de Montfort on the Mariology of Pope John Paul II]. In Ziegenaus, *Totus tuus*, 47–69.

———. "Die pseudoaugustinische Schrift 'De assumptione beatae Mariae virginis': Theologische Argumentationskunst und dogmengeschichtlicher Kontext" [The Pseudo-Augustinian Document "De assumptione beatae Mariae virginis": The Theological Art of Its Argument; Context in the History of Dogma]. In Ziegenaus, *Volksfrömmigkeit und Theologie*, 75–103.

Riestra, José A. "Bibliografia sobre la 'Mulieris dignitatem'" [Bibliography on "Mulieris dignitatem"]. *Estudios Marianos* 62 (1996): 267–90.

———. "El titulo 'Mater Ecclesiae' en los manuales recientes de mariología" [The Title "Mater Ecclesiae" in Recent Manuals of Mariology]. *Annales theologici* 10 (1996): 449–69.

———. "La contestación de la paternidad de Dios y la mariología feminista" [The Debate on the Fatherhood of God and Feminist Mariology]. *Estudios Marianos* 66 (2000): 389–430.

———. "La maternidad de María en la mariología feminista" [The Motherhood of Mary in Feminist Mariology]. *Estudios Marianos* 68 (2002): 221–76.

———. "Los movimientos feministas y su significación teológica: La mariología feminista" [Feminist Movements and Their Theological Significance: Feminist Mariology]. *Estudios Marianos* 72 (1996): 3–42.

Rigato, Maria-Luisa. "Maria di Nazaret di stirpe levitico sacerdotale" [Mary of Nazareth, of the Levitical Priestly Line]. *Theotokos* 8, no. 1 (2000): 275–304.

Righetti, Mario "Il culto mariano attraverso i secoli" [The Cult of Mary through the Centuries]. In *EMTheo* (1954): 417–26; (1958): 364–371.

———. *Storia liturgica* [Liturgical History]. Vol. 2. 2nd ed. Milan: Ancora, 1955.

Ripberger, Albert. *Der Pseudo-Hieronymus-Brief IX "Cogitis me,"* 57–113. Fribourg: Universitätsverlag, 1962.

Risse, Günter. "Maria, die Gottesfürchtige: Das Marienbild im Koran" [Mary the God-Fearer: The Image of Mary in the Koran]. *Sedes Sapientiae: Mariologisches Jahrbuch* 3, no. 1 (1999): 36–61.

Roberson, Ronald. "Assira, Chiesa, d'Oriente" [Assyrian Church of the East]. In Farrugia, *Dizionario enciclopedico dell'Oriente cristiano*, 82f. 2015.

Robert, André, PS. "La Sainte Vierge dans l'Ancien Testament" [The Holy Virgin in the Old Testament]. In du Manoir, *Maria*, 1:23–39. 1949.

Roberts, Alexander, and James Donaldson, eds. *Ante-Nicene Fathers 1885–1887* (*ANF*). 10 vols. Peabody, Mass.: Hendrickson, 1994.

Robichaud, Armand J., SM. "Maria, dispensadora de todas las gracias." In Carol, *Mariología*, 805–37. English original: "Mary, Dispensatrix of All Graces." In Carol, *Mariology*, 2:426–60.

Rocca, Giancarlo. *L'Adversus Helvidium di san Girolamo nel contesto della letteratura ascetico-mariana del secolo IV* [The "Adversus Helvidium" of St. Jerome in the Context of Ascetical-Marian Literature of the Fourth Century]. Bern: Peter Lang, 1998.

Röwekamp, Georg. "Timoteo di Gerusalemme" [Timothy of Jerusalem]. In Döpp and Geerlings, *DLCA*, 831.

Rosa, Pietro. "Aspetti della mariologia di Cirillo Alessandrino e di Nestorio" [Aspects of Mariology in Cyril of Alexandria and in Nestor]. *Theotokos* 12, no. 1–2 (2004): 255–85.

Roschini, Gabriele M. "Breve commento all'enciclica 'Ad coeli reginam'" [Brief Comment on the Encyclical "Ad coeli reginam"]. *Marianum* 16 (1954): 409–32.

———. "De natura influxus B.M. Virginis in applicatione Redemptionis" [The Nature of the Influence of the BVM in Application to the Redemption]. In AMI, *Maria et Ecclesia*, 2:223–95. 1959.

———. *Dizionario di mariologia* [Dictionary of Mariology]. Rome: Editrice Studium, 1961.

———. "Equivoci sulla Corredenzione" [Misunderstandings about Coredemption]. *Marianum* 10 (1948): 277–82.

———. *La Madonna negli scritti di Maria Valtorta* [Mary in the Writings of Maria Valtorta]. 2nd ed. Isola del Liri: Centro Editoriale Valtortiano, 1986.

———. *La Madonna: Secondo la fede e la teologia* [The Madonna: According to the Faith and Theology]. 4 vols. Rome: Libreria Editrice Francesco Ferrari, 1953–54.

———. *La mediazione mariana oggi* [Marian Mediation Today]. Rome: Marianum, 1971.

———. *Maria Santissima nella storia della salvezza: Trattato completo di mariologia alla luce del Concilio Vaticano II* [Mary Most Holy in the History of Salvation: Complete Treatise on Mariology in Light of the Second Vatican Council]. 4 vols. Isola del Liri: Pisani, 1969.

———. *Mariologia*. 3 vols. Milan: Belardetti, 1941–42.

———. *Problematica sulla Corredenzione* [Issues about Coredemption]. Rome: Marianum, 1969.

Rosini, Ruggero. *Mariologia del beato Giovanni Duns Scoto* [Mariology of Blessed John Duns Scotus]. Castelpetroso: Casa Mariana Editrice, 1994. English translation: *Mariology of Blessed John Duns Scotus*. Translated by Fr. Peter Damian Fehlner. New Bedford, Mass.: Academy of the Immaculate, 2008.

Rossi Espagnet, Carla. "La dignità della donna (Mulieris dignitatem—1988)" [The Dignity of Woman (Mulieris dignitatem, 1988)]. In *Prendere il largo con Cristo: Esortazioni e lettere di Giovanni Paolo II*, edited by G. Borgonovo and A. Cattaneo, 182–92.

Rosso, Stefano, SDB. "Anno liturgico" [Liturgical Year]. In De Fiores and Meo, *NDM*, 50–78.

———. "Mese mariano" [Marian Month]. In De Fiores and Meo, *NDM*, 935–45.

———. "Sabato" [Saturday]. In De Fiores and Meo, *NDM*, 1216–28.

Roten, Johann G. "Suarez." In Bäumer and Scheffczyk, *ML* 6:323–25.

Rouet de Journel, M.J., ed. *Enchiridion patristicum* [Patristic Handbook]. Freiburg im Breisgau: Herder, 1937.

Rovira, German, ed. *Der Widerschein des ewigen Lichtes: Marienerscheinungen und Gnadenbilder als Zeichen der Gotteskraft* [Reflection of the Eternal Light: Marian

Apparitions and Images of Grace as Signs of God's Power]. Kevelaer: Butzon and Bercker, 1984.

———, ed. *Die sonnenbekleidete Frau: Die leibliche Aufnahme Marias in den Himmel; Überwindung des Todes durch die Gnade* [The Woman Clothed with the Sun: The Bodily Assumption of Mary into Heaven; The Overcoming of Death through Grace]. Kevelaer: Butzon and Bercker, 1986.

———. *Im Gewande des Heils: Die Unbefleckte Empfängnis Mariens als Urbild der menschlichen Heiligkeit* [Clothed with Holiness: The Immaculate Conception of Mary as an Archetype of Human Holiness]. Essen: Ludgerus-Verlag, 1980.

———, ed. *Ungetrübter Spiegel: Maria, Mutter der Kirche* [Untroubled Mirror: Mary, Mother of the Church]. Essen: Ludgerus-Verlag, 1992.

Roy, Neil J. "Mary and the Liturgical Year." In Miravalle, *Mariology: A Guide*, 607–65.

Royo Marin, Antonio. *La Virgen María: Teología y espiritualidad marianas* [The Virgin Mary: Marian Theology and Spirituality]. 2nd ed. Madrid: Biblioteca de Autores Cristianos, 1997.

Ruiz Tintoré, Miguel. "La devoción al Corazón de María, corazón de las devociones a María" [Devotion to the Heart of Mary, Heart of the Devotions to Mary]. *Ephemerides Mariologicae* 63, no. 4 (2013): 467–88.

Rush, Alfred C., CSSR. "Mary in the Apocrypha of the New Testament." In Carol, *Mariology*, 1:156–84. Spanish translation: "María en los evangelios apócrifos." In *Mariología*, edited by J. Carol, 156–81.

Rzepkowski, Horst. "Dialog." In Bäumer and Scheffczyk, *ML* 2:184f.

———. "Kuan-yin." In Bäumer and Scheffczyk, *ML* 3:692f.

———. *Lexikon der Mission* [Dictionary of Mission]. Graz: Verlag Styria, 1992.

———. "Missiologie." In Bäumer and Scheffczyk, *ML* 4:472f.

Sacred Congregation of Rites. *Officium et Missa Pro Festo Immacolati Cordis Beatae Mariae Virginis.* AAS 37 (1945): 50.

Salgado, Jean-Marie. *La Maternité Spirituelle de la Très Sainte Vierge Marie* [The Spiritual Motherhood of the Most Holy Virgin Mary]. Studi Tomistici 36. Vatican City: Libreria Editrice Vaticana, 1990.

Sardi, Vincenzo. *La solenne definizione del Dogma dell'Immacolato Concepimento di Maria santissima: Atti e documenti* [The Solemn Definition of the Dogma of the Immaculate Conception of Mary Most Holy: Acts and Documents]. 2 vols. Rome: Tipografia Vaticana, 1904–5.

Sartor, Danilo. "Madre di Dio. III. Celebrazione liturgica" [Mother of God. III. Liturgical Celebration]. In De Fiores and Meo, *NDM*, 825–28.

———."Maria, Assunta III. Celebrazione liturgica" [Mary, Assumed. III. Liturgical Celebration"]. In De Fiores and Meo, *NDM*, 178–83.

———. "Pietà popolare" [Popular Piety]. In De Fiores, Schiefer, and Perrella, *DMar*, 944–53.

Sartor, Danilo, Aristide Serra, and Stefano De Fiores. "Regina." In De Fiores and Meo, *NDM*, 1189–1206.

Scanziani, Francesco. "Da Lumen gentium VIII ad oggi: Il trattato di mariologiain Italia" [From Lumen gentium VIII to Today: The Treatise on Mariology in Italy]. *La Scuola Cattolica* 132, no. 1 (2004): 75–121.

———. "Il manuale di mariologia dagli inizi dell'ottocento al Vaticano II" [The Manual of Mariology, from its Beginnings in the 1800s to Vatican II]. In Boaga and Gambero, *Storia della mariologia*, 2:783–816.

Schaff, Philip, ed. *Nicene and Post-Nicene Fathers*. First Series (*NPNF1*). 14 vols. (1886–89) Peabody, Mass.: Hendrickson, 1994.

———. *Nicene and Post-Nicene Fathers*. Second Series (*NPNF2*). 14 vols. (1886–89). Peabody, Mass.: Hendrickson, 1994.

Scharbert, Josef. "Hoheslied" [Song of Songs]. In Bäumer and Scheffczyk, *ML* 3:232–34.

———. "Propheten" [Prophets]. In Bäumer and Scheffczyk, *ML* 5:323–24.

Scheeben, Matthias J. *Handbuch der katholischen Dogmatik* [Handbook of Catholic Dogmatic Theology]. Gesammelte Schriften 2–7. Freiburg im Breisgau: Herder, 1958. 3rd ed. 1957.

———. *Immakulata und päpstliche Unfehlbarkeit: Sedes Sapientiae und Cathedra Sapientiae* [The Immaculate and Papal Infallibility: Seat of Wisdom and Cathedra of Wisdom]. Edited by Josef Schmitz. Paderborn: F. Schöningh, 1954, new edition.

Scheffczyk, Leo. "Canisius." In Bäumer and Scheffczyk, *ML* 1:647f.

———. *Das Mariengeheimnis in Frömmigkeit und Lehre der Karolingerzeit* [The Mystery of Mary in the Piety and Doctrine of the Carolingian Age]. Leipzig: St. Benno-Verlag, 1959.

———. "Die 'Marienweihe' in Leben und Lehre Johannes Pauls II: Unter systematischem Aspekt" ["Marian Consecration" in the Life and Teaching of John Paul II, in a Systematic View]. In Ziegenaus, *Totus tuus*, 109–24.

———. *Die theologischen Grundlagen von Erscheinungen und Prophezeiungen* [Theological Basis of Apparitions and Prophecies]. Leutesdorf: Johannes-Verlag, 1982.

———. *Ecumenismo: La ripida via della verità* [Ecumenism: The Steep Way of Truth]. Memoria via 1. Vatican City: Lateran University Press, 2007.

———. "Exegese und Dogmatik zur virginitas post partum" [Exegesis and Dogmatic Theology on the Virginity in Childbirth]. *Münchener Theologische Zeitschrift* 28, no. 3 (1977): 291–301.

———. "Fundamentalprinzip, mariologisches" [Fundamental Principle of Mariology]. In Bäumer and Scheffczyk, *ML* 2:565–67.

———. *Grundlagen des Dogmas: Einleitung in die Dogmatik* [Foundations of Dogma: Introduction to Dogmatic Theology]. Katholische Dogmatik 1. Aachen: MM Verlag, 1997.

———. *Il mondo della fede cattolica: Verità e forma; Con un'intervista a Benedetto XVI* [The World of the Catholic Faith: Truth and Form; Including an interview with Benedict XVI]. Translated by Alessio Musio. Milan: Vita e Pensiero, 2007. German original: *Katholische Glaubenswelt. Wahrheit und Gestalt.* Aschaffenburg: Pattloch, 1977.

———. "Konvenienzgründe" [Grounds of Fittingness]. In Bäumer and Scheffczyk, *ML* 3:637–39.

———. "Maria Assumpta—im Licht des Erlösungsgeheimnisses" [Mary Assumed, in the Light of the Mystery of Redemption]. *Sedes Sapientiae: Mariologisches Jahrbuch* 4, no. 1 (2000): 45–70.

———. *Maria, crocevia della fede cattolica* [Mary, Crossroads of the Catholic Faith]. CdM 1. Lugano: Eupress FTL, 2002.

———. *Maria, Mutter und Gefährtin Christi* [Mary, Mother and Companion of Christ]. Augsburg: Sankt Ulrich, 2003.

———. "Maria: Punto focale dei misteri della fede" [Mary: Focal Point of the Mysteries of the Faith]. *RTLu* 9, no. 2 (2004): 283–94.

———. "Nestorius." In Bäumer and Scheffczyk, *ML* 4:598f.

———. *Neue Impulse zur Marienverehrung* [New Impulses to Marian Devotion]. St. Ottilien: EOS Verlag, 1974.

———. "Privatoffenbarungen" [Private Revelations]. In Bäumer and Scheffczyk, *ML* 5:318–20.

———. "Prophetin" [Prophetess]. In Bäumer and Scheffczyk, *ML* 5:324f.

———. "Protoevangelium II: Dogmengeschichte" [Protoevangelium II: History of Dogma]. In Bäumer and Scheffczyk, *ML* 5:343–44.

———. "'Sitz der Weisheit': Maria–Bild vollendeten Menschseins" ["Seat of Wisdom": Mary, Image of Humanity Fulfilled]. *Sedes Sapientiae: Mariologisches Jahrbuch* 2, no. 1 (1998): 48–69.

———. "Tendenzen und Entwicklungslinien der Marienlehre im Mittelalter" [Schools of Thought in Marian Doctrine and Lines of Its Development in the Middle Ages]. In *Das Zeichen des Allmächtigen: Die jungfräuliche Gottesmutterschaft Mariens in ihrer Verbindlichkeit für das christliche Leben*, edited by German Rovira, 118–38. Würzburg: Naumann, 1981.

———. "Scholastik" [Scholasticism]. In Bäumer and Scheffczyk, *ML* 6:57–59.

———. "Weihe" [Consecration]. In Bäumer and Scheffczyk, *ML* 6:696–98.

Schenk, Richard. "Merkelbach." In Bäumer and Scheffczyk, *ML* 4:424.

———. "Thomas v. Aquin." In Bäumer and Scheffczyk, *ML* 6, 399–405.

Schmaus, Michael. *Katholische Dogmatik.* Vol. 5, *Mariologie.* 2nd ed. Munich: Hueber, 1961. Italian translation: *Dogmatica Cattolica.* Vol. 2, *La Madre del Redentore* [*Mariologia*]. 3rd ed. Turin: Marietti, 1969, 357–716.

———. "Maria." In *Sacramentum mundi*, edited by K. Rahner, 5:52–68. Brescia: Morcelliana, 1976. German original: "Maria." In *Sacramentum mundi,* ed. Rahner, 3:334–49. Freiburg: Herder, 1969.

Schmid, Josef. "Abstammung Mariens" [Lineage of Mary]. In Bäumer and Scheffczyk, *ML* 1:21f.

Schmidt, Axel. "Johannes Duns Scotus über die Immaculata Conceptio" [John Duns Scotus on the Immaculate Conception]. *Sedes Sapientiae: Mariologisches Jahrbuch* 8, no 2 (2004): 55–78.

Schmidt, Firmin M., OFM Cap. "Realeza universal de María" [Universal Queenship of Mary]. In Carol, *Mariología*, 867–920. English original: "The Queenship of Mary." In Carol, *Mariology*, 2:493–549.

Schmuck, N. "Katakombenmalerei" [Catacomb Painting]. In Bäumer and Scheffczyk, *ML* 3:523–26.

Schmucki, Octavian. "Franz v. Assisi." In Bäumer and Scheffczyk, *ML* 2:509–11.

Schnackenburg, Rudolf. *Il Vangelo di Giovanni.* 3 vols. Brescia: Paideia Editrice, 1973–81. German original: *Das Johannesevangelium.* Vols. 1–3. Freiburg im Breisgau, 1979 (4th ed.), 1980 (3rd ed.), 1979 (3rd ed.) English translation: *The Gospel according to St. John.* London: Burns and Oates, 1968.

Schneider, Gerhard, ed. *Evangeliae infantiae apocrypha* [Apocryphal Infancy Gospels]. Fontes christiani 18. Freiburg im Breisgau: Herder, 1995.

Schneider, Johannes. *Virgo Ecclesia facta: La presenza di Maria nel crocifisso di San Damiano e nell'Officium Passionis di san Francesco d'Assisi.* Assisi: Porziuncola, 2003. German original: *"Virgo Ecclesia facta": Die Gegenwart Marias auf dem Kreuzbild von San Damiano und im "Officium passionis" des heiligen Franziskus von Assisi.* St. Ottilien: EOS Verlag, 1998. English translation: *Virgo ecclesia facta: The Presence of Mary in the Crucifix of San Damiano and in the Office of the Passion of St. Francis of Assisi.* New Bedford, Mass.: Academy of the Immaculate, 2004.

Schönborn, Christoph. "Maria—Herz der Theologie—Theologie des Herzens" [Mary, Heart of Theology, Theology of the Heart]. In *Weisheit Gottes—Weisheit der Welt: Festschrift für Joseph Kardinal Ratzinger zum 60. Geburtstag*, edited by Walter Baier et al., 1:575–89. St. Ottilien: EOS Verlag, 1987.

Schürmann, Heinz. *Il Vangelo di Luca* [The Gospel of Luke]. Vol. 1. Brescia: Paideia, 1985. German original: *Das Lukasevangelium.* Vol. I. Freiburg im Breisgau: Herder, 1969.

———. "Maria im modernen Judentum" [Mary in Modern Judaism]. *Sedes Sapientiae: Mariologisches Jahrbuch* 2, no. 2 (1998): 102–19.

Schultze, Bernhard, SJ. "Theologi palamitae saeculi XIV de mediatione B.M. Virginis" [The Palamite Theologians of the 14th Century on the Mediation of the Blessed Virgin Mary]. In PAMI, *De mariologia et oecumenismo*, 355–422.

Schulz, Hans-Joachim. *Die byzantinische Liturgie: Glaubenszeugnis und Symbolgestalt* [The Byzantine Liturgy]. 2nd ed. Trier: Paulinus-Verlag, 1980. English translation: *The Byzantine Liturgy: Symbolic Structure and Faith Expression.* Translated by Matthew J. O'Connell. New York: Pueblo, 1986.

Schumacher, Joseph. "Maria, die Mutter Jesu, im Islam" [Mary the Mother of Jesus, in Islam]. *Sedes Sapientiae: Mariologisches Jahrbuch* 2, no. 1 (1998): 70–93.

Schwegler, Theodor. *Die biblische Urgeschichte* [Biblical Primeval History]. 2nd ed. Munich: Friedrich Pustet, 1962.

Schweitzer, Albert. *Geschichte der Leben-Jesu-Forschung* [The History of Research into the Life of Jesus]. 9th ed. Tübingen: Mohr, 1984. Originally published in 1913. Italian translation: *Storia della ricerca sulla vita di Gesù.* Brescia: Paideia, 1986. English translation: *The Quest of the Historical Jesus.* Minneapolis: Fortress, 2001.

Schwendimann, Friedrich. *Herz-Jesu-Verehrung heute?* [Devotion to the Heart of Jesus Today?] Regensburg: J. Habbel, 1974.

Scicluna, Charles J. "Criteri e norme della Congregazione per la Dottrina della Fede nel discernimento delle apparizioni mariane" [Criteria and Norms of the Congregation for the Doctrine of the Faith in the Discernment of Marian Apparitions]. *Marianum* 74 (2012): 229–81.

———. "Orientamenti dottrinali e competenze del vescovo diocesano e della Congregazione per la Dottrina della Fede nel discernimento delle apparizioni mariane" [Doctrinal Orientations and Competences of the Diocesan Bishop and of the Congregation for the Doctrine of the Faith in the Discernment of Marian Apparitions]. In *Apparitiones Beatae Mariae Virginis in historia, fide, theologia: Acta Congressus mariologici-mariani internationalis in civitate Lourdes Anno 2008 celebra-*

ti, edited by Stefano Maria Cecchin and Antonio Ligotti, 1:329–56. Vatican City: PAMI, 2010.

Scippa, Vincenzo. "Lettere ai Corinzi" [Letters to the Corinthians]. In *La Bibbia Piemme*, edited by Luciano Pacomio, 2717–93. Casale Monferrato: Piemme, 1995.

Scola, Angelo. *Il mistero nuziale*. 2 vols. Vatican City: Pontificia Università Lateranense, 1998–2000. English translation: *The Nuptial Mystery*. Grand Rapids, Mich: William B. Eerdmans, 2005.

Sebastian, Wenceslao, OFM. "Maternidad espiritual de María." In Carol, *Mariología*, 711–59. English original: "Mary's Spiritual Maternity." In Carol, *Mariology*, 2:325–76.

Second Vatican Council. Dogmatic Constitution on the Church *Lumen gentium* (*LG*). November 21, 1964.

———. Constitution *Sacrosanctum concilium*. December 4, 1963.

Sedlmeier, Franz. "Jes 7,14: Überlegungen zu einem umstrittenen Vers und zu seiner Auslegungsgeschichte" [Is 7:14: Considerations on a Disputed Verse and the History of Its Exegesis]. In "*Geboren aus der Jungfrau Maria*": *Klarstellungen*, edited by A. Ziegenaus, 13–43. Mariologische Studien 19. Regensburg: Pustet, 2007.

Segalla, Giuseppe. "Il bambino con Maria sua madre in Matteo 2" [The Child with Mary His Mother in Matthew 2]. *Theotokos* 4, no. 1 (1996): 15–27.

Seller, J. J., OSA, and Ildefons M. Dietz, OESA. "Emmerick." In Bäumer and Scheffczyk, *ML* 2:335f.

Sennott, Thomas M. *Acheiropoeta: Not Made by Hands; The Miraculous Images of Our Lady of Guadalupe and the Shroud of Turin*. New Bedford, Mass.: Franciscan Friars of the Immaculate, 1999. Reprinted San Francisco: Ignatius Press, 2011.

Serra, Aristide. "Alleanza" [Covenant]. In De Fiores, Schiefer, and Perrella, *DMar*, 40–48.

———. "Assunta I. Fondamenti biblici dell'Assunzione" [Mary Assumed. I. Biblical Foundations of the Assumption]. In De Fiores and Meo, *NDM*, 163–67.

———. "Bibbia" [Bible]. In De Fiores and Meo, *NDM*, 231–311.

———. *E c'era la Madre di Gesù: Saggi di esegesi biblico-mariana (1978–1988)* [And the Mother of Jesus Was There … Essays in Biblical-Marian Exegesis]. Milan and Rome: CENS and Marianum, 1989.

———. "'… e lo avvolse in fasce …' (Lk 2:7b). Un segno da decodificare." In *E c'era la Madre di Gesù: Saggi di esegesi biblico-mariana (1978–1988)* [And the Mother of Jesus Was There … Essays in Biblical-Marian Exegesis], 253–57. Milan and Rome: CENS and Marianum, 1989.

———. "Galati 4,4: Una mariologia in germe" [Gal. 4:4: A Mariology in Germ]. *Theotokos* 1, no. 2 (1993): 7–25.

———. "Immacolata e alleanza: Verso una verifica dei fondamenti biblici del dogma di Pius IX" [The Immaculate and Covenant: Toward a Verification of the Biblical Foundations of the Dogma of Pius IX]. In Toniolo, *Il dogma dell'Immacolata Concezione*, 223–69.

———. "Immacolata II. Fondamenti biblici." In De Fiores and Meo, *NDM*, 688–95.

———. *La Donna dell'Alleanza: Prefigurazioni di Maria nell'Antico Testamento* [The

Woman of the Covenant: Prefigurations of Mary in the Old Testament]. Padua: Messaggero, 2006.
———. "La 'Mulieris dignitatem': Consensi e dissensi" ["Mulieris dignitatem": Agreements and Dissents]. *Marianum* 53, no. 141 (1991): 144–82.
———. *Le nozze di Cana (Gv 2,1–12: Incidenze cristologico-mariane del primo "segno" di Gesù* [The Wedding of Cana (Jn 2:1–12): Christological-Marian Implications of the First "Sign" of Jesus]. Padua: Messaggero, 2009.
———. "Madre di Dio I. Fondamenti biblici" [Mother of God. I. Biblical Foundations]. In De Fiores and Meo, *NDM*, 806–12.
———. *Maria a Cana e presso la croce: Saggio di mariologia giovannea* [Mary at Cana and at the Foot of the Cross: Essay in Johannine Mariology]. Rome: Centro di Cultura Mariana 'Madre della Chiesa, 1985. 3rd ed. 1991.
———. *Maria presso la Croce: Solo l'addolorata? Verso una rilettura dei contenuti di Giovanni 19,25–27* [Mary at the Foot of the Cross: Only the Lady of Sorrows? Toward a Re-reading of John 19:25–27]. Padua: Messaggero, 2011.
———. *Maria secondo il Vangelo* [Mary according to the Gospel]. Brescia: Queriniana, 1987.
———. *Nato da donna: Ricerche bibliche su Maria di Nazaret (1989–1992)* [Born of Woman: Biblical Research on Mary of Nazareth (1989–1992)]. Milano and Rome: CENS and Marianum, 1992.
———. "Sapiente" [Wise]. In De Fiores and Meo, *NDM*, 1272–85.
———. "Testimonianze mariane in Luca e Giovanni" [Marian Witnesses in Luke and John]. In Dal Covolo and Serra, *Storia della mariologia*, 1:79–140.
———. "*Una spada trafiggerà la tua vita» (Lc 2,35a): Quale spada? Bibbia e tradizione giudaico cristiana a confronto* ["A Sword Will Pierce Your Life" (Lk 2:35a): Which Sword? The Bible and Jewish-Christian Tradition in Contrast]. Rome: Marianum, 2003.
———. "Vergine II: Testimonianza biblica" [Virgin. II. Biblical Witness]. In De Fiores and Meo, *NDM*, 1424–54.
Sesboüé, Bernard, SJ. "La doctrine de l'Immaculée Conception dans le dialogue oecuménique (Groupe de Dombes et accord luthéro-catholique de 1999)" [The Doctrine of the Immaculate Conception in Ecumenical Dialog: Ehe Dombes Group and the Lutheran-Catholic Agreement of 1999]. In Toniolo, *Il dogma dell'Immacolata Concezione*, 395–414.
Seumois, André V. "Maria nei paesi di missione" [Mary in the Mission Countries]. In *EMTheo* (1958): 212–20.
Seybold, Michael. "Unbefleckte Empfängnis I. Dogmatik" [Immaculate Conception. I. Dogmatic Theology]. In Bäumer and Scheffczyk, *ML* 6:519–25.
Sgreva, Gianni. *Le apparizioni della Madonna in Africa: Kibeho* [Apparitions of Our Lady in Africa: Kibeho]. 2nd ed. Camerata Picena: Shalom, 2004.
Sgubbi, Giorgio. *Dio di Gesù Cristo, Dio dei filosofi: Il cristico e il critico* [God of Jesus Christ, God of the Philosophers: The Christic and the Critical]. Bologna: EDB, 2004.
Shea, George W. "Historia de la mariología en la Edad Media y en los tiempos modernos." In Carol, *Mariología*, 267–306. English original: "Outline History

of the Mariology of the Middle Ages and Modern Times." In Carol, *Mariology*, 1:281–327.

Shoemaker, Stephen J. *Ancient Traditions of the Virgin Mary's Dormition and Assumption*. Oxford: Oxford University Press, 2002.

Siano, Paolo M., FI. "Uno studio su Maria Santissima 'Mediatrice di tutte le grazie' nel magistero pontificio fino al pontificato di Giovanni Paolo II" [A Study of Mary Most Holy "Mediatrix of All Graces" in the Pontifical Magisterium up to the Pontificate of John Paul II]. *Maria Corredentrice* 8 (2006):191–266.

Sigl, Paul Maria. *Die Frau aller Völker: Miterlöserin Mittlerin Fürsprecherin* [The Lady of All Nations: Co-Redemptrix, Mediatrix, Advocate]. Goldach, Switzerland: Familie Mariens der Miterlöserin, 1998.

Sileo, Leonardo. "Filosofia, medicina e teologia: Il concepimento di Maria nella svolta teoretica di Duns Scoto" [Philosophy, Medicine, and Theology: The Conception of Mary in the Theoretical Turn Wrought by Duns Scotus]. In *Giovanni Duns Scoto: Studi e ricerche nel VII Centenario della sua morte*, edited by Martín Carbajo Nuñez, 2:39–89. Rome: Pontificio Ateneo Antonianum, 2008.

Siudy, Teofil. ed. *La Vergine Maria nel magistero di Giovanni Paolo II* [The Virgin Mary in the Magisterium of John Paul II]. Vatican City: PAMI, 2007.

Sizonenko, Demetrius. "Fede e tradizione teologica della Chiesa ortodossa russa circa la Tuttasanta" [Faith and Theological Tradition of the Russian Orthodox Church on the All-Holy Virgin]. In De Fiores and E. Vidau, *Maria Santa e Immacolata*, 91–103.

Socias, James, ed. *Daily Roman Missal*. Woodridge, Ill.: Midwest Theological Forum, 2011.

Socci, Antonio. *Il quarto segreto di Fatima* [The Fourth Secret of Fatima]. Milan: Rizzoli, 2006.

Solá Carrió, Francisco de Paula. "Verdaderas y falsas Apariciones: Criterios de discernimiento" [True and False Apparitions: Criteria of Discernment]. *Estudios Marianos* 52 (1987): 115–34.

Söll, Georg. *Storia dei dogmi mariani* [History of Marian Dogmas]. Rome: Libreria Ateneo Salesiano, 1981. German original: *Mariologie* [Handbuch der Dogmengeschichte III/4]. Freiburg im Breisgau: Herder, 1978.

———. "Verehrung Mariens" [Marian Devotion]. In Bäumer and Scheffczyk, *ML* 4:596–99.

Spiazzi, Raimondo, ed. *Enciclopedia mariana "Theotocos"* ["Theotokos," Marian Encyclopedia]. Genoa: Bevilacqua e Solari; Milan: Editrice Massimo, 1954. 2nd ed. 1958.

Špidlík, Tomáš et al., eds. *Testi mariani del secondo millennio*. Vol. 2, *Autori dell'area russa: Sec. XI–XX* [Marian Texts of the Second Millennium. Vol. 2, Authors of the Russian Region: 11th to 20th Centuries]. Rome: Città nuova, 2000.

Spiteris, Yannis. *Salvezza e peccato nella tradizione orientale* [Salvation and Sin in Eastern Tradition]. Bologna: EDB, 1999.

Staid, Ennio D. "Rosario" [Rosary]. In De Fiores and Meo, *NDM*, 1207–15.

Stakemeier, Eduard. "De Beata Maria Virgine eiusque cultu iuxta reformatores" [The Blessed Virgin Mary and Her Cult, according to the Reformers]. In *De mariologia et oecumenismo*, edited by PAMI (Rome: PAMI, 1962), 423–77.

Starowieyski, Marek. "Le titre Theotokos avant le concile d'Éphèse" [The Title Theotokos before the Council of Ephesus]. *Studia Patristica* 19 (1989): 237–42.

Stauffer, Ethelbert. *Jesus: Gestalt und Geschichte*. Bern; Francke, 1957. English: *Jesus and His Story*. London: SCM, 1960.

Stawrowsky, Alexis. "La Sainte Vierge Marie: La doctrine de l'Immaculée Conception des Églises Catholique et Orthodoxe; Étude comparée par un Théologien Orthodoxe" [The Holy Virgin Mary: The Catholic and Orthodox Churches' Doctrine of the Immaculate Conception; Comparative Study by an Orthodox Theologian]. *Marianum* 35 (1973): 36–112.

Stefani, Piero. "Ebrei" [The Jews]. In De Fiores, Schiefer, and Perrella, *DMar*, 447–55.

Stegmüller, Otto. "Berengaudus." In Bäumer and Scheffczyk, *ML* 1:435.

Stegmüller, Otto, and Heinrich M. Köster. "Ekbert von Schönau." In Bäumer and Scheffczyk, *ML* 2:312.

Stegmüller, Otto, and Helmut Riedlinger. "Bernhard von Clairvaux I. Leben und Werk" [Bernard of Clairvaux. I. Life and Work]. In Bäumer and Scheffczyk, *ML* 1:445–47.

Stegmüller, Otto, and Richard Schenk. "Contenson." In Bäumer and Scheffczyk, *ML* 2:92.

Stegmüller, Otto, and R. Schulte. "Arnald von Bonneval." In Bäumer and Scheffczyk, *ML* 1:243f.

Steinhauer, Hilda. *Maria als dramatische Person bei Hans Urs von Balthasar: Zum marianischen Prinzip seines Denkens* [Mary as a Dramatic Figure in Hans Urs von Balthasar: The Marian Principle of His Thought]. Salzburger Theologische Studien 17. Innsbruck: Tyrolia, 2001.

Stern, Jean. "L'examen canonique des apparitions mariales selon Benoît XIV" [The Canonical Examination of Marian Apparitions according to Benedict XIV]. In PAMI, *De cultu mariano saeculis XVII–XVIII*, 5:341–63. 1987.

———. *La Salette: documents authentiques*. 3 vols. Paris: Cerf, 1984–91.

———. "La Salette I. Geschichte" [La Salette. I. History]. In Bäumer and Scheffczyk, *ML* 4:25–27.

———. "La Salette: Une affaire de discernement" [La Salette: A Matter of Discernment]. *Marianum* 72, no. 177–78 (2010): 535–46.

Stierli, Josef. "Jesuiten." In Bäumer and Scheffczyk, *ML* 3: 373–75.

Stiernon, David. "Marie dans la théologie orthodoxe gréco-russe" [Mary in Greco-Russian Orthodox Theology]. In du Manoir, *Maria*, 7:241–338. 1964.

Stimpfle, Josef. "Entschiedenheit für Gott: Begründung, Sinn, Ziel und Durchführung der Weihe an das Unbefleckte Herz Mariä" [Commitment for God: Basis, Meaning, Aim, and Implementation of Consecration to the Immaculate Heart of Mary]. In Stimpfle, *Im Dienste am Evangelium*, edited by Georg Schmuttermayr. Donauwörth: Auer, 1988.

Stock, Klemens, SI. *Maria, la Madre del Signore, nel Nuovo Testamento* [Mary, Mother of the Lord, in the New Testament]. 2nd ed. Rome: Edizione ADP, 2003.

Stöger, Alois. "Armut Mariens" [The Poverty of Mary]. In Bäumer and Scheffczyk, *ML* 1:242f.

———. "Glaube Marias" [The Faith of Mary]. In Bäumer and Scheffczyk, *ML* 2:646f.

Stöhr, Johannes. "Barmherzigkeit Mariens" [Mercy of Mary]. In Bäumer and Scheffczyk, *ML* 1:364–70.

———. "Charismen" [Charisms]. In Bäumer and Scheffczyk, *ML* 2:25–31.

———. "Corazón de Madre (Consideraziones teológicas sobre la Consagración a María)" [Heart of the Mother (Theological Considerations on Consecration to Mary)]. *Scripta de Maria* 2nd ser., 1 (2004): 141–80; see also a German version, "Sapientia cordis: Theologische Überlegungen zur Weihehingabe." *Sedes Sapientiae: Mariologisches Jahrbuch* 1, no. 1 (1997): 74–118.

———. *"Er hat sich für uns hingegeben" (Tit 2,14): Die Erlösungstat Christi und seine Kirche* ["He Gave Himself Up for Us" (Ti 2:14): Christ's Act of Redemption and His Church]. Weilheim-Bierbronnen: Books on Demand, 2007.

———. "Eucharistie und Maria." In Bäumer and Scheffczyk, *ML* 2:406–9.

———. "Gnadenfülle" [Fullness of Grace]. In Bäumer and Scheffczyk, *ML* 2:662–64.

———. "Herz Mariä III. Dogmatik" [Heart of Mary. III. Dogmatics]. In Bäumer and Scheffczyk, *ML* 3:167–69.

———. "Josef, der 'Gerechte,' jungfräulich mit Maria im Ehebund vereint" [Joseph the "Just Man," Virginally United with Mary in the Bond of Marriage]. *Sedes Sapientiae: Mariologisches Jahrbuch* 5, no. 2 (2001): 53–86.

———. "Maria in der christlichen Ehe nach päpstlichen Verlautbarungen" [Mary in Christian Marriage according to Papal Declarations]. *Sedes Sapientiae: Mariologisches Jahrbuch* 11, vol. 1 (2007): 84–126.

———. "Maria und die Einheit der Kirche" [Mary and the Unity of the Church]. *Sedes Sapientiae: Mariologisches Jahrbuch* 4, no. 1 (2000): 71–99.

———. "Mariologie." In Bäumer and Scheffczyk, *ML* 4:320–26.

———. "Mutterschaft, geistliche" [Motherhood, Spiritual]. In Bäumer and Scheffczyk, *ML* 4:560–63.

———. "Neue Hoffnungen in der Mariologie für die Anglikaner" [New Hopes in Mariology for Anglicans]. *Sedes Sapientiae: Mariologisches Jahrbuch* 9, no. 2 (2005): 91–98.

———. "Neuere Impulse zur Theologie und Verehrung des Herzens Mariä" [Recent Advances in Theology and Devotion of the Heart of Mary]. In PAMI, *De cultu mariano saeculo XX*, 2:397–427.

———. "Verdienst Marias" [Merit of Mary]. In Bäumer and Scheffczyk, *ML* 6:593–96.

———. "Zur Bibliographie der Immakulata" [Toward a Bibliography of the Immaculate.] *Sedes Sapientiae: Mariologisches Jahrbuch* 8, no. 1 (2004): 61–90.

Stramare, Tarcisio. *Gesù lo chiamò padre: Rassegna storico-dottrinale su san Giuseppe* [Jesus Called Him Father: Historical-Doctrinal Review of St. Joseph]. Vatican City: Libreria Editrice Vaticana, 1997.

———. "Giuseppe" [Joseph]. In De Fiores and Meo, *NDM*, 633–55.

———. "Il matrimonio della Madre di Dio" [The Marriage of the Mother of God]. *Divinitas* 46, no. 1 (2003): 19–52.

———. *Il matrimonio della Madre di Dio: I santi sposi* [The Marriage of the Mother of God: The Holy Spouses]. Verona: Edizioni Stimmatine, 2001.

———. *Vangelo dei Misteri della Vita Nascosta di Gesù (Matteo e Luca I–II)* [Gospel of the Mysteries of the Hidden Life of Jesus (Matthew and Luke 1–2)]. Bornato in Franciacorta (Brescia): Sardini, 1998.

Sträter, Paul, ed. *Katholische Marienkunde* [Catholic Marian Doctrine]. Vols. 1–3. Paderborn: F. Schöningh, 1947. (1962, 3rd ed.), 1947 (1962, 3rd ed.), 1951. Italian translation: *Mariologia*. Vols. 1–3. Turin: Marietti Editori Pontifici, 1952–58.

Studer, Basil. "Il concilio di Efeso (431) nella luce della dottrina Mariana di Cirillo di Alessandria" [The Council of Ephesus (431) in Light of the Marian Doctrine of Cyril of Alexandria]. In *La Mariologia nella catechesi dei Padri (età postnicena)*, edited by S. Felici, 49–67. Rome: LAS, 1991.

Stumpf, Gerhard. ed. *Maria: Mutter der Kirche* [Mary: Mother of the Church]. Landsberg: Initiativkreis Katholischer Laien und Priester in der Diözese Augsburg, 2004.

Suárez, Francisco. *Francisci Suarez … Opera omnia*. Vol. 19. Edited by Vivès. Paris: 1856–78.

Suh, Augustinus. *Le rivelazioni private nella vita della Chiesa* [Private Revelations in the Life of the Church]. Bologna: Edizioni Studio Domenicano, 2000.

Tanquerey, Adolphe. *Compendio di teologia ascetica e mistica* [Compendium of Ascetic and Mystical Theology]. 2nd ed. Rome and Paris: Desclée, 1930.

Testoni, Manuela. *Le apparizioni della Madonna di Guadalupe: Storia e significato* [Apparitions of Our Lady of Guadalupe: History and Significance]. Cinisello Balsamo: San Paolo, 1998.

Theas, Pierre M. *La fede di Maria* [The Faith of Mary]. Rome: Città Nuova, 1978.

Thomas Aquinas. *De regimine principum* I.1–2. In *St. Thomas Aquinas: Political Writings*, ed. R. W. Dyson. 5–10. Cambridge: Cambridge University Press, 2004.

Tineo, Primitivo. "Pío IX y la definición de la Inmaculada" [Pius IX and the Definition of the Immaculate]. *Scripta de Maria* 2nd ser., no. 1 (2004): 205–36.

Toniolo, Ermanno M., OSM. "Akáthistos" [Akathist Hymn]. In De Fiores and Meo, *NDM*, 16–25.

———. *Akathístos: Saggi di critica e di teologia* [Akathist. Critical and Theological Essays]. Rome: Centro di cultura mariana "Madre della Chiesa," 2000.

———. "Bibbia" [Bible]. In De Fiores, Schiefer, and Perrella, *DMar*, 199–216.

———. *Bibliografia mariana*. Vol. 9, *1990–1993*. Rome: Ed. Marianum, 1998. See the entry for Besutti, *Bibliografia mariana* for information on the series.

———, ed. *Il dogma dell'Immacolata Concezione di Maria: Problemi attuali e tentativi di ricomprensione* [The Dogma of the Immaculate Conception of Mary: Current Issues and Attempts at Reinterpretation]. Rome: Ed. Marianum, 2004.

———, ed. *Il magistero mariano di Giovanni Paolo II: Percorsi e punti salienti* [The Marian Magisterium of John Paul II: Pathways and Salient Points]. Rome: Centro di cultura Mariana "Madre della Chiesa," 2006.

———. *La Beata Vergine Maria nel Concilio Vaticano II: Cronistoria del capitolo VIII della costituzione dogmatica "Lumen gentium" e sinossi di tutte le relazioni* [The Blessed Virgin Mary at the Second Vatican Council: Chronicle of Chapter Eight of the Dogmatic Constitution "Lumen gentium" and Synopsis of All the Reports]. Rome: Centro di cultura Mariana "Madre della Chiesa," 2004.

———. "La forma impegnativa di culto mariano: La consacrazione personale a Maria" [The Commitment Form of the Cult of Mary: Personal Consecration to Mary]. In Toniolo, *La Vergine Maria nel cammino orante della Chiesa*, 237–50.

———, ed. *La Madre del Signore dal Medioevo al Rinascimento* [The Mother of the Lord, from the Middle Ages to the Renaissance]. Itinerari Mariani dei due millenni 3. Rome: Centro di cultura Mariana "Madre della Chiesa," 1998.

———, ed. *La Vergine Madre dal Rinascimento ad oggi* [The Virgin Mother from the Renaissance to Today]. Itinerari Mariani dei due millenni 4. Rome: Centro di cultura Mariana "Madre della Chiesa," 1999.

———, ed. *La Vergine Madre dal secolo VI al secondo millennio* [The Virgin Mother from the Sixth Century to the Second Millennium]. Itinerari Mariani dei due millenni 2. Rome: Centro di cultura Mariana "Madre della Chiesa," 1998.

———, ed. *La Vergine Maria nel cammino orante della Chiesa: Liturgia e pietà popolare* [The Virgin Mary in the Praying Pilgrimage of the Church: Liturgy and Popular Piety]. Rome: Centro di cultura Mariana "Madre della Chiesa," 2003.

———, ed. *La Vergine Madre nella Chiesa delle origini* [The Virgin Mother in the Origins of the Church]. Rome: Centro di cultura Mariana "Madre della Chiesa," 1996.

———. *La Vergine Madre di Dio nei primi padri della Chiesa* [The Virgin Mother of God in the Early Fathers of the Church]. Rome: Centro di cultura Mariana "Madre della Chiesa," 1988.

———. "Magnificat." In De Fiores, Schiefer, and Perrella, *DMar*, 785–90.

———. "Maria 'donna nuova' nella testimonianza liturgica: Maria nella liturgia orientale" [Mary, the "New Woman" in Liturgical Witness: Mary in the Eastern Liturgy]. In Hauke, *La donna e la salvezza*, 75–111.

———, ed. *Maria e l'Eucaristia* [Mary and the Eucharist]. Rome: Centro di cultura Mariana "Madre della Chiesa," 2000.

———, ed. *Maria nel Concilio: Approfondimenti e percorsi* [Mary at the Council: Insights and Pathways]. Rome: Centro di cultura Mariana "Madre della Chiesa," 2005.

———. "Maria nelle chiese orientali" [Mary in the Eastern Churches]. In Ferugia, *Dizionario enciclopedico dell'Oriente Cristiano*, 469–75.

———. "Padri della Chiesa" [Fathers of the Church]. In De Fiores and Meo, *NDM*, 1044–80.

———. "Testi mariani di Paolo, Marco, Matteo e Luca 1, 46–55" [Marian Texts of Paul, Mark, Matthew and Luke 1: 46–55]. In Dal Covolo and Serra, *Storia della mariologia*, 1:29–77.

Torelló, Johannes B. "Echte und falsche Erscheinungen: Besonnenheit und Offenheit vor den Marienerscheinungen" [True and False Apparitions: Prudence and Openness in View of Marian Apparitions]. In Rovira, *Der Widerschein des ewigen Lichtes*, 89–107. 1984.

Tosatti, Marco. *La profezia di Fatima* [The Prophecy of Fatima]. Casale Monferrato: Piemme, 2007.

Toso, Mario, ed. *Essere donna: Studi sulla lettera apostolica "Mulieris dignitatem" di Giovanni Paolo II* [Being a Woman: Studies in John Paul II's Apostolic Letter "Mulieris dignitatem"]. Turin: Elledici, 1989.

Trapp, Erich. "Geometres Johannes" [John the Geometer]. In Bäumer and Scheffczyk, *ML* 2:618.

Trenner, Florian. "Lukasbild" [Image in Luke]. In Bäumer and Scheffczyk, *ML* 4:183–86.

Truhlar, C. V. (Karel Vladimir), SJ. "Principia theologica de habitudine Christiani erga Apparitiones" [Theological Principle of the Christian Attitude toward Apparitions]. In *De apparitionibus virginis immaculatae*, edited by AMI. Virgo Immaculata 16. 1–17. Rome: AMI, 1956.

Tschochner, Friederike. "Königtum Mariens II. Kunstgeschichte" [Queenship of Mary. II. Art History]. In Bäumer and Scheffczyk, *ML* 3:593–96.

Tüskes, Gábor, and Éva Knapp. "Stephan der Heilige" [St. Stephen]. In Bäumer and Scheffczyk, *ML* 6:294f.

Twents, Simone. *Frau sein ist mehr: Die Würde der Frau nach Johannes Paul II* [To Be a Woman Is More: The Value of Woman according to John Paul II]. Buttenwiesen: Stella-Maris-Verlag, 2002.

Unger, Dominic J., OFM Cap. "Utrum secundum Doctores Ecclesiae Virgo Maria Filium suum Dei Filium esse nunzio angelico cognoverit" [According to the Doctors of the Church, Did the Virgin Mary Know Her Son to Be the Son of God through the Message of the Angel?]. In *Maria in Sacra Scriptura*, edited by C. Balić, 4:347–420. Rome: PAMI, 1967.

Valasek, Emil. "Philippsdorf." In Bäumer and Scheffczyk, *ML* 5:204.

Valentini, Alberto. "Magnificat." In De Fiores, Schiefer, and Perrella, *DMar*, 785–90.

———. "Maria canta la misericordia di Dio" [Mary Sings the Mercy of God]. In P. Di Domenico and E. Peretto, *Maria Madre di misericordia*, 122–45.

———. *Maria secondo le Scritture: Figlia di Sion e Madre del Signore* [Mary according to the Scriptures: Daughter of Zion and Mother of the Lord]. Bologna: EDB, 2007.

Van Ackeren, Gerald, SJ. "Maternidad divina de María" [Mary's Divine Motherhood]. In Carol, *Mariología*, 570–618. English original: "Outline History of the Mariology of the Middle Ages and Modern Times." In Carol, *Mariology*, 1:177–227.

Vanhoye, Albert. "Discussioni sulla Nuova Alleanza" [Debates on the New Covenant]. *RTLu* 1, no. 2 (1996): 163–78.

———. *La lettre aux Hébreux: Jésus-Christ, médiateur d'une nouvelle alliance* [The Letter to the Hebrews: Jesus Christ, Mediator of a New Covenant]. Jésus et Jésus-Christ 84. Paris: Desclée, 2002.

———. "La Mère de Dieu selon Gal 4,4" [The Mother of God according to Gal 4:4]. *Marianum* 40 (1978): 237–47.

Vekemans, Roger, SJ, ed. *Cor Christi: Historia, teología, espiritualidad y pastoral* [Heart of Christ: History, Theology, Spirituality and Pastoral Care]. Bogotá: Instituto Internacional del Corazón de Jesús, 1980.

Veraja, Fabijan. *Le cause di canonizzazione dei santi: Commento alla legislazione e guida pratica* [Canonization Causes of Saints: Commentary on the Legislation and Practical Guide]. Vatican City: Libreria Editrice Vaticana, 1992.

Vetten, C. P. "Giustino Martire." In Döpp and Geerlings, *DLCA*, 454–58. English translation "Justin Martyr." In *Dictionary of Early Christian Literature*, translated by M. O'Connell. 356f.

Viciano, Albert. "Antike versus zeitgenössische Exegese: Theodoret von Kyros' Kommentar zu Gal 1,19" [Ancient vs. Contemporary Exegesis: Theodoret of Kyros's Commentary on Gal 1:19]. *FKTh* 12 (1996): 285–89.

———. "Tertullian." In Bäumer and Scheffczyk, *ML* 6:373f.

Vidal Manzanares, César. "María en el Corán: Confluencia de los apócrifos cristianos con la polémica proselitista del Islam" [Mary in the Koran: Confluence of the Christian Apocrypha with the Proselytistic Polemics of Islam]. *Ephemerides Mariologicae* 42 (1992): 295–309.

Villafiorita Monteleone, Andrea. *Alma Redemptoris Socia: Maria e la Redenzione nella teologia contemporanea* [Beloved Companion of the Redeemer: Mary and the Redemption in Contemporary Theology]. CdM 8. Lugano and Gavirate (Varese): Eupress FTL, 2010.

Villar, José Ramón. "La madre de Dios en la teologia ortodoxa" [The Mother of God in Orthodox Theology]. *Scripta de Maria* 2nd ser., 7 (2010): 27–73.

Volken, Laurent. *Le rivelazioni nella Chiesa* [Revelations in the Church]. Rome: Ed. Paoline, 1963. French original: *Les Révélations dans l'Église*. Tournai and Paris: Ed. Salvator, 1961.

Vollert, Cyril, SJ. "María y la Iglesia." In Carol, *Mariología*, 921–66. English original: "Mary and the Church." In Carol, *Mariology*, 2:550–96.

———. "Principio fundamental de la mariología." In Carol, *Mariología*, 431–87. English original: "Fundamental Principle of Mariology." In Carol, *Mariology*, 2:30–87.

von Balthasar, Hans Urs. *Elucidations*. Translated by John Kenneth Riches. San Francisco: Ignatius Press, 1998. Italian translation: *Punti fermi*. Milan: Rusconi Editore, 1972. German original: *Klarstellungen: zur Prüfung der Geister*. 2nd ed. Freiburg im Breisgau: Herder, 1971.

———. *The Moment of Christian Witness*. Translated by Richard Beckley. San Francisco: Ignatius Press, 1994. Italian: *Cordula ovverosia il caso serio* [Cordula; or the emergency]. Brescia: Queriniana, 1968. German original: *Cordula oder der Ernstfall*. Einsiedeln: Johannes Verlag, 1967.

———. *Nuovi punti fermi*. Milan: Jaca, 1980. German original: *Neue Klarstellungen*. Einsiedeln: Johannes Verlag, 1979. English translation: *New Elucidations*. Translated by Sister Mary Theresilde Skerry. San Francisco: Ignatius Press, 1986.

———. *Teodrammatica*. Vol. 3. Milan: Jaca, 1992. German original: *Theodramatik* II/2. Einsiedeln: Johannes Verlag, 1978. English translation: *Theo-Drama* III. San Francisco: Ignatius Press, 1992.

von Balthasar, Hans Urs, and Joseph Ratzinger. *Maria Chiesa nascente*. Translated by Angelo Colacrai. Rome: Edizioni Paoline, 1998. 2nd ed. 2005. German original: *Maria–Kirche im Ursprung*. Freiburg im Breisgau: Herder, 1980. English translation: *Mary: The Church at the Source*. Translated by Adrian Walker. San Francisco: Ignatius Press, 2005.

von Campenhausen, Hans F. *Die Jungfrauengeburt in der Theologie der Alten Kirche* [The Virgin Birth in the Theology of the Ancient Church]. Heidelberg: Carl Winter, 1962. English translation: *The Virgin Birth in the Theology of the Ancient Church*. Translated by Frank Clarke. London: SCM, 1964.

von Gaal, Imre. "Die Marienerscheinungen in Robinsonville/Champion im Bistum Green Bay (Wisconsin, USA)" [Marian Apparitions in Robinsonville/Champion in the Diocese of Green Bay]. *Sedes Sapientiae: Mariologisches Jahrbuch* 16, no. 2 (2012): 35–59.

———. "Ein Weg von der Polemik zum Lobpreis: Die unbefleckte Empfängnis Mariens in der Sicht von Eduard Preuß (1834–1904)" [A Way from Polemics to

Praise: The Immaculate Conception of Mary in the View of Eduard Preuss]. *Sedes Sapientiae: Mariologisches Jahrbuch* 9, no. 1 (2005): 39–67.

von Le Fort, Gertrud. *Die ewige Frau.* Munich: Kösel, 1962. Originally published in 1934. English translation: *The Eternal Woman.* San Francisco: Ignatius Press, 2010.

Vrankic, Peter. "Der selige Pius IX, der Papst der Immacolata" [Bl. Pius IX, Pope of the Immaculate]. *Sedes Sapientiae: Mariologisches Jahrbuch* 8, no. 2 (2004): 79–99.

Wenger, Antoine. "Foi et piété mariales à Byzance" [Marian Faith and Piety in Byzantium]. In du Manoir, *Maria*, 5:923–81. 1958.

———. *L'Assomption de la Très Sainte Vierge dans la tradition byzantine du VI au X siècle: Études et documents* [The Assumption of the Most Holy Virgin in Byzantine Tradition of the Sixth to Tenth Centuries: Studies and Documents]. Paris: Institut français d'études byzantines, 1955.

Wensinck, A. J., and P. Johnstone. "Maryam." In *Encyclopédie de l'Islam*, edited by E. Van Donzel, 6:613–17. Leiden: Brill, 1996.

Willam, Franz Michel. *Storia del Rosario* [History of the Rosary]. Translated by Rodolfo Paoli. Rome: Orbis catholicus, 1951. German original: *Die Geschichte und Gebetsschule des Rosenkranzes.* Vienna (Wien): Herder, 1948.

Winter, Aloysius. "Das Werk der Maria Valtorta: Ein beliebtes Skandalon?" [The Work of Maria Valtorta: A Popular Scandal?] In Ziegenaus, *Volksfrömmigkeit*, 163–90.

Wittkemper, Karl. "Braut IV. Dogmatik" [Bride. IV. Dogmatics]. In Bäumer and Scheffczyk, *ML* 1:564–71.

———. "Dreifaltigkeit I. Dogmatik" [Trinity. I. Dogmatics]. In Bäumer and Scheffczyk, *ML* 2, 233–39.

———. "Eudes" [John Eudes]. In Bäumer and Scheffczyk, *ML* 2:411f.

———. "Herrin" [Lady]. In Bäumer and Scheffczyk, *ML* 3:161f.

Yasuda, Thomas T. "The Message of Mary Coredemptrix at Akita and Its Complementarity with the Dogma Movement." In Miravalle, *Mary Coredemptrix*, 3:235–49.

Zamberlan, Nereo. "La *Collectio Missarum de B. Maria Virgine:* Bibliografia ragionata (1986–2001)" [The "Collection of Masses of the BVM": A Critical Bibliography]. *Marianum* 65, no. 163–64 (2003): 49–99.

Zavalloni, Roberto, and Eliodoro Mariani, eds. *La dottrina mariologica di Giovanni Duns Scoto* [The Mariological Doctrine of John Duns Scotus]. Rome: PAA-Edizioni Antonianum, 1987.

Zedda, Silverio. "Lc 1, 35b, 'Colui che nascerà santo sarà chiamato Figlio di Dio.'" [Lk 1:35b: "He Who Is to Be Born Holy Will Be Called Son of God."] *Rivista Biblica* 33, no. 1 (1985): 29–43, 165–89.

Zelinsky, Vladimir. "Mary in the Mystery of the Church: The Orthodox Search for Unity." In *Mary Coredemptrix*, 2:177–225.

Zeljko, Ivan. *Marienerscheinungen—Schein und Sein aus theologischer und psychologischer Sicht: Dargestellt am Beispiel der Privatoffenbarungen in Medjugorje* [Marian Apparitions: Appearance and Reality from Theological and Psychological Viewpoints, Illustrated by the Example of Private Revelations at Medjugorje]. Hamburg: Dr. Kovač, 2004.

Ziegenaus, Anton. "Apokalyptische Frau" [Woman of the Apocalypse]. In Bäumer and Scheffczyk, *ML* 1:191.

———. "Auserwählung" [Election]. In Bäumer and Scheffczyk, *ML* 1:302f.

———. "Befestigung in der Gnade" [Firmness in Grace]. In Bäumer and Scheffczyk, *ML* 1:399f.

———. "Charakter Marias" [The Character of Mary]. In Bäumer and Scheffczyk, *ML* 2:19–24.

———. "Darbringung Jesu im Tempel II. Dogmatik" [Presentation of Jesus in the Temple. II. Dogmatics]. In Bäumer and Scheffczyk, *ML* 2:142f.

———, ed. *Das Marianische Zeitalter. Entstehung—Gehalt—bleibende Bedeutung* [The Marian Age: Development, Content, Enduring Meaning]. Mariologische Studien 14. Regensburg: Friedrich Pustet, 2002.

———. "Demut Marias I. Dogmatik" [Humility of Mary. I. Dogmatics]. In Bäumer and Scheffczyk, *ML* 2:167–69.

———. "Der Weg zu einem geschlossenen mariologischen Traktat in den dogmatischen Handbüchern des deutschsprachigen Raumes" [The Way to a Self-Contained Treatise on Mariology in the Dogmatic Handbooks of the German-Speaking Countries]. FKTh 12, no. 2 (1996): 102–26.

———. "Die Jungfrauengeburt im Apostolischen Glaubensbekenntnis: Ihre Interpretation bei Adolf von Harnack" [The Virgin Birth in the Apostles' Creed: The Interpretation by Adolf von Harnack]. In *Divergenzen in der Mariologie: Zur ökumenischen Diskussion um die Mutter Jesu*, edited by H. Petri, 35–55. Regensburg: Pustet, 1989.

———. "Die vollkommene Hingabe an Jesus durch Maria nach Ludwig-Maria Grignion von Montfort" [Total Consecration to Jesus through Mary according to Louis Marie Grignion de Montfort]. In Ziegenaus, *Totus tuus*, 31–45.

———. "Ehe III. Dogmatik" [Marriage. III. Dogmatics]. In Bäumer and Scheffczyk, *ML* 2:284–86.

———. "Engel II. Dogmatik" [Angel. II. Dogmatics]. In Bäumer and Scheffczyk, *ML* 2:339.

———, ed. *"Geboren aus der Jungfrau Maria":* Klarstellungen ["Born of the Virgin Mary": Elucidations]. Mariologische Studien 19. Regensburg: Friedrich Pustet, 2007.

———. "Häresie" [Heresy]. In Bäumer and Scheffczyk, *ML* 3:67–69.

———. *Jesus Christus: Die Fülle des Heils; Christologie und Erlösungslehre* [Jesus Christ: The Fullness of Salvation; Christology and Doctrine of the Redemption]. Katholische Dogmatik 4. Aachen: MM-Verlag, 2000.

———. "Jungfräulichkeitsgelübte" [Vow of Virginity]. In Bäumer and Scheffczyk, *ML* 3:481–83.

———. *Maria in der Heilsgeschichte: Mariologie* [Mary in Salvation History: Mariology]. Katholische Dogmatik 5. Aachen: MM-Verlag, 1998.

———, ed. *Marienerscheinungen: Ihre Echtheit und Bedeutung im Leben der Kirche.* [Marian Apparitions: Their Authenticity and Meaning in the Life of the Church]. Mariologische Studien 10. Regensburg: Friedrich Pustet, 1995.

———. "Ohnmacht" [Helplessness]. In Bäumer and Scheffczyk, *ML* 4:683–85.

———. "Schönheit" [Beauty]. In Bäumer and Scheffczyk, *ML* 6:51f.

———. "Socia" [Associate]. In Bäumer and Scheffczyk, *ML* 6:194f.

———. "Stellvertretung (der Menschheit durch Maria)" [Representation (of Humanity by Mary)]. In Bäumer and Scheffczyk, *ML* 6: 292f.

———, ed. *Totus tuus: Maria in Leben und Lehre Johannes Pauls II.* [Totally Yours: Mary in the Life and Teaching of John Paul II]. Mariologische Studien 18. Regensburg: Friedrich Pustet, 2004.

———. "Unvollkommenheiten" [Imperfections]. In Bäumer and Scheffczyk, *ML* 6:547.

———. "Unsündlichkeit" [Impeccability]. In Bäumer and Scheffczyk, *ML* 6:545f.

———, ed. *Volksfrömmigkeit und Theologie: Die eine Mariengestalt und die vielen Quellen* [Piety and Theology: The One Figure of Mary and Its Many Sources]. Regensburg: Friedrich Pustet, 1998.

Zielinski, Andrzej Kazimierz. *Maria–Königin der Apostel: Die Bedeutung Mariens nach den Schriften des Palottiner-Theologen Heinrich Maria Köster für das Katholische Apostolat und die Neuevangelisierung in Lateinamerika* [Mary, Queen of Apostles: The Significance of Mary for the Catholic Apostolate and the New Evangelization in Latin America, according to the Pallottine theologian H. M. Köster]. Frankfurt am Main: Peter Lang, 2000.

Zmijewski, Josef. *Die Apostelgeschichte* [Acts of the Apostles]. Regensburg: Pustet, 1994.

———. *Die Mutter des Messias: Maria in der Christusverkündigung des Neuen Testaments* [The Mother of the Messiah: Maria in the New Testament's Proclamation of Christ]. Kevelaer: Butzon and Bercker, 1989.

Index of Scripture

Old Testament

New Testament

Index of Names

Index of Topics

Introduction to Mariology was designed in Adobe Caslon and composed by Kachergis Book Design of Pittsboro, North Carolina. It was printed on 55-pound Natural Offset and bound by Maple Press of York, Pennsylvania.